THE WAR OF NERVES

ALSO BY MARTIN SIXSMITH

The Lost Child of Philomena Lee

Russia: A 1,000-Year Chronicle of the Wild East

THE WAR OF NERVES

INSIDE THE COLD WAR MIND

MARTIN SIXSMITH

PEGASUS BOOKS
NEW YORK LONDON

THE WAR OF NERVES

Pegasus Books, Ltd.
148 West 37th Street, 13th Floor
New York, NY 10018

First Pegasus Books cloth edition July 2022

ISBN: 978-1-63936-181-6

10 9 8 7 6 5 4 3 2 1

Printed in the United States of America
Distributed by Simon & Schuster
www.pegasusbooks.com

AUTHOR'S NOTE

There is a long and ignoble tradition of writers who devour the work of their researchers and publish it as their own. Academics are notoriously inclined to put their name on papers substantially written by their students. Acknowledgements can be slight and grudging. But I have the opposite problem. So brilliant and assiduous has the work of my researcher been that I would dearly wish to see him given a co-author credit for this book. The fact that he is my son, Daniel Sixsmith, of whom I am rather fond, plays no part in my unbounded admiration for his historical knowledge, scholarly expertise and endlessly creative originality.

London, February 2021

CONTENTS

PREFACE

The Cold War pitted the United States of America and the Soviet Union against one another for the best part of fifty years. From the end of the Second World War to the dissolution of the USSR in 1991, the psychodrama playing out between the superpowers held the world in thrall. The Cold War, both sides declared, was a contest of competing social, economic, political and ethical systems, each of them professing a monopoly on wisdom and the keys to humankind's future. Washington and Moscow explored and constructed their own identities in opposition to and competition with each other; each sought to persuade, cajole or intimidate the rest of the globe to support their cause. It was a conflict in which the battleground was, to an unprecedented extent, the human mind: the aim was control not just of territory, resources and power, but of loyalties, belief and the nature of reality.

Histories of the Cold War – charting facts and dates, speeches and events, stalemates and stand-offs – are not in short supply. But what strikes me as most remarkable – and what this book proposes to examine – is the way this extraordinary period shaped not just the experiences but the *thinking* of millions of people, from the politicians at the top to the ordinary men and women scurrying down the steps to their basement fallout shelters; and how some of the mental processes inculcated by the Cold War continue to influence the way we see the world today.

With no direct military confrontation between the two superpowers, neither side could achieve physical domination over the other.*

---

*In 1945, George Orwell used the term 'Cold War' to describe the stagnant conflict that might develop between nuclear powers (George Orwell, 'You and the Atom Bomb', *Tribune*, 19 October 1945. www.orwellfoundation.com/the-orwell-foundation/orwell/essays-and-other-works/you-and-the-atom-bomb/).

Instead, regimes in East and West deployed psychological means to keep their domestic population – and sometimes their enemies' population – convinced of their superiority. The timing was propitious. At the start of the twentieth century, the once arcane science of psychology had begun to percolate into popular awareness. Freudian psychoanalysis penetrated modern culture; behavioural psychology colonised the economy, administration and government. Companies used it for the organisation of their workforce and factories, governments in the planning of their educational systems, the army for intelligence and aptitude tests. For the competing powers, psychology was a tool: a means to convince the world, perhaps at times themselves, of their own righteousness and their enemy's iniquity. They used overt propaganda – state media; radio, television, posters – but also more nuanced messages conveyed through ostensibly independent channels. Literature, art, music and cinema were co-opted by both the USSR and the USA (the former more blatantly than the latter, but both with stubborn persistence) to embody the message that *we* are right and *they* are wrong.

Each side strove to understand the thinking of the other in an ongoing guessing game that at times strained the boundaries of what psychologists call Theory of Mind – the ability to understand that others may think differently from oneself. Confirmation bias, the tendency to select only that information which confirms our own beliefs, abounded: the minutes of meetings stored in government archives showed ministers, generals and bureaucrats sifting the evidence of enemy thinking – then unerringly selecting only those pieces that supported what they had already decided to be the case.

In both East and West, shorn of direct experience of what life was like across the divide, people largely believed what they were told about the 'other', albeit with fluctuating degrees of conviction. Both

---

It was taken up by the Americans Bernard Baruch and Walter Lippmann, who applied it to the specific circumstances of the Soviet–American confrontation (Andrew Glass, 'Bernard Baruch coins term "Cold War"', *Politico*, 16 April 2010. www.politico.com/story/2010/04/bernard-baruch-coins-term-cold-war-april-16-1947-035862). Although it is true that uniformed American and Soviet soldiers never fought each other, proxy wars were stoked, funded and supported by the opposing sides. Countries across the globe, particularly in the developing world, counted the dead, while Americans and Soviets experienced the largely bloodless version of the Cold War.

sides experienced a pervasive fear stemming from a global tension between two systems, each with the means to destroy the planet. Years of rumbling international hostility affected individual mental well-being, manifesting in social paranoia, catastrophising, and surges of collective hysteria.

In 1969, twelve months after Soviet tanks had crushed the Prague Spring, I travelled as a schoolboy through a divided Europe. The drama of the Sputnik years had persuaded our school to hire an adventurous young Cambridge graduate to teach us Russian. That summer he took us on a series of trains through France, Belgium, West Germany, then on into the Soviet Union. We were bolshie grammar school boys going boldly, boorishly to the mysterious land whose language we had been learning, eager to meet the Russian *babushkas*, *soldaty* and *studentkas* we had been declining in number, gender and case for the past two years.

When our train crossed the border from Poland into the Soviet Union at Brest, in what is now Belarus, we shuffled onto a windswept platform to see our carriages hoisted aloft while new bogies for the wide-gauge Soviet tracks, selected long ago to baffle western invaders, were shunted under them. Eighteen hours later we were on a smoke-spewing Intourist bus rattling down Moscow's traffic-free six-lane boulevards to our hotel beside the Kremlin.

Howard Cooper was allocated room 107, where we deciphered a plaque to its previous occupants, Vladimir Lenin and Nadezhda Krupskaya. To our great delight, we were woken in the night by phone calls from sultry-voiced ladies proposing things more interesting than a history lesson. When our teacher warned us under no circumstances to accept, Linklater said, 'But sir, what if we just want to practise our Russian?'

We stood out from the locals because we wore bright t-shirts and jeans, chewed chewing gum and had biros to write with. We had them, they wanted them; fraternisation ensued. 'Shooing gum? Shooing gum?' said the urchins. 'You got jeans? You like icon?' said the men in leather jackets. 'You want change me money?' said the alluring *blondinkas*. After the first week we had empty suitcases and a good grounding in the economics of the Eastern Bloc. Years later I was unshocked to discover in socialist Romania that packs of Kent cigarettes had replaced the worthless Leu as the favoured unit of currency.

Russia became a part of my life. I studied its language, history and culture at university in England, then as a postgraduate in the United States. After that first eye-opening foray, I went back regularly. I saw how Leonid Brezhnev's pathological fear of change and blind commitment to the arms race was bankrupting the country. People struggled to get life's necessities, including food and adequate clothing. Luxury goods such as TVs were as rare as a green Soviet flag. Even getting on the waiting list for a fridge was an achievement. Jokes were a psychological prop that kept people sane: there was a popular one about a man who does finally get on the list, and when he asks when he can collect his fridge the official says, 'On the tenth of August the year after next.' But the man looks in his diary and says, 'That day's no good.' The official asks him why, and the man says, 'Because that's the day the plumber's coming to fix my heating.'

As a student at Harvard in the late 1970s I saw the other side of the coin. The Americans in my class had their own humour, much of it aimed at the 'commies'. They had grown up in the era of duck-and-cover drills anticipating nuclear war; memories of paranoia-inducing McCarthyism remained fresh and, thanks to Stanley Kubrick's *Dr. Strangelove*, they knew exactly how the apocalypse would be played out. My academic thesis was about Russian poetry, but it was impossible to avoid the politics.

I spent the endgame of the Cold War flitting between East and West as a correspondent for the BBC. Between 1980 and 1997 I was based for four years in Brussels, three in Warsaw, four in Washington DC and five in Moscow. In the USA I found fear, mistrust and hatred of the Soviet enemy; few were the voices that praised the communist system. In the USSR I saw the same things in reverse, but with an added dimension of envy and sneaking admiration. The extraordinary 'kitchen debate' of 1959, later broadcast on Soviet television, when Nikita Khrushchev and Richard Nixon traded barbs about which country made the better dishwashers, had encapsulated the swaggering braggadocio of two opposed systems. But for ordinary Russians it was the sight of American homes with fitted kitchens – which certainly weren't fixtures in their own homes – that made the most lasting impact.

When Soviet communism collapsed, after seventy-four years of the greatest social experiment the world has ever seen, the West spectacularly misjudged the psychology of the times. After decades of misery under communism, the Russian people were willing to do almost anything to share in the freedoms and economic success of the West. Boris Yeltsin renounced the past, threw open Russia's borders and secrets. Friendship was the name of the game. But the victors spent little time reflecting on the sensitivities of the defeated: the West treated Russia with condescension, and in the years following 1991 trod on every one of its exposed nerves.

By the time I left the BBC to go and work for the newly elected prime minister, Tony Blair, the Cold War was yesterday's news; the psychology of Soviet–American confrontation seemed a subject of merely historical interest. Unrestricted capitalism had come to Moscow; a select few made billions, while the rest of the country descended into corruption, poverty and violence, culminating in a series of catastrophic financial and constitutional crises. By 2000, Russians had had enough. Western-style democracy seemed to bring only chaos and suffering. Vladimir Putin, then almost as unknown to Russians as he was to the wider world, set out to restore stability and pride to a country in crisis.

Two decades on, he has largely achieved his aims, but at the cost of relations with the West. Moscow once again blusters and threatens, flexing its muscles on the international stage, eliminating its enemies at home and abroad. We read how the Russians are spying, hacking, sabotaging and subverting; and we can be sure that we are doing the same to them. Mass nuclear drills in Russia's cities are a salutary sight for all to behold.

In the West, too, the icy chill re-descending on international relations has resurrected elements of Cold War thinking, or at least a nostalgia-tinted version of it; a harking back to a time when we knew who our enemy was, when our own problems and failings could be blamed on the malevolent 'other' seeking to do us harm. The thinking of Truman and Stalin, Kennedy and Khrushchev, Nixon and Brezhnev, Reagan and Gorbachev, the men who led the world to the brink; their hopes, fears and devious designs; the methods they used to mould the psyche of their populations; and the devastating emotional impact on the millions who lived in daily terror of nuclear conflagration, are things of which we would do well to remind ourselves.

INDIVIDUAL OR COLLECTIVE –
TWO NATIONAL PSYCHES

Long before either the advent of communism or the twentieth-century antagonism that pitched them into bitter rivalry, Russia and America were already identified as competing poles of social and spiritual values. In 1835, the French historian Alexis de Tocqueville predicted with uncanny precision the global dominance the two would achieve:

> There are, at the present time, two great nations in the world … I allude to the Russians and the Americans. Both of them have grown up unnoticed; and whilst the attention of mankind was directed elsewhere, they have suddenly assumed a most prominent place amongst the nations; and the world learned their existence and their greatness at almost the same time. All other nations seem to have nearly reached their natural limits … but [Russia and America] are proceeding with ease and with celerity along a path to which the human eye can assign no term.[1]

In 1835, Moscow and Washington seemed content to plough their non-intersecting furrows, but de Tocqueville foresaw a future in which the world would be divided between their irreconcilable visions of human nature. 'The Anglo-American relies upon personal interest to accomplish his ends, and gives free scope to the unguided exertions and common-sense of the citizens; the Russian centres all the authority of society in a single arm: the principal instrument of the former is freedom; of the latter servitude.'[2] That distinction between the individual and the collective sits at the heart of the values America and Russia would come to represent. It would condition their beliefs, their motivation and their national character. It would define how they viewed themselves, and each other – and in each, it would foster the messianic drive to prove that *their way* was best.

For a millennium, Russia has been an autocracy with power concentrated in the hands of an all-powerful leader or leadership group. Strong centralised rule has held together a disparate, centripetal empire and preserved it from the predations of powerful foreign enemies. Sporadic attempts at democracy have ended in a return to the same default mode of governance; the cause of the state has taken priority over the interests of the individual.

In the twenty-first century, Vladimir Putin sits at the head of what he terms a 'power vertical', governing from the top, appointing figures loyal to the state to key positions where they implement policy decisions. The federal centre controls the appointment of regional governors, judges and security chiefs. The president's friends run the major state industries, enriching themselves and him. Putin refers to it as 'managed democracy' – under the communists it was called 'democratic centralism' – but it began in the time of Ivan the Terrible. In the sixteenth century, Russia was a capricious autocracy, with the tsar at the top, the people at the bottom and few civic institutions to mediate power between them. Corrupt, often uneducated placemen appointed through personal connections wielded unchecked authority over justice, taxes and daily life. The system of *kormlenie* – literally 'feeding' – saw a succession of tsars give their favourites responsibility for administering a geographical region or a sector of the economy. The appointee would receive no salary, but would have the right to enrich himself from the cash flow his activities generated. It was a licence to fleece the people. It brought great loyalty from those the tsar had appointed and great power for the monarch who held their fate in his hands.

The United States, since 1776, has been a democracy, with moderating institutions, checks and balances and a division of powers that enshrine the right of the people to oversight and control of their elected representatives. The state has foregone absolute power and freed the individual to exercise his or her initiative in the pursuit of private gain and happiness.

At times in America, too, governors, sheriffs, city mayors, local and national officials have abused their powers for personal gain. But graft has never been endemic in the fabric of national government.

Because the state does not enjoy absolute political power, neither does it enjoy economic impunity. The years since 1776 have been characterised by a devotion to the notion of liberty, implanted first by a rejection of the civic curtailments enforced by Britain, then maintained by a population wary of a return to tyranny.

The concept of liberty in the US has been based on the protection of natural rights, presumed to be inherent in the nature of man. It has offered guarantees for the self-governance of local communities, protected economic autonomy, defined social justice and underpinned moral freedoms in areas of personal conscience.

There have been challenges. Anti-federalist campaigners contended that freedoms were best preserved at local level or at the level of individual states, rather than by national government. The dispute played a role in the outbreak of civil war; slavery was a stain on the lofty ideals of the young nation. It surfaced in continuing opposition to 'big government' and surprising (at least, to European eyes) anger about federal initiatives such as Barack Obama's plan for national healthcare. But at all times, liberty was at the heart of the debate and at least some of the people had a say in it. Citizens neither laid down nor were pressured to lay down their individual rights to the collective cause of the state.

Unlike America, Russian lands were vulnerable, not shielded by protecting oceans, open on all sides to hostile forces: from the twelfth century, fierce nomadic tribes in the southern steppes had been raiding Kievan Rus'* to pillage, murder and kidnap. The wild dangerous steppe and the dark forces contained within it became an enduring terror myth in the national psyche.†

This conviction that Russia is vulnerable helps explain behaviour that can seem strange to the West – the readiness to sacrifice the individual, the subjugation of personal interests to the good of the whole, the collectivist ethos that enshrines the state as the supreme national priority. It's seen in the unflinching expenditure of Russian lives in battle, the aggressiveness of a military stance that flows from the certainty of national weakness, and the widespread acceptance

---

* The medieval forerunner to what would become the Russian state.
† From their depths would come forth the Mongol hordes that ruled over much of European Russia for two hundred years.

that the state has the absolute right to murder its enemies abroad. When the Kremlin suppresses dissenting voices, jails opposition candidates and closes critical media outlets, the outcry within the country is minimal. Independent polls show that the majority of Russians support Vladimir Putin because they buy into the millennial credo that only a powerful state can guarantee order at home and protection from hostile outside forces.

The Russian state's reliance on the readiness of the individual to sacrifice him or herself in the cause of the collective supposed a benevolent view of human nature, in which mankind was held to be cooperative, altruistic, ready to forego selfish aims in furtherance of the common good. This concept was explicitly posited in the years of Soviet communism (though Moscow frequently had to 'enforce human goodness'). The American model, in contrast, held that human nature was innately competitive, programmed to seek the ultimate personal benefit from life. If government were to be truly of the people, by the people and for the people, it would have to accept the reality of human selfishness and harness it for the success of the nation.

The American conservative thinker and political commentator Charles Krauthammer, a qualified psychiatrist who experienced life in the White House from the inside, wrote that the supposition of human virtue plays no part in the American concept of governance.

> I would say, unlike a lot of other political systems, which are based on the notion of the virtue of the individual, the American system is constructed in a way that it requires it the least. In fact, to me the American system was and is the most realistic in understanding the fallen condition of the human being and expecting very little of the individual.[3]

Krauthammer concluded that the American understanding of human nature – flawed, selfish and competitive – produced a more successful, more enduring system of governance than those predicated on idealised notions of human goodness. The American conception of individual economic liberty, thought of by Krauthammer as Smithian capitalism, grew directly from the concept of natural rights and underpinned the construction of nineteenth-century America. The main duty of government was to get out of the way of the citizen, allowing him or her to shape his or her own personal and economic well-being; individual economic enterprise was the key to the vigour and prosperity of the whole.

With the exception of the brief, failed experiments with democracy that occurred sporadically in her history, Russia has experienced no comparable discussion of the merits of individual rights. The unquestioned predominance of the state dates back to the occupation of Russian lands by the Mongols between 1237 and 1480, during which Russia's population was subjugated, her economy disrupted and her development set back. The nineteenth-century political philosopher Pyotr Chaadayev identified the Mongol occupation as the genesis of Russia's enduring failure to develop as a western nation:

> Our history began in barbarity and backwardness, followed by brutal foreign oppression whose values were imbibed by our own rulers. Cut off from the rest of humanity, we failed to acquire the universal values of duty, justice and the rule of law. When we finally threw off the Mongol yoke, the new ideas that had blossomed in Western Europe did not penetrate our state of oppression and slavery, because we were isolated from the human race. We fell into a condition of ever deeper servitude. While the whole world was being rebuilt and renewed, nothing was built in Russia.[4]

In the two centuries of Mongol rule, the Russian princes grew to admire the Mongol model of an autocratic, militarised state. When the Mongols left, they adopted it for themselves. Civic participation and respect for the law, glimpsed in some of the Russian princedoms before 1237, were replaced by an all-powerful state that crushed freedoms but brought strength and political unity. In the centuries ahead, it would become Russia's default position.

In contrast, by the end of the eighteenth century, when the tenets of governance for the new nation of America were being laid down, the century of Enlightenment had pushed those values already inherited from Europe further along the road to democracy. The French Revolution of 1789 enshrined the principle that individuals are free to do what they wish, as long as they do not violate the rights of their neighbour. 'Liberty consists in the ability to do whatever does not

harm another,' asserted the *Déclaration des droits de l'homme*. Thomas
Jefferson, who had been in Paris and had helped the French to draft
the *Déclaration*, promoted its principles in America. 'Rightful liberty
is unobstructed action according to our will,' he wrote to a correspondent in 1819, 'within limits drawn around us by the equal rights
of others. I do not add "within the limits of the law" because law is
often but the tyrant's will, and always so when it violates the rights
of the individual.'[5]

Russia was presented with her own opportunity to enter the
community of democratic nations in early 1917. The provisional government of Alexander Kerensky, which took power after the popular
February Revolution, began to introduce western-style parliamentary reforms, with free elections to a national constituent assembly, a
body that was intended to pave the way for a constitution and a parliament based on universal suffrage. After a largely peaceful election, in
which two-thirds of the population voted, the constituent assembly
convened in the Tauride Palace in St Petersburg on 5 January 1918. But
by then, Kerensky's government had been forcibly removed by the
Bolsheviks' October coup, and Lenin, whose party had not done well
in the elections, wasn't about to let democratic niceties threaten his
hold on power. The Bolshevik deputies walked out after the first votes
went against them, then sent soldiers with guns to evict everyone
else. 'Everything has turned out for the best,' Lenin wrote afterwards.
'The dissolution of the Constituent Assembly means the complete
and open repudiation of democracy in favour of dictatorship. This
will be a valuable lesson.'[6]

The Russian people's striving for freedom and self-government
in 1917 had delivered them up to a new and even more oppressive
despotism that would endure until the collapse of the Soviet Union
in 1991. In the course of those seventy-four years, relations between
Moscow and Washington would evolve through tension to crisis to
the brink of war. At the root of it was a conflict between two inimical
systems: the American way of individualism and liberty versus the
ingrained Russian heritage of collective endeavour and subservience
to the state. In the second half of the twentieth century, vast swathes
of humanity would be forced, cajoled or seduced into conforming to
one or the other.

2

TWO NATIONS; TWO MISSIONS

At the end of the Second World War, the economic and military might of the US and the USSR outstripped that of other nations by such a margin that the only threat they faced was from each other. Emerging from the war with a clear conception of their own achievements and power, each became gripped by fear of the rival beyond their borders, and concluded that the threat must be controlled. To do so, they would need to convince as many countries as possible, using any methods necessary, that their way of doing things was the right one.

The Bolsheviks had assumed communism was right for, and would be welcomed by, humankind. But the failure of worldwide revolution led Stalin to promote the isolationist policy of 'socialism in one country', before the war brought it to a dramatic end. The Americans, for their part, exported democratic capitalism with a relentless assurance that would endure into the twenty-first century. In the war of nerves that developed after 1945, each side championed their cause with a quasi-religious zeal while struggling to understand that the other might think differently. In cold war as in hot, there is a premium on deciphering the enemy's motives and intentions. But Washington and Moscow fell into the trap of imputing their own reasoning to the other. *How could anybody not think like us?*

The resulting misunderstandings and misinterpretations would lead to a decades-long period of international tension that benefited neither the superpowers nor the rest of the world. Why did Moscow and Washington convince themselves that postwar international politics was a zero-sum game?

Even in 1945, the facts hardly supported the fear. By any objective measure, the USSR was no threat to the US; its industrial base had been ravaged and its population decimated. Three hundred thousand Americans had died in the war, but the Soviets lost over 20 million people. The US economy was thriving; the Soviet Union was a shell of what it had been. As late as 1959, Nikita Khrushchev would still vainly be promising that with time the USSR would 'catch up' with America.

'The Soviet Union was never the *other* superpower,' writes the Cold War historian Odd Arne Westad. 'The gap that separated the communist regime from the United States in economic achievement, technological innovation, and overall military capability was so great that it is impossible to place the two in the same category.'[1]

The reason Washington so feared the prospect of Soviet dominance was to do with the way each side perceived the other, and how they allowed their preconceptions to colour what they saw. The opacity of Soviet politics meant the West had no clear view of what went on in Moscow, meaning that western observers superimposed templates from their own experience. Both Washington and London took for granted, for instance, that there would be a range of political forces in the Kremlin pushing for different things. Western intelligence reports from the time refer, mistakenly, to hardline elements in the politburo that were supposedly forcing Stalin to act more aggressively than he himself wished.

The Soviets, on the other hand, *could* follow the goings-on of American politics through the western media and the open reporting of policy discussions. But they too refracted what they saw through the prism of their own experience. The Kremlin concluded that western democracy was a pretence, an act put on for show, and that the levers of power were in reality pulled by the hidden hand of sinister industrialists and millionaires.

The tendency to attribute one's own thoughts and practices to the other side characterised political discourse in both countries and has continued into modern times, where legitimate concerns about the manoeuvring of the other are magnified by pre-digested stereotypes. Notions of Russian chicanery shaped American responses to Donald Trump's 2016 gambit towards Moscow, in particular the assumption that he was being manipulated by Kremlin blackmail. A history of exaggerated assessments of Washington's ability to spread hard and soft power made it easy for the Kremlin to attribute domestic reverses and unrest to the covert hand of the CIA.

Russophobia emerged much later in America than it did in Europe. Before the nineteenth century, the two countries felt a degree of mutual affinity, viewing one another as a mirror image across the

Pacific. As late as 1881, Walt Whitman could write that Russia and America 'so resemble each other' in a whole list of national characteristics, including their sense of 'historic and divine mission'.[2] Through much of the nineteenth century it was against Europe that Russia had measured herself. Defining herself by comparison to the Great Powers, Germany, France and the United Kingdom, Russia had developed a complex mixture of inferiority and superiority complexes.[3] From the early twentieth century, and unmistakably in the years after the Second World War, the role of dark shadow alter ego was taken over by an increasingly powerful United States.

In 2017, historians from America and Russia attempted to trace the origins of the misconceptions that have characterised relations between the two countries. In a paper titled 'A Genealogy of American Russophobia', Sean Guillory, from the Russian and East European Studies Center at the University of Pittsburgh, argued that the American portrayal of bogeyman-Russia had its roots in America's own self-image. 'In American eyes, Russia appeared as a distortion of the American self, reflected through a carnival mirror. It's a distorted, disfigured, inchoate, even horrifying image, but still an enigmatic source for American self-juxtaposition and psychological displacement.'[4] Ilya Budraitskis, of the Russian Academy of Sciences, wrote that Soviet anti-Americanism 'gradually developed as a dynamic combination of the political and the moral. If the first was defined by the confrontation of superpowers, the second addressed the fight for the soul of every individual Soviet person.' According to Budraitskis, the US was viewed as 'a power awakening dark, instinctive sides: greed, unbridled sexuality, a taste for primitive culture stirring up base passions and desires'.[5] America was an inimical, corrupting influence, 'a virus infecting a Soviet society whose immune system had been weakened',[6] undermining the morale of Soviet citizens and the stability of the Soviet system.

Different viewpoints; different perspectives: but both advanced with a messianic energy, driven by the conviction of their own exceptionalism. According to the American historian David Foglesong, such obsession and passion could be generated only between two societies that were more alike than they cared to admit.

Since Russia could be seen as both like and unlike America –
both Christian and heathen, European and Asiatic, white and

dark – gazing at Russia involved the strange fascination of looking into a skewed mirror. The commonalities such as youth, vast territory and frontier expansion that made Russia seem akin to the United States for much of the nineteenth century served to make Russia especially fitted for the role of 'imaginary twin' or 'dark double' that it assumed after the 1880s and continued to play throughout the twentieth century ... Thus, more enduringly than any other country, Russia came to be seen as both an object of the American mission and the opposite of American virtues.[7]

America strove to rescue Russia from the error of her ways with the hurt feelings of a sibling horrified by the other's betrayal. In the atheistic era of Soviet socialism, religion became a focus of the American 'mission', key to the assertion of its influence.[8] Church leaders blessed the crusade to save souls in the heathen empire, and President Franklin Roosevelt predicted that the Soviet Union would be swept by a religious revival. The diplomat George Kennan reported that the Bolshevik regime had failed to eradicate religious sensibility and had 'lost moral dominion over the masses of the Russian population'.

In 1630, John Winthrop had characterised his ideal America as 'a shining city upon a hill', populated by free men, open to all religious creeds and beliefs. By the twentieth century, 'the shining city' had become a byword for the American dream. John Kennedy spoke of it before his inauguration, and Ronald Reagan made it an article of faith for his time in the White House.[9]

That 'shining city upon a hill' is what Americans strove to bring to Russia. But Russia had its own messianic mission, dating back considerably further. In 1453, the destruction of Christian Byzantium by the Turks left Muscovy as the sole remaining bastion of the Orthodox faith, directly exposed now to the expanding empire of Islam. The emerging nation embraced the God-given mission to defend the civilised world against the infidel. A mystical prophetic text known as *The Legend of the White Cowl* circulated, claiming to consecrate Moscow as the 'Third Rome', the true guardian of God's rule.[10]

After 1917, the idealist despots of Leninist socialism recast this myth for their own purposes. Moscow the Third Rome became Moscow the Third International, destined to redeem the world through the new religion of communism. Just as Christian Russia

A LIGHT THAT WILL NEVER FAIL!
—Cargill in the Kansas City *Journal-Post*.

At the heart of the Cold War lay two faiths. One asserted that Jesus could
show man the way to Heaven in the afterlife, the other that Marxism–
Leninism could create such a paradise on Earth.

believed for centuries that it had a God-given mission to bring truth
and enlightenment to mankind, so Russian communism believed
in its own holy destiny to change, educate and perfect the human
species.

Whether American or Russian, burnishing a nation's credentials
as a global champion of truth and goodness requires an adversary
against whose failings such behaviour can be validated.[11] As George
Kennan remarked, neither the American self-image nor the Soviet
self-image could exist without the other: 'to cultivate the idea of
American innocence and virtue … requires an opposite pole of
evil'.[12] Similarly, to Georgy Arbatov, the Kremlin's leading expert
on America, 'the United States needs the Soviet Union to satisfy the

American psychological need for a villain. In this way, Americans can see themselves as a shining city on the hill.'[13] The American obsession with dark Russian forces was a mirror image of how Russians themselves have thought about the US: a paroxysm of paranoia and conspiratorial thinking, putting the blame for internal problems on sinister outside agents. The two countries remain locked in an embrace of interdependence that has defined the way each thinks about the other for over a hundred years.

3

KISSING STALIN'S BUM

As the Second World War drew to a close, the preoccupations of both sides came into focus. Having suffered the greatest human and material losses, the Soviet Union's priority was to ensure that such a tragedy could not be repeated. Future security and concrete measures to prevent another invasion from the west were accompanied by a burning desire for the USSR to obtain its just reward for the sacrifices it had made. The US wanted to create a system of effective world governance that would guarantee future peace and secure America's place at the forefront of it.

With the benefit of hindsight, it may seem that the aims of the US and Russia were destined to bring them into conflict. But that is not the view of many, on either side of the East–West divide. Accounts of the past are coloured by emotions, prejudices and unwitting or deliberate distortions. For a historian, that is a burden; for a psychologist, a blessing. Differing interpretations of the past shed light on national psychologies; examining the thoughts and intentions of the individuals who led those nations illuminates misapprehensions and misinterpretations that would exacerbate those tensions. America and Russia were the 'dark twins' of twentieth-century geopolitics – and psychology loves the study of twins, allowing as it does the comparison of how different outcomes can emerge from shared makeups.

The received western view that the Cold War was triggered by Soviet expansionism is disputed by historians and politicians. 'I think that all the way through the Soviet period,' said Robert Service, author of *The End of the Cold War, 1985–1991*, 'there was controversy in the West about how to handle Soviet communism, and the more powerful the Soviet Union became, the more contested the whole question became. But the polarity between accommodation and confrontation – you can already see it in the early years of the Soviet regime. In that sense, the Cold War didn't start after the Second World War; it started in the early 1920s.'[1]

In the view of Grigory Karasin, a long-serving deputy foreign minister and ambassador to the United Kingdom from 2000–5, the postwar years offered an opportunity to reset relations with the USSR. But, he says, the Allies spurned it, and western belligerence was at least in part to blame for the failure of the USSR to evolve in the direction of liberal democracy.

> It is natural to suppose that the USSR, in having paid such a dreadful price to achieve victory, was willing to play by the rules and to compromise with its former allies ... If the West had taken a more constructive line of engagement with the Soviet Union in 1946, things might have turned out differently in the Soviet Union. This would probably have given Stalin no choice but to proceed with social and political reform. It would have removed his excuse for refusing reform and developing a system centred on his own person – his cult of personality.[2]

The claim that Russia might have escaped its centuries-old history of centralised autocracy sounds improbable. But complaints of western insensitivity towards Russia, a failure to recognise those historical moments when she might have been drawn out of isolation and into the community of nations, are not new. They surfaced in the nineteenth century and again, powerfully, after the 1991 collapse of Soviet communism.

It is undoubtedly true that millions in the Soviet Union blamed the USSR's wartime allies for the advent of the Cold War. Their sense of disillusionment with the West was real, although this needs to be placed in context of a closed society where people's views are formed by information from rigidly controlled state media. But even Stalin himself genuinely seemed to believe that the West was responsible. As divisions grew over the postwar fate of central Europe, he wrote in the margins of a briefing document, 'We are not waging Cold War. It is the United States and its allies who are doing this.'[3] His comment, and others like it, were not intended for public consumption and appear to represent Stalin's real conviction that Moscow was open to compromise.

Both sides were bent on exporting their vision of the future. But

Vladimir Pechatnov, the head of the State Institute of International Relations of the Russian Foreign Ministry, says conflict might have been avoided if the West had paid more attention to Soviet sensitivities. It was, he says, psychologically important for Stalin that the West should recognise the suffering endured by the Soviets in winning the war. He needed the USSR to be acknowledged as a great power, with the status and the rewards it was due, as well as the security it craved for the future.[4] 'Russia was used to winning wars,' Vyacheslav Molotov complained, 'but was unable to enjoy the fruits of her victories. Russians are remarkable warriors but they do not know how to make peace. They are deceived and underpaid.'[5]

Stalin was determined that things would be different this time. He dwelled on the western Allies' failure to open a second front against the Germans when the USSR had been in danger of defeat. He suspected the West would have been happy to leave Nazis and Bolsheviks to fight each other into the ground. And now, having been beaten to Berlin by the Red Army, the West was trying to use diplomacy and geopolitics to claim the territory for which it had failed to fight. It rankled.[6]

The United States had emerged from the depression of the 1930s believing that its future depended on playing a greater role in the world, ensuring the growth of international trade that would benefit its economy. The attack on Pearl Harbor in 1941 had convinced Roosevelt that only the institution of a new global political and economic order would stop the repetition of the mistakes of the past:[7] it was time to reshape the world in America's political and economic image. 'We shall not again be thwarted in our will to live as a mature nation,' Roosevelt declared. 'We shall bear our full responsibility, exercise our full influence, and bring our help and encouragement to all who aspire to peace and freedom.'[8]

With a striking lack of self-awareness, neither side seemed to comprehend the suspicion and animosity with which their attempts to advance their benevolent ideologies were perceived from beyond their borders. The British, positioned between the two superpowers, struggling to maintain their global influence and place at the top table, were more self-aware. Alexander Cadogan, permanent undersecretary at the Foreign Office when the war ended, wrote in his diary that the Big Three were now in reality a 'Big Two and a Half'.[9] Britain had fallen behind its larger, younger rivals; it needed America's help,

but it strove for cooperation rather than subservience. Harold Macmillan recognised this when he described Britain's position in 1943 as
being the 'Greeks in this American empire. You will find the Americans much as the Greeks found the Romans – great big, vulgar,
bustling people, more vigorous than we are and also more idle, with
more unspoiled virtues and also more corrupt. We must run AFHQ
[Allied Forces Headquarters] as the Greek slaves ran the operations
of the Emperor Claudius.'[10]

British relations with the USSR had never been rosy. Mutual suspicion dated from the years after 1917, when London had sent troops
to help the anti-Bolshevik Whites. When Stalin agreed the Molotov–
Ribbentrop Pact in August 1939, pledging Soviet cooperation with the
Nazis, he did so after months of stalled negotiations with Britain and
France. And Soviet mistrust of the British remained even after they
became allies in 1941: as late as 1944, Stalin remained suspicious that
Churchill had engineered Rudolf Hess's flight to Scotland in May 1941
in order to plot a British–German alliance against the USSR,[11] and
Soviet feature films, such as the postwar *Secret Mission*, continued to
portray British agents collaborating with the Nazis.[12]

Conferences in Yalta in February and Potsdam in July 1945 were
intended to secure a lasting global peace and a new, functioning system
of international cooperation, but they took place against this background of hurt and resentment. The British, Americans and Soviets
had been thrown together in a somewhat unlikely wartime alliance,
and only common effort and common sacrifice had advanced it from
a matter of convenience to a relationship of nascent respect. By 4 February 1945, when Stalin, Roosevelt and Churchill gathered in Yalta's
Livadia Palace, there was a certain willingness not to throw away the
gains that had been made.

But history is not always made through the logical development
of policy. Policies are made by men and women, and the personalities of the leaders of the Big Three Allied powers and the interactions
between them would do much to determine the shape of the postwar
world, at times retreating from, at times hastening, the advent of the
Cold War. Stalin had taken a conscious decision to use charm and
cunning to extract what he could from the face-to-face discussions
with his fellow leaders.[13] At times he would be aggressive, at others
conciliatory, but always focused on achieving his goals. Roosevelt and
Churchill, the latter from an increasingly weakened position, had

other aims and other negotiating styles. In this clash of wills and egos, history would judge that the British and Americans allowed themselves to be bullied and intimidated by Stalin.

Was that the case? And if so, how did it come about? The first thing to say is that, although Roosevelt and Churchill were intelligent, sharp and experienced, Stalin was no fool either. The peasant from Georgia was an autodidact, widely read, gifted with a sharp mind and native cunning. He could be charming as well as ruthless, admired by his own team for the flexibility of his methods and the force of his will. In the inter-war years, he had a record of convincing the few foreigners he spoke to that he was straightforward and trustworthy. The Pulitzer Prize-winning *New York Times* correspondent Walter Duranty wrote countless articles assuring the US public of Stalin's good intentions. H. G. Wells had high praise after a visit to the Kremlin. 'I never met a man more sincere, decent and honest,' Wells wrote. 'There is nothing dark or sinister about him ... He is completely lacking in cunning and craftiness ...'[14]

It seems extraordinary with hindsight that Wells could describe one of history's most devious despots as 'sincere, decent and honest', but the power of face-to-face interaction should not be underestimated. From the earliest times of evolution, human beings learned to interpret visual signals in the movements and facial expression of an interlocutor: a skill so important to the well-being of our prehistoric ancestors that it became embedded in our social relationships. But those clues could also be faked, allowing for the manipulation of others. And Stalin was adept at this.[15]

Lenin is said to have had a name for those westerners who came to the USSR and reported that they had found everything to be rosy: he called them 'useful idiots'.* But it is clear that Wells was not an idiot. He was intelligent, educated and opinionated. And it may have been this latter quality that led him so spectacularly to misjudge Stalin: the human brain can convince itself so thoroughly of one

---

*It is disputed whether Lenin actually used the term. It is equally possible that it was a construct developed in the West to tarnish the reputation of anyone who visited a socialist country and failed to condemn what they saw there. It has, though, entered the political lexicon. See, for example, William Safire, 'On Language', *The New York Times*, 12 April 1987. www.nytimes.com/1987/04/12/magazine/on-language.html.

truth that it becomes incapable of absorbing an alternative, more convincing one.

> [S]elf-deception, by its very nature, is the most elusive of mental facts. We do not see what we do not see. Self-deception oper- ates both at the level of the individual mind and in the collective awareness of the group. To belong to a group of any sort, the tacit price of membership is to agree not to notice one's own feelings of uneasiness and misgiving, and certainly not to ques- tion anything that challenges the group's way of doing things.[16]

There is no suggestion that he deliberately falsified his views to meet the requirements of his peers, but the fact that H. G. Wells belonged to a 'group' – the Fabian socialism of Sidney and Beatrice Webb – may have contributed to the self-deception described by Goleman. His self-deception was sincere; of the self, by the self.

In contrast, when Winston Churchill set off in 1942 for the first of his two wartime visits to Moscow, he was deeply suspicious of the man he had publicly excoriated for two decades. Yet Churchill, too, showed signs of falling under the Soviet leader's influence. 'Poor Neville Chamberlain believed he could trust Hitler. He was wrong,' Hugh Dalton records Churchill as saying. 'But I don't think I'm wrong about Stalin.'[17] Anthony Eden came to fear that Churchill was 'under Stalin's spell'.[18]

Stalin's success is all the more surprising considering he spoke no foreign languages and neither did the senior members of his team. Few of them had ever travelled abroad. None of them seemed well placed to deal with the outside world; yet they made a success of some of the most high-profile international encounters of modern times.

Stalin and the rest of the Kremlin leadership had come to political maturity during the Russian civil war, a time when western aid to the Whites and the threat of western spies increased hostility towards the outside world. It had reinforced their wariness and formed Stalin's modus operandi for dealing with westerners – 'never trust them, rec- ognize their cunning but try to outfox them, exploit the differences that exist between them. Never forget that they want to destroy the Soviet Union and will take any opportunity to do so.'[19]

Churchill was a principal target of their mistrust. They believed he had had a hand in the plot to assassinate Lenin in 1918 and they knew he had participated in British attempts to defeat the Bolsheviks during the civil war.[20] Even when Germany invaded the Soviet Union in 1941 and the Russians became allies in the fight against Hitler, Churchill's speech on the radio remained strikingly critical:

> No one has been a more consistent opponent of Communism than I have for the last twenty-five years. I will unsay no word that I have spoken about it. But all this fades away before the spectacle which is now unfolding ... It follows therefore that we shall give whatever help we can to Russia and the Russian people.[21]

Even Roosevelt, no communist himself, was wary of the intensity of Churchill's hatred for the Bolsheviks. When Churchill was planning to fly to Moscow to meet Stalin in 1942, Roosevelt wrote to him,

> Stalin must be handled with great care. We have got always to bear in mind the personality of our ally and the very difficult and dangerous situation that confronts him. No-one can be expected to approach the war from a world point of view whose country has been invaded. I think we should try to put ourselves in his place.[22]

It seems that Churchill made an effort to do so. The British ambassador in Moscow, Archibald Clark Kerr, attended the 1942 meetings between Churchill and Stalin and left a wry, perceptive sketch of the thawing of personal relations.

> It was interesting to watch the impact of the two men. Clash and recoil and clash again, and then a slow but unmistakable coming together as each got the measure of the other, and in the end, much apparent understanding and goodwill. To me who am in a way responsible for the meeting it meant some very anxious moments. But at the end of today's meeting, I felt satisfied that it had been abundantly wise. Now the two men know each other and each one will be able to put the right value on the messages – and they are very frequent – that pass between them. At times both were very blunt, as if each one sought by

his bluntness to make a dint upon the other. I think that each succeeded and that the dints were deep.[23]

The two leaders took their time to feel each other out. Stalin asked for regular breaks, during which he would ostentatiously smoke his British-made pipe. Churchill, meanwhile, wandered about, 'pulling from his heated buttocks the seat of his trousers which had clearly stuck to them …'

Despite the immense stature he had achieved as a statesman and war leader, Churchill was prone to self-doubt. After his first session with Stalin, he muttered, 'I want that man to like me', and later cabled back to London the hope that he would 'establish a solid and sincere relationship with this man'.[24]

His hopes were not immediately realised. After the cordiality of the first day's meetings, a very different Stalin appeared the next morning, 13 August. He launched into an angry torrent of reproaches against the British, and against Churchill in person, over the Allies' failure to open a second front against the Germans in the west, which Moscow needed in order to reduce the strain on Soviet forces in the east. Having made that point with considerable force, Stalin broadened the attack, complaining about the quality of western military equipment furnished to the Red Army, accusing the British navy of cowardice and, most heatedly, criticising the Allies' failure to recognise the extent of Soviet sacrifices in confronting the Nazis. The language was crude and the Soviet interpreter, Vladimir Pavlov, did nothing to soften it.[25]

Stalin's anger was real. But at the same time he was a skilful negotiator and he knew such an outburst would be unsettling for Churchill. Valentin Berezhkov, Pavlov's colleague, was convinced that it was a deliberate tactic:

> All those people that came to [Stalin] they immediately believed him, everything that he said. He could be very severe, very unpleasant. And the next day he could be very cordial, very nice. This happened with Churchill for example, when he came in '42 and I translated. Stalin was angry and he offended Churchill, saying the British were afraid of the Germans, that they would never win this war. Churchill also became angry and it was very unpleasant, both trying to offend each other. Then the next day

Stalin [acted] like nothing happened, he was so cordial. Churchill said he couldn't believe that this was the same Stalin that he'd seen the previous day. I think he [Stalin] was a great actor.[26]

Unpredictability is a powerful negotiating tactic, putting one's interlocutor on the back foot, making it impossible for him or her to find solid ground for his or her own arguments and assumptions.* Churchill wrote later that this had been 'a most unpleasant discussion', in which Stalin had 'kept his eyes half closed, always avoiding mine, uttering at intervals a string of insults'.[27]

Lord Tedder, accompanying Churchill, suggested there may have been an additional reason for Stalin's wrath. The Moscow dacha where Churchill was staying, said Tedder, was almost certainly bugged.† In the time between the first and second meetings, Churchill had let rip about how Stalin was 'just a peasant' and that he 'knew how to handle him'.[28] Given Stalin's lifelong inferiority complex and his resentment of better-educated, intellectual colleagues, whom he constantly suspected of looking down on him, Churchill's sneering could hardly have been more damaging.[29]

But Stalin was not the only leader with a thin skin. Churchill, too, felt insults keenly. Clark Kerr found him the next morning, the 14th, struggling to digest the mauling to which he had been subjected. 'He was like a wounded lion,' Kerr wrote in his private journal, declaring he was 'damned' if he would keep his engagement to attend Stalin's state dinner that evening.[30] US Ambassador to Moscow Averell Harriman, as always, was sensitive to the prime minister's need for reassurance. When Churchill complained of a headache, laying his head on the table seemingly in despair, Harriman soothed him. Churchill responded by taking his hand and saying, 'I'm so glad, Averell, that

---

*It is intriguing to note the similarity of such tactics to the so-called 'madman theory' elaborated later in the century by Richard Nixon and Henry Kissinger (see Chapter 32).

† Churchill seems to have learned his lesson. At the Yalta Conference, he wrote in his memoirs that his Soviet hosts gave 'kindly attention' to 'every chance remark' that was made in rooms occupied by the British delegation. When an official commented that a large fish tank had no fish in it, it was quickly filled with goldfish. When someone complained that they had no lemon peel to put in their drinks, 'a lemon tree loaded with fruit' appeared the following day. Winston S. Churchill, *Triumph and Tragedy*, Boston: Houghton Mifflin, 1953, p. 347.

Churchill (in his beloved 'siren suit'), Stalin and Averell
Harriman. Moscow, 14 August 1942.

you came with me. You are a tower of strength.' Clark Kerr, whose
lack of sympathy evoked only hostile glances from his boss, wrote
that Churchill was like a small child, lapping up Harriman's 'sustained
bumsucking' with relish.[31]

Clark Kerr found Churchill temperamental and difficult, although
there was grudging respect and a shared sense of wry humour
between them. What Clark Kerr did not know was that Churchill
suffered from lifelong mental fragility, manifesting in several of the
symptoms of manic depression, now known as bipolar disorder. As
the prime minister's personal physician, Lord Moran, would later
confirm, Churchill had told him that he was aware of the seriousness
of his condition.

> I don't like standing near the edge of a platform when an express
> train is passing through. I like to stand back and, if possible, get a
> pillar between me and the train. I don't like to stand by the side
> of a ship and look down into the water. A second's action would
> end everything. A few drops of desperation.[32]

Churchill's confidant, Lord Beaverbrook, reported that Winston was
always 'at the top of the wheel of confidence or at the bottom of

intense depression'. He would alternate extended periods of debilitating despair which left him unable to get out of bed with manic
phases, where he would become charged with excessive levels of
energy. During these periods he would stay awake until two or three
in the morning, demanding that his secretary stay awake, too, while
he dictated the scores of books he wrote in his lifetime, or spoke
incessantly of new ideas and new plans for potential projects in the
future. For much of his life he turned to alcohol and drugs to keep
away, or at least manage, the darkness that hung over him.

Depression and self-medication through alcohol have a statistically
significant incidence of comorbidity and Churchill was no exception.
His capacity for drink was legendary. Lord Moran struggled to limit
his intake, but concluded that there was little chance of reducing
it. When depressive episodes threatened to incapacitate Churchill
during the war years, when Britain could hardly afford to have its
leader out of commission, Moran agreed to prescribe amphetamine
to keep him functioning during the day and barbiturates to help him
sleep at night. Professor Richard Lovell, Moran's biographer,[33] identified these as quinalbarbitone tablets, which Churchill referred to as
'reds', and d-amphetamine sulphate, dubbed 'Morans' or 'Majors'.
According to Lovell, Moran 'believed that he had a rather negative
reputation with Churchill as what he called "a vendor of nostrums"'.[34]

The British leader's background of mental fragility, alcohol abuse
and medication helps explain the alternating moods he exhibited
during the 1942 Moscow summit, swinging from exhilarated optimism to gloom and back again. He did in fact turn up to dinner,
but dressed inappropriately in his trademark overall-like 'siren suit'. It
was a childish show of defiance, a two-finger gesture to the man who
had humiliated and harangued him.

Churchill told the doctor accompanying him, Sir Charles Wilson,
'I ought not to have come ... I am going to leave this man [Stalin]
to fight his own battles.'[35] Clark Kerr had to spend the following
morning persuading him not to abandon the mission, pointing out
that the Russians were crude and unrestrained in their language at
the best of times; Churchill would be wrong to take Stalin's remarks
too personally. He should use his charm to put things right; he, of all
people, had the power to 'nobble' Stalin.[36]

Churchill nodded his agreement. A final meeting was scheduled
for 7 p.m. in the Kremlin. It was 15 August, the last night of the visit and

the last chance to end the summit on a friendly note. Much depended on it, including the future tone of military and political cooperation between East and West. Churchill remained quietly angry; his parting remark as he left for the meeting was, 'I shall not leave the Kremlin until I have that man in my pocket.'[37]

The talks began in a large Kremlin conference room, in which the two leaders were alone with their translators. Churchill opened by thanking Stalin 'for all the courtesy and hospitality' and apologised for not bringing better news about Allied operations in the west.[38]

Stalin replied that 'the personal exchange of views' referred to by Churchill had been 'of the greatest importance ... the fact that we have met is of very great value'. There had been disagreements, said Stalin, but 'the ground has been prepared for future agreement'.[39]

Churchill was ready to leave, but Stalin detained him, asking when they would meet again. 'You are leaving at daybreak. Why should we not go to my house and have some drinks?' Churchill replied that he was 'in principle always in favour of such a policy'[40] and they walked through a late-night, deserted Kremlin to Stalin's apartment, where they were joined by Molotov and Stalin's daughter, Svetlana. When the British Foreign Office representative, Sir Alexander Cadogan, came looking for his boss at 1 a.m., he found a scene of inebriated jollity, 'as merry as a marriage bell'.[41] 'I think the two great men really made contact and got on terms. Certainly, Winston was impressed and I think that feeling was reciprocated ... Anyhow, conditions have been established in which messages exchanged between the two will mean twice as much, or more, than they did before.'[42]

Clark Kerr, with characteristically sardonic humour, described Churchill's glee on his return from the Kremlin.

> The P.M. began to chuckle and to kick a pair of gay legs in the air. I can't remember the words he used, but it had all been grand. He had cemented a friendship with Stalin. My God! he was glad that he had come. Stalin had been splendid. What a pleasure it was to work with 'that great man'. ... He was like that dog with two cocks.[43]

In the view of the British embassy's chief interpreter, Hugh Lunghi, it was the marathon Kremlin drinking session that changed Churchill's view of Stalin. Having excoriated him as a distant, impersonal enemy for nearly two decades, Churchill now saw him as man; and, more-over, a man with shared passions – love of country, personal sensitivity, sense of humour, fondness of late-night drinking.[44]

It doesn't take a psychologist to know that the empathy engendered by face-to-face human contact is the most powerful means to defuse prejudices or, on the contrary, to deceive a doubting interlocutor. As the nineteenth-century Russian writer Mikhail Lermontov wrote, 'We almost always forgive that which we think we understand.'[45] In Churchill's case, the belief that he *understood* Stalin would play a central role in judgements made at later conferences, crucially in Yalta, that would affect the course of the Cold War to follow the hot one.

4

YALTA AND THE PSYCHOLOGY
OF BETRAYAL

Churchill felt – or, at least, hoped – that the Moscow summit of 1942 had cemented a positive relationship with Stalin. He came to rely on the personal chemistry he sensed between them in the vital decisions America, Britain and the Soviet Union would be called upon to make about the future of the globe. The United Kingdom was no longer the international player it had once been; by creating a human bond with the man in the Kremlin, Churchill believed he could shore up London's role in determining that future.

The 1942 summit had ended in high spirits. Clark Kerr embellished the ribald text of his private journal with a ribald sketch of his delighted-looking boss, smoking a cigar and wearing only a skimpy vest that signally fails to preserve his modesty.[1]

In his more manic phases, it seems that Churchill did indeed appear before colleagues improperly dressed, failing at times to button his pyjama flies.* For Clark Kerr, it was all part of the scatological humour that characterised his relationship with the prime minister; and Churchill himself was happy to respond in kind. When, in the run-up to the Teheran Conference of November 1943, Clark

---

* In Jill Rose's *Nursing Churchill: Wartime Life from the Private Letters of Winston Churchill's Nurse* (Stroud: Amberley, 2018) Doris Miles speaks of him strolling down the corridor 'with only a towel around him'. Another of his nurses, Dorothy Pugh, records similar instances in her wartime diary. Terry Waite recalls, 'We had a conversation in which she [nurse Pugh] mentioned that she had been the Matron to Churchill. She told me that Churchill wore the pyjamas of that period with the open fly, which sometimes showed his private parts, and she would say, "Put it away, Winnie!" I feel they had a great closeness, God rest her soul.' Commenting in 'A Unique WWII Archive from Churchill's Nurse', 2 August 2016. blog.churchillbook-collector.com/uncategorized/a-unique-wwii-archive-from-churchills-nurse-2/.

Archibald Clark Kerr's sketch of the prime minister
leaves far too little to the imagination.

Kerr requested clearer guidance on British policy towards Russia, he got a sparky reply. 'You want a directive?' Churchill asked. 'All right: I don't mind kissing Stalin's bum, but I'm damned if I'll lick his arse!'[2]

The leitmotif references to bumsucking, bum kissing and arse licking could send a Freudian into rhapsodies of analytic ecstasy, and at the least suggest a shared argot born in the chummy dormitories of Britain's public schools. It is unlikely that a Soviet ambassador would have dared to make a drawing of Stalin with his pants down. Similar misdemeanours were enough to have others sent to the camps.* Stalin and his closest collaborators had developed their own

---

*Clark Kerr remained a connoisseur of risqué repartee, contributing to Foreign Office folklore later that year, when he wrote a plangent letter to his friend, Reginald, Lord Pembroke, bemoaning the tedium of being posted for so long in the grey wastelands of Moscow:

6th April 1943. My Dear Reggie,

In these dark days man tends to look for little shafts of light that spill from Heaven. My days are probably darker than yours, and I need, my God I do, all the light I can get. But I am a decent fellow, and I do not want to be mean and selfish about what little brightness is shed upon me from time to time. So I propose to share with you a tiny flash that has illuminated my sombre life and tell you that God has given me a new Turkish colleague whose card tells me that he is called Mustapha Kunt. We all feel like that, Reggie, now and then, especially when spring is upon us, but few of us would care to put it on our cards. It takes a Turk to do that. Yours, Archie.

common vernacular while in Siberian exile, taking part in a world-altering revolution and waging a civil war. It had little in common with that of the British or the Americans.

A reliance on personal psychology, and a belief in personal recognition and face-to-face friendship, persisted through the years of conflict. Churchill wrote that if he could just dine with Stalin once a week then 'all the difficulties would be capable of resolution'.[3] Franklin Roosevelt has been accused of sweeping political priorities under the carpet for the sake of short-term strategic unity, but the early conferences show that Churchill and, up to a point, Stalin were doing so before Roosevelt entered the equation. Ideological issues were put to one side and the relationship framed as a 'warrior alliance', overriding other considerations in the quest for victory. On his journey back from the tripartite Teheran Conference, on 1 December 1943, Churchill cabled the Foreign Office that, 'the greatest goodwill prevailed and for the first time we got on to easy and friendly terms. I feel that I have established a personal relationship which will be helpful.'[4]

Such was the trust in that personal relationship that on his next visit to Moscow, in October 1944, Churchill allowed himself to be drawn into Stalin's vision of the postwar world, agreeing the relative influence in percentage points that each side would have in Romania, Greece, Yugoslavia, Hungary and Bulgaria. Once the list was drawn up, Stalin read it, ticked it in blue pencil and handed it to Churchill to keep as a souvenir.[5] While still in Moscow, Churchill drafted a remarkable letter to Stalin (though he did not send it), expressing his own hopes for the future:

> Hitler has tried to exploit the fear of an aggressive, proselytising Communism which exists throughout Western Europe, and he is being decisively beaten to the ground. But, as you know well, this fear exists in every country, because, whatever the merits of our different systems, no country wishes to go through the bloody revolution which will certainly be necessary in nearly every case before so drastic a change could be made in the life,

---

Reported in 'Notebook: Diplomatic News, by Geoffrey Wheatcroft', *Spectator*, Vol. 240, issue 2, 1978, p. 5.

habits and outlook of their society … We have the feeling that, viewed from afar and on a grand scale, the differences between our systems will tend to get smaller, and the great common ground which we share of making life richer and happier for the mass of the people is growing every year. Probably if there were peace for fifty years the differences which now might cause such grave troubles to the world would become matters for academic discussion.[6]

Could this be the same Churchill who before June 1941 had declared communism to be on a par with Nazism, 'devoid of all theme and principle except appetite and racial domination'? It is perhaps not surprising that Stalin was wary of such a sea change. In a meeting with the Yugoslav communist Milovan Djilas, Stalin let rip with the suspicions that tormented him, announcing that 'there's nothing [the English] like better than to trick their allies … Churchill is the kind of man who will pick your pocket of a kopeck if you don't watch him.'[7]

Stalin's cynicism is unsurprising. His inherent distrust of foreign leaders had been exacerbated by his bungled dealings with Hitler. In the summer of 1941, Soviet intelligence had repeatedly warned him that German troops were massing on the border, preparing to abrogate the Nazi–Soviet pact that had hitherto kept them out of the war. Stalin refused to believe that Hitler would betray him and failed to prepare for the onslaught that ensued. He was determined not to be outmanoeuvred again, certainly not on the basis of a few shared drinks with Churchill.

When the three leaders met for dinner at the Teheran Conference, Stalin was intent on probing his fellow diners with tests of their character. Following the formal toasts and exchange of gifts, he spoke with apparent nonchalance about measures that would need to be taken after the (victorious) end of hostilities. It would be necessary, Stalin said, for the Allies to execute between 50,000 and 100,000 German officers, so that Germany could never again launch another war. Believing that Stalin was speaking in jest, Roosevelt replied that 'maybe 49,000 would be enough'. But Churchill took him seriously. He expressed outrage that Stalin should suggest 'the cold blooded execution of soldiers who fought for their country' instead of proper, impartial trials, and stormed out of the room. Only when Stalin said

Soviet wartime propaganda reflected the ephemeral united
front the Allies formed against the 'Fascist beast'.

he had been joking did Churchill agree to return and even then he felt
(correctly) that Stalin had been testing him.[8]

Where Churchill vacillated between optimism and despair,
unsure whether the Soviets needed comforting or confronting, Roosevelt took a more detached view. Aware of the paranoia that could
engulf the Kremlin, he went out of his way to convince Stalin that
there was no American–British plot against him.

There were suspicions and resentments between all three leaders,
not just between East and West. According to his son's memoirs,
Roosevelt was reluctant to alienate the Soviets, while his reported
remarks show him, equally, to be wary of British attempts to maintain their power in the world and unwilling to fight a war to prop up
'their archaic, medieval empire ideas … I hope they realised they're
not senior partner.'[9]

When Anthony Eden heard that Roosevelt was refusing to plan a coordinated strategy for handling Stalin in Yalta, he was appalled. He complained to Harry Hopkins that they were 'going into a decisive conference and had so far neither agreed what we would discuss nor how to handle matters with a Bear who would certainly know his mind'.[10]

William Hayter, at the time a rising star of the British Foreign Office, later to become Britain's ambassador in Moscow, was a perceptive observer of the psychological complexities that conditioned relations between the Big Three. The Americans, Hayter wrote, were hampered by a historical reluctance to cooperate with powers beyond their borders, deriving from 'George Washington's association of the pejorative adjective "entangling" with the concept of alliances': 'Foreigners are, of course, un-American. And to be un-American is, we all know, bad.'[11]

As for the Soviets, Hayter suggested that centuries of isolation from the world had made Moscow blinkered and unwilling to compromise. The handicaps of Soviet diplomacy were 'principally ideological', concerned with 'advancing a missionary creed ... on a scale and of an intensity which other diplomacies do not require'.[12]

> It never seems to occur to [the Russians] that the proper object of a negotiation is not to defeat your opposite number but to arrive at an agreement with him which will be mutually beneficial ... Dealing with the Soviet Ministry of Foreign Affairs may be compared to dealing with an old-fashioned penny-in-the-slot machine. You put in the penny – your question – and in the end, probably, you will get something out; perhaps not what you wanted, an acid drop when you hoped for chocolate, but something; and you can sometimes expedite the process by shaking the machine. It is, however, useless to talk to it.[13]

Hayter concluded, perhaps unsurprisingly, that 'British diplomacy is the best'. But he acknowledged that in the straitened circumstances of 1945, Britain needed the cooperation of international allies and one of the priorities of the wartime conferences was to secure it.[14]

With twenty-first-century hindsight, it appears that the Big Three viewed each other through national psychological stereotypes. The British suspected Roosevelt of being too trusting and open, verging

on the naive; Stalin was convinced that British courtesy and recti-
tude was a cover for deceitful double dealing; and both Churchill and
Roosevelt were aghast at the Soviets' unrelenting insistence on confrontation. As with most stereotypes, there is a superficial truth in
such interpretations; the challenge was to see the reasons behind the
behaviour and, where appropriate, make allowances for them.

Stalin's mistrust of foreigners reflected injustices inflicted on
Russia in the past; but it also embodied a national and personal sense
of inferiority before the polished, self-confident West. Stalin was an
adroit statesman with a powerful memory, inexhaustible tenacity and
quick-thinking reactions, but he was deeply insecure. His daughter
Svetlana described his inner life as one of 'spiritual devastation and
bitterness'.[15] His inner rage found expression in crudity, defiance and
aggression. He disdained the etiquette of polite discussion and his
style was copied by those around him. Niceties and subtleties were
not the priority; demands were repeated and repeated until results
were obtained.

Stalin's insecurities found expression in defiant sneering, intended
to demonstrate that although Russians may be uncivilised, they
make fearsome enemies.* It was rumoured that Stalin carried in his
pocket a copy of the foul-mouthed reply sent by seventeenth-century
Cossacks to the Ottoman Emperor's ultimatum demanding their surrender. 'O sultan, Turkish devil and damned devil's kin that canst not
slay a hedgehog with his naked arse,' the Cossacks wrote.

> The devil shits, and your army eats. Thou shalt not, thou son
> of a whore, make subjects of Christian sons; we have no fear
> of you. Thou goat-fucker of Alexandria, swineherd of Egypt,
> pig of Armenia and fool of all the world; idiot before God, the
> crick in our dick; pig's snout, mare's arse – go screw thine own
> mother! The Zaporozhe Cossacks declare, You can kiss our arse!

---

* It was a common attitude. The poet Sergei Yesenin, visiting Paris in 1922, wrote:
'Even if we Russians are poor, even if we do have famine and cold and cannibal-
ism, yet we also have a soul, which people here hire out to others as something
unwanted. Even if we are Asiatics, even if we are foul-smelling and scratch our
backsides in public, yet we do not stink as much as it stinks here. The only thing
that can save the West is an invasion of barbarians such as ourselves. Russia should
prepare itself for an invasion of Europe!' M. Sixsmith, *An Unquiet Heart*, London:
Simon & Schuster, 2019, p. 410.

After difficult negotiations with the British, Stalin is said to have pulled the Cossacks' riposte from his pocket and declared, 'We sure screwed those English!'[16]

The Soviets perceived western representatives through an equally distorting lens of prejudice and stereotype. They were upper-class, deceitful capitalists, untrustworthy and bent on self-interest. 'They may strangle one,' said Andrei Gromyko about western diplomats, 'but they will do so wearing kid gloves, with a smile, almost gently.'[17] Stalin himself expressed his contempt for the practitioners of international diplomacy at an early stage of his career, a view that was reinforced by his subsequent dealings with the West.

> When a Minister of Foreign Affairs begins to wax eloquent in favour of a 'peace conference', you can take it for granted that 'his government' has already issued contracts for the construction of new dreadnoughts and monoplanes. A diplomat's words *must* contradict his deeds – otherwise, what sort of a diplomat is he? ... A sincere diplomat is like dry water, or wooden iron.[18]

Suspicion and counter-suspicion; prejudice and misapprehensions. Such was the tangled psychological framework in which the three nations approached the second, pivotal meeting of the war, where the future of central Europe would be decided and decisions made that would cause rancour and resentment for decades. By February 1945, the conflict had turned decisively in the Allies' favour. The Red Army had triumphed at Stalingrad and Kursk and driven the Germans from Soviet territory; the British and Americans had pushed forward from the beaches of Normandy; the Battle of Berlin was approaching. Decisions taken at previous conferences had been made more in hope than expectation. Now they would have the weight of measures that would become reality.

The venue for the conference was the Black Sea resort of Yalta. The Germans had been expelled from Crimea only ten months earlier and the region had not recovered from the devastation of the fighting. With a nod to the fickle hand of history, Stalin had chosen the Livadia Palace, a former holiday estate of Nicholas II and his family, as the main conference location. Other former royal palaces, transformed into workers' sanatoria under the Bolsheviks, were allocated

to accommodate the delegations. The Soviets were billeted in the
Yusupov Palace, the British in the Vorontsov and the Americans in
the Livadia itself, to save the ailing, wheelchair-bound Roosevelt from
having to travel to plenary sessions. As the Germans had plundered
or burned most of the fittings, the Soviet air force had to fly in new
furniture, new carpets and curtains, door handles and even wallpaper.
Two thousand workers were assigned to repair the damage.[19]

From the opening session, on 4 February 1945, the leaders
engaged in psychological skirmishes, some petty, others with potentially world-altering consequences, a pattern that would be repeated
throughout the Cold War. The pre-war order of importance had been
clear, but in 1945 it was no longer set in stone: each of the leaders
was staking a claim to influence in the postwar world. On the first
morning, Stalin made a point of arriving late. According to Rostislav
Sergeev, a Soviet diplomat at the conference, it was done deliberately
'to set the tone' and let the others know who was boss.

Of the two western leaders, Churchill had done the most to
create a working relationship with the Soviets. His two visits to
Moscow had given him an insight into the workings of the Kremlin
and, he thought, the character of the Soviet leader. But Stalin knew
that Britain was a fading force and that Roosevelt was the key to the
future. He went out of his way to treat the American president with
deference, demonstratively showing him more respect than he did to
Churchill.

Roosevelt was aware of the sensitivities of the situation. He styled
himself as an honest broker, attempting to balance the demands of
the British and the Soviets. Roosevelt wanted to trust Stalin; Churchill
was America's ally, but the two countries did not share all the same
postwar aims; Stalin sensed the tension between the Anglo-Saxons
and was aware that Churchill was pressing Roosevelt to take London's side against Moscow. The personal relationships were complex.
Suspicion hung over the conference.

'The impression was that Stalin was better disposed towards
Roosevelt than he was towards Churchill,' wrote Cold War historian
Vladimir Pechatnov.

But, for all the antipathies and difficulties, [the three leaders] felt
they knew what to expect from each other. It was in their interest to preserve a situation in which all things could be agreed on

this personal basis. In Yalta, Stalin had good reason to declare, 'As long as we three are alive, we need not fear for the future, for we shall not allow dangerous divisions to appear between us!' There was an element of rhetoric in Stalin's claim, but there can be no doubt that the factor of personal relations was one of great importance.[20]

As well as personal relations, personal capacities – and incapacities – played a part. Roosevelt was ill, confined to a wheelchair and at times struggling to follow the complexities of the proceedings. He said little and relied on advice from his officials. Churchill, on the other hand, spoke at great length. According to the US general Laurence Kuter, who sat with Roosevelt, 'Stalin spoke with simple unquestionable finality. In watching and listening to him, one had no doubt that he was the authority, but also no clue in his stature or deportment to how he obtained that authority.'[21] Hugh Lunghi, translating for Churchill, was equally struck by Stalin's powerful presence. 'He was very brief in what he said, so you had to catch it quickly. He didn't like being asked to repeat anything. Or if Churchill or someone was going on for rather a long time, then paused slightly before continuing, he'd chip in and say "Is that all?", so that the person would stop talking.'[22]

The formal photographs from the Livadia Palace, so familiar to postwar generations, reflect something of this in the body language of the participants. Churchill appears animated and not totally at ease; Roosevelt, lifted from his wheelchair for the group portraits, looks anxious, his legs atrophied, fingers bent around a cigarette. But Stalin is the master of proceedings. He sits four-square, staring confidently ahead, betraying no need to look to others for reassurance.

Stalin had good reason to feel confident. In the weeks before the conference, Soviet intelligence had supplied him with copies of the British strategy documents for the meeting. It meant Stalin knew London's aims and weaknesses, and he knew the negotiating strategy Churchill planned to adopt. Correspondence between Churchill and Roosevelt, provided by the Cambridge spies Guy Burgess and Donald Maclean, revealed the western Allies' disagreements about the postwar Europe they wanted to see. Forewarned, forearmed, Stalin held the psychological advantage and used it to decisive effect.[23]

He knew, in particular, that the Americans and British were unsure

At Yalta, Stalin projected the calm, focused confidence of a man
who knew exactly what Churchill and Roosevelt had in mind.

about the solidity of their alliance and divided on their postwar aims.
And he knew that the British feared Soviet military might enough to
avoid confrontation on some of the key divisive issues that would
arise. The minutes of Churchill's War Cabinet Post-Hostilities
Planning Sub-Committee on 6 June 1944, revealed long afterwards,
concluded that Britain should make 'a real endeavour to secure the
full and friendly participation of the USSR in any system of world
security,' in furtherance of which, 'we should not oppose any reasonable demands of the USSR where they do not conflict with our vital
strategic interests'.[24]

The Soviets were in no doubt of their own priorities. The proposed means of achieving them had been set out a year earlier in a
document titled 'On the desirable foundations for the future'. Written
by Ivan Maisky, former ambassador to the United Kingdom and now
a deputy foreign minister, it set itself the daunting task of establishing
'the desired future of the world'.

Top Secret. Note from Deputy People's Commissar
for Foreign Affairs of the USSR, I. M. Maisky

I briefly summarize thoughts on the basic elements of the
desired future of the world:

1. The overall aim: It is necessary for Soviet Union to ensure peace in Europe and in Asia for a period of 30–50 years.
2. In accordance with the above, USSR should come out of this war with strategically advantageous borders, the basis of which should be the borders of 1941.[25]

Maisky does not say it, but the 'strategically advantageous' borders of 1941 were the result of Moscow's pact with Hitler. The German–Soviet Border and Commercial Agreement of January 1941 had confirmed the de facto division of Europe between Germany and the USSR, with the Soviets gaining the Baltic States and the eastern part of Poland.

The strategically advantageous borders negotiated by Stalin had gone out of the window in June 1941 when Hitler launched Operation Barbarossa. Now, with Allied victory in sight, Moscow viewed Yalta as an opportunity to reinstate lost advantages. 'In postwar Europe,' Maisky concluded, 'there must remain just one mighty land power – the USSR, and only one strong naval power – Britain.'[26]

If Stalin went to Yalta believing he could foment such discord between the western Allies that London would come running to Moscow, he was misguided. While it was true that Roosevelt and Churchill did not always see eye to eye, only a blinkered Marxist could convince himself that the West could so easily be split. Maisky was more realistic about the potential dangers of a cold war succeeding the hot one.

> Between the USSR and the United States lie two oceans. This makes our country relatively invulnerable even to American aviation, at least in the first postwar period. If there are any sharp contradictions between the USSR and the United States in the more distant future, however, America could create many serious challenges for the Soviet Union … They could also begin to assemble an anti-Soviet bloc in Europe.[27]

In response, Maisky wrote, Moscow must become a rallying point for the rival pole of Cold War ideology, with 'the transformation of the USSR into a centre of attraction for all genuinely democratic medium and small countries, and genuinely democratic elements in all countries, especially in Europe'. To do so effectively, the USSR would need

friendly states on its western borders, the biggest and strategically
most important of these being Poland. Under Soviet plans, Polish
lands in the east, long disputed between Warsaw and Moscow, would
be ceded to the USSR, while former German lands in the west would
be tagged onto Poland's western borders. The whole of the resulting
state would be drawn into the Soviet sphere of domination. Churchill
was determined to secure Polish independence: as the Yalta Conference approached, it was clear that the question of Poland would be
divisive. The issue dominated the conference; it was debated at seven
of the eight plenary sessions[28] and the outcome would have a decisive
influence on the postwar world order.

With the benefit of his intelligence reports, Stalin knew that
Poland was not Roosevelt's priority. The Americans' key aims were
to get the Soviets to join the war against Japan and to ratify the creation of an international body that would become the United Nations.
Stalin sensed he could play Churchill and Roosevelt against each
other, hoping to leave Churchill isolated.

Churchill spoke of Britain's moral obligation to the Poles: 'That is
how we started the war and we are committed to a democratic, free,
and strong Poland.'[29] But for Stalin, the USSR's security depended
on a pro-Soviet Poland to act as a buffer against the risk of future
invasion; he could hardly allow the historically anti-Russian Poles the
freedom to undermine it. He countered that for the Soviets, Poland
was a question of honour *and* of security.

Churchill and Stalin were using the same terms – honour, security, freedom – but they were speaking different languages. And each
was backing a different Polish government. Churchill championed
the Polish government in exile, pre-war ministers and politicians who
had taken refuge in London. But Stalin had set up an alternative Polish
government, dominated by communists, based in the Soviet-liberated
Polish city of Lublin. Churchill forced the issue. 'If we separate still recognising different Polish Governments,' he declared, 'the whole world
will see that fundamental differences between us still exist ... If the Conference is to brush aside the existing London Government and lend all
its weight to the Lublin Government there will be a world outcry.'[30]

Stalin did not blink. Buoyed by his understanding that Roosevelt
would not go to the wall over Poland, he stood his ground. In a show
of magnanimity, Stalin agreed that the Lublin government could be
broadened to include non-communist representatives from within

Vast quantities of tobacco and alcohol helped soothe nerves
during often tense deliberations over the world's future.

Poland or living abroad, creating a provisional government of national
unity. Elections could be held as soon as possible, preferably within a
month or two. But, in a harbinger of what was to come, he rejected
out of hand Churchill's suggestion that these should be overseen by
the Great Powers to ensure fairness.[31] With only lukewarm backing
from Roosevelt, Churchill was not going to win the argument.

The import of Stalin's victory at Yalta was to leave Poland in
thrall. The bitterness it created endured for decades. When I arrived
to live in Warsaw in 1986 I found it a byword for acrimonious betrayal.
'Yalta' would be spat out as if it were a swearword. In the America
of McCarthyism and anti-communist witch-hunts, Yalta was cited as

proof that accommodating the Soviet Union led to ineluctable disaster. A *Time* magazine cover of 1951 called the conference a 'milestone on the road to lost peace'.[32] In reality, the division of Europe was more or less a fait accompli determined by the forces on the ground. It would have been impossible to remove the Red Army from land they had conquered. But western opinion came to think of Yalta as an act of appeasement on a par with Munich.*

The conference moved towards its conclusion with none of the three leaders completely satisfied, but with Stalin having achieved most of his objectives. In toasts at the farewell dinner in the Yusupov Palace, Churchill spoke of the atmosphere of friendship and intimacy and praised Stalin as a great conqueror. But he struck a note of warning, expressing the hope that the fruits of victory would not be thrown away in 'the troubles that follow ... wars. I must say that never in this war have I felt the responsibility weigh so heavily on me, even in the darkest hours, as now during this Conference ... Do not let us underestimate the difficulties. Nations, comrades in arms, have in the past drifted apart within five or ten years of war.'[33] Stalin's response was a masterclass in sincere insincerity. He had spent much of the conference deceiving his fellow participants; now he laboured the protestations of his own honesty.

> I am talking as an old man; that is why I am talking so much. But I want to drink to our alliance, that it should not lose its character of intimacy, of its free expression of views. In the history of diplomacy I know of no such close alliance of three Great Powers as this, when allies had the opportunity of so frankly expressing their views. I know that some circles will regard this remark as naive.[34]

Linguistic psychologists have a concept known as 'face'. It distinguishes between the words someone speaks (the semantic or informational

---

* Churchill himself knew he had lost out to Stalin. He would later defend himself in vain before the House of Commons, 'I repudiate any suggestion that we are making a questionable compromise or yielding to force or fear. The Poles will have their future in their own hands, with the single limitation that they must honestly follow a policy friendly to Russia. That is surely reasonable. I know of no government which stands to its obligations more solidly than the Russian Soviet Government.'

content of an utterance) and the unspoken emotional impact with which the speaker loads them (their social-emotive import).[35] Positive face reflects a wish to be accepted and liked by others; negative face indicates an intention to act in a way that might not meet approval.[36] The language used by Stalin in the continuation of his seemingly improvised speech manifests both of these. His repeated insistence on his own naivety suggests that, like Gertrude in *Hamlet*, he really doth protest too much.

> Experienced diplomatists may say, 'Why should I not deceive my ally?' But I as a naive man think it best not to deceive my ally even if he is a fool. Possibly our alliance is so firm just because we do not deceive each other; or is it because it is not so easy to deceive each other? ... May [our alliance] be strong and stable; may we be as frank as possible![37]

Stalin was far from 'naive'; and he had been anything but 'frank'. In the extract quoted above, his veiled but evidently inimical semantic content is an example of negative face; his repeated claims not to be a deceiver dare his interlocutors to challenge the blatant implausibility of his words. Churchill, characterised by Eden as 'liking to talk, but not to listen', seemed willing to overlook the disconnect in Stalin's words for the sake of Allied harmony.

> There was a time when the Marshal was not so kindly towards us, and I remember that I said a few rude things about him, but our common dangers and common loyalties have wiped all that out. The fire of war has burnt up the misunderstandings of the past. We feel we have a friend whom we can trust, and I hope he will continue to feel the same about us.[38]

With the three leaders willing, at least publicly, to play down their differences and pledging to continue their wartime cooperation, the prospects for postwar discord seemed remote. Churchill was in celebratory mood; according to Alexander Cadogan, 'drinking buckets of Caucasian champagne which would undermine the health of any ordinary man'. And the mood spread to the rank and file. British, American and Soviet sailors who had come to Yalta with their national delegations fraternised in the bars and cafés. Captain Mikhail Kruk of the Russian navy was among those instructed to mingle with the foreigners in the fashionable Hotel Crimea, and saw that it was possible to get on with these representatives of the capitalist West.

> We had everything you could ask for on tap. Champagne, cognac, food to eat … We talked away with the Brits and the Americans – no politics; just about women, being at sea, the great life we all had; that sort of thing. We didn't really speak each other's language, so we were waving our hands around so much that they ached. It was a marvellous time. I liked the Americans best, because the British didn't really loosen up. They were always a bit stiff and a bit up themselves. The Americans were more like us – more open, less reserved; lots of arm wrestling, that sort of thing.[39]

But for all the positive talk, the legacy of Yalta would be divisive. The leaders of the capitalist and socialist worlds may have thought they understood each other, but they remained in large measure incapable of seeing things through the other's eyes. On 13 February 1945, British and American bombers began the firebombing of Dresden, and within forty-eight hours the city and much of its industry were wiped out. According to Soviet diplomat Rostislav Sergeev, the Kremlin perceived the bombing – coming so soon after the Yalta celebrations – as an act hostile to the USSR.

> For seven days [at Yalta], we had discussed the postwar arrangements in Europe, and only one issue caused serious disagreement – the question of reparations from Germany. Stalin insisted that Germany must compensate us for all our material losses, to the tune of ten billion dollars. Churchill leapt up out of his seat and spoke very sharply. A heated argument broke out. Stalin yelled that Churchill did not know what he was talking about and who he was talking to – he was talking to the victors [the USSR]! There was, as they say, a sharp exchange of views … By the end of the conference, things were mended. Everyone laughed and drank together. But the Allies soon revealed their dissatisfaction with the agreements they had signed and the true colours of their attitude towards the USSR. They did it within a day. Between 13 and 15 February, they 'wiped Dresden from the face of the earth' – and with it, vast quantities of the industry

and materiel that the Yalta accords had just agreed would go the Soviet Union.[40]

A month after the Dresden raids, relations between East and West were further undermined in what again appears to have been a misunderstanding, amplified by mutual distrust. At the end of February 1945, with the Nazis facing defeat, SS General Karl Wolff, the commander of German forces in Italy, contacted American officials to ask if they would negotiate a local surrender and ceasefire. Talks took place in Switzerland in early to mid March between Wolff and Allen Dulles, an OSS (Office of Strategic Services) agent, later to become Director of the CIA. US and British military commanders were involved in the meetings, but the Soviets were not. The Kremlin leapt to the conclusion that the western Allies were manoeuvring to reach a separate peace with the Germans, in which the USSR's interests would not be represented.

It seems in retrospect that the Wolff meeting was deliberately instigated by the Germans to sow dissension between the Allies. It nearly worked. On 3 April 1945, Stalin wrote to Roosevelt accusing the West of pursuing a deal under which the Germans would permit western forces to advance to the east, thus allowing the British and Americans to occupy Germany before the Red Army could get there.[41] '[This affair] has developed an atmosphere of fear and distrust ... Why was it necessary to conceal this from Russians, and why were your allies, the Russians, not notified? ... I would never have taken such a step.'[42]

Churchill wrote to Stalin to say that Britain was 'astonished and affronted' by the 'most wounding and unfounded charges' made by the Kremlin.[43] The back-slapping of Yalta, just six weeks earlier, had given way to renewed acrimony.

The Wolff affair illustrated how quickly the tone of personal discourse between the three leaders deteriorated. After the Yalta Conference, it had ultimately seemed that the three-way alliance was solid, with a genuine commitment to peaceful coexistence. As individuals, they had been able to forge an understanding, at times even displaying affection for one another. But as representatives of opposing systems, each with their own inherited values and psychological frameworks, they struggled to truly understand how the other viewed the world. Within a few months, suspicions and recriminations would escalate until hot war was replaced by Cold.

5

POTSDAM AND PARANOIA

In the mid 1970s, when I was a student in Russia, state television showed war films on two evenings every week with an extra one at weekends. The Second World War had left hardly a family untouched, and the obsession with the conflict was deep seated and long lasting.

But *Seventeen Moments of Spring* stood out. It was a war story that became a classic, with a plot involving espionage, deceit and suspicion among the Allies. Its hero, played by the handsome Vyacheslav Tikhonov, is a Soviet agent who has infiltrated the German High Command. Known to the Nazis as Max Otto von Stierlitz, his task is to report on Axis military plans. In early 1945, Stierlitz finds out about an approach the Germans are making to conclude a separate peace with the British and Americans. If successful, it would leave the Nazis free to concentrate all their firepower against the Red Army, while the western Allies would take possession of central and eastern Europe. Stierlitz learns that the German Karl Wolff and the American Allen Dulles are plotting together in Switzerland. Stierlitz risks his life to expose their machinations. It seems that he will be betrayed and executed, but he manages to foil the plot and avert the danger to the Soviet Union.

The series, which ends with Red Army troops advancing on Berlin, was a sensation. Eighty million people watched it, with the surge in electricity consumption as TVs were switched on forcing power stations to increase their output; streets would empty and the crime rate drop. For decades afterwards, *Seventeen Moments* would be re-broadcast annually on Soviet, then Russian television; Leonid Brezhnev is said to have watched it twenty times, postponing politburo meetings so as not to miss an episode. To this day, songs from the series are heard on the radio and nearly all Russians know its most famous quotes.

'The alcohol went straight to his head.' Stierlitz, played by
Vyacheslav Tikhonov, was the embodiment of a Soviet spy in the
Second World War, as seen from the 1960s. He defeated the Nazis,
while simultaneously foiling the duplicitous western allies.

It may seem odd that one of the greatest Soviet war movies was about
betrayal by the USSR's allies. But *Seventeen Moments* came out at the
height of the Cold War, when mistrust of the West was at its sharp-
est and Soviet culture was engaged in an exploration of its origins.
The official Soviet line was to lay the responsibility squarely at the
West's door, but Russian historians even then accepted, in private at
least, that Moscow had not been without blame.[1] Much of the suspicion had stemmed from the character of the man at the top. By the
time of the late war conferences, Stalin was convinced that both sides
would take any opportunity to gain the upper hand. If he, Stalin,
were capable of infiltrating, spying on and undermining the West,
then the West *must* be doing the same to him, he assumed: a classic
example of projection.

Soviet intelligence reports, some accurate, others exaggerated,
deepened Stalin's mistrust. His responses grew increasingly vehe-
ment. He made threats that were in turn viewed by the West as
disproportionate and antagonistic. The self-amplifying cycle of antip-
athy pushed Washington and London towards the very hostility that

Stalin had begun by imagining in them. Psychological isolation and suspicion of others nudged him into obsession. 'He was depressed by his aloneness,' Nikita Khrushchev said, 'and he feared it.'

The British seemed genuinely nonplussed. Recalling Stalin's insistent suspicions about the Rudolf Hess affair (see Chapter 3), Churchill at first dismissed the Soviet leader's paranoia as an aberration: 'Remembering what a wise man [Stalin] is, I was surprised to find him silly on this point.'[2] In the month after Yalta, Archibald Clark Kerr played down Moscow's growing mistrust against the West in a dispatch to his boss, Anthony Eden, writing:

> The Soviet Union tends to disport herself like a retriever puppy in somebody else's drawing room. We must expect her thus to rampage until she feels that she is secure from any unpleasant surprises in neighbouring countries, and then we may, I think, foresee that she will emerge from her puppydom and settle down to the serious and respectable business of collaboration with her major allies.[3]

Despite the smug tone of the missive, London evidently understood that much of the Soviets' behaviour was the result of genuine concern about the safety of their borders.

Poland would quickly re-emerge as a bone of contention. When London and Washington expressed concern about Soviet intentions, Stalin was quick to cry foul. 'You evidently do not agree that the Soviet Union is entitled to seek in Poland a Government that would be friendly to it,' he wrote in April 1945.

> I cannot understand why in discussing Poland no attempt is made to consider the interests of the Soviet Union in terms of security. One cannot but recognise as unusual a situation in which two Governments – those of the United States and Great Britain – reach agreement beforehand on Poland, a country in which the U.S.S.R. is interested first of all and most of all, and place its representatives in an intolerable position, trying to dictate to it.[4]

In an act of undisguised coercion, Stalin ordered the arrest of the leaders of Poland's Armia Krajowa (AK), the non-communist resistance that had fought heroically to free their homeland from the Nazis. Because Stalin recognised only the communist resistance movement, the Armia Ludowa, he tarred the AK with false accusations of collaborationism and anti-Soviet sabotage. Sixteen of its senior commanders were imprisoned in the Lubyanka, tortured, and made to sign false confessions. Of the twelve found guilty, several would die in Soviet jails.

Stalin was pushing at the boundaries of western compliance, testing the willingness of its leaders to stand up to aggression in the new era that was dawning. Churchill could no longer dismiss Stalin's behaviour as harmless. He wrote to him with a stark warning of the future that would emerge from a breakdown in East–West trust.

> There is not much comfort in looking into a future where you and the countries you dominate, plus the Communist Parties in many other States, are all drawn up on one side, and those who rally to the English-speaking nations and their associates or Dominions are on the other. It is quite obvious that their quarrel would tear the world to pieces, and that all of us leading men on either side who had anything to do with that would be shamed before history.[5]

By now Churchill was aware of Stalin's personal touchiness and did his best to assuage it.

> I hope there is no word or phrase in this outpouring of my heart to you which unwittingly gives offence. If so, let me know. But do not, I beg you, my friend Stalin, underrate the divergences which are opening about matters which you may think are small to us but which are symbolic of the way the English-speaking democracies look at life.[6]

Symbolic divergences encapsulated the growing resentment between the sides. The western Allies announced that they would celebrate VE (Victory in Europe) Day on 8 May each year. The Soviets replied that since the German surrender was signed at 11 p.m., when it was already the following day in Moscow, they would celebrate it on the 9th. Four days after the end of hostilities, Churchill wrote to the new man in the White House, Harry Truman.

What is to happen about Russia? I have always worked for
friendship with Russia, but, like you, I feel deep anxiety because
of their misrepresentations of the Yalta decisions, their attitude
towards Poland ... the combination of Russian power and the
territories under their control ... and above all their power to
maintain very large armies in the field for a long time ... An
iron curtain* is drawn down upon their front. We do not know
what is going on behind ... the issue of a settlement with Russia
before our strength is gone seems to me to dwarf all others.[7]

Truman had been thrust into the presidency less than a month earlier,
following the death of Franklin Roosevelt on 12 April 1945. The exertions of the trip to Yalta had weakened his predecessor's already
fragile health. On 1 March, he had been pushed onto the floor of the
US Congress in a wheelchair to give his report on the conference. He
said his long journey had left him tired, but dismissed rumours of his
poor health. He felt 'refreshed and inspired', ready to make the 'great
decisions' that lay ahead. He was looking ahead to the end of the war
and the plans he was promoting for an international body that would
become the United Nations.

The founding conference of the UN had been fixed for 25 April,
but Roosevelt would not live to see it. On 29 March, he went to his
country retreat at Warm Springs in Georgia. In the early afternoon of
Thursday 12 April, he was sitting for a portrait by the artist Elizabeth
Shoumatoff when he mumbled, 'I have a terrific headache', and fell
forward from his chair. The president was dead of a cerebral haemorrhage at the age of sixty-three.

In the years after his death, Roosevelt's character was subjected to
revisionist scrutiny that did not enhance his posthumous reputation.
Critics who blamed him for the West's failure to halt Soviet expansionism and the subsequent onset of the Cold War sought out his

---

* This seems to be Churchill's first use of the term 'iron curtain'. He would use it
again, famously, in his Fulton, Missouri, speech the following March. But it had
already been used by the Russian philosopher Vasily Rozanov to describe the cata-
clysm of the 1917 Bolshevik revolution: 'With a clank, a squeal and a groan, an
iron curtain has descended over Russian history: the show is over, the audience has
risen. It's time for people to put on their coats and go home. But when they look
around they see there are no coats any more, and no more homes.'

Critics were convinced FDR's weakened physical state, clearly
visible during his final State of the Union Address in January
1945, enabled Stalin to outmanoeuvre him at Yalta.

psychological flaws. FDR was undoubtedly sick at the time of the
Yalta Conference and there were suggestions that he had allowed
Stalin to seize the advantage because of his illness. But eyewitnesses
at the negotiating table reported that this was not the case. Charles
E. Bohlen, the US diplomat who served as Roosevelt's interpreter,
wrote, 'While his physical state was certainly not up to normal, his
mental and psychological state was certainly not affected ... Our
leader was ill at Yalta ... but he was effective.'[8]

So, if Roosevelt was well enough to know what he was doing, did
he demonstrate personal naivety – or an overly sympathetic view of
Soviet socialism – in allowing Stalin to get his way? Sir Frank Roberts,

later to become the British ambassador in Moscow, thought that 'Roosevelt and Churchill were susceptible to Stalin because he did not fit the dictator stereotype of the time. He was not a demagogue; he did not strut in flamboyant uniforms. He was soft-spoken, well organized, not without humour, knew his brief – an agreeable façade concealing unknown horrors.'[9] According to Arthur Schlesinger, the Democratic adviser and White House insider, Roosevelt 'responded to what he saw of Soviet behaviour in the world, and he never saw very far into the Soviet Union. Always an optimist, he hoped that the wartime alliance would bridge the ideological chasm and create a new reality for the peace. Even with the benefit of hindsight, this still seems a hope worth testing.'[10]

Schlesinger gave the president the benefit of the doubt,* but others were less forgiving. Charles Bohlen described Roosevelt as weak, failing to support Churchill's more realistic assessment that Moscow had to be confronted with strength. 'His apparent belief that ganging up on the Russians was to be avoided at all cost was, in my mind, a basic error stemming from Roosevelt's lack of understanding of the Bolsheviks … In his rather transparent attempt to dissociate himself from Churchill, the President was not fooling anybody and in all probability aroused the secret amusement of Stalin.'[11] The revisionist assessment of Roosevelt's character would grow as the Cold War escalated: by 1960, George Kennan, the deputy head of the US Mission in Moscow, would write that Roosevelt's assumption that Stalin would melt if 'exposed to the charm of a personality of FDR's caliber' was 'so childish that it was really unworthy of a statesman of FDR's standing'.[12] The new man in the White House seemed intent on reversing his predecessor's policy of accommodation. Beginning with the Potsdam Conference of July 1945, Harry S. Truman was willing to talk tough.

---

* Roosevelt himself argued that his emollient approach to Stalin was not born of weakness. It was, rather, a means to an end – the establishment of a lasting international order that would ensure America's leading role in global politics, without attracting accusations of coercion. He spelled this out in his fourth and final inaugural address in January 1945: 'We have learned the simple truth, as Emerson said, that "the only way to have a friend is to be one". We can gain no lasting peace if we approach it with suspicion and mistrust or with fear.' Franklin D. Roosevelt, 'The Fourth Inaugural Address', Washington DC, 20 January 1945. avalon.law.yale. edu/20th_century/froos4.asp.

The choice of Potsdam, a leafy suburb of Berlin, for the final summit of the wartime Allies was redolent with history. Churchill arrived on 16 July to find a city that 'was nothing but a chaos of ruins'.[13] It was his first chance to meet Truman, and the prime minister wrote that he was 'impressed with his gay, precise, sparkling manner and obvious power of decision',[14] a pointed contrast with the irresolute, debilitated Roosevelt. '[Truman] invited personal friendship and comradeship and used many expressions at intervals in our discussions that I could not easily hear unmoved. I felt that here was a man of exceptional character and ability ... simple and direct methods of speech, and a great deal of self-confidence and resolution.'[15]

Churchill and Truman made separate tours of the defeated city, shepherded by Russian minders through the ruins of the Reichstag and Hitler's bunker. It was Stalin's way of impressing on them that it was he who had conquered Berlin and that possession was ten-tenths of the law. Seeing the suffering of the German people seems to have softened Churchill, perhaps with half an eye on the looming rivalry with the Soviet Union. 'In the square in front of the Chancellery there was a considerable crowd. When I got out of the car and walked about among them, except for one old man who shook his head disapprovingly, they all began to cheer. My hate had died with their surrender and I was much moved by their demonstrations.'[16]

Stalin, never well disposed towards Churchill, had been watching with keen interest the general election that was being held in the UK. Results were expected the following week and Churchill's fate hung in the balance. At a private dinner on 18 July, Stalin played down the prospects of the Labour Party, despite its decidedly socialist manifesto, and expressed the hope that Churchill would be re-elected.

Perhaps liberated by the sense that his days in power were numbered, perhaps emboldened by a piece of news that he and Truman were expecting from Allied scientists in the New Mexican desert, Churchill enunciated the fear that was haunting the West – that, far from supporting freedom in Europe, Stalin was spreading communist domination ever further westwards, by political oppression or, in the worst scenario, the continued advance of the Red Army. Stalin's response was a mixture of bluff and lies.

> Stalin said ... On the contrary, he was withdrawing troops from the West. Two million men would be demobilised and sent

home within the next four months. Further demobilisation was only a question of sufficient railway transport ... He said that Russia was ready to talk about trade with Britain. I said that the best publicity for Soviet Russia abroad would be the happiness and well-being of her people.[17]

Despite occasional outbursts, the meeting at Yalta had been conducted in an atmosphere of goodwill. Potsdam, according to Hugh Lunghi, was 'a bad-tempered conference'.[18] The alliance of personalities, the human glue that held things together when politics were tearing them asunder, was dissolving. Roosevelt was dead; within a few days Churchill would be out of office, replaced by Clement Attlee. By the end of the Potsdam gathering, only Stalin would remain from the wartime Big Three leaders.

To Soviet ears, western concerns over the fate of eastern Europe sounded hypocritical, points of contention artificially manufactured to put Moscow on the back foot. Stalin was worried about the future security of the Soviet Union – he admitted as much – but there is no indication that he felt he was reneging on the agreements he had made at Teheran and Yalta. Had he and Churchill not agreed a division of Europe? Had they not written it down at their meeting in October 1944? Had Churchill not kept the list as a souvenir?*

Stalin's deep-seated mistrust, frequently and not always accurately described as paranoia, made him quick to lose faith in people and in the promises they made.[19] His response was to convince himself that he was better, and almost certainly smarter, than they were; he was convinced that he could see through his deceivers and that he must play them at their own game. He needed to believe – and seemingly did believe – that he held enough cards to trump his adversaries' hand. It was a tenet of Marxist–Leninist doctrine that capitalism would ultimately destroy itself, but dogmatic faith in ideological infallibility was a poor basis on which to construct a foreign policy.

As the Potsdam negotiations got under way, an event occurred that would test the relationship between the Big Three leaders. Churchill received a message that changed everything.

---

*Stalin would, with some justification, point to the way British troops intervened in Greece in 1944, supporting the fight against left-wing partisans who had fought against the Germans.

On July 17 world-shaking news arrived. In the afternoon Stimson*
called at my abode and laid before me a sheet of paper on which
was written: 'Babies satisfactorily born'. By his manner I saw
something extraordinary had happened. 'It means,' he said, 'that
the experiment in the Mexican desert has come off. The atomic
bomb is a reality.'[20]

Churchill had known that research on the bomb was nearing comple-
tion, but he had not been told how or when it might be tested. Now
he learned from his American colleagues of the terrible force that had
been unleashed on the earth.

The bomb had been detonated at the top of a pylon 100 feet
high. Everything had been cleared away for ten miles round, and
the scientists and their staffs crouched behind massive concrete
shields … The blast had been terrific. An enormous column of
flame and smoke shot up to the fringe of the atmosphere of
our poor earth. Devastation inside a one-mile circle was absolute. Here then was a speedy end to the Second World War, and
perhaps to much else besides.[21]

The immediate discussion between Churchill and Truman centred on
Japan, where war was still raging. 'To quell Japanese resistance man
by man and conquer the country yard by yard might require the loss
of a million American lives and half that number of British,' Churchill
wrote. 'In its place was the vision – fair and bright indeed it seemed
– of an end of the whole war in one or two violent shocks.'[22] Their
thoughts then turned to the man waiting to meet them the following
morning. Possession of the bomb meant there was no longer any
need to plead for Soviet assistance in the fight against the Japanese.
And no longer being beholden to Moscow meant the western Allies
held a stronger hand in Europe: 'Stalin's bargaining power, which he
had used with such effect upon the Americans at Yalta, was therefore
gone.'[23]

Both men were at pains to observe Stalin's reaction. If they were
expecting horror or dismay, they were to be disappointed. Truman
waited a week before giving him the news.

---

*Henry L. Stimson, US secretary of war.

On July 24 I casually mentioned to Stalin that we had a new weapon of unusual destructive force. The Russian Premier showed no special interest. All he said was that he was glad to hear it and hoped we would make 'good use of it against the Japanese'.[24]

In reality, Stalin had been taken aback, but his skill at concealing his emotions came to his aid. The Soviet general Georgy Zhukov, who was accompanying him, wrote that Stalin had tried to downplay the impact of the news.

Churchill and many other Anglo-American authors subsequently assumed that Stalin had really failed to fathom the significance of what he had heard. In actual fact, on returning to his quarters after this meeting, Stalin, in my presence, told Molotov about his conversation with Truman. The latter [Molotov] reacted almost immediately. 'Let them. We'll have to talk it over with Kurchatov and get him to speed things up.'[25]

Igor Kurchatov was the scientist who had been heading the project to produce a Soviet atomic bomb. Since 1942, he had benefited from information provided by Soviet spies in the British and American research programmes, but the first Soviet test would not happen until August 1949, partly because of Stalin's paranoia: he suspected that the technical data received from the West might be deliberate disinformation.[26]

Before the successful US bomb test, the USSR had held the advantage, with its apparently endless resources of manpower and conventional equipment deployed in the European theatre. Suddenly, it seemed to the Kremlin that the world had become alarmingly unbalanced. The psychology of East–West relations had shifted and Stalin knew he had to act.

After the use of nuclear weapons against Japan, he would send an urgent message to the managers of the Soviet atomic programme. 'Hiroshima has shaken the whole world. The balance has been broken. Build the Bomb – it will remove the great danger from us.'[27] In the minds of many Soviet citizens, the demonstration of western nuclear might represented an imminent threat. As the Cold War took hold and allies were transformed into foes, Soviet state media did little to assuage their fears. Yuli Khariton, a leading physicist in the Soviet weapons programme, wrote after the Hiroshima explosion, 'The Soviet Government interpreted it as atomic blackmail against the USSR – as a threat to unleash a new, even more terrible and devastating war.'[28]

While there was little evidence that the Americans genuinely intended to use nuclear weapons against the USSR, it undoubtedly gave the West renewed confidence. Harry Truman was emboldened in his determination to reverse Roosevelt's policy of accommoda-tion. He was considerably more suspicious of Stalin and of Soviet intentions than his predecessor had been.* Soviet actions in eastern Europe were now unequivocally framed as aggressive expansionism, incompatible with the undertakings Stalin had given at Yalta. Mos-cow's demands for influence and control were compared to Hitler's escalating ultimatums of the 1930s. There was a determination not to make concessions or cede territory in the way that had happened before the outbreak of the Second World War.[29] The stage was set for the emergence of the Truman Doctrine, in June 1947, with its Manichean division of the globe into spheres of democracy and totalitarianism, colouring foreign policy decisions and raising the temperature of international relations. The question of the future of Germany would lie at the heart of it. Britain and America cham-pioned reconstruction and recovery; Russia, with French backing, demanded dismantling and punitive reparations.

Ultimately, and ironically, the Cold War would grow from disagreements about the best way to maintain prosperity and peace, not from a desire on either side to fight.

---

* Although, the image of Truman as a 'tough guy' willing to slug it out with the Soviets owes much to retrospective myth-making, not least in Truman's own record of events (see Chapter 8).

6

STALIN THE NEUROTIC

When the Yugoslav communist and political theorist Milovan Djilas was introduced to Stalin at the end of the war, he expected to meet a god. The reality was less prepossessing.

> He was of very small stature and ungainly build. His torso was short and narrow, while his arms and legs were too long. His left arm and shoulder seemed rather stiff. He had quite a large paunch and his hair was sparse, although the scalp was not entirely bald. His face was white, with ruddy cheeks. Later I learned that this coloration, so characteristic of those who sit long in offices, was known as the 'Kremlin complexion' in high Soviet circles. His teeth were black and irregular, turned inward. Not even his moustache was thick or firm ... with those yellow eyes ...[1]

Stalin was aware of his own ugliness and sought to hide it from the world. He wanted people to see him as something he was not. According to Valentin Berezhkov, the Kremlin's chief interpreter at the Teheran Conference of 1943, Stalin was so concerned about the impression he would make on Roosevelt and Churchill that he personally arranged the seating plan 'with the lights not coming straight on his face, because his nose and cheeks were dotted with smallpox. He always had his photographs painted so people didn't know about his very unpleasant appearance.'[2]

In the Cold War years, each side weighed every signal from the other, attempting to read their opponent's mind and intentions: understanding or misunderstanding the state of Stalin's mental health. Daniel Rancour-Laferriere, who used the tools of Freudian psychoanalysis to explore the motivations of Russian writers and public figures, concluded that many of Stalin's thoughts and actions stemmed from his complex attitude towards himself. 'In adulthood, Stalin had to live with two affective extremes: he worshipped himself and he hated himself. The first he dealt with by promoting a narcissistic cult of personality. The second he dealt with by instituting a reign of terror, by turning the hatred outward.'[3]

An American diplomat, Robert Tucker, who worked at the US embassy in Moscow in the early 1950s, observed Stalin at first hand. Tucker's observations led him to the conclusion that the Soviet leader was suffering from a dangerous psychological disorder.

> A person who experiences 'basic anxiety' resulting from adverse emotional circumstances in early life may seek and find a rock of inner security by forming an idealized self-image ... for example, as a great warrior [or] as saint-like. Repressed self-hatred is experienced as hatred of others. The particular others on whom it is projected are likely to be those who have incurred the neurotic person's vindictive animosity by somehow failing to affirm him as the idealized self that he mistakenly takes himself to be ... a need for 'vindictive triumph'.[4]

Tucker based his diagnosis on the theories of the German-American post-Freudian psychoanalyst Karen Horney. Seeking a psychological explanation of Stalin's behaviour, Tucker concluded that Stalin must be 'a neurotic personality ... possessed [of] an unprecedented plenitude of political power'.[5]

Tucker communicated his diagnosis to the State Department, but his bosses showed little interest. The USA continued to frame its dealings with Moscow on the assumption that Stalin was a rational man whose actions were based on ruthless but lucidly calculated realpolitik. Relying on a political consensus formed by years of western reporting from the Soviet capital, US officials and politicians broadly accepted the opinion of journalists such as Walter Duranty, the Pulitzer Prize-winning Moscow correspondent of *The New York Times*, who thought he was 'a man of steel ... his life-work is the robot system of flesh and blood'.[6]

When western observers in Moscow expressed surprise at the cult of personality that surrounded Stalin, Soviet officials assured them that the popular adulation was genuine; a little overenthusiastic, perhaps, but a spontaneous outpouring of love from the Soviet people. Washington swallowed the official line that Stalin tolerated the hero-worship with bemused self-deprecation. But Robert Tucker saw through it. He became convinced that Stalin was the architect of his own personality cult and that it was the result of deep-seated paranoia, a projection of 'his own monstrously inflated vision of himself as the greatest genius of Russian and world history. It must be an institutionalization of his neurotic character structure.'[7] Tucker identified what he called Stalin's 'enemy complex', a belief that he was surrounded by dangerous foes at home and abroad, so needed at all times to be on his guard. He argued against Washington's belief that Stalin was merely the mouthpiece of the politburo, *primus inter pares* and a moderating factor on the more extreme elements in the Kremlin. In fact, Tucker wrote, Stalin was an archetypal arrogant 'vindictive neurotic', as defined in Karen Horney's seminal work, *Neurosis and Human Growth*.

> Motivated by an 'impelling need for triumph' the arrogant vindictive neurotic cannot tolerate anybody who knows or achieves more than he does, wields more power, or in any way questions his superiority. Compulsively he has to drag his rival down or defeat him. Even if he subordinates himself for the sake of his career, he is scheming for ultimate triumph.[8]

The official short biography of Stalin, *Kratkaia Biografiia*, which first appeared in 1947 and was intended to be read by every citizen of the USSR, described him as follows:

> Everyone knows the indefinable, shattering force of Stalin's logic, the crystal clarity of his intellect, his steel will, devotion to the party, ardent faith in the people and love for the people. His modesty, simplicity, sensitivity to people and mercilessness to enemies are well known to everyone. His intolerance for sensation, for phrase-mongering and chatterboxes, for grumblers and alarmists is well known. Stalin is wise, unhurried in the solution of complex political questions.[9]

Robert Tucker noted that even that level of extravagant praise was not enough to satisfy Stalin's thirst for acclaim. The unassuageable

self-doubt of the inadequate personality led him to personally intervene to add more praise, while also denying the very 'vanity and
self-adulation' from which he so evidently suffered.

> Stalin personally edited the glorifying *Short Biography* of himself
> published in 1947, and in so doing marked the very places where
> he thought that the praise of his services was insufficient. Thus
> he inserted the following sentence: 'Although he performed his
> task as leader of the party and the people with consummate skill
> and enjoyed the unreserved support of the entire Soviet people,
> Stalin never allowed his work to be marred by the slightest hint
> of vanity, conceit, or self-adulation.'[10]

Stalin's insecurities about his perceived personal inadequacies seem
insufficient explanation for all of this; such is the experience of nine-
tenths of the human race, after all, and most do not seek vindication
through aggression and megalomaniacal self-aggrandisement. Psychologists seeking for clues to Stalin's character have, unsurprisingly,
rummaged in the formative years of his childhood.

Growing up in Tsarist Georgia, the young Joseph Dzhugashvili
contended with poverty, violence and illness. Bouts of smallpox and
other infections scarred his face, stunted his growth and left him
physically weak. He was run over by a horse and cart, with the result
that his left arm was shorter than his right and partially paralysed,
while the toes on his left foot were fused together, resulting in a lifelong limp.

He seems to have been frequently beaten by his cobbler father
and his schooling was irregular and unhappy. He was, though, nurtured by a devoted mother, whose insistence that he was destined for
great things instilled in him a conviction of personal superiority. At
the same time, the setbacks and humiliations of his youth fostered a
desire for vindication and revenge on those who had mistreated him.
The son of Stalin's Bolshevik comrade Vladimir Antonov-Ovseyenko,
historian Anton Antonov-Ovseyenko would later write a devastating
deconstruction of the roots of the dictator's psychological flaws.

> An individual's character is formed, of course, in early child-
> hood, in the first years of life. What did little Soso [Georgian
> diminutive of Joseph] experience in his family, in his preschool

years, and at school? Beatings, cruelty, rudeness, and constant humiliation ... The roots of Stalin's inexhaustible cynicism are to be sought here [in his formative years, when] Stalin faced constant violence.[11]

Antonov-Ovseyenko, who is not an impartial witness, suggests that Stalin's tormented self-image led him to demand absurdly exaggerated recognition – not just political power, but reverence for his intellectual, moral and personal prowess. Stalin's claim to be a heroic battler for the rights of the downtrodden Russian people is interpreted as a sublimation of his driving need to struggle for personal vindication, to prove himself and muffle the repressed terror of being exposed as unworthy.[12] The quest for vengeance on his perceived enemies necessitated lengthy periods of dissimulation, during which Stalin would wear the mask of compliance and civility, while continuing to nurture the sense of personal injustice that remained always with him. Alan Bullock wrote of 'his vindictiveness, his unfailing memory for an insult or injury, with an implacable determination to be revenged, however many years might pass'.

> One of the best-known stories about Stalin is told by Sere-bryakov, a party member who had known him since the time of the civil war. When a group of comrades was discussing everyone's idea of a perfect day, Stalin said, 'Mine is to plan an artistic revenge upon an enemy, carry it out to perfection and then go home and go peacefully to bed.'[13]

All human beings interpret the world around them in terms of how they think of themselves and it is natural to project our own self-perceptions onto others. But most people understand that not everyone thinks precisely as they do. According to Robert Tucker, Stalin lacked this perspective: he attributed his own thoughts and behaviour to those around him, with the consequence that he regarded the world as a place of fakes and hypocrites, wearing masks in order to deceive. His refusal to trust anyone had far-reaching consequences in the era of domestic purges, but his suspicion extended equally to the West. As early as 1923, he wrote, 'The wolves of imperialism who surround us are not dozing. Not a moment passes without our enemies trying to seize some little chink through which they could crawl and do us harm.'[14]

Acute paranoia combined in Stalin with a violent temper. Robert Tucker speculates that he internalised the cruelty of his father, while the fear of a violent, unpredictable parent expanded first into a mistrust of all fathers and, eventually, of all men.[15] The daring Stalin displayed in his early years – planning and executing bank robberies, taking part in political demonstrations and street fighting – wilted as he grew to fear the world. His later years would be mired in debilitating anxiety, employing teams of bodyguards and carrying a revolver at official meetings. He never flew, rarely travelled through Moscow and dispatched convoys of decoy cars when he had to do so.

For long periods Stalin would remain cooped up in the Kremlin, or at his fortified dacha outside Moscow, avoiding human contact but simultaneously fearful of being alone. Politburo colleagues would be made to spend hours sitting with him, often being mocked and humiliated, while he brooded on the enemies, real and imagined, that he had on his execution lists. Robert Tucker concluded that Stalin had psychopathic qualities – his willingness to condemn millions to death without visible remorse suggested a profound absence of empathy for the sufferings of others; he would sign death sentences then laugh unconcernedly as he watched Charlie Chaplin movies in his private cinema. His inability to be satisfied with the choruses of praise heaped upon him, and his reported fretting over the sincerity or otherwise of the Stalin cult (*do they really love me, or merely fear me?*), spoke of a blinding self-obsession.

There is, though, disagreement over the state of Stalin's mental health. It has become customary to attribute many of his actions to paranoia, but Antonov-Ovseyenko disagrees.

> That means attributing all of his crimes, which cost millions of lives, to mental illness. Would a sick or mentally unbalanced person have been able so masterfully to hamstring all his political rivals and build such a model apparatus of power? ... No, Stalin was unquestionably of sound mind. Neither schizophrenia nor paranoia has any hold over such malicious natures. But his boundless ambition might seem maniacal to an outsider.[16]

Antonov-Ovseyenko may be right to query the traditional diagnosis of psychotic paranoia, but that does not automatically mean Stalin was 'of sound mind'. A personality disorder such as sociopathy (previously termed psychopathy) certainly does not preclude high-functioning cold-blooded ruthlessness; in fact, it indicates it. In his magisterial exegesis of dictatorial derangement, *Hitler and Stalin: Parallel Lives*, Alan Bullock traces the development of Stalin's sociopathic behaviour and, initially at least, discerns method within the madness.

> Like Hitler, he paid great attention to timing and showed the same intuitive skill in probing an opponent's mentality and weaknesses ... He combined, for example, a remarkable capacity for detail with an instinctive suspicion, especially of allies and those who proclaimed their loyalty. Deceit and treachery were second nature to him.[17]

Bullock's diagnosis, so far as he makes one, is that Stalin suffered from debilitating narcissism, a psychological disorder in which a person becomes so absorbed with him or herself that nothing else matters. The result, says Bullock, is that 'only the person himself, *his* needs, feelings and thoughts, everything and everybody as they relate to *him* are experienced as fully real, while everybody and everything else lacks reality or interest'.[18]

In Freudian terms, this secondary narcissism (as opposed to the normal self-regard manifested by all humans) is the consequence of affection being projected outwards and rejected by the object at which it is directed. Affection rebuffed is turned back onto the self and festers in the unbalanced psyche; the individual becomes cut off from his fellows and uninterested in others. Unable to express love for another and thus to have it reflected back to him, he becomes weighed down by low self-esteem, shame and guilt. He becomes defensive and withdrawn, until all his thoughts and actions become an obsession with himself, his own qualities and his own achievements.[19]

In Stalin's case, the obsession seemed to be the acclaim and world-wide recognition he might attain if he succeeded in modernising and weaponising the USSR into a pre-eminent world power. He was aware that his crash industrialisation and collectivisation policies were causing human misery on an unprecedented scale, but his narcissism made the suffering unreal to him, a shadow world of irrelevancy. Bullock points to the moment Stalin became aware of his divine mission to achieve immortal greatness, underlining a passage in Napoleon's memoirs describing himself as 'an unusual person consumed with the ambition to do great things', and draws the connection between such beliefs and narcissism. 'Narcissistic personalities are convinced of their own special qualities and superiority over others, and any threat to this self-image – such as being criticised, shown up or defeated – produces a violent reaction and often a desire for revenge.'[20]

That fear of being 'shown up' was embedded in Stalin's psyche; the 'violent reaction' to criticism led to ever more ruthless acts of revenge. In December 1927, the president of the Congress of Russian Neurologists and Psychologists, Vladimir Bekhterev, was granted a three-hour appointment in the Kremlin to examine the Soviet leader and report on his mental state. No record of the meeting survives, but when Bekhterev returned to his colleagues he declared, 'I have just examined a paranoiac with a small, dry hand.'[21] Twenty-four hours later, he was dead. The cause was never revealed and Bekhterev, who had previously been in good health, was buried before a postmortem could be carried out. His name was subsequently removed from public documents and textbooks, with his reputation restored only after the fall of the USSR.[22]

Medical records show that Stalin suffered from a range of physical illnesses, exacerbated by the regular consumption of alcohol and chain smoking. His blood pressure was high; he complained of pains in his joints and he was a chronic insomniac. But he had a deep mistrust of doctors, becoming convinced in later life that they were intent on poisoning him. The chief Kremlin physician, the cardiologist Dmitry Pletnev, attended Stalin in the 1930s and allegedly told colleagues that the Great Leader was suffering from delusions of persecution. In 1937, Pletnev was arrested, charged with murdering the socialist writer Maxim Gorky, tortured and coerced into signing a false confession. He died in a labour camp.[23] In January 1953, two months before his own death, Stalin announced that another wide-ranging conspiracy had been uncovered: the health of the Soviet leadership was being undermined by the Kremlin's own medical staff, who were part of a 'Jewish Doctors' Plot', bent on political assassination. *Pravda* ran a front-page article under the headline 'Vicious Spies and Killers behind the Mask of Academic Physicians': 'The filthy face of this Zionist spy organisation and its vicious actions are now completely unmasked … Comrade Stalin has repeatedly warned us … We must liquidate sabotage and purge complacency from our ranks.'[24]

Hundreds of people were arrested and tortured. Stalin told the judge in the case to 'beat them, beat them and beat them again'. He warned the security minister that if the doctors did not all confess, he himself would be 'shortened by a head'.[25] When the arrested men were coerced into signing false admissions of guilt, Stalin told the secret police, 'See! You are like blind kittens! What would have happened without me? The country would perish because you don't know how to root out our enemies!'[26]

In the last decade before his death in March 1953, Stalin's fear of doctors made him wary of all medical treatment. Instead, he consulted veterinarians and treated his high blood pressure with self-administered iodine drops. As his mental state deteriorated, so did his physical health. On the balance of available evidence, the Canadian neuroscientist Vladimir Hachinski has argued that the cause of Stalin's paranoia was the cumulative effect of a series of lacunar strokes. These, Hachinski says, 'tend to predominate in the fronto-basal areas, and disconnect the circuits that underpin cognition and behaviour'.[27]

The few doctors who were allowed to examine Stalin tend to support Hachinski's hypothesis. Dr Alexander Myasnikov was part of the medical team that treated Stalin in his final days and was present at the dictator's autopsy, concluding that reduced blood supply caused by the hardened arteries exacerbated dangerous personality traits that had been present since his early years. His memoir of the events, written contemporaneously but published only sixty years later, confirms that Stalin suffered a progressive hardening of the arteries in his brain, diminishing his ability to think objectively. 'In essence a sick man ruled the state ... Stalin's cruelty and paranoia, his fear of enemies, his losing the ability to soberly assess people and events, as well as his extreme stubbornness, were all in large part the result of the atherosclerosis of the arteries in his brain.'[28]

While the influence of Stalin's mental state on his domestic policy decisions has been widely reported, less attention has been paid to the role it played in his relations with foreign countries. But if the Soviet leader really was 'unable to distinguish between what was good and bad and who is a friend and who is an enemy', it is certain that it would have impacted on his behaviour in the Cold War. The American psychologist Raymond Birt attempted a re-evaluation in his 1993 paper 'Personality and Foreign Policy: The Case of Stalin'.

Anyone who has ever worked in a bureaucratic setting knows how much of the decision-making process is devoted to ego-mania, pride, one-upmanship and other games that have nothing to do with the objective conditions the bureaucracy has to deal with ... [yet] apart from a few notable exceptions (Tucker 1971, 1990; Rancour-Laferriere 1988), it is seldom considered that Stalin's acts were the product of underlying psychological needs.[29]

Birt proposed that the evolution of 'the behaviour of the Soviet Union', its purges and Cold War suspicions, can be linked to 'the development of Stalin's personality': 'Stalin used the Soviet bureaucracy as an ego defence, making the state at a crucial juncture little more than an extension of one man's personality. Explanations of the behaviour of that state that do not take Stalin's personality into consideration as an intervening variable are ... inadequate.'[30] Almost seventy years after Stalin's death, historians continue to debate exactly what blend of paranoia, insecurity and ideology fuelled his, and by extension the Soviet Union's, conduct in the early Cold War.[31] For much of his reign, the western Allies struggled to account for the impact of the Soviet leader's personality, underestimating both the extent of Stalin's personal power and the depth of his mental aberration, calamitously failing to account for the influence they had on Soviet policy. In such a context, Churchill and Roosevelt's attempts to create a personal bond with him – to charm him into concessions – and the West's obstinate belief in the normality of his decision-making appear to be doomed miscalculations.

7

THE LONG TELEGRAMS

Charles Bohlen, a senior US diplomat who served in Moscow before, during and after the Second World War, was fond of saying, 'There are two "famous last words". One is, "alcohol doesn't affect me"; and the other is, "I understand the Russians".'[1] The puzzlement was not confined to the West. After the conclusion of the war, both sides struggled with the same questions – who are we facing now that allies are turning to foes? What exactly is this 'other' power? What are its motivations? What does it want, and how far will it go to achieve it?

Sometimes the opposing sides got it right, but more often they were wrong; sometimes spectacularly so. Two crucial texts, written by men with experience of living in the 'other's' land, set the parameters for the Cold War guessing game. Both were telegrams composed in the pivotal year of 1946, one sent by a US diplomat in Moscow, the other by a Soviet diplomat in Washington. Both exhibit signs of a phenomenon we will encounter frequently as we consider the efforts of each side to decipher the thinking of the other: confirmation bias, the tendency to interpret the mind of others according to the preconceptions of our own.

The questions were urgent – the future of the world depended on them – and deeply perplexing. One man better placed than most to answer them was the deputy head of the US mission in Moscow. George Kennan had followed the evolution of the US–Soviet relationship since the early 1930s, serving in Latvia and Czechoslovakia as well as in the USSR. He had witnessed the vagaries of Stalin's decision-making at first hand, expressing disgust at the dictator's mass purges and condemning the cynicism of his international manoeuvrings. In the heat of war, East and West had grown to think of each other as military confederates, thrown together by circumstances if not by ideological conviction. But Kennan doubted the sincerity of the Soviets' commitment to cooperation, and his doubts grew in the months following Yalta and Potsdam.

Kennan empathised with the Russian people, but he harboured no illusions about the Soviet leadership: they were slippery customers who would take whatever they could get in diplomatic exchanges and give nothing in return. He went to great lengths to inform his bosses in the State Department of his misgivings. By failing to reshape postwar western policy towards the Soviet Union, he wrote, America and her allies were 'in danger of losing, like the dog standing over the reflecting pool, the bone in our mouth without obtaining the one we saw in the water'.[2]

Kennan's views were supported by evidence, but perhaps because of the mutual sacrifices of the war, perhaps because Washington feared rocking the boat with Stalin, the State Department filed Kennan's reports and did nothing. The secretary of state, James Byrnes, continued to counsel accommodation, trusting his own ability to strike deals with his Soviet counterparts.

By February 1946, Kennan was exasperated. He decided to resign. In what he thought would be his final dispatch, he sat down to put on record his assessment of the psychological underpinnings of the Soviet state. It might never be acted on, but it would stand as his Cassandra prophecy, his message to posterity.

> I had to go right back to Page One and try to tell them things that they had forgotten during the war. This all hangs together with this question that this was the same group of people (Stalin and his colleagues) who had tried to make a deal with Hitler at our expense and never had changed their views about us [the West].[3]

Far from being ignored, Kennan's Long Telegram, as it became known, would become a turning point in postwar diplomacy. Its dissection of the workings of the Soviet mind, the thoughts and desires of the Soviet leadership, the fears and emotions of the Soviet people, remains the Ur-text of the forty-five chilly years that would follow.

Kennan wrote that he was convinced the USSR was shucking off its wartime conciliation in favour of a return to the systemic hostility of the post-revolutionary years. In evidence, he quoted the propaganda with which the Kremlin was moulding the mental outlook of the Russian people.

George Kennan's Long Telegram would set the tone for the United
States' attempts to 'contain' the Soviets in the early Cold War.

Basic Features of Post War Soviet Outlook, as Put Forward by
Official Propaganda Machine:
(a) USSR still lives in antagonistic 'capitalist encirclement' with
     which in the long run there can be no permanent peaceful
     coexistence.
(b) Capitalist world is beset with internal conflicts, inherent in
     nature of capitalist society.
(c) Internal conflicts of capitalism inevitably generate wars.[4]

Kennan's opinion was that Stalin was bent on expanding Soviet
power. But, he wrote, in the minds of the Russian people themselves
there was little appetite for international aggression. 'Latter are, by
and large, friendly to outside world, eager for experience of it, eager
to measure against it talents they are conscious of possessing, eager
above all to live in peace and enjoy fruits of their own labor.' As a
result, the leadership was obliged to inculcate in them the fear of a
menacing foreign enemy. The Kremlin's insistence on the tenets of
Marxist dogma made belligerence and tyranny inevitable.

We have here a political force committed fanatically to the belief that with US there can be no permanent *modus vivendi*, that it is desirable and necessary that the internal harmony of our society be disrupted, our traditional way of life be destroyed, the international authority of our state be broken, if Soviet power is to be secure ...

In this [Marxist] dogma, they found justification ... for the dictatorship without which they did not know how to rule, for cruelties they did not dare not to inflict, for sacrifice they felt bound to demand. In the name of Marxism they sacrificed every single ethical value in their methods and tactics. Today they cannot dispense with it.

If Washington felt it could take the Kremlin's promises at face value, it should think again. The Soviets were practised in the art of dirty tricks, saying one thing in public while pursuing sabotage and aggression behind the scenes. 'Soviet policy ... is conducted on two planes: (1) official plane represented by actions undertaken officially in name of Soviet Government; and (2) subterranean plane of actions undertaken by agencies for which Soviet Government does not admit responsibility.' That Freudian-sounding 'subterranean plane of actions' would be a crucial weapon in a conflict where military confrontation would remain on the back burner. The Kremlin's expertise in psychological warfare, Kennan wrote, had the capacity to undermine the USA from within.

... to disrupt [our] national self-confidence, to increase social and industrial unrest, to stimulate all forms of disunity ... poor will be set against rich, black against white, young against old, newcomers against established residents, etc. ... all Soviet efforts on unofficial international plane will be negative and destructive in character.

In the field of psychological manipulation, Kennan concluded, Moscow was ahead of the USA. Far from being a phenomenon of the twenty-first century, fake news was already on the agenda in 1946. The Kremlin was adept at using lies and deceit, infiltration and disinformation to wrong-foot both its former allies and its own population: 'The very disrespect of Russians for objective truth – indeed, their disbelief in its existence – leads them to view all stated facts as instruments for furtherance of one ulterior purpose or another.'

Kennan stated his case in stark terms because he wanted Washington to take note of what he was saying. But he was far from being a simple warmonger. He understood why the Russians felt the need for belligerence on the international stage.

> At bottom of Kremlin's neurotic view of world affairs is traditional and instinctive Russian sense of insecurity. Originally, this was insecurity of a peaceful agricultural people trying to live on vast exposed plain in neighborhood of fierce nomadic peoples. To this was added, as Russia came into contact with economically advanced West, fear of more competent, more powerful, more highly organized societies in that area ... Russian rulers have invariably sensed that their rule was relatively archaic in form, fragile and artificial in its psychological foundation, unable to stand comparison or contact with political systems of Western countries. For this reason they have always feared foreign penetration, feared direct contact between Western world and their own, feared what would happen if Russians learned truth about world without or if foreigners learned truth about world within. And they have learned to seek security only in patient but deadly struggle for total destruction of rival power, never in compacts and compromises with it.

The Long Telegram set the tone for what would become known as 'containment' – a policy of limiting and countering the Soviet threat, later to be enshrined in the Truman Doctrine of 1947. Containment held that Moscow's aggression could be kept in check without sliding into another war.

> I would like to record my conviction that problem is within our power to solve – and that without recourse to any general military conflict ... Soviet power is impervious to logic of reason, and highly sensitive to logic of force. For this reason it can easily withdraw – and usually does when strong resistance is encountered at any point. Thus, if the adversary has sufficient force and makes clear his readiness to use it, he rarely has to do so ...

success will really depend on degree of cohesion, firmness and vigor which Western World can muster.

Moscow's psychological warriors, Kennan warned, were adept at provoking self-defeating emotions in their opponents, with the aim of clouding western judgement. Washington shouldn't step into the trap, maintaining 'the same determination not to be emotionally provoked or unseated by it, with which doctor studies an unruly and unreasonable individual'.

The coming struggle, Kennan predicted, would be for hearts and minds, not physical conquest. The Kremlin's monopoly on the provision of public information meant it could convince its own people of whatever it wished. But not so in the West. To keep the public onside, to avoid panic and discontent, the governments of free democracies would have to persuade and assure their own citizens.

Kennan's emphasis on moulding public thinking would be enthusiastically implemented in the years ahead, though the aim was rarely to deter anti-Soviet and anti-communist feeling. The West would have to show itself to be confident of its own moral values and the ethical rightness of its way of life. Even the smallest show of weakness could open the door to the insidious forces of communism, forever seeking to infiltrate its message into people's hearts.

> World communism is like malignant parasite which feeds only on diseased tissue … we must have courage and self-confidence to cling to our own methods and conceptions of human society. After all, the greatest danger that can befall us in coping with this problem of Soviet communism, is that we shall allow ourselves to become like those with whom we are coping.

Kennan's telegram was setting some key parameters for the coming clash of value systems. Democracy and communism were about to compete for global approbation. The winner would be the one who convinces the world of his nation's superior values; the loser the one whose self-belief and moral resolve falters and weakens.

> It is not enough to urge people to develop political processes similar to our own. Many foreign peoples, in Europe at least, are tired and frightened by experiences of past, and are less

interested in abstract freedom than in security. They are seeking
guidance rather than responsibilities. We should be better able
than Russians to give them this. And unless we do, Russians certainly will.

Kennan's words would have an impact way beyond his expectations.
Henry Kissinger would later say that 'George Kennan came as close
to authoring the diplomatic doctrine of his era as any diplomat in our
history'.[5] The message of the Long Telegram gained political trac-
tion because it arrived at a tipping point in US attitudes, the moment
when Washington was beginning to realise that there was no scope
for civil diplomatic relations with the Soviets.

    In politics, as in most things, facts gain in importance when they
chime with the mind-set of those interpreting them: Washington
was finally ready to hear the message Kennan had been sending. It
was not a changed reality that allowed George Kennan to influence
history, but a changed perception of it.

Less well known is another 'long telegram'. This one was sent by
Kennan's opposite number, Nikolai Novikov, who in September 1946
was the Soviet ambassador in Washington. Asked by Moscow to
assess US intentions in the dawning confrontation between the two
blocs, Novikov sat down to give his considered view of American
thinking. Like Kennan, he did his best to comprehend the psyche of
the opposition, but he fell into a very Soviet form of confirmation
bias.

    The parallels between the two telegrams are outweighed by their
differences. They are written by two men from different backgrounds,
each with a defined societal perspective on the world. Kennan and
Novikov see things through the prism of their own personal, historical and cultural preconceptions. There is no mistaking which of the
two is the product of a culture of free thinking, libertarian independence, where the individual is regarded as the supreme criterion and
the state's role to facilitate his or her pursuit of happiness. It is equally
evident which one comes from a society driven by communal values
and the overriding need to support the good of the state.

    Nikolai Novikov was a successful career diplomat. He had
progressed through the ranks to occupy the most coveted post in
Soviet diplomacy. And he had done so by adopting and reflecting the

world-view of his masters in the Kremlin. If Stalin believed that the capitalist world was riddled by internal contradictions that would lead inexorably to its imminent collapse, Novikov wasn't going to argue. He accepted that Marxist dialectical materialism had scientifically proved history to be marching relentlessly via class struggle to a socialist world. And he surveyed the American society he was living in to find the evidence to prove the theory.

'[C]urrent relations between Britain and the United States are quite conflictive and cannot be long-term,' Novikov writes, identifying the Middle East as a potential 'focal point of Anglo-American conflicts where the agreements currently reached … will be destroyed'. This prediction of conflict between the US and Britain was supported by little other than Marxist dialectics. London and Washington had had their ups and downs, but only a blinkered believer in the Hegelian model of a capitalist world doomed to collapse under its own contradictions could extrapolate that the western alliance was about to founder.

Novikov describes US policy towards occupied Germany as 'one of the most important facets of the overarching US strategy to limit the international role of the USSR in the postwar world'. Washington, he writes, 'is not taking measures to eliminate the monopolistic associations of German industrialists on which German Fascism depended in preparing aggression and waging war'. The policy is deliberate; it has 'a clear anti-Soviet edge'.[6]

When everything has to fit the template of capitalist–imperialist preparations for 'a third war' which would lead to the US 'winning world supremacy',[7] it is natural that Novikov should parse Washington motives as sinister and menacing: 'It ought to be fully realized that American preparations for a future war are being conducted with the idea of war against the Soviet Union, which in the eyes of American imperialists is the chief obstacle in the American path to world domination.'[8] Part of the build-up to war, Novikov reports, is the use of the American media 'to create an atmosphere of war psychosis among the masses'. Reflecting the belief of his Kremlin bosses, based on the relationship between politicians and media in the USSR, Novikov states confidently that the anti-Soviet editorial content of US newspapers is dictated word-for-word by the White House.

It was a feature of much Soviet analysis that the intelligence – including that gathered by KGB operatives at considerable risk to themselves – had to be tailored to support the views, often whimsically self-deluding, held by the Kremlin. Since Soviet socialism by definition could not be wrong, failings in industry, agriculture and food supply must be the result of foreign plots or sabotage, with the upshot that real problems were not dealt with, or discussed endlessly in the fruitless search for an ideologically correct solution. The aggressive policies of the United States were a useful explanation for much that is going, or has gone wrong in the Soviet Union, and Novikov makes the most of them.

> US foreign policy has been characterized in the postwar period by a desire for world domination. This is the real meaning of repeated statements by President Truman and other representatives of American ruling circles that the US has a right to world leadership [*rukovodstvo*]. All the forces of American diplomacy, the Army, Navy, and Air Force, industry, and science have been placed at the service of this policy. With this objective in mind broad plans for expansion have been developed, to be realized both diplomatically and through ... an arms race, and the creation of newer and newer weapons.[9]

There has been a hardening in US imperialism, Novikov reports, since President Truman succeeded Roosevelt in the White House. Truman, he says, is 'a politically unstable person with certain conservative tendencies'. That, and the subsequent appointment of Byrnes as secretary of state, have led to 'a strengthening of the influence on US foreign policy of the most reactionary circles'. There is nostalgia now for the Roosevelt era, and the late president's 'course for cooperation among peace loving countries', though this fondness does not extend to the still excoriated Churchill.[10] Novikov laments that Moscow's sincere desire for East–West cooperation is likely to be rebuffed by the new administration.

> The present policy of the American government with regard to the USSR is also directed at limiting or dislodging the influence of the Soviet Union from neighbouring countries. In implementing this policy in former enemy or Allied countries adjacent to the USSR, the United States attempts to support reactionary forces with the purpose of creating obstacles to the process of

democratization of these countries and to secure positions for the penetration of American capital into their economies.[11]

Before it went to Stalin, Novikov's telegram was further edited by Vyacheslav Molotov, with the result that Moscow was effectively telling its man in Washington what he should be reporting to Moscow.[12] The dispatches of Soviet diplomats, George Kennan would later claim, were little more than 'a way of saying to their masters in Moscow: "How true, sir!"'[13]

But, while it is true that Novikov's reading of the international situation seeks to fit selective information into a Marxist–Leninist interpretation of the world, several of his claims are supported by the facts. By the end of 1946, US rhetoric really had become more aggressive; expenditure on the military really had increased; many Nazi-era administrators and industrialists in Germany were indeed being allowed to remain in position; and US bases were being established across the globe, in positions from which they could launch strikes against the Soviet Union.

What Novikov's text reveals very clearly is that the Kremlin was afraid, genuinely concerned that the West, and specifically the US, represented a real and imminent threat. Khrushchev wrote that this fear stayed with Stalin until his death.

> In the days leading up to Stalin's death, we believed that America would invade the Soviet Union and we would go to war. Stalin trembled at this prospect. How he quivered. He was afraid of war. He knew that we were weaker than the United States. ... This fear stayed with him from the first days of World War II, when he said: 'Lenin left us a state and we turned it to shit.' Our victory in the war did not stop him from trembling inside.[14]

The questions posed by Kennan and Novikov were also exercising the Foreign Office in London. In July 1945, Sir Harold Orme Garton Sargent, the deputy under-secretary for foreign affairs, had expressed puzzlement over the prospects for British foreign policy in a world where the potential enemy was both inscrutable and unpredictable.

It is true that in the case of Nazi Germany Hitler kindly explained in *Mein Kampf* both his objectives and methods. But in the case of the Soviet Union Stalin is not likely to be as obliging. We shall have to try and find out for ourselves what is his plan of campaign and to anticipate the tactics which he intends to employ from time to time to carry it through. And this is not going to be easy, nor shall we always be able, even among ourselves in this country, to agree on the conclusions to be reached.[15]

Even before the war ended, ambassador Archibald Clark Kerr had offered his assessment of Soviet intentions, predicting that Moscow would seek to exert its influence well beyond its pre-war sphere of influence. In a lengthy memorandum on Soviet policy dated 31 August 1944, he forecast three likely outcomes of an Allied victory: the removal of any immediate threat to Soviet security, the consolidation of Stalin's dominant position, and the manipulation of communist movements in other countries to serve interests of 'Russia as a state, as distinct from Russia as a revolutionary notion'.[16]

Frank Roberts was British Minister to the Soviet Union after the war, and he worked closely with George Kennan. His dispatches in the weeks that followed the latter's Long Telegram echoed Kennan's views on the psychological origins of Soviet insecurity, pointing out that 'even after her greatest victories in the past, Russia has somehow found herself deprived of many of the fruits of those victories, and has never achieved the security which she thought her due reward'.[17]

Roberts did not underestimate Soviet leadership's ruthlessness, comparing their belief in their own ideology to that of the Jesuit zealots of the Counter-Reformation. Marxism, he wrote, was a genuinely held creed, not a bluff or a cynical pretence. 'They believe the ends justify the means and they are at the head of a chosen people, or rather a chosen group of peoples, with a chosen system designed to spread throughout the world.'[18] Like Kennan, Roberts pleaded for resilience – 'we must be strong and look strong' – in Britain's foreign policy, but also subtlety: 'this strength should always take account of Soviet susceptibilities and prestige. Above all, we should never rattle the sabre and make it difficult for the Russians to climb down without loss of face.'[19]

The recommendations of Clark Kerr and Roberts, together with that of George Kennan, which Washington had communicated to London, contributed to a hardening of British policy. Their pleas for understanding of the Soviet psyche, for sensitivity in dealing with Moscow's apprehensions, seem to have gone unheeded. In April 1946, C. F. A. Warner, the head of the Foreign Office's northern department, proposed an aggressive response to Moscow's expansionist ambitions. 'The Soviet Campaign Against this Country and Our Response to it' drew alarming parallels with the international situation Britain had faced in 1939.

> The Soviet Union has announced to the world that it proposes to play an aggressive political role, while making an intensive drive to increase its own military and industrial strength. We should be very unwise not to take the Russians at their word, just as we should have been wise to take *Mein Kampf* at its face value.[20]

The rhetoric acquired a sort of self-intensifying ferocity. Approving the work of the committee on 7 November, the Foreign Office section chief, Sir Nigel Ronald, wrote:

> It does no-one any good to remonstrate with a tiger. In such a case, it is well to remember that one is dealing with a tiger; not arguing with a professor of epistemology. The only rules of the game known to the tiger are those which he chooses to make up as he goes along. The only chance for the tiger's adversary is to be guided by those rules as soon as he is able to apprehend them and to play accordingly. Satisfactory relations can only be built up in this way and force opposed by equal or greater force if the tiger is to be dissuaded from further pursuing the contest.[21]

Heightened tensions with Moscow represented a challenge for the British Labour government, in power since July 1945. Clement Attlee and his ministers had initially attempted to maintain an independent British position in the world, beholden neither to Washington nor to Moscow. In March 1946, foreign secretary Ernest Bevin wrote, 'The other point which influences me in the European scene is that we are the last bastion of social democracy. It may be said that this now represents our way of life as against the red tooth and claw of American capitalism and the Communist dictatorship of Soviet Russia.'[22]

The policy led to accusations that London was 'going soft' on Stalin. But by January 1948, Bevin's views seemed to be shifting. He presented an outspoken memorandum to Cabinet, identifying the Soviet threat, and warning that 'we shall be hard put to it to stem the further encroachment of the Soviet tide'.[23]

Bevin's fear was not only of military peril, but of a moral and psychological threat that the West would struggle to contend with.

> It is not enough to reinforce the physical barriers which still guard our western civilisation. We must also organise and consolidate the ethical and spiritual forces inherent in this western civilisation of which we are the chief protagonists ... If we are to preserve peace and our own safety at the same time, we can only do so by the mobilization of such a moral and material force as will create confidence and energy on the one side and inspire respect and caution in the other. The alternative is to acquiesce in continued Russian infiltration and helplessly to witness the piecemeal collapse of one western bastion after another.[24]

Bevin saw Britain's role now as a conduit between the countries of western Europe and the United States. London would help to forge an alliance of western forces capable of providing a counterweight to the military and spiritual influence of the USSR, and offering 'political and moral guidance' to the 'countries of western Europe which despise the spiritual values of America'.[25]

There was, though, a recognition that the Soviets were difficult interlocutors who did not play by the rules of international diplomacy. Frank Roberts, in his dispatches to London, stressed the missionary zeal of the Bolshevik leadership and their obsessive determination to get their way; an unwillingness to compromise, a fear of giving ground to a superior opponent. When the Russians negotiate, Roberts wrote, their diplomacy resembles a litigant pursuing an aggressive lawsuit, wearing down their opponent with endless demands, forcing him to settle out of court, with much ground yielded, simply to put an end to the relentless struggle.[26]

William Hayter, who would serve as ambassador to Moscow in the years after Stalin's death, wrote perceptively and amusingly about the clash of world outlooks that made communication between East and West fraught. Hayter had understood much about the convolutions of the Soviet mind.

> No Soviet negotiator can ever persuade himself of the sincerity of his bourgeois interlocutor. The latter must *ex hypothesi* be hostile to the Soviet system and must wish to destroy it. Consequently it is useless and a waste of time to try to persuade or convince him by rational argument; what you [i.e. the Soviet diplomat] must do is to weaken his position, by the threat or the actual mobilization of a hostile public opinion in his rear, so that he has to make concessions willy-nilly.[27]

The Soviets held the advantage. They could appeal to public opinion in their opponents' countries, in a way that the West could not.

> The best way [for a Soviet negotiator] to do this is by making proposals which both you and he know to be utterly impracticable but which sound well, total disarmament, say, or a withdrawal of all foreign troops from this or that country; these will not be accepted and are not expected to be, but in rejecting them the bourgeois negotiator will have to make other concessions. For this kind of tactics to be effective [western] public opinion must be suitably worked up, and here the Soviet Government possesses undoubted advantages. The first is a total lack of inhibitions about truth or consistency. Probably most people lie a bit, more or less, sooner or later; but few people lie as often and as freely as a Soviet official. Capitalist diplomats lie too, of course. But they do not like being caught out, whereas Soviet diplomats will tell lies that they know everyone else will know to be lies. And for obvious reasons they do not need to worry about Parliamentary questions or press exposures of their untruths and their inconsistencies. All this is very helpful when you want to blacken your partner or opponent in a negotiation.[28]

Hayter's stark assessment of Soviet diplomacy was borne out by a memo – unearthed many years later – containing a pep talk from Stalin to his foreign minister, Vyacheslav Molotov, in April 1946.

> In your dealings with Byrnes you behaved wrongly. When Byrnes attacked, you went on the defensive. In fact, you should have attacked him back. You let Byrnes get away with accusations of USSR expansionism. You should have attacked the imperialistic tendencies of the USA and Britain [and stated that] accusing the USSR of expansionism is malicious slander. You should consider these instructions. At your next meeting with Byrnes or Bevin you should not justify or defend yourself, but be accusatory and go on the attack.[29]

William Hayter correctly diagnosed the brute strength of Soviet diplomacy. But, he wrote, it was hindered by equally important drawbacks, including an almost total lack of understanding of the western mind. The biggest handicap for a Soviet diplomat, Hayter concluded, was the ingrained confirmation bias drummed into him from the days of his earliest schooling:

> His Marxist training means, or seems to a non-Marxist to mean, that he cannot look objectively at the country on which he is reporting or the people with whom he is negotiating. They cannot be as they seem, they must be as Marx or Lenin told him that they ought to be. It is often supposed that Soviet ambassadors, in reporting conditions in their country of residence, will deliberately distort the picture in order to give pleasure to the Kremlin or to avoid censure from it. But more importantly the Ambassadors *themselves* cannot see straight; they report what they see, but what they see is not what is there, because their vision is distorted by their Marxist spectacles.[30]

As for the Americans, Hayter suggests they too struggled with a national mind-set clouded by preconceptions and misinterpretation. While American embassies were generally very good at amassing useful information, he wrote, 'there seems on occasion to be a curious inability to get inside the skin of a foreigner, and this can lead to odd misunderstandings'.

A psychological handicap is the American temperament. This is notoriously mercurial. The curve is always going up and down in dizzying zigzags. Everything is black or white. One day America is invincible, on top of the world, the next in despair, defeated, out of date. A foreign nation, say China, is America's darling one day, the root of all evil the next. Americans are not good at the observation of subtle gradations, the long-term calculations, the patient endurance of irremediable inconveniences that are part of the diplomatic substance. They want quick and definite solutions.[31]

We know broadly what the British and Americans thought of each other's psychological flaws and we know what they thought of the Soviets'. We know less of what the Soviets thought. In the atmosphere of fear and secrecy maintained by Stalin, his diplomats were largely unwilling to write or say anything other than the party line. Only many years later, in the era of glasnost, did former officials begin to reflect on the misconceptions of the postwar years. In a 2006 interview, historian Vladimir Pechatnov claimed that the end of military operations in 1945 was followed by a genuine conviction in diplomatic circles that Moscow's former allies were bent on turning partnership into animosity.

As late as 1946, Stalin continued to hope that the Americans would grant us favourable economic loans to help with our postwar recovery. But the USA gave us the run-around and led us up the garden path. We kept up cultural contacts [with the West] – I would remind you that the jamming of foreign radio stations did not begin until 1947. But as early as autumn 1945, the American military were planning on the Soviet Union being their main future opponent. As for the British General Staff, they had already been told by Churchill to produce plans for a war with the USSR.[32]

While the British and Americans were busy convincing each other of Stalin's expansionist intentions and characterising their own moves as reactive and defensive, Pechatnov says the Soviet view was very much the opposite – that it was the western Allies who first moved towards aggression.

It seems to me that the policy of the West towards the USSR changed much more than the policy of Stalin towards the West. The key turning points were in the spring and the winter of 1946 with the 'long telegram' of George Kennan setting out the future strategy of 'containment' against the USSR, followed by Churchill's Fulton speech and the sharply expressed anti-Soviet direction that their military planning then began to take. The decisive shift was made by the Americans and the British. And after the launch of the Marshall Plan there was already no way back.[33]

Weighing the evidence from both sides of the Iron Curtain, it could plausibly be argued that the world was plunged into forty-five years of Cold War because each of them held psychological preconceptions about their opponent's inherent aggression that led to an ultimately fatal misunderstanding.

George Kennan was aware of the scope for misinterpretation and its potential consequences. 'The Russians are a nation of stage managers,' he told an interviewer, 'and the deepest of their convictions is that things are not what they are, but only what they seem.'[34] But if the Soviets were prone to misreading the mind of their opponents, the Americans were equally guilty. When Washington spoke of its mission to export democracy or to bring freedom to the Russian people, it was seeking to impose its own prejudices on a nation it had signally failed to understand. 'It would be pointless for the West to try to ... produce in short order a replica of the western democratic dream. Of one thing we may be sure: No great and enduring change in the spirit and practice of government in Russia will ever come about primarily through foreign inspiration or advice.'[35]

Disappointed and annoyed by the Truman administration's co-opting of his Long Telegram to justify its hardline approach to the Soviet Union, Kennan sought to redress the balance. In an article published anonymously in 1947 in the journal *Foreign Affairs* ('The Sources of Soviet Conduct' by 'X'), he stressed the psychological factors that had shaped Soviet foreign policy thinking and repeated his belief that only a sensitive reading of these would allow the US to influence the Kremlin leadership.

The political personality of Soviet power as we know it today is the product of ideology and circumstances: ideology inherited by the present Soviet leaders from the movement in which they had their political origin, and circumstances of the power which they now have exercised for nearly three decades in Russia. There can be few tasks of psychological analysis more difficult than to try to trace the interaction of these two forces and the relative role of each in the determination of official Soviet conduct, yet the attempt must be made if that conduct is to be understood and effectively countered.[36]

Kennan's pseudonymous article dissected the Soviet persecution complex that rejects rational consideration of outside attempts at influence, but stressed that rebarbative rhetoric did not automatically mean the Soviets were seeking violently to overthrow the capitalist world.

It lies in the nature of the mental world of the Soviet leaders, as well as in the character of their ideology, that no opposition to them can be officially recognized as having any merit or jus tification whatsoever. Such opposition can flow, in theory, only from the hostile and incorrigible forces of dying capitalism. This means we are going to continue for a long time to find the Russians difficult to deal with. It does not mean that they should be considered as embarked upon a do-or-die program to overthrow our society by a given date ... There is no trace of any feeling in Soviet psychology that that goal must be reached at any given time ... these precepts are fortified by the lessons of Russian history: of centuries of obscure battles between nomadic forces over the stretches of a vast unfortified plain.[37]

Washington, said Kennan, should adopt the same resolute patience displayed by the USSR, avoiding challenging Soviet notions of pride and honour in a way that would provoke a hostile response.

In these circumstances it is clear that the main element of any United States policy toward the Soviet Union must be that of long-term, patient but firm and vigilant containment of Russian expansive tendencies. It is important to note, however, that such a policy has nothing to do with outward histrionics: with threats or blustering or superfluous gestures of outward 'toughness'.[38]

Kennan warned that the 'Russian leaders are keen judges of human psychology', 'quick to exploit evidence of weakness' such as displays of temper. Instead, demands should be made in a way that allowed the Russians to preserve a sense of pride, leaving 'the way open for a compliance not too detrimental to Russian prestige'.[39]

The coming conflict, Kennan warned, would be a test of American resolve and of American values:

> The issue of Soviet–American relations is in essence a test of the overall worth of the United States as a nation among nations. To avoid destruction the United States need only measure up to its own best traditions and prove itself worthy of preservation as a great nation. The thoughtful observer of Russian–American relations will find no cause for complaint in the Kremlin's challenge to American society. He will rather experience a certain gratitude to a Providence which, by providing the American people with this implacable challenge, has made their entire security as a nation dependent on their pulling themselves together and accepting the responsibilities of moral and political leadership that history plainly intended them to bear.[40]

In his 1947 article, Kennan twice used the word 'containment', the policy forever associated with his name. But Truman's conception of containment – a policy of harsh, unyielding threats – neglected the psychological nuances of Kennan's exegesis. His message was to be used in ways he had not intended.

Policy paper NSC-68, 'United States Objectives and Programs for National Security', adopted in April 1950, effectively militarised the containment doctrine, rejecting negotiation in favour of a substantially expanded military budget, the development of a hydrogen bomb and preparation for regional confrontation with communist forces across the globe. NSC-68 was drafted by men with little or no direct experience of the Soviet Union. It lacked the psychological understanding of Kennan's writing, instead staking everything on the all-out arms race of the coming decade. 'I grew to feel like one who had inadvertently loosened a large boulder from the top of a cliff,' Kennan wrote, 'and now helplessly witnesses its path of destruction in the valley below, shuddering and wincing at each successive glimpse of disaster.'[41]

Speaking in 1996, he reiterated that he had not intended to portray the Soviets as a military threat:

> It all came down to one sentence in the 'X' article where I said that wherever these people, meaning the Soviet leadership, confronted us with dangerous hostility anywhere in the world, we should do everything possible to contain it and not let them expand any further. I should have explained that I didn't suspect them of any desire to launch an attack on us. This was right after the war, and it was absurd to suppose that they were going to turn around and attack the United States. I didn't think I needed to explain that, but I obviously should have done it.[42]

8

THREATS AND MIND READERS

It was February 1975. President Richard Nixon had resigned following the revelation of the Watergate affair, and trust in politics and politicians was at an all-time low. The rock band Chicago's hit single 'Harry Truman' caught the moment, with its plaintive lament for the former president. 'America needs you,' ran the lyrics, 'Harry, could you please come home?' Harry Truman had died in 1972 and his posthumous reputation was high: a nation's anxious yearning for a time of honesty, when life was straightforward and the country run by men you could trust, was loaded onto Truman's shoulders. He was remembered as decisive and forthright, the man who had dealt with the communist threat, overturning the conciliatory politics of his predecessor, FDR, and heeding George Kennan's advice of containment through strength. When Truman left office in 1953, the Cold War was under way, the US had invested heavily in the reconstruction of Europe and thousands of American troops were on the European front line. Washington had delivered on the Truman Doctrine's promise to support those who resisted totalitarian oppression; war was raging in Korea. He himself boasted of his willingness to take responsibility; a sign on his desk in the Oval Office announced, 'The buck stops here'.

It is a trope of American politics, when modern presidents vacillate, to compare them to Harry Truman, personification of the bold decision-maker. A poll of US political scientists ranked him the sixth-best president and one of the least divisive.[1] The truth, as ever, is more complicated than the myth. While in office, Truman had the lowest approval ratings of any modern president.[2] There is little evidence to suggest he ever read Kennan's policy documents, still less that he applied them as Kennan recommended. A revisionist psychological study has portrayed him as 'uncertain, vacillating, lacking a coherent philosophy of foreign policy and often unduly impressed by the last person he spoke to'.[3] If Truman's decisiveness is a myth, where did it come from? And how did the perception slide from the truth?

An episode in the very first days of Truman's presidency set the tone. Truman's version of it in his memoirs makes a point of stressing the hard line he took with the Soviets, who had been getting away with too much, failing to honour the agreements they made at Yalta. In self-congratulatory detail, he recalls how in April 1945 he traded blows with the Soviet foreign minister, Vyacheslav Molotov. The new president – thrust into office just a few days earlier – reportedly denounced Soviet actions over Poland in 'Missouri mule-driver's language'.[4] In an exchange that has entered Cold War mythology, Molotov is said to have complained, 'I have never been talked to like that in my life!', to which Truman boldly retorted 'Carry out your agreements and you *won't* get talked to like that!'[5]

The alleged drama was useful for both sides. Americans warmed to the idea of Truman as mild-mannered Clark Kent donning a Superman cloak to stand up to the Soviet villain. It chimed with America's assimilated self-image, the land of the free, leading the fight for freedom abroad. But it also served the Soviets, confirming Moscow's contention that America and the West were insensitive bullies, lacking in respect, unwilling to acknowledge the sacrifices the Soviet Union had made in saving the world from Nazism. It would allow Gromyko and Molotov to rehearse the tale as evidence that the death of Roosevelt had changed things for the worse, that the arrival of Truman was the turning point after which America made the Soviets their enemies – proof, in short, that the Americans had started the Cold War.

It seems, though, that the Truman–Molotov encounter may not have happened as it was portrayed; that the fiery confrontation was a myth. An examination of contemporaneous records by the British historian Geoffrey Roberts suggests the reality was quite different: only after Soviet–American relations had deteriorated later in the Cold War did the 'Molotov–Truman encounter [come] to be looked upon as a particularly negative event'. It was only in retrospect that this became 'one of the mythical, emblematic events of the early Cold War'.[6]

One assumption might be that Truman made up the story of himself as tough guy to boost his image. But the real explanation seems more complex. The confrontation story is one of several instances in which Truman's recollection of events is coloured by retrospectively acquired knowledge. While he would boast that his 'words of one syllable' had delivered a 'straight one-two to the jaw' of old 'Iron Ass' Molotov,[7] the reality of April 1945 was that the new president was timid and hesitant over foreign policy. For much of 1945 he remained content to continue Roosevelt's policy of placating the Soviets, seeking agreement rather than risk severing ties. Truman's unconscious reworking of the *actualité* fits a pattern outlined by the Russian-American theologian and psychologist Georges Florovsky in his 1969 work 'The Study of the Past'. 'In retrospect, we seem to perceive the logic of the events which unfold themselves in a regular or linear fashion according to a recognizable pattern with an alleged inner necessity. So that we get the impression that it really could not have happened otherwise.'[8]

Baruch Fischhoff, a one-time pupil of Daniel Kahneman, with whom he shares a professional interest in the subconscious aspects of decision-making, has explored the vexed relationship between foresight and hindsight. In his 2003 work 'Hindsight ≠ foresight', Fischhoff argues that the mind allows us to believe that we were aware of how situations would develop in the future. As a result, we tend to make the past conform to a pattern which in reality is only later revealed, persuading ourselves that we knew what the outcome would be all along.[9] 'It is argued,' he concludes, 'that this lack of awareness can seriously restrict one's ability to judge or learn from the past.'[10]

The mind's tendency to revolt against the thought that its existence in its current form is contingent on countless prior events and coincidences* persuades it that the randomness (of the present) was in fact conforming to the necessity of the past (viewed from a future 'now'): 'Finding out that an outcome has occurred increases its perceived likelihood. [We] tend to believe that this relative inevitability was largely apparent in foresight, without the benefit of knowing what happened.'[11] Thus the fact the Soviet Union and the United States broke decisively during Truman's presidency creates the belief that it was inevitable from the start. The experienced Truman of the memoirs recasts his inexperienced self in the light of what he would later learn.

---

* See Sartre's exploration of contingence in *Nausea* (1938) and *Being and Nothingness* (1956).

Florovsky's and Fischhoff's works investigate how the present shapes our memories of the past, but another model of perception, known as schema theory, suggests that past experience can equally condition the way we process the present. Put simply, the world presents us with such a multiplicity of simultaneously occurring data that the human brain is unable to assimilate in real time all the signals it is receiving. The mind therefore develops coping strategies, one of which is to contextualise current information in the light of the past. It means we unconsciously classify events into pre-determined categories, known as schemas, matching them with previous experience and extrapolating what might happen now from what happened in the past.

This phenomenon has intrigued psychologists, who have conducted controlled experiments to investigate it. Brewer and Treyens asked a series of individuals to stand in an office for thirty seconds. The subjects were then taken outside and asked to list what things they saw there. A surprising number said they had seen things that were not actually present, including books and files. The experimenters concluded that people have an assimilated representation of what an office consists of and that that 'schema' includes books and files.[12]

The key proponents of schema theory were a school of psychologists in the mid twentieth century, many of them refugees from Nazi Germany, who developed a model that became known as gestalt. Gestalt posited that human beings are endowed with innate cognitive structures, which allow us to make sense of the world by combining myriad pieces of perceptual data into a coherent whole ('gestalt' in German means a 'shape' or a 'form'). The mind moulds life's bewildering volatility into templates, something that has a pattern. But in doing so, it alters – and can falsify – the nature of the data it receives. As one of the original gestaltists, Kurt Koffka, famously said, 'The whole is something other than the sum of its parts.'[13]

When Franklin Roosevelt died on 12 April 1945, Truman had been vice president for just eighty-two days. He lacked experience in foreign affairs, had no college degree and felt 'a terrible inadequacy of education'. He told a group of reporters: 'Boys, if you ever pray, pray for me now. I don't know if you fellows ever had a load of hay fall on you, but when they told me yesterday what had happened, I felt like the moon, the stars, and all the planets had fallen on me.'[14]

Panicked, Truman sought reassurance in the past. History would be his prop and his guide, 'history [which] I considered far more than a romantic adventure. It was solid instruction and wise teaching which I somehow felt that I wanted and needed.'[15] History's inherited patterns would condition what Truman came to see as his presidential mission, colouring his decision-making. His manuscript notes for a planned autobiography show him both aware of the role history can play – 'I've read somewhere that Herodotus said a good historian makes the facts fit the event to make a good reading' – and convinced that he would be able to provide the unvarnished truth, unsullied by the effects of hindsight or embellishment – 'To save too many knowing spreaders of misinformation from going to hell on the present biography I guess I'll have to state the few interesting facts of my life without the introspective trimmings with which most so-called writers and half-baked essayists clutter up the printed page.'[16]

By the time he met Anthony Eden in May, Truman was relying on his intuition in a way that alarmed some of his interlocutors. 'I am here to make decisions,' he told the British foreign secretary, 'and whether they prove right or wrong, I am going to make them.'[17] An ingénu in international politics, aware he was out of his depth, Truman declined to admit weakness, creating a bluff of tough-talking decisiveness. At the Potsdam Conference in July, the British ambassador to Moscow, Sir Archibald Clark Kerr, voiced a level of concern over Truman's decision-making processes that was evidently shared by others.

> On first contact Mr. Truman made a very good impression, with those blue eyes magnified under heavy lenses, his energy and vitality, his directness and candour, his forthright subaltern air of do or die. But as the conference wore on his vacillations became rather trying. He would take up a point one day and say, 'No, no, no!' beating the table with the sides of his hands. Then everything would come to a halt. But the next morning, after he had talked to his advisers, he would come back and pass over the same point with a mere nod of approval. Pretty soon people stopped taking his snap judgements seriously.[18]

Having neither the knowledge nor the experience on which to make considered judgements brought the temptation to take mental short-cuts, rely on incongruous historical parallels, shoehorn information

into pre-adopted schemas. Under pressure, he settled on the first explanation, rather than seek the right one. 'I don't have to get anybody's
agreement but Harry Truman's,' he told an audience in Missouri in
1945, 'and sometimes I'm afraid that agreement comes too quickly.'[19]

The role of intuition in decision-making is one of the subjects of
Daniel Kahneman's 2011 book, *Thinking, Fast and Slow*. Kahneman
describes two modes of thought: system one, fast, instinctive and
emotional; and system two, slower, more deliberative and logical.
The first involves automatic thinking; decisions are made with little
conscious effort and no feeling of control, linking a 'sense of cognitive ease to illusions of truth and reduced vigilance'.[20]

System two, slow thinking, is more complex. It demands con-
centration and the exercise of agency. Decisions are made by the
conscious self, based on reflective choices, reasons and beliefs. It may
seem that system two is the better tool for making decisions, but
Kahneman suggests system one is the essential starting point at the
root of our choices. Its rapidity means that it will at times lead us
to false conclusions, or will be overwhelmed by the detail and complexity of the task, and that is when system two is activated. Where
system two processes doubt, system one is given to overconfidence.
Its over-reliance on hindsight creates an exaggerated belief in our
ability to order experience. 'Narrative fallacies arise inevitably from
our continuous attempt to make sense of the world ... we humans
constantly fool ourselves by constructing flimsy accounts of the past
and believing they are true.'[21] The belief that we understand the past
fosters an overconfidence in the ability to know the future.[22]

Truman's decision-making bears the hallmarks of Kahneman's
system one. For example, in the lead-up to Potsdam, he seems to
have based his assessment of Stalin on a schema drawn from his own
political mentor in Missouri. Tom 'Boss' Pendergast was the man
who set Truman on the road to the White House and Truman idealised him. He was Truman's mental image of 'the strong leader',
who, as he 'had learned from history', was 'a man who has the ability
to get other people to do what they don't want to do, and like it'.[23]
In Truman's mental representation, the Soviet leader was the incarnation of Pendergast – 'Stalin is as near like Tom Pendergast as any
man I know'[24] – and he incorrectly attributed Pendergast's qualities
to him. Because Pendergast had adhered robustly to 'the code of the
politician' – that a man must always keep his word – he assumed that

Stalin would do the same. It convinced him that Stalin was a reasonable man and a moderating influence on the communist extremists around him. 'If you could sit down with Stalin and get him to focus on the problem,' Truman wrote, 'Stalin would take a reasonable attitude, whereas if the problem never got around to Stalin ... it might be handled by the Molotov clique.'[25] Like Pendergast, Stalin was a 'big man' and 'it is always easy to understand and to get along with big men ... Little fellows, on the other hand, are a challenge, due to their egotism and desire to show off their knowledge and "strut their stuff".'[26] Truman's incorrect intuition that Stalin and Pendergast were cut from the same cloth did indeed reduce his vigilance, making him credulous and hesitant. Churchill found Truman weak. On the eve of the Battle of Berlin, he was urging the president to think again about Stalin.[27]

Churchill was the man who had foreseen the Second World War; now he seemed convinced the past was repeating itself. If, in his early meetings with Stalin, 'system one thinking' had led him to trust the Soviet leader, it would appear that system two had kicked in by 1945. 'All these matters can only be settled before the United States Armies in Europe are weakened,' he told his foreign secretary, Anthony Eden, on 4 May 1945. 'If they are not settled before the United States Armies withdraw from Europe and the Western world folds up its war machines, there are no prospects of a satisfactory solution and very little of preventing a third World War.'[28]

In the spring of 1945, under the shadow of earlier experience, Churchill exhibited some of the qualities he felt Truman lacked, making the first move in what would become a psychological dynamic of threats, guesses and pretence. Incensed at the Soviets' refusal to hold free elections in Poland – a betrayal of the Yalta agreement, Churchill said – he instructed his military commanders to produce a plan to 'save' central Europe. What the British chiefs of staff came up with in response to Churchill's request was so apocalyptic and so potentially damaging to East–West relations that it was hidden from public view for over fifty years. Only in 1998 did the National Archives deem that Cabinet File 120/691, dated 22 May 1945, was safe to release. It contained the plans for 'Operation Unthinkable', a plan to deploy British, American, Polish, even German troops if necessary, to push the Red Army out of Europe. It would have triggered a major renewal of hostilities. On the front page, the words 'Russia: Threat to

Western Civilisation' were written by hand in ink, followed by a bald statement of the plan's objective: 'To impose upon Russia the will of the United States and the British Empire.'

The paper explored the possibility of a pre-emptive strike against the Soviet Union. 'A quick success might induce the Russians to submit to our will at least for the time being. But if they want total war, they are in a position to have it … The only way in which we can achieve our object with certainty and lasting results is by victory in a total war.' Under the headings 'Decisive Defeat of the Russian Forces' and 'Occupation of Vital Areas of Russia', it discussed the pros and cons of Britain and the US committing to such a 'total war'. Not surprisingly, the need for discretion was paramount: 'Owing to the special need for secrecy,' it noted, 'the normal staffs in Service Ministries have not been consulted.'[29]

According to Sir Alan Brooke's war diaries, Churchill was 'completely carried away' by the announcement of the US acquisition of the atomic bomb. 'We now had something in our hands which would redress the balance with the Russians!' Brooke quotes him as saying. 'Now we could say, if you insist on doing this or that, well we can just blot out Moscow, then Stalingrad, then Kiev, then Kuibyshev, Kharkov, Sebastopol etc., etc.'[30]

Throughout May and into June, London slowed down the demobilisation of British forces on the territory of continental Europe controlled by the western Allies. Was an attack seriously being considered? The huge numerical superiority of the Red Army, who were estimated to have up to 6 million men in Europe, meant that any conflict would be lengthy and brutal. Churchill's hopes of a short sharp victory hardly seemed realisable. The British generals concluded with typical understatement that an invasion of the Soviet Union would be 'hazardous'.

'Operation Unthinkable' never took place, but Churchill's personal distrust of Stalin was evident; no longer did he consider him a 'wise fellow' with whom business could be done. The Soviet Union and the western Allies had fought together in a coalition of convenience and once the fascist threat had been defeated, the pre-war suspicion returned. Did Churchill fall into the trap of schema thinking? The most readily available comparison – Germany's actions in Czechoslovakia in 1938, an authoritarian leader demanding control over part of a central European nation – bore similarities to Soviet demands over

Poland in 1945. Churchill saw himself in the role of Cassandra, his warnings doomed to go unheeded. 'Last time I saw it all coming and cried aloud to my own fellow-countrymen and to the world, but no one paid any attention ... We surely must not let that happen again.'[31] But there were differences now. While the Soviet Union after the war was militarily strong, its industrial base was demonstrably crippled and its population decimated, its leadership and its people psychologically unnerved by the recent memory of a surprise attack from the West, carried out through the vulnerable Polish Corridor. Churchill – and Attlee after him – nonetheless reached the conclusion that Stalin was intent on conquering western Europe.

The work of the American political scientist and cognitive psychologist Herbert Simon, seeks to explain some elements of decision-making processes among leaders in the fields of economics and politics. Simon's 1956 work on rational choice in decision-making[32] outlined the constraints that limit logical thinking, coming up with the term 'satisficing' to convey the tendency among decision-makers to seek a satisfactory solution in place of an optimal one, sifting through available alternatives until an arbitrary threshold of acceptability is met. Perceptual satisficing is done not consciously, but based on a subject's ingrained – or, perhaps, most recent – schemas. A belief is formed not only by the information presented, but by the relative availability of the prototypes into which it can be fitted, including how readily those ideas come to mind – and that belief is not readily changed as new information is received.[33] Despite the differences between Nazi Germany in 1938 and the Soviet Union in 1945, a simplified, 'satisficed' analogy between the two seems to have lodged in Churchill's mind.

Western leaders, who had witnessed Stalin's propensity for paranoia at Yalta, responded with paranoia of their own. Churchill's flirtation with 'Operation Unthinkable' was the expression of suspicions that would spiral on both sides.

When Churchill made a speech in November 1945 praising Russia and Stalin personally, Stalin's kneejerk response was to dismiss it as a trick. 'Churchill does all of this because he needs to soothe his bad conscience,' he told the politburo, 'and needs to camouflage his hostile attitude to the USSR, in particular the fact that Churchill and his pupils from the Labour Party are the organizers of a British–American–French bloc against the USSR.'[34]

While the West fumed about Soviet behaviour in Poland, the Soviets increasingly felt that the new governments in the US and the UK were trying to row back on the agreements of Yalta and Potsdam by questioning Moscow's right to influence in Romania and Bulgaria and side-lining Soviet interests in the Far East.

The Soviets believed the West was trying to deprive them of the just rewards of their military triumph: an expression of Molotov's schema view that historically, 'Russians are remarkable warriors but they do not know how to make peace. They are deceived and underpaid.'

When, at a military parade at the Paris Peace Conference of 1946, Molotov felt his seat was too far down the pecking order, he walked out, with Stalin's approval. 'You behaved absolutely correctly,' Stalin wrote. 'The dignity of the Soviet Union must be defended not only in big matters, but also in minutiae.' Moscow's skin was thin and slights, real or imagined, hurt.[35] London was equally consumed by fear. After Attlee replaced Churchill in Downing Street, a meeting of senior ministers chaired by the prime minister on 5 November 1946 noted that, 'an examination of the European theatre of operations alone leads us to the conclusion that ... a conquest of Western Europe by the Soviet must be considered as a practical possibility, particularly in the next ten months'.[36]

A reflexive presumption that 'the other' was bent on aggression led to skewed thinking on both sides. Evidence was shoehorned into preconceived schemas. Actions were deemed to be aggressive, even if close examination showed them to be not dissimilar to one's own. Differences in the objectives of the two countries, wrote Dean Acheson, meant that 'many of the acts of the Soviet Government appear to the United States Government to be violations of the spirit of an international agreement although it is difficult to adduce acceptable evidence of literal violations'.[37]

The political scientist Robert Jervis has written about the influence of preconception on the way evidence is formulated into policy-making; in other words, how our existing beliefs, rather than the information we receive, shape the decisions we make:

[We] normally think that an actor's perceptions of others – their goals, intentions and characteristics – precede the development of his policy toward them. Although this logical progression

is correct for some cases, there are others in which causation
flows in the reverse direction – statesmen first set their policy
toward another state and then develop the image of the other
that supports and would have led to such a policy. The relationship between beliefs and policy is then one of rationalization
rather than rationality.[38]

Those perceptions that are useful for the adopted policy are shaped
and hardened into facts; evidence that does not accord with them is
ignored. Dean Acheson was well aware that western governments
depended on the electorate to keep them in power, but that the electorate had little time for nuances. Few voters had either the capacity
or the inclination to decipher complex issues of international politics.
'In the State Department we used to discuss how much time that
mythical "average American citizen" put in each day listening, reading
and arguing about the world outside his own country,' Acheson noted
ruefully. 'Assuming a man or woman with a fair education, a family,
a job in or out of the house, it seemed to us that ten minutes a day
would be a high average. If this were anywhere near right, points to
be understandable had to be clear. If we made our points clearer than
truth, we did not differ from most other educators and could hardly
do otherwise.'[39] The result was a simplification of debate, a hardening
of propaganda and a removal of caveats from the anti-Soviet message
that the White House felt compelled to disseminate. Making things
'clearer than truth' became a finely developed art in both East and
West.

By 1946, Churchill had lost the backing of the British electorate,
but he still had the ear of global opinion. His speech 'The Sinews
of Peace', delivered at Truman's invitation in Fulton, Missouri, on
5 March of that year, etched a stark image in the imagination of the
world that would define the psychological topography of a divided
Europe.

> From Stettin in the Baltic to Trieste in the Adriatic, an iron
> curtain has descended across the Continent. Behind that line
> lie all the capitals of the ancient states of Central and Eastern
> Europe. Warsaw, Berlin, Prague, Vienna, Budapest, Belgrade,
> Bucharest and Sofia, all these famous cities lie in what I must call
> 'the Soviet sphere', and all are subject in one form or another,

not only to Soviet influence, but to a very high, and, in some cases, increasing measure of control from Moscow ... The Communist parties have been raised to pre-eminence and power far beyond their numbers and are seeking everywhere to obtain totalitarian control ... This is certainly not the liberated Europe we fought to build up, nor is it one which contains the essentials of permanent peace ... I do not believe that Soviet Russia desires war. What they desire is the fruits of war and the indefinite expansion of their power and doctrines ... Our difficulties and dangers will not be removed by closing our eyes to them; nor will they be removed by a policy of appeasement.[40]

With the Truman White House continuing to hesitate between confrontation and accommodation, Churchill's proposed course of action was intended to influence public opinion in favour of the former.

From what I have seen of our Russian friends and Allies during the war, I am convinced that there is nothing they admire so much as strength, and there is nothing for which they have less respect than for weakness, especially military weakness. For that reason, the old doctrine of a balance of power is unsound.[41]

Truman distanced himself from the speech, claiming he had not known its contents before it was delivered. Given that they had spent so long together on the train ride from Washington to Missouri, Truman's claim is doubtful.[42] More likely, he feared the public would view him as a warmonger. When, a week after Churchill's address, opinion polls showed that 60 per cent of Americans felt their leaders were being too soft on the Soviets, Truman's stance began to harden.[43]

Stalin took Churchill's speech as a slander and a threat. In an interview in *Pravda* the following week, he railed against western imperialism's desire for war. 'Mr Churchill and his allies,' Stalin declared, 'resemble Hitler and his allies. They have concluded that the English-speaking nations should rule the world.'[44] With no access to news or information other than that provided by the state, the vast majority of Soviet people believed that Britain and America were now warmongers, most probably future enemies. Stalin's reply to Churchill's charge of 'Soviet expansionism' was one that every Russian understood: in the light of Russia's long history of foreign invasions, including the recent German invasion, the creation of 'buffer states' in the countries of eastern Europe was a natural objective.

Stalin's swagger masked an inner panic. Despite the Red Army's size and successes in the war, the Soviet Union did not possess what the US did: the nuclear bomb. The spectacle of what the new American weapon had done to the Japanese cities of Hiroshima and Nagasaki in August 1945 had convinced Stalin that the Red Army's numerical strength was now meaningless. Soviet society was gripped by the sudden, dreadful knowledge that the warmongers in London and Washington had the means to wipe out Moscow, Leningrad and innumerable other cities.

When the *Sunday Times* correspondent in Moscow asked Stalin about the bomb, the dictator had a studiously upbeat reply. 'Atomic bombs are meant to frighten those with weak nerves,' he told his questioner, 'but they cannot on their own decide the outcome of wars. Of course, monopoly ownership of the secret of the atomic bomb creates a threat. But there are at least two remedies. Monopoly ownership of the bomb cannot last for long. And use of the atomic bomb will be prohibited.'[45]

Stalin clearly did not trust prohibition. Moscow had declined to join Washington's newly created Atomic Energy Commission, which was given the task of regulating nuclear weapons. So, only one option remained. The Soviet Union would have to develop its own bomb, and quickly.

The need became even more pressing when, in March 1947, President Truman announced his doctrine of US support for nations struggling for liberty and democracy. The Truman Doctrine was aimed initially at preventing Greece and Turkey from falling into communist hands. Its wider aim, however, was clear: the US would offer support to the eastern European nations already under the Soviet yoke. Truman told congressional leaders that if Greece fell, it would be the first domino of many that would inevitably follow. There was little evidence for what would become known as the 'domino theory', and Truman probably knew it; but he had taken the advice of Senator Arthur Vandenberg that he should 'scare the hell out of the American people' to ensure the bill passed.[46] The starkness of his warning was an example of the politician's need to sharpen, simplify and dramatise his message for popular consumption. A Manichean vision of a world divided between freedom and oppression was crucial to the Truman

Doctrine. It needed to be painted in broad strokes to convince the average voter and to persuade Congress to vote through funds to save Greek democracy.

> At the present moment in world history nearly every nation must choose between alternative ways of life. The choice is too often not a free one … I believe that it must be the policy of the United States to support free peoples who are resisting attempted subjugation by armed minorities or by outside pressures. If we falter in our leadership, we may endanger the peace of the world – and we shall surely endanger the welfare of our own nation.[47]

Three months later, Washington announced a programme of economic and technical assistance to European states struggling to rebuild their economies after the war. The European Recovery Program, popularly known as the Marshall Plan, offered to make aid available to countries on both sides of the Iron Curtain. The total eventually exceeded $13 billion, or five per cent of the United States' annual GDP,[48] but Washington's largesse brought obligations. Recipient nations would have to furnish details of their national economy and cooperate with US advisers in a programme of modernisation and restructuring. After initially hesitating about taking part in discussions, Moscow ordered its satellites to steer clear. The Soviet deputy foreign minister, Andrei Vyshinsky, in a speech to the United Nations in September 1947, denounced the Marshall Plan as a capitalist ploy to divide the world into pro- and anti-Soviet camps.

> The Marshall Plan constitutes in essence merely a variant of the Truman Doctrine … the implementation of the Marshall Plan will mean placing European countries under the economic and political control of the United States and direct interference in the internal affairs of those countries … this plan is an attempt to split Europe into two camps … to complete the formation of a bloc of several European countries hostile to the interests of the democratic countries of Eastern Europe and most particularly the interests of the Soviet Union.[49]

When Czechoslovakia and Poland said they might take the American money, Stalin ordered them to refuse. He was determined to shape the previously capitalist economies of his 'buffer states' to the Soviet model of socialist central planning; American influence was seen as hostile interference.

To counter the Marshall Plan, Moscow created Comecon, the Council for Mutual Economic Assistance, in January 1949. The new body issued a defiant statement to the western powers:

> The Governments of the United States of America, of Great Britain, and of certain Western European states have imposed a trade boycott on the countries of People's Democracy and the USSR because these countries did not consider it appropriate that they should submit themselves to the dictatorship of the Marshall Plan, which would have violated their sovereignty and the interests of their national economies. In the light of these circumstances ... the countries of People's Democracy [Bulgaria, Hungary, Poland, Romania and Czechoslovakia] and the USSR, consider it necessary to create the Council for Mutual Economic Assistance, on the basis of equal representation between the member countries ... to accelerate the restoration and development of their national economies.[50]

The Eastern Bloc was pulling up the drawbridge. For Stalin, socialism would be safe only when Moscow had the bomb and, as we know, that would not happen until August 1949. Recently declassified documents suggest, however, that history might have been very different. In September 1945 the US secretary of war, Henry Stimson, sent a memorandum to President Truman suggesting that Washington should share the secret of the bomb with the Russians. Moscow was almost certainly working on its own atomic programme, Stimson wrote, but would it not be better for the West to 'voluntarily invite [the USSR] into the partnership upon a basis of cooperation and trust' in order to avoid 'what will in effect be a secret armament race of a rather desperate character'?

Stimson's gambit might have changed the world. Its success, as he acknowledged, would have depended on Washington making a leap of faith by placing its trust in Moscow's willingness to do the same. In the event, the secretary of the navy and future secretary of defense, James Forrestal, persuaded Truman to veto the idea. 'The Russians, like the Japanese, are essentially Oriental in their thinking,' Forrestal wrote. 'It seems doubtful that we should endeavor to buy their understanding and sympathy. We tried that once with Hitler. There are no returns on appeasement.'[51]

Forrestal's conviction that gambling on the goodwill of the other side was naively unrealistic would become the default position for East and West thinking throughout the Cold War, even if it had not been Truman's when he first entered office.

9

WAR BY INADVERTENCE

The meeting of Soviet and American troops on the Elbe River in April 1945 signalled the beginning of the end of Europe's costliest war. A new atmosphere of friendship and cooperation, anointed by the blood sacrifice of Allied nations east and west, seemed the inevitable outcome of years of toil and shared effort. 'We were like brothers. We had defeated the enemy together, we were united in fighting fascism and we'd won. The Americans gave us cigarettes, biscuits, whatever they had, even watches as souvenirs. The atmosphere was unbelievable.'[1] The photograph is staged – the two flags and the makeshift backdrop with the words 'East meets West' are the handiwork of US propaganda officials – but the sentiments of Red Army Lieutenant Alexander Silvashko are transparently sincere.

And 2nd Lieutenant William Robertson, the US soldier in the historic photo, is equally warm in his assessment of his new comrades. 'They were good people and we had no problem getting along with the individual Russian soldiers we met there at all. There was relief that the war was coming to a close and that the Allies had won. We were plain thankful that we were there and still breathing.'[2]

History, though, is rarely inevitable.

After the war, Alexander Silvashko returned to his job as a schoolteacher. In 1949, he was excited to hear that Mosfilm was making a movie called *Meeting on the Elbe*. He was looking forward to showing it to his students, but he would be sadly disappointed. Far from celebrating the joyous events that Silvashko remembered taking part in, the film was shaped by the new international climate that was darkening the world. It showed the Americans as duplicitous, potential future enemies, their generals in 1945 already planning for war with the Soviets. 'I remember seeing *Meeting on the Elbe*,' Silvashko would recall five decades later. 'I thought I'd find my character played

The warm embrace 2nd Lieutenant William Robertson and Lieutenant
Alexander Silvashko shared in May 1945 may have been staged, but
it reflected genuine feelings of mutual admiration between the
men who fought against Hitler. The warmth would not last.

somewhere in it. I was terribly upset when I realised that it was completely untruthful.'[3] Silvashko said he lamented the distortions that the postwar present had imposed on the victorious past, but he was reluctant to speak about them to his students. 'The atmosphere [in 1949] was one of fear. The children liked my tales of the war, but I never told them about the meeting on the Elbe. If I had discussed what had happened openly I would have been in trouble, pulled in and questioned by the secret police.'[4]

Silvashko was speaking in the perestroika years, when it was de rigueur to denounce the lies of the Stalinist era, and the present often colours the past – the Silvashko of 1996 was remembering the Silvashko of 1949 remembering the Silvashko of 1945. It seems farfetched that he would have been 'pulled in' by the secret police for his memories of the Elbe meeting, but it is not beyond the bounds of possibility. It is certainly the case that representations of the meeting between Red Army and American troops disappeared from view in the USSR. Smiling Americans embracing their Soviet counterparts no longer fitted the image of the new enemy.

For those who had fought in the war, who had witnessed the common struggle and shared the emotions of combat, there was puzzlement. Konstantin Simonov, the Soviet author whose novel *The Living and the Dead* would become one of the classic testimonies of the Second World War, was by no means a dissident voice. But in his 1947 novella, *The Smoke of the Fatherland*, his hero speaks bitterly of the dashed hopes felt by many in the Soviet Union.

> To many of us it seemed, especially towards the end of the war, that, yes, the last shot will have been heard and everything would change. Of course, in a way, people are right: everything has changed, there is peace, the guns are silent ... But they thought that there would be friends all around for the rest of their life. And now all around there are enemies.[5]

Spiralling mistrust led both sides to imagine 'enemies all around'.[6] And each was determined to show their resolve, to prove to the other that they would not be intimidated. While hopes for peace and coop-eration in the postwar years were now a pipe dream, Washington and Moscow had by and large managed to keep their fears and sus-picions in perspective. There was, though, one issue that threatened to undermine the fragile equilibrium. Differences over the future of Germany, and specifically over the status of Berlin, would become the first flashpoint of the Cold War, the source of international para-noia and escalating irrationality that threatened a resumption of open hostilities. Neither side wanted war, but prolonged friction inflamed tensions to the point where rational judgement was in danger of being swamped.

Berlin is the place where the War of Nerves, the continuous testing of the other side's resolve by non-violent means, began in earnest. East and West saw it as a proving ground for their competing ideologies, the turbulent hinterland between capitalism and commu-nism where each would strive to convince the people that their side represented the future. The Great Powers exerted their might, from public propaganda to covert psychological warfare to threats and dirty tricks.

Occupied Germany had been a rubbing point between the wartime Allies since it was partitioned at the end of hostilities. The British, French and Americans were finding it increasingly difficult to work with the Soviets and there had been confrontations at the inter-section of the occupied zones. While the West wanted to boost the German economy as a bulwark of European postwar recovery, Stalin wanted to keep Germany weak, to punish her and ensure she would never again be in a position to wage war.

Even before the blockade, Berlin was the focus of the world's attention. The German capital had been a psychological reference point throughout the Soviet war effort. *'Do Berlina!'* – 'On to Berlin!' – was painted on Red Army tanks, yelled by divisional command-ers, included in military bulletins. Soviet troops knew their work was not done until they had taken Hitler's capital. The Nazis had come to their homeland, murdered their wives and children; their revenge would be to capture Berlin, and they had done so. Now they felt the West was muscling them out of it.

For the West, Berlin was the key to the balance of power. With Poland lost to Soviet control and communist forces preparing to seize power in Czechoslovakia, the fear was that Moscow's next target would be Germany. In September 1946, secretary of state James Byrnes had committed the US to a policy of economic reconstruc-tion and a long-term military presence in Germany; the US would not sit back and watch while the people of Europe were once again overtaken by undemocratic forces. Byrnes's speech, to an enthusias-tic audience in Stuttgart, was an attempt to win German hearts and minds. It became known as the 'Speech of Hope'.

> I want no misunderstanding. We will not shirk our duty. We are not withdrawing. We are staying here … The American people want to return the government of Germany to the German people. The American people want to help the German people to win their way back to an honorable place among the free and peace-loving nations of the world.[7]

The Soviets, who wanted a socialist government in Germany as a guarantee of their own future security against attack from the west, regarded Byrnes's speech, with its suggestions that the border between Germany and Poland should be reassessed, as a provocation, a flagrant contradiction of the Yalta and Potsdam agreements.

Differences over Germany fostered suspicion and created scope for dangerous miscalculation. Moscow believed the slow rate of reparations being delivered from the western sectors of Germany to the USSR was a deliberate American ploy, an insult to the Soviet men and women who had given their lives to defeat Nazism; US economic aid to West Germany was a bribe, designed to seduce the German people. General Lucius Clay, the military governor of the American zone, acknowledged as much. 'There is no choice between becoming a Communist on 1,500 calories a day,' Clay wrote, 'and a believer in democracy on 1,000.'[8] The West needed to offer the Germans more than just idealistic talk of the benefits of democracy.

In those tinderbox years, each side studied the pronouncements of the other, trying to disentangle the truth from the bravado, straining to decode the reality behind the disinformation, the threats and the lies. Churchill's assertion that 'the truth is so precious that she should always be attended by a bodyguard of lies' fed the mistrust. In such febrile times, with national pride in play and the future of Europe at stake, the fear of war by inadvertence was high. The Pentagon's 1946 Joint Outline War Plan, code-named PINCHER, warned that the main risk was not that war would be started by the deliberate act of either side, but that an unspecified 'miscalculation' could trigger one, and 'no war with the USSR can be less than a total war, requiring the full utilization of the entire US and allied war potential'.[9]

As military governor of the US zone, Lucius Clay was as conscious as anyone of the risks both sides were running. 'This is a war of NERVES,' he wrote to his troop commander, 'and we must have the stout nerves. Any indication of weakness on our part would jeopardize our position in central Europe ... We must be as well trained as possible and on the alert to avoid a surprise action.'[10]

The British were supportive of the American strategy. Bankrupted by war, the United Kingdom could contribute little to the rebuilding of the West German economy, but it could offer its intelligence expertise. A Foreign Office report, 'Survey of Present Situation in Germany', dated 24 April 1946, showed a subtler understanding of Soviet sensitivities over Berlin and of the weaknesses of the Allied position.

> It should be remembered that the city was captured by Soviet troops and, on the principle that takings are keepings, it is not surprising that they should regard it as more theirs than anybody

else's ... An island in the Soviet zone, Berlin is largely dependent on Soviet goodwill. The three western Allies are responsible for the feeding of their respective sectors [of Berlin], but the food, the trains, the roads, must all pass through Soviet territory. For the Soviet Element it is the home ground. The western Allies are playing away.[11]

The report did not minimise what was at stake. 'In Berlin,' it concluded, 'the Russians are energetically creating a new order' to replace the defeated Nazi one; failure to maintain an Allied presence in the German capital could mean the spread of communism to West Germany, too.

If our foothold were lost, eastern Germany would be completely sealed off from the west. Such division would be purely one-sided, since the western Allies would find that they could not effectively seal off western Germany from the east – just as today Soviet views and news are exported to the world but little world news is imported into the USSR. In addition, our withdrawal from Berlin and the loss of prestige it must involve would go far to convince many Germans in the west that unity and security could only be achieved by accepting communism in their turn. They would surely feel that Soviet domination in the east had come to stay and they would wonder how long the western Powers would continue to hold on in western Germany ... Of one thing we may be sure. They will not rest content with organising their own zone. Already they are actively supporting the Communists in the western zones.[12]

Having read the report's conclusions, the foreign secretary, Ernest Bevin, formulated the approach that would guide British policy in the decades that followed. 'The danger of Russia has become certainly as great as, and possibly even greater than, that of a revived Germany,' Bevin wrote. 'The worst situation of all would be a revived Germany in league with or dominated by Russia.[13] ... Physical control of the Eurasian land mass and eventual control of the whole World Island is what the politburo is aiming at.'[14] While Moscow may have been dogged by the inherited fear of invasion from the west, Britain and other European states were haunted by the prospect of an alliance between Germans and Slavs. Losing Berlin could be fatal in the battle to stop the Soviets dominating the globe.

The tensions over the German capital were on the agenda at meetings of the Council of Foreign Ministers in Paris in 1946 and Moscow in 1947, but the participants left bitterly divided. The Kremlin was horrified by the western Allies' failure to act punitively against the defeated Germans. When Stalin accused them of reneging on their commitment to implement the so-called 'Four Ds' – demilitarisation, disarmament, denazification and democratisation – in their zones of occupation, his complaints were far from groundless. David Cornwell, later to become the author John le Carré, was serving as a field security officer in Austria. 'We were supposedly Nazi-hunters,' Cornwell wrote, 'and when you actually identified somebody who was a wanted figure of some sort with a disagreeable or hateful past, there was a question mark about his usefulness.' The West was willing to turn a blind eye to war crimes if it meant former Nazis could help with intelligence about the Red threat. 'We were already looking at the Communist enemy. To me it was bewildering. I'd been brought up to hate Nazism and all of a sudden to find that we'd turned on a sixpence and the great new enemy was to be the Soviet Union was perplexing.'[15]

Recriminations and misunderstandings increased the tension. By early 1948, each side seemed to be speaking to an interlocutor who had blocked his ears. Stalin announced that his aim was German unification and urged East German communists to draft a constitution that would be discussed and admired by the West. 'All the [German] people must be drawn into discussion of the constitution. This will form the psychological basis for the realisation of a united Germany.' In response, and without consulting the Soviets, the western powers declared that they intended to combine their three zones to establish a federal West German state.[16]

Even the steady nerves of General Lucius Clay had begun to fray. In March 1948 he sent a panicked telegram to the joint chiefs of staff in Washington hinting that war was close:

> Within the last few weeks, I have felt a subtle change in Soviet attitude which I cannot define but which now gives me a feeling that [war] may come with dramatic suddenness. I cannot support this change in my own thinking with any data or outward

evidence in relationships other than to describe it as a feeling of a new tenseness in every Soviet individual with whom we have official relations. I am unable to submit any official report in the absence of supporting data but my feeling is real.[17]

West Berlin, 'this island of capitalism in a sea of communism', had long rankled with Stalin. As Khrushchev later admitted, 'We wanted to exert pressure on the West to create a unified Berlin inside a GDR that would then close its borders.' The Kremlin, he said, was 'prodding the capitalist world with the tip of the bayonet'.[18] When Stalin met the East German communists Wilhelm Pieck and Otto Grotewohl in Moscow in March 1948, he was bullish about the possibility of forcing the Allies out of Berlin.[19] It was just three months before the commencement of the Berlin blockade; Stalin was evidently thinking ahead.

In June the Allies declared that a new currency, the Deutsche Mark, was being introduced in the western zones. The Soviets responded that it could not be used in Berlin, despite the occupying powers holding joint authority there. They announced the introduction of their own currency, the Ostmark, and decreed that only Ostmarks would be accepted in the capital. To underline the point, the Soviet authorities halted all western shipments into the city, citing unspecified 'technical difficulties' with transport links. Allied supplies to their zones of the capital had to travel by train across the hundred miles of Soviet-controlled territory that separated it from the West. Now, with train links blocked by Moscow, the western sectors of Berlin began to run out of food and coal.

The incomprehension between East and West was exacerbated by the impact of their contrasting approaches to diplomacy. Throughout their history as an opposition group, the Bolsheviks had traditionally dealt with problems through confrontation. They had little experience of, and seemingly no interest in, the niceties of diplomatic norms. Berlin was a good example of their propensity for making discomfiting moves – threats and swagger and outrageous bluff – to move a dispute in their favour. Lacking experience of such tactics and unsure about how to deal with them, the West tended to overestimate the earnestness of Soviet bullying. The chief Soviet representative in the Berlin encounters, Vyacheslav Molotov – nicknamed 'Football head' by British embassy staff in Moscow – made no bones about his lack of finesse. 'I regard myself first of all as a politician and not a diplomat,' he told Allen Dulles. The hardball techniques of Bolshevik party meetings – slander, filibustering, intrigue and spying – were his preferred operating methods. 'Winning someone's trust,' Molotov said, 'was only a tactical ruse; flexibility on policy was a sin, acknowledgement of mistakes a death sentence.'[20]

In reality, much of the posturing was simply bravado: Stalin was testing western resolve, gauging how far he could push the Americans and British without military confrontation, in a high-stakes game of chicken.* Vladimir Yerofeyev, Stalin's French-language interpreter from the Soviet Foreign Ministry, remembered that 'Stalin was very calm. He smoked; he didn't walk about like he usually did. Normally he would pace around like a cat in his soft boots, but this time he stayed seated.'[21]

The western powers, by and large, also remained calm. Stalin's imposition of the blockade on 24 June had taken London and Washington by surprise but, after the initial shock, cool heads prevailed. The Russia Committee of the British Foreign Office, meeting in July, concluded that the situation in Europe was now 'very largely a matter of war of nerves'. With the help of the latest military intelligence, William Hayter assured committee members that 'there were still no signs of preparation for war within the Soviet Union itself'.[22]

There were, though, pressures that could not be ignored. By August, the British embassy in Berlin was cabling London to say,

> Our position is fundamentally weak because we cannot stay in Berlin indefinitely in defiance of the Soviet Union ... With regard to the Soviet position, there is no doubt that they have lost ground heavily in the political field and have forfeited any chance of winning the majority of the Germans over to themselves for many years to come ... [But if] we can find a half-way house it would be better to accept it rather than admit a breakdown.[23]

The Americans were also looking to clarify their thinking about how to respond to Soviet aggression. A National Security Council report

---

* For more on such tactics, see Chapter 21, which explores the work of Nobel Prize-winning game theorist and nuclear strategist Thomas Schelling in detail.

of 18 August stated the obvious, that Russia 'has become for the time being the outstanding problem of US foreign policy' but lamented the lack of political leadership from the White House. 'There has,' concluded the report's authors, 'been no clear formulation of basic US objectives with respect to Russia.'[24]

Harry Truman was struggling to fill the gap. As soon as the crisis began, he had ordered sixty 'atomic capable' B-29 bombers to fly to US bases in Germany and Britain, hinting (falsely) that they were armed with nuclear weapons. It was an early example of the nuclear brinkmanship that would characterise the Cold War: the US didn't even possess sixty atomic bombs. At the same time, the British and US air forces were beginning to ferry in supplies to the blockaded city. In 1948 and early 1949, they flew over 1,500 flights a day, carrying more than 4,500 tons of cargo.[25]

Technically the Soviet blockade did not contravene any agreements over the shared city, as the western Allies had never formally secured road or rail access rights to their sectors of Berlin. The only right of access in the postwar agreements was by air, and Soviet air traffic controllers were – albeit grudgingly – continuing to guide Allied planes through their airspace. The ongoing Soviet cooperation, minimal as it was, seemed an indication that Moscow was not seeking all-out confrontation with war as its endgame. Without the controllers' assistance, the airlift would have been all but impossible.[26]

As it was, the western supplies were enough to spare West Berliners having to seek aid from the Soviets, a humiliation that would effectively have signalled an end to Allied control of their occupation sectors. The Red Army tried to impede the airlift, buzzing the incoming planes and shining spotlights to dazzle the pilots, but they stopped short of shooting them down. By the spring of 1949, the Berlin airlift had achieved its aim. Moscow gave up, announcing on 12 May that the blockade would be lifted.

The first flashpoint of the postwar years had confirmed the preconceptions of both sides, cementing each of them in their sense of blinkered self-righteousness. Demonstrations in West Berlin affirmed the narrative of western democracy fighting the good fight against the forces of communism. 'People of the world, look upon this city!' declared City Councillor Ernst Reuter to crowds in the Platz der Republik on 9 September 1948, the height of the crisis. 'You cannot,

Washington and Moscow competed to convince the defeated
Germans that they alone knew the way to a golden future.

you must not, forsake us! There is only one possibility for all of us: to
stand together until this fight has been won, until the fight has finally
been settled through victory over the enemies, through victory over
the force of darkness.'[27]

In the battle for the hearts of the German people, Moscow's show
of aggression had done little to bolster the Kremlin's cause. The West
may have been reluctant to risk a war for the people of West Berlin,
but it did its utmost to convince them that democracy offered a credible alternative to the communists. Berlin was the first skirmish in the
psychological war between the two sides and US propaganda stole
the show. From posters to radio messages, from economic largesse
to lessons in comportment for GIs on the ground, all was geared to a
single end – keeping Germany in the Allied camp.

Moscow trailed in the propaganda war. Its message lacked pur-
chase in western Germany. In the East, though, it was a different
story. Soviet communism exerted its grip on the sources of mass
information to mould and deceive its own population and that of the
satellite states. The veteran anti-communist Arthur Koestler wrote
in *The New York Times*: 'No political treaties and trade agreements
can guarantee peace as long as this world remains psychologically

divided into two worlds, with persecution-mania on one side, growing alarm on the other ... Psychological armaments should be made an object of international negotiations and of political bargaining just as armaments in the air and on the sea.' For Koestler, the communists' denial of freedom of information equated to a weapon of war, a barricade to liberty and a crime against the people it affected. He called, rather optimistically, for the West to demand intellectual openness and free media in return for the economic concessions that Moscow needed.

> A country which builds a Maginot line of censorship from behind which it fires its propaganda salvoes is committing psychological aggression ... Psychological disarmament should be made a bargaining object in all future negotiations, and given high priority on the political agenda. It should be made the pre-condition of concessions in the geographical, economic and scientific field. To get it accepted, the use of all levers of pressure, political and economic, would be morally justified.[28]

The US approached the struggle against communist influence with the panache of its Madison Avenue salesmen, the advertisers who influenced consumers' choices between brands at home and who would now do the same to the minds of Europeans and Asians faced with a choice between political ideologies. Nothing if not imaginative, the army's Education and Information Division engaged Theodor S. Geisel, better known as the cartoonist and children's author Dr Seuss, to produce documentary films on how the defeated peoples of the Axis powers could be persuaded to embrace western democracy. While Moscow's propaganda was focused on straightforward claims about the benefits of the communist system, Washington was less direct. Geisel's script outlines how the US intended to instil the illusion of free choice in its target audience – just so long as that choice fell in favour of the American idea: 'Let them think for themselves, talk for themselves and educate themselves. ... Let them set up whatever form of government they choose, provided it's a form of government we know will work for peace.'[29]

The aim of this ostensibly empowering psychological strategy is to convince the defeated populations that they are making their own choice of political system, but to ensure that their 'free choice' is also the one that Washington prescribes. It inculcates the impression of a democracy based on freedom and honesty, but is aimed squarely at achieving a specific, American-approved outcome.

The US and the USSR expended considerable effort in the struggle to guide, and where possible control, the way countries in their spheres of influence would develop. The Berlin airlift was accompanied by a fierce propaganda exchange, with each side accusing the other of being the cause of the crisis. The outbreak of a 'book war' saw the Americans, British and Soviets taking it in turns to publish documents suggesting their opponents were tarred by ties to the Nazis. Moscow accused the West of failing to purge civil servants who had worked for Hitler, while the Allies highlighted the Nazi–Soviet Pact of 1939, with Stalin's pledge to cooperate with the Axis powers. When talks over Berlin broke down in January 1948, the US State Department published a document titled *Nazi–Soviet Relations 1939–1941*. It revealed for the first time the Secret Protocol of the Molotov–Ribbentrop Pact, under which Moscow and Berlin agreed to carve up central Europe and suggested a 'friendly agreement' between them over whether or not they would allow Poland to continue to exist.[30] The documents had been discovered by British troops in the German Foreign Office archives and were released to cause maximum embarrassment for the Soviets. They made headlines worldwide, much to the delight of the State Department: 'The Soviet Government,' wrote the author of the department's bulletin, 'was caught flat-footed in what was the first effective blow from our side in a clear-cut propaganda war.'[31]

The release of the Secret Protocol signalled the end of restraint. Psychological warfare would no longer be shackled by ethical considerations; lies and fake news became as powerful as the truth, trust between East and West a thing of the past. Any means were fair in the struggle to convince Berliners that 'we' were on their side and 'they' were plotting their downfall. News bulletins released by the East German authorities announced that Allied planes were secretly dropping beetles on their crops in order to spoil the potato harvest. Posters appeared with cartoons of menacing-looking insects painted in the colours of the American flag.

Kafka's Gregor Samsa would have acknowledged the cunning absurdity of the ruse. With so little food available – and no other sources of news – people were conditioned to pin their economic hardship on a tangible enemy. 'Potatoes were the main thing we had to eat in East Germany at the time,' remembered Erhard Geissler, who grew up in Leipzig. 'My father and mother and I would share a single potato for breakfast. We were shocked to hear that our food supply was under threat.'[32] Official publications dubbed the beetles 'six-legged ambassadors of the American invasion' and 'a criminal attack by American imperialist warmongers on our people's food supply'. It permitted the authorities to inflame anti-western sentiment by urging young people to go into the fields and kill the insects, nicknamed *Amikäfer*, or Yankee Beetles, singing a popular song of the time with new words, 'Go home, Ami! Ami, go home!'

Not all East Germans were convinced. Ingo Materna, who was eighteen and had lived under all four occupying powers, saw through the deception. 'We didn't take it seriously at all. It was obvious that there were beetles in the field, but we didn't believe the Americans were dropping them. We'd known about the beetles for a long time. So we were quite sceptical.'[33] But the regime's propaganda machine insisted, reminding people of the terrible destruction wrought by Allied bombing raids during the war; why would Washington have any more scruples about dropping a few beetles?

It was, ironically, true that Colorado beetles, the insects destroying the German crops, had come from America. But they had arrived in Europe long before the Cold War, carried over on trade ships in the late nineteenth century. West Germany was able to control the infestation with the use of chemical pesticides. But in East Germany, any pesticide it did produce was shipped off straight to the Soviet Union.

For West Berliners, the materiel dropping from the cargo holds of American and British bombers was much more welcome. Mercedes Wild was a child in the American sector during the Allied airlift. Fifty years later she could still remember the excitement she felt at discovering the marvels of US candy. 'Something was floating down and many of the children knew what it was. Everyone was running and I started running, but there were not enough parachutes for everyone.' Disappointed, Mercedes wrote to the 'Chocolate Uncle' at Tempelhof airport, in reality an office of the US Information Service. She asked them to drop some chocolates at the house with the white chickens – 'it doesn't matter if it scares them' – and was delighted to find a package miraculously delivered to her front door. 'This was the first piece of chocolate I had had,' Mercedes remembered fondly. 'When I bit into it, it was heaven on earth.'[34]

The children dubbed the Allied planes the Candy Bombers or the Raisin Bombers: US Flying Fortresses and British Lancasters became associated in their minds with Hershey bars and mint humbugs. For such children, who had known only the hardship of the war and postwar years, an act of kindness, in the shape of sweets falling from the sky, would stay with them for the rest of their lives, conditioning their subsequent thinking.[35]

The airlift had the opposite effect in the East. Hearing the endless overflights bringing western luxuries to those 'on the other side' sapped the morale of the Soviet troops stationed there. 'We lived at Karlshorst,' recalled Yakov Drabkin, an official in the Soviet military administration, 'and we could hear the noise of the airplanes which delivered everything including Christmas presents and chocolate. We couldn't match it. We were poor and the West was rich. And, of course, this crazy blockade was bound to fail.'[36] Others, like the teenaged Vladimir Naiden, who described himself as 'completely conditioned by our powerful propaganda' remembered 'swearing and shaking my fist at the planes' swooping low over Alexanderplatz.[37]

The Allied airlift had been a demonstration of western determination, motivated by the conviction that weakness over Berlin would further embolden the Soviets. Stalin had poked the West with a bayonet and the West had not flinched. His blockade had backfired. Moscow looked to the world like an unprincipled aggressor and many Germans whom the Kremlin had been courting in its bid to secure a unified Germany were now alienated and hostile.

A meeting of the Council of Foreign Ministers was called, to meet in Paris in the spring, to try to salvage some vestiges of East–West cooperation. On the day it began, 23 May 1949, the western Allies announced the formation of the Federal Republic of Germany. There were to be no concessions on the currency reform. It was the last time the foreign ministers would meet for five years.

Seven weeks earlier, on 4 April 1949, twelve western countries had signed the founding charter of the North Atlantic Treaty Organisation, a move the future British ambassador to NATO, Frank Roberts, attributed directly to the bungled Soviet aggression in Berlin. 'The overall success of the Berlin airlift was first of all that it persuaded a lot of very frightened people throughout Europe that they had to come into the Atlantic Alliance, which provided security and a feeling that we are safe despite the presence of these very much larger Russian forces, which are next door.'[38] The first confrontation of the postwar years had left a legacy of bitterness and mistrust. Similar encounters in the future would be rendered more dangerous by the Soviet development of the nuclear bomb. With the goodwill of the war years consigned to the past, Silvashko and Robertson's warm embrace on the Elbe was nothing more than a distant memory.

10

TROUBLE AMONG SOCIALIST FRIENDS

In 2012, researchers at Stanford University furnished empirical proof of something parents have known since time began: that babies, from the earliest hours of their existence, process and respond to the human face long before they recognise any other object. Using real-time MRI scanning, the researchers were able to show that the infant brain's reaction to facial expressions was more advanced and more powerful than their assessment of any other visual cue.[1] It is a feature that remains with all of us for life. Human faces are the thing that has the greatest power to influence our thoughts and our emotions, a concept that the ideologues of the Soviet Union seem to have understood.[2]

For the USSR, the face of Joseph Stalin became a powerful tool that could be used to inspire loyalty, sacrifice and hard work, not just in the Soviet Union, but across the socialist world. Inconveniently, Stalin was far from beautiful. Scarred by smallpox, with yellow, bloodshot eyes, a withered arm and even shorter than Vladimir Putin (5 feet 5 inches), the Soviet leader presented a challenge to those Soviet artists charged with making him appear heroic. But just as there was no shortage of zealots willing to turn a blind eye to the faults of the regime, so there was no shortage of artists ready to gloss over the imperfections of the leader. Statues made him as tall as the powerfully built Tsar Alexander III; photographs were retouched to smooth his skin and give him the radiant visage of a saint. The implication was clear. Stalin was the hero the socialist world needed and there was no space for rivals.

After the Second World War, the sanctification of Stalin reached its preposterous apogee. It was motivated in part by his own vanity and insecurity, but it had a psychological significance far beyond personal inadequacy. A population bombarded with images of their handsome, noble leader, brave in battle but ready always to show

'Stalin's kindness illuminates the future of our children!'

kindness to children, absorbed a deep-rooted belief in his goodness, regardless of the fact that he was arresting, torturing and murdering millions. Posters declaring, 'We thank you, Comrade Stalin, for our happy childhood!' had hung in schoolrooms since the 1930s, colouring the consciousness of each generation with the conviction of Stalin's benign omnipotence. The regime understood that children were malleable. It worked hard to forge their socialist consciousness and the majority of them responded with loyalty to party, state and leader.

A curiously moving Soviet documentary of Stalin's seventieth-birthday celebrations at the Bolshoi shows young boys and girls in their Pioneer uniforms reciting verses in praise of the Great Leader.

Thank you for our happy childhood; there is no brighter one in the world! We promise to study well, to look to the future, to forget the word 'failure' ... Today we are Pioneers; tomorrow we will be engineers, tractor drivers, doctors, steel workers, weavers, agronomists and teachers. All roads are open to us, all paths![3]

Today, the 'happy childhood' slogans sound like ludicrous hyperbole, but in the narrow, secretive USSR of the 1940s and 50s, they rang without irony.

All political leaders seek to impress by the demonstration of personal strength and capacity. It is a tenet of the social contract that those who are led delegate their fate to the safekeeping of the leader. But the myth of personality – in Stalin's case, universally known as the 'cult of personality' – did more. It was a tool that shaped the thoughts and behaviour of a nation. In times of uncertainty, the politician who promises to keep his people safe is the one who gains support; the human mind seeks reassurance. The people may or may not truly believe that he will protect them from outside menaces, but even if they do not truly believe it, a collective process of self-convincing takes place.

A politician who promises salvation equally accepts the role of scapegoat. The assigning of a society's destiny to an individual covers failure as well as success. Catastrophes are more easily absorbed if the mind can pinpoint a cause for them (the external locus of control which is inherent in setbacks that cannot be explained is hard to digest), so part of the implied contract between a citizen and a leader who makes promises is that the promiser will bear some or all of the responsibility when things go wrong, just as he will take the glory if they go well. We blame an individual so that everyone else is exculpated.

The existence of a cult of personality in a communist society may be regarded as ironic, since Marx held that it is the dialectical march of history which guarantees the people's triumph, not the actions of individuals. But the reality is that 'the people' struggle to put their faith in an abstract idea; they crave a human face to embody it. In Orthodox Russia it had been the face of Christ; then it was Lenin, and now it was Stalin.

In the years following 1945 there seemed little for the leader to take the blame for, as all seemed to be ending well for the Soviet Union. The triumphs of the war years – coupled with the airbrushing of the glitches that history inconveniently throws up – imbued Stalin with an aura of infallibility. With the world divided between East and West, and with the threat from foreign powers trumpeted relentlessly in the Soviet media, it was seductive and comforting to accept the myth of personality offered by the state. Stalin had won the

World War; now he was winning the Cold War. Show him unquestioning obedience and he, in return, will guarantee that which you most desire – personal safety and national success. Even for those who doubted Stalin and questioned his record, the promise of protection and happiness was often sufficient to still the doubts. Such was the soil in which flowered the image of Stalin as superman, Stalin as trustworthy father, Stalin as god.

He was not unique. The 1930s had been a time of great anxiety and strongmen leaders had emerged in many countries. Hitler, Mussolini and others had failed, but Stalin had stood the test. Now he emerged as the Soviet saviour, his personal attributes unquestionable, without whom the USSR would founder. Now he accepted grandiloquent titles – 'The Father of Nations', 'The Brilliant Genius of Humanity', 'The Gardener of Human Happiness' – and was acclaimed as the leading authority on everything from agriculture to linguistics.

It stood to reason that such a man must be accorded unquestioning loyalty. During the war, Red Army soldiers were said to have hurled themselves into battle shouting '*Za rodinu! Za Stalina!*' – 'For my country! And for Stalin!' Even some victims of the regime, men and women arrested and tortured by the Kremlin's secret police, refused to blame him. Anguished letters to Stalin from the cells of the Lubyanka express certainty that he cannot be aware of the horrors to which they are being subjected, convinced that he would put a stop to them if only he knew. There was a naive, unwavering faith in Stalin's goodness that would unleash a national, painful outbreak of cognitive dissonance when the truth emerged after his death.

In the opening years of the Cold War, from 1945 until his death in 1953, Joseph Stalin had not only a Soviet Union of 170 million people to hold together, but an increasingly fractious empire composed of eastern and central European buffer states. Moscow's rejection of the Marshall Plan and the Berlin blockade had made clear that the wartime rapprochement of communism and capitalism was over. Both superpowers would keep a keen eye on each other; but their allies, too, had to be watched. The new 'communist bloc' would need to be Stalinised, a task that the man himself recognised as challenging. 'Introducing communism into Poland,' he complained, 'is like putting a saddle on a cow.'[4]

But the Stalin myth had currency not only in Soviet Russia. Even in those satellite countries that would cause him the greatest headaches there was, initially at least, an awed respect for his legend and his achievements. To many in the socialist camp, Stalin was the inspiration who gave them confidence that they could take on the forces of capitalist imperialism and win.

The psychological sway of the Stalin myth can be traced through the example of Yugoslavia. The Yugoslavs would become Moscow's first fraternal dissidents, expelled from the Cominform as early as 1948, but they were not always so. Milovan Djilas, the Yugoslav politician and political theorist who had been Tito's number two during and after the war, echoed the widely held reverence for Stalin's talismanic powers:

> We waxed enthusiastic not only over Stalin's views but also over the 'perfection' of their formulation. I myself referred many times in discussions to the crystal clarity of his style, the penetration of his logic … Sometimes the idolatry acquired ridiculous proportions: we seriously believed that the war would end in 1942, because Stalin said so, and when this failed to happen, the prophecy was forgotten – and the prophet lost none of his superhuman power. In actual fact, what happened to the Yugoslav Communists is what has happened to everyone in the long history of man who has ever subordinated his individual fate and the fate of mankind exclusively to one idea: unconsciously they described the Soviet Union and Stalin in terms required by their own struggle and its justifications.[5]

When Djilas first met Stalin in 1944, he viewed him as 'the man of wisdom' who 'all his life, and still now, looked after the success and happiness of the whole Communist race'. His description of the journey to Moscow sounds almost as if he is making an assignation with a lover.

> Finally a Soviet plane took us to the Soviet Union – the realization of our dreams and our hopes … I was gripped by a new, hitherto hardly suspected emotion. It was as though I was returning to a primeval homeland … I could not suppress my excitement. It sprang from the very depths of my being. I was aware of my own pallor and of my joyful, and at the same time almost panic-stricken agitation.

What could be more exciting than to be received by Stalin? … Stalin was the incarnation of an idea, transfigured in Communist minds into pure idea, and therefore into something infallible and sinless.[6]

As with any love affair, however, the deeper the initial passion, the greater the disillusion when things go wrong, the fiercer the resentment and the hatred. Yugoslav support for communist agitation in Greece brought a reprimand from Stalin; Tito defied Moscow's instructions and it escalated into a battle of wills. Relations soured to the point where military confrontation seemed possible. Stalin, used to omnipotence, inhabited a world 'in which there was no choice but victory or death,' wrote Djilas.[7]

Stalin did not invade Yugoslavia, but he did ostracise it and its ungrateful leadership. The West celebrated the first cracks in the socialist monolith, poking at the wound. When Tito announced that Yugoslavia would follow its own path to socialism, without the tutelage of Moscow, American and British news bulletins crowed that 'Portraits of Stalin have gone from public buildings. Today, Belgrade residents line up for hours to see American movies.'*

With a little emollience, Stalin could probably have patched things up; but emollience was not in Stalin's makeup. He regarded nonconformist thinking as a personal affront. Stalin told the politburo, 'I will shake my little finger and tomorrow there will be no Tito any more.'[8] According to the Soviet army general and military historian Dmitry Volkogonov, plans were laid to assassinate Tito with bubonic plague, although the plot was never implemented.[9]

On both sides, egos bristled, attitudes hardened. Tito went on to pursue what he labelled the 'Yugoslav road to socialism', a show of independence and a challenge to Soviet communist orthodoxy which relied on a fierce policy of political non-alignment, allowing him to court both communist and capitalist support.

The Yugoslav leadership were reviled in the Soviet media.

---

*The posters, in fact, revealed little about Yugoslavia's break with Moscow. The Tarzan films were widely shown and extremely popular in the Soviet Union at the time. Pathé News for 15 December 1949; 'Tito Faces Soviet Threat'. www. britishpathe.com/video/stills/tito-faces-soviet-threat.

Headlines habitually referred to them as 'Tito and his bloody clique'.*

By standing up to Stalin and living to tell the tale, Tito pulled off the trick that Hungary and Czechoslovakia would signally fail to do in the following two decades. Indeed, the memory of Yugoslavia's defiance almost certainly contributed to the Kremlin's determination to crush later revolts when they arose elsewhere. Moscow tried to lure Tito back into the socialist camp after Stalin's death, but he continued to benefit from US economic aid and was famously entertained at Buckingham Palace by Queen Elizabeth II in 1972, where he was awarded the Order of the Bath.

The Stalin myth – the overpowering cult of personality – had brought the USSR advantages in both East and West. It sent a message of uncompromising, intimidating resolution that friends and enemies alike would do well to respect. But Stalin the myth could be effective only inasmuch as Stalin the man retained a semblance of personal psychological balance. The signs in the remaining years of his life suggest that he did not.

Desperate not to allow others to follow Tito's example, Stalin ordered purges in other Soviet satellite states to remove potential rebels in the rest of the bloc. As with his approach to domestic opposition, it may be argued that Stalin's incipient paranoia determined the scale and ferocity of these. In Hungary and Czechoslovakia, there were show trials of the party leadership, reminiscent of the Soviet purges of the 1930s. In Prague, fourteen members of the politburo, including the party's general secretary, were convicted of 'Tito-ist' subversion and treason. The evidence was fabricated, but eleven of them were executed and the others sentenced to life in jail.[10]

Stalin's brutal retribution against those who questioned the infallibility of the Soviet state and its leader reflected his own need for personal vindication, but it also had a political rationale. The French historian Alexis de Tocqueville wrote that *any* concession by an autocratic regime threatens it with disintegration. 'Experience teaches

---

* This led to an amusing example of how the Soviet public, always eager to support the official line, could be wrong-footed by changing circumstances: in 1956, during a brief rapprochement, crowds turned out to welcome the Yugoslav leader on a visit to Moscow with banners enthusiastically proclaiming, 'Long live Tito and his bloody clique!'

us that the most critical moment for bad governments is the one which witnesses their first steps towards reform ... for evils which are patiently endured when they seem inevitable become intolerable once the possibility of escape from them is hinted at.'[11] Allowing Tito to diverge from Soviet orthodoxy would acknowledge that the monolith could be fallible; and fallibility would open the way for the whole project to be questioned. De Tocqueville concludes, 'The very redress of grievances throws a sharp light on those that are left unredressed, and adds fresh poignancy to their smart ... It is almost never when a state of things is the most detestable that it is smashed but, rather, when it begins to improve.'[12]

Dissenting subordinates in eastern Europe were not the only threat to Stalin's leadership. A new, powerful ally had appeared on the global stage who would in time present a much greater problem. At first sight, the triumph of Mao Zedong in China seemed an unalloyed win for the communist world. The Americans viewed the outcome of the Chinese civil war as a grave psychological blow to Washington's prestige. 'We felt that they [the Chinese] had betrayed all of our high hopes and our expectations of them,' lamented John Paton Davies of the US State Department. 'We had become emotionally involved with them, and then they had done this! They had gone off and become Communist!'[13]

For Stalin, Red China presented a different sort of challenge. Ever since his accession to power, he had been the uncontested leader of the socialist world. So the establishment of the People's Republic of China on 1 October 1949, a Marxist state with half a billion people, was greeted with mixed emotions. Unconvinced that Mao's uprising would be successful, Stalin was initially reluctant to back a losing cause. Even when Mao had emerged as leader, Stalin was less than generous in supplying him with aid. When Mao came to Moscow in December 1949, he was not given the welcome he thought he merited. Nikita Khrushchev recalled being informed that someone called 'Matsadoon'* had come to see him. When he asked 'Who?' he was told, 'You know, that Chinaman.'[14] Mao was made to wait six days for an appointment with Stalin. Holed up in a government guesthouse and aware he was being insulted, he shouted into the

---

*Khrushchev was well known for mangling foreign names, but even he should have been familiar with the leader of the world's largest socialist state.

microphones that he knew were monitoring him, 'I have come here to do more than just eat and shit!'[15]

Historians have usually regarded the scatological reference as a joke, but it appears that Stalin was indeed counting on Mao to empty his bowels. A former Soviet intelligence officer, Igor Atamanenko, claims to have found documents in the Russian security archives suggesting that Stalin was intent on collecting and examining Mao's excretions, collected via secret boxes connected to the toilet in his apartment. Stalin's secret police, says Atamanenko, had set up a special department with 'endocrinologists, physiologists, immunologists and psychonervologists [sic]' who would analyse samples of foreign leaders' faeces to help develop psychological profiles of them: a lack of potassium, for example, was thought to indicate a highly strung demeanour and possibly insomnia. The man in charge of the scheme, Arkady Rosenthal, later emigrated to the West and was allegedly recruited by the CIA to use the same trick against Nikita Khrushchev when he visited America in 1959.[16]

When Stalin and Mao did finally meet on 21 December, the atmosphere was chilly. Nikolai Fedorenko, Stalin's interpreter, noted the one-upmanship expressed in the two men's body language. 'Mao shook Stalin's hand for a very long time. Stalin came up to greet him quite slowly. He knew how to play the role of statesman, he was a very good actor, and didn't rush like Mao.'[17] Stalin was not alone in standing on his dignity. Mao, too, had a narcissistic streak, insisting on taking personal credit for his country's achievements. Philip Short, a former BBC Beijing correspondent and author of a study of the Chinese leader, summed him up: 'Mao is a biographer's dream. He was devious, tricky, complex, full of human failings, and either brilliant or mad or both.'[18]

The first summit between the communist giants ended in acrimony. Mao had come to ask Stalin for financial support to bolster communist power in China and left with the promise of a paltry $300 million. 'It was like wresting meat from the jaws of a tiger,' Mao told his aides. His humiliation in Moscow appears to have inculcated a lasting hatred of the Soviet Union.[19]

To western eyes, however, the loss of China and the emergence of a second communist leader of global stature seemed an augury of a Red alliance that threatened the world. British government records held in the National Archives in London suggest that the second half

Mao Zedong of China, Walter Ulbricht of East Germany, and Yumjaagiin Tsedenbal of Mongolia were among the socialist leaders who travelled to Moscow to celebrate Stalin's seventy-first birthday in December 1949.

of 1949 was spent in fevered discussions of how the West might tear the two socialist giants apart.

The West, by its own admission, had little influence over the rising forces of global communism. Efforts to provoke a Sino–Soviet split would be problematic and slow, had not events, as so often, intervened.

Within a year Stalin would be seeking Mao's help. In 1945 Korea had been divided along the thirty-eighth parallel, with Soviet troops occupying the north and US troops the south. Three years later, the north became the Democratic People's Republic of Korea and the south the Republic of Korea. In 1950, when North Korea's leader Kim Il-Sung asked Moscow's permission to invade the south, Stalin agreed. The Soviet Union offered to provide arms and equipment for the North Koreans, but made clear that Soviet troops would not play a direct role in the fighting.

When the Korean War began, on 25 June 1950, Kim's army won a series of quick victories and Seoul fell within three days, forcing the South Korean forces to retreat into a small zone in the south-eastern tip of the peninsula. But to the Soviets' surprise, the US came to the South's aid. Profiting from the absence of the Soviet ambassador to the United Nations,* Washington pushed through a resolution to

---

*Moscow had been boycotting the UN since the start of the year in protest at Taiwan's presence on the Security Council.

send UN troops to help the South Koreans. It was the opportunity for which Acheson and Bevin had been hoping, to test the solidity of the Moscow–Beijing relationship.

The American army helped the South to retake Seoul and then crossed the thirty-eighth parallel into the North. Stalin realised he had misjudged the situation: he must now decide if he was willing to risk all-out war with America. Kim appealed to Moscow for direct military help, but Stalin refused.

Instead, Stalin turned to China. He put pressure on Mao to send Chinese troops, disguised as volunteer units, into the combat zone, and Mao agreed. Fighting continued for over a year until a stalemate was reached at the end of 1951. It took another two years before an armistice was signed. The border dividing the two Koreas reverted to the thirty-eighth parallel. No formal peace treaty was ever agreed.

Despite Moscow staying out of the fighting in Korea, the West concluded that the Soviets were the architects of the invasion and the war. Evidence to the contrary was disregarded. A process of con- firmation bias reinforced Washington and London's conviction that Stalin was set on world domination, that he had the military means to achieve it and that he was plotting to deploy such means as soon as circumstances allowed.

With the benefit of hindsight – and with access to documents from the participants that were secret at the time – it is clear that a complex three-way dance in the dark was going on between the Soviets, the Chinese and the Anglo-Saxon West. In the absence of certainty, all sides attempted to read the intentions of the others, and all projected their own beliefs, fears and values onto their adversaries, often with misguided outcomes.

The West regarded Moscow and Beijing as allies in a menacing global communist partnership, noting the signs of disagreement between China and Russia, but playing them down. In fact, it had hurt Stalin's pride to go cap-in-hand to Beijing, although he portrayed his manoeuvring to make China do the fighting as a calculated strategy. Neither Stalin nor Mao publicised the damage that events in Korea inflicted on Sino–Soviet relations, but the effects would be felt in the years ahead.

Declassified US intelligence reports from the time help tell the story of how the West often misconstrued what was going on. The first months of 1949 had provided reasons for optimism. In April, the

CIA reported that America had 'checked the Soviet-Communist activities that were seeking to break down Western Europe'. But then, on 3 September, an American B-29 bomber on patrol over the North Pacific detected abnormal levels of radioactivity. Analysts concluded that this was the news they had been fearing but had not expected to come so early: the Soviet Union had exploded an atomic device.

The CIA's reaction bordered on panic. An Office of Research and Evaluation (ORE) report of 22 September concluded that 'the overall US security position is now subject to inevitable and fundamental modification'.[20] And the speed with which Moscow had developed the bomb prompted fears of leaks from within the US.

The CIA announced that the security of American intelligence would be tightened and warned the National Security Council to expect an intensified Soviet propaganda war against the West. Its director, Roscoe H. Hillenkoetter, drafted an interim directive outlining immediate measures to be taken. But the shock caused by Moscow's acquisition of nuclear capacity led to a deeper crisis of trust in the ability of the United States to defend its interests in a world where the balance of power seemed suddenly to have shifted. America's priorities in this new age of anxiety would need thoroughgoing reorganisation and fresh ideas. NSC-68, written in the first months of 1950, was the document that attempted to provide them.[21]

NSC-68 is one of the key texts of the Cold War. Drafted under the guidance of Paul Nitze, then the director of the policy planning staff, it set in stone the key assumption that would guide western thinking for almost four decades: that the free world is threatened by a monolithic and hostile communist alliance, coordinated and commanded by the Kremlin.

> The gravest threat to the security of the United States within the foreseeable future stems from the hostile designs and formidable power of the USSR, and from the nature of the Soviet system.
>
> The political, economic, and psychological warfare which the USSR is now waging has dangerous potentialities for weakening the relative world position of the United States ...
>
> In the light of present and prospective Soviet atomic capabilities, the action which can be taken under present programs and plans becomes dangerously inadequate ... A continuation

of present trends would result in a serious decline in the strength of the free world relative to the Soviet Union and its satellites.[22]

Nitze and his co-authors are convinced that Moscow has the means and the desire to spread communism and Soviet rule to the rest of the globe. The report bristles with the adrenaline of collective fight-or-flight, a call for action in the face of an existential threat.

> We must organize and enlist the energies and resources of the free world in a positive program for peace which will frustrate the Kremlin design for world domination by creating a situation in the free world to which the Kremlin will be compelled to adjust. Without such a cooperative effort, led by the United States, we will have to make gradual withdrawals under pressure until we discover one day that we have sacrificed positions of vital interest.[23]

And while Washington is cajoling and organising the thinking of the free world, it must simultaneously stiffen its own defences. Words are not enough. There needs to be the political will to devote unprecedented budget resources to a demonstration of military resolve, 'a rapid and sustained build-up of the political, economic, and military strength of the free world', the 'only means short of war which eventually may force the Kremlin to abandon its present course of action and to negotiate acceptable agreements on issues of major importance'.[24]

The CIA reports of the period indicate a growing conviction that the potential flashpoint in East–West tensions has shifted away from Europe. A much bigger proportion of the intelligence material is devoted to Asia, specifically to Korea. The automatic assumption of Moscow's guiding hand in the Korean conflict conditions CIA reporting for the remaining years of the 1950s. The traditional monthly review of intelligence becomes a weekly bulletin, and the focus shifts from political and ideological themes to overwhelmingly military concerns. The assumption that Moscow is acting as a puppet-master, orchestrating events around the globe, leads the agency analysts to predict renewed aggression in Europe. The bulletins for July 1950 warn of potential hostilities beginning in Albania or Bulgaria, which are said to be 'in better [military] condition than heretofore estimated'. They report that Hungary and Romania have been building new military airfields and that Moscow has been urging West European communist parties to sabotage America's military capacity in their countries.[25] 'Throughout the Soviet orbit,' says the summary on 10 August, 'the trend towards preparedness for war has continued. There is, moreover, evidence that certain phases of this program are being accelerated with some urgency.'[26]

British and American defence experts discussed at length the date by which the USSR would be ready to launch its offensive. The British were more sanguine than their American counterparts,[27] but the discussion is largely of 'when', not 'if'. When examined closely, the CIA reporting offers little in the way of concrete evidence for any imminent Soviet aggression; but it does not need to. In a political environment where the common assumption is one of inevitable conflict with a belligerent USSR, the reports are essentially reinforcing shared conclusions that have already been adopted.

The picture of an intelligence community entrenching its own preconceptions is not an unusual one. When your job is to pick up on signs that the other side is plotting against you, there is a natural tendency to jump to conclusions and ignore contradictory voices. But the CIA of the 1950s seems nonetheless to have contained at least a few independent thinkers willing to challenge the embedded wisdom. The BBC journalist Trevor Barnes, writing in 1982, suggests that the assumption of a malign Soviet Union bent on world domination and coordinating global forces to bring it about was questioned by several analysts within the agency.

> Ironically, a group of CIA analysts were seeking to undermine this assumption at about the same time as NSC-68 was being drafted. Project Jigsaw, a top secret review of world communism set up in late 1949, concluded there was *no* masterplan for global domination centred on Moscow, even if the Kremlin did manipulate the communist parties of other nations (the French and Italian in particular) ... The conclusions of Project Jigsaw were however so unorthodox they were smothered, even within the Agency itself.[28]

As the West argued with itself over the likelihood of Moscow launching an attack, Stalin was struggling to reconcile differences within the communist camp. Far from being the unified alliance that the West believed it to be, the Sino–Soviet entente was beset by disagreements between a gung-ho Beijing, exhilarated at having won a bruising civil war against the American-backed forces of the Kuomintang, and the more cautious, restraining hand of Moscow. The long-serving Soviet foreign minister Andrei Gromyko revealed in his memoirs that Mao pressed the Kremlin to use nuclear weapons against American targets later in the 1950s, arguing that China could survive a nuclear war even it lost 300 million people and would then 'finish off the capitalists with conventional weapons'.[29] It seems possible that Beijing was pushing Moscow for similarly draconian action in the aftermath of Korea. In August 1952, Stalin was forced to restrain the Chinese premier, Chou En-Lai, when he came on a visit to Moscow.

'The Americans are not capable of waging a large-scale war at all,' Stalin soothed his guest. 'They want to subjugate the world, yet they cannot subdue little Korea! No, the Americans don't know how to fight. They are fighting little Korea, and already people are weeping in the USA. What will happen if they start a large-scale war? Then, perhaps, *everyone* will weep!'[30] If Mao's scenario for unleashing nuclear war seemed improbable (200 million Chinese might survive, but the USSR, whose weapons Mao was asking to be used, probably would not), there appear to have been similar fantasies in the West.

In January 1952, Harry Truman's diary records in characteristically homely fashion the frustration he felt at dealing with the mendacious, untrustworthy communists, likening the experience to 'an honest man trying to deal with … the head of a dope ring!'

You can almost hear the president's exasperation. His irritation leads him to speculate on what he could do to make the racketeers and the dope dealers see sense.

> It seems to me that the proper approach now would be an ulti-matum with a ten day expiration limit, informing Moscow that we intend to blockade the China coast from the Korean border to Indo-China, and that we intend to destroy every military base in Manchuria, including submarine bases, by means now in our control, and if there is interference we shall eliminate any ports or cities necessary to accomplish our peaceful purposes … This means all-out war. It means that Moscow, St. Petersburg, Mukden, Vladivostock, Peking, Shanghai, Port Arthur, Dairen,

Odessa, Stalingrad and every manufacturing plant in China and the Soviet Union will be eliminated.[31]

In public, Truman never suggested anything of the sort. His diaries were a private repository of anger and frustration rather than a draft of future policy. His successor, Dwight Eisenhower, seemed more serious about it.

Memorandum of Discussion at a Special Meeting of the National Security Council on Tuesday, March 31, 1953

The President then raised the question of the use of atomic weapons in the Korean war ... the President and Secretary Dulles were in complete agreement that somehow or other the tabu which surrounds the use of atomic weapons would have to be destroyed. While Secretary Dulles admitted that in the present state of world opinion we could not use an A-bomb, we should make every effort now to dissipate this feeling.[32]

The 1950s was a decade of tough talking, with fingers crossed, hoping that the political bluff would not be called. Even Eisenhower seems never seriously to have considered using the bomb in a first strike. But, as George Kennan pointed out, politicians were under pressure to appear warlike:

In the early 1950s ... the exaggerated image of the menacing Kremlin thirsting and plotting for world domination came in handy. There was, in any case, not a single administration in Washington, from that of Harry Truman on down, which, when confronted with the charge of being 'soft on communism', however meaningless the phrase or weak the evidence, would not run for cover and take protective action.[33]

The manipulation of myth and image had become central to the Cold War. The elevation of Stalin to the status of god-like socialist behemoth, the symbol of insuperable Soviet power, had begun in the studios of the artists, sculptors and filmmakers charged with sanitising the blemished reality of his face. It had seemed a mere illusion, a confidence trick perpetrated by *trompe l'oeil* and sleight of hand. But it had become a tangible force, shaping the course of world affairs. Moscow benefited from it – the Soviet people bowed their heads to the authority of the Father of the Nation and fellow travellers around the globe rallied to the values it projected. Western leaders, too, made use of it. Truman and Churchill were able to exploit the fearsome power that the Stalin myth projected. The bogeyman of a terrible enemy can unite people as effectively as an inspirational leader. The psychology of myths and myth-making would be at the heart of the war of nerves.

11

STALIN'S GHOST – MEMORY, FEAR AND
THE MONSTER FROM THE GRAVE

The West continued to puzzle over what motivated Stalin and how to read his words and actions: while his slide into sociopathy represented a threat to the world – and a more immediate and personal one to the Russian people and his Kremlin colleagues – it was slow to take his mental state into account when formulating international policy. For those who lived in the USSR, the omniscience and omnipotence of Stalin was taken as gospel, a trope that the Kremlin used to influence and control the population. And so effective were the psychological methods deployed to inculcate the official image – the infallibility, the goodness, the ruthlessness in vengeance if one didn't obey – that the idea of Stalin wormed its way into people's brains.

Even after his death, Stalin lived on in the minds of millions, a figure of affection, or a demonic presence that many found impossible to eradicate. Russians would search in vain for ways to remove him from their collective memory, to dig up and incinerate the ghost that continued to haunt them.

One apparently firm foothold in the slippery landscape of Stalin's final years is that the Soviet leader was lonely. His wife had shot herself in 1932, after Stalin had humiliated her at a Kremlin dinner party – the culmination of years of mental and physical abuse – and relations with his surviving children were distant. His belief that he was surrounded by enemies dissuaded him from making any but the most unavoidable public appearances. He socialised almost solely with his colleagues in the politburo, often in the Kremlin or at his dacha. Several of them recorded their discomfort at being forced to eat, drink and dance with him long after they wanted to go home. He would ply his guests with alcohol, waiting for drunken remarks that he could use against them as proof of their disloyalty. He would mock his colleagues for their gluttony and alcoholism. Sometimes he would force the corpulent Nikita Khrushchev to dance the Ukrainian *gopak*. Khrushchev recalled in his memoirs:

> He suffered terribly from loneliness ... he needed people around him all the time. When he woke up in the morning, he would immediately summon us, either inviting us to the movies or starting some conversation which could have been finished in two minutes but was stretched out so that we would stay with him longer.[1]

To make matters worse, by 1952, his memory and native cunning were failing. At times he seemed lost. Khrushchev recalled one incident when Stalin, seemingly unaware of those around him, muttered over and over, 'I'm finished. I trust no one, not even myself ...'[2] Left alone with his thoughts, his paranoia grew.

Stalin took to spending long periods at his dachas in the south of the USSR. Molotov, Mikoyan, Beria, Khrushchev and the others ran the USSR on a day-to-day basis, but could make no changes to the country's strategic direction. Easing tensions with the West, improving living standards or reducing prisoner numbers in the Gulag would need approval from the boss – and he was not ready to give it.

Despite their caution, Stalin's mind filled with suspicions of what his colleagues were up to. He accused Molotov and Mikoyan of being 'capitulationists' to the West. He criticised them for their visits to the United States and began to exclude them from meetings and dinners. Initially, the other members of the politburo would inform Molotov and Mikoyan where they were meeting and the two would simply turn up; but eventually, Stalin exploded: 'Stop this! Stop telling them where I am! I won't tolerate it!'[3] Mikoyan believed that Stalin in the weeks before his death was planning to 'settle scores with us' as 'a matter not just of political but of physical annihilation'.[4]

In January 1952, Stalin sought medical help. Dr Vladimir Vinogradov had been Stalin's personal physician for several years. He had treated him after a heart attack he suffered in the summer of 1945, and had helped keep his illness secret. But now he faced a trickier challenge. The leader was showing signs of memory loss, mood swings, irrational behaviour and debilitating fatigue. Vinogradov told Stalin he was suffering from hypertension and atherosclerosis. It was a matter of urgency that both conditions should be treated, and for the treatment to be effective there would need to be complete rest. In other words, he said, if the leader of the Soviet Union wished to avoid the possibility of imminent death, he would have to retire from public activity.

Stalin flew into a rage. He ordered Vinogradov out of the room. He informed his aides that the doctor should be dismissed from his post and arrested. But Vinogradov was right. Stalin rarely exercised and his nocturnal activities meant he seldom got to bed before the small hours. All this and the stress of leadership had taken their toll. Where once he strode up the mausoleum steps on parade days, now he shuffled, struggling for breath.

The more Stalin's health deteriorated, the more he fell prey to paranoia. He had taken advantage of Lenin's long illness in the 1920s to usurp the old leader's power. Now he feared that those around him were doing the same to him.

Stalin moved from blaming his own doctor to distrusting *all* doctors. He had always feared assassination and now he believed that the doctors trying to preserve his health were bent on killing him. He convinced himself that malicious medics had already poisoned others in the leadership. 'They perish one after another,' he told a politburo colleague after several leading Bolsheviks had died from natural causes. 'Shcherbakov, Zhdanov, Dimitrov – all of them died so quickly! ... We must replace the old doctors with new ones!'[5]

In Stalin's fevered imagination, Vinogradov's suggestion that he should retire became a plot to remove him from power. He ordered the arrests of other physicians who had treated the party leadership, and it was no coincidence that a high proportion of those detained were Jewish. The year 1952 was the high-water mark of anti-Semitism in postwar Russia: in August, the members of the Jewish Anti-Fascist Committee would be wiped out; in December, the defendants chosen by Moscow to be executed in the Prague trials would also be Jewish.

By January 1953, Stalin had announced the discovery of the 'Jewish Doctors' Plot'. A show trial was being prepared for the doctors, but its aim was to draw in many more victims, up to and including top party leaders. At the Nineteenth Party Congress in October 1952, Stalin had attacked Mikoyan and Molotov for their 'shoddy work', seemingly paving the way for their replacement.* Beria, too, had reason to fear the dictator was planning to remove him from his post. Stalin seemed to be preparing a repeat of the so-called Leningrad Affair of two years earlier, in which party leaders whom Stalin perceived as rivals were accused of corruption and embezzlement. Six of them had been executed and over 2,000 removed from their posts.

But Vinogradov, his fellow doctors and the hundreds of others under arrest would never come to trial. On 5 March 1953, Stalin died.

On 17 February, Stalin had left the Kremlin to spend time at his dacha in the Kuntsevo district on the western outskirts of Moscow. Late at night on Saturday 28 February, he told his guards to go and get some sleep. 'I'm also going to bed,' he said. 'I won't be needing you today.'⁶

Stalin usually rang the bell for attention when he woke. But on the morning of Sunday 1 March, there was silence. The staff were in a quandary: the boss's instructions were not to come into his room until he rang, but as the hours went by they began to worry. At 6 p.m. a light came on in his room, much to everyone's relief. But Stalin still did not emerge or call them in. Only at ten o'clock in the evening was Pavel Lozgachev, the deputy commissioner of the dacha, selected to go in. He found Stalin slumped on the floor, barely conscious, in a pool of his own urine. The leader of the Soviet Union had been lying helpless for hours: the terror he instilled in those around him meant that any chance of saving his life was ruled out.⁷

According to Lozgachev, Stalin was conscious but unable to speak. They lifted him onto the chaise longue from which he had fallen and called the Kremlin. The news caused panic. The first minister who received the call refused to take it. Eventually, Beria came on the line and asked for details, but it was over two hours before he and Malenkov finally arrived at the dacha. By then, Stalin was lying unconscious with his eyes closed, and the two men approached him cautiously on tiptoe. Lozgachev recalled Beria telling Malenkov to

---

*When Molotov's Jewish wife, Polina Zhemchuzhina, met with Golda Meir in Moscow and expressed sympathy with the cause of the nascent state of Israel, she was arrested on baseless charges of treason and banished to the steppes of Kazakhstan. In a vain attempt to prove his loyalty to the party and to Stalin, Molotov repudiated her; but to no effect. He was soon removed from his post and marginalised from the leadership group.

'wake him up!' When Malenkov refused to do so, Beria turned round to those present and said, 'What are you looking at? Can't you see that Comrade Stalin is sleeping? You're all panicking for nothing. If anything happens, then you can ring me.'[8]

No doctor was called until mid morning on Monday 2 March, by which time it was too late. After lying unconscious for another three days, Stalin suffered a brain haemorrhage and on the morning of 5 March he vomited blood. Those present took turns to pay their final respects. According to Stalin's daughter, Svetlana, Beria kissed the dying man's hand and sobbed pitifully, but immediately afterwards seemed full of glee. Svetlana's account of her father's final moments is horrifying:

> For the last twelve hours the lack of oxygen became acute. His face and lips blackened as he suffered slow strangulation. The death agony was terrible. He literally choked to death as we watched. At what seemed like the very last moment, he opened his eyes and cast a glance over everyone in the room. It was a terrible glance, insane or perhaps angry, and full of fear of death. He suddenly lifted his left hand as though he were pointing to something up above and bringing down a curse on all. The gesture was incomprehensible and full of menace.[9]

The lurid image of a Stalin possessed of demonic powers, capable of calling down vengeance even from beyond the grave, would linger in the Russian psyche. The man who had ruled over the largest empire in the world for nearly thirty years had become in the popular imagination a superhuman behemoth inspiring both terror and love. Newspapers were printed with black borders and Soviet radio replaced its transmissions with funereal music. Yuri Levitan, the USSR's most famous newscaster, announced Stalin's passing:

> The heart of Lenin's comrade-in-arms and the inspired continuer of Lenin's cause, the wise leader and teacher of the Communist Party and the Soviet people, has stopped beating ... The immortal name of Stalin will live for ever in the hearts of the Soviet people and all progressive mankind. Long live the great, all-conquering teachings of Marx, Engels, Lenin and Stalin![10]

The immediate grief of the Soviet people was genuine. The Great Leader, the Father of the Nation, the man whom generations had thanked for their 'happy childhood', was gone. A huge crowd braved the elements to attend the ceremonies, covering Red Square with a carpet of flowers. Many spoke of feeling 'orphaned' by Stalin's death, fearing that the Soviet Union without his guiding hand would be overwhelmed in a world of menacing foreign enemies. The novelist Alexander Zinoviev would later comment on the mass hysteria that shaped people's thoughts and would reshape them again in future years:

> The Soviet people, conditioned by decades of lies and pretence, effortlessly, freely and gladly made themselves feel sincere grief … just as they would later, and with all the ease of well-trained creatures of Communism, put themselves into a state of sincere rage at the thought of the evil actions of their former idol and his vile henchmen.[11]

Stalin's funeral was accompanied by its own terrible tragedy, the first indication in the minds of a superstitious nation that his power over them may not have ended with the beating of his heart. As hundreds of thousands of mourners converged on Red Square, the police erected barriers of trucks across the approach roads. Crowds built up and people became trapped. More than five hundred were crushed to death. News of the catastrophe was suppressed; it became a taboo subject. The poet Yevgeny Yevtushenko said it was the moment he realised something was very wrong in his country:

> We were caught between the walls of houses on one side and a row of army trucks on the other. 'Get the trucks out of the way!' people howled. 'Get them away!' 'I can't. I've not been given any orders,' a very young, bewildered police officer called back, almost crying with desperation. People were being crushed against the trucks by the crowd; their heads were being smashed; the sides of the trucks were running with blood. And all at once I felt a savage hatred for everything that had given birth to that 'I have no orders', when people were dying of someone's stupidity. For the first time in my life I thought with hatred of the man we were burying. He could not be innocent

of the disaster. It was that 'I have no orders' which had caused the chaos and the bloodshed.[12]

The target of Yevtushenko's anger was the controlling, manipulating Soviet autocracy that Stalin had embodied, the way in which society had been deprived of the capacity to think for itself, and the sinister ease with which popular compliance had allowed Stalin and his henchmen to inflict the horrors of lies and repression upon them. Decades of Stalinist purges, murder and war had left the population traumatised. Now, looming over everything was the question of how to address the legacy of the man who had run the country so brutally for so long.

In 1953 the Cold War was at its height. The Soviet people had been taught that their country was under threat and it was only the genius of Comrade Stalin that kept them safe. It was a message designed to secure unquestioning obedience. But it neglected to address the impact on people's minds that would ensue when the Great Leader was gone. Even Yevgeny Yevtushenko felt bereft, identifying 'a sort of general paralysis' affecting the whole country, making him and his fellow Russians weep 'sincerely with grief and perhaps also with fear for the future'.[13]

Stalin, and the myth of Stalin, was a tool of psychological power, moulding a generation, persuading them to accept the Cold War world-view that the state constructed for them. 'That day was a turning point in my life,' wrote Yevtushenko. 'I realized that there was no one to do our thinking for us now, if indeed there ever had been ... A feeling of responsibility, not only for myself but for our whole country, came upon me and I felt its crushing weight on my shoulders.'[14]

The physical death of Stalin could not undo the psychological harm. The spectre of the dictator would linger in the nation's collective consciousness. Yevtushenko's poem 'The Heirs of Stalin' captured Soviet Russia's 'death of God' moment, followed, harrowingly, by the realisation that God had been not a benign father but a demonic impostor. Even the marble slabs of the mausoleum in which he was interred could not suppress his power.

Mute was the marble. Mutely glimmered the glass.
Mute stood the sentries, bronzed by the breeze.

Smoke rose from the coffin
And breath seeped through its cracks
As they bore him through the mausoleum doors.
Inside he was silent, watching,
His embalmed fists just pretending to be dead,
So that later he might gather strength
For a sortie from the grave ...
I fancy there's a phone-line in that coffin

When 'The Heirs of Stalin' was first published, in 1962, Nikita Khrushchev had already made his historic 'secret speech' denouncing Stalin's crimes. Stalin was removed from the mausoleum in 1961 and his statues – thousands of them, all over the USSR – were dismantled as part of the Khrushchev Thaw. But it was done surreptitiously, as if those doing it were still in dread of the dictator's retribution, or someone pointing out that they too had been complicit in his deeds. Squads of engineers would appear during the night, and the following morning the towering bronze Stalins that had watched over city squares and people's lives were gone.

Yevtushenko's poem distinguishes between that (in many ways rather superficial) physical iconoclasm, and the complex, painful memory-work that would need to go on if the tentacles of Stalinism were to be excised from the national psyche. Soon after 'The Heirs of Stalin' appeared, Khrushchev got cold feet and the de-Stalinisation process faltered. The poem disappeared from print for a quarter of a century.

Where the politicians quailed, Russian culture stepped forward. For centuries the arts have stood as Russia's other world, a garden of liberty, offering Russians a better vision of themselves when political discourse was choked and repressed. Now they took up the task of exorcising Stalin's ghost. Literature, poetry, music, painting and film were ways of digesting and exorcising the man whose all-too-living memory continued to trouble and oppress. A distinctly Gogolian story began to circulate of how art might triumph over the dark forces of dictatorship. As with so many Russian tales, no one can say for certain if it is true or wishful fabrication. But it has become rooted in the collective memory of society and, according to the musicologist Solomon Volkov, it was believed by the composer Dmitry Shostako-vich. 'In his final years,' Volkov quotes Shostakovich as saying, 'Stalin seemed more and more like a madman, and I think his superstition grew.'[15] According to Shostakovich's reported account, Stalin let no one in to see him for days at a time, spending hours listening to the radio. 'Once, Stalin called the State Radio Committee ... and asked if they had a record of Mozart's Piano Concerto No. 23, which he had heard on the radio the day before. "Played by Yudina", he added.' The concerto had been performed by the distinguished, eccentric Russian pianist Maria Yudina, a forceful personality and a devout Orthodox Christian. Hearing the dictator's voice – 'Genghis Khan with a telephone', as Bukharin described him – the representative of the State Committee panicked and told Stalin that of course they had the record. In fact the concert had been live and no recording existed.

> But they were afraid to say no to Stalin; no one ever knew what the consequences might be. A human life meant nothing to him. All you could do was submit, be a yes-man to a madman. Stalin demanded that they send the record with Yudina's performance to his dacha. The Committee were in a panic, but they had to do something. They called in Yudina and an orchestra to record it that night. Everyone was shaking with fright ...

The single, unique copy of the record was rushed out to Stalin's dacha in time for the next morning and he put it on the turntable. So pleased was he, the story goes, that he sent Yudina a reward of 20,000 roubles. But instead of gratefully accepting, the headstrong pianist wrote him a reply that amounted to a suicide note: 'I thank you Josif Vissarionovich, for your aid. I will pray for you day and night and ask the Lord to forgive your great sins before the people and the country. The Lord is merciful and He will forgive you. I gave the money to the church that I attend.' The warrant for Yudina's arrest was duly drawn up but, amazingly, Stalin did not give the order for it to be carried out. Did he recognise the truth of Yudina's charges? Did the mighty dictator fear the Almighty? Did he acknowledge the power of art to bear witness when earthly power is gone? The story concludes with the heartening thought that music has the capacity to defeat the darkest evil. 'Nothing happened to Yudina. And they say her recording of the Mozart was going round on the turntable when the Leader and Teacher was found dead in his dacha. It was the last thing he heard ...'[16]

The role of culture in the process of psychological de-Stalinisation took many guises. Black humour – subverting and debunking – was a powerful weapon, depicting Stalin in ways that took away his dignity. The poet and singer Bulat Okudzhava used mockery to address the legacy of fear. In his poem 'The Black Cat', Stalin is ugly, with 'dirty claws' and 'yellow eyes', but at the same time menacing.

> A black cat lives in our yard,
> Lurking in the dark,
> Smirking through his whiskers.
> A grinning moustache upon his snout
> …
> Asking little, demanding nothing,
> Day or night he utters not a sound.
> We all may bring our food to him,
> But we thank him as we go.*

Shrinking Stalin to a tomcat, then to a pair of whiskers, is a scornful, belittling metonymy, reducing the dictator to unseemly physical attributes. In Kornei Chukovsky's poem 'Tarakanishche' – 'The Giant Cockroach' – Stalin appears as an insect. Written as a children's fairy tale, the tone is mocking and playful. It was turned into a musical cartoon for TV and remained a favourite through the Soviet years and beyond. But Chukovsky's killer cockroach has chilling undertones. 'A dreadful giant, the big bad cockroach, raged and twitched his moustache. "I'll gobble you up; I'll gobble you up; I'll show you no mercy!"' The whole of the animal kingdom, from mighty tigers, to bears and hippopotamuses, prostrates itself before him, fearing for their lives. When a kangaroo points out the absurdity of bowing down to a little bug, the animals tell her to go away, 'or misfortune will descend upon us'. Eventually, a sparrow calls the cockroach's bluff. 'It pecked and gobbled the cockroach, who turned out not to be such a giant after all … though his whiskers stuck out from the sparrow's beak to the last. And how overjoyed were all the beasts of the animal kingdom that

---

* Though Okudzhava never stated explicitly that the cat was Stalin, the implication is clear. When asked directly, he preferred to smile mysteriously and assert that the poem was about the inhabitants of the building, rather than the cat they so feared. Were they, and thus the Soviet people, to blame for creating this monster? D. Bykov, *Bulat Okudzhava*, Moscow: Molodaya Gvardiya, 2009, p. 168.

he was gone!' For those who had eyes to see, the cockroach's identity was no secret – and the fate reserved for him was what the arts were aiming to do to the memory of Stalin.[17]

In the 1980s, with the reforming Mikhail Gorbachev in the Kremlin, de-Stalinisation brought new revelations and new interpretations of the past. When, in the late eighties, near the start of my posting as BBC correspondent in Moscow, I asked a group of schoolteachers how they were coping with all the changes, they showed me instructions they'd received from the Education Ministry. The Kremlin was directing them physically to remove eighty pages from the standard textbooks and glue in a new, revised section that the ministry had provided. There was a popular joke that 'Communism made the future certain, but the past unpredictable'.

In 1991, after the coup that ended Soviet power, the old communist statues were laid out in a Moscow park to be reviled by the public. I saw people kick and spit on the images of the men who had oppressed Russia for seven decades. But, even then, there was a lurking feeling that the past does not die easily. 'Night Watch', a song from earlier years by the poet Alexander Galich in which the Stalin statues come back to life and march through the streets, trampling once again on the Russian people, was still resonant.

History in Russia is endlessly malleable; and some pages of the past are nowadays being replaced once again, this time by a Kremlin seemingly more favourably disposed towards the old dictator. Images of Stalin started appearing in the mid 1990s as an icon of protest against the disastrous capitalism of the Yeltsin years. The banners then were carried by elderly people nostalgic for Soviet times, and by Russian nationalists opposed to the West.

Since 2000, Vladimir Putin has allowed a new version of Stalin to emerge, celebrating his victory in the Second World War and toning down the condemnation of his repressions. Critics accused him of promoting a positive image of Stalin to appeal to old beliefs and prejudices. In 2008, in a popular poll, Stalin was voted as one of the most representative heroes of Russia, together with the medieval prince Alexander Nevsky, ahead of Pushkin and Dostoevsky. Putin has unbanned celebrations marking Stalin's birthday. The first new Stalin monuments for decades have appeared recently in Yalta and Tver, while items documenting his crimes were removed from the Gulag museum in Perm.

'Bring back Stalin!', a tub-thumping song by Sergei Kurochkin, met with great approval in certain quarters when Crimea was annexed by Moscow from Ukraine in 2014. 'Bring back Stalin to us, He is our generalissimus!' demand the lyrics, 'And bring back Stalin's statues on our streets!'[18] The song was not endorsed by the Kremlin, but neither was it banned.

The idea, the memory, the ghost of Stalin remains powerful. Even in his own lifetime he was a work of fiction, polished and packaged by the official Soviet machine, and his myth has been preserved by the very act of exorcising it. Since his death, Stalin's image has been appropriated by a multiplicity of groups with very different views of Russia's past, and different ideas of what they want Russia to be. It serves different purposes, different goals and different aspirations. In the twenty-first century, Stalin has become a highly pliable fantasy figure of popular imagination. After the straightforward outrage of earlier years, authors have vied to outdo each other in the grotesque surrealism of their descriptions, portraying him as a baboon, a cross-dresser, a sexual pervert. It is, perhaps, a way of saying that there *was* no real Stalin, that he was always a projection of popular longings, desires and ideas about how Russia should be.

12

A PSYCHOLOGICAL VACUUM

In his 1963 'Behavioral Study of Obedience', the Yale psychologist Stanley Milgram explored the disconcerting processes that play out between the givers of orders and those who must choose whether or not to obey them.[1] His experiments were prompted by the realisation that hundreds of thousands of ordinary German men and women had carried out actions during the Second World War that were barbaric, immoral and inhuman. Were all these people monsters? Or had something happened that made them act against nature?

At the Nuremberg war trials in 1945–6, several defendants had argued that they were not guilty, because they were carrying out the instructions of their superiors. The defence of 'only obeying orders' – *Befehl ist Befehl*, in German – was used again by the Nazi functionary and Holocaust organiser Adolf Eichmann when he was tried by an Israeli court in 1961. The principle has been debated by lawyers, ridiculed by British satirists, and was disallowed as mythical by Article 8 of the Charter of the International Military Tribunal drawn up for Nuremberg. But it shed a troubling light on the fact that seemingly ordinary people can be persuaded to do extraordinary things. Milgram's experiment for the study of obedience was described in an article in the *American Psychologist* journal:

> In Milgram's basic paradigm, a subject walks into a laboratory believing that s/he is about to take part in a study of memory and learning. After being assigned the role of a teacher, the subject is asked to teach word associations to a fellow subject (who in reality is a collaborator of the experimenter). The teaching method, however, is unconventional – administering increasingly higher electric shocks to the learner. Once the presumed shock level reaches a certain point, the subject is thrown into a conflict. On the one hand, the strapped learner demands

to be set free, he appears to suffer pain, and going all the way
may pose a risk to his health. On the other hand, the experimenter ... insists that the experiment must go on. In sharp
contrast to the expectations of professionals and laymen alike,
some 65% of all subjects continue to administer shocks up to the
very highest levels.[2]

Milgram's conclusion was that instructions issued by a figure confidently expressing authority have a powerful coercive effect. The
majority of people found it hard to disobey, even when their conscience told them that what they were doing was wrong. Milgram
concluded that once 'a person comes to view himself as the instrument for carrying out another person's wishes, he therefore no longer
sees himself as responsible for his actions ... Relatively few people
have the resources needed to resist authority.'[3]

The abdication of personal values occurs when individual
accountability is ceded to a higher authority – a person, organisation
or government claiming to know what is best for the group. Sigmund
Freud identified it in his 1921 work *Group Psychology and the Analysis of
the Ego*, where he talks of how an individual might substitute loyalty
to a leader for their own sense of self and agency. This figure need
only 'possess the typical qualities of the individuals concerned in a
particularly clearly marked and pure form, and need only give an
impression of greater force': the psychological need for a leader is
so strong that it will invest them with 'a predominance to which he
would otherwise perhaps have had no claim'.[4]

It is fair to say that more than one twentieth-century leader recognised and exploited the concept Freud describes. Milgram had at
the forefront of his thoughts the regime of Adolf Hitler, but his conclusions were just as applicable to that of Stalin. 'Control the manner
in which a man interprets his world, and you have gone a long way
toward controlling his behavior. That is why ideology, an attempt
to interpret the condition of man, is always a prominent feature
of revolutions, wars, and other circumstances in which individuals
are called upon to perform extraordinary action.'[5] Among several
features reinforcing the authority of an order-giver, Milgram notes
the 'scientist's white coat' worn by the experimenter in his study.
Subjects seemed impressed or cowed by such outward symbols of
authority and it is no surprise that authoritarian regimes the world

ВКП(б)

ВОСПИТАЕМ ПОКОЛЕНИЕ, БЕЗЗАВЕТНО
ПРЕДАННОЕ ДЕЛУ КОММУНИЗМА!

The Soviet boast that they were 'raising a generation to be utterly
devoted to the cause of communism' suggested something of
the psychological methods at work on Young Pioneers.

over have power-dressed their own authority figures – army, police,
prison officers, civil service. Uniforms intimidate those who are
subject to their authority and de-individuate those who wear them.
They invest the wearer with both the shared authority of a self-
bolstering group and the cloak of anonymity: a uniform to hide
behind, a reassurance that you can get away with anything. In Soviet
times, uniforms were everywhere. Even the children were dressed in
the white shirts and red bandanas of the communist Young Pioneers,
imbuing them early in life with the communal ethos of obedience,
belonging and authority.

Milgram described the way controlling autocracies subsume
individuals into the unthinking whole.

> Each individual possesses a conscience which to a greater or
> lesser degree serves to restrain the unimpeded flow of impulses
> destructive to others. But when he merges his person into an
> organizational structure, a new creature replaces autonomous
> man, unhindered by the limitations of individual morality,
> freed of humane inhibition, mindful only of the sanctions of
> authority.[6]

The leaders of the USSR, Stalin chief among them, were adept at exploiting the psychological levers of obedience. But Milgram's 'tendency to obedience' can be undermined if enough people at a given time find enough cause for dissatisfaction. The Kremlin's physical repression of independent views (the Russian for 'dissidence', *inakomyslie*, means literally 'thinking differently') testified to the leadership's fear that resentful thinking might tip into resistance. The obedience compact meant sustaining the belief, by force if necessary, that the emperor's clothes were not missing.

For Joseph Stalin, the charade became his life. World leaders, like the rest of us, get set in their ways. Part of it is just getting old; our brains are less open to the assimilation of new possibilities. But Stanley Milgram concluded that once we have committed ourselves to a course of action, even if we know in our own mind that it is dubious or wrong, we are unlikely to retreat from it, because doing so would mean having to accept that we were at fault in the past, that we had lied or acted badly. We tend to persevere in a course of action, and maintain that it is acceptable, in order not to have to admit the guilt already accrued. The British sociologist Peter Marris writes of belief perseverance, or conceptual conservatism, the tendency to maintain a conviction despite new information that contradicts it. The process of giving up a belief, he says, is similar to the working out of grief, because 'the impulse to defend the predictability of life is a fundamental and universal principle of human psychology ... a deep-rooted and insistent need for continuity'.[7]

To accept compromises so late in life, to release the men and women he had sent to the Gulag, to acknowledge that the capitalist world might not be the epitome of evil or that communism might not be building the people's paradise, would have meant Stalin admitting he had been wrong all along. And that is something that few human minds can cope with.

To the very end, Stalin maintained his contention that the capitalist world would collapse into infighting, paving the way for the global triumph of communism. In 1952, when the evidence suggested this was becoming increasingly far-fetched, he covered his ears and rebuked the doubters.[8]

While Stalin was alive, the old rigidity of thinking, the belief perseverance that made it impossible to break with the past, remained entrenched. His death opened a window on the West that promised to let fresh air into the fetid atmosphere of a claustrophobic USSR. But old thinking persisted in both camps and not everyone was ready to accept change. Decades of propaganda, the psychological warfare waged by the Kremlin at home and abroad, was a constraint on new thinking. Could things be different now? Nikita Khrushchev's daughter Rada, who was twenty-four at the time, felt anything was possible. 'We looked to the future with optimism. We believed that we could do everything, that in our country everything would turn out all right.'[9]

But Washington and London, just as much as Moscow, were affected by conceptual conservatism. Restoring the trust that was needed to move forward would meet resistance in both East and West. In the event, it was Stalin's successors who made the first move.

Unwilling to contemplate change and wary of discussing a future without him, the old dictator had made no plans for what would happen after his death. His temporary absences from Moscow had allowed a loose collective leadership to take shape, but no heir apparent. The first roster of the Communist Party Presidium announced in March 1953 contained ten names, of which Malenkov, Beria, Molotov, Khrushchev and Bulganin were the most influential. With Stalin gone, the Presidium pressed ahead with a number of popular measures, including more spending on the civilian economy, a reduction in the repressive powers of the police and the release of those who had been arrested under Stalin's so-called 'Doctors' Plot'. Moscow put out feelers to the United States about the prospects for easing tensions between the two blocs. In July, an armistice was signed to end the Korean War.

But Soviet politicians were far from immune to the claustrophobia and paranoia they had instilled in the population. Khrushchev called it 'Stalin's mental disease', the xenophobia that made the Soviet leadership 'regard every foreigner as an unmasked enemy, who came only with the goal of recruiting Soviet people for espionage'.[10] A malevolent military–industrial complex was seen as controlling western decision-making, secret cabals of warmongers fostering dark forces bent on the destruction of the USSR. Kremlin reformers struggled at times to make their voices heard. It was a divergence of view that contributed to an acrimonious, at times deadly rivalry and it would continue until Khrushchev emerged as *primus inter pares* three years later.

For its part, the West recognised that Stalin's death presented an opportunity. But Washington's initial hope was less for rapprochement than for Soviet collapse. A CIA report speculating on the consequences of Stalin's death had concluded that 'the absence of Stalin's prestige and personality might give rise to manifestations of personal rivalry among politburo members that could result in the rapid disintegration of the Soviet regime',[11] and had called on the Psychological Strategy Board to undertake 'active measures' to help bring this about.[12] Khrushchev later revealed his own fears that hardliners on both sides might use the uncertainty to tip the world into armed conflict. 'In the days leading up to Stalin's death,' he wrote, 'we believed that America would invade the Soviet Union and we would go to war.'[13]

The rhetoric from Moscow, however, made Washington pause. The Kremlin's message was one of change and renewal, backed by the overt suggestion that West and East might choose cooperation over confrontation. Georgy Malenkov, then seen as the leading voice in the Presidium, set the tone in his contribution to Stalin's eulogy on 12 March.

> It is not true that humanity is faced with a choice between two alternatives, either a new world war or the so-called Cold War. The Soviet government decisively opposes Cold War, since that policy is the policy of preparing a new world war, which with modern weapons means the end of world civilization.[14]

Five months earlier, *Time* magazine had depicted him on its front cover as Stalin's puppet, little more than a mouthpiece for his master. So the fact that he was now the man suggesting peace with the West carried weight. Malenkov repeated his message in a speech to the Supreme Soviet on 8 August 1953, telling deputies, 'We consider that there are no objective grounds for a collision between the United States and the USSR.'[15] Proceedings were carried live by Soviet radio as a signal to audiences at home and abroad that this was an important policy announcement.

Washington was listening. The CIA report on the speech concluded, '[I]t is now quite clear that, at least for some time to come, the Communist Party of the USSR and the Soviet government is Georgy Maksimilianovich Malenkov ... Coexistence is possible, Malenkov believes, as far as the Soviet Union is concerned.'[16] The CIA seemed to think that the softening in Moscow's stance was 'an official answer to the Western psychological warfare campaign',[17] the result of the 'active measures' carried out by the USA's Psychological Strategy Board (PSB), which had been set up in 1951 and tasked with waging psychological warfare against the country's enemies.

But the agency was non-committal on whether or not Washington should trust the apparent olive branch from the Kremlin.

> However, it is a Soviet axiom that the capitalist West, by its very nature, is doomed to destruction. Whether the highest Soviet rulers sincerely believe this is difficult to say. The point is that they force their followers to believe in the axiom and are quite successful in this task. That is all that counts ... They think it is quite sufficient to seize every opportunity to weaken capitalist countries from the inside.[18]

The fact that Malenkov also used his speech to announce the successful development of a Soviet hydrogen bomb suggested that the Soviets were wary of being seen to have gone soft, as the CIA was quick to point out. 'Unfortunately, the Communist Party and the government of the USSR sincerely believe the West is preparing for an aggressive war against the USSR, and that they will spare no effort to put over this idea to the people.'[19] The writer of the report speculates on how the Soviets gained access to the secrets of the hydrogen bomb ('it has been proven that much top-secret information concerning the research and production of the atomic bomb fell into Soviet hands. How can we be sure that this was not repeated in the case of the hydrogen bomb?') but, given the dramatic developments in Malenkov's speech, the tone of the report is remarkably measured. Amid much frenzied and unsubstantiated speculation in the intelligence reporting of the time, the document is restrained and largely factual. With both sides desperate to look into the mind and intentions of their adversaries, the quality of the inferences drawn is unusually high.

The British, too, were speculating on how the USSR would evolve in the post-Stalin era. A Foreign Office memorandum issued on 9 April 1953 accepts that there has been a shift in Soviet attitudes, but is dubious about the Kremlin's motives, attributing the new rhetoric to political manoeuvring rather than a genuine desire for peace.

TNA, PREM 11/540 CONFIDENTIAL
SOVIET POLICIES AFTER STALIN'S DEATH ...
A desire for a détente could be explained in terms of the problems which faced the Soviet leaders when they took over power. There are no grounds for believing that there have been any changes in the ultimate objectives of Soviet policy, that is to say: in the short term, the disruption of N.A.T.O. and the promotion of revolution in colonial and 'semi-colonial' territories; in the long term, the establishment of a world system of Communist States under Soviet leadership.[20]

The writer is reluctant to believe that the leopard is capable of changing its spots. Such is the level of suspicion that had grown between East and West since the end of the war that the Foreign Office questioned whether the Malenkov overtures might be a trap, 'better calculated to divide the Governments opposed to them (above all to divide the United States and its allies) ... than the bludgeoning xenophobia displayed by Stalin since 1946'.[21]

Stalin had been dead for a little over a month; it was early days to draw long-term conclusions. In the uncertain times that lay ahead, the report recommends cautious engagement – avoiding 'both in policy and propaganda any action that would give the Soviet people the impression that the West is implacably hostile whatever conciliatory gestures their leaders make'[22] – and no let-up in military preparedness in the event of Soviet treachery.

The context in which the Foreign Office memorandum was written helps explain its cautious tone. Less than two months before the death of Stalin, the United States had inaugurated a new president. Dwight Eisenhower, former supreme commander of the victorious allied forces in Europe, was a war hero, a Republican and a patriot. The public expected him to be tough on the Soviets and opposed to détente. Eisenhower's campaign materials had spoken of a 'policy of political boldness' that would 'roll back' Soviet domination of eastern Europe, marking the end of 'the negative, futile, and immoral policy of "containment"'.[23] John Foster Dulles, who would become Eisenhower's hawkish secretary of state, was calling for active US intervention to foment anti-Soviet rebellion in Moscow's satellite states.

Liberation from the yoke of Moscow will not occur for a very long time and courage in neighboring lands will not be sustained unless the United States makes it stubbornly known that it wants and expects liberation to occur. The mere statement of that wish and expectation would change, in an electrifying way, the mood of the captive peoples. It would put heavy new burdens on the jailers and create new opportunities for liberation.[24]

But Eisenhower hesitated. Ever since Churchill's time in opposition at the turn of the decade, the British leader had been lobbying him for 'jaw before war'. On 11 March 1953, Churchill renewed his plea.

[N]ow when there is no more Stalin ... I have the feeling that we might both of us together or separately be called to account if no attempt were made to turn over a leaf so that a new page would be started with something more coherent on it than a series of casual and dangerous incidents at the many points of contact between the two divisions of the world.[25]

In further messages, Churchill added, 'It would be a pity if a sudden frost nipped spring in the bud ... Would it not be well to combine the re-assertions of your and our inflexible resolves with some balancing expression of hope that we have entered upon a new era?' ... '[W]e think, as I am sure you do also, that we ought to lose no chance of finding out how far the Malenkov regime are prepared to go in easing things up all around.'

Eisenhower remained dubious. 'I tend to doubt the wisdom of such a meeting,' he wrote in reply, 'since this would give our opponent the same kind of opportunity he has so often had ... to make of the whole occurrence another propaganda mill for the Soviet.' It was the height of the McCarthy era: like Truman before him, Eisenhower was under domestic pressure to act tough and reluctant to open himself to accusations of being 'soft' on the Soviets. Neither could he be certain that the Soviet olive branch was genuine. The USSR had just successfully tested a hydrogen bomb and there was no guarantee that the Kremlin leadership – still an enigma to observers in the West – was united behind Malenkov's suggestions of détente.

Oleg Troyanovsky, later to become a distinguished Soviet ambassador, but then a junior Foreign Ministry official and translator, remembered the frustration felt in Moscow. '[The US] did not seem to appreciate moderation and refused to acknowledge the obvious truth that constructive steps by one party required a similar response from the other side ... They did not show any signs of encouragement to those sections of the Soviet political spectrum that stood for better relations with the West.'[26] In a classic example of each side misreading the other, what Moscow perceived as American intransigence was actually the result of hesitation, indecision and incompetence. In the early 1950s, the then president Harry Truman had instructed the Psychological Strategy Board to develop a plan specifically to exploit the psychological vacuum that Washington knew would follow the eventual death of Stalin. 'Operation Cancellation' would have the aim of sowing strife among the new Kremlin leadership and provoking a breakdown in government by disseminating black propaganda among the Soviet population. When Stalin died, Eisenhower told the National Security Council that 'the moment is propitious for introducing the right word directly into the Soviet Union', but no action was taken. The State Department counselled against propaganda that could be 'interpreted as an appeal to the Soviet people to rise up against their rulers in a period of mourning'.[27]

When Eisenhower asked for an explanation he was angered to discover that, while much discussion had been devoted to the opportunity that Stalin's death would offer the US, little had been done in terms of concrete planning. At a Cabinet meeting on 6 March, he berated those present.

> For about seven years, ever since 1946, I know that everybody who should have been concerned about such things has been sounding off on what we should do when Stalin dies – what difference it would make, how it would affect our policies. Well, he died – and we went to see what bright ideas were in the files of this government, what plans were laid. What we found was that the result of seven years of yapping is exactly ZERO. We have no plan. We don't even have any agreement on what difference his death makes. It's – well, it's criminal, that's all I can say.[28]

This muddled policy – rather than any strategic decision – prevented Washington from exploiting the psychological advantage of Stalin's death. But neither did the US use it as an opportunity to create better relations. A month after the dictator's demise, General Charles Jackson, Eisenhower's adviser on psychological warfare, wrote in his diary, 'We have given a virtual monopoly to the Soviets over the minds of people all over the world – and in that month, they have moved with vigor and disarming plausibility.'[29]

Only on 16 April, six weeks after Stalin's death, was Eisenhower ready to lay down the broad outline of US policy towards the new USSR that was taking shape. His speech, to the American Society of Newspaper Editors in Washington DC, was titled 'Chance for Peace'. It offered a constructive response to the overtures from the Kremlin, while challenging the Soviets to back up their gestures with tangible concessions.[30]

> This is one of those times in the affairs of nations when the gravest choices must be made, if there is to be a turning toward a just and lasting peace. The world knows that an era ended with the death of Joseph Stalin ... the new Soviet leadership now has a precious opportunity to awaken, with the rest of the world, to the point of peril reached and to help turn the tide of history. Will it do this? We do not yet know. Recent statements and gestures of Soviet leaders give some evidence that they may recognize this critical moment. We welcome every honest act of peace. We care nothing for mere rhetoric.[31]

Eisenhower's speech was translated and published in both *Pravda* and *Izvestiya*, a signal that the Kremlin was taking his proposals seriously. A *Pravda* editorial on 25 April rejected Eisenhower's criticism of Soviet foreign policy, but responded to his call for cooperation by emphasising Moscow's willingness to negotiate on outstanding international problems.[32]

There were, though, divisions in DC. John Foster Dulles, the anti-communist zealot at the head of the State Department, while claiming to support the president, made a point of contradicting nearly everything Eisenhower's speech had outlined. 'All will know,' Dulles said, 'and I am confident that the Soviet leaders know best of all, that what we plan is not greater weakness but greater strength ... We are not dancing to any Russian tune.'[33]

A few months later, Dulles repeated his misgivings about détente and called for a strengthening of the policy of maximum military (nuclear) deterrence.[34]

> The Soviet Communists ... seek, through many types of maneuvers, gradually to divide and weaken the free nations by over-extending them in efforts which, as Lenin put it, are 'beyond their strength, so that they come to practical bankruptcy'. Then, said Lenin, 'our victory is assured'. Then, said Stalin, will be 'the moment for the decisive blow'.
>
> ... there is no local defense which alone will contain the mighty land power of the Communist world. Local defenses must be reinforced by the further deterrent of massive retaliatory power ... [Our] basic decision was to depend primarily upon a great capacity to retaliate, instantly, by means and at places of our choosing.[35]

When British and American officials met to coordinate their plans for the post-Stalin era, the differences in their approach came to a head. With Anthony Eden undergoing surgery for a damaged bile duct, Lord Salisbury, as acting foreign secretary, expressed alarm at the belligerent tone Washington was adopting. In particular, he noted the danger of unbridled US rhetoric encouraging popular but futile uprisings in the Soviet-dominated satellite states of eastern Europe.

> TNA, CAB 129/61/37
> C.(53)187 CABINET SECRET
> POLICY TOWARDS THE SOVIET UNION AND GERMANY
> 3 July 1953
> (...)
> Anglo-American differences about the Soviet Union.
> There seems now to be a new and more dangerous American tendency, which has its roots in the Republican election campaign and was illustrated in a recent statement by Mr. Dulles, to interpret the situation behind the Iron Curtain as already very shaky and therefore to advocate new although unspecified measures to encourage and even promote the early liberation of the satellite countries. It is my intention to resist American pressure for new initiatives of this kind. A policy of pinpricks is calculated to exasperate the Russians and is most unlikely to help the

unhappy peoples of the occupied countries. The last thing we want to do is to bait the Russian and satellite Governments into taking violent measures against them. We must of course keep the spirit of freedom alive in Eastern Europe, but we should also counsel prudence and restraint.[36]

The situation in the Soviet satellite countries was about to take centre stage, with tragic consequences. And some of the blame would lie with the loose rhetoric and lack of psychological insight displayed by politicians in both East and West.

By the early summer of 1953, everyone knew that Stalin's death had opened the way for change. But no one knew what form that change would take. In the USSR and abroad people strained to interpret the signs coming out of Moscow. In the absence of clarity, many of them shaped the evidence to fit the future that they wished for. Most tragically, the people of East Germany decided that the end of Stalin meant the end of Stalinism. They glimpsed a chance for liberation, and in June 1953 they took to the streets.

The immediate cause of the unrest was a series of mixed signals from the Kremlin. In mid 1952, with Stalin's backing, the East German government had increased work norms to improve output. The Programme for the Accelerated Construction of Socialism, meaning more work for the same pay, was unpopular. In the first four months of 1953, 120,000 East Germans fled to the West. With Stalin gone, the new men in the Kremlin ordered the authorities in Berlin to abandon the new work quotas.[37]

The move backfired. Instead of mollifying public opinion, the appearance of concessions from the previously unyielding authorities convinced people that change was possible and they demanded more of it. As Alexis de Tocqueville had pointed out a century earlier, 'the moment of greatest danger for an authoritarian regime is when it begins to reform itself'.*

---

* A. de Tocqueville, *L'ancien régime et la révolution* (1856). In this case, the East German authorities did not, in fact, reduce the work quotas. They did, however, publish a 'New Course' in the official party newspaper, admitting past mistakes, opening the door for further criticism from the public. C. Ostermann (ed.), *Uprising in East Germany 1953: The Cold War, the German Question, and the First Major Upheaval Behind the Iron Curtain*, Budapest: Central European University Press, 2001, p. 20.

The sight of Soviet tanks on the streets of East Germany
brought back painful memories of the past and sparked
anxieties over what was to come for many Germans.

On 17 June 1953, hundreds of thousands of workers went on strike in all the major cities of the German Democratic Republic. Forty thousand protestors gathered in East Berlin. Their initial demands for lower work quotas took on a political character, with calls for the resignation of the government. Late in the afternoon, the authorities called on Soviet forces based in the GDR to suppress the protest. Twenty thousand troops with tanks and machine guns quickly cleared the streets. Casualty figures are disputed, but at least fifty-five people were killed and hundreds more were arrested and sent to penal camps.

The German Communist Party newspaper, *Neues Deutschland*, blamed the uprising on 'western agencies' bent on disrupting the stability of East Germany. And, in a way, they were right. There had already been disturbances in Czechoslovakia and Hungary after Stalin's death, as people sensed an opportunity to win greater freedom from Soviet domination. The exponents of US psychological warfare had incited the uprisings in speeches, radio broadcasts and propaganda. But when it came to the crunch, the West did not send the material support the rebels believed they had been promised. Having resisted attempts to improve relations with Moscow, Washington's politician-warriors also failed to support the uprisings they had helped foment in the USSR's satellite states. The psychological vacuum triggered by Stalin's death was not limited to the Soviets. Leadership groups on both sides of the Iron Curtain would struggle to adapt their thinking to new realities.

13

THE SECRET SPEECH AND THE PSYCHOLOGY OF THE CROWD

Then came something unexpected – a windfall in the form of Nikita Khrushchev's secret report about Stalin to the 20th Party Congress, a copy of which came into American hands and was published in the *New York Times* on June 5, 1956.[1]

For Robert Tucker, the American diplomat-psychologist who had spent the early 1950s analysing Stalin's character from the US embassy in Moscow, publication of Khrushchev's secret speech shone new light on the psyche of the man who had puzzled and intimidated the West.

In this lengthy document, most significantly called 'On the Cult of Personality and its Consequences,' a one-time admiring protégé, who had become one of the dictator's lieutenants and observed him at close hand from the late 1930s to his death, offered abundant first-hand testimony that Stalin was a man of colossal grandiosity along with profound insecurity that caused him to need constant affirmation of his imagined greatness.[2]

Khrushchev's speech was a windfall not only for psychologists seeking to understand the nature of Stalinism; it also gave the West ammunition with which to criticise the Soviet state. Washington broadcast the text of the nominally secret report to all the countries of Soviet-dominated eastern Europe, with a consequential acceleration of their demands for political change.

Khrushchev was probably aware that the contents of his address would not remain secret. He was certainly aware of the iconoclastic impact it would have both in the USSR and abroad. So why did he make it? Stepping up to the podium of the Twentieth Party Congress on 25 February 1956 was the biggest gamble of a man whose political life would be based on throwing the dice, and whose risk-taking would come to define this second phase of the Cold War. The reasons behind it are comprehensible only in the context of the psychology of the man and his times.

In the confusion that followed Stalin's death, Lavrenty Beria, Vyacheslav Molotov, Georgy Malenkov and Nikita Khrushchev declared themselves a collective leadership. The atmosphere reeked of fear and ambition: all of them were eyeing the leading role, all trembling at the heresy of usurping 'the boss', and all had been involved in the excesses of Stalinism. They rifled through records and papers that might incriminate them. Beria stole the safe holding documents from Stalin's dacha to destroy whatever the dictator had on him and acquire compromising material on his colleagues. Ostensibly a partnership of equals, the 'collective' leadership were a sack of ferrets: divided, distrustful, on the brink of panic.

The arch-Stalinist Malenkov was the early favourite, with Khrushchev at his side in an uneasy duumvirate. All feared Beria, skulking in the shadows with his secret policemen and an intimate knowledge of where the skeletons were buried. They suspected he had poisoned Stalin,* and when an autopsy was carried out, the results were conveniently lost. Beria declared an amnesty for convicts serving less than five years and by the summer the streets were full of thousands of petty criminals, whom Beria was said to be recruiting to sweep him to power.

Khrushchev couldn't delay. The stakes were high and, gambler that he was, he played the odds. With the collusion of Marshal Zhukov, he ambushed Beria at a meeting of the Central Committee Presidium, accusing him of being a British spy.† Beria could only

---

* In his memoirs, Molotov claims Beria boasted he had done so, telling the politburo that Stalin had been planning to remove them, and that he – Beria – had 'saved us all'.
† Beria was certainly not a British spy, but his fate should not inspire pity. In 1998, when Beria's house on Moscow's Garden Ring became the Tunisian embassy, the bones of five women were unearthed in the garden. Declassified archives revealed that Beria was in the habit of raping and murdering young girls that his bodyguards snatched for him from the street. www.gazeta.ru/science/2019/08/12_a_12572749. shtml.

mumble, 'What's going on Nikita Sergeyevich?' before Zhukov and a band of armed officers burst in to arrest him. Convicted of terrorism and counter-revolutionary acts, Beria was executed in December.

The mood of the country changed. There was a collective sigh of relief. In prisons and labour camps, political inmates greeted the news of his death by throwing their caps in the air. Stalin's demise, and now Beria's downfall, removed the fear and emboldened thoughts of resistance. There were uprisings. At Kengir camp in Kazakhstan, 13,000 prisoners went on strike. The prison officials didn't know what to do; the god-like authority that had instructed *Homo Sovieticus* how to live his life was gone. 'They had no idea what was required of them,' Solzhenitsyn wrote, 'and mistakes could be dangerous. If they showed excessive zeal and shot down a crowd they might end up being punished as henchmen of Beria. But if they weren't zealous enough, and didn't energetically push the strikers out to work – exactly the same thing could happen!'[3] After forty-two days of hesitation, Red Army tanks crushed the revolt, killing 700 prisoners.[4]

Even the men in the Kremlin didn't know if they had done the right thing. They had relied on Stalin for everything, but he was gone now and they were on their own. They set up a committee. Pyotr Pospelov, secretary of the Communist Party Central Committee, was instructed to enquire into abuses of power in the USSR, including Stalin's purges and executions, going back as far as the 1930s. But when Pospelov delivered his report in early 1956, it put the leadership in a quandary. If they suppressed it, would they be seen to be covering up the crimes of Stalinism? If they published it, would people realise that they too were complicit in them? The Twentieth Party Congress, the first since Stalin's death, was scheduled for February 1956, less than a month away. A decision had to be made, and Khrushchev made it.

Nikita Sergeyevich Khrushchev did not appear to have the mind of a Machiavelli. Far from it. In early life, he had been a shepherd, then a miner in the Donbass region of his native Ukraine. He'd been a union official during the First World War, fought for the Reds in the revolution and joined the Bolsheviks in 1918. His rise through the party's ranks seemed to owe more to being in the right place at the right time than to talent. By 1938 he was first secretary of the Ukrainian Communist Party, served as a political commissar in the war and in 1949 was brought to Moscow, where he was appointed central committee secretary.

According to William Hayter, British ambassador to the Soviet Union in the 1950s, Khrushchev did not lack for native wit or energy and ambition. But he was no intellectual, Hayter told me three decades later; Khrushchev's character was rough and unrefined. At a dinner in the Kremlin, Hayter thought Khrushchev struggled to follow the conversation. 'He needed Malenkov to explain things to him in words of one syllable.'[5] His modest background and lack of refinement led rivals to discount him as an uneducated *muzhik*; but he was a survivor, who would wrong-foot opponents with colourful, scabrous quips. Hayter admitted that he had initially underestimated Khrushchev, misled by his peasant-like manners.[6] In his memoirs, Hayter acknowledged Khrushchev's qualities – a dogged perseverance and a very thick skin. 'He was like a little bull who, if aimed in the right direction, would charge along and be certain to arrive with a crash at his objective, knocking down anything that was in his way.'[7] By the time of the Party Congress in February 1956, Khrushchev had knocked most obstacles – including most of his rivals – out of his path.

Threatened by an alliance between Malenkov, Molotov and Kaganovich, Khrushchev moved to head them off. The Pospelov report was a useful weapon. His opponents were more implicated in the purges of the 1930s than he was, so they had the most to lose if the report came out. Khrushchev began to argue in favour of publishing it. 'If we don't tell the truth at the Congress,' he told them, 'we'll be forced to do so at some time in the future. And then we won't be the people making the speeches – we'll be the people under investigation.'[8]

Malenkov objected, but on the final day of the Congress, 25 February, Khrushchev announced an unscheduled, closed session, without foreign delegates or outside observers. His speech to the audience of communist officials would become known as 'The Speech on the Personality Cult and its Consequences', or simply 'The Secret Speech'. Stalinism, Khrushchev declared, had perverted the ideals of communism. Allowing one man to become so powerful, to make decisions as if he were a god, had brought the party into disrepute.

> Comrades, it is foreign to the spirit of Marxism–Leninism to elevate one person, to transform him into a superman possessing supernatural characteristics, akin to those of a god. Such a

man supposedly knows everything, sees everything, thinks for everyone, can do anything, is infallible in his behaviour. Such a belief about a man, and specifically about Stalin, was cultivated among us for many years. The cult of Stalin became the source of a whole series of exceedingly serious perversions of party principles, of party democracy, of revolutionary legality ...'[9]

The psychological impact of the charges could hardly be more shattering. The Soviet people had been conditioned to rely on their god-like leader in almost all respects. The national psyche had learned to cede responsibility to an all-powerful party, led by an all-knowing leader. Discouraged from thinking for themselves, many had lost the will to do so. The mental prop of Stalinist infallibility had sustained them; to learn that it was wrong all along was alarming and disorienting.

In Khrushchev's analysis, the 'personality cult' of Stalin was what had undermined the socialist experiment – the unchecked lawlessness and injustice, the repressions and mass murder. After four gruelling hours, his speech rose to an inflammatory climax.

> Comrades! Stalin was a very distrustful man, full of sickly suspicions. He would look at a man and say. 'Why are your eyes so shifty today?' or 'Why are you not looking me directly in the eyes?' Everywhere he saw 'enemies', 'two-faced deceivers' and 'spies' ... There was the cruellest repression against anyone who in any way disagreed with Stalin. 'Confessions' were acquired through physical pressures. Innocent individuals – who in the past had defended the Party line – became victims. Mass arrests and deportations of many thousands of people, execution without trial and without normal investigation created conditions of insecurity, fear and even desperation.[10]

When Khrushchev finished speaking, there was a 'deathly hush'. Those present, party members who had followed the will of Stalin all their lives, had just been told that their life was based on a lie; they had devoted their existence to the ravings of a madman. The audience dispersed, hardly knowing what to say to each other. Communists were faced with the impossible choice between faith in the infallibility of Stalin and faith in the infallible leadership of the Communist Party of the Soviet Union. In the weeks that followed, there were reports of heart attacks and delegates committing suicide.*

The speech was a gamble. Khrushchev knew it risked turning the party against him. It questioned the authority on which the Bolsheviks had ruled for decades. There were fiery discussions. Unwilling or unable to jettison the past, voices were raised against the 'slurs' on Stalin's good name.

It is no easy task to restructure the psyche of a nation. Stalin's sudden fall from grace triggered conflicting emotions for one speaker at the Mari regional party (*obkom*) meeting. That Stalin's transgressions were finally being discussed in public was cause for happiness and satisfaction, but this was overshadowed by 'bitter indignation' at the party's own history of wrongdoing. At the same time in Krasnoyarsk, Sidov, a senior engineer, noted that 'all the greatness of Stalin, about which so much was said for more than twenty years, has evaporated into thin air'.[11]

Other party members worried about the effect these revelations would have on the public. 'What happens if those [outside the party] do not believe us [when we tell them the] opposite of what we have told them in the past?'[12] A young Mikhail Gorbachev was shocked at how many people persisted in regarding Stalin as their protector, not their oppressor. In Georgia protesters chanted, 'Down with Khrushchev!' Years of misinformation had left people incapable of differentiating truth from lies, as the head of the local party school in Bashkiria made clear when the speech was read to an audience of party members. The 'cult of personality', he explained, was 'so lodged in our psychology ... that only a major reform (*krupnaia perestroika*) would be able to uproot it'.[13]

Khrushchev seemed to have reduced Stalin to a caricature, a

---

* 'Kak Zapad uznal o doklade Khrushcheva' ('How the West learned about the Khrushchev report'), BBC Russian Service, 6 March 2006. news.bbc.co.uk/hi/russian/in_depth/newsid_4741000/4741094.stm. In recent years, doctors have learned more about stress-induced heart attacks, known as Takotsubo cardiomyopathy. These can be triggered by severe emotional shock, most commonly the sudden loss of a child. In the case of delegates at the Twentieth Party Congress, the equivalent shock would have been the sudden undermining of the foundation of much of their lives. Deepak Bhatt, '"Stress" cardiomyopathy: A different kind of heart attack', *Harvard Health Blog*, Harvard Medical School, 3 September 2015. www.health.harvard.edu/blog/stress-cardiomyopathy-a-different-kind-of-heart-attack-201509038239.

one-dimensional tyrant who could be dismissed and forgotten. But the reality was much more intricate: the identification between the person of the ruler and the soul of the nation noted by Robert Tucker[14] meant that any attack on Stalin was perceived by millions as an attack on their own being. Far from being imposed on a captive people, the sway of the dictator is a compact willingly entered into by both sides, his adherents an intensely loyal, psychologically tight-knit band, impervious to criticisms of him or his policies. On the contrary, their loyalty thrives on collective rejection of criticism, which has the effect of entrenching it ever deeper. Stalin's hold on the Soviet mind lasted way beyond his physical demise and would be hard to break.

The social theorists of the Frankfurt School, led by Theodor Adorno and Leo Löwenthal, examined the psychological origins of the surprisingly intimate bond between leader and people in their 1950 book *The Authoritarian Personality*. As refugees from Nazi Germany, their immediate subjects were the fascist dictators of western Europe, but their conclusions can just as well be applied, *mutatis mutandis*, to Stalin. Adorno and Löwenthal drew on Freudian explanations of 'mass psychology' to illuminate the devotion that authoritarianism inspired. They questioned previous models of the leader as a kind of hypnotist, deluding a credulous, childlike people. Gustave Le Bon's seminal work of 1895, *The Psychology of Crowds*, had concluded that 'the crowd wishes to be ruled and oppressed and to fear its masters', who rule through strength and violence.[15] But Freud amended Le Bon's model to suggest that the crowd is more effectively ruled through the simulacrum of love than by the application of violence:

> [The leader] at the very beginning of the history of mankind, was the *Superman* whom Nietzsche only expected from the future. Even to-day the members of a group stand in need of the illusion that they are equally and justly loved by their leader; but the leader himself need love no one else, he may be of a masterly nature, absolutely narcissistic, but self-confident and independent. We know that love puts a check upon narcissism, and it would be possible to show how, by operating in this way, it became a factor of civilisation.[16]

In his 'Freudian Theory and the Pattern of Fascist Propaganda' (1951), Adorno developed the argument of identification between leader and followers. It is not only the narcissism of the leader which binds them in the social compact, but that of the followers themselves; the people come to idealise the leader, as they once idealised themselves. The demagogue's success (in rising to the heights of power, carrying the honour of the nation, etc.) is a balm to the disillusioned narcissism of the people, helping them overcome the regret that torments them at having failed to meet the standards they once set themselves. The leader, says Adorno, achieves this by possessing the archetypal qualities of those who follow him: superman thus has to resemble the follower and 'to appear as his *enlargement*, completing the follower's self-image, a collective projection of himself'.[17] And there is no easier way to build collective narcissism than by conjuring the spectre of a powerful external evil bent on destroying the cohesion of the group.

Prominent thinkers, including Pyotr Chaadayev, Nikolai Karamzin, Alexander Radishchev and Mikhail Speransky, grappled with the seeming enthusiasm Russians have shown for the acceptance of authoritarian rule, from the time of the tsars to the communists to the modern era. The novelist Vasily Grossman, writing shortly after the death of Stalin, identified two brief chances of freedom in Russia – the liberation of the serfs in 1861 and the 'bourgeois' revolution of February 1917 – both of which were rejected. Explanations have been advanced for the spurning of democracy – that Russia's geopolitical conditions make western-style parliamentary liberalism difficult; that the vast size of the country requires a strong, centralised power to hold it together. But the same argument might, for example, be applied to India.

In Russia's case, there appears to be an additional factor – a collective psychology, imbibed and nurtured over centuries, dating back to the Mongol occupation, which inclines her people to prioritise strong leaders and authoritarian leadership.* Adorno's analysis of the western European dictators is useful in explaining this aspect of Stalinism's potency. The authoritarian leader, Adorno suggests, is in harmony with the psyche of the nation. He discerns his people's psychological wants and needs because he resembles them psychologically. What distinguishes him is not any personal superiority, but the capacity to turn their unconscious desires into action – to express without inhibitions that which is latent in them. The leader meets the

---

* See Chapter 1 for more detail.

unconscious wishes of his audience by turning his own unconscious outward, by making rational use of his irrationality. 'The leaders are generally oral character types ... The famous spell they exercise over their followers seems largely to depend on their orality: language itself, devoid of its rational significance, functions in a magical way and furthers those archaic regressions which reduce individuals to members of crowds.'[18]

The conviction that an attack on Stalin was an attack on Russia, indeed, an attack on every single Russian person, was deep seated. Khrushchev himself, for all his bravado in exposing the crimes of Stalinism, could never overcome the reverence he felt for Stalin's 'greatness'. At the Central Committee Plenum in June 1957, which marked his ultimate triumph over Malenkov and his other rivals, Khrushchev declared, 'All of us taken together aren't worth Stalin's shit!'[19] Khrushchev had been careful to distance himself from the actions of his predecessor, while attempting to limit the damage to the Communist Party's reputation. But his behaviour in dealing with the West revealed how difficult it was for him to escape the paranoia and suspicion ingrained in Bolshevik thinking, the conviction that the world outside was irredeemably hostile.

At their first postwar summit, in Geneva in July 1955, the US, the USSR and the UK had set themselves the goal of reducing international tensions and lessening the threat of war. Although Premier Nikolai Bulganin was the nominal head of the Soviet delegation, Khrushchev took the lead. Alongside him was Marshal Zhukov, present in part because he and Eisenhower had developed a cordial relationship in their time as war commanders. The two military men were frank with each other. Zhukov told Eisenhower that the Soviets were worried about the possibility of NATO aggression and concerned that the western media were painting a distorted picture of Soviet intentions. Far from thirsting for confrontation, as the American press would have it, the Soviet people were 'fed up to the teeth with war'. 'No one in the Soviet government or the Central Committee of the Party has any such intentions,' Zhukov said. The two superpowers 'should work very seriously towards détente', which would enable them to reduce tension and cut military spending.[20] Eisenhower told Zhukov that he agreed with him. He, too, would like to reduce tensions, but he had to take account of public opinion in the USA. He could not be seen to be caving in to Soviet demands. It would, he said, 'take some time until the present psychological state of distrust and fear were overcome ... What was necessary were some events or series of events which might change the psychological climate.' What might help, Eisenhower said, would be an agreement on an 'Open Skies' arrangement, whereby each side would grant the other access to its airfields, long-range bombers and missile factories. Such openness would help reduce the fear and uncertainty that prevailed both in the US and in the USSR. Zhukov told Eisenhower that he saw the value of such a move. He would report it to Khrushchev and give it his backing as a military man. But when he did so, Khrushchev flew into a rage. How could Moscow accept such a deal, he said, when it would reveal that the true state of Soviet forces was far weaker than Soviet propaganda claimed?[21] At the summit's closing ceremony, Khrushchev approached Eisenhower, cocktail in hand, and sneered, 'Who are you trying to fool with such a transparent espionage trick? ... You surely don't expect us to take any of that seriously, do you?'[22]

For a man who was about to denounce Stalin's 'sickly' para-noia – 'everywhere he saw enemies, two-faced deceivers and spies' – Khrushchev himself remained painfully mistrustful of the capital-ist world. He warned at the end of his 1956 speech that 'We cannot let this matter get out of the Party, especially not to the press ... We must know the limits; we must not give ammunition to the enemy; we must not wash our dirty linen before their eyes.'* Like all the party leadership, Khrushchev been a loyal Stalinist, no matter how he sought to reframe his past, and a partial reappraisal of history would not be enough to dispel the psychological hold Stalin had on their minds. It would take more than a change of leadership to unblock the logjam of suspicion in East–West relations.

---

* Khrushchev was also mistrustful of those around him and would soon turn on those who helped him seize power in the Kremlin. In October 1957, Zhukov would be removed from his post as defence minister for developing his own 'cult of per-sonality', accused of inflating his role in the defence of Stalingrad and the defeat of Nazi Germany. The accusations were ludicrous but Khrushchev persevered, saying Zhukov's behaviour 'degrades and offends people who demand truth, who want the truth to be spoken'. Khrushchev, like Stalin, was content to create the 'truth' that helped him. Unlike under Stalin, those removed from power were exiled rather than executed. C. Hooper, 'What Can and Cannot Be Said', *Slavonic and East European Review* 86:2 (2008), 306–27, pp. 312 and 316.

14

PSYCHOLOGICAL WARFARE

At noon on 24 January 1946, Admiral William Leahy and Rear Admiral Sidney Souers were summoned to the Oval Office. They had been told that the president had new responsibilities for them and Harry Truman, with his lifelong love of ceremony, wanted to mark the occasion. To their surprise, he greeted them with a black hat, a black cloak and a wooden sword. He handed these to Souers and told him to put them on. Truman then stuck a black moustache on his upper lip. He was, he wrote in a jocular memo, inducting them into the cloak-and-dagger world of international subterfuge.[1] 'By virtue of the authority vested in me as Top Dog, I require and charge that Front Admiral William D. Leahy and Rear Admiral Sidney W. Souers receive and accept the vestments and appurtenances of their respective positions, namely as Personal Snooper and as Director of Centralised Snooping.'[2] Truman's somewhat idiosyncratic way of inaugurating the United States' Central Intelligence Group – soon to become the Central Intelligence Agency – was in tune with the national mood. The war had been won and America had emerged – unlike the other Allied countries – militarily and economically strong. It was time for some fun after the suffering and pain.

Things were different in the Soviet Union. The years between 1945 and the death of Stalin in 1953 marked a descent into national paranoia. The Soviet leadership knew that the USA and its allies held the upper hand in the burgeoning East–West rivalry; the Soviet people learned to fear the aggression of the imperialist warmongers. To some extent this was justified: in the USA and Britain, there was concern that a wounded Soviet Union with an unstable leadership may be prepared to risk everything on an unwinnable war. While the official policy towards the USSR remained containment, the undisguised aim of some in Washington was world domination and the obliteration of communism.

The CIA was to be the key tool for achieving this. The agency was tasked with integrating psychological warfare into America's foreign policy framework. The art of influencing people's thinking, emotions and behaviour without resorting to military means would range from the relatively benign and overt – information campaigns to promote policy decisions, for example – to the malevolent and secret – the dissemination of deliberately false information via opaque sources to undermine foreign governments.

The founding documents of the Psychological Strategy Board in 1951 were suitably vague, defining 'psychological operations' as 'a cover name to describe those activities of the United States in peace and in war through which all elements of national power are systematically brought to bear on other nations for the attainment of US foreign policy objectives'.[3]

The scale of operations was made clear, with the US joint chiefs of staff declaring the intention to 'develop and rapidly implement a large-scale program of psychological warfare, including special operations, comparable in scope to the Manhattan District project of World War II' (which produced the nuclear bomb).[4]

The CIA's Psychological Operations (PSYOP) were intended to shape the way foreigners perceived America. But the increasing reliance on deception abroad would have the unintended consequence of undermining trust in institutions at home.

It was simpler for the Kremlin – a monolithic communist state manipulating the sources of public information – to control the thoughts of its population than it was for the White House. Americans believed they thought for themselves and in an atmosphere of postwar euphoria, there was little appetite for conflict, plenty for relaxation and enjoyment. New car sales rocketed, as did the tourist industries of Florida and Southern California.

Harry Truman faced an uphill task to convince the nation it must gear up for new hostilities. But there were powerful voices lobbying him to do so. The secretary of state, James Byrnes, advised the president that Moscow needed to be confronted. In his Stuttgart speech of September 1946, Byrnes had challenged Moscow over its designs in Europe and pledged that US forces would remain stationed there; instead of punitive economic measures against Germany, there would be generous US aid to help rebuild the country as a liberal democracy. The aim, as Byrnes readily acknowledged, was to keep the Germans in the western sphere of influence and neutralise Soviet attempts to turn it to communism. 'The nub of our program was to win the German people ... It was a battle between us and Russia over minds.'[5]

In public, speaking as a politician, Harry Truman's rhetoric was firm. 'We cannot sit idly by and see totalitarianism spread to the whole of Europe,' he wrote. 'Only our strength will save the world.'[6]

As a man, he wavered. Those around him felt he was unsure how to reconcile the warnings of a growing Soviet menace with the scepticism of Congress and a public mood unreceptive to demands for sacrifice in the cause of a distant and uncertain conflict. Arthur Schlesinger concluded that Truman spent much of his presidency in a 'genuine torment of indecision'.[7] If the unpalatable consequences of military engagement were to be avoided, other methods would have to be adopted and psychological warfare would become chief among them.

Psychological warfare, sometimes called 'political warfare', was not new. In May 1948, in a briefing to the National Security Council, George Kennan sought to explain Washington's current needs in the context of the history of undeclared political combat. 'Political warfare,' Kennan wrote, 'is the employment of all the means at a nation's command, short of war, to achieve its national objectives. Such operations are both overt and covert.' In Kennan's view, the US needed to improve quickly to match the Soviets.

> Lenin so synthesized the teachings of Marx and Clausewitz that the Kremlin's conduct of political warfare has become the most refined and effective of any in history. We have been handicapped however by a popular attachment to the concept of a basic difference between peace and war ... Having assumed greater international responsibilities than ever before in our history and having been engaged by the full might of the Kremlin's political warfare, we cannot afford to leave unmobilized our resources for covert political warfare.[8]

Psychological warfare in this new era of undeclared hostilities would have both constructive and destructive aims. It would seek to

Countries such as the Philippines became the battleground
for competing American and Soviet psychological warfare
programmes, often descending into vicious proxy fighting.

convince the world that western democracy represented the forces
of good. And it would use all methods to undermine the forces of
the enemy, including overt and covert support for anti-Soviet liberation movements in communist countries. The CIA would be given
responsibility for the latter.

Harold Lasswell, one of the founding fathers of propaganda
studies and author of the 1930 treatise *Psychopathology and Politics*, recognised psychological warfare as a new name for an old game: 'The
basic idea is that the best success in war is achieved by the destruction
of the enemy's will to resist, and with a minimum annihilation of
fighting capacity.'[9] In Kennan's conception, it would mobilise not just
armies in the field, but the resources of the whole nation. 'Psychological warfare,' wrote the Cold War historian Kenneth Osgood,

erased distinctions between the front line and the home front,
and made the mobilization of the masses an indispensable

feature of modern conflict ... Virtually every aspect of American life – from political organizations and philosophical ideals, to cultural products and scientific achievements, to economic practices and social relationships – was exposed to scrutiny in this total contest for the hearts and minds of the world's peoples.[10]

By the spring of 1950, many of the ideas adumbrated by Kennan had been codified in a weighty strategy document, NSC-68, 'United States Objectives and Programs for National Security'. Its opening paragraphs set the tone.

Practical and ideological considerations ... both impel us to the conclusion that we have no choice but to demonstrate the superiority of the idea of freedom by its constructive application, and to attempt to change the world situation by means short of war in such a way as to frustrate the Kremlin design and hasten the decay of the Soviet system.[11]

There now existed, said the authors of NSC-68, a Manichean battle between the two superpowers. It was not of America's making, but America must face up to it:

Unwillingly our free society finds itself mortally challenged by the Soviet system. No other value system is so wholly irreconcilable with ours, so implacable in its purpose to destroy ours, so capable of turning to its own uses the most dangerous and divisive trends in our own society, no other so skilfully and powerfully evokes the elements of irrationality in human nature everywhere, and no other has the support of a great and growing center of military power.[12]

Considering the Soviet Union's range of activities, the State Department in 1950 recommended that the United States must 'encourage ... the emergence of satellite countries as entities independent of the USSR' and 'the revival [in the Soviet Union] of the national life of groups evidencing the ability and determination to achieve and maintain national independence'.[13] It was a call for the direct fomentation of unrest, not only in the Soviet vassal states, but on the sovereign territory of the USSR itself – not something that Washington could easily admit to under international law. But legal and moral considerations held little sway. One of NSC-68's leading proponents, Paul Nitze, then director of the State Department Policy Planning Staff, later to become one of the Cold War's most hawkish warriors, pressed energetically for the enactment of all measures of psychological warfare, regardless of ethical principles.

> The integrity of our system will not be jeopardized by any measures, overt or covert, violent or non-violent, which serve the purpose of frustrating the Kremlin design. Nor does the necessity for conducting ourselves so as to affirm our values in action as well as words forbid such measures, provided only they are appropriately calculated to that end and are not so excessive or misdirected as to make us enemies of the people instead of the evil men who have enslaved them.[14]

On 20 April 1950, two weeks after he had been handed an advance copy of NSC-68, Truman launched what he labelled a 'Campaign of Truth'. Its aim, he wrote, was to 'make ourselves heard round the world ... This task is not separate and distinct from other elements of our foreign policy. It is a necessary part of all we are doing ... as important as armed strength or economic aid.'[15] The rhetoric grew heated. Dean Acheson spoke of the need 'to demonstrate that our own faith in freedom is a burning and a fighting faith ... [It is] the most revolutionary and dynamic concept in human history and one which properly strikes terror into every dictator.'[16] The Voice of America radio network, government funded and government controlled, would be tasked with weakening the Soviet hold on satellite states, 'making the captive peoples realize they still belong with us. This means weakening the will of the Red Army officers and Red officials at home and abroad. It means keeping the Soviet Bear so busy scratching its own fleas that he has little time for molesting others.'[17]

By the time of the 1952 presidential election, the psychological arm-wrestling between East and West was central to the political debate. The Korean War was in its third year, Joseph McCarthy was fanning the flames of paranoia about communist infiltration and

'Cold War' was established as the defining political concept of the time.

'Our aim in the "Cold War",' Eisenhower repeated in his speeches on the campaign trail, 'is not conquering of territory or subjugation by force. Our aim is more subtle, more pervasive, more complete. We are trying to get the world, by peaceful means, to believe the truth. That truth is that Americans want a world at peace, a world in which all people shall have opportunity for maximum individual development.' Political warfare, he concluded, would be Washington's weapon of choice in the struggle ahead. 'The means we shall employ to spread this truth are often called "psychological". Don't be afraid of that term just because it's a five-dollar, five-syllable word. "Psychological warfare" is the struggle for the minds and wills of men.'[18]

In the course of the electoral campaign, Eisenhower and the Republicans attacked Truman's uncertainty, his handling of the conflict in Korea and blamed him for failing to prevent communist subversion at home. Despite growing doubts about Joe McCarthy's scaremongering, Eisenhower failed to condemn it. Eisenhower's achievements in the war had endowed him with an aura of firmness, almost invincibility. His campaign slogan was 'I like Ike', and America agreed.

The new president appointed Charles Douglas (C. D.) Jackson to the post of special adviser to the president for psychological warfare. His task was to elaborate a 'policy blueprint and plan for US psychological warfare' in order to 'win World War III without having to fight it'.[19]

Jackson was critical of the outgoing Truman administration's inability to project American values on the world. There had been, he said, 'an absolute paucity of policy' that jeopardised the USA's dynamic of global leadership. Things would be different now. 'There must be a product,' Jackson wrote, 'a new note sounded from America that will ring through the Free World and echo behind the Iron Curtain. A complete change from the present USA, on [the] defensive, afraid, wallowing in [our] own materialism, with overtones of [a] worldwide fear of [the] US getting belligerent and plunging the world into atomic war.'[20] Jackson was a salesman and the product he would be selling was American values – freedom, democracy, business and individual rights. The means for its dissemination would include the press, radio (in particular the CIA-funded Radio Liberty and Radio Free Europe), television and Hollywood. There would be other, covert methods, with ends far removed from the peaceful promotion of harmony and goodwill.

Jackson's public role was, in all but name, Minister of Propaganda. Behind the scenes he acted as a go-between with the Pentagon and with the outfit that would take the lead in America's efforts to subtly, or at least anonymously, influence the world – the CIA.[21] As the decade progressed, the efforts of the branches of government became more coordinated; the constraints on action by the CIA and others weakened. It had taken several years for the machinery of psychological warfare to be constructed; now that it had been, it seemed to have a life of its own.

In July 1954, a new document sought to widen the parameters of US policy towards the Soviet Union. Kennan's Long Telegram and subsequent X Article had recommended containment of the USSR in the expectation that Soviet communism, given time, would collapse from within. NSC-68 had upped the stakes to a policy of gradual coercion. Now the 'Report on the Covert Activities of the Central Intelligence Agency', known after its chief author as the Doolittle Report, went much further. The threat to the United States, the report claimed, had become so acute that all principles of fair play and political restraint must be abandoned in favour of untrammelled psychological force. 'It is now clear that we are facing an implacable enemy whose avowed objective is world domination by whatever means and at whatever cost. There are no rules in such a game. Hitherto acceptable norms of human conduct do not apply. If the US is to survive, longstanding American concepts of "fair play" must be reconsidered.'[22]

The Doolittle Report, for reasons not hard to understand, was classified as top secret, not to be revealed to the public. It recommended that the CIA be given carte blanche to carry out whatever acts of psychological warfare its operatives deemed necessary. The times demanded 'an aggressive covert psychological, political and paramilitary organization more effective, more unique, and if necessary, more ruthless than that employed by the enemy. No one should be permitted to stand in the way of the prompt, efficient, and secure accomplishment of this mission.'[23] The threat from Moscow was considered existential. The British planners, too, were shaken out of their usual pragmatism into paranoia. Increasingly strident strategy papers quoted Lenin's musings on psychological coercion as if they proved the imminent triumph of the Soviet will.

> Lenin wrote in his *Selected Works* that 'The method of imposing the will of one nation upon another may in time be replaced by purely psychological warfare ... the corruption of human mind, the dimming of the intellect, and the disintegration of the moral and spiritual fibre of one nation by the influence of the will of another is accomplished.' The time Lenin refers to has to a considerable degree arrived.[24]

Then, in 1956, Khrushchev made his so-called 'secret speech',* appearing to open the door for change, both in the USSR and in eastern Europe.

What followed, instead, was an example of unintended consequences, triggered by factors known to psychologists as 'motivated irrationality phenomena' – essentially, the human tendency to interpret events in accordance with one's own desires.[25] Khrushchev's motives for initiating the debate on de-Stalinisation are still contentious today, even with the benefit of hindsight. But what he was *not* doing – and there was good evidence of this even in 1956 – was signalling the abandonment of communist orthodoxy or a willingness to give up Soviet domination of eastern Europe. In some quarters, however, that is exactly how it was perceived. Millions in Hungary, Poland, Czechoslovakia, the GDR and elsewhere had dreamed for so long and with such fervour of liberation from Moscow, and politicians in Washington and London had spoken so encouragingly of their efforts to free themselves, that there was a rush to interpret Khrushchev's speech as the starting gun for change. According to Patrizia Pedrini, in her 'Philosophy of Self-Deception', intense desire for a specific outcome is frequently enough to override even a developed awareness of the true state of reality.

> Its disconcerting hallmark lies in the fact that we come to believe a proposition that we should at least doubt is likely to be true, and that we seem to do that because of a strong motivation to

* See Chapter 13 for details.

acquire that false belief. That is why self-deception is included among the so-called 'motivated irrationality phenomena', to which other phenomena also belong, e.g., wishful thinking, cases of precipitate believing under the influence of strong emotions, and so on.[26]

In 1956, 'motivated irrationality' would have tragic consequences. Responsibility would attach to all involved, from the actors on the ground to the autocrats in the Kremlin to the armchair warriors in the Eisenhower White House.

The Stalin era had endured for so long and inculcated such an impression of monolithic solidity that few had dared to challenge it. Stalin himself had seemed impregnable, almost immortal. As soon as he was gone, the illusion of infallibility weakened. Voices were raised, seizing on the perceived opportunity for change.

Hungary was the crucible in which the hopes, theories and deceptions clashed. A year earlier, in 1955, a reformist prime minister, Imre Nagy, had unsuccessfully attempted to slacken the grip of Stalinist orthodoxy, only to be dismissed and replaced by a hardline Stalinist. But Khrushchev's speech in February 1956 changed things. The message of de-Stalinisation spread through the Eastern Bloc. Workers' demonstrations in Poland toppled the government and brought a reformer, Władysław Gomułka, to power. The Hungarians followed suit, taking to the streets to demand Nagy be freed and reinstated. Back in office, Nagy disbanded the secret police and declared that Hungary would be leaving the Warsaw Pact, the socialist equivalent of NATO controlled by Moscow. It was a step too far.

On 1 November 1956, 75,000 troops and 2,500 tanks of the Warsaw Pact entered Hungary over the Romanian border. At dawn on 4 November, they entered Budapest. Imre Nagy, speaking first in English then in Hungarian, made an impassioned broadcast on national radio. 'This is Imre Nagy speaking. Today at dawn Soviet troops attacked our capital with the obvious intention of overthrowing the legitimate Hungarian government.' Street fighting left 3,000 dead, buildings burned and the revolution crushed. Nagy and his colleagues were arrested, taken to Moscow and later executed. It would be another three decades before Hungary would bc free.[27]

There was some justification for the Hungarian reformers' belief that the circumstances were propitious. Khrushchev's secret speech was ambiguous. He did not make clear the limits of what he was proposing, or that his call for change was intended more for internal communist consumption than for the outside world. In addition, Moscow's reaction to the first stirrings of liberalisation in eastern Europe had been conciliatory. The Kremlin had allowed Gomulka to introduce reforms in Poland. As late as October 1956, Khrushchev had personally flown to Warsaw and agreed to much of Gomulka's programme in return for a pledge of loyalty to communist principles.

The Hungarian reformers also believed that the West would come to their aid. Washington had spoken so encouragingly, and so belligerently. Nagy and his colleagues were convinced – or at least hoped – that NATO forces would stand up to the Soviets. To the very last minutes of the uprising, they were appealing to the US, to NATO and to the United Nations. The final broadcast from Hungarian radio before Soviet troops broke into the building and shut it down was heard around the world.

> Civilized people of the world! On the watch tower of 1,000-year-old Hungary the last flames are dying. Soviet tanks are roaring across our land. Our women – our mothers and daughters – sit in dread, remembering the terrible events when the Soviet army last came here in 1945 … Save our souls! Save our souls! This may be the last word from the last Hungarian freedom station. Listen to our call! Help us! Not with advice, not with words, but with action; with soldiers and arms! Help Hungary! … Help us! Help! Help![28]

The expectation of help from the West was not unrealistic. Washington had assiduously spread the message of hope. The CIA-funded Radio Free Europe (RFE) had been told to broadcast the full text of Khrushchev's secret speech, so that all the Comecon countries could hear it. The station had been founded in 1949, when Washington first adopted the policy of destabilising the Soviet bloc: it was well practised in the black arts of political warfare. By 1956, its annual budget was a considerable $21 million, of which $16 million came directly from the CIA.[29] Its goals were defined as preventing the integration of the Iron Curtain countries into the Soviet empire; deploying the talent and the views of émigré political figures, writers and journalists living in the US; serving as a 'voice of internal opposition'; and the psychological goal of 'contributing to the liberation of the nations imprisoned behind the Iron Curtain by sustaining their morale and stimulating in them a spirit of non-cooperation'.[30] This last goal was apparently served by RFE's subsidiary, Free Europe Press, sending thousands of helium balloons carrying leaflets into Czechoslovakia, Poland and Hungary, and placing toilet paper bearing the face of the Hungarian communist prime minister on trains bound from Vienna to Budapest.[31]

By 28 October, with Soviet tanks already massing, RFE was encouraging revolt and resistance. Broadcasts called on the Hungarians to engage in armed struggle, advised on how to attack tanks and how to sabotage railways and communications. When fighting began, RFE urged the Hungarians to set up a central military command and not to surrender.

Hungary was seen as a test by both sides of how far each was prepared to go to achieve their aims: for Washington, that of liberating the satellite states from Soviet domination; for Moscow, of keeping them within their orbit, thus maintaining the vital buffer against western aggression. Vice President Richard Nixon's remarks, reported in the minutes of a National Security Council meeting, reflect the ambiguous, at times mendacious tenor of the debate over American support for the rebellion. 'After all, we are not saying that we are going to initiate uprising and violence in the satellites. We are merely saying that we will not always discourage such uprising and violence if the uprisings should occur spontaneously ...'[32]

The tone from the White House was reminiscent of Henry II's 'Who will rid me of this turbulent priest?' No direct order was recorded for posterity, but the CIA got the message.

Allegations that RFE and the CIA had pushed the Hungarians into an unwinnable revolt by raising unrealistic hopes of western military assistance were quick to surface after the uprising was crushed. There was a period of soul-searching among those responsible. C. D. Jackson, the special adviser to the president for psychological warfare, issued a categorical denial. 'Over the years, Radio Free Europe has never, in a single broadcast or leaflet, deviated from its essential policy, and did not broadcast a single program during the recent Polish and Hungarian developments which could be described as an "incitement" program.'[33] Allen Dulles was more open. 'RFE broadcasts went somewhat beyond specific guidances,' he wrote in a report at the end of November, 'in identifying with Hungarian patriot aims, and in offering certain tactical advice to the patriots.'[34] At least sixteen scripts were identified that might have misled the revolutionaries into expecting western help. Many of these, said the report, had been written by Hungarian political exiles employed by RFE, many of whom had radical anti-Soviet views. The CIA lacked employees with good enough spoken Hungarian to check on the contents of what was being broadcast.[35] The Hungarian-born Charles Gati, who was in Hungary at the time of the revolution, wrote that Eisenhower and Dulles' rhetoric 'combined the best techniques of Hollywood with those of Madison Avenue. The United States was offering a product – liberation – that it could not deliver. The advertising was misleading; but it convinced the oppressed peoples of eastern Europe that their cause was America's cause, and it reinforced their Soviet oppressors' belief that in America they had an implacable enemy.'[36]

Allen Dulles downplayed the impact of America's psychological warfare in an effort to absolve the CIA of blame. 'The uprising resulted from ten years of Soviet repression,' Dulles wrote, 'and was finally sparked by the shooting on 23 October of peaceful demonstrators, and did not result from any external influence, such as RFE broadcasts or Free Europe leaflets.'[37] The CIA's deputy director of plans, Frank Wisner, who oversaw the RFE broadcasts and approved the use of the sign-off, 'Freedom or death!', had a nervous breakdown and would later commit suicide.[38]

Whatever the private recriminations about Washington's role, the invasion of Hungary was a substantial propaganda opportunity for the US. Moscow had shown itself capable of aggression, murder and the flouting of international law in pursuit of a political system which clearly did not enjoy the support of those who lived under it. As early as 24 October, a week *before* Soviet forces would invade Hungary, the US secretary of state, John Foster Dulles (Allen's brother), had requested a meeting of the UN Security Council to highlight the Hungarian crisis.

But on 29 October those plans were thrown into disarray when Britain, with the participation of France and Israel, invaded Egypt. Trouble had been brewing since July, when the Egyptian president, Gamal Nasser, had nationalised the Suez Canal, threatening British military and economic interests in the region. The US had sympathised, but counselled London strongly against precipitate action.

The counsel was ignored. Prime Minister Anthony Eden sent in the troops without informing Washington. Richard Nixon lamented the lost opportunity. 'We couldn't on one hand complain about the Soviets intervening in Hungary and, on the other hand, approve of the British and the French picking that particular time to intervene against Nasser.'[39] The unlikely upshot was that, instead of coming to blows over Hungary, the United States and the Soviet Union were united in denouncing the events in Egypt. In an extraordinary diplomatic note, Bulganin even proposed joint Soviet-American action. Any mention of Hungary by the UK, France or even the US was dismissed by the Soviets as a western smokescreen to divert attention from their imperialism in Egypt. The Suez debacle, said the British representative to the UN, Sir Pierson Dixon, was a humiliation. 'I remember feeling very strongly that we had by our action reduced ourselves from a first-class to a third-class power.'[40]

The received wisdom has been that Khrushchev seized on the Suez invasion as a useful cover for his invasion of Hungary – Suez happened on 29 October; Hungary on 1 November – relying on the furore over the first to swamp recriminations about the second. But recently released minutes of the Soviet politburo suggest his motivation was very different. In late October, Khrushchev appears to have decided *against* military action, opting instead for the same mixture of concessions and arm-twisting he had used in Poland. But when the politburo convened on 31 October he had changed his mind, seemingly unwilling to allow Soviet timidity to be contrasted with the boldness shown by the imperialists in Egypt.

> We should take the initiative in restoring order in Hungary. If we depart from Hungary it will give a great boost to the Americans, English and French – the imperialists. They will perceive it as weakness on our part and will go on the offensive. We would then be exposing the weakness of our position. Our party will not accept it if we do this. To Egypt they will then add Hungary. We have no other choice.[41]

In a meeting with Tito on 3 November, Khrushchev repeated the same message: 'What was there left for us to do? If we let things take their course, the West would say we are either stupid or weak, and that's one and the same thing. We cannot possibly permit it.'[42]

The psychology was symptomatic of Cold War thinking – an innate unwillingness to be seen to be weak and to risk losing influence to a rival, even if it comes at the cost of reputational damage. This time, though, things worked out. Khrushchev emerged from the 1956 events reassured that he could bluff the West, that he had handled the crisis adroitly, avoiding the disastrous outcome that had once seemed inevitable. It would embolden him to a dangerous degree when future confrontations arose. The CIA, for its part, had learned that failing to deliver on perceived promises created the impression of impotence and undermined faith in America. In future, American influence would be exerted covertly, hidden from the eyes of the world, achieving policy aims without claiming the glory.

15

MCCARTHYISM AND WITCH-HUNTS

In 1947, Irving Berlin's song 'The Freedom Train', performed by Bing Crosby, was heard by millions of Americans.* And the freedom train was not simply a poetic image: pulled by a brand-new red, white and blue locomotive named the *Spirit of 1776*, it carried historic exhibits, including the original Declaration of Independence, George Washington's notes on the Constitution, the Gettysburg Address and the Emancipation Proclamation, from town to town across America, its priceless contents protected at all times by an honour guard of US Marines.[1]

This being America, the train was sponsored by General Electric, Standard Oil and Paramount Pictures, but its instigator and ideological patron was the US attorney general, Tom Clark. Clark's motivation was somewhat complicated. The freedom train was, of course, a celebration of a nation's pride at the role it had played in the recently ended war. But, at the same time, it also represented underlying anxieties. Clark said, with a note of misgiving, that he wanted the train to 'reawaken in the American people the loyalty it is known they have for the American way of life'.[2] 'With the war's end, the American people cast off their singleness of purpose. In true democratic fashion they began to move in many directions – talked and acted as suited their fancy. That is a characteristic of democracy.'[3]

President Truman was one of the 3.5 million visitors to board the freedom train during its eighteen-month journey across the country. He had a sincere wish, he said, 'that every person in this country,

---

*The song carried particular weight because of the man who sang it. Bing Crosby was named 'the most admired man alive' by a poll carried out that same year. G. Giddins, *Bing Crosby: A Pocketful of Dreams: The Early Years, 1903–1940*, Boston: Little, Brown and Company, 2001, p. 6.

America's leaders, intimidated by the Soviets' apparent ability to unify and mobilise their people around ideology, turned to their own past for a rallying cry.

and in every country, for that matter, could see those documents and appreciate just what they stand for – freedom of the individual and liberty to live as that individual sees fit, as long as he lives in harmony with his neighbors.'[4] There was, though, an inherent problem with such a Voltairean commitment to personal liberty. It implied that Americans were free to propound views that did not conform to American ideals, and that was a contradiction that Tom Clark struggled to accept. 'Peddlers of pernicious propaganda take advantage of our right of free speech. They would pit class against class, and race against race, in order to destroy in peace-time the unity that characterized this nation in war … We must stay alert!'[5]

In an era when both communism and democratic capitalism were beginning to define themselves not just as political systems, but as discrete ways of life with their own values, mentality and moral underpinnings, America faced a challenge. While Soviet communism had no qualms about instructing its people what to believe and how to live, it was an unfortunate 'characteristic of democracy' that it denied itself the right to compulsion. Clark thought that the best defence against the 'wicked forces at work all over the world that would snuff out Freedom' was to 'make the ideal of democracy a living fact, a way of life such as to enlist the loyalty of the individual in thought, in feeling, and in behavior'.[6]

In the end, however, when 'greedy, careless or complacent people' failed to recognise the obligations and limits of American freedoms, they would – paradoxically – have to be compelled to do so. In order to protect liberty, Clark concluded, America would have to limit it.

In March 1947, worried by reports that communists were infiltrating government positions, Clark convinced Truman to approve Executive Order 9835, under which the FBI director, J. Edgar Hoover, would set in motion a hunt for 'subversive' elements in American society. In the decade that followed, the so-called 'Loyalty Order' would see 4.5 million government employees scrutinised by the FBI, 27,000 of them subjected to further investigation and more than 5,000 accused of disloyalty. Those identified by the investigators would be dismissed or pressured to resign. They had no right to see the evidence in their case and no real prospect of finding another job. Not one of the dismissal procedures led to a single charge of espionage.[7]

A democracy that publicly espoused the values of liberty yet committed itself to such a policing of minds laid itself open to accusations of Orwellian doublethink. With fear spreading like an epidemic, passed from mind to mind by men who stood to gain from it, America was in the throes of a full-scale identity crisis. Moral panic at the top induced paranoia in the public. Rumour and speculation conjured the spectre of a secretive, powerful evil that must be eradicated by any means and at any cost if the nation were to survive. The restrictive values of the Soviet enemy – the very constraints that America was pledged to combat – were projected deep into the collective mentality of the American people.

It was not done unknowingly. The preamble to Executive Order 9835 navigates the moral and legal dilemmas with a slightly shamefaced parade of moral legalese. '[E]ach employee of the Government of the United States is endowed with a measure of trusteeship over the democratic processes which are the heart and sinew of the United States,'[8] the document begins; therefore:

> [I]t is of vital importance that persons employed in the Federal service be of complete and unswerving loyalty to the United States ... the presence within the Government service of any disloyal or subversive person constitutes a threat to our democratic processes ... maximum protection must be afforded the United States against infiltration of disloyal persons into the ranks of its employees.[9]

It is almost certainly the case that small groups of communist sympathisers had indeed been passing information to the Soviets during the Second World War, a time when the USA and the USSR were allied in the fight against Nazism. By 1947, the level of suspicion had grown out of proportion to the threat. Hoover's testimony before the House Un-American Activities Committee in March 1947 reflected the level of disquiet in official circles. 'The Communist movement in the United States ... stands for the destruction of our American form of government; it stands for the destruction of American democracy; it stands for the destruction of free enterprise; and it stands for the creation of a "Soviet of the United States" and ultimate world revolution.'[10] The Communist Party of the United States was, in fact, a negligible force. By the 1950s, it had around 10,000 members, of whom 1,500 were estimated to be informers for the FBI.[11] But this didn't deter Hoover.

> Victory will be assured once communists are identified and exposed because the public will take the first step of quarantining them so they can do no harm. Communism, in reality, is not a political party. It is a way of life – an evil and malignant way of life. It reveals a condition akin to disease that spreads like an epidemic; and like an epidemic, a quarantine is necessary to keep it from infecting the nation.[12]

'Arousing public opinion', it seems, was a conscious aim of Hoover's – and the government's – strategy. The language of the witch-hunt was present from the beginning; 'identifying and exposing' the hidden menace lurking 'malignantly' among us was the cue for suspicion and paranoia. Prior involvement in protests or strikes became grounds for investigation, anonymous testimony sometimes enough to lose someone their job.

The explanation was, at least in part, to be found in the tenor of the times. The initial spike in American self-confidence following victory in war had dissipated with alarming rapidity. Instead of the world fit for freedom many had expected, postwar politics were throwing up threats from every quarter – a seemingly aggressive Soviet Union in Europe and a growing communist threat in Asia. The 'loss' of China to Mao Zedong's communist forces in October 1949 ratcheted domestic fears. The US had made substantial efforts to keep China in the western camp; that it had failed to do so seemed inexplicable. As John Service of the US State Department recalled,

> It seemed incredible to most uninformed Americans that this country [China] that we had lavished so much care and affection on, and we thought was so friendly – so many of their people had studied in America and so on – should turn Communist, should turn to the other side. Many people felt that there had to be some explanation – there had to be some sort of a conspiracy, some sort of a plot.[13]

Within months of Mao's triumph, the conspiracy that allowed it to happen had become a reality in the American mind. At an event in West Virginia in February 1950, the Republican senator Joseph McCarthy drew on the catastrophising rhetoric of looming calamity to describe the state of affairs in which America found herself.

> At war's end, we were physically the strongest nation on earth and, at least potentially, the most powerful intellectually and morally. Ours could have been the honor of being a beacon in the desert of destruction, a shining living proof that civilization was not yet ready to destroy itself. Unfortunately, we have failed miserably and tragically to arise to the opportunity.[14]

McCarthy's language tapped into the national mood, addressing and inflaming the perception that America was weak and morally contaminated, rotting from within. Despite knowing of the traitors in their midst, those at the top, McCarthy intimated, had become complicit in their evil machinations.

> The reason why we find ourselves in a position of impotency is not because our only powerful potential enemy has sent men to invade our shores, but rather because of the traitorous actions of those who have been treated so well by this Nation … The State Department is infested with communists. I have here in my hand a list of 205 – a list of names that were made known to the Secretary of State as being members of the Communist Party and who nevertheless are still working and shaping policy in the State Department.[15]

The fear of communism was not new in America. There had been Red Scares following the 1917 Russian Revolution and the subsequent western military intervention against the Bolshevik regime. Mistrust had endured throughout the inter-war years and, emerging again now, found fertile soil in the national psyche. But the new scare would become dangerously pervasive, challenging the very freedoms and liberties it claimed to protect. It was spread and amplified both by politicians who genuinely believed the dire predictions of communist infiltration, and by those adroit enough – cynical enough – to exploit them for their own advantage.

Before his West Virginia speech, McCarthy had been a little-known first-term senator facing a tricky re-election campaign. His 'unmasking' of communists at the heart of government catapulted him into the limelight; in the minds of many, he was the nation's protector against the 'enemy within', a celebrity, politically all but untouchable.

In a gambit of considerable psychological nous, McCarthy coupled his denunciation of communist subversives with an exegesis of the spirit of national weakness that had allowed them to infiltrate the body politic. His rhetoric captured the lurking fear of many Americans that their country had lost its way, forfeiting its wartime strength for a morally and physically weakened peacetime America, effeminate and no longer able to protect itself. McCarthy laced his fulminations with heavy-handed hints that the highest security risks in government were homosexuals, what he called the 'prancing minions of the Moscow party line'.[16] But it went further. The Red Scare was accompanied by a deliberately fomented 'Lavender Scare' that targeted gay men and women in all walks of life. McCarthy and his fellow thinkers drew the battle lines with considerable acuity: America had gone soft, they said, forsaking its former virility and manhood for limp-wristed acquiescence. Her young generation was weak, open to communist influence, and homosexuality was a symptom of that weakness. 'If you want to be against McCarthy, boys,' he told the press, 'you've got to be either a Communist or a cocksucker.'[17] Appealing to the deeply conservative America of the 1950s, where homosexuality was illegal and subject to vicious prejudice, McCarthy pointed to his own straightforward, reliable manliness. 'McCarthyism,' he declared, with a casual adoption of his own -ism, 'is Americanism with its sleeves rolled.'

The prophecy of decay chimed with public perceptions. Evidence was furnished to prove that McCarthy was right. Conservative commentators opined that America's young could do with rolling up their sleeves and performing some physical exercise. Out of 4.7 million draftees between 1950 and 1957, they reported, 1.6 million were 'found unfit for duty' for physical or mental reasons. American youth was in decline, while Soviet youth was getting fitter and stronger; a 'muscle gap' was growing with the Soviet Union and urgent action was needed to correct it.[18] A report to President Eisenhower by his psychological warfare panel would warn that the growing Soviet dominance in international sport was convincing the world that 'communists are young, vigorous, full of promise for the future; while democrats or Americans are effete, decadent, dissipated, and destined for early extinction'.[19]

Fear led to irrational thinking. Conspiracies were seen everywhere, some run by the communists, others simply presented as fact. Many were swallowed by a public conditioned now to believe the worst, convinced that the American body was at risk of subversion. Public health scares multiplied. Vaccination programmes and the fluoridation of water were denounced as covert plots to poison, undermine or control American lives, with the right-wing, Los Angeles-based 'Keep America Committee' predictably declaring them the work of 'the Communistic World Government' and 'international Jewry'.

Just as Lenin had purged Soviet schools and universities of unreliable, old-regime sympathisers, replacing them with Bolshevik 'red' professors, McCarthy announced that education was the key to stopping subversion in the USA. In his widely read 1952 book, *McCarthyism: The Fight for America*, he demanded as a first step the removal of the 'countless' communists currently working in American colleges, poisoning children's minds with their malignant propaganda. 'We cannot win the fight against Communism if Communist-minded professors are teaching your children,' he wrote, neglecting to provide evidence of who and where these professors might be. 'We cannot lose the fight against Communism if loyal Americans are teaching your children.'[20]

The renowned developmental psychologist Erik Erikson, who had spent the first thirty years of his life as a Jew in Germany and Austria, recognised the symptoms of mass hysteria. Erikson was not a

This 'Keep America Committee' pamphlet shows that paranoia surrounding public health, vaccines and political conspiracies is no recent phenomenon,

communist, but he deplored McCarthy's right-wing populism and the politicisation of education. When he was asked to agree to a loyalty oath being inserted into his professorial contract at Berkeley, Erikson refused and resigned. His statement to Berkeley's Committee on Privilege and Tenure critiqued the attempts to subjugate intellectual discourse to political dogma, to seize the minds of America's young and mould them to an enforced world-view.

The gesture of this contract will not allay public hysteria ... I know that the general public at the moment indulges (as it always does when it is confronted with change) in a 'bunching together' of all that seems undefinably dangerous: spies, bums, Communists, liberals, and 'professors'. A few politicians always thrive on such oversimplification, some out of simplicity, some out of shrewdness. But who, if the universities do not, will lead the countermove of enlightenment? Who will represent, in quiet work and in forceful words, the absolute necessity of meeting the future (now full of worse than dynamite) with a conviction born of judiciousness?[21]

In addition to, or perhaps because of, his personal experience of fanaticism in Germany, Erikson had spent time teasing out the roots of hysteria in public life. He was a powerful voice deploring its emergence in America.

> My field includes the study of 'hysteria', private and public, in 'personality' and 'culture'. It includes the study of the tremendous waste in human energy which proceeds from irrational fear and from the irrational gestures which are part of what we call 'history'. I would find it difficult to ask my subject of investigation (people) and my students to work with me, if I were to participate without protest in a vague, fearful, and somewhat vindictive gesture devised to ban an evil in some magic way – an evil which must be met with more searching and concerted effort.[22]

As a developmental specialist, Erikson is remembered for his influential model of the stages of human growth. His books *The Life Cycle* and *The Life Cycle Completed* chart the phases of mental and emotional progression that characterise the life-journeys of individuals. In 1950, he saw that life-journey in terms of the nation. The 'tremendous waste in human energy which proceeds from irrational fear' that Erikson witnessed being played out in the American people corresponded to the developmental crisis he identified as a transitional stage in the lives of adolescents. His book *Childhood and Society*, published six months after McCarthy's speech in West Virginia, elaborated his concept of the teenage identity crisis, the period in which adolescents on the cusp of physical and sexual maturity struggle to form a coherent image of the self and of their role in the world. Teenagers, he said, waver between secure-identity and role-confusion. It is a conflict they must resolve for themselves before they can move on to the next stage of their development; but Erikson suggests that parents also play an important role. If they allow the child freedom to explore him or herself, he or she will determine their own identity. But if parents continually push a child to conform to their view of the world, the teenager will be plunged into identity confusion.

With McCarthy and the US government in the role of normative parents, the American people had become confused adolescents, unsure what to believe, uncertain how to live and anxious about their future in a menacing, unpredictable world. While the Soviets noisily proclaimed their fixed sense of ideology and clarity of mission, America seemed to lack what Erikson called the security of identity.

The novelist Harold Brodkey captured the permeating air of disquiet. McCarthy's strident, 'parental' demands for obedience troubled the collective psyche, dividing thought between bewildered acquiescence and the fog of uneasy conscience.[23]

> [M]oral cowardice and personal safety and corruption and self-doubt and unlimited greed became national characteristics and national virtues. No one knew how to act. It felt as if this were a country consisting entirely of recent converts, and everyone went on tiptoe. McCarthyism came – first it was an attack on the upper-caste white Protestants that Roosevelt distrusted, and then on show business figures, and then it became a move toward a popular coup. It was not an era of clear thought.[24]

Deepening the nation's cognitive dissonance were the other voices of authority that McCarthy recruited to his cause. The Catholic Church, never any slouch in anathemising the godless creed of socialism, threw in its lot with his message of nation, church and heterosexuality. The Kennedy family became his personal friends. The Catechetical Guild of America produced lurid comic-book propaganda supporting his warnings of the perils of communism.

On 1 May 1950, the town of Mosinee, Wisconsin, elected to drive the message home. It would show itself to be a worthy disciple of the new McCarthyite gospel. The town authorities announced that they would be holding a 'Communist takeover day' to dramatise the horrors awaiting a nation that failed to defend itself. 'Red Commissars' would be out patrolling the streets, instructing the townsfolk how to act in a proper communist fashion. Sidewalk soup kitchens would dish out communal food to the hungry people, left destitute by the new centrally planned socialist economy. A summons to an evening meeting on Mosinee's main square – imaginatively renamed 'Red Square' – would bring the play to an end. The vivid staging of the harsh realities of communist life stirred widespread interest; even the Soviet news agency TASS sent a reporter. Unfortunately for Mosinee's mayor, Ralph Kronenwetter, the realism was a little too real – on being dragged out of his bed by a squad of 'Red guards', he suffered a cerebral haemorrhage and died in hospital.[25]

By the mid 1950s, America seemed to be following the model of the Soviet Union, which had long promoted political commitment in its young people. The communist youth organisation, the Komsomol, taught its fledgling recruits that they must prize loyalty to the state more highly than loyalty to friends and family. Its poster boy was a thirteen-year-old named Pavlik Morozov, who in 1932 denounced his father as an enemy of the people. Pavlik's father was sent to die in a labour camp, while Pavlik himself was subsequently murdered by angry, bourgeois-lackey relatives. The story of his noble self-sacrifice was learned by every schoolchild, his portraits and statues installed in schools and colleges.

Textbooks in American schools began to be similarly endorsed with instructions to children on how they should root out the communists in their classrooms, teachers as well as students. For the 1955 school year, the textbook *Exploring American History*, carried the following advice to pupils.

> The FBI urges Americans to report directly to its offices any suspicions they may have about Communist activity on the part of their fellow Americans. The FBI is expertly trained to sift out the truth of such reports under the laws of our free nation. When Americans handle their suspicions in this way, rather than by gossip and publicity, they are acting in line with American traditions.[26]

For an America struggling to define itself, McCarthy's simplistic prescription – that we define ourselves by opposition to the 'other' of Soviet communism – had a seductive appeal. His explanation for America's woes – that they are the work of the hostile 'other' – was reminiscent of Stalin's policy of exculpating the nation for its own failings by ramping up a unifying hostility to an external bogeyman. The witch-hunt was a staple of Soviet life, where saboteurs and wreckers were always to blame; in the US, the role would be taken by Reds under the bed.

McCarthyism nurtured moral panic. The sociologist Howard Becker described him as a 'moral entrepreneur', raising the spectre of 'deviant' subcultures in order to persuade others to join his crusade, to create new societal rules and to promote themselves in the process.[27] McCarthy, said Richard Hofstadter, was 'an old and recurrent phenomenon in our public life', the paranoid conspiracy theorist who spreads fear and panic to gain notoriety.[28]

As the months passed and the initial impact of his 'revelations' threatened to diminish, McCarthy redoubled his accusations and turned up the volume of his rhetoric. A year on from his West Virginia debut, he had moved from talk of communist sympathisers in the bureaucracy to claims of a sinister cabal of politicians at the very top of the government, deliberately plotting the downfall of their own country.

> How can we account for our present situation unless we believe that men high in this government are concerting to deliver us to disaster? This must be the product of a great conspiracy on a scale so immense as to dwarf any previous such venture in the history of man. A conspiracy of infamy so black that, when it is finally exposed, its principals shall be forever deserving of the maledictions of all honest men ... What can be made of this unbroken series of decisions and acts contributing to the strategy of defeat? They cannot be attributed to incompetence.[29]

There was no room for nuance in McCarthy's view of the world. He saw himself as *the* defender of civilisation, all others either with him or against him; he talked in apocalyptic terms, total triumph or total defeat. When his warnings were not heeded – or, worse, mocked – he turned on those who doubted him, demonising them as agents of the 'enemy'. His raison d'être depended on maintaining the illusion of the end of days, the ultimate disaster that, without him, would assuredly destroy the world. Richard Hofstadter's description of the paranoid spokesman's vision of 'the foe' has an alarming number of hallmarks of the James Bond villain.

The enemy is clearly delineated: he is a perfect model of malice, a kind of amoral superman – sinister, ubiquitous, powerful, cruel, sensual, luxury-loving. Unlike the rest of us, the enemy is not caught in the toils of the vast mechanism of history. He wills, indeed he manufactures, the mechanism of history, or tries to deflect the normal course of history in an evil way … Very often the enemy is held to possess some especially effective source of power: he controls the press; he has unlimited funds; he has a new secret for influencing the mind.[30]

The paranoid politician portrays his enemy as an evil superman in order to justify his own existence, to persuade society that they need Joseph McCarthys. According to Hofstadter, the paranoid warrior's lurid imagining of the powerful-malignant 'other' likely contains elements of his own psyche.

It is hard to resist the conclusion that this enemy is on many counts the projection of the self. Both the ideal and the unacceptable aspects of the self are attributed to him … The enemy may be the cosmopolitan intellectual, but the paranoid will outdo him in the apparatus of scholarship, even of pedantry … the sexual freedom often attributed to the enemy, his lack of moral inhibition, his possession of especially effective techniques for fulfilling his desires, give exponents of the paranoid style an opportunity to project and express unacknowledgeable aspects of their own psychological concerns.[31]

In the light of McCarthy's insistent characterisation of the enemy as 'homosexual cocksuckers' it is tempting to ask what 'unacknowledgeable aspects of *his* psychological concerns' were in play. For Arthur Miller, who was himself caught up in the Red Scare, targeted as a putative communist sympathiser, the time was surreal, like 'being trapped in a perverse work of art, one of those Escher constructs in which it is impossible to make out whether a stairway is going up or down'.[32]

Rifling through its history to discover a prototype for the collective madness of contemporary America, Miller alighted on the Salem witch trials of 1692–3. For Miller, the naked unreason of the Salem witch-hunts was a manifestation of an inherent paranoia within the human psyche. At most times it lies dormant, waiting to be kindled into life at moments of panic and collective fear. 'There was something marvellous in the spectacle of a whole village, if not an entire province, whose imagination was literally captured by a vision of something that wasn't there.'[33] In both Salem of 1693 and Washington of 1953, evidence was less important than suspicion. To be suspected was to be guilty. The episodes took place two and a half centuries apart, but that was Miller's point: there is a force in the psychology of man, something disturbing and darkly lurking that does not change with time.

The Crucible unmasked Congress's hypocrisy on the stage; the House Un-American Activities Committee (HUAC), which had been set up in 1938 to investigate disloyalty and subversive activities by US citizens, responded by denouncing Miller in the real world. Miller diagnosed a society in which the moral compass had been demagnetised.

> In any play, however trivial, there has to be a still point of moral reference against which to gauge the action. In our lives, in the late nineteen-forties and early nineteen-fifties, no such point existed anymore. Gradually, all the old political and moral reality had melted like a Dalí watch. Nobody but a fanatic, it seemed, could really say all that he believed.[34]

McCarthyism's early target had been the State Department, but its apotheosis came with the assault on Hollywood. HUAC's choice of Hollywood was not accidental. It encompassed anti-Semitism and the not entirely unfounded conviction that European refugees from Nazism who peopled the big picture houses had brought with them a stealthy fondness for Nazism's Soviet conquerors. But the underlying motive was fear: fear of the cinema's effortless ability to mould the thoughts of millions, to sway the minds of audiences in intimate darkened rooms through the unmediated medium of image and emotion. The American people may listen to the words of politicians, but it was the power of art that shaped their minds. Control the cinema, control the means of persuasion and – like the men in the Kremlin – you control the people.

Reading the speeches of Joseph McCarthy today is a lesson in fiery rhetoric and psychological inducement, but the moral emptiness at their heart is apparent. Like Arthur Miller's witch-finder Hale, Joseph

McCarthy was driven by demons. He had acquired an addiction to fame, to the thrill of personal attention that comes from the stirring of controversy and, when that thrill became harder to attain, to the consolation of alcohol. He sought out bigger targets; HUAC went after bigger scandals and bigger scalps, until McCarthy overreached himself. In 1954, he accused the US Army of communist subversion. President Eisenhower called for a public investigation. Broadcast on national television, the spectacle laid bare the real McCarthy. The American people saw him for a bully who intimidated witnesses and squirmed with embarrassing coyness when questioned himself. An intemperate attack by McCarthy on a young lawyer prompted the army's chief attorney, Joseph Welch, to turn on him. 'Until this moment, Senator,' Welch declared, in words carried all over America, 'I think I never really gauged your cruelty or your recklessness. Have you no sense of decency, sir, at long last? Have you left no sense of decency?'[35]

Censured by the Senate for his behaviour and for the way he ran his investigations, McCarthy's career was over. He died of hepatitis three years later, in 1957, at the age of forty-eight. The long-serving chairman of the Senate Foreign Relations Committee, Senator J. William Fulbright, reflected with some bewilderment on the power of inculcated dogma that had driven a whole society out of its mind.

> Our leaders became liberated from the normal rules of evidence and inference when it came to dealing with Communism. After all, who ever heard of giving the Devil a fair shake? Since we know what he has in mind, it is pedantry to split hairs over what he is actually doing ... Our 'faith' liberated us, like the believers of old, from the requirements of empirical thinking.[36]

By comparison to the millions who suffered and died in the years of Stalin's Terror, the impact of McCarthyist persecution on its victims was less severe. A few hundred were imprisoned; 10 or 12,000 lost their jobs.[37] The lasting damage was the fear that gripped the nation and left its imprint in the minds of the American people. That, and the realisation that a country which considered itself the brightest, purest democracy, the proudest defender of liberty, could so easily be drawn into the same evil manoeuvring as the tyranny it loudly decried.

16

BRAINWASHING

In October 1962, at the height of the Cuban missile crisis, American cinema audiences flocked to see Frank Sinatra in the role of a returning US prisoner of war from the conflict in Korea. Captain Bennett Marco has survived his captivity physically unscathed, but he is plagued by terrifying nightmares. In his dreams, Marco remembers sitting with other members of his platoon listening to a middle-aged woman lecturing about hydrangeas; but when the camera cuts away, we see that the men are actually being held by uniformed communist guards. 'I have conditioned them,' says a menacing-looking official addressing an audience of Soviet and Chinese officers, 'or *brainwashed* them, which I understand is the new American word.'

The communist official cites five (real) scientific papers by US researchers on how psychological conditioning can turn subjects into violent criminals; then he offers a practical demonstration. He orders the platoon sergeant, played by Laurence Harvey, to strangle one of the men. Brainwashed into an obedient, unthinking automaton, Harvey does so. When he returns to America, he will be a pawn of his communist masters, eventually to be infiltrated into the US Senate, where he will carry out the malevolent orders of Moscow and Beijing.

The Manchurian Candidate provoked much debate about the mechanics of brainwashing. Psychologists were broadly sceptical about the film's clinical accuracy, but the plot struck a chord in US society. The years of 'Reds under the bed' paranoia from Joseph McCarthy and his followers had convinced many that the enemy possessed covert means of undermining America from within, so it was understandable that Americans would believe the communists were brainwashing their unsuspecting compatriots. The fear of brainwashing would figure prominently in the propaganda of the Cold War. But what, if any, psychological basis lay behind it?

*

The Korean War had ended nine years before *The Manchurian Candidate*, the film that has become synonymous with Cold War brainwashing, appeared in cinemas. The fighting had reached a stalemate as early as 1951, but peace talks had dragged on for another two years. The negotiations were held up by the question of what should happen to the thousands of prisoners on either side. North Korea and China insisted that their men should be returned to them immediately; the western combatants wanted captives to be offered the choice of where they would settle. If thousands of Chinese troops could be persuaded to choose capitalist Taiwan over 'Red' China it could be trumpeted as a victory for the West, proof that socialism governed only through oppression.

In the event, it was agreed to let prisoners of war choose their destination. When the armistice was signed, on 27 July 1953, more than 20,000 Chinese and Koreans refused to return to their homelands. The world's attention, though, fell on the twenty-one men who 'turned their backs' on the USA and opted to go and live in China. There was outrage in the US media; anger and confusion in the minds of Americans. How could these young men – sergeants, privates and corporals; representatives of 'the land of the free' – choose communism in preference to returning to their home? Since the adoption of the Truman Doctrine in 1947, America had proclaimed it was fighting to free the 'captive peoples' suffering under the yoke of communism; now Americans were faced with evidence that they themselves were not immune to its lures.

The acuteness of the psychological challenge to US society was manifested in the extravagant language used to describe the defectors and in the frantic, baffled search for an explanation of their behaviour – anything that would pin the blame on inadequate or vindictive individuals, rather than ills inherent in western democracy. 'Never before in history,' thundered *Newsweek*, had Americans chosen to remain with their captors. They were 'the sorriest, most shifty-eyed and grovelling bunch of chaps', with many 'bound together more by homosexuality than communism'.[1]

The anger endured. Private David Hawkins, from Oklahoma City, was only seventeen when he was taken prisoner. Held in squalid conditions for three years, he became one of the twenty-one men who chose to settle in China. When he returned to America four years after the war's end, he was grilled by Mike Wallace on prime-time TV.

WALLACE: What was so awful in the United States? ... you made the tremendous step of turning traitor to your country. What was it inside you that made you want to do that?

HAWKINS: ... I felt that in getting sent so far away from home to fight on a barren rock, against something that I didn't fully understand, that I got a raw deal. I didn't know what I was fighting for. I felt that the States had made a big mistake, that we had no business over there.

WALLACE (summing up): After the Korean War, Marine Colonel General Shepherd said that our ultimate weapons against communism were, as he put it, 'Faith and Courage'. Those weapons obviously couldn't be issued by the army to David Hawkins when he went into battle and was captured. Faith and courage are instilled by home, in church, in school, and in that sense David Hawkins' problem certainly has become our own.[2]

The language is telling. Wallace sets out to discover what was 'wrong' with men like David Hawkins; but throughout their conversation, and made explicit at the end, his remarks betray the underlying insecurity about the American way of life that has gripped US society.

One explanation put forward immediately and insistently by the press was convenient, but deeply unsettling – these men had been brainwashed; their captors had employed devilish methods to wipe their minds, replacing their healthy American patriotism with implanted communist propaganda.

Even the etymology of the term, it was claimed, smacked of the Orient. Edward Hunter, the journalist who helped spread panic and fear about brainwashing, maintained the word was a translation of the Chinese *hsi nao*, meaning 'to cleanse the mind'. *Hsi nao* had indeed been the expression used for Maoist indoctrination in China; but there was no evidence to link it with the pre-existing western concept. Hunter was far from disinterested. He had worked for the OSS in Korea, the predecessor of the CIA, and the sensational claims of his book *Brain-Washing in Red China* suggest he was out to make a name for himself.[3]

Red China, Hunter declared, was a giant insane asylum where the Communist Party acted as controlling, manipulative psychiatrists. The regime was adept at both 'brain-washing' and 'brain-changing',

which he declared to be two distinct processes. 'Brainwashing is indoctrination, a comparatively simple procedure, but brain-changing is
immeasurably more sinister and complicated. Whereas you merely
have to undergo a brain-cleansing to rid yourself of "imperialist
poisons", in order to have a brain-changing you must empty your
mind of old ideas and recollections.'[4] In Hunter's terms, the men
of Bennett Marco's platoon – perhaps also the twenty-one GIs who
defected to Red China – had been subjected to the 'sinister and complicated' operation of brain-changing. The big question, which took
a terror-inducing grip on the US imagination, was, 'How many more
of them are there among us?'[5]

Korea wasn't the first time the US had suspected the communists
of messing with American minds. In 1949, Robert Vogeler, an American businessman, was arrested and tried for sabotage in Hungary,
giving an oddly worded confession that raised suspicions.* Americans
regarded themselves as uniquely resilient, immune to the psychological weaknesses of those foreign folk who let themselves be enslaved
by communism, so Vogeler's capitulation could be explained only
by the malign operation of mind-altering techniques such as drugs
or hypnotism. 'The mind, spirit and body are attacked over and over
again,' Vogeler told an interviewer on his return to the US, 'until
the will is slowly ground away. The very body is forced into league
against one's personality ... The thought kept running through my
head, *You can't do this to an American!*'[6]

Americans had traditionally valued 'open-mindedness' as an
attribute peculiar to the countries of liberal democracy. The 'open
mind' was tolerant, flexible, broad, realistic and unprejudiced; the
'closed mind', by contrast, the mind of the totalitarian East, was
rigid, intolerant, narrow, conformist, ideological and prejudiced.
Open-mindedness was seen as a tool to fight communist authoritarianism and help unite American society. But was it also the quality
that made Americans vulnerable to brainwashing?[7] David Hawkins,
the 'turncoat' GI, claimed that it was his open-mindedness, his curios-
ity about the world, that made him open to his captors' suggestion

---

* 'I was sent from a big country, America, to Hungary, a small country, to interfere
and undermine its efforts in rebuilding and rehabilitating itself from the effects of
war.' Cited in S. Carruthers, *Cold War Captives: Imprisonment, Escape, and Brainwashing*, Berkeley: University of California Press, 2009, p. 146.

of moving to China. 'I don't think it ever occurred to the US or the army that there would be GIs who would choose to go somewhere other than their own country,' he recalled. 'My reasoning was, they really have embraced this socialism so let me see what it is like – let me check it out.'[8]

The suggestion embraced by US conservatives was that an open mind might not be such a good thing after all. As early as 1950, the National Security Council had suggested that instead of the liberal consensus that all men should be free to think and believe as they like, there should be a greater effort to shape their thoughts, warning against the excesses of 'a permanently open mind'. The 1955 Department of Defense Report on the Korean experience identified this lack of ideological education as a weakness: the communists taught their people that they must love communism, so why not teach ours that they must love democracy. 'The uninformed POWs were up against it,' the report concluded. '[They] couldn't answer arguments in favor of communism with arguments in favor of Americanism, because they knew very little about their America.'[9] Brainwashing, it seemed, might be best applied at home.

To avoid acquiescing in the stigma of American weakness, US politicians and the media sought to paint a picture of a powerful, monolithic communist machine, devoid of doubt, irresistible in its zeal and commitment to brainwashing the capitalist enemy. But the reality was that the brainwashers, too, were human. The testimony of Wu Henian, a former camp instructor, revealed that some Chinese guards were themselves unconvinced by the attraction of ideology.

> We were trying to tell the POWs that capitalism was doomed to collapse, and that socialism was bound to win. But after a couple of months we found that such a theory was untenable, unacceptable to almost all the POWs ... We changed by telling them that such a war was unnecessary, was dirty. Some POWs began to think that the American government should not have been involved in such a war.[10]

'Turncoats' like Hawkins may simply have been curious to see another part of the world; some African-American GIs were reluctant to return to a life as second-class citizens; others feared they'd face criminal charges for their behaviour in the camps. But none of these explanations calmed the fears that haunted America. As Hawkins and others returned from China, worries grew that they would bring their 'sickness' with them. Hawkins himself told Mike Wallace that they had been groomed by the Chinese so that 'in the event of a revolution in the States ... we would return to the US to take part in that revolution'.

> WALLACE: It sounds cloak and dagger-ish ... but how can we be sure that you yourself have not been sent back here in some manner to work on behalf of the Red Chinese?
> HAWKINS: You wouldn't know for sure![11]

All those who were captured in Korea now seemed questionable, potentially untrustworthy and suspicious. Quite apart from those who chose to remain behind, other POWs had provided more information than the required name, rank and number. Some had made false confessions about war crimes, including the US Marine Colonel Frank Schwable. In captivity, Schwable had confessed to taking part in germ warfare bombings, before recanting his confession when he returned to America. He struggled to explain the complex psychological process that had led him to do something that now seemed outlandish and shameful. 'The words were mine, but the thoughts were theirs,' Schwable said. 'This is the hardest thing I have to explain: how a man can sit down and write something he knows is false, and yet, to sense it, to feel it, to make it seem real.'[12]

Schwable's experience became a test case for the responsibility attaching to those who acceded to the demands of the enemy: were they responsible for their actions and therefore guilty of a crime, or were they compelled by complex, perhaps inexplicable psychological factors that exculpated them from guilt? The Dutch psychologist Joost Meerloo gave evidence in Schwable's defence to the board of inquiry, and he was categorical. 'Each man has his own limit of endurance, but that this limit can nearly always be reached and even surpassed is supported by clinical evidence ... Nearly anybody subjected to the treatment meted out to Colonel Schwable could be forced to write and sign a similar confession ... Anyone in this room.'[13] The team of psychologists engaged by the US military's Study Group on Survival Training agreed. I. E. Farber, Harry Harlow and Louis Jolyon West concluded that the men had been reduced to conditions of debility, dependency and dread (DDD). They had been subjected to sleep deprivation, isolation, malnutrition and threats. When combined with occasional rewards for good behaviour, the psychologists testified, a state of 'complete compliance' is created that induces detainees to change their beliefs and behaviour.[14] 'Far from furnishing proof of the operation of some unnatural process of "brainwashing",' their report concluded, a prisoner cooperating 'is a predictable consequence of the operation of laws of normal human behavior.'[15]

> Such behavior in persons whose intelligence, integrity or patriotism can scarcely be doubted has suggested to many a mysterious power or knowledge that enables Communists to manipulate the thoughts and actions of others in a manner ordinarily reserved to characters in the more lurid sorts of science fiction. Accordingly, such terms as 'brainwashing', 'thought control', 'menticide', and so on, have been applied to the process or product of this manipulation.[16]

Farber, Harlow and West rejected the claims of communist brainwashing. Their report located the causes of prisoners' willingness to collaborate in other, less exotic psychological mechanisms. They were writing in 1957, when American academic psychology was dominated by the school of Behaviorism. Behaviorists held that all behaviour is the result of environmental conditioning: a subject responds to external stimuli – some positive, some negative – and acquires behavioural patterns in the same way that mice in a maze are conditioned by rewards and punishments. Like Pavlov's dogs or B. F. Skinner's rats, human beings were believed to be subject to the unconscious force of operant conditioning. The Behaviorists rejected the concept of a human mind making independent decisions in the name of individual volition. There were stimuli, reactions and behaviour, with no agency in between. B. F. Skinner, who by the 1950s was the movement's leading proponent, maintained that *all* our actions and *all* our thoughts are determined by these external environmental factors.

The most radical Behaviorists contended that, with the right conditioning, any person can potentially be moulded to perform any task. There is no point in probing our mental states, they claimed, because our thoughts do not determine our behaviour. There *is* no mind, said Skinner, no 'little man inside' that steers the physical body; the concept of free will is merely self-delusion.

If there is no mind, it follows that there can be no mind-tampering, no brainwashing. The Behaviorists dodged the issue of responsibility, but if there is no free will, the question arises of whether there can be guilt. Farber, Harlow and West, though, do not ascribe the willingness of US prisoners to collaborate with their captors simply to a Behaviorist-style stimulus–response process.

> While these speculations [about brainwashing] have an undeniable romantic appeal, more sober analyses of factors influencing the behavior of prisoners under Communist control indicate that they are neither mysterious nor indicative of any unusual amount of psychiatric sophistication on the part of the Communists. Indeed, considering the extraordinary degree of control the Communists maintain over the physical and social environments of their prisoners, it is rather surprising that their efforts to indoctrinate and convert have not been even more successful.[17]

Farber, Harlow and West understood that the unconscious nature of the process made it difficult, perhaps impossible, for POWs to explain their feelings and actions to people back home.

> The familiar stimuli of home reinstate different verbal responses, both overt and implicit, that affect recall. The returnee feels different, talks differently, and thinks differently than he did in the former context. Since, like all of us, he is unaware of many of the cues to his former behavior (as well as his current behavior), it is as useless to ask him to explain his earlier reactions as it is to ask a person why he once disliked olives or is for the moment unable to recall the name of an old acquaintance.[18]

The charges against Colonel Schwable and others were dropped, but the stigma remained. The US military recoiled from accepting that the enemy could force compliance from even the toughest Americans, tending instead to write off those who 'broke' under pressure as flawed. Sensation-seeking alarmists such as Edward Hunter took the opposite view. The communists, he told HUAC, were able to suborn vast numbers of Americans because America itself had lost its moral backbone. 'The objective of Communist warfare is to capture intact the minds of the people and their possessions, so they can be put to use ... The Communists are being abetted in their brainwashing program in the United States by the collapse of traditional American ideals of self-reliance and individual integrity.'[19]

A film made immediately after the end of the Korean War had sought to depict in a realistic fashion the suffering of the men in the camps. *Prisoner of War* (1954) starred Ronald Reagan as a POW. It had official cooperation from the US Army in the form of a technical adviser, Captain Robert Wise, who had himself spent several years in what he described as 'constant mental anxiety' in a 'hell on earth'. Just before the film was released, however, the US military withdrew its support. The Department of Defense, which was at the time investigating hundreds of returning POWs for collaboration, was alarmed by Reagan's character, Webb Sloane, repeatedly saying, 'Every man has his breaking point.' The Defense Department was struggling to quash the idea that the communists, with the psychological techniques at their disposal, could force 'every' American to submit to their will. Accepting the premise would imply a systemic weakness in the American character or, worse, in the values on which America had based its collective identity. Instead, the military put the blame on individuals, 'weaklings' with flawed characters. 'There has been no evidence in the U.S. Army that every man has a breaking point. Generally speaking those with weaker character break.'[20]

There was considerable official anxiety that the world would interpret the instances of US prisoners collaborating with the enemy as an inherent national weakness. POWs who had acquiesced in the communist 're-arrangement of thought' were 'intellectual eunuchs', declared Henry Cabot Lodge Jr., the US ambassador to the United Nations. Professional psychiatrists were enlisted to back up the campaign of invective directed against the individual soldiers who had failed to resist. Dr J. C. Moloney, addressing the American Psychoanalytic Association Convention, put forward a specious Freudian explanation of why the men had cracked. 'Any POWs who accepted Communist propaganda as a result of Soviet "mind washing" techniques,' Moloney theorised, 'were men who, as children, gave up the struggle to be themselves or abandoned themselves to the dictates of father or mother.'[21] It was meaningless and insulting, but it served the

purposes of the administration. The army's own psychiatrists, such as
Dr William E. Mayer, went even further.

> The disease that killed most of the men in Korea and per-
> mitted the rest to be coerced in this way was the disease of
> non-commitment. They believed in nothing. They didn't dis-
> believe, they just didn't believe. They were committed to no
> system of values, they bought the idea that there was an infinite
> variety between good and bad and there's no point trying to
> make out which is which.*

There was a pervasive, unsettling feeling that America had gone soft.
The belief that the nation as a whole had lost its moral backbone,
and that this had resulted in the 'weakness' shown by the men in the
Korean camps, was widely discussed. The number of collaborators
was cited as evidence that a generation of American men had been
sapped by psychological and physical degeneracy. The terms 'collapse thesis', 'give-upitis' and 'Momism' gained currency. Momism
was a term coined by Philip Wylie in his 1942 polemic *Generation of
Vipers*. The book was an overarching and at times hysterical critique
of American society as a whole, but Momism – the contention that

---

* *'Every Man Has His Breaking Point': Reagan, Brainwashing and the Movies*, dir. Phil
Tinline, Hidden Persuaders/Wellcome Trust, 2017. The fear that Americans were
especially weak was unfounded. It overlooked the fact that so many Chinese and
Korean soldiers had also 'turned their backs on their homeland'. Much like the
communists, there were reports that the US had exerted psychological and physical pressure on captives to 'choose' Taiwan over a return to Red China. 'My time
in prison was by far the worst I experienced during the Korean War,' recalled one
Chinese POW, Zhang Da. 'We were under terrible pressure to choose Taiwan.
Those who dared to declare openly their wish to return to China were persecuted, even killed [by pro-Taiwan officers]. The Americans knew what was going
on and encouraged it.' 'We were used as pawns,' said another, Zhang Zeshi. 'The
Americans wanted a "free choice"', not because they cared for us or for human
rights, but because they just wanted to make a point: Look how many of them
wanted to come to the free world. [As for China], I don't think they cared about our
individual interests. It would just look bad if so many POWs did not come back.'
Cited in Calum and Lijia MacLeod, 'China's Korean War POWs find you can't go
home again', *Japan Times*, 28 June 2000. www.japantimes.co.jp/news/2000/06/28/
national/history/chinas-korean-war-pows-find-you-cant-go-home-again/#.
WfhVwxOoOHo.

American men had been deprived of their natural virility by a cult of namby-pamby mother-love – is what people remembered. 'Megaloid momworship has got completely out of hand,' Wylie complained.

> Mom is everywhere ... a new slave population continually goes to work at making more munitions for momism ... the Oedipus complex has become a social fiat and a dominant neurosis in our land ... The nation can no longer say it contains many great, free, dreaming men. We are deep in the predicted nightmare now and mom sits on its decaying throne ... Momism is a human calamity, a cause for sorrow, a reproach, a warning siren.[22]

The refrain against Momism was taken up elsewhere: a work of popular science examining the role of women in postwar America, *Modern Woman: The Lost Sex*,[23] claimed that smothering mothering had left two-thirds of all Americans neurotic or on the brink of neurosis. And a 1956 bestseller, *The Crack in the Picture Window*, reinforced the myth of Momism, adding that it also affected husbands, turning them into 'a woman-bossed, inadequate, money-terrified neuter'.[24] As late as 1963, Betty Friedan, in her book *The Feminine Mystique*, was still quoting the spurious theory that overly protective mothers could make their sons gay.[25]

Momism and other alarmist theories about America's weakening resolve were deconstructed and rejected by academics and thinkers, but continued to influence public opinion. Brainwashing, too, was questioned, but belief in its sinister power endured: as the historian and psychoanalyst Daniel Pick pointed out, it was 'a kind of mirror onto perceived vulnerabilities in American society itself ... a way of capturing a sense of alarming fragility in "us", or at least in some of "us"'.[26]

For the politicians, the spectre of a psychic threat was an expedient means of reinforcing the need for patriotic vigilance. The CIA director, Allen Dulles, whose agency was itself conducting experiments in the techniques of mind control, pointed an agitated finger at the USSR. 'The Soviets are now using brain perversion as one of their main weapons in prosecuting the Cold War,' he told a Princeton conference in 1953.

> Behind the Iron Curtain a vast experiment is underway to change men's minds, the perversion of the minds of selected

individuals who are subjected to such treatment that they are
deprived of the ability to state their own thoughts ... Soviet
science made rapid strides in the nefarious art of breaking down
the human mind ... the human mind becomes a phonograph
playing a disc put on its spindle by an outside genius over which
it has no control.[27]

It was hardly any wonder that the fear of hidden forces influencing
people's lives became a trope in the American psyche. Suspicion
grew that agencies at home and abroad were up to no good, everyone from the CIA to advertising firms to Ma Bell, the telephone
company. The fears were self-reinforcing, verging on national psychosis as more and more respondents claimed that they felt their
minds were being messed with. Vance Packard's book *The Hidden
Persuaders* (1957) deepened the atmosphere of suspicion. Packard
revealed how subliminal messages were used by advertising companies to 'force' you to buy their products, or by political campaigns
to push their candidate. They were 'showing up nationally,' said
Packard, 'in the professional politicians' intensive use of symbol
manipulation and reiteration on the voter, who more and more is
treated like Pavlov's conditioned dog'.[28] The unwitting public were
being taken for a ride by symbol manipulators who prey on psychological weaknesses to fill the minds of consumers with 'needs' they
didn't know they had. For them, Packard claimed, we the public
were just 'bundles of day-dreams, misty hidden yearnings, guilt
complexes, irrational emotional blockages ... we please them with
our growing docility in responding to their manipulation of symbols
that stir us to action.'[29]

The Polish sociologist Zygmunt Bauman drew an explicit parallel
between the hidden persuasion that occurs in everyday civilian life
and the alleged 'brainwashing' carried out by communists. 'Brainwashing' was merely a convenient term, Bauman argued, a simplistic
explanation of a phenomenon that appeared inexplicable. Western
polemicists such as Edward Hunter used it to highlight

the mystery of people being converted, the passage from one
fixed system of beliefs to another fixed system of beliefs. [So]
there must be some external force of a very powerful kind to
accomplish the fact of conversion. [Brainwashing] was a concept

which you assign to someone you don't like. No-one would say, 'I am a tremendously good brainwasher', even if they are ...

Edward Hunter applied it to communists; and communist powers in Poland applied it to capitalists. It was simply a nasty, dirty, unprepossessing concept, which you use in order to put a stigma on what other people are doing.'[30]

In communist Poland, Bauman reported, the regime accused the West of brainwashing its own citizens: it was manifestly impossible that a proletariat so heinously exploited by capitalist industry could still profess a love of capitalism; the only possible explanation was that the American masses must have been brainwashed.[31] What is certainly true is that Washington was not slow to explore the potential of brainwashing. On 13 April 1953, just three days after Allen Dulles had told his Princeton audience in lurid detail about the Soviet abuses of psychological manipulation and the techniques of mind control, he instructed CIA scientists to do exactly the same.[32]

'Project MK-ULTRA' was the code name for the CIA's mind control programme, run in tandem with the US Army Biological Warfare Laboratories. Dulles had procured the budget for a team of psychologists and brain researchers who would undertake experiments on human beings with the aim of developing drugs and techniques to be used on hostile subjects during interrogation. These would weaken the subject's will, subvert his ideological convictions and influence him to confess or defect to the societal system of his interrogator.

Because the experiments were to be carried out on humans rather than animals, and because they involved the administration of psychotropic drugs whose effects were as yet unpredictable, the agency acknowledged that it would be hard to find enough willing participants. Considerations of secrecy made the task even harder. Dulles therefore took the decision to authorise experiments on unwitting subjects, US and Canadian citizens who would be lured into situations where they could be used as guinea pigs. The subjects were never informed that they were being manipulated by the CIA; neither was their consent ever sought.[33] The experiments were illegal, but Dulles regarded the research as so vital to national security that the law could and should take second place. A society that claimed it was fighting for individual freedoms and the rule of law worldwide was consciously disregarding both at home.

Some subjects were drawn from hospitals and prisons, with agents told to select 'people who could not fight back'. Mental patients, prisoners, drug addicts and prostitutes were plied with experimental narcotics. One patient in Kentucky was given LSD continuously for 174 days. The declared objective was to manipulate people's mental states and alter brain functions. Hypnosis, sensory deprivation, isolation and verbal and sexual abuse were also applied.[34]

Those who worked for Project MK-ULTRA, including its director, Sidney Gottlieb, were not unaware of the dubious morality of what they were doing. The paradox of a freedom-loving country abusing the freedoms of its own people was not easy to rationalise, but the perceived enormity of the Soviet threat went some way towards it. John Gittinger, the CIA's chief psychologist between 1950 and 1974, admitted that 'a great fear' had taken hold of the agency. He and Gottlieb and the other programme directors were convinced they must prevent the communists from gaining any greater advantage than they already possessed. 'We were in a World War II mode,' Gittinger wrote. 'The war never really ended for us.'[35]

The unethical activities of MK-ULTRA might have remained a secret but for a tragic episode involving a young biochemist who worked for the project. Frank Olson was nominally on a business trip to New York in 1953 when he fell to his death from a window in the Statler Hotel. Olson's family were unaware that he was working for the CIA and his death was initially ruled a suicide. Alarmed by journalist enquiries into the nature of MK-ULTRA, the CIA destroyed all the files relating to the project in 1973, including those about Frank Olson. But in 1974, the investigative journalist Seymour Hersh wrote in *The New York Times* that the CIA had conducted illegal experiments on US citizens, and in 1975 a congressional committee was tasked with looking into the allegations. Its report revealed that a CIA colleague had secretly slipped LSD into Olson's Cointreau shortly before his death. This, said the committee, had triggered a psychotic reaction that led to his fall from the window. Olson's family were invited to the White House for a personal apology from President Gerald Ford and a meeting with the new CIA director, William Colby. Seymour Hersh, however, was convinced that Olson was pushed to his death because he was threatening to blow the whistle on the things he had witnessed in his time at MK-ULTRA, including 'terminal' experiments carried out on captured spies and enemy prisoners. 'Frank was viewed as a dissident ... He was letting them know that he was marching to a different drummer and you couldn't do that back then. He was a man who was profoundly distressed about what he was learning.'[36] Olson's children made an effort to draw a constructive lesson from their father's death. His son Eric described the CIA cover-up as symptomatic of 'the position the United States found itself in in the postwar period, for which it wasn't prepared, and it began to do things that put its own democratic institutions in great jeopardy. How can you have a democracy if its institutions are doing things that the public can't know about?'[37] Eric's brother, Nils, concurred. 'America fundamentally wants to think of itself as being good ... if America does have a darker side, it threatens your hold on your view of America and it's kind of like, "Gee, if I pull out this one underpinning of the American consciousness, is this a house of cards? Does it threaten the fundamental nature of America?"'[38]

The CIA's misguided attempts to exploit the inherent weaknesses of the human psyche were ultimately fruitless. As John Gittinger acknowledged, they 'had been chasing a phantom, an illusion – that the human mind was more capable of manipulation by outside factors than it is'.[39] It did little to protect America's freedom and even less to preserve its peace of mind. They exacerbated the very fears of covert enemy plots, brainwashing and hidden threats – that they had sought to allay. And, when suspicions of their activities became public, they did more to undermine confidence in America's institutions and values than anything achieved by Moscow.

17

SPUTNIK AND THE PSYCHOLOGY OF FEAR

In 1957, Little Richard was big. 'Tutti Frutti', 'Long Tall Sally' and 'Lucille' had made him a millionaire, and won him fans on both sides of America's racial divide. Outraged white moralists spluttered at the spectacle of mixed audiences dancing to 'licentious' black music. Richard revelled in it. But in October, he shocked the world with the announcement that he was quitting show business to become an evangelical minister in the Church.

'I was in Australia and I saw Sputnik and I got afraid,' he explained later, in his trademark rhymed couplets. 'When I was quitting, I was admitting I was scared of Sputnik. You know I came from the country; I'm not from the city – what a pity. I was scared to death to get back on the plane to come home. I was scared Sputnik would run into our plane – Russia done set this thing up. I had read about the Tower of Babel.'[1]

Little Richard's absence from the stage lasted little more than a year, but the vision of Sputnik lodged in his memory. It seemed to him a terrible warning from on high, a ball of light hurtling through the sky sent by God to make him change his ways. Sputnik had that effect. The writer Tom Wolfe captured the shock:

> The panic reached far beyond the relatively sane concern for tactical weaponry. Sputnik took on a magical dimension ... It seemed to dredge up primordial superstitions about the influence of heavenly bodies. It gave birth to a modern, i.e. technological, astrology. Nothing less than *control of the heavens* was at stake. It was Armageddon, the final and decisive battle of the forces of good and evil.[2]

On 5 October 1957, short-wave radio operators across the world had heard a new signal in the sky, a *beep beep beep* that grew stronger, faded and returned with unnerving regularity. They didn't know it, but Earth's first artificial satellite was travelling high above them, orbiting the globe at 29,000 kilometres per hour. It had been put into space from a launch pad in the steppes of Kazakhstan, on the back of a rocket designed to carry nuclear warheads.

Sputnik came as a surprise, but it shouldn't have. Nineteen fifty-seven had been designated as the International Geophysical Year (IGY), a project that brought together scientists from sixty-seven countries in a spirit of international cooperation, and both the US and the Soviet Union had included satellites as part of their programmes. In late September, reports from Moscow had suggested the Soviets were on the brink of a launch. But delegates to the IGY Special Committee Conference, meeting in Washington DC, received the news with barely disguised incredulity.

The politicians were equally flummoxed. At a White House press conference on 9 October, President Dwight Eisenhower was assailed by anxious, reproachful questions.

Mr. President, Russia has launched an earth satellite. They also claim to have had a successful firing of an intercontinental ballistic missile, none of which this country has done. I ask you, sir, what are we going to do about it? ...

Mr. President, Khrushchev claims we are now entering a period when conventional planes, bombers, and fighters will be confined to museums because they are outmoded by the missiles which Russia claims she has now perfected ...

Do you think our scientists made a mistake in not recognizing that we were, in effect, in a race with Russia in launching this satellite?

Eisenhower did his best to play things down.

Now, so far as the satellite itself is concerned, that does not raise my apprehensions, not one iota. I see nothing at this moment, at this stage of development, that is significant in that development as far as security is concerned ... The Russians, under a dictatorial society where they had some of the finest scientists in the world who have for many years been working on this, have put one small ball in the air. I wouldn't believe that at this moment you have to fear the intelligence aspects of this.

The reality of the Cold War may not have changed, but its psychology had; Eisenhower himself acknowledged that it was possible that 'the Soviets have gained a great psychological advantage throughout the world'.[3] Sputnik gave Russians succour and pride; it exacerbated American fears of the outside world. As the Greek philosopher Epictetus had pointed out nineteen hundred years earlier, 'It is not events that make us anxious; it is the way we think about them.' And Eisenhower had a job on his hands to calm the anxieties of a troubled nation.

To show that he himself was not perturbed, the president went to play golf. It didn't impress. The *Birmingham News* ran the banner headline, 'Ike Plays Golf, Hears the News'. The Democrat governor of Michigan, Mennen 'Soapy' Williams, composed a mocking ditty to 'little Sputnik, flying high' while 'Uncle Sam's asleep'.

Opposition politicians stoked the paranoia as a means to do down the Republicans. Lyndon Johnson, never one for measured rhetoric, proclaimed the advent of war in space.

> The Roman Empire controlled the world because it could build roads. Later – when it moved to the sea – the British Empire was dominant because it had ships. In the air age we were powerful because we had airplanes. Now the Communists have established a foothold in outer space. It is not very reassuring to be told that next year we will put a better satellite into the air. Perhaps it will also have chrome trim and automatic windshield wipers.[4]

The fear of satellites was not new. As early as 1952, *Collier's* magazine had warned that 'the first power that builds and occupies a space satellite will hold the ultimate military power over the Earth'.[5] Now newspapers were quick to point out that the R-7 rocket used to launch Sputnik could also deliver a nuclear warhead. If the Soviets could put missiles into space, they would hold the world hostage. Two months earlier, in August 1957, the Soviet Union had fired an R-7 over 6,000 kilometres and declared a successful test of a multi-stage Intercontinental Ballistic Missile (ICBM). The science-fiction writer

Arthur C. Clarke declared that with the advent of Sputnik 'the United States became a second-rate power'.[6]

Large numbers of Americans began reporting that they had seen Sputnik passing over their homes. In fact, the 58-cm metal sphere was imperceptible to the naked eye. Scientists suggested that what people were seeing might be the bigger second-stage of the Soviet rocket that had also achieved orbit, but the more likely explanation was the effect of worried self-delusion, a symptom of the ongoing war of nerves.

The White House fretted that the new admiration for Soviet technological superiority would tilt global public opinion away from Washington towards Moscow. When the United States Information Agency (USIA) and the State Department were commissioned to survey attitudes in western Europe, they returned with worrying news.

> The technologically less advanced – the audience most impressed and dazzled by the sputnik – are often the audience most vulnerable to the attractions of the Soviet system. The crux of the long-range Soviet propaganda effort may be its ability to win acceptance for the validity of the Soviet system, especially among the newly independent or dependent peoples ... The satellite, presented as the achievement of the Soviet system, helps to lend credence to Soviet claims – particularly if it is followed by comparable achievements unmatched by the West.*

---

*United States Information Agency report: 'World Opinion and the Soviet Satellite: A Preliminary Evaluation', 17 October 1957. White House Office of the Special Assistant for National Security Affairs files, Eisenhower. archive.org/stream/nasa_techdoc_20040045203/20040045203_djvu.txt.

The report went on to say that the Sputnik launch had had major consequences on world opinion:

'1. Soviet claims of scientific and technological superiority over the West and especially the U.S. have won greatly widened acceptance.

2. Public opinion in friendly countries shows decided concern over the possibility that the balance of power has shifted or may soon shift in favor of the USSR.

3. The general credibility of Soviet propaganda has been greatly enhanced.

4. American prestige is viewed as having sustained a severe blow, and the American reaction, so marked by concern, discomfiture and intense interest, has itself increased the disquiet of friendly countries and increased the impact of the satellite.'

In Britain, a public opinion poll conducted by Gallup soon after Sputnik's launch seemed to confirm that the US was losing the battle for hearts and minds. The poll asked, 'What is your reaction to the Russian success in launching a satellite?' with respondents allowed to select more than one answer: 48 per cent ticked, 'Made me wonder what the future holds'; 36 per cent said it 'Increased my respect for the Russians' and 27 per cent said it 'Made me wonder why the Russians have beaten the Americans to it'. Only 16 per cent said Sputnik had 'Increased my fear of war'; only 14 per cent ticked, 'Made me frightened of the Russians'; only 8 per cent said it 'Increased my hopes of peace'.[7] When asked separately who they thought was winning the Cold War, 36 per cent answered 'Russia' against only 9 per cent who said 'The West'.[8]

In the Soviet Union itself, a similar mix of reality and psychology was at work. Unlike in the West, public opinion had no influence on the decisions of the leadership. The key players were the politicians and the experts. But both had an eye on the psychology of propaganda, and both used psychology in trying to get their way.

In the years after Stalin's death in 1953, the Kremlin's interest in rocketry had been confined to military purposes, specifically the deployment of missiles that would dissuade an enemy attack. The leadership cared little about exploring the cosmos, and that presented Sergei Korolev, the head of the Soviet aerospace programme, with a problem. Korolev had struggled to impress the politburo sufficiently to gain the funding he needed. Writing many years later, Nikita Khrushchev acknowledged that he and his fellow politicians had been slow to understand what was on offer.

> Not too long after Stalin's death, Korolev came to the politburo to report on his work ... To tell the truth, the leadership of our country looked at the missile back then like a ram will look at a new gate that's been put in. The ram stares blankly at the gate. We couldn't get it into our heads that this huge cigar shaped tube could fly somewhere and blow someone up ... We walked around it like peasants at a bazaar getting ready to buy some calico, poking at it and tugging to test its strength. You might say, 'Look what a bunch of technological idiots has gathered'. We weren't the only ones who were such ignoramuses in those days.[9]

When he did accept that Korolev's 'huge cigar' could actually fly, Khrushchev wanted it loaded with explosives. He didn't see the point of using it to go into space. It was a blow for the space programme's engineers. Recently released archives from the period show that, unlike the politicians, they were enthused by the scientific, not the military potential of satellites.

May 1954. MEMORANDUM ON AN ARTIFICIAL EARTH SATELLITE.

The importance of such a satellite is hard to overestimate. It might be a laboratory for an entire series of scientific research, and have enormous economic importance, for example, [and] permit the observation of processes occurring on the Earth for a long time ... Finally, it might be a jump-off station for research of the Moon and other planets.[10]

Only at the very end of the discussion paper do the engineers turn to military matters, in a somewhat belated appeal to the leadership's overriding concerns.

Sergei Korolev needed to convince a reluctant party leadership to back a non-military space programme, and he did so by tapping into the Cold War rivalry that conditioned much of the Kremlin's thinking. Korolev published a series of speculative articles about the prospect of Soviet space travel, even announcing the creation of a fictitious Soviet commission to explore the possibility of putting a satellite into orbit. It was done without official sanction, but it drew the attention of US scientists, the CIA and the American press.

Washington's reaction was to declare that America, too, intended to launch its own satellite, which was precisely what Korolev had been hoping for. He wrote at once to Khrushchev and Bulganin, attaching a folder with press reports of Eisenhower's announcement of government funding for a US space effort and asking, in a masterfully understated manner, if the USSR really wanted to fall behind its Cold War rival.

Korolev's note was discussed at a meeting of the Presidium of the Soviet Communist Party three days later. The outcome was precisely what Korolev had intended: approval for the establishment of a Soviet satellite scheme.

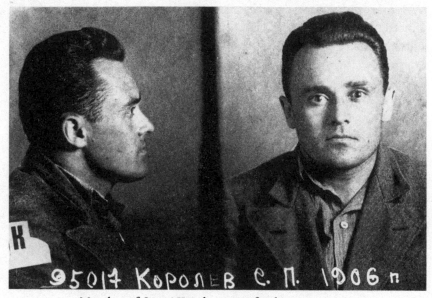

Mugshot of Sergei Korolev soon after his arrest in 1938
for wrecking and sabotaging state industry.

Sergei Korolev was a man of vision and steely determination, qualities that would secure him the pre-eminent position in the history of Soviet spaceflight. But his behaviour was driven by lessons learned in the course of a difficult life. Arrested in 1938 while in his early thirties, during one of Stalin's purges, he had been tortured and sentenced to death, then sent instead to a labour camp in Siberia. Punishment beatings led to injuries that included the loss of most of his teeth. Only his technical expertise saved him. He was transferred to a specialist camp to work on the war effort. Ludicrously, considering his dedication to scientific progress, Korolev had been accused of sabotaging technological research, charges that would be dropped only in 1957.

Anatoly Abramov, a colleague in the space programme design bureau, wrote that malnutrition and beatings had left Korolev with permanent damage to his jaw and neck, forcing him to turn his whole body in order to face someone and leaving him unable to open his mouth fully.

Korolev's experiences meant that he struggled to trust those in power. He had been forsaken by the party and betrayed by colleagues who implicated him in false accusations that led to his imprisonment.

He feared it could happen again. He was committed to building a successful Soviet space programme, but he did it through ploys and bargaining, taking calculated risks and playing the system. The Kremlin's stake in Korolev's work was based squarely on *being the first*. He had to deliver and deliver quickly. He decided to go for speed and simplicity, a design he half-jokingly labelled PS-1, meaning *Prosteishyi Sputnik*★ or Simplest Satellite. It would be a hollow, polished ball with four short antennae that could be ready in a matter of weeks. It was cheap to build. If the first launch failed, another could be ready at once.

Georgy Grechko, speaking in the 1990s, confirmed that Sputnik had no intrinsic scientific or military value; it was done solely for the psychological impact it would make, showing the world that the Soviets were at the forefront of science and discovery. It was for this reason that one of the very few major design guidelines was that its radio signal be powerful enough to be picked up by amateur listeners, allowing the entire world to track its progress around the globe.[11] 'We made it in one month, with only one reason: to be the first in space.'[12]

Right up to the eve of the launch, the project's directors were nervous. In a classified report to the Communist Party Central Committee, they betrayed anxiety about the reliability of the technology and, in particular, the possibility that components of the rocket might fall on 'capitalist countries'. Such an eventuality, especially if it were to cause civilian casualties, would have global consequences.

In the event, the technology worked. Nikita Khrushchev's son Sergei was with his father at an official dinner on the evening Sputnik was launched, 4 October 1957. He remembered how Nikita was called away for an urgent phone call and the delight on his face when he returned to the table. '"So, Korolev has just reported that today, a little while ago, an artificial satellite of the Earth was launched." Father looked triumphantly around at those present. ... he hoped that it would demonstrate the "advantages of socialism in practice" to the world, and to the Americans in particular.'[13] When Khrushchev called Korolev to the Kremlin to congratulate him, he was frank enough to admit he had been slow to realise what a psychological triumph Sputnik would be.[14]

There was uproar in the West, but coverage in the Soviet press was oddly muted. *Pravda* carried an announcement in the right-hand

---

★ 'Sputnik' in Russian means literally a companion or fellow traveller.

corner of its front page listing the satellite's technical specifications, but failing to highlight its ground-breaking significance.[15]

The cautious tone was the result of factors specific to the Soviet system. The space programme, as part of the military establishment, had always been shrouded in secrecy. Few outsiders knew what was going on or understood the magnitude of its achievement. And the media had learned from long experience to be circumspect. Events were never interpreted for readers or listeners, because the interpretation could turn out to be wrong. If an editor expressed views that did not coincide with the official line that later emerged from the Kremlin, he would have reason to be fearful. In the absence of instructions from the top, it was safer to wait.

When Sputnik garnered lavish coverage in the foreign media, the Soviets responded. The 6 October issue of *Pravda* was effusive. Its banner headline celebrated the 'Triumph of Soviet science and technology', with sub-heads proclaiming, 'A pinnacle of science'; 'The most audacious dreams of humanity now a reality'; 'Whole world follows with spellbound attention'; 'Progressive humanity warmly welcomes latest scientific triumph of Soviet Union'; '*They did it first*, says US expert'. There was even a poem, not a very good one, but nonetheless a signal of the magnitude of the moment in a society that worshipped and continues to worship the arts:

> Nay! This is no 'falling star',
> No wonder of wonders,
> But the fruit
> Of human toil unleashed,
> The free flight of thought.
> [...]
> Glory to the men who have illuminated space,
> Penetrated the depths of our native skies!
> Glory to the heroes of my land!
> Glory to the Communist Party of the USSR!
>
> by Sergei Vasiliev[16]

In the West, the demonstration of Soviet technological prowess seemed to give the lie to capitalist propaganda about Russian peasants in baste shoes, reduced to starvation by the absurdities of communist

Despite the fact Sputnik's beeps had been beamed to the world
on 4 October 1957, the Soviet press waited for Kremlin approval
before celebrating the achievement on 6 October.

economics, ploughing the fields with horses because they couldn't
afford tractors. Edward R. Murrow, the veteran CBS News commentator, declared that Sputnik had changed the American vision of
Soviet Russia.

> [It] has shattered a myth ... We failed to recognise that a totalitar-
> ian state can establish its priorities, define its objectives, allocate
> its money, deny its people automobiles, television sets, and all
> kinds of comforting gadgets in order to achieve a national goal.
> The Russians have done this with the intercontinental missile,
> and now with the Earth satellite.[17]

Sputnik was attaining a heroic, almost mythical resonance in the world's thinking. It had come, seemingly, from nowhere, the product of a society that the West at once feared but also complacently dismissed as backward.

The Soviet media contributed to the magical aura. Their coverage of the space programme was anonymous and secretive, never revealing specific plans for launches or commenting on rumoured failures, never naming any of the scientists or engineers involved. The key figures were referred to by cryptic titles that gave them a *Wizard-of-Oz*-like presence in people's imaginations. Korolev was 'The Chief Designer'; his colleague Mstislav Keldysh was 'The Chief Theoretician'; and Valentin Glushko was 'The Chief Constructor of Rockets'. For some Americans, including Tom Wolfe, it seemed to give the Soviets an air of invincibility. 'Every time the United States announced a great space experiment,' Wolfe wrote, 'the Chief Designer accomplished it first, in the most startling fashion.'[18]

Khrushchev assured the Soviet people that, in time, 'the names and photographs of these illustrious people will be made public', but for the moment, 'in order to ensure the country's security and the lives of these [people], we cannot yet make known their names'.[19]

The secrecy surrounding the Soviet space programme mystified and impressed the West, but for those involved it became wearisome. The space journalist Yaroslav Golovanov commented wryly, 'Secrecy was necessary so that no one would overtake us. But later when they did overtake us, we maintained secrecy so that no one knew that we had been overtaken.'[20] Such was the assimilated insecurity of those in charge that an extensive coded language was imposed on employees. The rocket and spacecraft were never to be referred to directly, but called instead the 'product' and the 'object', while the missile forces were called the 'customer'. Cosmonauts were told to use code in their radio communications with mission control, in case outsiders were listening in. On-board malfunctions were referred to in botanical terms; dahlia, oak, elm and mountain ash signified different technical problems. If a cosmonaut were to feel unwell, he was instructed to say, 'I see a thunderstorm', so when Pavel Popovich on Vostok 4 in 1962 really did report seeing a thunderstorm on Earth, ground control panicked thinking he'd vomited into his helmet.[21]

The obsession with secrecy allegedly led Nikita Khrushchev to reject the Nobel Committee's offer to nominate Korolev for a prize, insisting that it was the achievement of 'the entire Soviet people'. Sergei Khrushchev said his father thought singling out Korolev would anger other rocket designers and hamper the missile and space programmes. 'These people were like actors; they would all have been madly jealous at Korolev,' he said. 'I think my father's decision was psychologically correct. But, of course, Sergei Korolev felt deeply hurt.' Korolev's daughter, Natalia, recalled that the veil of secrecy vexed her father. 'We are like miners – we work underground,' she recalls him saying. 'No one sees or hears us.' The Soviet Union and the rest of the world learned Korolev's name only after his death in 1966.[22]

In 1957, Korolev had made it clear to the Kremlin leadership that Sputnik had little if any military value. But Nikita Khrushchev did little to lessen the fears of the American public, many of whom equated the Soviets' ability to launch a satellite with a capacity to launch ballistic missiles at the US. As Khrushchev's son Sergei explained in 2007,

> It was a signal to the United States, that now you have to be very cautious if you decide to attack us. You have to remember that in the 1950s, [US Air Force General Curtis] LeMay sent one memo after another that the Soviet Union must be destroyed before it is too late. We feared that one day, a US president would say: 'go ahead', instead of throwing them away. So this was not an escalation, it was more like a cold shower to the opposite side.[23]

In the US, even as President Eisenhower was playing down the importance of Sputnik, classified intelligence reports reveal that the CIA had grasped the importance of what had happened. The satellite itself was a sitting-duck target that the American military could shoot down with ease. But the rocket technology to put it into space meant that Moscow was way ahead in the nuclear missile game: a 'stupendous scientific achievement' which meant that 'the USSR has perfected an ICBM which they can put on any desired target with accuracy'.[24]

And the CIA was aware that the perception of Soviet military advantage was accompanied by a psychological win for Moscow: 'If the Soviet Union's scientists, technicians and industrialists were apparently to surpass the United States and first explore outer space, her propaganda machine would have sensational and convincing evidence of Soviet superiority.'[25] The Soviet technological triumph had triggered soul-searching, if not a full-blown crisis of confidence in the American way of life. *Newsweek* said Sputnik was a 'defeat in three fields: in pure science, in practical know-how, and in psychological Cold War'.[26] Eisenhower would admit, eight years later, that his apparent sang froid was a pretence and that he too knew how damaging the Sputnik launch had been. He confided to his secretary of state, John Foster Dulles, 'We need some vehicle to ride to suggest to the world, even if ever so briefly, that we are not stuck in the mud.'[27]

The reality was that the US was militarily equal, in many respects superior, to the USSR. But as the future secretary of defense, Thomas Gates, would point out, the facts were powerless in the face of perception. 'The mere reality of power in your inventories and arsenals will not do. There must be a public image in the minds of the people of the world of that reality of power, and there is no image. Therefore, we are short of one of the two legs that we must have.'[28] With a troubling perception of a 'missile gap' between a dawdling USA and a go-ahead USSR beginning to dominate public opinion, the White House was eager for an immediate response. A dramatic 'vehicle to ride', in Eisenhower's words, that would eclipse the achievements of the Soviets.

The US Vanguard satellite, rushed to launch by the US Navy in order to counteract the propaganda victory of the Soviets, was the focus of global attention. On 6 December 1957, two months after the successful Sputnik launch, the countdown was broadcast over loudspeakers for the thousands who had come to watch and the millions watching live on national television. The booster rockets ignited and the shiny cylinder rose four feet into the air, before a sudden loss of thrust brought it sinking back down in a plume of black smoke, its nose cone shaken loose, stumbling like a drunken man unsure of his footing. Ruptured fuel tanks exploded, destroying the rocket and much of the launch pad. The satellite itself was thrown clear and rolled on the ground with its transmitters still sending out a signal.[29]

Stayputnik, Oopsnik, Flopnik and Kaputnik were among the names bestowed on Vanguard by US newspapers. 'Failure to launch test satellite,' headlined *The New York Times*, 'assailed as blow to US prestige.' Lyndon Johnson called it 'most humiliating'. Eisenhower was mocked. The Russians gloated. A Soviet delegate to the United Nations asked, with a smile, if the United States were interested in receiving aid earmarked for 'undeveloped countries'.[30] *Time* magazine

US officials were desperate for an image to capture the success
of their own rocket and space programme. Instead, their first
attempted launch heightened feelings of inadequacy.

gave its Man of the Year accolade to Nikita Khrushchev.

A few weeks later, Wernher von Braun, the father of the Nazi
V-2 rocket programme and now the director of the US Army Ballistic
Missile Agency, used a Redstone missile to send the Explorer 1 satellite into space. But in terms of public perception, it was too little, too
late. Edward Teller, the chief developer of the US hydrogen bomb,
declared that US had lost 'a battle more important and greater than
Pearl Harbor'.[31] It was a blatant exaggeration, but Teller knew what
he was doing. Appealing to the collective memory of America's military humiliation was a powerful weapon. If Korolev had leveraged

Khrushchev's fears of falling behind in the Cold War, American scientists now did the same, urging the government to fund their research.

When Dr Lloyd Berkner, one of the directors of the International Geophysical Year project, addressed the Council on Foreign Relations in New York in January 1958, it marked a crucial point in the superpower space race. It was, he said, a race that the Soviets were already winning, gaining influence in the world through their daring – and peaceful – exploits.[32]

> In view of the reduced effectiveness of both military power and national wealth as instruments of policy, a kind of power vacuum has appeared. Clearly, the side that can effectively develop a new instrument will enjoy a powerful advantage. The Soviet Union seems to have found one in *scientific achievement as a basis for claiming intellectual leadership.*[33]

As it would emerge, the space race and the struggle for intellectual supremacy were not so much a military competition as a contest for hearts and minds, the arm-wrestling of two systems determined to prove their moral superiority. A later report to the White House by the National Aeronautics and Space Council touched deftly on Eisenhower's sorest nerve: Soviet achievements in space were giving 'new credibility' to Soviet ideology in other fields.

> From the political and psychological standpoint the most significant factor of Soviet space accomplishments is that they have produced new credibility for Soviet statements and claims. Where once the Soviet Union was not generally believed, even its baldest propaganda claims are now apt to be accepted at face value, not only abroad but in the United States. The Soviets have used this credibility for the following purposes:
> a) To claim general superiority for the Soviet system on the grounds that the sputniks and Luniks demonstrate the ability of the system to produce great results in an extremely short period of time.
> b) To claim that the world balance has shifted in favor of Communism.
> c) To claim that Communism is the wave of the future.[34]

Having been surprised by Sputnik and embarrassed by the Vanguard fiasco, Eisenhower was wary of losing out again. He warned the National Security Council that 'the US had better not undertake space activities for psychological, political or propaganda advantage unless we are able to compete with the Russians. Otherwise we would be in a poker game with a second-best hand.'[35] When he came to Congress to give the State of the Union address on 9 January 1958, he revealed just how shaken he had been by the Soviet triumphs and the fear of more to come.

> The threat to our safety, and to the hope of a peaceful world, can be simply stated. It is communist imperialism ... most of us did not anticipate the psychological impact upon the world of the launching of the first earth satellite. Let us not make the same kind of mistake in another field ... I am fully confident that the response of the Congress and of the American people will make this time of test a time of honor. Mankind then will see more clearly than ever that the future belongs, not to the concept of the regimented atheistic state, but to the people – the God-fearing, peace-loving people of all the world.[36]

A new front had been opened in the Cold War. The quest for dominance had expanded from the ground beneath people's feet to the contents of their minds and now to the limitless expanse above their heads. By framing all global politics as a competition for supremacy, the politicians had made US–Soviet rivalry in space a surrogate for hostility on earth. The fear of losing face at home and internationally left neither side with any margin for failure. The final years of the 1950s and the first years of the 1960s would see the race quicken dramatically on all fronts.

18

THE KITCHEN: COMPETING UTOPIAS

In 1812, the invading forces of Napoleon's Grande Armée captured Moscow. The emperor's invasion plans had been vindicated; his troops could supply themselves from the city's resources of food and fuel and clothing, while imposing their will on the Russian nation. Napoleon, though, had failed to reckon with the will of the Russian people. His adjutant, le Comte de Ségur, watched in horror as Muscovites ran through the streets setting fire to their own city.

> Napoleon was woken by the double light of day and conflagration ... He was in a state of extreme agitation ... after striking at the heart of an empire, to find it exhibit any other sentiment than that of submission. He felt himself conquered and surpassed in determination of will. Every moment he was starting from his seat, rushing to the windows, all the while exclaiming: 'What a terrible thing! To have done this to themselves! What a strength of character! What a people! They really are Scythians!'[1]

Napoleon had come face to face with a defining facet of the Russian character: a ruthless, self-sacrificing determination that surfaces at times of national crisis. Napoleon and his troops would be on the receiving end of it as they turned tail and retreated from Moscow.

A year later, Russian forces were at the French border. In March 1814, Tsar Alexander I led the Russian and Coalition troops into Paris. For the vast majority of the Russian soldiers who had never been outside their own country, the brief but triumphant occupation of French territory was an eye-opener. They glimpsed a world their rulers would have preferred them not to see – a world of liberty and prosperity. It stayed with them when they returned home. It set them wondering why their own country should not enjoy the same benefits. The bacillus of discontent had infected an important class of Russian society.

When Alexander I died in December 1825, 3,000 soldiers, many of them veterans of the French campaigns, gathered in St Petersburg's Senate Square, demanding an end to autocracy, civil freedoms and the liberation of the serfs. They would go down in Russian history as the Decembrists. Their revolt was crushed, their leaders arrested, executed or exiled. But they left a legacy of inspiration for future generations of rebels against tyranny and repression.

The Soviet Union emerged from the Second World War triumphant but in tatters. Millions had died, with entire cities annihilated. A devastated economy left much of the population in poverty, with families living on top of one another in communal apartments. Red Army soldiers advancing across Europe had seen the wealth of the West and, just like the Decembrists of 1825, felt that their homeland offered little reward for their heroism.

The novelist Konstantin Simonov whose poem 'Wait for Me' would become the great anthem of human emotions in time of war, saw service in Europe East and West, witnessing at first hand the Battle of Berlin. He wrote of his comrades' surprise at and envy of western prosperity.

> The contrast between the standard of living in Europe and that of our own people, a contrast that millions of our soldiers had come face to face with, was a moral and psychological blow that wasn't easy to take, despite the fact that we had triumphed ... Millions of them were telling millions more what they, the victors, had seen there, in Europe. [It was] a difficult psychological state for the victors to find themselves in ...[2]

The Soviet leadership was aware of the danger. 'Stalin feared a new Decembrism,' Simonov wrote. 'He had shown Ivan to Europe and Europe to Ivan, as Alexander I did in 1813–1814.'[3] People wanted the rewards of the sacrifices they had made, but the Soviet state struggled to provide them. The Cold War was dawning and the Kremlin had decided that arms production must take precedence over the comfort of the people. Ironically, the West's bellicose rhetoric towards the USSR proved a propaganda blessing for a state that needed to explain why the promises of the radiant socialist future had to be put on hold. 'The people forgave us a lot, because of the Cold War,' wrote

Vladimir Semichastny, later to become chairman of the KGB. 'The West didn't only hurt us, it helped us, because by frightening us it played into our hands. We could say to the people "Tighten up your belts! Be patient! We have to wait for a better life and prepare for the worst!" And we used that.'[4]

The people waited. But by the mid 1950s, Nikita Khrushchev sensed that the material shortcomings of the world's largest country would have to be addressed, that housing fit for a world superpower would have to be built. One of the key psychological ambitions of Khrushchev's 'Thaw' (a term coined from the title of Ilya Ehrenburg's 1954 novel of social and mental renewal in the USSR) was to eliminate the Soviet Union's inferiority complex.

In 1957, Khrushchev said he was making it his mission for the USSR to 'catch up with and overtake the United States', and that by 1980 the people of the Soviet Union would live in the utopian state of full communism. The US became the reference point for all the nation's striving. Soviet pride was at stake – the target of 'beating the Americans' was intended to boost performance in all sectors of the economy. Posters implored the Soviet people to work together to 'Catch up and overtake the United States in per capita production of meat, milk, and butter'. As Soviet leader, Khrushchev had at least a broad grasp of the economic realities on both sides of the Iron Curtain and he knew how far Moscow was trailing behind; but his enthusiasm and pugnacity got the better of him. It was a gamble: putting a date on the achievement of communist nirvana meant that failure to achieve it would be evident and damaging, failure to match the capitalist enemy humiliating. Ehrenburg himself pointed out the contradiction at the heart of a rhetoric which endlessly denigrated America, only to admit that Moscow was struggling to catch up with it. 'Unending talk about one's superiority is linked with grovelling before things foreign – both of these are different aspects of our insecurity complex.'[5]

As part of his campaign for change, Khrushchev went some way towards lifting the veil of secrecy about the world outside the USSR. In the postwar years, Stalin had not spent a single day outside the countries of the socialist camp. His fear of what would happen should Soviet citizens learn the realities of life in the West meant that they lived their lives in a hermetically sealed world. The state controlled all sources of information and fed its people a crudely distorted vision of life in capitalist countries. Unlike the reclusive Stalin, Khrushchev was naturally curious; he was keen to travel, to see and learn and to talk to people. By 1958, he had signed agreements for student exchanges and increased trade between East and West.

For President Eisenhower, confident of the superiority of material life in the US, the growth in East–West visibility was a welcome development. 'If we are going to take advantage of the assumption that all people want peace, then [we need] methods by which people can gradually learn a little bit more of each other,' he told a conference on people-to-people relations.

> I am talking about the exchange of professors and students and executives and of the ordinary traveler abroad ... In short, what we must do is to widen every possible chink in the Iron Curtain and bring the family of Russia, or of any other country behind that Iron Curtain, that is laboring to better the lot of their children – as humans do the world over – closer into our circle, to show how we do it, and then to sit down between us to say, 'Now, how do we improve the lot of both of us?'[6]

Eisenhower's public rhetoric was of peace and reconciliation. But a classified report to the National Security Council in June 1956 revealed Washington's secret hope that exposing the Soviet people to the outside world would hasten the downfall of their communist government.

STATEMENT OF POLICY ON EAST–WEST EXCHANGES
Department of State, S/P–NSC.

> Our foreign policies are necessarily *defensive*, so far as the use of force is concerned. But they can be *offensive* in terms of promoting a desire for greater individual freedom ... within the Soviet Union, and greater independence within the satellites. East–West exchanges should be an implementation of positive United States foreign policy:
> – To increase the knowledge of the Soviet and satellite people as to the outer world so that their judgments will be based upon fact and not upon Communist fiction.
> – To stimulate their desire for more consumer's goods by

> bringing them to realize how rich are the fruits of free labor
> and how much they themselves could gain from a gov-
> ernment which primarily sought their well-being and not
> conquest.
> –   To encourage freedom of thought by bringing to the Soviet
>   and satellite peoples challenging ideas and demonstrating
>   to Soviet and satellite intellectuals the scope of intellectual
>   freedom which is encouraged within the United States.[7]

Strikingly, and seemingly without having thought through the consequences, Khrushchev had signed an agreement for the USSR and
the USA to put on exhibitions of their own economic achievements
in each other's largest city. Soviets and Americans would showcase
their vision of themselves and their futures in a display of material
exhibits. For Washington, it meant that the triumphs of American
technology would be displayed directly to the citizens of their rival,
with no Kremlin filter to lessen the impact of dishwashers, colour
TVs and other luxuries unknown in the USSR. For the US ambassador in Moscow, Llewellyn Thompson, it was a windfall opportunity
to convince the Soviet people of the superiority of American system.
'[We should] endeavor to make the Soviet people dissatisfied with
the share of the Russian pie which they now receive.' Done properly, it could be 'the most productive single psychological effort ever
launched by the US in any Communist country'.[8]

The Soviets seemed more concerned about getting access to
western science and technology, promoting the fiction that they
were the equal of the USA and, if possible, securing valuable foreign
currency.

The American Exhibition in Moscow was fixed for July 1959. As
the date approached, it seemed to dawn on Khrushchev's advisers that
there were inherent dangers in allowing the Americans unfettered
access to the Soviet public. Georgy Arbatov, a leading expert on US
politics, warned, 'An underlying US policy is the so-called "erosion"
of our social system. As a professional student of the United States, I
feel that this is a basic United States policy line and that it distorts all
good proposals, including those regarding contacts.'[9]

Vice President Richard Nixon, who would be representing the
US in Moscow, consulted widely on how he should approach his
meeting with Khrushchev. Senator Hubert Humphrey, who had met

Khrushchev in Moscow the previous year, spoke enthusiastically about 'a man who is very much up our line' and with whom America could have a constructive relationship. 'This guy has a great sense of humor, and he's very clever ... Believe me, you're not dealing with a nonentity. This boy was born early and leaves late.' But, he warned, Khrushchev 'is a man who is insecure, who thinks we are rich and big and keep picking on him ... defensive in an offensive way, insecure in a superconfident way ... he has to pretend that he is secure and consequently demonstrates his insecurity in overstatement.'[10]

The hypersensitivity identified by Hubert Humphrey stemmed at least in part from Khrushchev's humble origins and a tendency to overcompensate for his uncultured manners and provincial accent by a challenging stance towards those he suspected of considering themselves his superiors. Richard Nixon had things in common with him. He too came from a poor, rural family – his father had been a failed lemon farmer turned grocer – and feelings of inferiority seemed to drive both men. Both had to work hard to make up for their perceived backwardness; both felt the need constantly to prove themselves. But there were differences. Where the affable Khrushchev was able and willing to talk to anyone and take on any topic, Nixon was private and reserved, avoiding unscripted interactions and speaking openly only with his most trusted allies.*

Their encounter on 24 July 1959 in the exhibition halls of Sokolniki Park on the outskirts of Moscow would be one of the most extraordinary interactions of the Cold War. Followed by journalists from all over the world and filmed by TV cameras, the two leaders paraded through rooms packed with the latest US domestic technology, including fridges, washing machines, movie cameras, televisions and dishwashers. The theme of the exhibition was 'a transplanted slice of the American way of life', laid out to give visitors the impression they were walking through the rooms of a middle-class family house.[11]

The series of impromptu exchanges between Khrushchev and Nixon – what would become known as the Kitchen Debate – shone a light on the competing images of modernity and civilisation in East

---

* After their famous presidential campaign debate, John Kennedy would comment perceptively, 'Nixon must always be thinking about who he is. That is a strain. I can be myself.' J. Farrell, *Richard Nixon: The Life*, Brunswick: Scribe, 2017, p. 283.

Nixon did his best to impress Khrushchev with America's amazing
kitchens, but his Kremlin counterpart refused to be awed. A 'young'
Leonid Brezhnev, standing to Nixon's left, looked more interested ...

and West, throwing into perspective the material and psychological
distance between the capitalist and communist systems.

What was meant to be a ceremonial photo opportunity descended
into a public spat. Khrushchev, rightly, refused to believe Nixon's
claim that the average American could afford a home equipped with
all the devices on show and argued fiercely but implausibly that
Soviet television sets were better than American ones. He mocked
the American obsession with 'gadgets' and asked if they had invented
a machine to 'stuff food into people's mouths'. As the argument grew
more heated, Khrushchev famously told his guest that 'we'll show
you Kuzma's mother!' – a piece of Russian slang meaning roughly,
'We'll show you what for!'

In light of the legendary character of the exchange, the importance it bore for the psychological interaction of East and West, and
the vexed character of their mutual perceptions, it is worth quoting at
some length from the transcript of the debate that the CIA compiled
for circulation to its officials.[12]

[Both men enter kitchen in the American exhibit.]
Nixon: I want to show you this kitchen ... which is built in thousands

of units for direct installations in houses. In America, we like to make life easier for women …

Khrushchev: *Your capitalistic attitude toward women does not occur under Communism!*

Nixon: *I think that this attitude towards women is universal. What we want to do, is make life more easy for our housewives … This house can be bought [by] most American [veterans from the Second World War] … any steel worker could buy this house. …*

Khrushchev: *… Your American houses are built to last only 20 years so builders can sell them new houses again at the end. We build firmly. We build for our children and grandchildren! … I do not think that this exhibit and what you say is strictly accurate … I hope I have not insulted you.*

Nixon: *I have been insulted by experts. Everything we say [on the other hand] is in good humor. Always speak frankly.*

Khrushchev: *The Americans have created their own image of the Soviet man. But he is not as you think! You think the Russian people will be dumbfounded to see these things, but the fact is that newly built Russian houses already have all this equipment right now! … And in Russia, all you have to do to get a house is to be born in the Soviet Union. You are entitled to housing. In America, if you don't have a dollar you have a right to choose between sleeping in a house or on the pavement. Yet you say we are slaves under Communism …*

Nixon: *This exhibit was not designed to astound but to interest. Diversity, the right to choose, the fact that we have 1,000 builders building 1,000 different houses is the most important thing. We don't have one decision made at the top by one government official. This is the difference.*

Khrushchev: *On politics, we will never agree with you …*

Nixon: *You can learn from us, and we can learn from you. There must be a free exchange. Let the people choose the kind of house … the kind of ideas that they want …*

Nixon: *I can only say that if this competition which you have described so effectively, in which you plan to outstrip us, particularly in the production of consumer goods, is to do the best for both of our peoples and for people everywhere, there must be a free exchange of ideas. There are some instances where you may be ahead of us – for example in the development of the thrust of your rockets for the investigation of outer space. There may be some instances, for example,* *color television, where we're ahead of you. But in order for both of us to benefit ...*

Khrushchev: [interrupting] *No, in rockets we've passed you by, and in the technology ...*

Nixon: [continuing to talk] *You see, you never concede anything ... You must not be afraid of ideas.*

Khrushchev: *We're saying it is you who must not be afraid of ideas! We're not afraid of anything!*

Nixon: *Well, then, let's have more exchange of them ... And this increase in communication, will teach us some things, and you some things, too. Because, after all, you don't know everything.*

Khrushchev: *If I don't know everything, then you know absolutely nothing about Communism, except for fear! ... But our dispute will be [reported] on an unequal basis. The TV apparatus is yours ... What I say to you won't be translated, and so your people won't hear it ...*

Nixon: *There isn't a day that goes by in the United States when we can't read everything that you say in the Soviet Union ... Never make a statement here that you don't think we read in the United States.*

Khrushchev: *Well, if that's the way it is, I will hold you to it! Give me your word ... that my speech will also be taped [and broadcast] in English! ...*

Nixon: *Certainly it will be. And by the same token, will everything that I say also be recorded and ... carried all over the Soviet Union? That's a fair bargain!* [They enthusiastically shake hands.]

Khrushchev: *We are businessmen, we came to an agreement right away!*[13]

What emerges from the transcript of the Kitchen Debate is the level of both understanding and incomprehension between the two sides: ultimately, it seems as if there is a psychological barrier that makes it all but impossible for capitalist and communist to see with each other's eyes. Nixon has been well briefed. He understands the limitations of the Soviet system – the technological backwardness, the secrecy, the fear of the West – and he exploits them with subtlety and restraint. Khrushchev also lands a number of blows. He accurately skewers the Americans' arrogant belief that a collection of gadgets will be enough to convert the Soviet people to their way of life. He is on safe ground criticising the materialism at the heart of America and comparing it to the noble aims the Soviet state declares it supports.

But Khrushchev ventures into difficult territory when he belittles America's production of consumer goods. His claims that the USSR already possesses the sort of technology on show in the US exhibit are patently false. He makes them, it seems, because he is swept along by the heat of the argument and by his own ebullience and swagger. His unwillingness to concede any point, to admit to any weakness, is a token of the insecurity complex identified by Ehrenburg. Communism was a shaky behemoth. It relied for its survival on the vast confidence trick that persuaded people of its infallibility. Admitting even one flaw would destroy the illusion, putting it in danger of collapse.

With little contact between East and West, tantalising peeks into the other's society could be both informative and misleading. Official representations revealed as much about who each country thought they were, and how they wanted to be perceived, as about the lived reality. The conclusion of the conversation, with both men agreeing that the recording of their exchange would be shown in full on their national television channels, is particularly revealing. It is evident from the tone of Khrushchev's voice that he is convinced he has won the argument. But Nixon has scored a series of psychological points: the Americans had little to fear from showing the debate on US television, while Khrushchev, in the heat of the moment, seems not to realise that broadcasting his remarks to the Soviet people would be freighted with danger. The audience would, at the very least, be aware that they did *not* possess the domestic luxuries that Khrushchev boasted were commonplace in Soviet homes. Catching him out in one lie would confirm the widespread conviction that the Kremlin leadership could not be trusted to tell the truth in other areas as well.

Despite Khrushchev's promise, Soviet television showed only an edited version of the debate. A selection of Nixon's less inflammatory remarks was translated and dubbed in Russian. Khrushchev's bluster remained evident. There was a sense of embarrassment among viewers at their leader's peasant manners and lack of culture. Nixon, meanwhile, admitted that 'Khrushchev knocked me out of the ring … All the briefings in the world could not have prepared me for [his] unexpected, unpredictable conduct.' When moving from the kitchen display to the Ampex room, the tension was so great that, 'I felt actually physically weak.'[14] Coverage of the encounter on US television showed Nixon struggling to deal with an aggressive Khrushchev. The

US press, however, selected those photos where Nixon appears to be taking the initiative, jabbing a finger into Khrushchev's chest, an image that played well with conservative opinion at home.

The following day, Khrushchev invited his guest to his private dacha outside Moscow. They took a trip along the Moscow river, during which Khrushchev stopped to accost local people, demanding to know, 'Are you captives? Are you slaves?' When they said no, he turned to Nixon and said, 'See how our slaves live!', smiling as if he had refuted all the American arguments.[15] He reminded Nixon of what he had said the previous day: that the Soviet people were proud of their achievements, and none too tempted by the blandishments of capitalism. The same theme permeated the reports of the exhibition in the Soviet media. Under the headline 'We will overtake America', the labour newspaper *Trud* reported Khrushchev as saying, 'By advertising the superiority of private enterprise the exhibition set out to place a bomb beneath the socialist order of the Soviet state and to arouse in the Soviet people the desire to return to the capitalist system … This merely displays how little they understand the Soviet people.'[16]

There was, though, widespread public interest in the American Exhibition. Over 2 million visitors came to see it during its six-week run. They got a rare glimpse of the outside world; and the sophistication of the exhibits impressed those who saw them. The jazz musician Alexei Kozlov wrote: 'It was very difficult to get in. Thousands of people queued endlessly. The Communist Party lost their hold over so many by raising the Iron Curtain even for a month. It was as if we were discovering a new planet, stepping into the future. We were stunned and couldn't believe that people actually lived like that.'[17] The free glasses of Pepsi-Cola handed out to visitors were a hit. A popular joke recounted how people asked for their opinion of this capitalist drink would reply 'Revolting!' before running to the back of the queue to get another glass.*

Public comments in the visitor books were more guarded, partly from the fear that they would be read by the Kremlin, but also because the exhibition failed to inspire a good number of Soviet visitors. One

---

*Thirteen years later, Pepsi would sign a reciprocal deal with Stolichnaya vodka to sell their products in each other's country. Throughout the Brezhnev era, Pepsi was one of the few western commodities that could be freely bought in the USSR.

person felt that the US was condescending to them, as if they were helpless bumpkins desperate for consumer goods:

> The exhibition shows how little the American organizers know about Soviet people. They wanted to astound us with trinkets ... They do not speak about [American] shortcomings, but a certain place should be set aside for them. We still have many short-comings, but if we were living with you in peace and friendship there would be fewer shortcomings ... Let us live in friendship and cease making atomic and hydrogen bombs; it is better if we improve our welfare.[18]

Another decried American materialism, lamenting the absence of 'culture' or 'spiritual values' in the US. 'The American standard of living is very high but the culture is on a low level. The Americans pay great attention to styles, kitchens, hair-dos, etc., as if that were all of life.'[19]

In a submission to the State Department in June 1959, the US embassy in Moscow sought to probe 'the real attitude of the Soviet people towards the regime and the society in which they live'. The Report on Soviet Attitudes and Public Opinion suggested that there was increasing acceptance, even enthusiasm, for Khrushchev's pro-gramme of reform. Most Soviet citizens still had grievances but 'there is almost no mass concern in the country over the lack of individual opportunity for effective political expression'. Most people accepted the Kremlin's assurances that the western way of living was worse, said the report, with a 'dictatorship of the wealthy, political repres-sion of the masses, racial discrimination, and gross inequalities'. This was in line with 'the idea that the US is still well ahead of the USSR in economic matters, an idea which the regime now officially sanctions in combination with the pledge that the gap is narrowing and will sooner or later be overcome'.[20]

It is not easy to assess the veracity of such assessments. Public opinion in an authoritarian state is notoriously hard to monitor. It was true that the Soviet Union was entering a time when its people did have hope for the future. The terrors of the Stalin years were gradually fading. But material shortages continued and there was an envious fascination with rumoured American abundance. Having trailed in the race for space and nuclear dominance, the ability to provide domestic comfort and quality of life was opened up by the Americans as a new front in the Cold War. The aim was to foster the envy and desire of the Soviet people, to make them demand what Americans already had. The endgame was the hope that public discontent would force the Kremlin to switch resources from military spending to domestic luxuries. Khrushchev's seven-year plan of 1958 included the aim of overtaking the US in terms of domestic appliances,[21] so the Kitchen Debate was of vital importance to him. He was trying to convince his people that their ideologically bright future would be just as comfortable as the one Nixon was selling them, a message that hardly chimed with current conditions.

One of Khrushchev's biggest problems was that the Soviet Union was struggling with a catastrophic housing shortage, the legacy of the destruction caused by the war. He had ordered the construction of thousands of concrete tower blocks across the country, but the build quality was low and living space severely restricted.* As late as 1965, the average Soviet city dweller still had only nine square metres of living space and more than half the urban population was still living in the cramped *kommunalki* (communal flats).[22] The scale of the building programme was remarkable, but new apartments had been put up fast and some suffered for it. Many of the prefabricated multi-storey blocks would need replacing only a few years later, and they quickly gained the nickname of *khrushcheby* – 'Khrushchev's slums'. The building boom inspired jokes and urban myths; even Shostakovich was moved to use it as the subject of an operetta, *Cheryomushki*, which captured the spirit of Khrushchev's great housing drive. Sasha and Masha dream of having a place of their own rather than living with their families. The Soviet state makes their dream a reality, although they have to struggle to overcome a meddling bureaucrat. As they picture themselves dancing in their future apartment, the consumer goods they wish to own – a modern fridge, furniture and a nice vase – come to life and dance alongside them. The piece premiered in Moscow in early 1959, a matter of months before the Kitchen Debate.

---

* A Soviet joke from that time reports that the annual meeting of the State Housing Construction Committee had two topics on the agenda, 'The building of new apartment houses and the building of communism.' The chairman opens the meeting and says, 'In view of the fact that we have no bricks and no mortar, let us devote today's session to the discussion of the second question.'

Soviet newspapers ran features about the 'ideal' kitchens people could expect to find in their new tower block homes. The new kitchens were small and very basic, but Soviet propaganda painted this as a plus, highlighting how many fewer steps it would now take a woman to make borshch. In this new kitchen, she could simply turn to the sink or cooker without unnecessary expenditure of energy.

The Kitchen Debate of 1959 demonstrated the extent of the psychological gap between the two sides, but it also began a dialogue. In the years ahead, cultural and educational exchanges would help to build some measure of understanding. Between 1958 to the end of the Cold War, tens of thousands of Soviet citizens were allowed to visit the West – all carefully vetted and all forced to return if they were ever to see their families again. Among those who came were Alexander Yakovlev, who would go on to become one of Mikhail Gorbachev's key advisers, and Oleg Kalugin, a future KGB general. Yakovlev's time in New York prepared him for a career in foreign diplomacy, and would help ease Gorbachev's misgivings as his era of glasnost began to open the USSR to the rest of the world. Kalugin, too, recalled the impact of his first contact with the West. 'As we walked through the airport, I was to experience ... the shock of leaving the grey, monochrome world of the Soviet Union and landing in a place virtually exploding with colours and sights.'[23]

For Kalugin, the cultural exchanges of the 1950s and 60s were a western 'Trojan Horse': 'They played a tremendous role in the erosion of the Soviet system. They opened up a closed society. They greatly influenced younger people who saw the world with more open eyes, and they kept infecting more and more people over the years.'* The new understanding cut both ways: Sheila Fitzpatrick was one of the new generation of historians who benefited from the cultural opening of the Thaw years. A year spent in Russia as an exchange student shaped her version of history.

Through exchanges and contact, a younger generation of Western scholars, and subsequently policy makers, began to

---

*Bolshoi Ballet choreographer Igor Moiseyev was shocked by what he saw in the US: 'I'm amazed that all your workers are fat and all your millionaires are thin.' Yale Richmond, 'Cultural Exchange and the Cold War: How the West Won', *American Communist History* 9:1 (2010), 61–75.

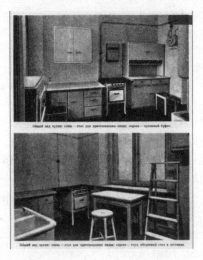

The ideal Soviet kitchen, its compact nature pitched as a
virtue, was said to dramatically reduce the number of steps
a woman would need to take to feed her family.

believe that 'The Russians are people, too,' something older
generations, who had had little direct experience of the Soviet
Union or its people, found harder to accept ... 'The Russians
are people' was a working assumption among young Western
'revisionist' scholars as well as a slogan popular with supporters of political détente. The reason this apparent truism seemed
important was that many of their seniors in Sovietology
appeared not to believe it.[24]

A visit by Khrushchev to the US later in 1959 did much to confirm
that the Russians – or at least, their leader – were very human. In
Los Angeles he went to the Twentieth Century Fox studios, where
he met Frank Sinatra, Gary Cooper, Elizabeth Taylor and Marilyn
Monroe, who had been told to wear her tightest, sexiest dress and
to leave Arthur Miller at home. Much to his chagrin, he was not
allowed to visit Disneyland, because the Los Angeles police said they
could not guarantee his safety. In a speech in Pittsburgh, Khrushchev
repeated his pledge to 'catch up with and overtake America', laugh-
ingly adding, 'I think this slogan has frightened some of you. But

why? ... We will stand up for ourselves and we will overtake you. We are warning you to buck your ideas up if you don't want to be lagging way behind us ...'[25]

When Khrushchev in his memoirs, written many years later, revealed the pride he felt at being invited to the USA, it was still the pride of a man and country with an inferiority complex.

> Who would have guessed it, that the most powerful capitalist country in the world would invite a Communist to visit? Who would have thought that the capitalists would invite me, a worker? This is incredible. Today they have to take notice of us. They have to recognise our existence and our power. Look what we've achieved ... From a ravaged, backward, illiterate Russia we have transformed ourselves into a Russia whose successes stun the world.[26]

Back in the USSR, Khrushchev's progress across the USA was given blanket coverage. His feisty treatment of his hosts played well with the hardliners, but others found it embarrassing. His competitiveness was widely mocked. A popular joke imagined Eisenhower responding to Khrushchev's jibes by suggesting they run a foot race to see who would 'catch up with and overtake' whom. When the athletic Eisenhower wins easily, the Soviet media are forced to find the correct gloss for it. 'Our leader Nikita Khrushchev has captured second place in a world-class field,' *Pravda* reports, 'while the US President finished second to last.'

This was gentle mockery, directed at a leader whom many in the Soviet Union regarded as flawed but well-intentioned; very different from the dark jokes born of fear that circulated about the terrifying Stalin. Khrushchev wanted to make life better for the people of the USSR. He was willing to show a more human face to the West to do so. The Moscow exhibition had offered each side an idealised and distorted glimpse of the other; but it had facilitated the sort of human contact capable of breaking down barriers at a time when mutual insecurities were throwing up mental and physical walls between them.

19

BRICKS IN THE WALL

The 1950s brought the modern media age a step nearer. Television began to replace cinema newsreels as the primary means by which populations – certainly in the West and selectively in the Eastern Bloc – were invited into the previously opaque world of politics. Visualising the news and the people who made it became an accepted, expected, activity in people's living rooms. Politicians' appearances, voices and personalities were accessible to all in a domestic setting, no longer hidden behind dry newspaper reports or impersonal accounts of speeches and debates, exposing them to the reflex responses, snap assessments of appearance and character, by which human beings have judged their fellows since the dawn of time. The character of nations was increasingly, ineluctably seen as encapsulated in the character of the men – and occasionally women – who represented them.

The chubby, bald, ebullient Khrushchev presented the West with an image of Soviet communism far removed from the beetle brows and menacing cockroach whiskers of his predecessor. It was a cognitive dissonance that the Allies struggled to reconcile. When Khrushchev made his first visit to the West – a nine-day trip to London in April 1956 – the mutual incomprehension was clear. 'Khrushchev is a mystery,' wrote the then British foreign secretary, Harold Macmillan. 'How can this fat, vulgar man with his pig eyes and ceaseless flow of talk really be the head – the aspirant Tsar – of all these millions of people of this vast country?'[1]

To lessen their perplexity, the British assigned two officials to follow Khrushchev. W. Barker of the Foreign Office and T. Brimelow, an interpreter, were asked to observe the 'aspirant Tsar' and report on what made him tick. The assessment they filed at the end of Khrushchev's visit was full of psychological insights ('at pains to make a good impression' … 'very conscious of his dignity')[2] but they are stumped by the contradictions of his character.

His expression is often one of cunning; less frequently one of impatient contempt. Outside the conference room, he proved to be arrogant, boastful and confident of his ability to outwit his opponents. With his son he was pleasant and kind … Even when Khrushchev was at his most serious, his earthy confident sense of humour kept breaking through … When he relaxes, his humour is rollicking and vulgar. He tells broad jokes and roars at them.[3]

The irrepressible Khrushchev signally failed to fit the staid British template of what a serious international statesman should be. They were baffled by his evangelising zeal for the system he represented ('His every thought seems to conform to the mould of Communist ideology … he does not give the impression of having an open mind') and by his genuine belief that his way was best ('His optimism about the future of the USSR seems to be unlimited'), even as they approached him with the same unwavering confidence in their own social system.

But in April 1956, Khrushchev had grounds for optimism. His 'secret speech' two months earlier had begun to lift the shadow of Stalinism; the successful test of a thermonuclear bomb in 1955 and recent successes with ballistic missiles gave him an injection of confidence. When challenged in a meeting with Rab Butler, the lord privy seal, about the sincerity of Moscow's doctrine of peaceful coexistence, Khrushchev had the assurance to respond with a teasing vein of humour.

Mr Khrushchev asked whether Mr Butler would not wish to see all Socialist countries disappear, if this could be brought about without war. Would he not welcome it, if the Supreme Soviet were to meet one day and proclaim that the policy of Socialist construction had failed and that they were reverting to private enterprise?[4]

Wrong-footed by the Ukrainian banter, Prime Minister Anthony Eden could respond only that 'he would have to think that one out very carefully'.

Khrushchev's next bilateral visit to the West was a twelve-day trip to the United States in September 1959. Khrushchev's daughter Rada, who accompanied him to Washington, recalled many years later that the American public appeared to feel the same bafflement as had Macmillan. 'It was an absolutely astonishing sight. Crowds of people were standing on the sides of the road. They waved their flags, but they were silent. Dead silence. We, the delegation, and Khrushchev were for Americans just like some aliens from the Moon. This is how I understood the feelings of these people.'[5] By the early 1960s, mutual misunderstanding had led to increasing tension. The sketchy promise of détente in the years following Stalin's death had been replaced by ill-tempered exchanges and growing international friction. By now, Khrushchev was perceived as unpredictable, irrational, perhaps unbalanced. The French foreign minister, Antoine Pinay, declared himself close to despair over the mind of 'this little man with his fat paws'.[6]

On the other side, the question of the future of Germany brought out all the Soviet leader's neuroses. He was obsessed by the need to maintain a socialist government in at least part – preferably in all – of the country that had inflicted so much suffering on the USSR. For Khrushchev it was an issue not only of strategic but of paramount psychological importance.

In a speech in 1958 he had denounced the existence of West Berlin – a western enclave surrounded by the socialist East – and told reporters that he considered it a 'malignant tumour of fascism and revanchism … That's why we've decided to do some surgery.'[7] With his customary bluster, Khrushchev told colleagues that controlling the access routes to Berlin meant he could 'squeeze the testicles of the West' whenever he wanted. But, in reality, he was haunted by the impact the West's Trojan Horse was having on the minds of the socialist subjects in the East. Since the airlift of 1948, East Germany had suffered a damaging brain drain. Several million of the GDR's most highly educated men and women had fled to the West via Berlin, where international agreements meant the border remained open.

The extent of the *Republikflucht* (desertion of the Republic) drove the East German leader, Walter Ulbricht, to badger the Kremlin to broker a solution. Khrushchev's aides joked that 'Soon there will be nobody left [in the GDR] except for Ulbricht and his mistresses',[8] but Khrushchev didn't find it funny, and, in a foretaste of the brinkmanship he would later deploy with growing abandon, he demanded that the US, Britain and France withdraw their forces from Berlin within six months and turn it into a free, demilitarised city.[9] He raised it with Eisenhower during his 1959 trip to America and got a non-committal response. With a comforting display of confirmation bias, he reassured the Soviet officials who greeted him on his return to Moscow, 'I can tell you in all frankness, dear comrades, that as a result of my talks with the US president, I have gained the impression that he sincerely wishes to see the end of the Cold War ... I am confident that we can do a great deal for peace ... Long live Soviet-American friendship!'[10]

But the shooting down of Gary Powers' U-2 spy plane over Soviet territory on 1 May 1960 meant that all bets were off. Eisenhower's admission of responsibility for the intrusion into Soviet airspace – and, undoubtedly, for other more widespread spying missions – dismayed the Soviet leader. He thought he had found an American he could trust. 'I am a human being and I have human feelings. I had hopes and they were betrayed ... you must understand that we Russians always go whole hog: when we play, we play and when we fight, we fight.'[11]

Ulbricht lobbied for aggression. A Soviet diplomat in Berlin reported that East German activists were champing at the bit, ready to 'invade' West Berlin.[12] Alarmed, Khrushchev summoned Ulbricht to Moscow and announced in no uncertain terms that Soviet forces would never take part in such an action. Instead, he told him, 'We will work out with you a tactic of gradually crowding out the western powers from West Berlin, but without war.'[13] Moscow, he said, would 'have to put our rockets on military alert'. It would be a provocative move that would inflame international tensions; but Khrushchev, the gambler, was willing to trust his own judgement of how the West would react. 'Luckily, our adversaries still haven't gone crazy,' he concluded. 'They still think. And their nerves still aren't bad ...'[14] Khrushchev was willing to stake much on the accuracy of his psychological assessment.

With relations with Eisenhower fatally damaged, he resolved to wait until 1961 and the election of a new American president before putting his plans for Berlin into action. When the new man in the White House turned out to be the relatively inexperienced John F. Kennedy, the youngest elected president in American history, Khrushchev's optimism increased.

Khrushchev, the son of a coal miner, and Kennedy, son of a millionaire, would meet for the first time at a hastily arranged summit in Vienna in June 1961. If Khrushchev approached the meeting with the conviction that he could bully his young interlocutor, Kennedy was ready for a fight. The first months of his presidency had been marred by economic and social problems at home; appearing on the international stage was an opportunity to show his mettle. 'I have to show him [Khrushchev] that we can be just as tough as he is,' Kennedy told his aide, Kenneth O'Donnell. 'I'll have to sit down with him, and let him see who he's dealing with.'[15]

To try to figure out who *he* was dealing with, Kennedy asked the CIA to produce a psychological profile of the Soviet leader. A panel of twenty psychiatrists, psychologists and medical professionals was assembled. They went through the psychological observation work done by western security agencies during Khrushchev's trips to the US in 1959 and the UK in 1956. Then they studied films, speeches and interviews with the Soviet leader, identifying salient personality traits, seeking for weaknesses, the psychological buttons that the president might wish to press. The panel's report, a fifteen-page 'personality sketch', was included in Kennedy's briefing papers for the summit. Its lead author, the psychiatrist Bryant Wedge, informed him that Khrushchev was a 'stable hypomanic character', a 'chronic optimistic opportunist' and 'impulsive' too.[16] 'He feels that he himself and his nation, with which he has increasingly identified his own person, have acquired a station which entitle them to acceptance and respect, if not affection.'[17] Worryingly for Kennedy, the CIA psychologists also confirmed the widely held understanding that Khrushchev was a powerful negotiator, a psychological bully in one-to-one exchanges, adept at adapting his behaviour to wrong-foot his interlocutor.

> He has acquired a reputation as a formidable figure in face-to-face encounter … There is an inclination to call Khrushchev an excellent role player, which means, in psychological parlance, that he can alter his behavior to fit many situations. Actually, Khrushchev excels as a 'character actor,' for his skill is not in adapting to meet new situations, but in forcing situations to conform to the role he can play. He has often achieved psychological advantage with this technique.[18]

Perhaps a little intimidated,[19] Kennedy sought the counsel of men more experienced at dealing with the Soviets. The French president, General de Gaulle, mindful that France was on the front line of any future conflict over Berlin, urged him not to give ground. 'Your job, Mr President, is to make sure Khrushchev believes you are a man who will fight. Stand fast … Hold on, be firm, strong.'[20] The former US ambassador in Moscow, Averell Harriman, suggested Kennedy might respond to Khrushchev's teasing humour – an effective weapon in his negotiating armoury – with some humour of his own.

> Don't be too serious, have some fun; get to know him a little, don't let him rattle you. He'll try to rattle you and frighten you, but don't pay any attention to that. Turn him aside gently. And don't try for too much. Remember that he's just as scared as you are ... His style will be to attack and then see if he can get away with it. Laugh about it, don't get into a fight. Rise above it. Have some fun.[21]

Unfamiliar with European politics and lacking experience of international diplomacy, Kennedy had shown signs of underestimating the psychological significance of the German question. 'We're stuck in a ridiculous situation,' he told his aides. 'It seems silly for us to be facing an atomic war over a treaty preserving Berlin as the future capital of a reunified Germany ... that will probably never be reunified.'[22] But de Gaulle was unbending. Berlin, he said, was a problem that could not be ignored. 'It is annoying to both sides that Berlin should be located where it is; however, it is there.'[23]

When the two leaders met in Vienna, Kennedy took a leaf from his opponent's book, attacking before he could be attacked. 'Look, Mr Chairman,' he told Khrushchev, 'you aren't going to make a communist out of me and I don't expect to make a capitalist out of you, so let's get down to business.'[24] Khrushchev, however, was not ready to forego the to-and-fro of ideological confrontation. He relished the clash of systems and felt that Kennedy lacked the dogmatic certainty he himself possessed. Dragged into a discussion he had been advised not to have, Kennedy accused the Soviets of 'seeking to eliminate free systems' across the world and backing communist parties that 'do not express the will of the people'.[25] It was hardly a new accusation. Khrushchev parried it with a mirrored charge of repression against the US. 'The United States wants to build a dam,' he said, 'preventing the development of the human mind and conscience.'[26]

When the agenda turned to Berlin, Khrushchev tried to hustle Washington into concessions. He went on the attack, as Harriman had predicted, declaring that Moscow was prepared to sign a peace treaty with the GDR, with or without the West's consent. It would be a provocative act, signalling the end of any hope of a unified Germany. 'Berlin is the most dangerous spot in the world,' Khrushchev said.

JFK found discussions with Khrushchev in Vienna hard
going. 'Like dealing with Dad. All give and no take.'

'The USSR wants to perform an operation on this sore spot to eliminate this thorn, this ulcer.'[27] His proposal that Berlin should become
a 'free city' hid the Kremlin's true aim of squeezing the western Allies
out of it. In accordance with Harriman's advice to turn Khrushchev
aside gently, Kennedy replied that Berlin was 'of the greatest concern
to the US' and US forces were not there on 'someone's sufferance'.
'We fought our way there,' Kennedy said. 'I did not assume office to
accept arrangements totally inimical to US interests.'[28]

Khrushchev hit back with a characteristic mix of disingenuous reassurance and a menacing upping of the ante, claiming that 'US prestige
will not be involved [if Washington were to accept Moscow's terms];
everybody will understand this'. If the US wanted a war over Germany,
he said, 'then let it begin now.'[29] ... 'The calamities of war will be shared
equally. War will take place only if the US imposes it on the USSR. It is
up to the US to decide whether there will be war or peace.'[30]

Khrushchev wore the mask of a poker player; impossible to tell if
his threats were real or bluff. Kennedy later told Hugh Sidey of *Time*
magazine, 'I never met a man like this. [I] talked about how a nuclear
exchange would kill seventy million people in ten minutes and he just

looked at me as if to say, "So what?" My impression was that he just didn't give a damn if it came to that.'[31] In a more intimate exchange with his brother Robert, he complained that dealing with Khrushchev was 'like dealing with Dad. All give and no take.'[32] He had endured

> the roughest time in my life. I think he [Khrushchev] did it because of the Bay of Pigs. I think he thought that anyone who was so young and inexperienced as to get into that mess could be taken. And anyone who got into it and didn't see it through had no guts. So he just beat the hell out of me ... I've got a terrible problem. If he thinks I'm inexperienced and have no guts, until we remove those ideas we won't get anywhere with him.[33]

At the end of the conference, Kennedy – who had been suffering from a bad back – was physically and mentally shattered. It was an outcome that the CIA's pre-summit 'personality sketch' had predicted with startling precision. 'Putting other persons on the defensive by forcing them to become unduly preoccupied with their own role-playing, is one of [Khrushchev's] primary methods of psychological manipulation. He has the uncanny ability of making people depart evaluating their own performance rather than describing his.'[34]

The CIA were not the only ones to favour psychological profiling. Ahead of the Vienna Conference, Moscow had commissioned the Soviet embassy in Washington to compile a profile of John Kennedy. The resulting document, authored by the chargé d'affaires, Mikhail Smirnovsky, was a typically Soviet concoction of dogma and desire to please the Kremlin – adopting the official line in all things, characterising the American leader in the language of Marxist ideology. But it also raised concerns that existed in the West about JFK. 'Kennedy is a typical pragmatist ... not governed by any firm convictions' whose '"liberalism" is rather relative',[35] noting that he failed to either condemn or support the McCarthyite witch-hunts. While his supporters wanted to paint him as 'a leader of the new generation able to lead the country to new heights', Smirnovsky was unconvinced.

> Judging by the strength of the available evidence about him, Kennedy ... lacks a certain breadth of perception, the ability to think over a matter philosophically and make appropriate generalizations. By the make-up of his mind he is more of a

good catalyst and consumer of others' ideas and thoughts, not a creator of independent and original ideas ... Temperamentally, Kennedy is a rather restrained, dispassionate, and reserved person, although he knows how to be sociable and even 'charming'.[36]

That the American leader had a weakness of character that would leave him susceptible to bullying was just what Khrushchev wanted to hear; indeed, that was largely Smirnovsky's reason for writing it. Alarmingly, though, the report suggested that the same weakness of character made Kennedy vulnerable to manipulation by his own generals and the American military–industrial complex. Despite his visits to the West, Khrushchev was obsessed by the belief that malevolent forces of capital controlled political decision-making there. Eisenhower had warned against the military–industrial complex as recently as January and Khrushchev feared their influence over his successor. The failed attempt to overthrow the Cuban regime in April, when Cuban exiles trained and backed by the CIA were routed at the Bay of Pigs, had indeed convinced him that Kennedy was weak, in thrall to his generals and military-industrialists. What might they push him to do if confrontation were to break out over Berlin?

Kennedy's martial rhetoric on his return to the US did little to calm things. He was determined to prove his mettle, and to prevent Khrushchev edging the Americans out of their legal right to remain in the German capital. 'I hear it said that West Berlin is militarily untenable. And so was Bastogne. And so, in fact, was Stalingrad. Any dangerous spot is tenable if men – brave men – will make it so ... We do not intend to abandon our duty to mankind to seek a peaceful solution. We seek peace – but we shall not surrender.'[37]

The stand-off had become a game of claim and counterclaim, bluff and threat, in which the ability to read the character and intentions of the opponent took on critical significance. He who could more accurately 'guess at what is on the other side of the hill' would have a powerful advantage. Khrushchev felt that, with Kennedy a potential pawn of the hawks in the military or, on the contrary, likely to blunder into war simply to display his own virility,* it was incum-

---

* He was not the only one worried by Kennedy's lack of experience. Harold Macmillan, seeing Kennedy in London immediately after Vienna, was shocked by the

bent on him – the elder, wiser statesman in the Kremlin – to seek a solution that would avert the risk of conflagration.

In a telephone call to Walter Ulbricht on 1 August 1961, Khrushchev acceded to what Ulbricht had long demanded – a border wall to stop the exodus to the West. In Khrushchev's assessment, a physical barrier would end, or at least suspend, the Berlin crisis without war and with minimal damage to the Soviet Union.[38] 'If we had decided to have a military confrontation, the question would quickly have been resolved in our favour,' Khrushchev concluded, with a slightly artificial swagger. 'But this would have been only the starting point. It would have meant shooting on some scale, large or small. War might have broken out.'[39]

The American psychologists tasked with explaining Khrushchev's character and motivations had told Kennedy that the Soviet leader was a man of decisive action. 'Khrushchev,' they wrote, 'is a person with little capacity for detecting nuances and subtleties ... He has the self-confidence of a man who knows what is right and what is wrong and is relatively invulnerable to subtle persuasion or moderately involved intellectual reasoning.'[40] There was, though, a caveat. 'He is a man of action and decision when he can see issues clearly, as black or white; but becomes confused and hostile when confronted by shades of grey.'[41] Khrushchev could evidently see 'shades of grey' in the Berlin situation: the British ambassador to Moscow, Frank Roberts, sensed that ordering the building of the wall had put him under mental strain. At a drinks reception in Moscow a day or two before construction began, Khrushchev announced to Roberts that a new Soviet military commander had been sent to Berlin. Roberts was intrigued – the Soviets were not in the habit of sharing military information with the West – but he didn't reply. Khrushchev, who had evidently intended his remark to impress or alarm his interlocutor, seemed disproportionately upset by the lack of response.

> He lost his temper: 'Well, if you take it like that, let me just tell you that I can destroy your country with eight of our nuclear

---

president's youth, and expressed severe doubts in his diary. 'I "feel in my bones" that President Kennedy is going to fail to produce any real leadership ... We may drift to disaster over Berlin – a terrible diplomatic defeat or (out of sheer incompetence) a nuclear war.' *American-British-Canadian Intelligence Relations, 1939–2000*, David Stafford and Rhodri Jeffreys-Jones (eds.), London: Frank Cass, 2000, p. 135.

bombs!' I [replied], 'I think that would be a mistake, you know, we're a rather small country, I think six would be enough. But don't forget … the RAF can come and bomb Moscow, and about nineteen of your other cities and destroy them, and that wouldn't be very good either, would it?' So Khrushchev said 'Well, maybe you're right, let's have a drink.' A kind of extraordinary conversation. But, of course … looking back on it, he must have thought that I knew or that our people in Berlin knew and had informed me that there was a plan to build a wall in Berlin. And this was the warning that if we reacted to that, he already had made his arrangements …[42]

If the wall were to be effective, it had to be built quickly; delay could allow many more East Germans to seize the opportunity for flight to the West. Dubbed 'Operation Rose', construction began in the early hours of 13 August 1961. When complete, the wall would encircle the entire perimeter of West Berlin, including its border with East Berlin and with the surrounding territory of the GDR. It would cut across 192 streets, 32 railway lines, 12 S-Bahn and U-Bahn lines and three autobahns, leaving West Berlin not just an island in a socialist sea, but an island surrounded by its own fence. Crucially, though, the three railways and three highways connecting West Berlin with West Germany were left untouched. The intention was not to isolate West Berlin from the world, but to isolate East Germans from the West.[43] With a touch of unconscious irony, the regime called it an 'Anti-Fascist Barrier', claiming that its purpose was to keep out malignant influences from the West. But according to Hagen Koch, the Stasi official in charge of mapping the course of the wall, everyone knew exactly what it was for.

> After our report and after I handed my notes to my commander, they started building the Wall and stealing building materials from all kinds of construction sites, whatever they could find … The Western Allies had three days to watch and realized in those three days that the action was not meant against them but against the population of the GDR. [For the Allies], it was 'not our problem'.[44]

In practical terms, little had changed for the West. The access routes to West Berlin remained open and there had been no attempt to

The Berlin Wall went up rapidly in August 1961,
sealing in the inhabitants of East Berlin.

interfere with Allied traffic using them. The real change was a psychological one. Western public opinion saw the wall as the physical
embodiment of the systemic division of Europe and the world, the
Cold War schism literally set in concrete. The challenge was ideological: would Kennedy stand by his championing of freedom, not only
for the peoples of the West, but for those of the GDR? Most of all, it
was a test of his commitment to the inhabitants of West Berlin, who,
he said, were 'badly shaken by the events of the week'. He proposed
to Macmillan and de Gaulle that they release a joint statement affirm-
ing their determination 'to maintain and preserve at whatever costs
[our] fundamental rights in Berlin and [our] obligation to those under
their protection'. Macmillan, less bullish, deleted 'at whatever costs'.*

Khrushchev knew he would get a bad press and he came out
punching, blaming others before they could blame him. The wall was
necessary, the Kremlin explained in a cable to the British government,
because 'West Berlin has been turned into a den of adventurers,

---

* Macmillan was also very reluctant to send more men to Berlin, pointing out that
they would merely be extra 'hostages' should the vastly stronger Soviet forces ever
decide to take West Berlin. The National Archives, PREM 11/3349.

Within a year of its erection, the Wall was a tourist attraction in
West Berlin. For many East Berliners, however, the 'anti-fascist
barrier' remained a source of fear and psychological distress.

rogues, paid agents, terrorists and other criminals serving the intelligence agencies of the whole Imperialist world'.[45]

On 24 August 1961, a twenty-four-year-old tailor, Günter Litfin,
was shot dead by GDR border guards as he tried to escape into West
Berlin. Kennedy was caught between a storm of public outrage and
Allied wariness over a response that might precipitate confrontation.
It was a low point in his presidency. When a journalist announced
he was writing a book about him, Kennedy wondered, 'Why would
anyone write a book about an administration that has nothing to
show for itself but a string of disasters?'[46]

Events on the ground forced the politicians' hand. Seeking to for-
malise the definitive separation between GDR and FRG, Ulbricht
announced that all Allied officials crossing into East Berlin would henceforth have to provide identification. It was a deliberate breach of the
four-power agreement and Ulbricht did it without informing Moscow.
General Lucius Clay, Kennedy's personal representative in Berlin, recognised the challenge to western resolve. He sent a US diplomatic car
through Checkpoint Charlie with instructions not to stop. One shot from
a border guard's rifle could have sparked war. In the event, the diplomats

took a brief spin in the East and returned safely. 'The Russians understand one thing,' Clay concluded, 'and that's strength. You must never negotiate with the Russians without having a position of strength.'[47]

The problem was that the Soviets also believed in Clay's strategy of strength. T-54 tanks were drawn up on the East German side of Checkpoint Charlie (Grenzübergang Friedrichstraße as it was known in the GDR), while American M48 Pattons appeared in the West. The former Allies in the fight against Nazism were facing each other with loaded weapons on the territory of the defeated foe. Anatoly Gribkov, a member of the Soviet Army High Command, was the conduit through whom the order to fire would pass. 'The tanks sat facing each other ... Khrushchev ordered the commander of Soviet troops in Germany that if the West used force, they should respond with force. I had a phone by one ear receiving information from Soviet military headquarters in Germany. The other phone was connected to the Kremlin.'[48]

This was war the modern way – with a live, global audience watching on television. CBS reported from the front line. 'The scene is weird, almost incredible. The American GIs stand by their tanks, eating from mess kits, while West Berliners gape from behind a rope barrier and buy pretzel sticks, the scene lit by flood lights from the eastern side while the Soviet tanks are almost invisible in the dark of the East.'[49] The truth was that western forces were hugely outnumbered. Khrushchev had been right that 'a military confrontation ... would quickly have been resolved in our favour'. If Kennedy wished to contest the outcome, he would have only one option and the idea of 'going nuclear' appalled him. Because all public communications between Washington and Moscow were coloured by considerations of face and prestige, a back-channel was used for negotiations. The US attorney general, Robert Kennedy, acted as a go-between, liaising with a senior GRU (Soviet foreign military intelligence) official, Georgi Bolshakov. Both sides had proved they were willing to stand up for what they considered rightfully theirs; they had paraded their manhood to the world. Now, with war looming, both agreed to de-escalate. 'It wasn't a good enough reason to start a war,' Gribkov later recalled. 'Khrushchev himself said "We're not unleashing a third world war because of Berlin." The Americans realised that too.'[50]

The tanks withdrew and the immediate crisis was over, but tension endured. For both sides, the wall was a symbol of failure; a reminder of how much things had changed since the cooperation of the war

The sight of Soviet and American tanks coming face to face terrified the world.

years. Each sought to blame the other; propaganda battles took the place of a battle of bullets. Kennedy called the wall 'the most obvious and vivid demonstration of the failures of the Communist system, for all the world to see'.[51] When the East German border guard Konrad Schumann was photographed leaping across the barbed wire to escape the GDR, the CIA helped circulate the image around the world.

While West Germans were eventually permitted to visit East Berlin – day passes were issued that expired at midnight and a minimum amount of East German currency had to be bought at exponentially inflated exchange rates – there was no movement in the other direction. The suffering was conspicuously asymmetrical. The composer György Ligeti called West Berlin a 'surrealist cage where those inside are free'.[52] In the cage of the East, freedom was a long-forgotten commodity. One hundred and forty people were shot, suffered fatal accidents or committed suicide after failed attempts to cross the wall. Thirty of them were not even trying to escape, falling victim to accidents or misunderstandings.[53]

The effect on the minds of those living behind the wall was far reaching. The East German psychiatrist Dietfried Müller-Hegemann identified so many symptoms that he posited a new psychiatric disorder, *Mauerkrankheit* or wall disease. There was, he said, a clear correlation between the incidence of psychosis, schizophrenia and irrational fears in his patients and the distance they lived from the wall. Rage, dejection, alcoholism and suicide were disproportionately common, notably among those who lived alongside the border.[54]

Gitta Heinrich was one of them. She grew up in Klein-Glienicke, a village that sat in a bend in the boundary between East and West. The wall, she said, surrounded the village on all sides; it 'felt like a prison. Wherever you went, you had to see the Wall.' Gitta acquired a pervasive anxiety that filled her life with a sense of unease. She described her *Mauerkrankheit* as 'an illness with a deep impact on the psyche. It was this real feeling of narrowness.' Even after the fall of the wall, she struggled to escape from the mental torment.[55]

A different condition, dubbed '*Mauer im Kopf* ('wall in the mind') by psychologists, was rooted in the disparate ways of thinking that developed between Germans in the West and those in the East. The hermetic border, the insistent political propaganda – persuasion in the West, indoctrination in the East – moulded minds. In the same fashion that the French language of Quebec, isolated from the mother country, remained close to that of Molière's time, so the mentality of the isolated GDR clung to distinctive ways of thinking.

For Anita Moller, because there was nothing to compare her life with – the West was an unknown mirage – it was hard to comprehend the abnormality of the way people lived and thought in the East. She became aware of it only after her brother, who was already in the West, arranged for her to join him by travelling through a secretly excavated tunnel. 'It was frightening down there. In the middle, directly below the wall someone had put up a sign saying "You are leaving the Eastern sector". And I thought "I'm in the West!" When I got to the other side I could hear a film camera running and thought "What's going on? This really is the evil West! Everything for the press and television!"'[56] Mental suffering, by definition, is all in the mind: as Epictetus pointed out, 'it is not events that make us sad, but the way we think about them'. In the GDR, those who could adopt the right mind-set – who could think about events in the 'right' way – found little to fret about. For men like Major Peter Bochmann, a platoon leader of the East German border guard who worked at Checkpoint Charlie for fifteen years, the wall was a source of reassurance, even of pride. 'I always had the opportunity to leave the GDR illegally by stepping one metre further but I never even considered that ... In my opinion the Wall in 1961 was a means to peace and quiet. ... The Wall, even though it seemingly imprisoned the people of the GDR, also gave them a serenity that they did not have anymore after the collapse of the Wall.'[57]

Divided Berlin became a subject for culture – novels and films full of symbolic meanings and psychological undertones. The novelist Peter Schneider called it 'the Siamese city', where each side saw its Jungian shadow reflected in the omnipresent wall that separated them: 'For Germans in the West, the Wall became a mirror that told them, day by day, who was the fairest one of all. Whether there was life beyond the death strip soon mattered only to pigeons and cats.'[58] In his novel *The Wall Jumper*, Schneider explores the experience of travelling to the 'other side'. His narrator finds crossing the wall a disorienting experience, 'familiar', akin to discovering another self, a version that he might have become but somehow did not.

> This was the shadow city, the afterbirth, the emergency edition of West Berlin. Yet, the tendency to recognition was contradicted by the impression of having abruptly landed on another planet. Life there didn't differ simply in outward organization; it obeyed another law. To attribute this to a different social order and pace of development was to label it too hastily.[59]

When, in the 1960s, the American neurologists Roger Sperry and Michael Gazzaniga severed the two hemispheres of the brain of a patient with severe epilepsy,* they found each hemisphere acting independently, competing with the other, almost, Gazzaniga recalled, as if two people were fighting over performing the same task.† Similarly,

---

* A band of fibres at the base of the brain, the corpus callosum, connects the hemispheres. By cutting it, Sperry and Gazzaniga were hoping to reduce the patient's epileptic symptoms. After the procedure, they were able to observe the ways in which each hemisphere might operate separately.

† As well as highlighting the physical functions of each hemisphere – language in the left, motor skills in the right, and so on – Sperry and Gazzaniga discovered differences in the way each side of the brain 'thinks' and perceives the world. Recognising implicit meaning; humour, tone, facial expression, body language; the contextual understanding of an utterance were all found to be located in the right hemisphere. The left hemisphere was found to be more mechanical and 'literal'.

in Berlin, that sense of puzzlement over the sudden deprivation of one half of the city's self resulted in disorienting experiences on both sides of the wall. Writing much later, the journalist Ernst-Michael Brandt described how a father in the East tried to explain to his daughter – born after 1961 and familiar only with the post-division world – what it might mean to be 'in the West'.

> He soon realized however that it's easier for a five-year-old child to grasp the rotation of the earth, sunrise and sunset, than to understand the grotesque situation of a divided city, especially when one part is also an island. Neither television from the West nor the daily encounters with the Wall on the way to her kindergarten made any difference. West Berlin was The West, and it was as far away as Africa, which after all was where bananas came from.[60]

Berliners would have to live with it for almost three decades. Within a year, another confrontation between the Great Powers, influenced and informed by the unresolved conflict over Berlin, would once again bring the world to the brink of disaster.

The author in Berlin, August 1970.

Roger W. Sperry, 'Hemisphere Deconnection and Unity in Conscious Awareness', *American Psychologist* 23:10 (1968), 723–33. people.uncw.edu/puente/sperry/sperrypapers/60s/135-1968.pdf.

20

THE SPACE RACE

By mid 1958, the Americans were ready to respond to the blow to their prestige inflicted by Sputnik. The presidential directive to the National Security Council establishing the National Aeronautics and Space Administration, NSC 5814/1, made clear what was expected. NASA must 'judiciously select' projects that would have 'a favorable world-wide psychological impact'.[1] Political and scientific think tanks were tasked with assessing what measure of psychological triumph by the US it would take to trump Moscow's initial successes. The recommendation of the Aeronautics and Space Council was clear: manned spaceflight.

> To the layman, manned space flight and exploration will represent the true conquest of outer space and hence the ultimate goal of space activities. No unmanned experiment can substitute for manned space exploration in its psychological effect on the peoples of the world. There is reason to believe that the Soviets, after getting an earlier start, are placing as much emphasis on their manned space flight program as is the US.[2]

They were indeed. As early as November 1957, the Soviet 'chief designer', Sergei Korolev, had followed up his Sputnik triumph with another first. When Nikita Khrushchev asked if Sputnik-2 could be ready for launch by the fortieth anniversary of the Bolshevik revolution on 7 November, Korolev replied that it could and, what's more, he could offer something extra – a dog.

Khrushchev saw the potential for headlines. His initial scepticism about Korolev's space programme had evaporated as he witnessed the discomfort it caused the West. He told Korolev to spend whatever it took. Sending a dog into space was the first step towards sending a man, and both Moscow and Washington knew that was the target to aim for.

Laika was a three-year-old mongrel, part husky, part terrier, that

Laika in 1957, preparing, or rather being prepared, for her final journey.

the space scientists had found wandering the streets of Moscow.[3] They knew she wasn't going to come back – there was as yet no means of re-inserting a spacecraft safely into the Earth's atmosphere – but they didn't know how or when she would die. In the absence of experimental evidence, the effect of spaceflight on living organisms was uncertain, and some of Korolev's engineers thought humans would not be able to survive in space. On 3 November 1957, at the Baikonur Cosmodrome in southern Kazakhstan, Laika was strapped into her capsule. A technician, Yevgeny Shabarov, kissed her on the nose, wished her bon voyage and closed the hatch.[4]

In the moments after lift-off, as the rocket reached peak acceleration, Laika's pulse soared from 103 to 240 beats per minute, returning to normal after approximately three hours of weightlessness in orbit. The monitors indicated that she was agitated, but that she was eating the food that had been provided for her. After seven hours, all signs of life ended. The following April, five months and 2,570 orbits later, Sputnik 2 (and Laika's remains) disintegrated as it re-entered the Earth's atmosphere.[5]

As with Sputnik 1, the new mission drew a gasp of admiration at home and abroad. This second Sputnik was bigger and more advanced than the previous 'hollow, polished ball'. If it was capable of carrying a dog, it was probably capable of carrying a warhead. But it was Laika that captured the popular imagination. In New York, a columnist for *Newsday* christened her 'Muttnik'. *The New York Times* on 5 November 1957, wrote, 'Although it was reported that the dog was a husky, it was suggested it might be an air-dale ... the second satellite puts the United States deeper in the dog-house.'[6]

Moscow prevaricated over Laika's fate, but many assumed – correctly – that she must have died. In Britain, traditional concerns for animal welfare tempered public approbation. 'I can't get that dog out of my thoughts,' one reader wrote to the *Daily Herald*. 'I feel terrible about it. If they must send up living things, why not collect a few child murderers.'[7] In the USSR, Laika and her fellow space dogs became stars, their image appearing on matchboxes and stamps, chocolates and cigarettes, razor blades and greeting cards.

Belka and Strelka, who went into space in 1960, were brought back alive and went on to have several litters of puppies. Khrushchev would later present one of them to John Kennedy, who crossed it with his own dog and produced four *pupniks*. It was fluffy, feel-good propaganda that played well with people alarmed about the increasing risk of nuclear war.

Kennedy had used Soviet space successes in his 1960 election campaign against Richard Nixon. His message was that the Republicans had allowed America to fall behind in many aspects of the Cold War and that he would turn things around:

> [B]ecause we failed to recognize the impact that being first in outer space would have, the impression began to move around the world that the Soviet Union was on the march, that it had definite goals, that it knew how to accomplish them, that it was moving and that we were standing still. That is what we have to overcome, that psychological feeling in the world that the United States has reached maturity, that maybe our high noon has passed.[8]

When he entered the White House in 1961, and subject to a barrage of prompting from politicians, experts and the media, Kennedy discovered that it is easier to criticise from without than rectify from within. He inherited a pessimistic prognostication of US prospects in space, including a table of dates by which each side might be capable of reaching certain landmark achievements. On all of them, Moscow was in the lead.

The turning point came in the spring of 1961. On 12 April, at 9.06

a.m. Moscow time, Yuri Gagarin climbed into his Vostok spacecraft at the tip of an R-7 rocket built by Sergei Korolev, turned the launch key to the 'go' position and lifted off from the Baikonur Cosmodrome, shouting '*Poekhali!*' ('Let's go!'). 'I heard a whistle and an ever-growing din,' Gagarin recalled. 'I felt how the gigantic rocket trembled all over, and slowly, very slowly, began to tear itself off the launch pad. The noise … had such a range of musical tones and timbres that no composer could hope to score it, no musical instrument or human voice could ever reproduce its magnificence.'[9]

For 108 minutes, Gagarin orbited the Earth at 18,000 mph, shooting eastwards across his homeland, then onward over the Pacific and North America. Above West Africa, Vostok's retro-rockets kicked in for a jolting forty-second burst and the spacecraft decelerated. Gagarin felt the ship turn and then begin its descent back to Earth's atmosphere – to its everlasting place in the history of scientific endeavour and human achievement.

When the Soviet media announced the mission's success, it was the first time the Soviet people had heard of the project. So fearful of failure were the Kremlin leadership that the very existence of a manned rocket had been kept secret. Gagarin's own parents learned that their son had become the first man in space only when they heard the news on the radio.[10]

In the event, Gagarin ejected from Vostok and landed safely in the countryside near Saratov in central Russia. He found himself surrounded by villagers who approached him with fear and suspicion. They took him for a spy. He had to point to the letters 'CCCP' on his helmet to reassure them. 'I am Russian,' he said. 'And you have just met the world's first spaceman!'

A second event that month helped spur President Kennedy to action. On 17 April 1961, just five days after Moscow had conquered space, the White House had sent a US-backed force of Cuban exiles to reconquer their homeland. The landing, at the Playa Girón in the Bay of Pigs, was a disaster. More than a hundred Cuban and American personnel were killed.*

---

* Those who survived the beach landing and the subsequent wave of executions, over a thousand men, were held in Castro's jails for a year and a half before being exchanged for a $53 million ransom of baby food and medicine from Washington. www.jfklibrary.org/learn/about-jfk/jfk-in-history/the-bay-of-pigs.

A composed Yuri Gagarin prepares to shock the world
by becoming the first human in space.

The Cuban fiasco infuriated Kennedy. In public, he took responsibility; in private, he lambasted the military and the CIA for persuading him that the operation had a chance of success. The CIA director, Allen Dulles, and members of his senior staff took early retirement. While Fidel Castro and Ché Guevara looked on with glee, Nikita Khrushchev cabled from Moscow to say that the USSR would not allow the US to enter Cuba, hinting that a further attempt would bring nuclear retaliation against US cities. The Bay of Pigs made America look mendacious, untrustworthy and – worst of all – incompetent and weak.*

Without Gagarin and without the Bay of Pigs, Kennedy might have left space to the Soviets. Now he was ready to stake his future on it. Back in the USSR, the celebrations – and the gloating – were under way. Yuri Gagarin was paraded through the streets in an open-top

---

*Guevara wrote Kennedy a cheeky note of congratulations – 'Thanks for Playa Girón. Before the invasion, the Revolution was weak. Now it's stronger than ever' – and told an interviewer that instances of counter-revolutionary activity, previously fierce and frequent, had fallen 'to zero'. Jon Lee Anderson, *Che Guevara: A Revolutionary Life*, New York: Grove/Atlantic, 1997, pp. 509 and 520.

'The Nation Rejoices! Hail to the Intrepid Son of Our Homeland!'

limousine, with Nikita Khrushchev at his side. At a reception in the Kremlin, he toasted the new cosmonaut, anointed him a Hero of the Soviet Union and mocked the Americans' misplaced faith in their own superiority.

> Arrogant commentators told us that Russians with their baste-shoes and footcloths would never be a great power. But once-illiterate Russia has pioneered the path into space. That's what you've done, Yuri! Let the whole world look and see what our country is capable of, what our great people and our great Soviet science can do. Let everyone who has sharpened their claws against us know this![11]

For three consecutive days, the front page of *Izvestiya* ran splash headlines above its masthead, proclaiming, 'The Supreme Triumph of our System, of our Science, our Technology and our Courage!'; 'The Feat of our Nation, the Glory of our Fatherland, the Pride of the World!'; 'The Nation Rejoices! Yuri Gagarin in Moscow! Hail to the Intrepid Son of Our Homeland!'

To rub in the fact that this was a socialist triumph, Khrushchev announced to a plenum of the Communist Party Central Committee that, 'Gagarin flew into space, but saw no God there.' As a practising member of the Russian Orthodox Church, it is unlikely that Gagarin reported any such thing; but the remark gained wide currency as a poke in the eye for the religious superstition of capitalist societies.

From a beleaguered White House, John Kennedy watched

the Soviet rejoicing and came to a decision that would define his presidency. 'The adversaries of freedom possess a powerful inter-continental striking force, large forces for conventional war and long experience in the techniques of violence and subversion,' he told the US Congress on 25 May. 'It is a contest of will and purpose as well as force and violence, a battle for minds and souls as well as lives and territory. And in that contest, we cannot stand aside.' The priority was to win the present war of nerves in order to avoid ceding the commanding heights in a future war of arms.

> If we are to win the battle that is now going on around the world between freedom and tyranny … it is time for a great new Amer-ican enterprise – time for this nation to take a clearly leading role in space achievement. For while we cannot guarantee that we shall one day be first, we can guarantee that any failure to make this effort will make us last … I believe the nation should commit itself to achieving the goal, before this decade is out, of landing a man on the Moon and returning him safely to the Earth.[12]

Meanwhile, Yuri Gagarin was on a global tour, visiting Brazil, Bulgaria, Canada, Cuba, Czechoslovakia, Finland, Great Britain, Hungary, Iceland and India. More than a million people lined the streets of Calcutta to greet him.[13] In Britain, he mingled with factory workers in Manchester and met Queen Elizabeth II at Buckingham Palace. *The Times* reported that he received 'a welcome bordering on hysteria'.[14]

Gagarin was a powerful ambassador for Soviet collectivist values, saying repeatedly that he may have been the man in the capsule, but that his success would have been impossible without the dedicated work of thousands of Soviet scientists, workers and technicians over many years. His modesty, open nature and good looks made him a celebrity. The power and immediacy of television were ushering in the era of politics by perception, in which a winning smile could soothe the harshest fears of dictatorship and a politician's scowl undo months of policy-making.

Gagarin's bravery was underlined by reminders of the perils of his mission. No one knew exactly how the module would cope with its fiery re-entry into the Earth's atmosphere, and there was an initially unacknowledged moment of drama when he became con-vinced that Vostok was about to burst into flames. 'I'm burning up.

'Socialism is our launchpad.'

Farewell, comrades!' he radioed as surface material began to burn off his capsule.[15] The possibility of death was a real one and Gagarin had left behind a letter to his wife and two daughters, to be opened should he not return.

> Hello, my sweet, lovely Valechka and Lenochka and Galochka. I wanted to write you a few lines to share the joy and happiness I am feeling. Today, the Government Commission decided to send me as the first man into space. Dear Valyusha, I am so happy! And I want you to be happy with me. The nation has entrusted me, a simple man, with such a vital task – to blaze the trail into space! Is there anything bigger or better one could wish for? This is history, a new age!

I trust the technology ... But there is always the chance of some accident. I don't believe it will happen. But if it does, Valyusha, I ask you – I ask all of you – not to waste yourself with grief ... Take care of our girls; love them like I do. Please, do not spoil them; raise them as people who can handle anything life throws at them. Make them worthy of the new society – of Communism. The State will help you.

... I have lived an honest life. I have served the people, even though my service was small.

I want to dedicate my flight to the people of the new society, the society of Communism that we are creating, to our great motherland and to our science ...

Goodbye, my dear ones. I hug you and kiss you. Your Dad. Your Yura. 10 April, 1961.[16]

Yuri Gagarin was worth a hundred ICBMs and the Kremlin knew it. Not until February 1962 did John Glenn emulate his feat of going into space orbit. He was given a ticker-tape parade in New York and awarded the NASA service medal. But America had come late to the party; and things that a closed society, with a planned economy run by autocratic rulers, could achieve with the stroke of a pen took longer in a democracy. The 'great adventure' of space, as Kennedy called it, had to be paid for. Not everyone was convinced. Dwight Eisenhower declared, 'anybody who would spend $40 billion in a race to the moon for national prestige is nuts'. Scientists told the Senate Aeronautical and Space Sciences Committee that manned space exploration had limited scientific value, its alleged importance was unrealistic and the rush to get to the Moon ate up scientific resources that could be better used elsewhere.[17] There were also questions about just who these achievements served, in a time of economic downturn and racial tension. Later, the jazz poet Gil Scott-Heron's work 'Whitey on the Moon' would sum up the discontent felt by many African Americans struggling to stay clean, fed and healthy while billions were spent on sending white astronauts into space.[18]

The estimated cost of sending a man to the Moon worked out at around $225 per American citizen, and Gallup polling suggested that 60 per cent of them were unhappy at having to pay it.[19] NASA's own chief historian, Dr Roger Launius, admitted that the Apollo programme was never popular. It had 'general acquiescence', he wrote, only because it existed for 'hard-edged' Cold War prestige reasons, as 'a surrogate for face-to-face military confrontation'. It was, he concluded, for 'very real Cold War objectives' that America embarked on the Moon programme.[20]

When asked if space was value for money, Kennedy's vice president Lyndon Johnson had a pithy answer. 'I, for one, don't want to go to bed by the light of a Communist moon.'[21] John Kennedy broadly agreed. 'The Soviet Union has made this a test of the system,' he told the NASA administrator James Webb on 21 November 1962. 'So that's why we're doing it.'[22]

In Kennedy's telling, two political systems* were being pitted against each other – the highly secretive and the somewhat more open; the centralised command economy and the democracy where people have to be persuaded, materials paid for and taxpayers convinced. NASA was a civilian-based organisation explicitly separated from the military; the Soviet space programme rode on the back of the country's ICBMs, overseen by the Defence Ministry. Cosmonauts were assigned military ranks, won military medals and were considered a part of the forces defending the socialist system.

The differences played into the psychological demands that each side placed on its spacemen. The Soviet selection process specified stringent psychological criteria that applicants were obliged to meet, set out in guidelines provided to selection boards: 'Low anxiety level; emotional stability and balance; extroverted personality; strong intellectual and perceptual abilities; acceptance of boredom and repetitive

---

* At a press conference on 12 April 1961, Kennedy had outlined his conception of the two 'systems' that would be competing in the battleground of space – collectivist 'dictatorship' versus individualist democracy: 'I do not regard the first man in space as a sign of the weakening of the free world, but I do regard the total mobilization of men and things for the service of the Communist Bloc over the last years as a source of great danger to us, and I would say we are going to have to live with that danger and hazard through much of the rest of this century.

'My feeling is that we are more durable in the long run. These dictatorships enjoy many short-range advantages that we saw in the Thirties. But in the long run, I think our system suits the qualities, and aspirations of people, the desire to be their own masters – I think our own system suits better. Our job is to maintain our strength until our great qualities can be brought more effectively to bear. But during the meantime, it is going to require a united effort.' www.jfklibrary.org/Research/Research-Aids/Ready-Reference/Press-Conferences/News-Conference-9.aspx.

tasks; vigilance and ability to focus attention; flexibility; memory; ability to control one's own reactions (self-control).'[23] There were questions related to work habits, personal habits and character. Applicants' responses were assessed by clinical psychiatrists, and western-developed personality tests, such as the Minnesota Multiphasic Personality Inventory (MMPI) and Cattell's 16 Personality Factor Test (16PF), were sometimes used. But there were also criteria of social background and political beliefs. Candidates were rated according to the social class from which they came – sons of workers and peasants were favourably regarded – and on their own political history, with membership of the party or of the communist youth organisation, the Komsomol, being close to obligatory. Psychiatric assessors would question them on a series of 'moral and political traits' such as their understanding of 'Soviet patriotism, military duty, hatred of the Fatherland's enemies, vigilance, and socialist internationalism'.[24]

Soviet psychologists were tasked with ensuring that only those candidates were selected who would be certain to put the collective success of the mission ahead of their own personal needs. The guiding principle was always that the mission took priority. 'Under this concept, an individual's personal goals and values are subordinated to the goals and values of society at large. Consequently, cosmonauts are aware that their activities not only affect each other but also reflect social principles that take precedence over their own individual desires and interests.'[25] Selected candidates were then subjected to physical tests designed to expose psychological weaknesses. Yuri Gagarin's main competitor, Gherman Titov, was a more experienced pilot who scored just as highly on the tests. When it came to separating them, and thus determining who would be the first man in space, Gagarin's background became the deciding factor. He was from rural peasant stock. He had grown up in Soviet territory occupied by the Germans during the war (later, there would be unlikely claims that, as a child, he had carried out courageous acts of sabotage against the Nazi invaders). And he had worked in a foundry before joining the Soviet air force. Gagarin ticked all the boxes. He was brave, honest and handsome, a true Soviet man inspired by the values of socialism. Titov, equally (perhaps better) qualified for the role, was from an educated, literary family and this apparently counted against him. He had annoyed his superiors by reciting Pushkin to himself while he was in the isolation chamber.

NASA also subjected its own prospective astronauts to psychological testing, in order to ensure that those selected could cope, both physically and mentally, with the strains of spaceflight. 'High level of general intelligence; drive and creativity; relative freedom from conflict and anxiety; self-sufficiency; adaptable; predictable behaviour patterns; motivated by the mission as a whole, not just personal advancement; no excessive impulsivity.'[26] The US emphasis on 'drive and creativity' contrasts with the Soviet requirement for 'acceptance of boredom and repetitive tasks', partly because American astronauts expected to play a bigger role in piloting their spacecraft, while Soviet missions were run largely from the ground and by on-board computers over which the pilot had no control. In fact, the American Mercury missions were run in a similar fashion to Soviet ones, with early astronauts were expected to 'act as back-up to fully automated systems', leading to them being mocked as 'spam in a can' by their air force rivals.[27] The space programme was far too important for either side to entrust missions to a fallible individual, no matter how thoroughly trained or composed they might be.

But, like the cosmonauts, US astronauts had to be representative of their country: Charles Donlan, the head of NASA's Space Task Group (STG), said, 'We looked for real men and valuable experience'; they were in search of 'the epitome of American masculinity'.[28] When the seven men selected for the Mercury Program were presented at a press conference on 9 April 1959, the questions they were asked barely touched on their abilities as pilots. Instead, the nation wanted to know what qualities they had as representatives of the American Way: What churches did they attend? How did their families feel about them going into space? What beliefs did they hold? All of them knew the role they had to play; all of them stood up for the values of nation and God.[29]

Moscow and Washington kept a wary eye on each other's use of psychological testing, speculating, sometimes rather wildly, on what their opponent might be up to. The two men in charge, Dr Oleg Kuznetsov, the leading psychiatrist in the Soviet space programme, and his American counterpart, Dr George Ruff, who led the psychological assessment in the selection of the Mercury astronauts, met at the 1966 International Congress of Aviation and Space Medicine in Prague. Kuznetsov confided to Ruff that the Soviet Union was worried about the high-level, classified psychological research that

NASA was carrying out. Ruff, knowing that there *was* no high-level research, asked how Kuznetsov had come to believe this. Simple, said Kuznetsov, unconsciously projecting the Soviet way of doing things: the very fact that NASA was 'pretending' to do no psychological research proved they must be working on something of extreme importance![30]

Both sides seemed determined to make their spacemen into heroes, representing the whole nation in a proxy combat between the two sides. 'The forgotten term, left behind in the superstitious past,' writes Tom Wolfe, 'was *single combat.*' Each side was sending its bravest men to decide the fate of the war.

> In single combat, the mightiest soldier of one army would fight the mightiest soldier of the other army as a substitute for a pitched battle between the two forces[31]... During the Cold War period, small-scale competitions once again took on the magical aura of a 'testing of fate', of a fateful prediction of what would inevitably happen if total nuclear war did take place ... Surveys showed that people throughout the world looked upon the competition in launching space vehicles in that fashion, i.e. as a preliminary contest proving final and irresistible power to destroy ... [I]n these neo-superstitious times it came to dramatize ... the entire technological and intellectual capability of the two nations and the strength of the national wills and spirit.[32]

Just as Yuri Gagarin was the epitome of the True Soviet Man, so the Mercury astronauts were a supreme version of the American 'Everyman', whose hard work, determination and moral character had seen him rise through a fair and egalitarian society, which they would now represent in space. They were predominantly from modest backgrounds, from regular schools, former GIs who served in the Second World War; and all, of course, were white. American society, as the Soviets accurately and unfailingly pointed out, was still one where African Americans were treated as second-class citizens, struggling for their right to travel freely on buses, let alone on spaceships. Where Soviet society viewed the ideal cosmonaut as an ideologically sound, peace-loving man who would show the degenerate West that communism was the future, America seemed to imagine its astronauts as modern-day cowboys, simultaneously conquering the Wild West of outer space while ridding it of the communist menace. And cowboys do not suffer from doubts or fear, as Roger Launius explained:

> From the beginning, the press was never motivated to dig up dirt on the astronauts; rather, reporters sought confirmation that they embodied America's deepest virtues. 'They wanted to demonstrate to their readers that the Mercury seven strode the Earth as latter-day saviors whose purity coupled with noble deeds would purge this land of the evils of communism by besting the Soviet Union on the world stage.' Today, people look back longingly to a simpler era when good was good and evil was evil, and, at least in memory, heroes did not disappoint. Psychological research or, worse yet, the faintest possibility that a mission would be compromised by psychological factors could be a public relations nightmare.[33]

The sheer bulk of the NASA spacesuit added to the astronauts' mystique. It made them appear larger, more powerful and more capable than normal humans. With their visors down, they became blank canvases, on which the common man could see his own image projected on a heroic scale.

But being a spaceman wasn't all adulation. There was a real risk to life, as astronauts on both sides would discover, as well as a psychological impact. Some were positive: follow-up studies of astronauts' mental health after they returned to Earth speak of an enduring impact, often associated with feelings of greater contentment and acceptance of life. Tests carried out on returned cosmonauts found their mental health had improved after they returned to Earth, becoming 'less anxious, hypochondriacal, depressive, and aggressive'.[34] But taking part in the space programme, East or West, brought sudden fame, and some struggled to cope with it. Others felt let down when the fame ran out. Gagarin felt guilty about taking the credit for a flight that was largely automated, heavily dependent on the work of engineers and designers whose identities could not be disclosed.

The cognitive dissonance of praise and celebration juxtaposed with feelings of unworthiness led to confusion, stress and crises. Men on both sides turned for solace to alcohol or to the oblivion-inducing thrill of daredevil stunts. Drink-driving incidents abounded. The head of cosmonaut training, Nikolai Kamanin, reported that by the end of

1961 both Gagarin and Titov were 'showing bad behaviour, drinking too much and insulting others'. In his private diaries, Kamanin notes that the two of them were indulging in 'high living' and consorting with 'loose women'. In July 1962, Kamanin writes that Titov was 'driving his Volga [car] all over the countryside at high speed', eventually being involved in a crash that resulted in the death of a motorist. Gagarin nearly died tumbling out of a window when his wife walked in on him drunkenly trying to seduce a nurse. He cracked his skull and needed emergency surgery.[35]

In public, Gagarin remained in control, but reports by British diplomats of his first press conference hint already at his struggle to adapt to the demands of sticking to the strict propaganda dictated to him by the Kremlin spin machine.

> Transcript: 'What were your feelings on landing?' 'My feelings were very complex and not at all easy to describe. I felt happiness, pride and joy that the flight was successfully completed.' [Then consults notes.] 'I was proud of having accomplished the task entrusted to me. I was happy in the knowledge that the flight had been achieved in the Soviet Union and that Soviet science had made yet another advance.'[36]

From the outset, Gagarin seems to have found fame a burden. He derived little pleasure from touring the world and resented being barred from further space flights by a Kremlin leadership terrified he might not return. He felt the pressure of being 'made to feel like some kind of super, ideal man. Everything I have done has always turned out okay, but just like everyone else I make lots of mistakes.'[37]

The American astronauts were thrust into the public spotlight at a time when their country was experiencing increasing levels of national self-doubt. Frank Borman, who orbited the Moon in 1968 on board Apollo 8, would later recall how he was booed and heckled when he appeared at speaking engagements at American colleges and universities. Viewed as a representative of Richard Nixon's administration, which had vowed to cut public spending but leave NASA's budget intact, Borman was met by hostile demonstrations. 'Everywhere I went, I met with antagonism and even hatred. I think I represented to these people "the establishment" ... at Columbia I was run off the stage by a guy in a gorilla suit. They threw marshmallows at me. It was unbelievable.'[38] The antagonism of the radical opposition in the US intensified the urgency with which the astronauts were shaped into national champions.

The Soviet Union was also in a state of transition, but theirs was a time of hope. The country was at last recovering from the worst ravages of the war, and now, it seemed, it was ready to challenge the Americans for leadership of the world. Cosmonauts were the embodiment of this success; young, healthy, peaceful and brave. 'Our space epic has convincingly revealed to the world the upbringing of a New Person – spiritually beautiful, courageous, devoted to communist ideals, and having a high sense of internationalism,' wrote *Pravda* on 4 November 1968.

The Kremlin rushed out what it said was Gagarin's autobiography, Road to the Cosmos,' charting his rise to fame from 'the most ordinary' Soviet family of workers and peasants, whose paths in life were opened wide and straight by the October Revolution.[39] The tone suggests that the Kremlin lent Gagarin a helping hand with the writing.

> While I was in space, my thoughts turned to America and its astronauts who would follow us into the cosmos. Will they be serving the cause of peace, like we are, or will they be slaves of those who are preparing for war? How good it would be if the peoples of the Earth would heed the wise and reasonable words of Nikita Sergeyevich Khrushchev and put all their strengths into achieving a universal and lasting peace.[40]

Gagarin sanctified Khrushchev and Khrushchev returned the compliment:

> Our Hero-Cosmonauts are people who even now already embody the wonderful traits of men belonging to the future Communist society [*Khrushchev had promised that communism would be achieved in the Soviet Union by 1980, auth.*] – high intellectual culture, moral purity, and perfect physique. Their deeds are driven by the love for Motherland, sense of public duty, and the true, noble ideals of Communism.[41]

When Gagarin visited London, *Pravda*, with its usual ideological extrapolation, reported that the occasion was helping to turn western public opinion against capitalism.

> The reception for Gagarin showed the great desire of the British people to live in friendship with the Russians. Public figures openly exposed what the papers fail to say, that Gagarin's reception demonstrates how sick the British people are of the Cold War and that the successes of socialist countries have not gone unnoticed by the British public, who do not often have the chance to show their real attitude toward them. For the British people Gagarin represents the New Man produced by the socialist system.[42]

Harold Macmillan thought that Laika would have got a bigger audience,[43] but there was concern.

An article by Lord Altrincham placed in the *Guardian* claimed that, 'Gagarinitis is a superficial disease, but it could have the most serious complications. We have to disabuse Mr Khrushchev of the hope that our fitful jealousy of the United States will give us a pro-Russian twist, or that our vulnerable position will incline us to seek peace at any price.'

Foreign Office papers from the time reveal a fear among officials that they were being portrayed as gullible dupes who fell into the Soviet propaganda trap. A working document was drawn up with arguments to defend themselves against the charge and prove they were not 'going soft' on the Soviets.

> We have been trying to counter this with the following points:
> The reception was that naturally due to anybody brave enough to do what he did.
> Lindbergh and Amy Johnson got equally rapturous receptions here when they made their flights.
> London's reaction was nothing political in it and was a spontaneous popular reaction, with perhaps a large dash of bobby-sox.
> If Commander Shepard were to come here he would get an equally enthusiastic reception, obviously modified in the light of the lesser nature of his achievement.
> There is doubtless a certain element of a frustrated desire

to fraternise with Russia: rebuffed at the Khrushchev level, the British turn with relief and consequent enthusiasm to a simple, warm and friendly Russian whom they can approach and who reciprocates ...

[But] *the trouble with most of this is that it is simply not true.*[44]

For its next propaganda coup, the Kremlin decided to send a woman into space. It would demonstrate that the socialist system prioritised equality between the sexes (a claim that anyone who lived in the patriarchal society of the USSR might find somewhat contentious) and that women could expect greater opportunities under communism than under capitalism.

The woman chosen by the all-male space hierarchy was Valentina Tereshkova. She was twenty-six years old when she went into orbit on 16 June 1963, picked from over 400 qualified candidates partly for her impeccable proletarian background and her father's heroism as a tank commander in the Second World War. Tereshkova spent three days in space, longer than all previous flights combined and, like Gagarin, she was feted as a symbol of Soviet superiority. Between 1964 and 1970, Tereshkova made forty-two trips abroad, taking a break only to marry a fellow cosmonaut and give birth to a daughter. She was appointed head of the Soviet Women's Organization and sent as a delegate to international women's conferences all over the globe. 'In that role,' said Nikolai Kamanin, 'she will achieve a thousand times more for our country and our Party than she could ever do in space.'*

Valentina Ponomareva, who trained alongside Valentina Tereshkova and later became a historian of cosmonautics, wrote about the unease cosmonauts felt at being treated like cogs in the machine:

> Our unconditional reliance on automation ... is not a random error or a conceptual mistake; it is a natural course of events.

---

* S. Gerovitch, 'The Human Inside a Propaganda Machine: The Public Image and Professional Identity of Soviet Cosmonauts', in James Andrews and Asif Siddiqi (eds.), *Into the Cosmos: Space Exploration and Soviet Culture*, Pittsburgh: University of Pittsburgh Press, 2011, p. 92.

Tereshkova continued to faithfully serve the leadership of her country into the twenty-first century. As a deputy of the United Russia Party, she proposed the 2020 constitutional change that allowed Vladimir Putin to serve further terms as president.

'The emphasis on automation' is the result of an inherent part of the total mistrust of the individual, the mistrust peculiar to our ideology ... Propaganda tried to impose on people's minds that technology decided everything. From this it directly followed that the individual was small and insignificant, only a tiny 'screw' in a giant mechanism ... They trusted the machine and did not trust the human being.[45]

In the years that followed Tereshkova's flight, the race to put the first man on the Moon drove the Kremlin to take ever greater risks with the safety of both its machines and its people. Korolev was ordered to launch the first multi-manned space missions and did so by stripping Vostok of all its safety features, cramming three men into a capsule designed for one and sending them into orbit with no means of rescue in an emergency.

In March 1965, Alexei Leonov became the first person to 'walk' in space during the Voskhod 2 mission, but once again Korolev had been hurried into launching a spacecraft before its technical problems had been properly tackled. A flimsy detachable airlock attached to the side of an old capsule left Leonov stranded in space as his suit expanded and prevented him re-entering. No longer able to feel his feet in his boots or to use tools effectively with his hands, he had to manually bleed oxygen from the suit in order to get back into the airlock, entering feet first, using considerable effort and more time than planned, and losing 12 lbs in sweat in the process. Knowing the authorities' reluctance to allow cosmonauts to use their initiative, Leonov decided not to communicate any of this to the ground.[46]

The historic walk was being covered live by Soviet radio, but when it was clear that Leonov was in difficulty the coverage was halted without explanation and replaced by Mozart's Requiem.* To

---

*Leonov explained later why he didn't tell ground control about the difficulties he faced on his spacewalk: 'It all depended on me. This was all being done for the first time and depended on my decisions. I felt as though someone was watching me from above and thinking to themselves: "It will be interesting to see how he gets out of this!" I was supposed to report every step I took, because below, on Earth, if something went wrong they needed to know how it all ended, in other words, why you died. Korolev told me: "No one knows where you are going, nor what awaits you on your journey. Therefore, you need to keep us informed at every step." But I decided not to report [my problems] over the radio. When I was

make matters worse, Voskhod's automatic guidance system then failed and the cosmonauts were forced to pilot their way home manually, eventually landing in a remote spot on the snowy taiga, several hundred kilometres from their target. Unable to contact the rescue party, Leonov and crewmate Pavel Belyayev spent a day and a night huddled together in freezing conditions.

By now, the whole Soviet space programme was flying on a wing and a prayer. In October of that same year, Leonov, Gagarin and Titov wrote a letter to the Soviet leadership warning that 'the situation has changed: the US has caught up and even surpassed us in certain areas … Unfortunately in our country there are many defects in the planning, organisation and management of vital work.' They received no reply.[47]

In January 1966, Sergei Korolev died at the age of fifty-nine, his life shortened by the beatings he had suffered in the Gulag. It was the beginning of the end. The space scientists had been working towards a flight that would see two Soyuz crafts meet and dock in space, but the programme had been dogged by technical problems. The Kremlin insisted that the mission must go ahead to coincide with the 1967 May Day celebrations, and the experienced cosmonaut Vladimir Komarov was chosen to lead it. Komarov knew the ship was not space-worthy. His KGB minder, Venyamin Russayev, spoke to him shortly before the launch and later recalled the conversation:

> As [Komarov] was seeing us off, he said straight out, 'I'm not going to make it back from this flight.' I asked him, 'If you're convinced you're going to die, why don't you refuse the mission?' He answered, 'Because if I don't make the flight, they'll send Yura [Gagarin], and he'll die instead of me. We've got to take care of him.'[48]

Film of the launch pad on 23 April 1967 shows an unsmiling Komarov,

asked why, I explained that anyone could have been listening in to our comms, and, if I reported difficulties, it could have been turned into a scandal. They only learned about my troubles after we landed, when I told them all about it in person.' Nuño Dominguez, 'There is no God, but sometimes he can punish you.' Interview with Alexei Leonov, *Público*, 7 May 2011. www.publico.es/ciencias/dios-no-existe-veces-castigar.html Accessed 14 June 2020.

a downcast Gagarin and some subdued technicians. Soon after take-off, the craft's guidance computers crashed and mechanical failures began to occur. Komarov complained to ground control: 'This devil ship! Nothing I touch works properly.'[49] After twenty-six hours, the mission was aborted and Komarov was told to re-enter the atmosphere, but when he tried to alter course he found it impossible to line the ship up correctly. The automatic attitude control and the solar panels had failed. With Soyuz's parachute system failing to deploy effectively, Komarov plummeted into the steppe at 400 mph.

After the Soyuz tragedy, Gagarin returned to his former job as a fighter pilot, and on a routine training flight the following year was involved in a near collision which sent his plane crashing to the ground. His remains were cremated and his ashes placed in the Kremlin wall close to those of Komarov, his friend and comrade. The Soviet space programme was in meltdown. The dead hand of central planning, excessive meddling from the leadership and a focus on propaganda victories at the expense of long-term development had undone all the scientific achievement and all the individual heroism. In 1969, when the Americans put the first men on the Moon, no Soviet cosmonaut would follow in their footsteps.

The psychological advantage now lay with the USA. Having led the space race for so long, Moscow had to cope with the same perception of being second best that had long troubled American minds.

The Soviets had crowed and the Americans did the same. A story widely circulated in US political circles claimed that on 20 July 1969, as an estimated 500 million people around the world watched the US Moon landing, Soviet TV elected to rerun a 1941 black-and-white musical comedy about the love of a shepherd for a swineherd on a collective farm. The story is not, in fact, true – the Moon landing took place at 6 a.m. Moscow time and Soviet TV didn't begin broadcasts until 8 a.m. – but it was a neat riposte to Moscow's public mockery of the US Vanguard failure. Two days later, on 22 July, *Pravda* carried a broadly accurate account of the US success,[50] but there was disappointment in Soviet society and, according to Nikita Khrushchev's son Sergei, a 'very similar feeling among Americans to when Gagarin went into orbit'.[51]

The fulfilment of John Kennedy's 1961 promise to 'land a man on the Moon and return him safely to Earth' marked the finishing line in the space race. In the intervening years, both the military and the psychological balance had tilted in Washington's favour. The time seemed to have come for cooperation to replace rivalry. As early as the Vienna summit of 1961, Kennedy had proposed a joint space mission with the Soviets, and he did so again in a speech to the UN General Assembly on 20 September 1963.[52]

Soviet self-assurance at the time and Kennedy's assassination two months later meant a joint Moon mission would not happen. But contacts at the level of science – and between astronauts and cosmonauts – continued. In 1969, Frank Borman visited the USSR and found a warm welcome. 'They were very, very friendly,' he recalled.

> My family and I spent two weeks there, travelled all over the country. They couldn't have been more nice to us ... The Soviet cosmonauts wished us well, as we wished them well for all of their flights ... The intellectuals there understood that their system was corrupt and couldn't last. But they were afraid to talk about it, unless you got them all by themselves. It was that kind of society. And I like to think that the Apollo Program had a lot to do with the subsequent dismantling of the Soviet Union.[53]

21

BRINKMANSHIP

The practice of nuclear deterrence is the shadow-boxing of hostile minds, the conjuring and interpretation of perception. You must persuade your opponent that you are prepared to use the weapons at your disposal, thereby dissuading him from using his. The persuasion must not be *so* effective, however, that the enemy comes to believe you are capable of wielding your weapons indiscriminately and concludes that he must wield his first. There is a fine line to be trod; an overstep is a step into eternity.

The art of brinkmanship, 'the threat that leaves something to chance',[1] was formulated by Eisenhower's secretary of state, John Foster Dulles. 'The ability to get to the verge without getting into war,' Dulles told *Time* magazine in 1956, 'is the necessary art. If you cannot master it, you inevitably get into war. If you try to run away from it, if you are scared to go to the brink, you are lost.'[2] The benefits were potential, the risks real; and Dulles' critics were unhappy with the trade-off. The Democratic presidential candidate Adlai Stevenson blasted Dulles for 'boasting of his brinkmanship – the art of bringing us to the edge of the nuclear abyss'.[3]

But by 1960, brinkmanship as a tactic was enshrined in the political lexicon. 'Brinkmanship is the deliberate creation of a recognizable risk,' Thomas Schelling wrote in his defining work, *The Strategy of Conflict*, 'a risk that one does not completely control.'[4] The risk was inherent in the by no means certain premise that one could predict the reaction of the other side, that one could expect rational thinking in both camps, and that the mind of the enemy could be reliably read. Given the grossly distorted image each side had developed of the other, it was a dangerous combination.

In Berlin, a military conflagration had been averted because neither side thought the former German capital important enough to go to war. It brought the world a reprieve, not a resolution. Tension remained high. Both Washington and Moscow feared the next crisis; should it break out in an area of strategic importance, the escalation to nuclear confrontation seemed more likely than ever.

The fourteen months between the stand-off in Berlin and the Cuban missile crisis of October 1962 were fraught with a sense of impending catastrophe. The weapon that had put an end to the Second World War, now in the armoury of both superpowers and dramatically more destructive than the Hiroshima and Nagasaki bombs, had reshaped humanity's mental representation of war. Few thought in terms of protracted terrestrial campaigns; modern war would be short, aerial and total.

Early twentieth-century thinkers had speculated that abolishing the 'civilised' rules of warfare – chivalry towards women and children, avoidance of chemical weapons, respect for the captured enemy – would make populations aware of the unbridled atrocities that could be committed in their name, with the result that war would become unthinkable.* The atomic bomb seemed at a stroke to have produced the same effect. Bernard Brodie, the elaborator of many of the key tenets of nuclear deterrence, wrote that the new capacity to inflict unlimited war would make war itself impossible. 'Thus far the chief purpose of our military establishment has been to win wars. From now on its chief purpose must be to avert them. It can have almost no other useful purpose.'[5]

Not everyone agreed: fourteen years on from the Geneva Conference on 'humane warfare', Albert Einstein was despondent about humanity's psychological inability to grasp the lesson of the nuclear age. 'The unleashed power of the atom,' he wrote in a telegram to mark the launch of the *Bulletin of the Atomic Scientists*, 'has changed everything save our way of thinking, and thus we drift toward unparalleled catastrophe.'[6] Washington acknowledged the psychological value of the bomb – that much was evident – but the generals and civil servants who formulated policy clung to the idea that it could and might be used for war. An undated Eisenhower-era report from

---

* Attending the 1932 Geneva Conference on the rules for 'humane warfare', Albert Einstein concluded, 'One does not make wars less likely by formulating rules of warfare … War cannot be humanized. It can only be abolished.' H. Zinn, *The Zinn Reader: Writings on Disobedience and Democracy*, New York: Seven Stories Press 2009, p. 243.

the US Department of Defense set out the administration's twin-track thinking.[7]

> Effective deterrent weapon systems must be shaped by political
> and psychological considerations as well as military effectiveness
> … They should combine just the right balance – and it can be a
> very subtle balance – of threat and assurance. What deters is not
> the capabilities and intentions we have, but the capabilities and
> intentions the enemy thinks we have. The central objective of a
> deterrent weapons system is, thus, psychological. The mission
> is persuasion.[8]

The advent of nuclear weapons changed people. The incalculable
might they could unleash cast a spell over otherwise rational thinkers. The British-American nuclear physicist Freeman Dyson sensed it
and fought against it. 'I have felt it myself,' he wrote,

> the glitter of nuclear weapons. It is irresistible if you come to
> them as a scientist, to feel it is there in your hands to release this
> energy that fuels the stars, to let it do your bidding, to perform
> these miracles, to lift a million tonnes of rock into the sky. It is
> something that gives people an illusion of illimitable power and
> it is in some ways responsible for all our troubles I would say.
> This technical arrogance that overcomes people when they see
> what they can do with their minds.[9]

Emboldened by the success of his scientists, Eisenhower decreed
that cuts could be made in conventional military spending, as the US
would now rely on a strategic nuclear response to any act of Soviet
aggression. The Eisenhower doctrine of Massive Retaliation – sold to
the American people as 'More Bang for Your Buck' – was a sketch-
ily constructed vision of deterrence that put Washington's eggs in a
single basket. Not only did it fail to account for 'less-than-total' challenges such as the Soviet invasion of Hungary (which was never going
to be met with a full-scale US onslaught on the USSR), it simultaneously gave Moscow a powerful incentive to strike first in the event of
a spiralling crisis. By the time of John Kennedy's presidency, it was
widely accepted – including by the public in both East and West – that
should either side launch a nuclear strike, it would trigger devastating

retaliation verging on annihilation. The concept of Mutually Assured Destruction – MAD – was predicated on that understanding. But it depended on each side acting rationally to avoid its own downfall; the lurking thought that one or other of them might not be so rational was the stuff of nightmares. 'Today, every inhabitant of this planet must contemplate the day when this planet may no longer be habitable,' Kennedy warned the UN General Assembly in 1961. 'Every man, woman and child lives under a nuclear sword of Damocles, hanging by the slenderest of threads, capable of being cut at any moment by accident or miscalculation or by madness.'* It was not a comfortable space for humanity to inhabit.

Lacking Washington's firepower, Nikita Khrushchev adopted a two-pronged strategy to keep the Soviet Union in the race for world domination. In public, the Kremlin called for de-nuclearisation, blaming the US (with some degree of credibility) for failing to engage. But behind the scenes, Soviet policy was just as provocative as that of the White House. In January 1962, Khrushchev told his politburo colleagues that Moscow was lagging in the superpower arms race, but could compensate by adopting an aggressive mind-set in the international arena. 'We should increase the pressure,' he declared. 'We must not doze off and, while growing, we should let the opponent feel this growth.'[10] The aim should be to maximise the state of tension in the world to the point where the next step would be military confrontation. It would put the Americans on the spot, in a position where they would be forced to back down. Using one of his trademark colourful similes, Khrushchev said it would be 'like a wineglass, filled to the brim', when a meniscus forms at the top and a single drop may cause it to overflow.[11] He may not have used the word 'brinkmanship', but it was as good a definition as anything so far proposed.

Manufacturing an unwinnable confrontation in order to intimidate one's opponent was the instinct of a gambler, and Khrushchev was nothing if not a gambler. His willingness to play for high stakes had been boosted by a conviction that it was his threat to use nuclear weapons, rather than Eisenhower's economic warnings, that forced

---

* The work of military strategist Herman Kahn helped introduce terms such as MAD, Doomsday Device and Megadeath (100 million deaths) into the popular lexicon. www.jfklibrary.org/learn/about-jfk/historic-speeches/address-to-the-united-nations-general-assembly.

Britain to back down over Suez in 1956. Written years later, Khrushchev's memoirs are full of bravado – it is the exceptional man who does not seek to justify his past behaviour – but he seems genuinely convinced of this. He dwells on a psychologically revealing vignette from a dinner party during his visit to London six months before the Suez invasion, in which he uses a conversation with the prime minister's wife, Clarissa Eden, to 'crudely' threaten the British.

> During dinner, Eden's wife asked a question. 'What kind of rockets to you have? Do they go far?' I answered her, 'Yes, they go far. Not only can our rockets reach the British Isles; they can go even farther.' She bit her tongue. My remark came across rather crudely and could have been interpreted as a threat. We actually *did* have that kind of purpose in mind ... we wanted to show that we had not come as supplicants, that we were a strong country.[12]

Khrushchev's fierce conviction that he could bully the West, despite knowing the USSR was far from matching western economic and military strength, was an example of the cognitive scripts that influence and distort human behaviour. All of us use mental maps derived from past experience to guide us through present and future challenges, and Khrushchev's cognitive script derived at least in part from the perceived success of his risk-laden gambits over Suez and Berlin. The past, however, can exert a disproportionate hold; reliance on it can lure us into irrational behaviour. According to the early proponents of cognitive theory David Krech and Richard Crutchfield, the effect is especially marked at moments of pressurised decision-making. 'There is a narrowing of the cognitive organization at the moment; the individual loses broader perspective, he is no longer able to "see" essential aspects of the situation and his behavior becomes consequently less adaptive.'[13] Three decades later, Amos Tversky and Daniel Kahneman would investigate the unconscious influence the past exerts and conclude that the power of unrecognised cognitive scripting is greater than we imagine. 'The production of a compelling scenario is likely to constrain future thinking. There is much evidence showing that, once an uncertain situation has been perceived or interpreted in a particular fashion, it is quite difficult to view it in any other way.'[14]

Khrushchev seems to have been particularly prone to such

rigidity of thinking, compounded by an exaggerated belief that his way was the only way. Oleg Troyanovsky identified Khrushchev's single-minded 'conviction decisions' as both a strength and a weakness. 'Khrushchev possessed a rich imagination and when some idea took hold of him, he was inclined to see in its implementation an easy solution to a particular problem, a sort of cure-all. In such instances, he could stretch even a sound idea to the point of absurdity.'[15] All those factors – reliance on templates from the past, single-mindedness, personal hubris and the inability to adapt to changing circumstances – would lead Khrushchev inexorably towards the next great global crisis. In the year before the Cuban showdown, his behaviour was unpredictable. The people of the world were spectators at an international game of bluff and counter bluff, and some leading thinkers were moved to question the rationality of their leaders' behaviour. 'Since the nuclear stalemate became apparent, the Governments of East and West have adopted the policy which Mr Dulles calls "brinkmanship",' wrote Bertrand Russell. 'This is a policy adapted from a sport which, I am told, is practiced by some youthful degenerates.'

> As played by irresponsible boys, this game is considered decadent and immoral, though only the lives of the players are risked. But when the game is played by eminent statesmen, who risk not only their own lives but those of many hundreds of millions of human beings, it is thought on both sides that the statesmen on one side are displaying a high degree of wisdom and courage, and only the statesmen on the other side are reprehensible. This, of course, is absurd ... The moment will come when neither side can face the derisive cry of 'Chicken!' from the other side. When that moment is come, the statesmen of both sides will plunge the world into destruction.[16]

The inherent flaw of brinkmanship is to assume that each side agrees where the brink is. But as Washington and Moscow pushed each other into increasingly aggressive stances, it was never completely clear that the Soviets and Americans truly knew where or when the tipping point might come. The bravado of 'youthful degenerates', fearful of being called chicken, lured them into slippery territory. Thomas Schelling, who would go on to win a Nobel Prize for his work on game theory, wrote that the brink of war is 'not the sharp edge of a cliff where one can stand firmly, look down and decide whether or not to plunge. The brink is a curved slope that one can stand on with some risk of slipping; the slope gets steeper and the risk of slipping greater as one moves towards the chasm.' The anxiety in Schelling's diagnosis is evident.

> The slope and the risk of slipping are rather irregular; neither the person standing there nor onlookers can be quite sure just how great the risk is or how much it increases when one takes a few more steps downward. One [protagonist] does not, in brinkmanship, frighten the adversary who is roped to him by getting so close to the edge that if one *decides* to jump one can do so before anyone can stop him. Brinkmanship involves getting onto the slope where one [protagonist] may fall in spite of his own best efforts to save himself, dragging his adversary with him.[17]

Even America's closest allies were confused. The British ambassador in Washington reported that he believed there was 'no element of bluff' to the American position, that the White House was 'inclined to play to the end of the game of chicken'.[18] But the art of the bluff, as Schelling points out, is to persuade people that it is not a bluff at all.

> Brinkmanship is ... the tactic of deliberately letting the situation get somewhat out of hand, just because its being out of hand may be intolerable to the other party and force his accommodation. It means intimidating an adversary and exposing him to a shared risk, or deterring him by showing that if he makes a contrary move he may disturb us so that we slip over the brink whether we want to or not, carrying him with us.[19]

In the early part of the 1960s, the psychology of nuclear brinkmanship spawned a thriving industry of elucidation and speculation. People racked their brains to understand what might be going on in the minds of the men making the life-and-death decisions that would determine their future. All agreed that deterrence could be framed in the language of logical thinking; what concerned many was the suspicion that decisions may be influenced by irrational emotions, hubris and fear.

Added to that was the fact that direct communication between the two sides was limited. Washington and Moscow frequently found themselves dancing with shadows, communicating by deed and gesture rather than word. Outlining demands or drawing red lines through statements to the media – TASS communiques, comment pieces in the *Washington Post* and *The New York Times* – depended on the other side noticing and correctly interpreting what was required. Each camp was prone to draw inaccurate conclusions or base its response on mistaken 'lessons' drawn from past confrontations. In their study of game theory, information processing and decision-making in international relations, Glenn Snyder and Paul Diesing pointed out that the paradox of nuclear fear was that it 'faces two ways; it induces caution in oneself but also the thought that the opponent is cautious too, and therefore will tolerate a considerable amount of pressure and provocation before resorting to acts that seriously risk nuclear war'.[20]

The result was a widespread belief that the rules of nuclear deterrence were qualitatively different from the conventional stand-offs of earlier times. Because the outcome of war would now be so devastating, the impression took hold that the bar for conflict had been raised, that leaders on both sides would exercise more caution before committing to war. But the contrary could also be true; that diplomats and politicians might feel that the enormity of nuclear warfare permitted them a wider margin for provocation. Thomas Schelling sought to explain the psychology of global confrontation in terms of the psychology of individuals. His account highlighted the ease with which the intentions of 'the other' may be misinterpreted.

> If I go downstairs to investigate a noise at night, with a gun in my hand, and find myself face to face with a burglar who has a gun in his hand, there is a danger of an outcome that neither of us desires. Even if he prefers just to leave quietly, and I wish him to, there is a danger that he may *think* I want to shoot, and shoot first. Worse, there is a danger that he may think that *I* think *he* wants to shoot. Or he may think that *I* think *he* thinks *I* want to shoot. And so on. 'Self-defense' is ambiguous, when one is only trying to preclude being shot in self-defense.[21]

Like the homeowner and the burglar, the US and the USSR had become trapped in a series of mirror-image perceptions of one another, with a 'mirror' that seemed increasingly warped. Writing a year before the Cuban crisis, the Russian-born American social psychologist Urie Bronfenbrenner, sought to define the effect of such a self-reflexive reinforcement of mutual stereotyping.

> Herein lies the terrible danger of the distorted mirror image, for it is characteristic of such images that they are self-confirming; that is, each party, often against its own wishes, is increasingly driven to behave in a manner which fulfils the expectations of the other ... Seen from this perspective, the primary danger of the Soviet–American mirror image is that it impels each nation to act in a manner which confirms and enhances the fear of the other to the point that even deliberate efforts to reverse the process are reinterpreted as evidence of confirmation.[22]

Mental stereotypes were reinforced by the language that attached to them. The Soviet regime employed two or even three Russian terms for what the West classed interchangeably as nuclear deterrence. The first of these, сдерживание (*sderzhivanie*), equates most closely to the English 'restraint' or 'containment'. It was an objective signifier of a desire to avoid destruction and was predominantly used in connection with Soviet nuclear policy. The far more threatening ядерное устрашение (*yadernoe ustrashenie*) means literally 'nuclear terrorising' or 'nuclear threatening'; and сдерживание путем устрашения (*sderzhivanie putyom ustrasheniya*) translates as 'restraint or containment by means of menacing'. These two formulations were more emotively charged, visceral and aggressive. Not surprisingly, they were the terms used to describe American nuclear policy. The choice was deliberate, imposed by the official-speak of the Kremlin, although not without some quotient of genuine belief. The effect was to condition public opinion through the shaping of language. Psychologists have shown that the more one repeats or hears repeated a specific formulation, even if it clashes with personal beliefs, the more the brain tends to flee the cognitive dissonance by conforming belief to language.

For the public on both sides of the Iron Curtain, the idea that the other side – the enemy – would have need of a nuclear deterrent seemed outlandish. It didn't enter people's minds. The 'enemy' was an aggressor, possessing *offensive*, not defensive, aims and weapons.

He would have no need for a deterrent because 'we' are peaceful and reasonable. The image was mirrored in each camp; few cared to address the thought that it could not be true of both.

Khrushchev's own characteristically colourful use of language shaped perceptions in East and West. His flamboyant claim that the USSR was 'producing missiles like sausages' (in fact, they had far fewer and of greatly inferior quality than the Americans) stirred the already boiling cauldron of western angst.

Placing weapons on Cuba would antagonise the US, but it was a way of addressing worries in the communist world – including in Beijing, where the government of Mao Zedong was showing itself to be particularly trigger-happy – that the Kremlin didn't have the nerve to confront the Americans. 'What about putting one of our hedgehogs down the Americans' trousers?' Khrushchev is reported to have asked his military commanders.[23]

'The idea of deploying nuclear missiles in Cuba,' Oleg Troyanovsky recalled, 'was conceived by Nikita Khrushchev himself. It was his brainchild, and he clung to it in spite of all the dangers and warnings.'

> What prompted him to take such a risky step? ... I had the impression that Khrushchev constantly feared that the United States would compel the Soviet Union and its allies to retreat in some region of the world. Not without reason did he believe that he would be held responsible for that. In conversations he sometimes recalled the words supposedly spoken by Stalin not long before his death: 'When I am not around, they will strangle you like kittens' ... since the two superpowers were in the throes of Cold War psychology, or even psychosis, many people regarded that [US] superiority as a serious threat.[24]

In May 1962, with his plan approved by the Presidium, Khrushchev sent a Soviet delegation to convince Castro to take the missiles, telling envoys that only by placing weapons there could they scare the US, restrain their aggression and 'save Cuba'.[25]

The 42,000 troops and forty-two missiles that Khrushchev dispatched in the autumn of 1962 were the greatest gamble of his life. He planned to announce the Cuban 'deterrent' to Kennedy after the November midterms; but in September, US planes spotted the Soviet ships sailing to Cuba and warned Moscow to turn them around. Khrushchev's response was to double the stakes. He added submarines, also now armed with nuclear weapons.[26]

The White House's initial uncertainty over exactly what the Russian vessels were carrying was resolved in mid October, when a U-2 spy plane brought back reconnaissance photos from Cuba. The images showed that launch sites were being built for ballistic missiles capable of hitting the United States. When the national security advisor, McGeorge Bundy, came to inform the president, he found him sitting on the edge of his bed in a bathrobe and slippers. Kennedy's response was succinct. 'We're probably going to have to bomb them!'[27]

Kennedy moved the US Strategic Air Command to DEFCON 2, the second-highest state of alert. For the first time, all long-range missiles and bombers were readied for action; the prospect of military action was imminent.[28]

Hearing that Kennedy was planning to address the nation on 22 October, Khrushchev jumped to the conclusion that Washington was ready to announce an invasion. Somewhat surprisingly, it took him aback. 'The point is we didn't want to unleash a war,' he lamented to a meeting of the Presidium in advance of Kennedy's speech. 'All we wanted to do was to threaten them ... The tragedy is that they can attack, and we shall respond. This may end in a big war.'[29] He had called Washington's bluff and Washington was about to call his. In Khrushchev's imagination, wild and at times irrational, the gamble he took had seemed sensible.

> My thinking went like this ... the United States could knock out some installations, but not all of them. If a quarter or even a tenth of our missiles survived – even if only one or two big ones were left – we could still hit New York, and there wouldn't be much of New York left ... The main thing was that the installation of our missiles in Cuba would, I thought, restrain the Unites States from precipitous military actions against Castro's government.[30]

Khrushchev's optimism was shared by few of his colleagues. Mikoyan and others had warned him that the missiles would almost certainly be detected before they were installed. The then Soviet ambassador in Washington, Anatoly Dobrynin, was caught between loyalty to his boss and incredulity at what he had done. 'Frankly,' Dobrynin told a 1989 conference called to look back at the Cuban crisis, 'I don't have the impression that everything was thought through to the last move, as in a game of chess. Undoubtedly, there was a conception, steps were taken, but there was improvisation as things unfolded.'[31]

Unravelling the factors that convinced Khrushchev he could get away with it is not simple. He seems to have felt that nuclear threats had worked in Suez and Berlin, so would probably work again in Cuba. And he was a man of great personal confidence, his self-belief reinforced by wartime successes in achieving victories through taking risks. The Cold War was a time of heightened intensity, when the highest stakes were fought for and the mentality of unwavering resolution was a crucial requirement. But the impression remains that there is something abnormal – something extraordinarily brave, irresponsible or perhaps sociopathic – about a man who can stake the future of the world on the throw of a dice; who is ready to destroy humanity in the name of an ideology whose declared aim is to save humanity. In retrospect, the psychological profile of Khrushchev produced by CIA experts ahead of the 1961 Vienna summit seems prescient. It suggested that even Khrushchev himself could not always distinguish between 'calculated bluffing' and the irrational attachment to an idea he has espoused and is unwilling to renounce. Struggling with details, said the report, he manifested a propensity to stake everything on a cure-all solution from which he is psychologically unable to back away: 'His ideas on how to achieve this ultimate goal, disarmament, are presumably of the foggiest nature, with few if any of the practicalities thought through.'[32]

Khrushchev's son Sergei observed his father at first hand. He understood the underdog mentality that drove many of his decisions. Having suffered so much at the hands of foreign aggressors, it was only natural that Russia would wish to demonstrate to others the pain of vulnerability. Cuba was the opportunity to do that. Resentment of past injustices and fear of losing face in the future combined to push Khrushchev in directions that a less emotionally driven man might have avoided.

I remember the tension of the days ... Cuba became to the Soviet Union the same as West Berlin to the United States: a

small, useless piece of land, deep inside hostile territory, but if
you will not defend it, even risking nuclear war, you will lose
face as a superpower ... We lived all the time here with enemies
on the gates [while] Americans were surrounded by two oceans,
they were protected. So, when they found that it is the missiles in
Cuba, the American public started panicking. It was an American
psychological crisis ... they found, 'We're also vulnerable. We
can be killed.' In the Berlin crisis, if we start a nuclear war, Russia
will kill Europeans – Germans, British, French – and Americans
will watch it on TV. Now, they saw that they were the same.[33]

In the event, Kennedy's speech to the nation on 22 October did not
announce immediate military action against the Soviet forces in Cuba,
but neither did it rule it out. More media-savvy than his opponents
in the Kremlin, Kennedy knew the power of appearances, the sway
that perception exerts over public opinion. However much he might
have panicked in private, he maintained an image of composure and
authority via his televised addresses. The president's purpose was to
persuade audiences in the US and across the world that the American
tiger had not lost its claws. With Kennedy, just as with Khrushchev,
pride and the fear of looking weak were influencing factors. The times
were given to catastrophising; showing weakness over a confrontation today seemed to presage the fall of dominoes and tomorrow's
ineluctable global triumph of the enemy.

Neither the United States of America nor the world community of nations can tolerate deliberate deception and offensive
threats on the part of any nation, large or small. We no longer
live in a world where only the actual firing of weapons represents a sufficient challenge to a nation's security to constitute
maximum peril ... this secret, swift, and extraordinary build-up
of Communist missiles cannot be accepted by this country, if
our courage and our commitments are ever to be trusted again
by either friend or foe.[34]

If the motivations for Khrushchev's gambit in Cuba had their roots
deep in the painful experiences of Russian history, Kennedy too
looked to America's past. He pledged to ensure that the same mistakes would not be made again.

The 1930s taught us a clear lesson: aggressive conduct, if allowed to go unchecked, ultimately leads to war. This nation is opposed to war ... But now further action is required – and it is under way. And these actions may only be the beginning. We will not prematurely or unnecessarily risk the costs of worldwide nuclear war in which even the fruits of victory would be ashes in our mouth – but neither will we shrink from that risk at any time it must be faced.[35]

The crisis was close to boiling point. Over the next few days, tension remained high. For the millions across the world who watched events unfold on their TV sets, it would leave a psychological wound that would take years to heal. For many of them who experienced the spectacle of humanity stumbling towards the brink of extinction, the memory remained vivid and troubling. John Guerrasio was a child in Brooklyn.

I remember sitting down with the family and watching Kennedy's speech and thinking the world was going to end any time now, and my mother called all of her six children into the kitchen and said, 'We may not see each other again. The world may end this afternoon.' And we said a prayer and [she] kissed us, and we all walked off to school thinking that that was the end of it ... And I was pretty amazed when three o'clock came and I got to go home and watch the Three Stooges again.[36]

Hoping to probe the weakness he thought he detected in the young American president, Khrushchev went on the offensive.* On 24 October, he wrote to Kennedy in terms that eschewed the decorum of diplomatic communication, blaming Washington's ultimatum to the Soviet flotilla for sparking the crisis and raising the threat of nuclear conflagration.

---

*Khrushchev undoubtedly believed that Kennedy was a lightweight who was being pushed towards war by the hawks around him. '[He] is a person of little authority in circles that decide and give direction to the policy of the United States of America. He is of no authority to both Rockefeller and du Pont.' (Remarks to Presidium colleagues at a meeting on 8 January 1962, cited in Aleksandr Fursenko and Timothy Naftali, *Khrushchev's Cold War: The Inside Story of an American Adversary*, New York: W. W. Norton, 2006, p. 413.)

The actions of the United States with regard to Cuba constitute outright banditry or, if you like, the folly of degenerate imperialism ... The Soviet Government considers that the violation of the freedom to use international waters and international air space is an act of aggression which pushes mankind toward the abyss of a world nuclear-missile war.[37]

How much did Khrushchev genuinely believe that the blame for the crisis lay with Washington? Did he in his own mind acknowledge that he was its instigator? Was his threat of war a real one, or merely the propensity for 'calculated bluff' noted by the CIA psychologists? And if it were a bluff, how conscious was he of the peril it contained; how confident that his bluff would not be called, with unimaginable consequences for mankind?

On 26 October, Khrushchev sent two further letters. His tone wavered between the inflammatory language of the previous communication and a new note of cautious conciliation. 'You can be calm in this regard,' he wrote, 'that we are of sound mind and understand perfectly well that if we attack you, you will respond the same way ... If war were to break out, then it would not be in our power to stop it, for such is the logic of war.'[38] The second letter hinted at a potential compromise: if the US were to agree to remove the Jupiter missiles it had secretly stationed in Turkey – and which presented as much of a threat to the USSR as Soviet missiles in Cuba would to the USA – then Moscow might be willing to makes concessions.

[If] you have not lost your self-control and sensibly conceive what this might lead to, then, Mr. President, we and you ought not now to pull on the ends of the rope in which you have tied the knot of war, because the more the two of us pull, the tighter that knot will be tied. And a moment may come when that knot will be tied so tight that even he who tied it will not have the strength to untie it, and then it will be necessary to cut that knot, and what that would mean is not for me to explain to you, because you yourself understand perfectly of what terrible forces our countries dispose.[39]

Kennedy was under pressure from his military commanders to 'show guts'. General Curtis LeMay, chief of staff of the US Air Force, lobbied him to sanction a pre-emptive bombing campaign to destroy the missile sites, warning the president, 'You're in a pretty bad fix.' Kennedy pushed back, reminding LeMay that, 'You're in there with me,' and joking with his defense secretary, Robert McNamara, 'These brass hats have one great advantage in their favor. If we listen to them, and do what they want us to, none of us will be alive later to tell them that they were wrong.'[40] The Executive Committee of the National Security Council, convened to advise the president, referred to 27 October as 'Black Saturday'. McNamara recalled later, 'It was a perfectly beautiful night, as fall nights are in Washington. I walked out of the President's Oval Office, and as I walked out I thought I might never live to see another Saturday night.'[41]

Now, at the very height of the crisis, Kennedy demonstrated a character trait that may have saved the world. Where Khrushchev had been obsessively intransigent in pushing ahead with his Cuban missile plan, dismissing the rational objections of Mikoyan and others, Kennedy showed the ability to analyse large amounts of ambiguous, inconsistent evidence under severe time constraints, with the knowledge that miscalculations may have serious consequences. Psychologists have demonstrated the rarity of such a talent: in their 1985 study 'Cognitive Perspectives on Foreign Policy', Tetlock and McGuire identified the tendency to exclude most incoming evidence that does not rapidly confirm decisions that are already favoured in the politician's mind. 'As crises intensify, particularly crises that culminate in war, images of environment and policy options appear to simplify and rigidify. Policymakers are more likely to ignore alternative interpretations of events, to attend to a restricted range of options, and to view possible outcomes of the conflict in terms of absolute victory or defeat.'[42]

Henry Kissinger pointed out that for much of the time – and especially in moments of crisis – foreign policy-makers 'work in darkness'.[43] Like the rest of us, politicians make decisions for the world as they perceive it, a simplified world coloured by a tendency towards confirmation bias. Laboratory experiments, case studies and simulations support the 'disruptive-stress' hypothesis: that high levels of pressure reduce the complexity and quality of a subject's information processing, pushing individuals to rely on old, often inappropriate problem-solving strategies.[44]

Disruption is exacerbated by exhaustion. Both sides in the Cuba crisis complained of lack of sleep. Dean Rusk reported, 'We had to go on a 24-hour basis here in the Department of State', while Khrush-chev recalled that, 'I slept one night in my studio fully dressed on the sofa. I did not want to be in the position of one western diplomat who, during the Suez crisis, rushed to the telephone without his trousers.'[45] In times of extreme stress, concluded the American political scientist Ole Holsti, 'there is a narrowing of the cognitive organiza-tion at the moment; the individual loses broader perspective, he is no longer able to "see" essential aspects of the situation and his behavior becomes consequently less adaptive'.[46]

Kennedy appears to have been an exception. He was able to resist the lure of a simple solution to a complex problem. Having consid-ered the military men's vaunting of the 'cure-all' pre-emptive strike, he rejected it in favour of patience, in the hope that it would allow Khrushchev to back down without feeling himself excessively humili-ated. Robert McNamara's account of the key hours of Black Saturday highlights Kennedy's ability to empathise with his opponent.

> We had two Khrushchev messages in front of us. One had come in Friday night and it had been dictated by a man who was either drunk or under tremendous stress. Basically, he said, 'if you'll guarantee you won't invade Cuba, then we'll take the missiles out'. Then, before we could respond, we had a second message that had been dictated by a bunch of hardliners, that said in effect, 'if you attack, we're prepared to confront you with masses of military power'. So, what to do? We had what I'd call the soft message and the hard message.[47]

The easy response for Kennedy would have been to rise to the hard-liners' challenge, to heed his own generals' insistence that Moscow must not be allowed to 'call us Chicken'. Indeed, Kennedy's initial thoughts seem to have been leading him in that direction.

> Tommy Thompson [Llewellyn Thompson, former US ambassa-dor to Moscow, who knew Khrushchev well] said, 'Mr President, I urge you to respond to the soft message.' The President said, 'We can't do that, it'll get us nowhere.'
>   Tommy said, 'Mr President, you're wrong' – and that takes a lot of guts – 'The important thing for Khrushchev, it seems to me, is to be able to say, "I saved Cuba; I stopped an invasion."'[48]

To Kennedy's credit, he took the time to think. Instead of insisting on the correctness of his own first inclination ('We can't do that, it'll get us nowhere'), he had the presence of mind to listen to the advice Thompson was giving him.

In Thompson's mind was this thought, 'Khrushchev's got himself into a hell of a fix and would then think to himself, "If I can get out of this with a deal that I can say to the Russian people that Kennedy was going to destroy the Cuban people and I prevented it!"' Thompson, knowing Khrushchev as he did, thought that Khrushchev would accept that, and Thompson was right. That's what I call empathy. We must try to put ourselves in their skin and try to understand how they see us, just to understand the thoughts that lie behind their decisions and their actions.[49]

Following Thompson's advice, Kennedy responded only to the Kremlin's first, 'soft' letter. He agreed that the US missiles could be removed from Turkey, but only several months down the line and with no public acknowledgement. The next morning, a response was received from Khrushchev: Moscow was willing to accept Kennedy's offer; the USSR would 'dismantle ... and return the missiles'.[50]

The world perceived the outcome as a victory for the West. In August 1961, 35 per cent of Britons surveyed in a Gallup opinion poll had said they thought Russia was winning the Cold War, while only 9 per cent said the West. By January 1964, Gallup found the figures had been reversed, with just 8 per cent now believing Russia was winning, and 26 per cent saying it was the West.[51]

On 30 October, three days after Black Saturday, *Pravda* hailed the Soviet government's 'calm and wisdom' for averting 'nuclear catastrophe'.[52] Khrushchev claimed victory but it was a hollow one. The Soviet leadership knew they had been humiliated. A whispering campaign began, accusing Khrushchev of 'adventurism', an archetypally Soviet term denoting rashness or irresponsibility. The whispers at home were *sotto voce*, but abroad – especially in Beijing and Havana – the charge was spoken loud and clear. 'We were irate,' Castro fumed. 'It really was a disgraceful agreement. It never crossed my mind they would do anything like this [remove the missiles without our consent].'[53]

To Kennedy's credit, he refrained from gloating in public. He knew in any case that the 'victory' had been achieved only at the cost of a reciprocal withdrawal of US missiles from Turkey. The American media showed less restraint. Newspaper headlines spoke of 'a humiliating defeat for Soviet policy' and unattributed quotes leaked from the White House, including one supposedly from Kennedy himself, exclaiming 'I cut his [Khrushchev's] balls off!'[54]

Robert McNamara recalled the relief in the administration at the end of the crisis. 'At the end, we lucked out. It was luck that prevented nuclear war! We came that close to nuclear war at the end … The major lesson of the Cuban missile crisis is this: the indefinite combination of human fallibility and nuclear weapons will destroy nations.'[55]

McNamara learned how right he was thirty years later. At an unprecedented meeting in Havana, Fidel Castro told McNamara that there had been 162 nuclear warheads on the island at the time of the crisis and that he, Castro, had lobbied Khrushchev to launch them against the United States. 'I couldn't believe what I was hearing!' McNamara recalled. 'It's almost impossible for people today to put themselves back into that period … Cold War? Hell, it was a Hot War!'[56]

22

DUCK AND COVER

There was a turtle by the name of Bert
And Bert the turtle was very alert,
When danger threatened him he never got hurt,
He knew just what to do ...
He'd duck! And cover!
Duck! And cover!
He did what we all must learn to do –
You, and you, and you, and you –
Duck and cover![1]

Had the Soviets fired their missiles from Cuba in October 1962, as Castro was urging them to do, schoolchildren all over America would have slid down from their chairs and hidden under their desks. For the previous decade, at the insistence of the US authorities, teachers had instructed young Americans to 'duck and cover' as soon as they heard the sound of the nuclear air-raid sirens in their cities, towns and villages. The drill had been repeated so often that for many children it became a Pavlovian response – an instinctive, unthinking reaction to a learned stimulus. The bouncy refrain of the 'Bert the Turtle' song, with its breezy doo-wop backing, made it sound like a jolly jape, but for those it was aimed at, duck and cover would leave a disturbing aftertaste.

The retrospective mockery with which Americans later spoke of duck and cover, and of the hapless inadequacy of Bert the Turtle's prescriptions for survival, was in part a coping mechanism. Neither Bert's turtle-shell nor the flimsy shelter of a school desk would have mitigated the effects of a 15-megaton bomb. Dropping to the floor and shielding your face may have protected you from the initial blast wave, but there would be no defence against the nuclear fallout that followed. Radioactive particles sucked into the explosion's fireball would be scattered for miles on the wind.

If Bert could hide in his shell, why did he need a helmet?
Civil defence policies were full of inconsistencies …

I, and my fellow baby boomers, grew up in the later stages of the
Cold War. Tensions were easing and adversaries talking, but fear
remained. Arriving to work as the BBC's correspondent in Geneva
in the mid 1980s, I found that the house we rented – like all houses in
Switzerland – had a nuclear fallout shelter in the basement, stocked
with canned food, water and air filters. Declaring that 'neutrality is
no guarantee against radioactivity', the Swiss government from the
1960s onwards had insisted on providing bunker space for all its citizens. We used the shelter as a bedroom for our youngest child and
slept peacefully, knowing that he at least would survive any nuclear
attack. For earlier generations the legacy of nuclear paranoia was
less benign. Living for so long under the constant menace of nuclear
bombardment, knowing that destruction from above could descend
at any moment and that little control could be exerted by the individual to protect themselves, took its toll, fostering anxiety and neuroses.
Amy Morris-Young, educated at St Euphrasia Elementary School in
Granada Hills, California, grew up in what she calls the 'thick soup of
post-World War II paranoia'.

Hiding under desks was unlikely to protect anyone from a nearby strike,
but the fear triggered by the drills could stay with children for life.

We girls were told by the Carmelite nuns ... that we were to
manage this lifesaving maneuver [of Duck and Cover] while
ensuring our panties never showed from under our plaid uniform
jumpers. Because, I suppose, modesty is paramount, even as one
is being vaporized. The threat of nuclear annihilation was just as
real to me as was the likelihood of meeting Satan around every
corner. ... I spent a lot of time and energy ... worrying about
my sudden doom, whether spiritual or physical, or both.

The paradigm of existential anxiety that the Cold War drills instilled
in a generation of Americans would remain with them. Many years
later, a nearby test firing of space shuttle engines produced a bang
and a rumble that reignited Amy Morris-Young's childhood terror.
By this time, the first generation of atomic weapons that had sent
Bert scurrying for cover had been superseded by devastating thermonuclear bombs, capable of turning entire cities to dust. Morris-Young
would have known that hiding was futile. But old habits die hard.

I ... looked down and saw [daughter] Chelsea's baby seat
trembling slowly across the vinyl floor. My hands shook as I
unbuckled the plastic clasp of her tiny seat belt, scooped her

out of her chair, crushed her to my chest and ran straight for the closet in my bedroom. How ludicrous is it that in that horrible moment, when I knew that it had finally happened, that an atomic bomb had been dropped on us and it was the end of the world, all I could think of was Bert the Turtle? Dum dum deedle dum dum … I crouched on the floor of the closet, holding my tiny girl, rocking and praying … saying, over and over and over: 'I'm sorry. I'm so sorry.' Because I was. So sorry. So ashamed that … we grown-ups, time after time, throughout history, seemed to have done such a poor job of taking care of each other, and the earth. We couldn't seem to stop hurting each other, playing war games with real casualties, and now it was too late.[2]

The psychological impact of governmental preparations for war differed from country to country. The Strath Report, commissioned in utmost secrecy by the British government in late 1954, had concluded that 'the hydrogen bomb presents problems of a revolutionary character for the defence of this country and a threat of the utmost gravity to our survival as a nation'.[3]

> The entire nation would be in the front line. Failure to provide adequate protection against radio-activity from fall-out would be disastrous. To remain in the open during fall-out would be suicidal in an area of 1,000 square miles for each bomb … The public should be thoroughly instructed in peacetime on the effects of hydrogen bombing and on the precautions necessary to minimise casualties.[4]

The report's author, Sir William Strath, recommended the building of shelters to protect the population from at least some of the dangers of radioactive fallout. He urged governmental transparency, including an open public discussion of the effects of nuclear war and the way society could best respond to them. Both recommendations were ignored. The Strath Report was classified and remained unpublished until 2002. The government baulked at the cost of shelter-building and shied away from the risks involved in a frank public information campaign. Instead, it embarked on an exercise of psychological manipulation designed to suppress discussion of thermonuclear weapons and of the limitations of civil defence, encouraging citizens instead to buy their own nuclear bunkers or simply to designate a 'fallout room' in their homes. It was a deliberate choice, made in the knowledge of the potential consequences. 'The objective,' wrote the minister of defence, Selwyn Lloyd, 'should be to limit the level of expenditure on home defence to the minimum needed to maintain public confidence.'[5]

Maintaining public confidence meant keeping people in the dark. The Strath Report's stark depiction of a Britain where half the population would die and the other half struggle on in a devastated land beset by the breakdown of civil society was considered unhelpful.[6] The government appeared to fear panic almost as much as war, and Britain had recent first-hand experience of its effects. The horrors of the Blitz had been partially concealed by an insistence on the British stiff upper lip, but the government remained concerned about the psychological damage to the population. The psychoanalyst Edward Glover had been tasked with assessing the extent of mental suffering and potential 'psychic casualties'.

> The whole atmosphere of modern war is likely to revive those unreasoning fears that the human race has inherited from its remotest ancestors; gas masks that make us look like strange animals; underground shelters; enemies overhead and unseen; wailing sirens; screaming air bombs ... Small wonder, then, that we are afraid lest in the face of a real danger our first impulse should be to behave like little children ... We are afraid of being afraid.[7]

Glover's warning of mental collapse coloured the government's thinking. The Joint Intelligence Committee (JIC) conceded that the next war would be infinitely more terrible than the Blitz. 'The Russians will regard the UK as such a threat,' wrote the JIC in 1955, 'that they will aim to render it unusable for a long period, and will not hesitate to destroy large parts of the UK to achieve this aim.'[8] But that was not the message the government wanted communicated to the people. With public fear needing to be managed and controlled, they revived a tool from the past:

> In the UK, the Civil Defence Service, disbanded at the end of the war, was revived as the Civil Defence Corps. Recruitment

advertisements were placed in national newspapers, emphasising the importance of the task at hand: 'In the H-bomb age ...
Civil Defence is part of our essential national preparedness.'[9]

'Civil Defence is Common Sense' was the snappy slogan. Recruits
would receive training that would enable them to live with the bomb.
'Learn to live with your eyes open in the same world as the H-bomb',
said the brochures.

The peace movement dismissed these measures as a ruse to
desensitise the population to the threat of war. If citizens were conditioned to believe that nuclear fallout could simply be washed off their
houses using a garden hose, or their fruit and veg decontaminated by
removing the skin, they were less likely to oppose their government's
participation in the arms race. It was, they said, a psychological con.

Washington, too, was concerned about the emotional stability
and moral self-control of the American people in the face of the
nuclear threat. In April 1953, the Federal Civil Defense Administration
(FCDA) compiled a thirty-four-page analysis, 'Civil Defense Implications of the Psychological Impact and Morale Effect of Attacks on
the People of the United States'. It concluded that the success of an
enemy attack depended not only on its destruction of the American
economy, but also – crucially – on the degradation of the nation's psychological equilibrium. The authors studied the range of reactions
that psychologists would expect among survivors of a nuclear attack
and arrived at some disturbing results.

The extreme stress of an attack, said the FCDA report, would
tip some people into irrational and dangerous behaviour, responding
with random acts of violence against convenient scapegoats at home,
in place of the absent enemy. Ethnic minorities were the likeliest
targets, the report claimed. Such violence risked setting off a chain
reaction of 'extraordinary flights of inappropriate behaviour'.[10]

Others would attempt to escape from the horror they found
themselves in by retreating into an inner fantasy world, denying the
reality of what had happened and becoming incapable of taking the
necessary steps to survive. A severe outbreak of violence and apathy
could trigger 'social chaos', achieving what the FCDA viewed as the
enemy's key aim of 'break[ing] our will to resist and to fight back'.

The despairing population would become easy prey to sects,
visionaries and fake prophets 'promising salvation from nuclear

terror' in mystical worlds beyond the horizon. In such conditions, Soviet psychological warfare would be impossible to resist, weakening American morale to the point of total surrender. 'The serious potentialities of panic, demoralisation and national paralysis,' the FCDA concluded, 'may suddenly be converted into actualities.'[11]

Frederick Peterson, the FCDA's administrator under Eisenhower, declared that panic was the greatest threat facing America.[12] Despite being citizens of the most powerful nation on earth, he wrote, Americans were also the most panic-prone; and panic was the psychological weakness at the heart of the nation's security.

> What will you do if one day an atomic bomb blasts your town? Will you take calm emergency action – or will you dash screaming into the ruined streets, a victim of your own horror? In a war, the whole country's survival could depend on your reaction to disaster ... because mass panic may be far more devastating than the bomb itself. We must not let uncontrolled fear conquer us in an emergency ... Like the A-bomb, panic is fissionable. ... Mass panic – not the A-bomb – may well be the easiest way [for the Soviets] to win a battle, the cheapest way to win a war.[13]

In 1950s America there was a distinct, probably deliberate, lack of public information about the physical effects of the bomb or what might happen in the event of an attack. Instead of alarming people about what lay in store, the authorities lectured them on how they should behave. There were, said the New York Board of Education, 'three Rs: Rights, Respects, and Responsibilities' that children should be taught to follow. 'The child should know what to do in school, at home, in the street, or in the playground. He should be trained in self-reliance, imbued with faith in his ability to survive, no matter what the danger.'[14]

Millions of copies of *You and the Atomic Bomb* were produced, distributed 'In the Interest of Human Welfare', telling people, 'What to do in case of an atomic attack'. Letters were sent to all homes, quoting reassuring comments from 'competent experts in the atomic field', aiming at bolstering public resolve. 'As devastating as the atomic bomb is,' a leaflet distributed in Los Angeles declared, 'there is no evidence to justify a feeling of hopelessness in the event of such a bombing.'[15] The claims were misleading; their purpose transparent.

The eminent British Freudian psychoanalyst and veteran of the First World War, Wilfred Bion, described the experience of coping with the constant fear of attack as a 'true war of nerves ... the opposite of a psychotherapeutic procedure'. Because the individual experiences personal anxiety of such unremitting intensity and duration, he is in danger of becoming detached from the aims and principles of his society. Once this happens, he becomes a 'casualty', his value to society neutralised by the enemy's might.

> The 'war of nerves' is an attack directed at the individual personally; if he can dissociate himself from the mass movement of a nation at war he may escape some of the effects. But then, from the point of view of an enemy, he has become a casualty. Or he can remain a member of his society; in which case, the more emotionally bound the members are, the more strongly will he feel that the attack is being launched at himself. Only if he remains at once both a member of his community and yet unaffected by the enemy's attack ... can he be said to remain psychologically not a casualty.[16]

To stiffen public resolve the FCDA felt it must 'sell' civil defence on a 'calm, long-range, common sense basis', making it 'a permanent part of our way of life in an atomic age'. In a letter of 27 February 1953, J. M. Chambers of the FCDA described the campaign as 'an issue of practical mass psychology ... an action programme' that was necessary because 'not enough people as yet visualize civil defense as something which intimately affects them as individuals, and in their families and communities'.[17] People, said Chambers, must be persuaded 'to learn to live with the bomb' and the psychological levers to get them to do so would be through appeals to patriotism, to enlightened self-interest and a rationally controlled fear of nuclear war.[18]

In retrospect, it is evident that the authorities' efforts to maintain public calm resulted in considerable mendacity. The perceived need to prevent panic was advanced as justification for obfuscation and, at times, downright lies. Irving Janis, a psychologist who would later become famous for his ground-breaking concept of 'groupthink', was at the time employed by the RAND Corporation. Asked to elaborate a psychological strategy to minimise public panic, Janis proposed that the authorities allow a certain level of openness, both about the effects of nuclear attack and about the limitations of civil defence. Drawing on the experiences of survivors of Hiroshima and Nagasaki, Janis warned that a close escape from such a destructive attack can 'have the effect of temporarily shattering the individual's psychological defences ... There will probably be a sizable minority who will not recover promptly from the harrowing, traumatic experience of the disaster. Such persons will not be capable of productive work and will have a demoralizing effect upon others in the community.'[19] In part, Janis said, the high level of 'psychological casualties' in Japan may have resulted from mental unpreparedness: people felt hopelessly overwhelmed by a phenomenon for which nobody had attempted to ready them. But if the public were allowed to have 'realistic expectations' about their prospects for survival, he suggested, they would be able more readily to combat 'feelings of helplessness'. By deploying 'emotional-training techniques that build up a tolerance for insecurity', civil defence would be a way of 'channclizing' apprehensions about nuclear attack in order to minimise 'disruptive fear reactions'. The 'emotional inoculation' against panic could not be total, but this in itself need not be a disadvantage, as 'a slight dose of insecurity often serves as a powerful motivation for participating in group activities which are designed to ward off the danger'.[20]

Janis claimed that even the lack of public shelters could be turned to psychological advantage. By encouraging people to build their own domestic shelters you could at once lessen any resentment towards central government's lack of action and imbue the individual with a sense of control over his or her chances of survival.[21]

It is evident that the real objective of the programme is not security, but the illusion of security. 'Even though surprise attacks may preclude their usefulness for some people,' Janis concludes, 'shelters will probably be psychologically advantageous' because 'non-rational factors' would endow domestic shelters with 'considerable symbolic value' in reducing anxiety.[22] As it happens, Americans took to the idea of building their own shelters with considerable enthusiasm. A thriving market grew up, with products ranging from a '$13.50 foxhole shelter' to a $5,000 deluxe model equipped with a phone, beds, toilets and a Geiger counter. A headline in *Life* magazine declared that 'Fallout Can Be Fun', making much play of a young couple who held a romantic honeymoon in their own nuclear bunker.[23]

'Survival Under Atomic Attack', Department of Civil Defense, City of Boston, Official US Government Booklet, 1951.

If the idea of a society learning to love the bomb to the extent of it becoming an accessory to fun and romance now seems grotesque, it was in part a function of the lack of popular understanding that surrounded the likely effects of a nuclear strike. Janis's suggestion of an honest discussion of the impact of a nuclear attack was largely rejected. In official government communications, the physical and psychological threat of the bomb was downplayed. *Survival Under Atomic Attack*, a booklet published by the Executive Office of the President in 1950, portrayed nuclear weapons as little more than slightly bigger conventional bombs with a touch more radioactivity, 'the only way besides size in which atomic bombs differ from ordinary ones'. The implication was that this was a quantitative increase in an already familiar weapon, rather than something qualitatively different and altogether more horrifying.

You Can SURVIVE!
You can live through an atom bomb raid and you

won't have to have a Geiger counter, protective
clothing, or special training in order to do it.
The secrets of survival are:
KNOW THE BOMB'S TRUE DANGERS.
KNOW THE STEPS YOU CAN TAKE TO ESCAPE THEM.[24]

Five years later, in *Facts about Fallout*, a public information film produced by the Office of Civil Defense, the reassuring narrator cheerily
recommends that houses exposed to nuclear fallout can be sprayed
down with a hose and the entire family should 'shower thoroughly'.[25]
'Dangerous radioactive fallout is like dust and can be removed like
dust,' says the commentary. 'If necessary you could drink water
containing fallout particles without worry or immediate harm. The
chances are you wouldn't have to for long. Water helps to wash itself
through the natural process of sedimentation.'[26] All of this would
go on in an orderly fashion, the film implies, with services such as
electricity and water continuing to function. The unspoken message
is that if panic and despair can be avoided, American society would
survive unharmed.

Civil defence was as much about managing emotions as it was
about saving lives. By engaging people in the common cause of the
nation, by persuading them that their efforts could make a difference,
or simply by giving them something to do rather than leaving them
to think, brood and despair, the authorities hoped to limit defeatism
– even if few truly believed in the actions being taken.

Wilfred Bion, writing during the Second World War, spoke of 'the
simple act of having to buckle on a belt and equipment before standing to arms' being enough in itself to instil confidence and boost the
perception of self-worth 'even when the objective situation appeared
desperate and the enemy commenced an attack'. For the most part
these measures were effective in keeping people sane.[27] Only when
the ineluctable realities of nuclear destruction began to dawn and the
soothing reassurances of official propaganda were exposed as baseless did people start to question the value of *any* action in the face of
Armageddon. John Hunter, a civil defence volunteer from Yorkshire,
was initially enthusiastic about his training as an emergency medic,
treating casualties of a nuclear strike.

We'd go right through from arriving at the scene to rescuing

them, treating them, giving first aid, removing them to casualty centres and then they'd be categorised and moved on, either
dead or needing further treatment ... I think we all thought
that we were going to save the world, initially. After some time
and watching films and seeing the increase of the power of the
bombers as the years went on, we realised there'd be nobody
surviving and these civil defence exercises were no good at all –
'cause we'd all be dead![28]

The Soviets, too, were concerned with civil defence. Like the rest
of the world, they were planning for the worst and hoping for the
best. There was a perception in Washington that Soviet preparations
were more advanced and more sophisticated than those of the USA.
American analysts reported that Moscow had spent the equivalent
of $20 billion on civil defence,[29] with the centralised nature of the
state allowing for better training, distribution of tasks and discipline.
Washington estimated that Soviet adults underwent training sessions
totalling sixty-four hours of instruction and that nuclear shelters were
at an advanced stage of construction.[30]

The opinions and to some extent the mood of the Soviet people
were easier to mould for an autocratic state that controlled the
sources of public information, but scepticism and fear existed in the
USSR just as they did in the West. The Russian historian Vladislav
Zubok recalled being at school in the Soviet Union and learning 'ludicrous survival skills' in civil defence classes, feeling 'very skeptical of
gas masks and bomb shelters', suspecting that gases would 'somehow
penetrate the clumsy masks and that we would be buried alive in the
so-called safe havens in the basements of our apartment houses'.[31]

The reality was that Soviet civil defence preparations were almost
as chimerical as those of the West, going through the motions in part
to bolster public confidence, but lacking in substance and unlikely to
change much in the event of a nuclear conflict. The man in charge
of civil defence, the deputy defence minister General Alexander
Altunin, was realistic about the prospects in his (confidential) 1976
annual report. '[Training] took place after a delay, and at times at a
low methodological level. Many people assembled for such sessions
and were led through the various points of a demonstration exercise,
but the trainees did not receive what was necessary. The practical
portion was poorly organised and in a stereotyped manner.'[32] General

Valentin Larionov, who had served with distinction in the Red Army's European campaigns in the Second World War, spoke many years later about the attitude of the Soviet leadership. Like their counterparts in the West, they too knew that a show of preparedness was more important for public morale than for any practical impact it might have. 'The [Soviet] leaders were guided by the idea that as there might not be a nuclear war,' he told a western documentary crew, 'why spend money that we were so short of? On the other hand, if there was a war, civil defence wouldn't help. It was a very sensible, purely pragmatic attitude.'[33]

There was, however, a more concerted effort to construct public fallout shelters in the USSR. Large collective bunkers were built on the outskirts of the big cities, but not in smaller towns. The upshot was that evacuation to distant shelters would involve complex logistical arrangements in the event of an attack. The authorities did their best to prepare people for this, appealing to the Soviet collective spirit of communal effort, self-help and calm cooperation.

A journalist friend of mine discovered a poignant relic of that campaign in a bombed-out building in the Chechen capital, Grozny, while covering the war there in 1996. The set of six public information billboards (pictured overleaf), still attached to the walls all those years later, laid out the procedures to follow in the event of an American nuclear strike. They have a rather pathetic air to them, with grim, determined faces striving to express the courage and calm resolution that the authorities deemed necessary for the task.

The US Castle Bravo test at Bikini Atoll in March 1954 had proved the hydrogen bomb to be a deployable weapon, but it also alerted the world to its dangers. Rather than the expected 5-megaton yield, the bomb had released a massive 14.8 megatons, to this day the largest American nuclear test. Civilians 300 miles away, supposedly far outside the danger zone, were exposed to fallout. The crew of a Japanese fishing vessel experienced severe radiation sickness and one of them, Aikichi Kuboyama, later died in hospital. His last words were, 'I pray that I am the last victim of an atomic or hydrogen bomb.'[34]

Castle Bravo changed attitudes on both sides of the Iron Curtain. The Harwell scientist Greg Marley later recalled the 'stunned expressions around him when he presented a detailed scientific appraisal of the damage and loss of life after a hypothetical H-bomb attack on Britain's major cities'.[35] Philip Allen, the Home Office under-secretary

The possibility of a calm, ordered evacuation in case of nuclear attack was pitched to a largely disbelieving Soviet audience.

responsible for civil defence, admitted that the unimaginably greater destructive power of thermonuclear weapons made all preparations close to redundant.

> I can remember sitting on a committee working out the horrors of the H-bomb as distinct from the much more modest A-bomb. And, although it seemed like Never-Never Land at the time, we did work out these theoretical methods of keeping on the government setting up organizations. One had a feeling that, if it came to it, nothing would quite work out the way one was planning. But, nevertheless, one simply had to plan.[36]

The distance between man's ability to wreak global destruction and his powerlessness to mitigate its effects was now greater than ever.

Even the Soviet authorities accepted their much-vaunted kitchens
would not withstand an American nuclear strike.

The German philosopher Günther Anders called it the Promethean
Gap. Having stolen fire from the gods, mankind was realising the
torment its possession entails and the damage that such knowledge
can wreak on the human psyche. Unable to sublimate the consciousness of the unprecedented potential for violence, humans were falling
into despair or becoming inverted utopians. The mind, overwhelmed,
tends to shield itself by looking away, avoiding thought or succumbing to the magic thinking of hope against hope.[37]

In the face of societal denial, voices were raised seeking to hold
up the truth in ways people could not dismiss. Television proved the
weapon of choice. It was the medium from which the public was
least likely to turn away and it furnished some powerful messages.
Research by the behavioural psychologists Amos Tversky and Daniel
Kahneman has shown that we find it 'easier to picture an event

occurring if we think it is likely to happen', and what could bring an
event to life more vividly than a realistic depiction of it on millions of
TV screens?[38] While cinema had traditionally represented an escape
from real life, the viewer sitting in an unfamiliar darkened room
where the fantastic is made visible, television brought the reality of
the outside world into the once safe space of people's homes. Governments recognised its power and were understandably keen to
influence or control it, especially when its subject was the potential
annihilation of the nation under their watch. But, in the West at least,
their control was not absolute.

In 1965, the young British filmmaker Peter Watkins set out to
make a docudrama for the BBC. Its title would be *The War Game*.
Watkins would draw on evidence from Hiroshima and information
gleaned from government publications and nuclear scientists, with
the aim of revealing to the British public what the aftermath of a
nuclear attack would look like. Using mainly amateur actors, the film
included scenes of destruction, children being blinded by the flash
of the bomb, food riots, summary executions of looters and mercy
killings for radiation sufferers. Interspersed between the harrowing
cinéma-vérité were statements from government and other establishment figures explaining the need for ever more powerful bombs.

The Home Office refused to cooperate with Watkins, and civil
defence organisations were instructed to refuse his requests for information, though many are rumoured later to have used the film for
training.

The BBC had initially been supportive. 'So long as ... the facts are
authentic,' a spokesman had affirmed prior to filming, 'the people
should be trusted with the truth. There are views at experienced
levels that since nothing can be done to save Britain from annihilation, it is better not to portray such probable occurrences or to give
frightening facts ... The film is bound to be horrifying and unpopular
... but surely necessary.'[39]

The War Game was completed in the autumn of 1965, but before
it could be broadcast there were discussions in high places. On 24
November, the BBC issued another statement.

The BBC has decided that it will not broadcast *The War Game*
... This is the BBC's own decision ... taken after a good deal of
thought and discussion but not as a result of outside pressure of

any kind ... The effect of the film has been judged by the BBC
to be too horrifying for the medium of broadcasting.[40]

The War Game would not be shown on British television for another
twenty years. Despite the BBC's protestations to the contrary, outside
pressure had indeed been applied. Lord Normanbrook, the then
chairman of the BBC governors, had previously been cabinet secretary, a role in which he had been responsible for home defence related
to nuclear weapons policy. Normanbrook had taken the decision to
show the film to government officials, writing to his successor in the
Cabinet Office, Sir Burke Trend: 'The film is not intended as propaganda, it is intended as a purely factual statement and it is based
on careful research into official material ... [But] the showing of the
film on television might well have a significant effect on public attitudes towards the policy of the nuclear deterrent.'[41] Normanbrook's
caution would be supported by later studies showing that the more
people reflected on the issues surrounding nuclear war, the more
likely they were to engage in anti-nuclear activities.[42]

Having decided that the truth would be too big a burden for
the fragile national psyche, Trend wrote to Herbert Bowden, lord
president of the council: 'The difficulty, for the BBC no less than for
the Government, is to think of some reason for suppressing the film
which would not stir up controversy or provoke suspicion that it was
motivated by political prejudice.'[43] Shortly after, Lord Normanbrook
wrote to the BBC's liberal-minded and slightly incredulous director
general, Hugh Greene, saying 'Whitehall will be relieved if we do
not show it.'

The British press largely supported the decision to pull the film,
but Kenneth Tynan in the *Observer* excoriated the official BBC line,
expressing incredulity at the corporation's claim that the film should
not be shown as 'children, the very old, or the unbalanced in the audience might be seriously disturbed'.[44]

The War Game stirred me at a deeper level than panic or grief.
So long as adequate warning is given to depressives ... it should
not only be televised but screened in cinemas, not just here
but everywhere on earth, especially in countries that possess
(or would like to possess) the bomb. The BBC is like a doctor
withholding the truth from a patient who is suffering from a

potentially fatal disease; silence may preclude panic, but it also precludes cure.[45]

In 1984, the BBC tried again. *Threads*, written by Barry Hines, was a lower-budget but grittier, even more realistic depiction of how an atomic strike and the nuclear winter that would follow might sever the ties that hold a society together. Its stark images of burning cats, melting milk bottles and wild-eyed desperate mothers cradling dead babies in their arms, shocked the nation. *Threads* came at a time when Washington was shifting its nuclear stance from the wary stasis of Mutually Assured Destruction to the destabilising assertion that the US could win a nuclear war, and the film struck a chord. Its director, Mick Jackson, said his aim was to confront the viewer with the reality that the world could be irreversibly changed in a matter of minutes. His explanation of why it was important to do so echoed Tversky and Kahneman's work on the relation between the ease with which an image of an event is visualised and the acceptance of its probability of occurrence.[46] 'It seemed that people weren't able to visualise the unthinkable,' Jackson wrote, 'especially politicians. So I thought that if I acted this out for them as a television drama – not as a spectacle or disaster movie – that would give them a workable visual vocabulary.'[47]

The controversy over *The War Game* and *Threads* helped re-energise opposition to nuclear weapons and gave fresh ammunition to protestors. The peace movement itself, though, was not new. Some of its earliest leaders in the months following Hiroshima and Nagasaki had been the very physicists whose work had facilitated the development of the bomb. The newly founded *Bulletin of the Atomic Scientists* and the admonitory Doomsday Clock were part of their attempts to change the world's thinking. The Manhattan Project veteran Eugene Rabinowitch remembered how 'in the summer of 1945, some of us walked the streets of Chicago vividly imagining the sky suddenly lit by a giant fireball, the steel skeletons of skyscrapers bending into grotesque shapes and their masonry raining into the streets below, until a great cloud of dust arose and settled over the crumbling city … From this vision arose the weak and inadequate attempts that groups of scientists made to stop the hands of the clock before it struck the first hour of the atomic age.'[48]

The prospects for the peace movement did not look promising, and they were up against powerful forces. On 28 November 1951, the authorities in New York City carried out America's largest ever civil defence drill, with 12,000 police officers and 300,000 volunteers testing emergency procedures. Schools, offices and even the stock exchange were evacuated. The streets emptied as New Yorkers followed instructions to take shelter in basements and the subway. The small number of peace campaigners who refused to take part were detained by the police.

But the peaceniks had some things on their side. The sense of community that grows from a common purpose expressed in opposition to overwhelming odds drew them close. Shared values and the comradeship of adversity forged strong bonds. Humour helped. In place of duck and cover, they proposed their own slogan for civil defence: 'Bend over. Put your head between your legs, and kiss your ass goodbye.'[49]

In Britain, the campaign drew together people from different walks of life, bridging boundaries of class, age, politics and ethnicity in a society traditionally divided along those lines. Sally Doganis was one of the 4,000 people to participate in the first march to the Atomic Weapons Research Establishment in Aldermaston in 1958. The march, which would later become an annual event attracting hundreds of thousands, thrived on its spirit of shared idealism, common aims and beliefs.

> We felt we united everyone under our banner, that it avoided party divisions, that it avoided class and age divisions. And here we were for the first time, a united country behind one very simple idea and it was a wonderful feeling of excitement, and of a better world. I don't remember feeling it was particularly radical, it was just something exciting and new that everyone had to believe in because it was so obviously right.[50]

The philosopher Bertrand Russell, one of the early proponents of the Campaign for Nuclear Disarmament (CND), identified the psychological underpinnings of the nascent peace movement as a crucial factor in the survival of the human race. 'Whether science and indeed civilization in general can long survive depends upon psychology. That is to say, it depends upon what human beings desire.'[51] Speaking on the BBC in 1954, he asked if humans were 'so destitute of wisdom, so incapable of impartial love, so blind even to the simplest dictates of

self-preservation' that they could willingly carry out 'the extermination of all life on our planet'. 'War does not determine who is right,'
Russell concluded, 'only who is left.' There needed to be 'a way of
making the world understand the dangers into which it was running
blindly, head-on'.[52]

Counterintuitively, though, 'making the world understand the
dangers into which it was running' was not as simple as demonstrating the graphic consequences of nuclear war. The American social
psychologist, Rensis Likert, whose eponymous Likert Scale was developed to gauge people's perception of international affairs, argued
that individuals could be made so fearful of 'supernatural' atomic
forces that they would simply 'hide [their] heads in the sand'.[53] More
recently, Seymour Feshbach carried out research on the use of fear as
a tool of persuasion and reached a similar conclusion: '[In] attempting to persuade people to adopt a particular peace-oriented policy by
stressing and detailing the horrible consequences of a nuclear war if
such a policy is not pursued, we run the risk of provoking defensive
reactions, including subsequent avoidance of the topic and of our
policy recommendations.'[54]

Robert Lifton, who as a young man served as a US Air Force
psychiatrist in Japan and Korea before becoming active in the peace
movement, devoted much of his career to studying the psychological
causes of wars and political violence. His examination of the mental
impact of the Hiroshima and Nagasaki bombings on those who survived identified a phenomenon which he and others labelled 'psychic
numbing', 'a necessary defense mechanism, since they could not have
experienced full emotions in response to such scenes and remained
sane'.[55]

Lifton found that survivors of Hiroshima reported a cessation of
human feelings, saying such things as 'I simply became insensitive to
human death' or referring to a 'paralysis of the mind'.[56] The ability
to feel emotion gradually returned as they were given medical treatment. As the shock of the bombs receded, their testimonies began to
carry weight in the anti-nuclear movement. One survivor described
American and Soviet testing of nuclear weapons as 'utterly absurd.
Both countries seem to be playing a sort of game, because they didn't
grasp its terror.'[57] Another ascribed the pursuit of nuclear weaponry
to international madness. 'I know the scale of the Hiroshima bomb
but those recent tests were bombs of a much larger scale … With

such bombs ... there might not be anybody left in the world in the future ... the thought occurs to me that they must be mad.' And a third pointed out that only those who had suffered the effects of a nuclear strike could truly comprehend the danger; those supporting nuclear proliferation were deliberately blinding themselves to the reality of what they were enabling.[58]

Lifton himself made explicit the comparison between the psychic numbing of the Japanese survivors and the mental processes taking place in the minds of those who were now building, testing or advocating the use of nuclear weapons. 'Potential perpetrators,' Lifton wrote, 'simply cannot afford to imagine what really happens to people at the other end of the weapon.'[59]

The effect of America's pervasive nuclear anxiety, coupled with society's mental contortions in refusing to address the realities of nuclear danger, impacted particularly vividly on the minds of children. The child psychiatrist Carlos Salguero warned that young Americans were being damaged by their parents' refusal to talk openly and honestly about the nuclear danger. It was, he said, an 'existential absurdity ... like a family secret regarding which, because of our own denial, children are not allowed to ask, to know, to speak up, [and can't] learn coping behaviors to change fear into hope, death into life, passivity into activity.'[60] When 350 children and young teenagers were asked in 1960 to imagine the world in ten years' time, 70 per cent of them brought up the bomb. Sibylle Escalona, who specialised in the psychology of individuality and individual differences, identified a tendency towards helplessness and passivity – 'a sense of powerlessness and cynical resignation' – among the young generation.[61] A study sponsored by the US Institute of Medicine suggested that the source of such troubled thinking lay in the lack of certainty and information provided to young children about the likely effect of a nuclear war.[62]

The testimony of parents concerned about the effect on their children's mental well-being tended to confirm the hypothesis that it was fear of an unknown, and therefore limitless, danger that lay at the root of the child's mental anguish. Some parents attempted to remedy the perception of helplessness by demonstrating that the individual need not lack agency. On the contrary, the child could take positive action; the locus of control – responsibility for one's own destiny – was internal, not at the mercy of an ill-defined and insuperable external threat. 'On a number of occasions,' Eva Hanhardt told the *The New York Times* in 1982, 'my 6-year-old has said, "There is going to be a war and we'll be killed." I tell her it's not inevitable, that people can do something … I've taken the children to demonstrations. They see other people there and feel that their presence is helping, too.'[63]

By the end of the 1950s, as many as 60 per cent of American children had nightmares about the prospect of nuclear war.[64] One of them was Jim Carroll, later to become a poet and punk rocker. An entry in his teenage diary from 1965 summed up the nuclear dread he felt and his resentment of the adult world's reluctance to talk about the concerns that were tormenting their children.

> I used to have horrible dreams of goblins in tiny planes circling my room and bombing my bed most every night age six or seven; every time a fire truck or an ambulance passed the house I was pissing with fear in my mother's arms with the idea that it was the air raid finally come … The worst is the old buggers can't believe that it's real, that it could ever happen to us. Now there's a big peace move growing in this country and my old man and the rest are calling me a creep and saying it's all some Commie who brain-washed us all. [But] I think more about a fire truck passing at night than I do about Karl Marx when I'm out yelling for them to fuck your wars.[65]

Jim Carroll was not the only one who found that being part of the peace movement in 1960s America meant attracting abuse for 'being a communist'. An element of the authorities' policy of maintaining popular support for the development of nuclear weapons was to demonise communism and reduce the Soviet people to one-dimensional villains. Any expression of sympathy for the 'enemy' was viewed as subversive, in Britain almost as much as in the US. The emergence of the peace movement was itself attributed to the machinations of Red agitation, the Kremlin using its agents to stir up young, impressionable idealists, tricking them into doing Moscow's bidding. As late as 1972, the UK's Counter Subversion Committee was warning that, 'The objectives of Communist subversion are not merely to outflank the alliances of the West and to destroy Western influence amongst the developing nations, but to damage the West itself by confusing public opinion, lowering its morale and weakening its will to resist.'[66]

The paranoia endured for at least another decade. The British Home Office was horrified when, in 1983, the British Medical Association (BMA) questioned the official government position on what would occur in the event of a nuclear exchange. In their report 'The Medical Effects of Nuclear War', designed 'to give the reader an objective and scientific account of the medical consequences that would follow the explosion of nuclear weapons', the BMA's doctors estimated that tens of millions of Britons would die, far exceeding official Home Office figures. They dismissed civil defence preparations as 'failing to take account of the dreadful psychological shock that would certainly affect the survivors of a major nuclear attack'[67] and sounded a stark warning.

> We believe that (a 200Mt) nuclear attack would cause the medical services in the country to collapse. The provision of individual medical or nursing attention for victims of a nuclear attack would become remote. At some point it would disappear completely and only the most primitive first aid services might be available from a fellow survivor.[68]

The government's response was to try to suppress the report and to smear those who had compiled it. 'Clearly the BMA has swallowed hook, line and sinker the propaganda of the disarmament groups,' wrote the Home Office official J. A. Howard in an internal memo exploring how the doctors' claims might be discredited. 'The Government will need to say something in rebuttal ... for no other reason than that the Report is likely to have a seriously negative effect on civil defence attitudes within the National Health Service. Nor will it do us any good in our current task of introducing, defending and bringing into force the new civil defence regulations.'[69] Letters were dispatched to all regional scientific advisers in England and Wales, declaring that the BMA was imbued with 'a high degree of bias towards the CND case, and a lack of cogent arguments or analysis. The report ... cannot be regarded as an objective scientific document.'[70]

Unlike the thousands of peacenik teenagers smeared as communists, however, the BMA had the means and the public standing to fight back. Sir John Stallworthy, who had chaired the BMA working party and knew that the report was factually accurate, wrote to the Home Office threatening to publicise its 'infamous' behaviour.

The allegations are totally false. This is the last straw. I am not
a member of CND, I am not aware ... that any member of the
working party is a member of CND and we did not take any
evidence from CND.

I am deeply concerned about this. It is a most infamous way
of behaving to issue a letter like this. Before publication of this
report, I took out two pages of references to a discussion we
had with Home Office officials because it made them look like
a group of morons.[71]

The subsequent home secretary, Douglas Hurd, issued a formal
apology and Sir John withdrew his complaint.

The BMA were patently not agents of Moscow. Others, though,
were. The World Peace Council was a communist-backed organisation, and the British Communist Party was openly funded by Moscow.
It was perhaps not surprising that official suspicion extended to outfits
expressing divergent views. The CND fastidiously refused to accept
anonymous donations for fear of being accused of accepting money
from dubious sources, but were nonetheless widely accused of being
communist stooges, with their initials said to stand for 'Communist,
Neutralist, Defeatist'. CND's case was not helped by the actions of
Soviet intelligence agents in London, who liked to claim credit for
anything that made them look efficient. In 1982, Arkady Gouk, the
KGB section chief in London, boasted to Moscow that he was behind
a huge CND demonstration in Trafalgar Square. In reality, he had
had nothing to do with it, but Moscow liked to hear it and western
governments were willing to believe it.

Bruce Kent, CND's long-time general secretary, did not deny that
the Russians tried to influence them. '[But] it wasn't just the Russians.
We used to have the Americans coming round regularly, too, trying to
tell us the error of our ways. In fact, we had one situation where the
Russian arrived late and the American arrived early, and it would have
been incredibly embarrassing to have them bump into each other
in the lobby.'[72] Such was the alarm over Soviet fifth columnists that
a 1973 government circular titled 'Home Defence Planning Assumptions' prioritised securing 'the United Kingdom against any internal
threat' above mitigating 'the effects of any direct attack ... involving
the use of conventional nuclear, biological or chemical weapons'.[73]
By promoting unrealistic civil defence schemes, hiding the facts of

nuclear war from the public and responding to even reasoned criticism as the work of communist infiltrators, western governments appeared paranoid and disconnected from reality, undermining trust in democratic institutions. To that extent, the Kremlin might reasonably have concluded that its efforts were not in vain. In the war of nerves, the ever-present threat of nuclear annihilation put civilians on its front line, with nowhere to take cover.

23

DISINFORMATION

On 31 October 1986, *Pravda* carried a cartoon of a shifty-looking scientist and a grinning American military officer exchanging a test tube for a fistful of dollars. The vial is labelled 'AIDS virus' and is full of Swastika-shaped bacteria. The feet of dead bodies surround the two men. The implication is hardly subtle: the American fascists are at it again, murdering innocent people in their plot to dominate the world.[1]

Above the cartoon, readers would have noticed a brief explanation, labelled as a quote 'From newspapers': 'According to some western scientists, the virus of AIDS, a serious disease for which no cure has yet been found, was created in the laboratories of the Pentagon.' The first mention of what came to be known as *Operation Infektion* had appeared three years earlier in a pro-Soviet newspaper in India, claiming that American scientists had manufactured AIDS as part of their biological defence programme at Fort Detrick in Maryland. It was the opening shot in a campaign that would eventually see the story printed in more than thirty languages in the media of eighty countries, many of them citing 'scientific proof' from research carried out at Humboldt University in East Berlin, and some suggesting that the initial aim of the virus was to kill only people of African, Arab and Asian heritage. The US ambassador in Moscow, Arthur Hartman, denounced the cartoon as 'dreadful' and dismissed the allegations as 'nonsense'. But the story was out and, like the virus itself, would prove immensely hard to get rid of.

The effect of disinformation – what we would call fake news – is to create a climate of pervasive uncertainty, in which it seems no one can be trusted. The aim of Soviet disinformation in the Cold War years was to undermine the confidence of people in the West in the open nature of their 'free' society and in the probity of the men who

The suspicion that the Pentagon was behind the
AIDS virus remains in some quarters ...

ran it. Moscow sought out the potential weak points in a nation's psyche, applying pressure, hoping to speed its degradation. Tacitly, Washington acknowledged the importance of such methods. 'There are no rules in such a game,' concluded the Doolittle Report of 1954. 'Hitherto acceptable norms of human conduct do not apply.'[2]

The impact of fake news on the human mind is profound. The mind creates mental maps and finds it hard to redraw them once they are settled. Accepting the unreliability of a 'fact' on which others have subsequently been built throws the mind into intolerable doubt.[3] Perversely, the more unlikely an assimilated 'fact' might seem, the harder it is to dislodge. Conspiracy theories are psychologically appealing because their initially outlandish nature, once accepted, can provide an explanatory template for a huge amount of otherwise inexplicable or highly complex events. In the absence of the overarching theory, the mind would be forced to engage in an unsettling process of rethinking to explain each of them individually.[4]

Weak, disenfranchised individuals, or indeed nations, appear to be more likely to turn to conspiracy theories. It is comforting to be able to ascribe the troubles in their lives and the lack of control they have over their fate to a single outside factor that is not their responsibility and cannot be overcome by their own effort, relieving the individual of the (usually unavailing) effort of remedying them.[5] Soviet disinformation was particularly successful in societies in Latin America and Africa, caught between the Cold War demands of East and West, where pressure to conform fuelled suspicion of the Washington government. The African-American population of the US was similarly targeted. A 1953 assessment by the Psychological Warfare School at Fort Bragg reported that Moscow was deliberately inflaming the dissatisfaction and the demands of what they awkwardly termed 'non-whites' across the world. 'Soviet propagandists have capitalized on this unrest, stirring up hatreds and creating new ones.' The United States, said the report, was the 'principal victim' of such attacks.[6]

It is undoubtedly true that Soviet propaganda sought out sore points among 'non-white' populations and inflamed grievances through false rumours. The US response was to exaggerate its extent and effectiveness, attributing even genuine social dissatisfaction to subversive foreign forces. Just as the Kremlin blamed problems in Soviet society on western sabotage, so the West was obsessed with enemies in its ranks. It surfaced in Joseph McCarthy's witch-hunts, in the assertion that the peace movement was a Soviet front, and in the suggestion that the civil rights movement was an example of communist agitation turning African Americans against the government.[7] Such claims were wide of the mark, but all were evidence of the success of the Soviets in disturbing and disrupting, leaving people disoriented, uncertain of what was real. Disinformation did not need to persuade them to believe a story was true, merely to consider it. If they could be convinced that it, or something close to it, might actually be possible, they would already be conditioned to doubt what they heard and read from official sources. There would be a climate of public credulity, in which the population were willing to believe the worst of their government.

The very word 'disinformation' has an aura of deceit to it. Its first appearance, according to the *Oxford English Dictionary*, was in

Russian in 1949. But the Russian term 'dezinformatsiya' has a distinctly un-Russian sound to it. There have been suggestions that the word itself is a piece of disinformation, devised by Stalin's propagandists to make it sound French ('désinformation'),* thus creating the impression that the technique was an invention of the devious West. 'Propaganda' dates from an earlier time – Pope Gregory XV founded the *Propaganda Fide* in 1622 to propagate the Catholic faith – but in many ways, that is what the two sides in the Cold War were trying to do: convert the world to their political faith. Defined by the *OED* as 'information, especially of a biased or misleading nature, used to promote a political cause or point of view', propaganda aims to change the way a nation behaves by influencing the way its people think.[8] US analysts in the twentieth century would divide it into three types: white propaganda is any straightforward, attributed, attempt to promote a person or organisation by publishing positive information about them; grey, as its name indicates, is more opaque, with its source remaining unclear or disguised, and the veracity of the information supplied open to debate; black propaganda is pure disinformation – falsities designed to vilify or besmirch the reputation of an adversary, with the real source deliberately hidden.

Thanks to the testimony of Ladislav Bittman, we have an inside account of how the communist world disseminated black propaganda. Bittman was an intelligence agent in Czechoslovakia's state security service, the *Státní bezpečnost* or StB, who defected to the West in 1968. According to his description of the socialist intelligence services in his own country and in the USSR, disinformation was conceived as 'a carefully constructed false message leaked to an opponent's communication system in order to deceive the decision-making elite or the public'. To succeed, Bittman wrote, 'every disinformation message must at least partially correspond to reality or generally accepted views, [because] without a considerable degree of plausible, verifiable information, it is difficult to gain the victim's confidence.'[9]

---

* The *Oxford English Dictionary*, which defines disinformation as 'The dissemination of deliberately false information, esp. when supplied by a government or its agent to a foreign power or to the media, with the intention of influencing the policies or opinions of those who receive it; false information so supplied, cf. black propaganda', suggests that the first use of the term in French came five years after it had appeared in Russian (1949 versus 1954; and 1955 in English).

Bittman worked closely with the KGB's Department for Active Measures, created in 1959 to focus on black propaganda and disinformation. The KGB, Bittman testified, believed that 'the mass production of propaganda and disinformation over a period of several decades will have significant effect on the balance of power between the western Alliance and the Communist Bloc' by causing the 'internal demoralization and erosion of power in target countries'.[10]

> Our main objective was to note and dissect all the enemy's weaknesses and sensitive or vulnerable spots and to analyze his failures and mistakes in order to exploit them. The formulation of special operations might remind one of a doctor who, in treating the patient entrusted to his care, prolongs his illness and speeds him to an early grave instead of curing him.[11]

Bittman was personally involved in a number of black propaganda activities, the most remarkable of which was Operation Neptune in 1964. As a trained diver, he secured a role with a Czechoslovak TV company that was filming a documentary about Černé jezero, the 'Black Lake', on the Czech–German border. On one of his dives, Bittman reported that he had spotted four large, heavily corroded cases on the lake bed, with what appeared to be German lettering. When the cases were brought to the surface, they were found to be full of documents that the Czechoslovak authorities confirmed to be Nazi files, dumped in the lake at the end of the war. Among them was a list of Gestapo collaborators, including a number of people still active in West German politics and the intelligence services. The ensuing scandal saw accusing fingers pointed at senior figures in the West German establishment and helped influence Bonn's decision to extend the statute of limitation for prosecuting war crimes. Speaking after his defection, Bittman took great delight in revealing the ingenuity of the scheme.

> This was a unique opportunity to use it [diving] as a beginning of a major campaign against West Germany by declaring that Czechoslovak television discovered a number of big Nazi chests filled with original Nazi documents. That was the beginning. Later I came back with my team, with the boxes, and placed them at the bottom of the lake. And then a few days later I came

as a diver for the television and helped them to 'discover' these boxes.[12]

The files consisted of some genuine documents mixed in with many fakes. The files had long been in the possession of the Soviet and Czechoslovak authorities, who were waiting for the optimum time to release them to cause maximum embarrassment to the West. 'It was necessary,' said Bittman, 'to create a first-grade sensation to bring them to the attention of the public.'[13]

In his memoirs, Bittman claimed that the StB and KGB had carried out 'hundreds' of similar 'games against the United States'

> ... mainly in developing countries troubled with high unemployment, complicated social, linguistic, tribal, and economic problems, aggressive nationalism, influence of military officers on political affairs, and considerable naiveté among political leaders. Latin America, with strong anti-American sentiments, was particularly fertile and responsive to Eastern European provocations.[14]

The US, while professing shock at Bittman's revelations, was not averse to spreading its own disinformation. In the two decades following the end of the war, Latin America was a key battlefield in the clash between propagandists from either side of the Iron Curtain. The United States, regarding its southern neighbours as part of its own sphere of influence, had sought to remove more than one regime with which it had fallen out. The standard modus operandi involved the CIA spreading rumours of communist plots and Moscow-backed politicians in order to soften up public opinion, before covert operations led to the departure of the unwanted government.

In 1954, the democratically elected president of Guatemala, Jacobo Árbenz, had introduced a new code of workers' rights and begun to reform land ownership. It made him popular with Guatemalans, but very *un*popular with the US-owned United Fruit Company (UFCO), which controlled the main Atlantic ports and enjoyed close ties with a number of US politicians, including secretary of state John Foster Dulles. Unhappy with Árbenz's reforms, UFCO complained to Washington. Árbenz, the company reported, was a dangerous communist, seeking to align himself with Moscow. The former

US assistant secretary of state, Adolf Berle, backed UFCO's claims, writing that Guatemala was undergoing a 'clear-cut intervention by a foreign power, in this case the Soviet Union'.[15] When Árbenz assured the American ambassador to Guatemala, John Peurifoy, that he was not in fact a communist, the ambassador shrugged. 'If he is not a communist,' Peurifoy reported to Washington, 'then he will certainly do until one comes along ... normal approaches will not work in Guatemala.'[16]

With disinformation deployed to prepare the ground, Washington dispatched a CIA-backed force of exiled Guatemalan army officers to drive Árbenz's government from power. A psychological warfare campaign, using local press and radio, convinced the Guatemalan people of the futility of opposing the invasion. A radio station, the Voice of Liberation, was set up to broadcast fake news about the supposedly desperate situation in the country. *Reader's Digest*, *US News*, Hearst press, *Time* and *Life*, *Harper's*, *The Nation*, *The New York Times* and the *New York Herald Tribune* all published articles denouncing Árbenz and defending UFCO. *Harper's* called Árbenz's Guatemala 'a nation run by party-line Communists under Comintern supervision'.[17] With victory won, Dulles declared that 'patriots rose up in Guatemala to challenge the Communist leadership and to change it', while Eisenhower spoke of 'the people of Guatemala throwing off the yoke of Communism'. Writing many years later, Dean Acheson acknowledged Washington's use of disinformation.

> The task of a public officer seeking to explain and gain support for a major policy is not that of the writer of a doctoral thesis. Qualification must give way to simplicity of statement, nicety and nuance to bluntness, almost brutality, in carrying home a point. ... If we made our points clearer than truth, we did not differ from most other educators and could hardly do otherwise.[18]

Disinformation, though, was a two-way street. The Kremlin hit back at Washington's duplicity with its own black propaganda. When a military coup d'état overthrew the government of Brazil in April 1964, rumours circulated of US involvement. There was, though, little in the way of concrete proof, until a letter surfaced, allegedly from the director of the FBI, J. Edgar Hoover, to one of his agents.

Hoover's smug congratulations to 'Agent Brady' on his role in 'Operation Overhaul' seemed finally to prove Washington's guilt. But for a missive celebrating secrecy and discretion, its wording seemed rather less than subtle:

> Dear Mr Brady,
> I want to take this means to express my personal appreciation to each agent stationed in Brazil for the services rendered in the accomplishment of 'Overhaul'.
> Admiration for the dynamic and efficient manner in which this large scale operation was carried out, in a foreign land and under difficult conditions, has prompted me to express my gratitude ... I am especially pleased that our participation in the affair was kept secret and that the Administration did not have to make any public denials. We can all be proud of the vital parts the FBI is playing in protecting the security of the Nation, even beyond its borders.[19]

Careful readers of the 'Hoover' letter would not have failed to detect the fingerprints of the KGB. Moscow's decision to implicate the FBI in a foreign plot, however, seemed odd; the CIA would have been a more natural target. Once again, Bittman had the explanation: the Kremlin didn't have any samples of CIA stationery to write on, so it settled for the FBI letterheads that it had in its possession! In the months that followed, Soviet operatives posing as diplomats, journalists or trade representatives in western countries were instructed to do whatever it took to get hold of a letter from the CIA. The result was an upsurge in greetings and Christmas cards received by CIA officials, clearly hoping for signed replies on letterheaded stationery.[20]

US efforts seemed more formal. The Defense Department's Psychological Operations Divisions (PSYOP) produced field manuals that were updated annually, setting out the aims and techniques of psychological warfare. The manuals were classified, but it was recognised that they may become public, so their contents related largely to 'white' or 'grey' PSYOP, while 'black' operations were less well documented.

> PSYOP resources to operate in general, limited, and Cold war ...
> to influence people so that they will behave in a desired manner.

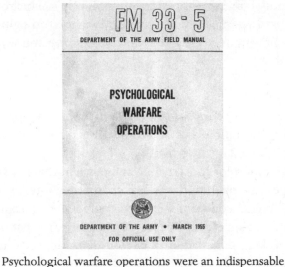

Psychological warfare operations were an indispensable
part of the Cold War arsenal.

> To influence the emotions, attitudes, or opinions of a target
> audience to achieve desired behavior at an appropriate time
> ... directed at large segments of the target nation's population
> using themes which exploit economic, military, psychological,
> and political vulnerabilities ... usually designed to reduce the
> effectiveness and internal control apparatus of the target govern-
> ment, defame the image of its leadership, destroy the military's
> will to fight, and exploit morale conditions which weaken the
> unity and strengths of the target country.[21]

A training film made by the American Army Pictorial Center in 1968
showed PSYOP in action.[22] US operatives in 'Hostland', a mythical,
vaguely Latin American country, are helping to protect 'this nation
seeking its own independent path to progress but stalled in its forward
march by a subversive force that grows more malignant with each
passing day ... a country in which outside forces have planted the seeds
of subversion.' In the campaign to counter communist destabilisation,
the PSYOP officer is seen using 'the tools which are essential to his job:
insight, a look into the minds of a people, a working knowledge of
their individual and group needs, attitude and ambitions'. Especially at
risk, says the film, are nations with a 'doubtful sense of national unity'.
Without US intervention, they are easy prey for communist agitation

and insurgence. PSYOP experts must encourage nation-building, making the individual citizen less vulnerable to outside influence. They must capture one mind, one heart, at a time, because:

> The 'average citizen' ... totals a billion, when added to all his counterparts all over the world. In the final analysis he will decide the future of the world. Because his importance is clearly recognised by forces that seek world domination, his mind has become a target. When he pledges his allegiance, when he decides in which direction he should pledge his loyalty, the issue in Hostland and many real countries in the world today will have been largely resolved. ... Who can say with certainty what he will decide, but given an effective, comprehensive Psychological Operations campaign as part of the background, we could logically make an optimistic forecast.[23]

In the absence of military confrontation, Washington and Moscow fought a murky, hidden war for hearts and minds that fostered anxiety and suspicion. From the earliest years of the Cold War, Washington and London had a tendency to overestimate the power and efficiency of the KGB. Writing in 1949, the British diplomat and later ambassador to the Soviet Union, William Hayter, reported that, 'Soviet policy in all parts of the world outside the Soviet orbit is to promote discord and confusion. Wherever civil or international disturbances arise, the malevolent purposes of the Kremlin are inferred to be at work.'[24]

There is less evidence about the Soviet equivalents of Washington's PSYOP manuals, but one that did surface, in 1989, recommended measures strikingly similar to those of the US.

> The conspiratorial promotion to the enemy of fabricated news, especially prepared materials and documents, so as to lead him into confusion and motivate him to decisions and actions that meet the interests of the Soviet state. Disinformation measures are undertaken to undermine the positions of imperialism in various countries of the world, increase the contradictions among imperialist states, bourgeois political parties and individual figures, to weaken their positions, counteract the unleashing of anti-Soviet campaigns and also for the purposes of influencing the outcome of negotiations.[25]

While the US and Britain feared Soviet subversion, the Kremlin was convinced that the USSR was the victim of disinformation from the West. Moscow's sense of victimisation, which continues in the twenty-first century, is based on the belief that the capitalist world is bent on undermining and holding back Russia's progress. While never achieving the same level of success as the KGB, the CIA certainly planted stories in the media of other countries, designed to discredit the Russians. During the Soviet occupation of Afghanistan in the 1980s, for instance, notices carrying the Soviet military seal would appear in newspapers across the Muslim world announcing, much to Moscow's embarrassment, 'Invasion Day celebrations' scheduled to take place at the local Soviet embassy.[26]

Historically, Britain has been a particular target of the Kremlin's suspicions. Soviet intelligence officials were convinced that the British were the unrivalled experts in psychological warfare, spreading false myths about Russia to undermine its morale. 'The palm of supremacy in the use of methods of black propaganda undoubtedly belongs to the English,' wrote Major General Rem Krasilnikov of KGB counter-intelligence.

> They are the masters of the art of political and moral discrediting, of disinformation, deception and slander ... The 'black' propaganda carried out by the English special services has contributed no small share to the creation of a negative, repulsive image of our country, beginning with autocratic Russia and ending with the contemporary Russian Federation. Her discrediting, irrespective of the form of rule existing in Russia, is the strategic aim of the ruler of Great Britain.*

In fact, the closed nature of Soviet society and the state's monopoly control of Soviet media made it considerably harder for Britain and

---

* It is perhaps worth adding that similar rhetoric was used by the Kremlin and its media outlets when they sought to dismiss accusations surrounding the poisonings of Alexander Litvinenko in London and the Skripals in Salisbury, viz. that they were an elaborate ruse concocted by British intelligence to besmirch Russia. J. Fedor, 'Chekists Look Back on the Cold War: The Polemical Literature', in Michael Herman and Gwilym Hughes (eds.), *Intelligence in the Cold War: What Difference did it Make?*, Abingdon: Routledge, 2013, p. 96.

the US to spread disinformation in Russia than it was for Soviet operatives to manipulate the free press of the West. In spring 1949, the Soviet Communist Party Central Committee's Department of Propaganda and Agitation (Agitprop) laid out a 'Plan for the Intensification of Anti-American Propaganda in the Near Future'.[27]

> To organise ... the systematic printing of material, articles and pamphlets exposing the aggressive plans of American imperialism, the anti-popular/inhumane character of the social and state order of the Unites States of America, debunking the fable of American propaganda about the 'prosperity' of America, revealing the deep contradictions of the American economic system, the deceitful nature of its bourgeois democracy, and the asininity of the culture and customs of America.[28]

Radio programmes, speeches, plays and public lectures criticising America were to be encouraged. The Central Committee listed the key themes to focus on.

> The capitalist monopolies in America that inspire the politics of aggression;
> NATO as a tool of Anglo-American imperialism;
> American ruling circles work to prohibit international understanding;
> American imperialists smothering the freedom and independence of people across the globe;
> Democracy in America – the hypocritical cover of all-powerful capital;
> USA – the country of ethnic and racial discrimination;
> The myth of high standards of living for all classes in America;
> The degeneration of culture in America;
> The propagation of amorality and brutal psychology in America.[29]

The overarching theme for the campaign was captured in a phrase that would characterise the official Soviet view of the capitalist world for many decades: *Zagnivayushchii Zapad*, the 'decaying, rotting West', was the term used to instil in the minds of the Soviet people that capitalism was falling apart.

An example of Kremlin black propaganda was the so-called 'Dulles Plan'. This was a lengthy document allegedly written by Allen Dulles in 1945 that surfaced towards the end of the Cold War. The 'Dulles Plan' appeared to lift the lid on the underhand dirty tricks deployed by Washington to help bring down the Soviet Union, providing copious details of a wide-ranging US government disinformation campaign, seemingly embarked upon as soon as the Second World War ended.

> We shall throw everything we have – all the gold, all the material might and resources into making the [Soviet] people into fools and idiots. It is possible to change the human brain, the consciousness of people. After sowing chaos there [in Russia], we shall imperceptibly replace their values by stealth with false ones ... Thus we shall find like-minded people, our own helpers and allies in Russia itself. Episode by episode, the tragedy will be played out, grandiose in scale, of the death of the most intractable people on Earth, of the definitive, irreversible dying out of its self-consciousness.[30]

The (fictional) 'Plan' revealed the West to be a malevolent, corrupting force, determined to undermine all that is good and valuable in Soviet society. The choice of Allen Dulles as its figurehead was no accident; he was a bogeyman for Khrushchev, and stories of his devilish plotting appeared regularly in the Soviet media, not least in the wildly popular spy drama *Seventeen Moments of Spring*.[31] The document attributes to Dulles the sort of intemperate fulminations that would arouse indignation and revulsion in Russian minds, positioning the USSR as the Cold War's good guys, assailed by the forces of evil.

> Literature, theatres, cinema – everything will depict and glorify the basest human emotions ... We shall support and raise so-called artists, who will begin to instill and drum into [Soviet] consciousness the cult of sex, violence, sadism, treachery – in a word ... immorality ... Honesty and decency will be mocked. Insolence, lies and deception, drunkenness and drug addiction, an animal fear of one another and shamelessness, treachery ... Nationalism and enmity of peoples, first and foremost enmity and hatred towards the Russian people – all of this we shall

cultivate deftly and imperceptibly, all this will blossom wildly ...
We shall debase and destroy the foundation of spiritual morality
... We shall corrupt, deprave, violate them.[32]

The document is full of inconsistencies. It is alleged to have origi-
nated in 1945, but Dulles did not become CIA director until 1953.
Entire sections of text have been lifted directly from a 1981 novel by
the Soviet author Anatoly Ivanov, while others are adapted from Dostoevsky's *The Demons*.* The fake 'Dulles Plan' nonetheless continues
to enjoy widespread credence in Russia, with Oscar-nominated filmmaker Nikita Mikhalkov declaring in 2012 that Vladimir Putin was
the only man capable of preventing the Plan's implementation.[33] It
has been cited in support of post-Soviet conspiracy theories naming
Mikhail Gorbachev and Eduard Shevardnadze as covert agents of
the West, dispatched to bring the Soviet Union to its knees. The fact
that significant parts of Russian society are willing to believe such
elaborate conspiracy theories helps the Kremlin to shrug off international criticism of its actions. Condemnation of its seizure of Crimea
or accusations surrounding the downing of the commercial airliner
MH17 by Russian-backed separatists in eastern Ukraine are explained
as further evidence of an orchestrated foreign disinformation campaign, designed to undermine the nation and marginalise Russia.

The longevity of the 'Dulles Plan' deception is not an isolated
case. The most enduring conspiracy theories are those that soothe
minds and mitigate personal blame for the failures of a society, in this
case the 'loss' of the Cold War. When Ullrich Ecker, a professor at the
School of Psychological Science of the University of Western Australia, conducted research into the psychology of misinformation,
he found how hard it is to correct them: if responsible authorities
ignore a story, it goes unchallenged and continues to circulate. But
denying a falsehood gives it further exposure, endowing it with a
subjective credibility comparable to the denials brought against it.

---

*Dostoevsky's anti-hero Pyotr Verkhovensky says, '... we'll make use of drunken-
ness, slander, spying; we'll make use of incredible corruption; we'll stifle every
genius in its infancy ... But one or two generations of vice are essential now; monstrous, abject vice by which a man is transformed into a loathsome, cruel, egoistic
reptile. That's what we need!' Fyodor Dostoevsky, *Demons*, translated by Constance
Garnett, London, 1913, extract from Part II, Chapter VIII: Ivan the Tsarevitch.

Misinformation continues to condition the way people remember events, their reasoning and their decision-making, even after false claims have been credibly corrected.[34]

Once a piece of information has been assimilated into the brain, it becomes hard to dislodge, especially if the correction takes a conventional form.[35] CBC News's rebuttal of the claims advanced by *Operation Infektion*, for instance, opened with a statement of the false allegations before explaining the caveats about them, with the overall effect of reinforcing rather than undermining their credibility. 'A Soviet military publication claims the virus that causes AIDS leaked from a US army laboratory conducting experiments in biological warfare. The article offers no hard evidence but claims to be reporting the conclusions of unnamed scientists in the United States, Britain and East Germany.'[36] The presentation of the false claim at the beginning of the news story colours all subsequent information. *Operation Infektion* is dignified by a national TV channel bestowing consideration on it, despite the report being about its unreliability. Like the best disinformation, *Operation Infektion* drew its legitimacy from being 'somewhat' credible. Those predisposed to believe it could point to similar cases of real misbehaviour in the US medical establishment, such as the Tuskegee Study, when doctors knowingly failed to treat African-American sufferers of syphilis in order to monitor how the disease progressed,[37] or the Special Operations Division of the chemical and biological warfare research facility at Fort Detrick, which had created germ weapons for the CIA.[38]

Psychologists Karen Douglas, Robbie Sutton and Aleksandra Cichocka tried to explain why so many people are predisposed to believe stories such as *Operation Infektion* and concluded that conspiracy theories, even those that appear to reveal the unethical behaviour of one's own government, can be comforting, serving a 'need for people to feel safe and secure in their environment and to exert control over the environment as autonomous individuals and as members of collectives'.[39] Signing up to a belief in the most improbable conspiracy theory creates a positive image of the self, as someone who 'knows better', who understands how the world functions, while others are left struggling with seemingly incomprehensible or irreconcilable facts.

As Ecker pointed out, people like to feel that they comprehend the world. They build mental models that fit their experience and they 'want these mental models to be *complete*'. 'They want to understand what's going on. They don't like incomplete models and they are willing to accept information that is maybe not very reliable or valid, if that allows them to build complete models of the world so they have what feels like a complete understanding.'[40] Once such an explanation has been accepted, they are unwilling to reject it even when credible proof of its falseness is offered, because they don't want their models to collapse.[41]

In 1992, Russia's director of foreign intelligence, Yevgeny Primakov, publicly admitted that *Operation Infektion* was a deception cooked up by the KGB. There was no truth to the rumours of a CIA plot. But even then, some people continued to believe that the US had deliberately manufactured AIDS,* dismissing Moscow's denial as a subterfuge and persisting in the conviction that they knew better than the facts. 'Once the AIDS conspiracy theory was lodged in the global subconscious,' wrote Thomas Boghardt, a senior historian at the US Army Center of Military History, 'it became a pandemic in its own right.'

> Studies have shown that whoever makes the first assertion about an event or occurrence has a large advantage over those who deny it later. When AIDS emerged in the early 1980s, Soviet bloc disinformation specialists quickly recognized the opportunity the mysterious epidemic offered, acted with alacrity, and planted disinformation only months after the scientific community had coined the term AIDS. Equipped with an intuitive understanding of the human psyche, Soviet and East German disinformation specialists applied the techniques that stimulate the growth and spread of rumors and conspiracy theories – simplistic scapegoating, endless repetition, and the clever mixing of lies and half-truths with undeniable facts … Like any good story, it traveled mostly by word of mouth, especially within the most affected subgroups. Having effectively harnessed the dynamics

---

* In 1992, 15 per cent of randomly selected Americans considered definitely or probably true the statement 'the AIDS virus was created deliberately in a government laboratory'. African Americans were particularly prone to subscribe to the AIDS conspiracy theory. In T. Boghardt, 'Operation INFEKTION: Soviet Bloc Intelligence and Its AIDS Disinformation Campaign', *Studies in Intelligence* 53:4 (2009), p. 19.

of rumors and conspiracy theories, Soviet bloc intelligence had
created a monster that has outlived its creators.[42]

Astoundingly, the Cold War paranoia of the Soviet authorities
extended to feeding disinformation to their own population. It has
emerged that for over fifty years, official maps of the USSR were deliberately falsified. In the same way that wartime Britain had reversed
signposts and changed road signs to confuse potential German invaders, so Soviet maps distorted the representation of highways, railway
lines and city boundaries. With the advent of glasnost, the Soviet
Union's chief cartographer, Viktor Yashchenko, revealed in 1988 that
it was done to conceal sensitive locations, to portray an idealised
future version of a Soviet city, or simply because maps were never
updated.

> We received numerous complaints. People did not recognize
> their motherland on maps. Tourists tried in vain to orient them-
> selves on the terrain ... A process that had started under the
> secret police in the 1930s continued in the post-Stalin time. It
> continued as a requirement of the work of our administra-
> tion ... Roads and rivers were moved. City districts were tilted.
> Streets and houses were incorrectly indicated ... This work
> became senseless with the appearance of space photography,
> but nevertheless it continued.[43]

When the truth was revealed, the newspaper *Vechernyaya Moskva*
asked, 'From whom, one wonders, are we keeping secrets? From ourselves?'[44] It was a pertinent question. For the most part, the Kremlin's
version of world events was accepted by ordinary people in the USSR.
There was, though, a level of suspicion about the trustworthiness of
official information that surfaced quite frequently during the Soviet
period. Inadvertent glimpses of the outside world allowed people
to compare western reality with the descriptions of it promoted by
their own government. When Nikita Khrushchev unwisely allowed
footage of luxurious American kitchens and domestic appliances to
be broadcast on national television while claiming that 'we already
have such things', during the so-called 'Kitchen Debate' of 1959, it
revealed to millions how unreliable the Kremlin's claims could be.
The cumulative result of such *aperçus* was a sort of weary cynicism

among sectors of the population. Some adopted a blanket attitude of disbelief.

> One relatively sophisticated assumption which leads at times to the acceptance of the opposite of what is found in the Soviet press is that the Soviet government projects its own motives onto foreign governments. Thus, a middle-aged bookkeeper says, 'The Soviet press interprets events in Korea as American aggression, when in actual fact the contrary is true and it is really Soviet aggression.' Another, a Ukrainian dairy technician, says, 'If they wrote that our enemies abroad were arming for war, I knew that the Soviet Union was arming.'[45]

The above is from a survey of Soviet society carried out by Harvard sociologists in 1959. The authors of *The Soviet Citizen: Daily Life in a Totalitarian Society* quizzed men and women who had fled the Soviet Union about how they evaluated claims in the official state media regarding international events.

> Another assumption about Soviet news policy ... was that the Soviet government would always attempt to prepare the populace in advance to accept unpleasant developments. 'If there were going to be a famine in the Ukraine, we always used to hear that there was hunger in Germany and Austria, and that children were picking food out of garbage cans. When I saw such examples I knew that soon we would have a famine.'[46]

The level of scepticism about the Kremlin's mendacity at times reached exaggerated proportions. A tendency to 'over-interpret' the news led to misunderstanding and confusion.

> One story that had wide general circulation in the Soviet emigration suggests the strange mixture of acceptance and rejection of the content of Soviet communications. ... It concerns a newsreel of race riots in Detroit, shown in the Soviet theatres to demonstrate the degree of racial discrimination in the United States. In one scene a Negro is shown being thrown through the air. There is a pan shot of his shoes as his feet pass the camera. The Soviet audiences, the story goes, noticed the quality of the

shoes. Accepting the plight of the Negro in America, they concluded that no American Negro would be wearing shoes of the
quality shown in this shot. Therefore, they reasoned, the Negro
must have been a professional Soviet actor, and the film the propaganda effort of a Soviet studio.[47]

The Harvard survey's appearance in 1959 came hard on the heels of
the McCarthyite hysteria in the US, and the authors temper their revelations about public mistrust in the USSR with a telling warning
against American smugness. 'It will perhaps come as a great surprise
to many,' write the book's publishers, 'that there is a close correspondence between the pattern of experience and attitudes of Soviet
citizens … and their counterparts on the same level of education or
occupation in a variety of other large-scale industrial societies having
markedly different culture and history and possessed of quite dissimilar political institutions.'[48]

No matter how 'advanced' a nation might consider itself to be,
people remain vulnerable to the effects of disinformation; skilled
propagandists can manipulate the inherent weaknesses of the human
mind to inculcate fake news; and the increasingly sophisticated technology of twenty-first-century social networks makes the process
ever more insidious.

24

DOUBLE AGENTS, DOUBLE
DEALING, DOUBLETHINK

It is widely reported that half the population of the world has seen at least one James Bond film.[1] The success of the franchise has conditioned the way people across the globe think about spies and spying, nudging conscious and subconscious perceptions towards an Anglocentric world-view, reinforcing western fears of the threat from the East and fostering the image of the gentlemanly British agent, playing tough but fair, a Cold War warrior who behaves like a medieval knight, rescuing damsels and his country from the distress in which they find themselves.

In the nineteenth century the Duke of Wellington declared that '[All] the business of war, and indeed all the business of life, is to endeavour to find out what you don't know by what you do; that's what I called "guessing what was at the other side of the hill."'[2] In the Cold War, more than any other, knowledge meant power. Infiltrating the enemy, exposing and disrupting his plans, was a vital, dangerous and seemingly glamorous business.

The Soviets had their own James Bonds. The hero of the 1974 film *The Starling and the Lyre* battles a western plot to sow discord between the USSR and her allies, makes long speeches about the US military–industrial complex and enjoys a weepy romance with a female spy. In *The Shield and the Sword*, a title drawn from the KGB's service emblem (overleaf), secret agent Belov is pitched into action against the Nazis. By the time of his fourth film appearance, he was the poster boy of Soviet postwar espionage in the minds of millions, including that of the sixteen-year-old Vladimir Putin, who went straight from the cinema to volunteer his services to the KGB.[3] Novel-readers and filmgoers enthralled by the unruffled professionalism of the fictional Bonds and Belovs – charming, hard-drinking and fearless

The KGB's sword and shield struck fear into countless hearts,
while inspiring others, including Vladimir Putin.

figures who became staples of Cold War mythology – might have
raised an eyebrow at the reality that lay behind them. The author
John le Carré worked as an intelligence officer early in his career and
was far from impressed by what he saw. 'Great ability rubbed shoulders with breath-taking incompetence,' he wrote later, 'and when
you were new you never knew which to expect. For a while you wondered whether the fools were pretending to be fools as some kind of
deception.' Perhaps there was 'a real efficient service ... somewhere
else,' le Carré mused. 'Later in my fiction, I invented one.'[4]

Intelligence was as good – or as bad – as the men and women who
gathered it. Acquiring information about the enemy's secrets, then
assessing its reliability, called for a developed understanding of the
opponent's thinking. Signals Intelligence (SIGINT), the majority of
intelligence work, involved the sifting of intercepted communications
to root out deliberate misinformation. But it was Human Intelligence
that required the greatest psychological awareness. HUMINT needed
to be handled with care. Relying on fallible individuals led to frag-
mentary, partial and frequently misleading information.

To make matters worse, politicians and officials who used intelligence to shape their decisions were prone to distorting it, discounting
facts that contradicted their preconceptions and emphasising points

that supported their view of the world. Sir Percy Cradock, the former chairman of the Joint Intelligence Committee, maintained that the 'main source of weakness [of the Soviet intelligence system] was the attempt to force an excellent supply of information from the multifaceted West into an oversimplified framework of hostility and conspiracy theory',[5] a view seemingly borne out by the testimony of Colonel Mikhail Lyubimov of KGB Foreign Intelligence. 'When we'd draw up reports,' Lyubimov acknowledged, 'we'd dramatize those bits that pointed up the threat to the Soviet Union. By emphasising the right things I'd ensure that my report went straight to the top, to the Politburo. If the report was dull and boring it would just get filed away. This was the problem with all suppliers of information – we'd tailor it to get a high rating from Moscow.'[6]

Markus Wolf, for thirty-five years the head of the Stasi's Main Directorate for Reconnaissance (HVA) and widely believed to be the prototype of Karla in le Carré's George Smiley novels, would not have been surprised. However great the courage, brilliance and suffering of agents gathering information, Wolf wrote, 'the efficiency of a service depends much more on the willingness of those who receive its information to pay attention to it when it contradicts their own opinions'.[7]

Intelligence in the Cold War could both reassure and unsettle its recipients. In his memoirs, Wolf concluded, somewhat self-servingly, that 'the intelligence services contributed to a half century of peace … by giving statesmen some security that they would not be surprised by the other side'.[8] Governments deployed spies to convince themselves of their own safety. But by doing so, they also magnified the spectre of penetration by the opposing side. The response was to increase counter-intelligence activities, ratcheting up the spiral of paranoia. Genuine fears of the enemy within, working unseen in the shadows, undermined confidence and trust. Regimes on both sides of the Iron Curtain played on public anxieties by exaggerating the threat. The American historian Vojtech Mastny recalled the self-fulfilling psychology of fear in his native Czechoslovakia. 'Reports showing vast penetration by western spies were not merely invented for public consumption to justify repression of imaginary enemies, but were taken seriously by the security services as working assumptions.'[9]

The double agent was the nightmare of all secret services. In 1985, with the Cold War once again threatening to turn hot, the

KGB scored a stunning success, arresting CIA and MI6 agents across the Soviet Union. More than a dozen key sources of information – 'assets' – were executed or imprisoned. With the search under way to identify the mole who had compromised its informants, the CIA decided it must make a concerted effort to uncover the motivations that inspire double agents. 'Project Slammer', run by the Defense Personnel Security Research Center (PERSEREC), was set up to identify at an early stage the psychological characteristics that might influence people to turn against their country. The CIA had traditionally associated treachery with somewhat simplistic motives: greed and fear, or occasionally self-aggrandisement, summed up in the acronym MICE (Money, Ideology, Coercion, Ego). But the task of identifying double agents was further complicated by the psychological attributes that all spies must possess as the very tools of their trade. Those attracted to and suited for intelligence work are ipso facto thrill-seekers, willing and able to operate on their own, good at deceiving others in order to succeed. Such character traits make the double game of betrayal appear exciting and challenging; their professional skills make it easier to conceal their guilt.[10]

Project Slammer examined thirty arrested spies, subjecting them to many hours of psychological testing and in-depth interrogation, both amicable and aggressive. Based on their results, the CIA investigators suggested they could identify the psychological profile of a potential turncoat.

> [A traitor] tends to perceive him- or herself as special, even unique, not a bad person, deserving yet dissatisfied with his or her situation, having no other (or easier) option than to engage in espionage [used throughout the report to specifically denote the activities of spies who betray their agencies] and, at any rate, simply doing what others frequently do.[11]

There was a special sort of egotism attaching to such characters, wrote the investigators, a sense of self that makes them feel above the law. 'The spy believes security procedures do not apply to him or her, and that security programs have no meaning unless they connect to something with which he or she can personally identify.'[12] But in many cases, self-belief was not enough to silence the voice of conscience. The double agent is forced into complex post facto rationalisations to maintain the pretence of behaving well. A spy will interpret their behavior in a way that leaves espionage as the "only option" and an essentially victimless crime. Once the spy commits to espionage, he or she reinforces their rationalizations by belittling the security system and highlighting the ease with which they are able to fool others and bypass safeguards.'[13] With time, however, the psychological strain of living with deceit becomes hard to bear. This is the traitor's moment of greatest danger, the moment when the authorities are most likely to uncover his or her treachery. '[T]he initial excitement of their deception fades, while stress increases. Nevertheless, they are reluctant to attempt to break out of their situation because the risks of punishment are too high. Interestingly, spies do not consider themselves traitors, finding some self-justification for their actions, and do not display remorse until after they are apprehended.'[14]

The US authorities uncovered so many moles in 1985 that it became known as the 'Year of the Spy'. One of the most notorious double agents of the Cold War, however, was just getting started. Aldrich Ames was a CIA agent with alcohol issues and tastes beyond his means, who turned to the Soviets for a solution to his problems. In exchange for several million dollars, he provided information that would lead to the deaths of numerous CIA assets. Markus Wolf made the point, however, that heavy drinking and accumulated debts are not enough in themselves to indicate a potential traitor.[15] Instead, he suggested that constant exposure to the psychology of the enemy actually fosters empathy for his world-view.

> Intelligence workers are encouraged by the secretive milieu in which they live or work to feel that the rules governing others do not apply to them. Members of a department that worked as intensely as the CIA's Soviet team must have come to know the enemy's mind-set so well that it became easier and easier to slip into his way of thinking, especially if, as in Ames' case, the bonds to one's country and agency have been whittled away by feelings of inferiority and frustration.[16]

The declared aim of Project Slammer was to help the CIA root out potential traitors at the recruitment stage, but its conclusions contain few practical suggestions for doing this. They point, rather, to factor convergences at later stages in agents' careers, 'psychological perfect storms', when job dissatisfaction, money problems and other stresses make them feel overwhelmed to the point that betraying their masters appears a way out, a means to gain respect or money or a sense of self-worth. The problem is that by this late juncture, the agent has become entrenched in the organisation, with concealment and self-defence mechanisms so well developed that it is difficult to penetrate his or her cover. '[S]pies usually do not consider committing espionage,' concludes the Slammer report, 'until after they are in a position of trust.'[17]

A case in point is that of Oleg Penkovsky. Penkovsky was a colonel in the GRU who became one of the West's most productive double agents. The detailed information on Soviet nuclear missile development that he provided in the early 1960s proved crucial for Washington's decision-making during the Cuban missile crisis. The CIA's official website describes Penkovsky's arrest with an unusual sense of drama. 'On the afternoon of October 22, 1962, a nondescript man was suddenly seized off the streets of Moscow by the KGB. He had been under surveillance on suspicion of treason. Thus ended Oleg Penkovsky's career of spying for the United States and Great Britain. Penkovsky is considered one of the most valuable assets in Agency history.'[18]

Penkovsky's early life may hold some clues to his behaviour. It seems his career in the GRU stalled following the revelation that his father, whom he had never known, had fought against the Bolsheviks in the civil war. This, together with some minor disciplinary indiscretions, appears to have blocked his path to promotion above the rank of colonel. The psychiatrist David L. Charney and the former CIA psychological operations officer John Alan Irvin posit that his decision to betray his country was fuelled by 'an intolerable sense of personal failure, as privately defined by [him]'. His approach to the Americans was an attempt to deal with this failure; having been snubbed by his countrymen, he turned elsewhere for 'personal validation'.[19]

Penkovsky tried to get in touch with the CIA through the US embassy in Moscow, pressing a note into the hands of an American student near the Kremlin. The text of his letter reveals a man expressing high ideals, seeking recognition for himself as 'a soldier-warrior for the cause of Truth, for the ideals of a truly free world and of Democracy for Mankind, to which ideals your – and now my – President, government and people are sacrificing so much effort'.

I wish to make my contribution, perhaps a modest one but in my view an important one, to our mutual cause, and henceforth as your soldier to carry out everything which is entrusted to me ... At the present time I have at my disposal very important materials on many subjects of exceptionally great interest and importance to your government ... I request that you 'relieve' me as quickly as possible of this material which I have prepared ... I ask that in working with me you observe all the rules of tradecraft and security, and not permit any slipups. *Protect me.*[20]

When the Americans failed to respond, Penkovsky turned to the British. His GRU role gave him access to foreign trade delegations and he used this to approach the British businessman Greville Wynne, asking to be put in touch with MI6. Penkovsky was due to travel with a Soviet trade delegation to London, where he was duly introduced to the British and American operatives who would become his handlers. CIA records of the meeting reveal a man expressing enthusiasm for the West and bitterness towards his own country, where he felt marginalised and slighted. 'I'll never be made a general, since my father was a White Officer ... They don't trust me ... My problem now is to do our work and be ready to fulfil your orders.'[21] His handler seems cautious, perhaps torn between excitement at the prospect of recruiting an important asset and doubt about the genuineness of what he is being offered. 'I want you to realize that the most basic consideration we have towards you is humanitarian,' the anonymous official responds, skilfully recognising Penkovsky's plea to be loved. 'Irrespective of how important you may be as a source of information. We regard you as an individual first of all.'[22]

Penkovsky offered to prove his bona fides by providing a sample of the information to which he had access. It turned out to be of such startling significance, unmasking two Soviet agents working in London under diplomatic cover, together with documents detailing the deployment patterns of Soviet missiles, that the CIA and MI6 struggled to believe it. Maurice Oldfield, who would go on to serve as the director of the Secret Intelligence Service, wrote that Penkovsky seemed 'the answer to a prayer. What he provided seemed like a miracle, too. That is why for so long he was mistrusted on both sides of the Atlantic. It seemed incredible that he could take such risks – not merely photographing top secret documents, but actually giving us the original documents in some instances.'[23]

Comments in the CIA and MI6 records of subsequent meetings show that Penkovsky's handlers remained puzzled by his motives. In defiance of the CIA's MICE categories, he was moved neither by great greed nor by any form of coercion. His overriding concern seemed to be a deep and rather naive desire for acceptance, placing an exaggerated value on the symbolic rewards that would provide the personal validation refused him in the USSR. 'You should not laugh at my request to kiss the Queen's hand,' he is recorded as telling his MI6 contact. 'All you need to say is that I have not yet reached such a stature to deserve this and in that case all I have to do is to work, work, work.' When he is told that a royal meeting will not be possible, Penkovsky displays an exaggerated sense of personal slight.

> Although my morale is excellent, after all, I am a soldier, not a young girl, I do feel slightly hurt and at a loss to understand why … I am refused this gesture which would mean so much to me in the sense of my morale … Why couldn't some … encouragement be shown to me in exchange for my work by your leaders in the West?[24]

Penkovsky's early enthusiasm for the West began to wane as he realised that here, too, he would face snubs and he would no more be fully accepted and valued in the West than he had been in Russia. He continued to pass on ever more sensitive intelligence, seemingly hoping to increase the approbation of his handlers. According to Wynne, the more information Penkovsky provided, and the greater the risks he took, the more he thirsted for extreme forms of validation.[25]

To soothe the hurt he felt at being refused a meeting with the Queen, the authorities appointed him to the rank of colonel in both the British and American militaries and agreed that their next meeting would be held in full military dress. Penkovsky had photos taken showing him in his new uniforms, which he appears to have treasured as a token of escape, a way to imagine himself as a different person in a different life. Astoundingly, and surely knowing the risk he was running, he kept them in a drawer in his Moscow flat. When he was eventually arrested, the photographs would become damning evidence at his trial.

Colonel Penkovsky in the British and American uniforms he treasured, and which ultimately precipitated his downfall.

In the last year of his life Penkovsky became ever more brazen in his brush-pasts and dead drops, neglecting to take the precautions he had agreed with his handlers. A sense of fatalism seemed to descend on him, a subconscious desire for the stress and deceit to be over. The risks Penkovsky took would lead to his downfall, and he probably knew it.

In Charney's formulation, 'All insider spies wind up imprisoned by the same psychology: Fear of being caught; constant grinding uncertainty, waiting for the other shoe to drop; yearnings for deliverance and relief; despair and hopelessness about the ultimate direction their lives will take.'[26] As the fear grows and the noose tightens, the agent enters the world of *Crime and Punishment*'s Raskolnikov, struggling with the compulsion to confess, knowing that being caught and convicted would at least put a stop to things.

Following his arrest in October 1962, Penkovsky was intensively interrogated. At his trial in May 1963, he was found guilty on all charges and sentenced to death. The official record showed that he was shot in the Lubyanka Prison in Moscow and cremated, although a former GRU officer who defected to the West later claimed Penkovsky had been bound to a stretcher and burned alive as a warning to other potential traitors.[27]

The psychology of the double agent's calvary was universal. Christopher Boyce, a CIA agent who worked as an informant for Moscow before being caught and sentenced to forty years in jail, spoke about his mental ordeal to a sub-committee of Congress,[28] explaining the difference between the romantic vision he was sold by the KGB ('a whole potpourri of James Bond lunacy') and the reality of the ordeal he went through as his cover was progressively blown.

> Everything [the KGB recruiter] said was totally foreign to what was actually happening to me. Where was the despair? Where were the sweaty palms and shaky hands? This man said nothing about having to wake up in the morning with gut-gripping fear before steeling yourself once again for the ordeal of going back into that vault … There was no excitement, there was no thrill. There was only depression and a hopeless enslavement to an inhuman, uncaring foreign bureaucracy. You're never going to get away from it and it's never going to end … It is infinitely better for you to make the extra effort to ensure that your personnel understand beyond a shadow of a doubt how espionage wounds a man than for more and more of them to find out for themselves.[29]

Regular agents could at least hope to retire with a pension, but for the double agent there was no escape. Even those who were extricated by their foreign employers remained the prisoner of their actions. The Cambridge spies succeeded in fleeing to Moscow, but found they were never truly trusted. The KGB believed a man who betrayed his country once could easily turn again. In a rare television interview in 1959, Guy Burgess ruefully rejected the suggestion that escape to the Soviet Union had changed his life. 'Men don't have changes of life,' he told an interviewer from the CBC. 'We can't have that.'[30] Kim Philby discovered that the promises he had received of being made a colonel in the KGB with substantive intelligence duties were a lie. He was kept always on the outside, living a lonely existence in a Moscow flat, listening to the BBC World Service and reading the cricket coverage in *The Times*, under virtual house arrest with the KGB screening his visitors. The KGB told both Burgess and Philby that the other did not want to see him, so they never met, eventually drinking themselves to death in their Soviet exile.

Markus Wolf's memoirs are strident about the contempt in which double agents were held by all espionage agencies.

> Betrayal is poison for every intelligence service, against which the vaccines at our disposal have only limited effect ... The psychological culture of an espionage service resembles that of a clan or tribe, in which individuals are united by some greater goal and a shared sense of identity, ideological or otherwise. When this is ripped open, a poison of distrust enters the system ... A traitor within an intelligence service betrays ... the whole integrity of his service.[31]

According to Wolf, the best defence against disloyalty was to create an ethos of belonging, a sense of being part of a family that must not be betrayed. Services could do this by 'building on existing patterns of loyalty – ideological, political, geographical – that date from childhood, ensuring that any officer who thinks of turning traitor is made to feel that so doing would make him a traitor to himself'.[32] The CIA in its early years fostered such homogeneity by recruiting from the East Coast Brahmin class known as WASPs (White Anglo-Saxon Protestants). The KGB relied on family dynasties and class loyalties, rejecting candidates who did not have a family history of loyalty to Bolshevism. The British intelligence services took the principle to extremes, drawing almost exclusively on the country's old boy networks of public schools and Oxbridge.

Markus Wolf claimed that the preponderance of upper-class intellectuals in the top echelons of western intelligence backfired, playing in the East's favour when it came to recruiting double agents. He wrote,

> The feeling of belonging to a special community, an elite and secretive club fighting for a noble ideal, was of particular importance to westerners from upper-middle-class backgrounds with strong and complex personalities. Perhaps this goes some way towards answering the question I am incessantly asked about

why such people flocked to work for us. What we offered them
was the chance of mixing idealism with personal commitment,
something that is missing in many modern societies.[33]

A sense of idealistic commitment to the values of communism
played a part in the defection of many British agents, including the
Cambridge spies. George Blake, an MI6 case officer who passed information to Moscow for years before being caught, offered a similar
explanation for his decision to switch sides. 'I viewed Communism as
an attempt to create the kingdom of God in this world. The Communists were trying to do by action what the Church had tried to achieve
by prayer and precept.'[34]

Part of the difficulty in detecting double agents lay in the blinkered
insularity of the British Secret Intelligence Service. Received prejudice made MI6 reluctant to believe that a chap from public school
and Oxbridge could be a traitor. In 1951, David Floyd, who had been
a communist when at Oxford, admitted to supplying information
to the Soviets while a diplomat in Moscow. Despite his confession,
the director of public prosecutions bewilderingly decided that the
evidence was 'clearly insufficient' for criminal proceedings. The case
was hushed up and Floyd went on to work for the *Daily Telegraph* for
several decades. When the facts came to light, and the foreign secretary, Herbert Morrison, demanded to know, 'Why must we employ
such doubtfuls?', a senior colleague attested that Floyd – mired as
he was in treachery – was 'a simple person who could not possibly
conceal a double loyalty'.[35]

Well before their defections, there had been warnings about the
reliability of Guy Burgess and Donald Maclean, but their access to
sensitive material had not been withdrawn. When the two fled to
Moscow in 1951, MI6 set up a secret committee of enquiry under Sir
Alexander Cadogan, permanent under-secretary for foreign affairs.
Cadogan's eventual recommendations were bathed in the cosy complacency of the British establishment, redolent of the British public
school, the urgent need for radical change obscured by the disor-
dered shared mentality of a tight-knit clique. There should be some
vetting of future agents, the report concluded, but it would be wrong
to ask MI6 members to spy on their fellows. 'It would be distaste-
ful to encourage the notion that it is the duty of every member of
the Service to watch the behaviour of his colleagues and, in school

parlance, to "blab" about them to the "head".'[36] Cadogan, reluctantly, concedes that there had been the odd sign of misbehaviour ...

> It was alleged that Mr. Maclean had on a number of occasions, usually when drunk, expressed extremely left-wing views ... and that as an undergraduate he had had homosexual tendencies. In Mr. Burgess's case it was alleged that he had been an active Communist as a Cambridge undergraduate ... and had been in contact with Communists up to 1939; that he disliked the Americans and American foreign policy; that he was a heavy drinker; that he took drugs; and that he was a homosexual.*

But none of that seemed to trouble Cadogan. His report is less concerned with avoiding such things happening in the future than with excusing the chaps who allowed them to happen in the first place. 'None of this information, whether true or false, was available to the Foreign Office or the M.I.5. before the disappearance of the two men,' Cadogan writes with a sigh of relief. The committee had 'not found anything radically wrong with the arrangements in the Foreign Office ... This is a great relief to my mind.'[37]

Any changes introduced as a result of the Cadogan enquiry proved insufficient to prevent Kim Philby, Anthony Blunt and John Cairncross from carrying on spying. Philby's defection in 1963 and Blunt's confession in 1964 may have tightened vetting procedures, but not by much. There was no call for any psychological assessment of the men or women who would become Britain's front-line operatives in the world of espionage. When I was myself approached to join MI6 in 1979, officials contacted my friends to ask if they believed I was gay, or promiscuous, a gambler or living beyond my means. That was the extent of it. Nobody asked if my grandfather had been a member of the British Communist Party and I didn't volunteer that he had been.

An episode from 1961 indicates that my experience was far from

---

* The repeated references to homosexuality echoed the Lavender Scare of McCarthyite America. The supposition was that being gay left a spy open to blackmail from the other side, as well as indicating dangerous deviation from expected, 'normal' behaviour. The National Archives, TNA/CAB 301/120, Report of Cadogan Committee, p. 6.

unique. Suspicions had been raised that secrets were being leaked from the highly classified Underwater Detection Establishment (UDE) in Portland. In the late 1950s, the behaviour of a clerk, Harry Houghton, and of Ethel Gee, a secretary who was Houghton's lover, drew the attention of UDE security. Houghton had previously been sent home from a posting in Warsaw following episodes of drunken behaviour, including some in which he physically assaulted his wife, Amy. Amy had left him, warning MI5 that Houghton was passing classified information to the Eastern Bloc. He had large sums of money in cash, far beyond his modest salary.

Reading the Security Service Personnel files now declassified at the National Archives betrays a remarkable lack of psychological insight on the part of the authorities. The files acknowledge that Houghton had alcohol problems. They refer to him as 'a man who has a fair amount of conceit of himself and may be inclined to "talk big" ... not the type who would qualify for further promotion'. His profile includes several of the MICE qualities (Money, Ideology, Coercion, Ego) associated with a person likely to be vulnerable to hostile recruitment. But his assessors perversely conclude that there is 'no question of his integrity' and instead blame his former wife. 'It is considered not impossible that the whole of these allegations may be nothing more than outpourings of a jealous and disgruntled wife ... No further action other than discreet surveillance is being taken at this time.'[38] Even more patronising, and misogynistic, is the assessment that was made of Houghton's accomplice, Ethel Gee.

> Plain in appearance and speaking with a fairly strong Dorset accent, it would be hard to find someone further removed from the popular conception of the female spy than Miss 'Bunty' Gee ... She has ... access to secret information. However, for a person of her limited education it would be difficult, if not impossible, to extract information of any value from the material which she handles.[39]

It seems that British intelligence had slightly conflicted criteria for investigating potential double agents. Too much education meant you were above suspicion of treason, too little and you couldn't possibly be capable of it. It was only several years later, after Houghton's flaunting of his ill-gotten wealth became so conspicuous and his dealings with his Soviet contact so brazen, that the whole spy ring, run out of a semi-detached bungalow in suburban Ruislip, was arrested.[40]

If Cold War spy games at times resembled an intellectual chess match between jolly schoolboys, they nonetheless had tragic results. The actions of double agents led to great suffering and death. Information supplied by Kim Philby while he was still active in MI6 led to a number of British agents being picked up the instant they set foot in the Soviet Union, with some later being shot. It is highly probable that George Blake's betrayal led to the execution of Oleg Penkovsky. Blake himself claimed he had been given assurances by the KGB that no harm would come to the men and women he betrayed, but it is unclear how much he believed them. Major General Oleg Kalugin, the KGB chief of counter-intelligence, suspected he was simply refusing to contemplate the consequences of his actions. 'George Blake had that innocent mind,' Kalugin said. 'He didn't want to know that many people he betrayed were executed. I think we even discussed this subject at one point and he wouldn't believe it. He would say: "Well I was told this wouldn't happen." It did happen; he was not told.'[41]

The documentary filmmaker George Carey, who interviewed Blake at his Moscow home in 2015, speculated about the psychological coping mechanisms Blake had developed over the years and the effect they produced on his psyche. 'He's a friendly, charming person. Clearly, one part of him is a very nice guy. All spies are contradictory, they lead double lives. I think these lives gradually become more separated, living constantly in two worlds with your brain split. And in the end the two halves stop talking to each other because it's the only way of surviving.'[42]

What Carey saw in Blake suggests a certain compartmentalisation, a defence mechanism aimed at counteracting cognitive dissonance over past actions.[43] It would allow Blake to avoid confronting the consequences of what he had done, ascribing his own conduct to a desire to 'do good'. Unable to reconcile this with the 'bad' outcomes for other people, he refused to acknowledge the contradiction. On a wider scale, the Cold War itself followed a similar pattern, compartmentalising the world into simple categories that allowed each side to preserve its idealised self-conception: 'we' are good, so our actions must be good; 'they' are bad, so all they do must also be bad.

Rationalising the brutal human outcomes that stemmed from the decisions they made exercised the minds of men and women at all levels of authority, from the president down. 'I have come to the conclusion,' Dwight Eisenhower wrote in 1954, 'that some of our traditional ideas of international sportsmanship are scarcely applicable in the morass in which the world now flounders.'[44] John le Carré's fictional spy boss, Control, agonised about the relative morality of East and West in *The Spy Who Came in from the Cold*, with the author hinting at the anguished, self-knowing sophistry of a troubled conscience.

'We do disagreeable things so that ordinary people here and elsewhere can sleep safely in their beds at night. Is that too romantic? Of course, we occasionally do very wicked things.' He grinned like a schoolboy. 'And in weighing up the moralities, we rather go in for dishonest comparisons; after all, you can't compare the ideals of one side with the methods of the other, can you, now? ... I would say that since the war, our methods – ours and those of the opposition – have become much the same. I mean, you can't be less ruthless than the opposition simply because your government's *policy* is benevolent, can you now?'[45]

Le Carré had hoped his book would prompt readers to ask, 'For how long can we defend ourselves by methods of this kind and still remain the kind of society that is worth defending?'[46]

Markus Wolf, in contrast, felt the brutal behaviour of his agency was justified by the purity of its ideological goals. If anything, they could have been more brutal. 'We East German Socialists tried to create a new kind of society that would never repeat the German crimes of the past ... Our sins and our mistakes were those of every other intelligence agency. If we had shortcomings, and we certainly did, they were those of too much professionalism, untempered by the raw edge of ordinary life.'[47] To bolster his defence, Wolf quotes Bertolt Brecht's play *The Measures Taken*.

What baseness would you not commit
To stamp out baseness?
If you could change the world
What would you be too good for?
Sink in the mire,

Embrace the butcher, but
Change the world.[48]

There were those in the West who were willing to work with monsters
in order to fight the communist threat. Gestapo Hauptsturmführer
Klaus Barbie, dubbed the 'Butcher of Lyon' for his role in torturing
and deporting French Jews and resistance fighters, was captured by
the Allies in 1945. Instead of being put on trial for war crimes, he was
enlisted into the fight against communism. Major Eugene Kolb was
the American intelligence officer who recruited and then protected
Barbie.

> There's a world of difference between high moral standards,
> high intelligence and the ability to manipulate people as you
> have to do in the intelligence business, and that Barbie was
> extremely good at … The major reason why we did not want
> to give Barbie up was simply that he had recruited too many
> people, he knew names and we suspected very strongly at the
> time that the French intelligence services had been thoroughly
> penetrated by Communist agents and we were very, very fearful
> that the moment they got Barbie their first interrogation task
> would not be his work against the Resistance or his work in
> Lyon but rather his work for us and what are the names of the
> people whom you have recruited and that we could not afford
> to do.[49]

The climate of bluff and double bluff, double agents and double
dealing led to a paradigm of convoluted, at times self-defeating,
thinking. The mind-set of trusting no one, of questioning all claims
and all information, created a world in which the simplest answer
was routinely discarded. Because such a premium was placed on
unearthing the most sophisticated, the most cynical, Machiavellian
explanation of any phenomenon, the obvious solution was often
overlooked. When Mikhail Gorbachev introduced his programme
of liberalisation in the 1980s, the Joint Intelligence Committee under
the leadership of Sir Percy Cradock pooh-poohed the idea that the
reforms might be genuine. How naive, said the worldly-wise spooks,
to think we should trust anything those crooks in Moscow tell us. Margaret Thatcher's adviser Charles Powell was left to rue the inflexible

patterns of thinking that had blinded the JIC to the obvious, but *too* simple, truth.

> The biggest single failure of intelligence of that era was the failure of almost everybody to foresee the end of communism. It caught us completely on the hop. All that intelligence about their war-fighting capabilities was all very well, but it didn't tell us the one thing we needed to know – that it was all about to collapse. It was a colossal failure of the whole Western system of intelligence assessment and political judgement.[50]

The Foreign Office diplomat Sir Reginald Hibbert observed that the British secret services had done little more than argue 'that the future is going to be broadly like the present, only more so'.[51] Uncovering 'secrets' had become such an ingrained modus operandi that the intelligence agencies simply overlooked the abundance of evidence that was available to all. Whitehall had been seduced by a preference for secret sources over straightforward facts. It was, said Hibbert, 'a culture where secrecy comes to be confused with truth and where, after a time, contact is lost with earthly awkwardness'.[52]

25

INVENTING THE ENEMY
IN BOOKS AND FILM

In the autumn of 1957, the British architectural historian and biographer James Lees-Milne was staying at Roquebrune on the French Riviera. In his diary he records a visit to Winston Churchill and his wife, Clementine, who were occupying Lord Beaverbrook's villa five miles down the coast. Winston, he says, seemed 'very much older and rather pitiable'. He had stepped down from the leadership of the Conservative Party and had suffered a mild stroke the previous December. 'Much smaller, less broad and slighter,' Lees-Milne writes. 'He stumbled down the steps and shuffled across the terrace.'

By the end of the evening, Churchill is sitting 'slumped in an armchair in the middle of the room', making polite conversation. Lees-Milne's wife, Alvilde, asks him if he has read a newly published book called *On the Beach* by the popular novelist Nevil Shute. Churchill says he has, and it is evident that he has been shaken by it. Shute's book is set in Melbourne, Australia, in the days after a nuclear war has devastated the northern hemisphere. Radiation unleashed by the war has wiped out three-quarters of the globe and is now spreading inexorably southwards. Humanity's days will soon be over, and Shute describes the anguished thoughts of his characters as they await their inevitable death.

It emerges that the war has been triggered by a series of misunderstandings and miscommunications. It is a war by inadvertence, the nightmare scenario that preoccupied the British and other nations in the years after 1945. Churchill had been personally involved in the government's discussions of such a contingency, and Lees-Milne's account makes clear that he remained tormented by them.

'Alvilde told him how much she was impressed by Shute's book. [Churchill] said he was sending it to Khrushchev. She asked would he not also send it to Eisenhower. Sir W's retort? "It would be a waste of money. He is so muddle-headed now ... I think the earth will soon be destroyed by a cobalt bomb. And if I were the Almighty, I would not recreate it, in case they destroyed Him too the next time".'[1]

On the Beach encapsulated the pervading sense of doom that gripped the world as the nuclear rhetoric between East and West escalated, seeming to portend the end of days. It demonstrated the capacity of art to capture and focus the emotions of millions, to shape the discussion that politicians were having and, perhaps, to influence its outcome.

The arts have long been Russia's secret world of the mind, a flourishing mental garden of freedom when free speech was silenced. Early in the twentieth century, the Bolsheviks recognised the importance of art as a psychological weapon. Literature was controlled by the Soviet Writers' Union, whose bureaucrats defined what was acceptable and what was not. The doctrine of socialist realism decreed that all art must depict man's struggle for socialist progress. Culture was permitted only if it was socialist culture.

Stalin, too, acknowledged the power of writers, calling them the 'engineers of human souls'.[2] For a man who murdered millions with little compunction, he took an obsessive interest in the fate of individual poets and artists, personally weighing and meting out rewards and punishments. Under these conditions, poetry took on an almost religious significance. Boris Pasternak's son, Yevgeny, told me that his father knew the subversive power of what he wrote:

> The knowledge of free poetry was the only thing that could take the place of free speech. Poetry came to encompass everything that was most important to us; everything we believed in, everything we yearned for ... It allowed us to keep alive the freedom of memory and independence of thought in the dark years when 'they' were trying to reduce us to nothing.[3]

Nikita Khrushchev sought to tame art, to harness it for the aims of the state. 'Writers are like the artillery,' Khrushchev declared, 'because they clear the way for our infantry. They cleanse the brains of those who need it. You should fire at the enemy – not at your own side.'[4] It was a warning to Pasternak and writers like him: art should not be used for purposes other than those decreed by the Kremlin.

'Writers and artists are the hardest of all to deal with,' Khrushchev complained. 'They think they can govern the state much better than the Party can. So they keep trying to teach us what to do and how to do it; they'd like to be the spiritual leaders of society ... With people like that you have to be careful, to keep a sharp lookout.'[5]

The dissident satirist Vladimir Voinovich said there were two categories of writers in the Soviet Union,

> writers people wanted to read and writers people didn't want to read. No one published the ones people wanted to read, and the ones no one wanted to read were published ... They banned some writers, thereby assuring them popularity and stimulating great interest in their works. And others, on the contrary, they published in enormous editions, which was completely pointless because no one read them.[6]

In the Cold War years, that gap between desirability and availability was exploited by the West. Boris Pasternak fell into the first of Voinovich's categories, and as such he was useful to the ideologues in Washington and London. Khrushchev had banned Pasternak's novel, *Doctor Zhivago*, from publication because of its ideological failings. The official notification of its rejection made clear why. 'The spirit of your novel is one of non-acceptance of the socialist revolution. The general tenor of your novel is that the October Revolution ... did not give the people anything but suffering.'[7]

When the manuscript was smuggled to Italy in 1957, the CIA viewed it as a tool to deploy against the enemy. They ensured it was translated and distributed in great numbers, including – surreptitiously – behind the Iron Curtain. John Maury, the agency's Soviet Russia chief, wrote that the book would 'produce a psychological impact upon' Soviet recipients.

> *Dr Zhivago* is considered to be the most heretical literary work by a Soviet author since Stalin's death. Pasternak's humanistic message – that every person is entitled to a private life and deserves respect as a human being, irrespective of the extent of his political loyalty or contribution to the state – poses a fundamental challenge to the Soviet ethic of sacrifice of the individual to the Communist system.[8]

An internal CIA memo of April 1958 made clear that the aim was to shame and embarrass the Soviet state. 'We have the opportunity to make Soviet citizens wonder what is wrong with their government, when a fine literary work by the man acknowledged to be the greatest living Russian writer is not even available in his own country in his own language, for his own people to read ... This book has great propaganda value.'[9] When the files relating to the Zhivago affair were declassified in 2014, the extent of the CIA's machinations became evident: the agency considered that '*Doctor Zhivago* was an important Cold War-era success story for the CIA'.[10] The agency had funded the publishing of the book in vast numbers then bought thousands of copies in order to turn it into a bestseller. A memo of December 1957 explained why. '*Dr. Zhivago* should be published in a maximum number of foreign editions, for maximum free world discussion and acclaim and consideration for such honor as the Nobel prize.'[11]

When *Doctor Zhivago* did indeed help its author win the 1958 Nobel Prize for Literature, the CIA was quick to take the credit. The Kremlin threatened and bullied Pasternak, telling him that if he travelled to Stockholm, he would not be allowed to return. Soviet writers were instructed to denounce his 'literary weed' of a book and workers were told to stage demonstrations against him. The sheer cruelty of the Soviet regime's reaction was grist to the CIA's mill.

> The regime's outraged reaction to the rewarding of the Nobel Prize and the expulsion of Pasternak from the Writers' Union, demonstrated that Khrushchev's attitude toward the writers and intellectuals was not very different from Stalin's ... [Pasternak] has already become a symbol for every Soviet writer who wishes to express his own ideas and convictions.[12]

But the effect on Pasternak himself was devastating. His son, Yevgeny, told me that his father's health was shattered by the controversy over *Doctor Zhivago* and that he never recovered.

> He was delighted and happy when he got the letter offering him the Nobel Prize. He naively thought he'd be able to accept it. But the authorities threatened him ... I saw him that day, and it was clear what a terrible blow it had all been to him. I couldn't recognize my father. His face was lifeless, his eyes full of pain.[13]

Eighteen months later Pasternak was dead.

Although the covert US involvement in his book's success had been sanctioned by President Eisenhower and overseen by CIA director Allen Dulles, agency memos hastened to stress that the 'hand of the United States Government should not be shown in any manner'.[14]

The CIA had evidently grasped an important tenet of behavioural psychology – that people are most effectively manipulated when they do not realise they are being manipulated.[15] The deployment of 'nudge theory' in twenty-first-century politics has been a relatively benign example of the principle of unconscious influencing. 'Nudge units' have been set up by governments in Britain, Germany, Japan and elsewhere, based on the idea that by subtly altering the environment, you can guide people towards the desired outcome.* The CIA, however, was less concerned with persuading people to drive safely or stop littering than with the inculcation of hatred towards a Cold War opponent. They had created the environment in which Boris Pasternak could become a global literary star and at the same time effectively precipitated his crushing by the Soviet state. For the CIA it was a perfect turn of events, nudging people into 'understanding' the brutality of socialism.

The agency operated through front organisations, covertly funded by Washington. One of them, the Congress for Cultural Freedom, proclaimed itself to be the champion of every man's 'right to hold and express his own opinions, and particularly opinions which differ from those of his rulers'. At its peak, the congress had offices in thirty-five countries, running its own news service and organising international cultural events to bestow honours and prizes on favoured artists, musicians and authors. According to Frances Stonor Saunders, the historian of the CIA's cultural policy in the Cold War, its purpose was to 'nudge the intelligentsia of western Europe away from its lingering fascination with Marxism and Communism towards a view more accommodating of "the American way"'.[16]

As part of the CIA's bid to spread 'soft power', winning intellectual

---

* The initial name of 'nudge theory' was 'libertarian paternalism'. Its creators, Cass Sunstein and Richard Thaler, described it as a means to 'steer people's choices in welfare-promoting directions without eliminating freedom of choice'. C. Sunstein and R. Thaler, *Libertarian Paternalism is Not an Oxymoron*, available at SSRN: ssrn. com/abstract=405940 p. 1.

hearts and minds that might otherwise be attracted to Moscow, the agency arranged the first American abstract art exhibition in Europe and the Boston Symphony Orchestra's first European tour. It funded dozens of cultural and political journals, including the respected *Paris Review* and London's *Survey* magazine. Its overriding aim was to promote the message that 'West is Best' and it did it in a variety of ways, from the entirely innocent showcasing of western cultural achievement, to the subliminal planting of its ideological message in books and magazines. Editorial control seemed in most cases to be sensitive and largely non-interventionist. As long as a publication continued to highlight the USSR's (real) abuses of human rights and civic freedoms, and did not stray too far into criticisms of US policy, it remained broadly free to set its own priorities.

But the CIA did not limit itself to manipulating magazines. Institutes of higher education were also targeted, as I discovered when I returned to Oxford in 1979 from two years as a graduate student studying at Harvard. At St Antony's we were blessed with the most outstanding Russian tutors of our generation. There was no overt direction of what we should write or what political slant our graduate theses should take. But there were certainly rumours in the common room. We knew that Max Hayward, the doyen of Russian dons at the college, had previously been a diplomat in Moscow, expelled for unstated reasons in 1955; that he was outspokenly anti-Soviet and that he had been chosen as the English translator of *Doctor Zhivago* in 1957. In 1966 a donation to the college of $3.5 million from the Ford Foundation was widely believed to have come from the CIA, prompting the *Saturday Evening Post* to run an article claiming that Oxford had 'a school for spies ... disguised as St Antony's College'.[17] A CIA slush fund was later confirmed as the source of the money.[18]

Joel Whitney, the author of *Finks: How the CIA Tricked the World's Best Writers*, rejects the contention that the agency was simply showcasing western culture and intellectual learning. The cultural Cold Warriors, the book argues, 'again and again used anti-Communism as a lever to spy relentlessly on writers of all political inclinations, and thereby pushed U.S. democracy a little closer to the Soviet model of the surveillance state'.[19] 'The more liberal guys who were part of the brain trust that formed the CIA saw ... that culture itself was becoming a weapon, and they wanted a kind of Ministry of Culture too. They felt the only way they could get this paid for was through the CIA's black budget.'[20] The amounts of money flowing through the CIA's 'black budget' were large. As early as 1950, policy document NSC-68 had set aside $120 million* for psychological warfare. The use of 'counterpart funds', some drawn from the resources distributed under the Marshall Plan, acted as a conduit to finance covert activities in Europe. The US secretary of state, Edward Barrett, justified the expense, saying, 'In the contest for men's minds, truth can be peculiarly the American weapon. It cannot be an isolated weapon, because the propaganda of truth is powerful only when linked with concrete actions and policies … a highly skilful and substantial campaign of truth is as indispensable as an air force.' The CIA was able to pay authors handsomely for their contributions to its publications. The supposition was that the recipients would not know who was providing the funding, although some of them clearly suspected.[21]

The methods may have been clandestine, but there were powerful public voices insisting that the need was real and urgent. Prominent intellectuals, such as Melvin Lasky, editor of the literary magazine *Encounter*, clamoured that the West was losing the battle for hearts and minds. While the Soviet lie was travelling round the globe at lightning speed, Lasky complained, 'the [western] truth had yet to get its boots on'.[22]

Lasky's support for the CIA's endeavours was vociferous. What a surprise, then, when it emerged that he too was on the agency's payroll! Rumours of CIA backing for *Encounter* surfaced in 1966, but Lasky wrote an outraged letter to *The New York Times* denying the charges. The following year, the game was up. Sol Stern, a journalist on the California newspaper *Ramparts*, wrote an article alleging that the CIA had been secretly funding the US National Student Association (NSA), and other journalists quickly followed his lead.

> The newspapers described how legitimate tax-exempt foundations laundered millions of dollars from the CIA and passed the funds to an agency-designated list of civic and cultural groups, labor unions, magazines, and book publishers. It soon became clear that the CIA/NSA relationship was just one thread in an elaborate web of citizen front groups secretly supported, and sometimes even created, by the spy agency in the early days of

---

* Equivalent to approximately $1.3 billion in 2020.

the Cold War ... The top-secret project had been approved at the highest levels of the U.S. government.[23]

Melvin Lasky confessed privately that he had known about the CIA funding for years, but *Encounter*'s founding editor Stephen Spender was humiliated, unable to convince friends and colleagues that he had been oblivious.[24]

By funding publications such as *Encounter*, the CIA was aiming to influence western intellectuals unsure which of the two sides in the Cold War represented the lesser evil. Leading figures in France, including Jean-Paul Sartre, Pablo Picasso and Albert Camus, were talking openly of the moral equivalence of Washington and Moscow, or leaning towards the Kremlin's view of the world. In Britain, the novels of Graham Greene blurred the lines between the ethical values of West and East. When *On the Beach* sold 100,000 copies in its first six weeks of publication – it would eventually sell 4 million – Nevil Shute voiced a truth that the CIA must have found uncomfortable. 'A popular novelist,' Shute wrote, 'can often play the part of the *enfant terrible* in raising subjects which ought to be discussed in public and which no statesman cares to approach. In this way, an entertainer may serve a useful purpose.'[25]

Many were displeased by Shute's message in *On the Beach*. Republicans labelled it communist sedition. The *National Review* contended that the book's 'tiresome descriptions of vast atomic destruction' were 'designed to destroy whatever is left of American faith in the military'.[26] But *On the Beach* shines an unblinking light on the human consequences of the supposedly hypothetical discussions among politicians asserting the need for nuclear deterrence. In Shute's universe, the moment of death – and therefore the length of life remaining – is mercilessly defined. It recalls the writing of Kierkegaard, Sartre and Camus, each meditating on an existence rendered meaningless in a doomed universe. Shute's characters find their ways of dealing with the absurdity of inevitable death in much the same ways as do Sartre's.

Albert Camus had been shocked when he heard of the bombing of Hiroshima, writing in the leftist journal *Combat*:

We are told, in the midst of hundreds of enthusiastic commentaries, that any average city can be wiped out by a bomb the size

of a football. Our technical civilization has just reached its greatest level of savagery ... What will it bring to a world already
given over to all the convulsions of violence, incapable of any
control, indifferent to justice and the simple happiness of men
– a world where science devotes itself to organized murder?[27]

His greatest novel, *The Plague* (1947), reflects on the psychological
dramas people endure when life is darkened by unrelenting trauma.
Its conclusions, drawn from the pain of Nazi occupation, are equally
applicable to mankind's angst in the nuclear age.

> Everybody knows that pestilences have a way of recurring in
> the world; yet somehow we find it hard to believe in ones that
> crash down on our heads from a blue sky ... we tell ourselves
> that pestilence is a mere bogy of the mind, a bad dream that
> will pass away. But it doesn't always pass away and, from one
> bad dream to another, it is men who pass away ... they thought
> that everything still was possible for them. They went on doing
> business, arranged for journeys, and formed views. How should
> they have given a thought to anything like plague, which rules
> out any future, cancels journeys, silences the exchange of views.
> They fancied themselves free, and no one will ever be free so
> long as there are pestilences.[28]

In the cinema, Stanley Kubrick's 1964 film *Dr. Strangelove or: How I
Learned to Stop Worrying and Love the Bomb* took Nevil Shute's *enfant
terrible* role to comic extremes. Its plot – a nuclear apocalypse triggered by a deranged American general and an uncontrollable Soviet
doomsday device – undoubtedly thrust 'subjects that no statesman
cares to approach' into the public's face. Whereas promotional films
such as *Duck and Cover* were designed to convince the public that
nuclear war was something manageable (in effect, encouraging them
to 'stop worrying and love the bomb'), Kubrick's aim was to 'make
real' a subject that others would like to conceal behind theoretical
talk and misleading depictions. Kubrick understood that cinema has
the singular power of *poiesis*, the ability to make real that which had
hitherto been unimaginable.[29]

'The bomb has almost no reality and has become a complete
abstraction,' Kubrick told the *New Yorker*. 'It is very rare to find

anyone who can become emotionally involved with an abstraction. The longer the bomb is around without anything happening, the better the job that people do in psychologically denying its existence. It has become as abstract as the fact that we are all going to die someday, which we usually do an excellent job of denying.'[30] Kubrick had become obsessed with the political rhetoric surrounding the nuclear debate. He collected and read over seventy books on nuclear strategy,[31] growing increasingly aware of the comic absurdity of the language in which issues of life and death were framed. In a RAND Corporation memorandum, the nuclear strategist Bernard Brodie had compared the no-cities plan, which avoided striking population centres, to 'coitus interruptus', while the all-out destruction favoured by Curtis LeMay was equated with 'going all the way' and leading to a 'quick and messy climax'.[32]

Kubrick, a long-standing student of Freudian psychoanalysis, adopts and parodies the military's 'war as sex' argot, inflating it to satirical proportions. *Dr. Strangelove*'s opening credits show the penetrative mid-air refuelling of long-range bombers, before the world is imperilled by a single-sperm bomber slipping through Soviet defences as the rest are repelled. The denouement follows the rapturous ride of Major Kong straddling the nuclear bomb until it hits the ground, triggering the Soviet doomsday device and the orgasmic explosions which signal the end of the film … and the world. The drama of the intervening ninety minutes arises from the sexual frustration of US Air Force General Jack D. Ripper, convinced that the communists have sapped his and America's masculinity through 'foreign substances introduced into our precious bodily fluids'. It parodies Cold War paranoia over communist plots to contaminate the American body and body politic, including the 1959 scare over plans for the fluoridation of water, denounced in newspaper headlines as a 'Red Scheme for Mass Control'.[33] 'The real purpose behind water fluoridation is to reduce the resistance of the masses to domination and control and loss of liberty … Repeated doses of infinitesimal amounts of fluorine will in time gradually reduce the individual's power to resist … and make him submissive to the will of those who wish to govern him.'[34] Just as ill-intentioned communists were circulating undetected among 'real' Americans, so America's water was being infiltrated by 'communist' minerals. In Newburgh, New York, people began feeling the effects of communist fluoridation, even before it began. 'John

Kingsley of the Newburgh filtration plant revealed the extent of people's paranoia. "Our fluoride feeder machine had been unexpectedly delayed a month in delivery, and while people were being 'poisoned' and had headaches and couldn't get their water to stop fizzing, it was the same old water they'd always been drinking!"'[35]

Kubrick's film lampooned the irrationality, hysteria and panic that does the enemy's job for him, the insanity that puts the survival of the planet at risk. And he did it all with desperate, smiling humour. In *Dr. Strangelove*, Americans and Soviets are equally hapless, as human and as dangerous as each other, each capable of starting a war at any moment.

But the American establishment didn't get the joke. 'No Communist could dream of a more effective anti-American film to spread abroad than this one,' thundered the *Washington Post*. 'United States officials, including the President, had better take a look at this one to see its effect on the national interest ... If shown around the world, it might cause the United States as much harm as many a coup or revolution.'[36]

The fear was real. Cinema was a potent medium, attracting viewers from all walks of life, demanding little effort from its consumers, but packing a powerful punch. As early as the 1920s, the German filmmaker F. W. Murnau had identified cinema's potential to shape thoughts and opinions, correctly predicting the future ... give or take a streak of misplaced Panglossian optimism. 'The screen is as great a potential power as any medium of expression. Already it is changing the habits of mankind, making people who live in different countries and speak different languages, neighbors. It may put an end to war, for men do not fight when they understand each other's heart.'[37] The *Washington Post* evidently preferred the simple certainties of the majority of Cold War films, ditching psychological subtlety in favour of stereotypes, declining to examine the motivations of 'the other'. Most Cold War movies adopted the core message of their own society – Soviet filmmakers proclaimed the superiority of socialist values; US heroes fought for the American Way. Both Hollywood and Mosfilm eschewed shades of grey, opting instead for crudely drawn caricatures – communist infiltrators seeking to undermine American society or duplicitous imperialists bent on corrupting honest Soviet citizens.

Even before Joe McCarthy's rise to prominence, the House

Un-American Activities Committee (HUAC) had put Hollywood on notice. By the end of the Second World War, the Motion Picture Alliance for the Preservation of American Ideals (MPA) had united conservative moviemakers and film stars in the battle against communist infiltration, garnering support from Walt Disney, Gary Cooper, Clark Gable, Ayn Rand, Ronald Reagan, Ginger Rogers and John Wayne. The MPA's 'Statement of Principles' opined that US cinema should bring to life the abstract struggle of the Cold War, show what was being fought for, point out where danger lurked and reveal what the enemy looked like.

> We believe in the American way of life: the liberty and freedom which generations before us have fought to create and preserve; the freedom to speak, to think, to live, to worship, to work, and to govern ourselves as individuals, as free men. Believing in these things, we find ourselves in sharp revolt against a rising tide of communism that seeks by subversive means to undermine and change this way of life ... Motion pictures are inescapably one of the world's greatest forces for influencing public thought and opinion, both at home and abroad. We refuse to permit the effort of Communist, Fascist, and other totalitarian-minded groups to pervert this powerful medium into an instrument for the dissemination of un-American ideas and beliefs.[38]

The result was a torrent of clumsy quasi-propaganda. Between 1948 and 1962, Hollywood made over a hundred films about the fight against communism,[39] including *I Was a Communist for the FBI*, *My Son John*, *I Married a Communist* and many others. All depicted communists as corrupt, devious and racist, fomenting unrest, determined to undermine American democracy and replace it with a repressive communist regime. In many of the films, the villains are American communists, manipulated by the hand of Moscow, depicted with little or no psychological complexity.[40]

Films played a part in shaping attitudes in the US, as they did in the USSR. Stalin was himself a movie addict, often forcing his politburo comrades to sit and watch with him in his private Kremlin cinema late into the night. In his 'secret' speech to the Twentieth Party Congress in 1956, Khrushchev spoke of Stalin's inordinate dependence on films. 'Everything he knew about the country ... he learned from films ...

Stalin thought that was how things really were. He shut himself off from the people, not going out anywhere.'[41]

Believing that 'cinema is the most important means of mass agitation',[42] Stalin decreed that films should be made that showed 'the superiority of the Soviet order over bourgeois democracy'.[43] All movies in the USSR needed the approval of the party, so their message was more uniform even than that of Hollywood, with no scope for dissenting voices. Between 1946 and 1950, almost 50 per cent of the villains in Soviet films were British or American.[44]

Hollywood sought to celebrate the American way of living as right, decent and morally upstanding, while the communist threat was portrayed as a menacing, creeping disease, an illness that threatened to infect and overwhelm the body politic – Americans were good; Russians were bad.

The Soviet approach was different. Moscow's Cold War movies showed us that ordinary folk, no matter which country they came from, were the same. People were all human and all equal. The differences between them arose from the nature of the political regime under which they lived. So, while the superior Marxist ideology of the Soviet Union brought out the best in its citizens, inculcating selfless ideals of civic solidarity, cooperation and love for one's fellow man, capitalism did the opposite. It fostered selfishness, greed and a beggar-my-neighbour approach to life. The bulk of the population in the West was forced to become aggressive, self-seeking and immoral because they were trapped by the infernal system of capitalist oppression, while the minority who controlled the levers of power were fat-cat businessmen and corrupt militaristic politicians who grew rich from the sweated labour of the workers. The message was clear: if only the western proletariat would rise up and demand a socialist state, they too could know the joys already possessed by their counterparts in the East. It was a powerful message and the majority of Soviet viewers signed up to it. Even if they knew that their lived reality was far from the idealised depiction they saw on the big screen, people were generally proud of the contrast with the degenerate West.

Documents from the agitation and propaganda section of the Central Committee Secretariat of the Communist Party offer a glimpse of how Soviet thinking about the cultural depiction of their Cold War rivals evolved. In 1947, they produced an instruction manual for the various Soviet artists' unions, including cinema. The stated aim of *The Plan on Measures for Propagating the Idea of Soviet Patriotism among the Population* was to 'overcome the vestiges of capitalism' in the Soviet Union, and wipe out any lingering 'feelings of sycophancy towards the capitalist West and contemporary bourgeois culture'.[45] To do this, cinema and other art forms were instructed to contrast the downtrodden state in which capitalist populations were condemned to live with the 'moral superiority and spiritual beauty of Soviet man, who is working for the good of all society'. The 'image of the enemy' is most effective when it is the antithesis of the idealised vision of the self. If the ideal is honest and brave, then the enemy should be cunning and cowardly. Films and books should be sure to carry the words of Stalin, specifically that 'every last Soviet citizen, free of the chains of capitalism, stands with his head higher than any high-ranking foreign functionary, dragging on his shoulders the yoke of capitalist slavery'.[46]

The moral was that socialism was the future, the path to peace and happiness for *all* of mankind. The Soviet people should be encouraged to feel pride that they, under the guidance of the Bolshevik party, had succeeded in building socialism; that they had created the most egalitarian society on the planet, where questions of national and ethnic conflict had been eradicated. Theirs was a society where the worker had overcome the oppression of the exploitative class, and where women were truly emancipated. It was 'crucial to show that the hatred Soviet people feel for all oppression is inextricably linked to their ardent love of their socialist homeland'.[47]

Soviet cinema took up the challenge. The most widely viewed Soviet film of 1949 was Grigori Aleksandrov's *Meeting on the Elbe* (*Vstrecha na Elbe*). It sold over 24 million tickets and won a Stalin Prize for its depiction of Soviet and American soldiers meeting in Germany at the end of the war. The film is remarkable for its celebration of common purpose between East and West. 'Comrade, this is how the people of the whole world could live, in friendship and with trust,' announces a Soviet soldier to his American buddies. 'Yes, but only if certain people don't interfere,' interjects a Soviet infantryman. The message is clear: the ordinary folk of the USSR and the USA would be delighted to live in peace and harmony, as long as the capitalist-imperialists in Washington would stop their evil manoeuvring. The delightfully kitsch score (by a rather knowing, perhaps even sardonic Dmitry Shostakovich) pipes up with exaggeratedly sinister harmonies to underline the point of the dialogue and, right on cue, the capitalist warmonger, General MacDermott of the American High Command, arrives on the scene.

MacDermott is dead against East–West fraternisation, this 'most dangerous postwar development', and it doesn't take long for the audience to discover why. MacDermott is a typical American imperialist who hates socialism and is actively plotting to rescue former Nazis from the Soviet zone of occupation. His own men are embarrassed by his behaviour. Major Hill, a 'good American', shocked by the actions of his boss, strikes up a people's friendship with his Soviet opposite number, Major Kuzmin. Together they drink a toast to a time when the common people of the world can live in (socialist) harmony. 'We love America,' proclaims Kuzmin, 'the country of brave and honourable people. The country of Jack London, Mark Twain, Whitman, Edison, Roosevelt. We will never forget your courageous soldiers, who we met on the Elbe. We love and respect the people of America.' 'Yes,' says Hill. 'In the world, there are truths that are stronger than dollars.' Kuzmin doesn't disagree. 'Let us do everything in our power so that in the future we do not meet as enemies. Remember, the friendship between the people of Russia and America is the most important question facing humanity today.'

Poor Major Hill. How could he expect to get away with such fraternisation? He is told by his superiors that he will suffer for his friendly relations with 'that Russian'. Summarily dismissed from the army, he is summoned back to the US and hauled up before HUAC.

It is a knowing dig by Aleksandrov, a message from a Soviet filmmaker to his counterparts in the US. By 1949, with the support of the MPA, HUAC had subpoenaed dozens of screenwriters, actors and directors. Many had been blacklisted and were unable to work in Hollywood. Those who refused to inform on colleagues or answer HUAC's questions became known as 'Fifth Amendment Communists'.

One actor who had been coerced into 'naming names' was Sterling Hayden, who would go on to play the paranoid General Ripper in *Dr. Strangelove*. Hayden's story bore a remarkable similarity to that of Major Hill in Aleksandrov's film. Hayden had served in the Office of Strategic Services, a predecessor of the CIA, during the Second World War and had been posted to Yugoslavia. While there, he had been impressed by the communist partisans he fought alongside and on his return he briefly joined the Communist Party of

America. The FBI used this 'communist past' to blackmail him into collaborating with HUAC, threatening to end his career and ensure he lost custody of his children if he refused. The decision to inform tormented Hayden for the rest of his life. 'I don't think you have the foggiest notion,' he would write later, 'of the contempt I have had for myself since the day I turned into a stoolie for J. Edgar Hoover'.[48] He was appalled to receive a telegram from fellow actor Ronald Reagan, praising his decision to testify.

> Not often does a man find himself eulogized for behaving in a manner he himself despises … Most of the papers had nothing but praise for my one-shot stoolie show. Only a handful, led by *The New York Times*, denounced this abrogation of constitutional freedoms whereby the stoolie could gain status in a land of frightened people.[49]

Reagan himself had fewer qualms. He was an enthusiastic FBI collaborator, with the confidential code name of T-10, and met his future wife Nancy when he used his influence to get her removed from HUAC's list of communist sympathisers.

The pressure resulting from the HUAC hearings forced studio executives to disown wartime films, such as *Mission to Moscow, Song of Russia* or *The North Star*, that showed sympathy for America's then ally, the USSR. The head of Paramount Pictures dutifully proclaimed his studio's patriotism, announcing that Hollywood should seek to bring 'the truth' to audiences at home and throughout the world, even if it meant losing money by doing so.

> We, the industry, recognize the need for informing people in foreign lands about the things that have made America a great country and we think we know how to put across the message of our democracy. We want to do so on a commercial basis and we are prepared to face a loss in revenue if necessary.[50]

The profit motive regained the upper hand, however. When public enthusiasm for communist scare movies began to wane, Hollywood moved on to other topics. Their Soviet counterparts enjoyed no such freedom. The didactic content of Soviet films made them hard to sell to West European audiences and allowed US productions to corner the market. '[Soviet films] are too sober, not diverting like American films,' complained one Tuscan cinema manager. 'When Jane Russell and Gary Cooper are the stars, then my house is filled and a line waits outside. These Russian films! One hardly hears any laughter during an entire evening.'[51]

As Helmut Hanke, the East German sociologist, pointed out, socialism was an unrelentingly serious endeavour. Its set themes were revolution, war and the struggle against reactionary forces, with film regarded as just one more means of bringing those messages to the population. Unfortunately, very little attention was paid to making such films attractive to audiences. The idea of making life in socialist countries appear to be fun was regarded as rather outlandish. 'We thought we could help things along by trying to understand the issue through scholarly analysis,' recalled the story editor of the GDR's state movie studio, DEFA, Hans-Joachim Wallstein.

> Our biggest problem came from outside, in the form of a large and ever-growing influence of art and entertainment from the West. We had to find a socialist equivalent for all this, the musical included ... Naturally, the DEFA films had to have fantasy and the filmmakers were called upon to show a sense of fantasy in their work. But what does fantasy mean? Lenin said: 'The socialist artist must dream'. But what are dreams in Socialist Realism?[52]

The answer came from the very top of the East German Communist Party. 'Your films must show the democratic profile of our new state system! ... Catch the rising sun of the socialist consciousness in the lenses of your camera!' According to the leading GDR actress Karin Schröder, that was easier said than done. 'They wanted big audiences for their films but it just didn't work. Everyone flocked to see western films, while we wanted them flocking to ours.'[53]

Budgetary constraints meant Soviet filmmakers at times struggled to produce enough movies to fill the cinemas. One way to bridge the gap was the gradual release of western 'trophy films' (purloined from German cinemas during the war) and subtly (sometimes not so subtly) edit them. To illustrate the problems of western society, the original happy endings would be abruptly excised, leaving the film to end unexplainedly after the second act, with the hero forever suspended in a moment of anguished despair. Pirated Tarzan movies proved popular with Soviet audiences, earning the state revenue from ticket sales, with no money spent on production, while also framing western 'civilisation' in a negative light.[54]

When Hans-Joachim Wallstein and some of his more adventurous DEFA colleagues, in frustration, decided to write a comedy about the difficulty of making a comedy – and somehow got it through the state censor – it became one of the GDR's biggest ever hits. *Revue um Mitternacht* (1962) was a musical stuffed with songs about how complicated it was to make a successful musical. Audiences loved it. But the authorities seemed alarmed. 'The question remains whether it is advisable for DEFA to dedicate its efforts to the musical film,' wrote the official East German press. 'Frankly, this is the most flagrant offspring of the capitalist pleasure industry.'[55]

The real source of objection was more likely the film's all too accurate depiction of the politicisation of art and culture, something that both sides preferred to keep hidden from their respective publics.

26

ART, POSTERS AND JOKES

To mourn the death of Stalin in 1953, Pablo Picasso, a member of the French Communist Party since 1945, drew a stylised portrait of the Great Leader and sent it to Louis Aragon, editor of the communist weekly *Les Lettres Françaises*.

Under the headline, 'The Debt We Owe to Stalin', the paper's front page carried articles by France's leading socialist intellectuals from the worlds of politics, science, art and literature. Aragon's very personal editorial compared his grief at the death of the Soviet leader to the grief he felt at the death of his mother. A poem by the communist writer Henri Bassis lamented 'The news that plunges us into deepest despair; The ocean of silence that laps the Kremlin shores; The night that darkens; The world left orphaned.'[1]

The flood of sentiment owed much to the tropes of the Stalin personality cult. Today they sound ridiculously exaggerated, but in 1953 they were accepted as the Left's lingua franca. Picasso's idealised drawing, on the other hand, aroused contention. The leadership of the French Communist Party reprimanded him for creating it and Aragon for publishing it, leading to great glee in the capitalist media. 'Picasso Rebuked by Reds!' smiled *The New York Times*; 'Portrait of a Woman with a Moustache,' sneered the *Daily Mail*.[2]

For Picasso himself, the controversy seemed a slur on his socialist integrity. 'Can you imagine if I had done the real Stalin,' he fumed to his friend Pierre Daix, 'such as he has become, with his wrinkles, his pockets under the eyes, his warts? ... A portrait in the style of Cranach! Can't you hear them scream, "He has disfigured Stalin!"' According to Daix, Picasso launched into an angry, rambling monologue. Reading it now evokes the boiling tensions at the heart of the relationship between Cold War politics and Cold War art.

And then I said to myself, why not a Stalin in heroic nudity? ...

Yes, but Stalin nude? And what about his virility? If you take the pecker of the classical sculpture, it's so small. But, come on – Stalin? He was a true male, a bull! So, then, if you give him the phallus of a bull, and you've got this little Stalin behind his big thing they'll cry: 'But you've made him into a sex maniac! A satyr!' Then if you are a true realist you take your tape measure and you measure it all properly. That's worse: you made Stalin into an ordinary man. And then, since you are ready to sacrifice yourself, you make a plaster cast of your own thing. Well, it's even worse. 'What, you dare take yourself for Stalin!' After all, Stalin, he must have had an erection all the time … So, tell me, you who knows: Socialist Realism, is it Stalin with an erection or without an erection?[3]

The vexed love affair that Picasso carried on with Moscow was characteristic of the times. He had joined the party at the end of the Second World War, when East–West relations were still cordial. The Kremlin was happy to profit from his name and reputation, as well as from his generous cash donations. But his art was so far removed from the tenets of socialist realism that it was largely banned in the USSR. Not until 1949, when Picasso produced his marvellously memorable *Dove of Peace* as the emblem of the communist-run World Congress of Partisans for Peace, did the Soviet authorities relent. While Stalin was building a nuclear arsenal and crushing dissidence in eastern Europe, Picasso toured the world, attending Peace Congress events, distributing his beautiful doves as a token of Soviet pacifism.*

Moscow had recognised that the visual arts have an uncommon power to sway emotions and shape opinions; that in the battle for Cold War supremacy a picture was worth at least a thousand words.

Ever since his epochal *Guernica* (1937), Picasso had held that 'painting is not made to decorate apartments'. For the politically

---

* The actor Brian Blessed recalled attending one such event as a child in Sheffield. He cheekily asked Picasso to prove that he was a great artist and Picasso responded by drawing a Peace Dove for his young critic. Blessed responded by saying, 'That's not a dove!' and crumpling it to the floor, much to his own later regret. www. telegraph.co.uk/finance/personalfinance/fameandfortune/11977486/Brian-Blessed-Picasso-gave-me-a-50m-picture.-I-threw-it-away.html.

committed left-wing artist, it was a weapon against the enemy, a tool to advance the socialist cause. In his painting *Massacre in Korea* (1951), Picasso expressly contrasts the ominously occluded masks of the capitalist murderers with the naked, defenceless faces of their victims. He knew what he was doing; the image has a visceral impact.

Unfortunately for Picasso, though, the two sides in the Cold War had very different aesthetics. The political and financial independence of most artists in the West meant they were free to pursue their own conception of artistic beauty. Governments by and large did not issue decrees to the creative community, and the extent of official intervention was limited in most cases to the adjudication of obscenity charges or offences against religious sensitivities. The result was a flowering of variegated, individual styles.

In the Soviet Union, artistic style was dictated by the Kremlin. A regime bent on subjugating culture to its own political agenda feared that aesthetic pluralism might legitimise demands for ideological pluralism and insisted instead on a monolithic artistic style regulated from above. Socialist realism demanded an art stripped of complexity and abstraction, with any divergence from a realistic depiction of the workers' struggle denounced as degenerate. Picasso might have had the right message, but he had decidedly the wrong style; it could hardly be championed by a Kremlin leadership that kept its own artists in socialist realist handcuffs.

For painters caught between the two superpowers, the circle was hard to square. 'Official' artists in Cold War eastern Europe adopted an often contorted explanation for the superiority of socialist realism. In an act of unconscious projection, a Polish documentary of 1950 titled *Nowa Sztuka* ('New Art') accused the West of the very abuses the filmmakers knew were being carried out by the Soviet Union. Over pictures of Henry Moore sculptures, paintings by Salvador Dalí, Munch, Grosz and Dix, the voiceover denounces western 'imperialist' art, as if it were a product created on the orders of capitalist governments.

> Imperialism brutally uses art to serve its own ends. The ingrained pessimism of it turns people into cannon fodder and removes their desire to revolt or to fight for a better tomorrow. Future killers of women and children are excited by these pictures, which release their basest instincts. We contrast this degenerate

art with the world of our own painters who are creating a new epoch through socialist realism.[4]

Nikita Khrushchev expressed his feelings about experimental art in 1962, when he toured an exhibition of 'Thirty Years of Moscow Art' at the capital's Manezh Gallery. His thunderous, protracted rant against 'this dog shit' and the 'homos' who produced it was recorded and reproduced in a (CIA-funded) western magazine.[5] In the fifty years since, Khrushchev's monologue has become a staple of Soviet humour. It encapsulates the regime's fear of the power of art and the witlessness of the leadership's forlorn attempts to contain it.

> This is just a mess … as though some child had done his business on the canvas when his mother was away and then spread it around with his hands! … What is hung here is simply anti-Soviet. It's amoral. Art should ennoble the individual and arouse him to action. And what have you set out here? We should take down your pants and set you down in a clump of nettles until you understand your mistakes. You should be ashamed … All the state has spent on you, and this is how you repay it. This is an art for donkeys … You've gone out of your minds. You want to deflect us from the proper course. Gentlemen, we are declaring war on you![6]

A furious Khrushchev decided he had pinpointed the cause of the problem. The offending artists had been duped, infected with the degenerate aesthetic values of the West.

> They say you like to associate with foreigners. A lot of them are our enemies, don't forget … You are parasites. We have to organize our society so that it will be clear who is useful and who is useless. Give me a list of those who want to go abroad, to the so-called 'free world'! We'll give you foreign passports tomorrow, and you can get out! Your prospects here are nil … Live out there in the 'free world.' Study in the school of capitalism, and then you'll know what's what. The people and government have taken a lot of trouble with you, and you pay them back with this dog shit.[7]

In Nikita Khrushchev's USSR, philistine paranoia was government policy. And there were those in the West who would have liked to adopt it, too. Dunderheads in all countries denounce what they don't understand. George Dondero, a Republican Congressman from Michigan, was just as colourful as Khrushchev in his denunciation of abstract painting; the only difference was that he ascribed the abomination of modern art ... to communism! 'Communism is a hydra-headed serpent that attacks the true democracies on all fronts, political, social, economic, scientific, cultural,' Dondero railed in a speech to the House of Representatives. 'We have been blind to the fact that Communist undermining of our traditional values has made broad progress in one of our great cultural fields – the field of art.'[8] In diatribes titled 'Communists Maneuver to Control Art in the United States' and 'Modern Art Shackled to Communism', Dondero denounced 'communist' painters such as Vasily Kandinsky, who were leading 'a battalion of Cubists, futurists, Expressionists, Constructionists, Suprematists, Abstractionists'. They were, said Dondero, a 'germ-carrying art vermin' who had infected American society: 'Communist art, aided and abetted by misguided Americans, is stabbing our glorious American art in the back with murderous intent.'[9]

The Cold War was riddled with pleasing incongruities. The CIA, which might have been expected to agree with Dondero that modern American art was 'an unconsciously used tool of the Kremlin', took a different view. For them, the flowering of abstract expressionism was an opportunity. Few of the agents working on Langley's cultural warfare programme could have had much time for Jasper Johns, Jackson Pollock, Mark Rothko or Cy Twombly, but they could see their value as psychological propaganda. American expressionism was the diametric antithesis of Soviet official art. It had no political message, no ideological content, and its stylistic abstraction would horrify the proponents of proletarian realism. It was, said CIA official Donald Jameson, a powerful means to promote America's contribution to world art and undermine that of her opponents. 'We recognised that this was the kind of art that did not have anything to do with socialist realism, and made socialist realism look even more stylised and more rigid and confined than it was.'[10] The CIA channelled money to the Museum of Modern Art in New York, with the aim of promoting American expressionism abroad. The museum's director, Nelson Rockefeller, himself a committed anti-communist, took up the challenge. Exhibitions of American abstract art would tour the world, including 'Masterpieces of the Twentieth Century' in 1952, 'Modern Art in the United States' in 1955 and the ambitious 'New American Painting' which was shown in every major European city between 1958 and 1959. In Rockefeller's world-view, American expressionism represented 'Free Enterprise Painting'.

'The Central Intelligence Agency used American modern art as a weapon in the Cold War,' wrote the cultural historian Frances Stonor Saunders. 'In the manner of a Renaissance prince – except that it acted secretly – the CIA fostered and promoted American Abstract Expressionist painting around the world for more than 20 years ... in the propaganda war with the Soviet Union, Russian art, strapped into the communist ideological straitjacket, could not compete.'[11]

The CIA's strategy worked. Soviet commentators responded with just the right level of outrage. 'American Expressionism shows sterility of technique,' wrote Alexander Zamoshkin, director of the Pushkin Museum. 'It has transcribed a full circle.' It had failed to achieve anything that the Russian avant-garde artist Kazimir Malevich hadn't already done thirty years earlier.[12] For Donald Jameson, Moscow's indignation confirmed that the agency had hit a psychological nerve. 'In a way, our understanding was helped because Moscow in those days was very vicious in its denunciation of any kind of non-conformity to its own very rigid patterns. And so one could quite adequately and accurately reason that anything they criticised that much and that heavy-handedly was worth support one way or another.'[13]

As usual in the Cold War, one side's PSYOP activity brought a response from the other. In 1959, exasperated by the publicity the Americans were generating, Moscow sent a collection of its own art, some of the finest masterpieces of socialist realism, to the West. The official Soviet media claimed the show was a runaway success. Reporting on the exhibition's visit to the Royal Academy in London, the art journal *Iskusstvo* boasted that 78,000 visitors had admired the officially approved Soviet artworks. 'The huge interest of the English public in the exhibition is explained by one particular fact: the great prestige of the Soviet Union in the eyes of the population ... but English criticism keeps silent about the fine art of our native land.' Judging by the visitors' book at the exhibition, there might have been a reason for the silence. 'Dull and tedious' ... 'The biggest bore I have ever seen' ... 'Art cannot be chained but you have chained it' were just a few of the comments. *Punch* magazine ran a cartoon of a couple leaving the exhibition, with the wife saying to her husband: 'Well, it explains why they're so mad keen on science.'[14]

If Soviet painters were losing the battle for Cold War supremacy, Moscow felt it was doing better in a branch of art it had made peculiarly its own. Political cartoons and political posters had been a staple of Soviet propaganda since the revolution of 1917. Unlike in the West, where satirists had never enjoyed the backing of the authorities, the newly formed Soviet state took a keen interest in satirical posters because of their ability to convey easily understood, easily digested messages in the starkest, simplest terms. Their target audience was a poorly educated population, lacking sophistication, many of whom could not read. Because of the importance attached to posters by the regime, Russia's finest writers and artists devoted themselves to producing a body of high-quality work. Vladimir Mayakovsky wrote smart, snappy verses for billboards glorifying Lenin and the Soviet future. The Kukryniksy, a collective pseudonym for artists Mikhail Kupriyanov, Porfiry Krylov and Nikolai Sokolov, produced caricatures mocking the West, denouncing capitalist hypocrisy and the threat of imperialist aggression. In a series of books titled *Satire in the Fight for Peace*, the Soviet cartoonist Boris Yefimov explained why the Kremlin placed posters at the heart of its drive for global psychological influence.

> The pointed, fervent, proactive art of political satire is an effective and accurate weapon in the fight against enemies of peace and the security of the world … Political satire has the social responsibility to fight for peace, mercilessly unmasking provocateurs and those who seek to spark conflicts in all parts of our planet … Satirical laughter is like a surgical scalpel, which can make visible and plain the secrets that were hidden behind the screens of falsehood and curtains of smoke. The biting sarcastic oeuvre of artists tears off the enticing masks of the enemies of peace and socialism.[15]

Posters became an important weapon of Cold War psychological warfare, using striking images to implant ideological messages in the minds of those who saw them. Western politicians were portrayed as parasites, milking the Middle East and Latin America, fomenting political unrest, posing as benevolent peacemakers while preparing for war. The US was depicted playing NATO and the UN like an accordion, its leaders as nuclear maniacs with bulging eyes, the perpetrators of colonialism. Soviet posters found their way into the West European market and onto the streets in the Third World. Some viewers might smile at their simplicity, but in the minds of many in Africa and Latin America they planted the seeds of disgust with capitalism and sympathy for the socialist cause that would later grow to fruition in their own revolutionary movements.

The duplicity of the West is contrasted with Soviet integrity and candour in the 1977 poster *This Is the Nonsense One Draws from a Poisoned Well*. A smartly dressed elderly man, recognisably a capitalist with his gold cufflinks, frock coat and bowler hat, is seen writing a diatribe about the 'Soviet threat' while dipping his quill in the poisonous ink inside his own head. Viewers could hardly miss the message that the Soviet threat was an invention of western warmongers, desperate to foment conflict in order to fill their own pockets, oblivious to the death and destruction they spread across the world. The strikingly grotesque nature of the image ensured it would stick in the minds of those who saw it, returning to and conditioning their thoughts when the phrase 'Soviet threat' was next encountered.

The Soviets, however, did not have a monopoly on striking images. Picasso's 1949 *Dove of Peace* which had resonated in western minds, was used as the basis of some equally memorable posters aimed at exposing the hypocrisy of the Soviet peace programme.

Jo-Jo La Colombe ('Uncle Joe the Dove'), produced in 1951 by the French anti-communist movement *Paix et Liberté*, showed Stalin with the dove firmly on a string, preaching peace but wielding a flail with a ball in the form of a nuclear bomb. An earlier poster showed the dove to be a tank in disguise.

Political posters were plastered on Soviet streets, reproduced in books and displayed in art galleries. In 1977, Leonid Brezhnev personally inaugurated the 'Third International Exhibition of Satire in the Fight for Peace' in Moscow. Propaganda images ridiculed the Cold War enemy, deliberately creating a simplified, one-dimensional image of 'the other', reinforcing the perception of 'them' as evil and 'us' as good. According to the Jungian psychologist and philosopher Sam Keen, such images subtly change the way we think of a potential adversary. 'Caricatures allow us to gently dehumanise the enemy,'

JO-JO-LA COLOMBE

Western audiences needed reminding that good old
Uncle Joe wasn't just interested in peace ...

Keen concludes. 'Yes, he is dangerous and scary, but he is not quite
human, he looks and moves in strange ways, sufficiently different
from ourselves to either fear, despise or deride ... Before we make
war, even before we make weapons, we first create the idea of an
enemy whom we can fight.'[16]

In the same way that art and posters were deployed in the service
of the socialist message, so too was humour. But while art and posters
are public media, open to scrutiny by the state and utilised only by
the authorities, humour is a private, potentially subversive method of
communicating, open to both sides.

As a western schoolboy in the late 1960s, I can remember the
tatty, green-backed books with the thumbed pages and scribbles
in the margins that were handed out to us by our elderly Russian

language tutor. She had brought them with her when she left the Soviet Union; they were a memento of a world and a world-view she had left behind, and she delighted in teaching us to read them.

The books were full of Soviet anecdotes and short stories that purported to be light-hearted and humorous. Like regular jokes, they had a plot and a punchline. But they were stuffed with the most sinister political propaganda. One tale I remember reading in class recounted a shepherd's struggle to protect his flock from a predator. After diligently watching over them night and day, he uncovers the culprit:

> 'That is a wolf in sheep's clothing!' and he took the rope he had with him, threw it around the wolf's neck and hanged him from a tree. Two men who were passing by were amazed … 'What does this mean, comrade?' they asked the shepherd. 'Is it possible you hang sheep?' 'No,' said the watchful shepherd, 'but I hang wolves when I catch them, even when they are dressed in sheep's clothing!' When the two men understood their mistake … they congratulated him. 'You are quite right, comrade!' they said. 'The most dangerous enemies are those who disguise themselves and walk amongst us.'

In an era of state-fomented paranoia about capitalist saboteurs and unpatriotic citizens undermining Soviet society, the message was not hard to divine. The green books had other, more positive stories, such as the tale of the Soviet schoolboys who hear from their teacher about all the marvellous things the next Five-Year Plan is going to produce. The first boy says, 'I wish I could go to sleep and wake up in five years so I can see everything all built at once.' The second one says, 'No, I would like to witness the great Soviet nation building all these marvels.' But the third one, the wisest of them, says, 'I would like to build all the marvels with my own hands.'

Generations of Soviet children grew up on such stories. Their young minds absorbed the legitimate pride in the achievements of their country. But they also imbibed the Cold War bile, hatred and xenophobia that the anecdotes promoted. Like Mary Poppins's spoonful of sugar, the veneer of humour disguised the taste of the poison.

While western audiences were laughing at cartoons of Desperate

Dan and Yogi Bear, the most popular Soviet cartoon character of the postwar period was a fellow called Mister Twister, based on a poem from the 1930s by the satirical writer Samuil Marshak, titled 'Mister Twister in the Land of the Bolsheviks'. It is one of a series of charmingly rhymed tales about an evil US capitalist who travels to the USSR to amuse his fractious, spoiled daughter. In one episode, they discover that their hotel in Leningrad admits people of colour. They storm out in protest and spend the rest of the poem vainly seeking a Soviet hotel that practises racial bigotry. The verse-writing is amusing and catchy. Even now I can recite the opening lines by heart: *Meester Tveester, byvshii meenistr, Meester Tveester milyonyaire* ... (Mister Twister's a former minister, Mister Twister's a millionaire; Banker, broker, newspaper king ...)

As schoolboys visiting the USSR we were told that the Soviet equivalent of the British *Private Eye* (or for an older generation, *Punch*) was a magazine called *Krokodil*. Widely read and widely quoted, *Krokodil* was full of the same sort of jaundiced propaganda that filled our Russian teacher's little green books; but with the best will in the world, it really wasn't funny. Like all Soviet publications, *Krokodil* had to go through multiple layers of regulation and censorship, which was hardly conducive to big laughs. The Soviet comedian Yakov Smirnoff, who enjoyed some success in the United States in the 1980s after emigrating there, recalled how he had to get approval from the Ministry of Culture for his material: 'They got the least funny man in all of Soviet Union and he would review your jokes – to make sure that they weren't too good ...'*

In the USSR, the best jokes were to be found on the unofficial market, the whispered humour of ordinary folk keen to poke fun at the system and the regime. Freed from ideological control, it served as an outlet for frustrations, exposing the absurdities of socialist society, puncturing the tyrant, unmasking the lies and keeping hope

---

*When he moved to the US, most of Smirnoff's more popular jokes poked fun at the world he had escaped. He even appeared in a nationwide advertising campaign for Miller Lite: 'In America, there is plenty of light beer and you can always find a party – in Russia, Party always finds you.' Avi Steinberg, 'The impossible dream of Yakov Smirnoff', *Guardian*, 22 January 2015. www.theguardian.com/news/2015/jan/22/-sp-can-king-cold-war-comedy-make-comeback-yakob-smirnoff.

alive when all seemed darkness. Jokes were a release for downtrodden citizens; samizdat and the underground humour-mill kept folks sane in an insane society. 'What is socialism?' asked one familiar riddle, to which everyone knew the answer: 'A particularly long and painful transition from capitalism to capitalism.' 'What nationality were Adam and Eve?' asked another joke. 'Russian,' comes the reply. 'Why? Because they were both naked, had only apples to eat, and thought they were in paradise.'[17]

The West had its own jokes about the idiocy of Cold Warriors who prioritised spending on missiles over spending on people. Ronald Reagan was mercilessly pilloried for his alleged lack of intelligence and blinkered world-view. The British television satire show *Spitting Image* ran sketches titled 'The President's Brain is Missing', and newspaper cartoonists delighted in mocking his perceived senility.

But not for nothing was Reagan known as the Great Communicator. I remember him coming to Moscow for a summit in 1988. He was seventy-seven and had spent his political career excoriating the communist system; but now Gorbachev was in power and rapprochement was happening. At such a sensitive juncture in East–West relations, the US president would surely need to display tact and gratitude for Moscow's willingness to give ground. Instead, Reagan told jokes. They were the very jokes we knew Soviet citizens told each other in the privacy of their own homes, but here was the president telling them with the butt of the humour – the Kremlin leadership – standing right beside him:

> An American man, boasting to his Russian friend, says the USA is such a great country that anyone can walk up to the White House and shout 'The President of the United States is a liar and a crook!' But the Russian shrugs. 'So what?' he says. 'In my country, too, anyone can walk right up to the Kremlin and shout "The President of United States is a liar and a crook!"'

Reagan flashed his winning smile as he weaponised the humour of the Russian people to score ideological points off the Russian state.

The Soviet news agency TASS was not amused. It had already criticised Reagan's 'indelicate' humour, calling it 'an embarrassment to the US people and hardly becoming for the leader of a great country'.[18] But Gorbachev grinned and bore it. As the weaker party in the process of East–West bargaining and the economic supplicant in the drive for a Cold War settlement, he had little choice. Added to which, the glint in Reagan's eyes was convivial enough to soften the bite of his humour.

It wasn't until 2018, when the CIA began to declassify its files, that the full story of Reagan's Soviet jokes emerged.[19] Far from being the off-the-cuff humour of an irrepressible raconteur, the president's storytelling was a carefully calibrated campaign, masterminded by the agency's psychological warfare experts. CIA contacts in the USSR had been instructed to gather all the underground anecdotes they could find that poked fun at the Soviet system and revealed the discontent of the Soviet populace.[20] The former CIA analyst Peter Clement remembers, 'The US Embassy in Moscow would send in a "jokes cable", usually annually, listing some of the better jokes that they had picked up. At the end of year, they would do a kind of an annual round-up, kind of a holiday gift if you will. It was very reflective of the public mood. We all looked forward to getting it.'[21]

In 1984, doing a sound check for a radio address, Reagan came close to pushing the humour too far. 'My fellow Americans,' he intoned, not realising his microphone was switched on. 'I am pleased to tell you that I have signed legislation that will outlaw Russia forever. We begin bombing in five minutes ...' In retrospect it was hardly funny; at the time it was even less so. The Soviet embassy heard it and radioed the Kremlin, who scrambled the Soviet air force.

While much has been written about the role humour plays in our lives, there has been little in the way of satisfactory theories for what makes something funny. Freud viewed jokes as something intangible, analogous to dreams. Both are products of the unconscious mind, through which we can overcome inhibitions and communicate that which is repressed in normal conversation. He explored the process in his 1905 work *Jokes and Their Relation to the Unconscious*:

> We speak of 'making' a joke; but we are aware that when we do so our behaviour is different from what it is when we make a judgment or make an objection. A joke has quite outstandingly the characteristic of being a notion that has occurred to us 'involuntarily'. What happens is not that we know a moment beforehand what joke we are going to make, and that all it then needs is to be clothed in words. We have an indefinable feeling,

rather, which I can best compare to an absence, a sudden release
of intellectual tension, and then all at once the joke is there – as
a rule ready-clothed in words.[22]

For Freud, jokes are a glimpse into people's feelings about their lives,
emotions of which they might not be consciously aware. Depressing
realities too painful or too dangerous to address in normal discourse
are shared and defused with the balm of humour. The CIA took
the jokes circulating in the Soviet Union as evidence of the system's
increasing weakness and a widespread desire to see it end: but people
across the world delight in mocking their leaders, no matter how
free the society in which they live, without necessarily expressing
a desire, much less an intention, to topple the state. Such jokes are
about making sense of the world around us and maintaining order
in our minds.

Historian Jon Waterlow argues that while transgressive jokes
might have been a sign of resistance to the Soviet regime, they were
more likely to have been coping techniques that gave people a sense
of control over their mental space and allowed them to continue to
function within the system. Like the black market or the informal
economy of *blat* (the exchange of services between contacts), jokes
were non-sanctioned means of making things work in challenging
circumstances. In hard times, jokes can serve to prove to ourselves
and others that we understand how things work (or don't), reconcil-
ing the gap between discourse and reality and dampening psychic
distress. This was especially important in the Soviet Union, where the
lofty claims of the state were often distant from lived reality.

Jokes may not make the world better, but they can improve how
we think and feel about our place in it. Telling an inappropriate joke
was a powerful act of non-conformity for the powerless, and as such
daring jokes were not the preserve of dissidents and oppositionists.
When one Soviet citizen asked another why Lenin wore shoes and
Stalin wore boots, the punchline – 'Lenin knew where he was going'
– poked fun at Stalin's errors, rather than suggesting the whole Soviet
project should be junked.[23]

That it was possible to make fun of the state and still want it
to achieve its aims left analysts in the Harvard Project on the Soviet
System puzzled. Even in their survey group of Soviet émigrés and
refugees, which displayed a 'very high level of dissatisfaction with

an exceedingly wide range of Soviet institutions and practices', they were surprised that there was 'no direct and simple line leading from dissatisfaction with the conditions of life and hostility toward the regime to active disaffection from the whole form and practice of the Soviet system'.[24]

If Soviet citizens were largely willing to criticise but tolerate Soviet power, the reality was more complicated in eastern Europe. Here, the state was often viewed as the representative of an oppressive foreign power. On his world tour, Yuri Gagarin was received less enthusiastically in Poland than in other countries and jokes were told about his exploits. In one of them, a Polish worker calls to his mate, 'Hey Janek, the Russians have gone up into space!' 'What? All of them?!' 'No, only one.' 'Huh! So what are you wasting my time for?'

Unlike dreams, jokes are by necessity social; the teller needs an audience. Freud wrote that 'laughter is among the most highly infectious expressions of psychic states. When I make the other person laugh by telling him my joke I am actually making use of him to arouse my own laughter.'[25] In societies where a remark uttered in the wrong company can lead to adverse repercussions, this is a risk – even if the experience of oppression makes people need the release of illicit humour all the more. Conditions made trust hard to come by but, once achieved, the friendships that ensued were treasured in a way that few in the West could appreciate. According to the Soviet sociologist Vladimir Shlapentokh, creating one's own pocket of privacy and security in a paranoid state sealed lifetime bonds of intimacy.*

But being funny in serious times could have repercussions. The authorities were wary of networks of trust between individuals forged outside officially sanctioned social settings; jokes undermined their monopoly on control. The security services strove to put a stop to the wry smile they regarded as a weapon of resistance. An East German

---

* Shlapentokh points to survey data showing that Soviet citizens ranked friendship far higher in their system of values than their Western counterparts did. V. Shlapentokh, 'Final Report to National Council for Soviet and East European Research: Social Values in the Soviet Union: Major Trends in the Post-Stalin Period', 30 August 1984, pp. 61–2.

His personal account of friendship and trust from his experience of living in the Soviet Union and in America is also revealing. See V. Shlapentokh, *An Autobiographical Narration of the Role of Fear and Friendship in the Soviet Union*, Lewiston: Edwin Mellen Press, 2004.

Just because the Cold War threatened the continued existence of
the human race didn't mean it couldn't be used to sell cereal.

saying summed up the pleasures and the consequences. 'There are
people who tell jokes. There are people who collect and tell jokes. And
then there are people who collect people who tell jokes …'

Christoph Kleemann, an archivist who worked on the files left
behind by the Stasi, concluded that political humour flourishes best
in conditions of repression. 'Political jokes thrive in dictatorships.
Anyone who tells one or laughs about one creates democracy for a
brief moment, and brings the regime leaders down to his level.'[26]

But humour thrives in all adverse circumstances, not just dictatorships. Russia's troubled experiment with democratisation in the 1990s
had its own supply of wistful jokes. 'Everything our leaders told us
about communism was false,' one of them began. 'Unfortunately,
it turns out that everything they told us about capitalism was true.'

27

MUSIC

When I was a student in Leningrad in the 1970s, I made an effort to get into the Soviet spirit. The cult of Lenin was big in those days and I liked the kitschy Lenin teapots and miniature statues, the posters, the films, the Lenin poems and the sentimental Lenin songs. There was one song in particular that caught my ear. It was called 'Lenin Is Always With Us', and its big punchy tune, with blaring brass and rousing chorus, was hard to resist.[1] 'Lenin is always with you,' sings the basso profundo, 'In grief, in hope and joy,' proclaim the Red Army Ensemble. 'Lenin is your springtime, Your every happy day. In every moment Lenin is with us, Bringing joy to the world!'

The older generation loved the big heroic ballads celebrating the USSR's military exploits in the struggle against Nazi Germany. The Soviet Union referred to the Second World War as the Great Patriotic War and that summed up the feelings it evoked in many who had fought in it. To western ears, the music of 'Lenin Is Always With Us' may sound trite and overblown. To a veteran of Stalingrad, it had the power to fill the heart with pride and the eye with tears.

It was different for the younger generation. They mocked the music of their elders, just as we did in the West. When I met my first Russian girlfriend we were living in a very communal student dormitory at the Leningrad Polytechnic. I asked if there was somewhere we could be alone, but she told me with a straight face that we could never be alone *potomu chto Lenin vsegda s nami* – 'because ... Lenin Is Always With Us.'

In the Cold War years, music played its part in the ideological arm-wrestling. For a regime seeking to condition hearts and minds, emotional impacts such as those created by music are potentially powerful psychological levers. Each side vaunted the supremacy of its own and derided the inadequacy of its opponent's. Each tried to export its music to the other, with varying degrees of success. The right to listen to and admire the music of 'the other' became a contested issue. The USSR sent its composers, pianists, violinists to the West, where they were met with critical acclaim and political opprobrium. Western governments, for all they may have disliked the popular music of their younger generation, recognised its value as a tool of psychological influence. The Kremlin might try to ban western pop, but it couldn't stop Soviet teenagers wanting it and feeling resentful when they were told they couldn't have it. Music came to encapsulate the values of the two opposing societies, both official and unofficial, and to project their image to the world.

In Russia, the relationship between the arts and the state has always been tighter than in the West. The collective, the nation, the people have been preoccupations of Russian culture in a way that they have not been in the capitalist democracies. Russian composers have put their art at the service of their homeland. Tchaikovsky's *1812 Overture* is built on two themes that develop into a climactic confrontation and a resolution of cathartic intensity. The first of them, the French national anthem, paints a menacing sound picture of Napoleon's armies marching eastwards into Russia. But a new theme arises, the tsarist hymn, quiet at first, then growing in confidence until the overture erupts into patriotic fervour. The French defeat cues national rejoicing, a powerful musical embodiment of something visceral in the Russian psyche: the fear of invasion, an ever-present, ever-menacing nightmare.

In the seventeenth century an equally perilous moment saw Russia occupied by Polish armies from the West. The tsar was being hunted down by Polish troops, but a Russian peasant, Ivan Susanin, sacrificed his own life to throw them off the trail. Mikhail Glinka's opera *A Life [Laid Down] for the Tsar* makes the message clear – that the individual must sacrifice himself for the greater good; the state is necessary for the survival of the people and the individual is therefore bound to serve it.

The enshrinement of the common good as society's paramount ideal makes possible some of the best and the worst in the Russian nation. At one end of the scale, it informs the early idealism of twentieth-century communism and the continuing social solidarity of the Russian people. At the other, it underpins phenomena like the Red Army's reckless sacrifice of men in the Second World War and the postwar pillaging of the civilian economy to serve the needs of the military. The Bolsheviks didn't know what to make of the Susanin legend. At first they banned Glinka's opera because it glorified the tsar, but when they realised the power of its collectivist message, they relented. Its rousing final chorus, 'Slavsya Ty, Rus' Moya!', later to become briefly the Russian national anthem, is today a standard in the repertoire of the Red Army Choir.

In the communist era, the duty of composers to serve the state became an obligation. Prokofiev wrote cantatas in praise of the revolution; Shostakovich wrote choral works and symphonies that bolstered the Soviet message. But when they got things wrong, it had serious consequences. So appalled was Stalin by Shostakovich's musically daring, politically dubious *Lady Macbeth of the Mtsensk District* (1934) that he wrote a withering condemnation of the work in *Pravda* under the headline 'Muddle instead of Music'. It left Shostakovich in fear for his life.

The Nazi threat re-established the bond between music and the state, rehabilitating composers who not so long ago had been denounced. Shostakovich wrote his Seventh Symphony, a tribute to his native Leningrad, while he was serving as a part-time fire warden in the besieged city. 'All of us are soldiers today,' Shostakovich wrote. 'And those who work in the field of culture and the arts are doing their duty on a par with all the other citizens of Leningrad.'[2] The Soviet leadership announced that the symphony represented an artistic denunciation of the evils of Nazism. They ordered a bombardment of German positions to halt the shelling of the city during the first performance, which was broadcast on loudspeakers in the streets and subsequently around the world. Shostakovich would later claim that the 'Leningrad' was a denunciation of all dictatorships – communist as well as fascist – but it gave a powerful boost to Soviet morale.

Music can be both ideologically motivated and artistically successful. The semi-dissident poet Yevgeny Yevtushenko wrote verses that edged up to the very frontier of what was permissible in the Soviet era, criticising the excesses of communist authoritarianism. Several of his poems became successful popular songs, including one called 'Do the Russians Want War?'. Set to music by Eduard Kolmanovsky, it climbed the Soviet charts in 1961 as the world rushed to the brink of nuclear confrontation. 'Do the Russians Want War?' ask the lyrics:

If you think the Russians want war,
You should ask the silence in our fields,
Ask our sons who lie beneath them.
They fought and died not just for us,
But for all the people of the earth,
So all can sleep at night.
Ask our soldiers you met on the Elbe.
Ask our mothers and our wives.
We don't want our boys to die again.

It was propaganda, but it was potent stuff. And it was addressed directly to the West, casting 'the other' in the role of putative aggressor.[3]

Few western governments were able to call on the same quality of musical support that the Kremlin received from its composers and musicians. The 1950s and 60s produced a string of US hits with anti-communist themes, most of them from country music stars. Carson Robison's 'I'm No Communist' of 1952 ('Communists and spies are making monkeys out of us!') appealed to the conservative 'redneck' electorate that helped keep Eisenhower's Republicans in power.[4] Roy Acuff's 'Advice to Joe' (1951) was positively bloodthirsty in its call for Washington to use its monopoly of atomic weapons to wipe out communism before Moscow acquired the bomb. He too had something to say to the leader in the Kremlin, warning they would soon 'see the lightnin' flashin', hear atomic thunders roll!'[5]

In contrast to the self-righteous, religious-conservative bombast, other artists conveyed the anti-communist message with a modicum of humour. Bo Diddley's 'Mr. Khrushchev' (1962) used the tropes of the blues to give a black American perspective on the Cold War. In contrast to the stance that later black artists would take,* Diddley was broadly supportive of 'the white man's' politics, calling on Americans to back JFK and 'to unite and protect our land' from Soviet advances.[6]

Prescott Reed's 1958 'Russia, Russia (Lay that Missile Down)', written by folk singer Tom Glazer, was a pastiche of Russian musical cadences, with mock balalaikas churning out bubble-gum riffs.

---

* For example, Gil Scott-Heron's take on the space race in 'Whitey on the Moon', cf. Chapter 20.

It pointed an accusing finger at the Kremlin, but the references to shared interests, such as music, food and sports, served to humanise the Soviets and open the door for rapprochement. Not content to merely influence the opinion of the US public, the record label announced that they would be sending the first two copies of the record 'to President Eisenhower and Khrushchev'.[7]

While Reed extended the hand of peace to Moscow, others aided the Vietnam War effort by travelling to entertain the troops, although the number of overtly pro-war songs was not great. Merle Haggard wrote his 1969 'Okie from Muskogee' to support US soldiers who were 'giving up their freedom and lives to make sure others could stay free'. 'The Dawn of Correction' by the group The Spokesmen had a pro-war message, proclaiming the need to 'keep free people from Red domination', while – grotesquely – C-Company's 'The Battle Hymn of Lt. Calley' praised the American officer who in 1971 was convicted of massacring civilians in the Vietnamese village of My Lai; it sold over 2 million copies.[8]

If music could be enlisted to support the regime, it could also be deployed against it. Shostakovich exacted his revenge on Stalin by writing a scathing operetta titled *Antiformalisticheskiy Rayok* ('The Anti-Formalist Show'). Its moustachioed lead character belts out extracts from the Great Leader's illiterate cultural denunciations in an unmistakeable and ungrammatical Georgian bass, while the Poet retorts, 'Thank you comrade leader for that lucid and highly informed oration to elucidate such vital questions on the subject of music …'[9] But in the USSR, examples of dissident music had to be kept hidden. Performing them in public carried great danger. Shostakovich wrote his 'for the drawer' – a personal, private vengeance that could not be made public until long after his death.

In the West, things were different. A large number of politically minded Cold War songs carried an anti-state message. Paul Robeson, Woody Guthrie, Pete Seeger and – in Britain – Ewan MacColl were among those popular artists who were sympathetic to the communist cause. Their governments may have frowned on the message their music conveyed, but by and large they didn't ban it. Robeson, also the only black musician among the group, was the exception. His bass-baritone voice had captivated audiences from the Theatre Royal in London to the Bolshoi in Moscow, ensuring his words carried across the globe, and he was uncompromising in his views. 'The artist must take sides. He must elect to fight for freedom or for slavery. I have made my choice.'*

His, at times blind, loyalty to Moscow displeased his own government, but his denunciation of the treatment of African Americans exposed an injustice the self-proclaimed land of liberty preferred to hide. Having previously declared that he 'felt a full human being' the first time he stepped on Soviet soil, Robeson attracted the ire of the American establishment when he spoke at the communist-affiliated World Congress of Partisans for Peace in Paris in 1949.

> We in America do not forget that it is on the backs of the poor whites of Europe ... and on the backs of millions of black people the wealth of America has been acquired. And we are resolved that it shall be distributed in an equitable manner among all of our children and we don't want any hysterical stupidity about our participating in a war against anybody no matter whom. We are determined to fight for peace. We do not wish to fight the Soviet Union.[10]

When his words were misreported by the Associated Press, suggesting that African Americans would side with the Soviets in any future war, Robeson was branded an enemy of America.[11] The National Association for the Advancement of Colored People (NAACP) were pressured to distance themselves from him, and Robeson's next concert in the US, a civil rights benefit in Peekskill, New York, was targeted by violent, racist mobs. The FBI confiscated his passport, and for much of the 1950s he was unable to travel to perform abroad, or indeed to collect the International Stalin Prize he was awarded in 1952.

When summoned before HUAC in the summer of 1956, Robeson, a Columbia Law School graduate, ran rings around the committee, dismissing their suggestion that he should relocate to Moscow permanently.

---

* Speech given at an anti-fascist fundraiser at the Royal Albert Hall, 1937, in P. Foner (ed.), *Paul Robeson Speaks: Writings, Speeches, Interviews, 1918–1974*, London: Quartet Books, 1978, p. 118. Robeson, however, was more willing to turn a blind eye to the shortcomings of the Soviet Union.

[My] father was a slave, and my people died to build this country, and I am going to stay here, and have a part of it just like you. And no Fascist-minded people will drive me from it. Is that clear? … You gentlemen … are the non-patriots, and you are the un-Americans, and you ought to be ashamed of yourselves.[12]

In the 1960s, Bob Dylan, Joan Baez and others turned 'protest' music into a recognised, commercialised genre. Dylan's 'Talkin' World War III Blues' tackled the fear that the threat of nuclear annihilation had lodged in the human psyche. His 'Masters of War' protested the arms race. And 'With God on Our Side' mocked the self-righteous, hypocritical teachings of conservative American politics.

'A Hard Rain's a-Gonna Fall', premiered in 1962, was reportedly written in response to the Cuban missile crisis. In his memoirs, Dylan recalled the oppressive psychological burden of the times that prompted him to write it: 'After a while you become aware of nothing but a culture of feeling, of black days, of schism, evil for evil, the common destiny of the human being getting thrown off course. It's all one long funeral song.'*

'Let Me Die in My Footsteps' was inspired by the sight of construction workers beginning work on a nuclear fallout shelter.[13] As Dylan told the critic Nat Hentoff,

I was going through some town, and they were making this bomb shelter right outside of town … As I watched them building, it struck me sort of funny that they would concentrate so much on digging a hole underground when there were so many other things they should do in life. If nothing else, they could look at the sky, and walk around and live a little bit, instead of doing this immoral thing. I guess it's just that you can lead a lot of people by the hand. They don't even really know what they're scared of.[14]

Mainstream 'protest' songs with their serious-minded anti-war lyrics were accompanied by a subversive school of acerbic musical satire.

The apocalyptic nature of the subject seemed somehow reduced by the music's lightness, a subliminal lifting of the gloom that

---

* Bob Dylan, *Chronicles: Volume One*, Simon & Schuster, 2004, p. 85. The chronology doesn't quite fit, and it seems Dylan wrote the song before the October Crisis.

enveloped a menaced world. It chimed with the popular mood. Tom Lehrer's 'We Will All Go Together When We Go' carried a reassurance that we were 'all in this together', an implied pledge of human solidarity ('Universal bereavement, an inspiring achievement'), forlorn and despairing, but comforting nonetheless.

By the time of the Woodstock festival in 1969, Lehrer-esque humour had become the vernacular of the anti-war movement. Country Joe and the Fish performed their 'I-Feel-Like-I'm-Fixin'-to-Die Rag', with its burlesque music and *grand guignol* lyrics, to an audience of young people who had all been, or were about to be, subjected to the terrifying lottery of conscription to the Vietnam War. The song reflected the sense of hopeless, slightly out-of-control abandon that many Americans seemed to be experiencing in the face of the Cold War's unremitting terror: 'put down your books and pick up a gun, we're gonna have a whole lotta fun!'[15]

Feeling impotent in the face of an ineluctable external threat is known to psychologists as 'perceived external locus of control' and is recognised as a powerful instigator of depressive thoughts.[16] Russians, too, suffered from trauma-inducing anxiety over the ongoing threat to their survival, but Soviet musicians knew that lyrics touching on such delicate subjects would not be tolerated. Those who did explore the new nuclear realities did so in a remarkably sanitised fashion. Muslim Magomayev, once dubbed the 'Soviet Sinatra', had a catchy number titled '*Atomny Vek*' ('The Atomic Age'), whose words morph seamlessly from a meditation on nuclear power to a rather saccharine love song. Magomayev reassures his millions of listeners that despite being in 'the atomic age ... the globe still turns and turns, With music that plays'. This is 'an age of machines, an age of poetry, Of wisdom and of mischief', but no machine can answer 'the single, vital question: Do you love me or do you not?'[17]

In the psychological battle for Cold War musical supremacy, pop music was not Moscow's strongest suit. Few in the West had heard of Yevgeny Yevtushenko; even fewer of Muslim Magomayev. What they had heard of were the great nineteenth-century Russian composers, such as Tchaikovsky, Borodin and Rimsky-Korsakov. Contemporary Russian music had also burst onto the western scene following the wartime success of Shostakovich's Leningrad Symphony, championed by Toscanini and played frequently on the radio as a symbol of Allied solidarity.

Classical music was Russia's trump card, but the Kremlin was extraordinarily slow to realise it. From the mid 1920s onwards, Soviet musicians had been forbidden from travelling abroad for fear that a taste of capitalist luxury and freedom would tempt them to defect. By the 1950s, however, Moscow had understood the propaganda value of music and was sending its stars to dazzle the West. The pianists Emil Gilels and Sviatoslav Richter, the cellist Mstislav Rostropovich and the violinist David Oistrakh wowed audiences in Britain and the USA, winning rapturous notices on the arts pages and extensive, although not always positive, coverage in the political columns. Their consummate artistry and the shining humanity of their personalities put a human, cultured face on the Soviet Union, challenging western-manufactured stereotypes of the Russians as menacing, soulless robots.

For the musicians themselves, travelling to the West as official representatives of the Soviet regime could be stressful. The endearingly eccentric Rostropovich, invited to meet Harold Macmillan, took it in his stride, reportedly addressing the prime minister as Meester MacMillion and praising him for his leadership of Britain during the war. But Rostislav Dubinsky, the gifted leader of the Borodin Quartet, justified the Kremlin's fears by defecting to the USA.*

Dmitry Shostakovich found the task unnerving. Sent to New York in 1949 as a Soviet delegate to the communist-sponsored Cultural and Scientific Congress for World Peace, he was given an officially approved speech to read out at a press conference. Recordings of the event reveal how he struggled to parrot the propaganda of a regime he had come to loathe; when Shostakovich faltered, his interpreter simply took over and read out the rest of the text for him. The American playwright Arthur Miller, who was there, was perceptive enough to understand the composer's dilemma. 'God knows what he was thinking in that room,' Miller wrote, 'what splits ran across his spirit, what urge to cry out and what self-control to suppress his outcry lest he lend comfort to America and her new belligerence toward his country, the very one that was making his life a hell.'[18]

---

*He would later write a colourful autobiography that lifted the curtain on the relationship between Soviet officialdom, creative artists and the impact of music on public thinking. See R. Dubinsky, *Stormy Applause: Making Music in a Worker's State*, Boston: Northeastern University Press, 1992.

Shostakovich was forced to act as an international representative
of the Soviet Union, when he would much rather have been
watching his beloved Dinamo Leningrad play football …

Anti-communist demonstrators picketing the congress denounced Shostakovich for agreeing to lend his support to the Soviet
regime. At the end of the press conference, the Russian émigré composer Nicolas Nabokov rose to his feet and asked him if he concurred
with the Kremlin's recent denunciation of Stravinsky. Knowing that
Shostakovich would have no choice but to answer in the affirmative,
Nabokov declared that his answer proved he was 'not a free man, but
a tool of his government'.[19] Shostakovich, who admired Stravinsky's
music, felt himself exposed and humiliated.[20] 'I still remember with
horror my first trip to the USA,' he would recall many years later. 'I
wouldn't have gone at all if it hadn't been for intense pressure from
administrative figures of all ranks and colours, from Stalin down. I
felt like a dead man. I answered all the idiotic questions in a daze,
and thought, "When I get back it's over for me." Stalin liked leading
Americans by the nose that way. He would show them a man – here
he is, alive and well – and then kill him …'[21]

    In retrospect, there seems to have been a surprising level of
comprehension among the American public for the difficulty of Shostakovich's position. Many Americans who had come to love his music

were willing to sympathise with a beleaguered composer, struggling to remain true to his art in a restrictive society. The exchange with Nicolas Nabokov, the reaction of Arthur Miller and the evaluation of the US media throw a nuanced light on the West's perception of Soviet music and its place in the East–West jousting of the time. One of the anti-communist placards carried by demonstrators outside the congress read, 'Shostakovich, Jump Thru the Window!', seemingly an appeal for him to defect to the West. The American Federation of Musicians subsequently invited him to apply for residence in the US and forty-two prominent musical figures, including Aaron Copland, Serge Koussevitzky and Leonard Bernstein, presented him with a scroll of friendship. 'Music is an international language,' read the inscription, 'and your visit will serve to symbolize the bond which music can create among all peoples. We welcome your visit also in the hope that this kind of cultural interchange can aid understanding among our peoples and thereby make possible an enduring peace.'[22]

When Moscow's prestigious International Tchaikovsky Piano Competition was first staged a decade later, in 1958, the Cold War was at its height and the expectation was that the prize would be given to one of the many outstanding Soviet pianists in order to boost the USSR's image on the world stage. But a tall young American from Texas, looking like a 'runner bean with asparaguses for fingers',[23] played concertos by Tchaikovsky and Rachmaninov and got a standing ovation that lasted for eight minutes. Lavan 'Van' Cliburn was clearly the audience's favourite. His performances were on a par with those of his Soviet rivals, but the fact that he was American seemed to give the Moscow public an added incentive to take him to their hearts. Their applause was in part an expression of dissatisfaction with the Soviet leadership's cultural chauvinism, an affirmation of the universal values of music, and it put the judges in a dilemma. The chairman, Emil Gilels, himself a pianist of genius, turned to Khrushchev for guidance. 'May we give the prize to an American?' Gilels asked. Khrushchev, to his credit, replied, 'If he is the best, then give it to him!'

It seemed a defining moment. Music had united Soviets and Americans, momentarily bridging the chasm of politics and offering a glimpse of hope when East–West relations were in the deep freeze. Cliburn was feted by Khrushchev and lionised on his return to America. He received a ticker-tape parade in New York and was mobbed by fans. His records sold in the millions. 'I appreciate more than you will ever know that you are honouring me,' he told an audience in City Hall, New York, 'but the thing that thrills me the most is that you are honouring classical music. Because I'm only one of many. I'm only a witness and a messenger. Because I believe so much in the beauty, the construction, the architecture invisible, the importance for all generations, for young people to come that it will help their minds, develop their attitudes and give them values. That is why I'm so grateful that you have honoured me in that spirit.'[24]

We underestimate at our peril the power of great music to shape the human soul. On 21 August 1968, the day after his motherland had led the invasion that crushed Czechoslovakia's Prague Spring, Mstislav Rostropovich was due to play at the Proms in London's Royal Albert Hall. The orchestra was the Soviet State Symphony and there were public protests. Rostropovich – a lifelong champion of liberty and freedom of thought – played the cello concerto of the Czech composer Antonín Dvořák, rising to his feet at the final note and holding aloft the work's score in a gesture of solidarity with the Czech nation. His encore, the Sarabande from Bach's Suite No. 2 in D minor, was, he said, a piece he wished to offer to all those who were in sorrow. He was cheered to the rafters.

The Kremlin was willing to welcome Cliburn partly because he had played 'their' music and partly because Russia could claim much of the credit for making him famous. But most western music was frowned upon. In the socialist world, 'capitalist' pop was dismissed as decadent and degenerate, a reflection of the society that produced it. Classical music affected many people in Soviet Russia, but pop music appealed to many more. The authorities were aghast at its popularity. They struggled to stop their citizens from being 'infected' by the western diseases of jazz and rock. At the end of the war in Europe, Red Army soldiers had returned home with whatever they could carry, and some of their most treasured items were the jazz and blues records they had 'liberated' in the West. As with the returning Decembrists in the Russian armies that defeated Napoleon, their glimpse of western freedoms made a lasting impression. The sounds of Duke Ellington, Louis Armstrong and Glenn Miller began to be heard from the apartment windows of the socialist bloc. Western radio stations, including the BBC and Voice of America, broadcast programmes of jazz and invited Soviet listeners to write in with requests to London and Washington.

Official publications warned of the danger. *Kultura I Zhizn* ('Culture and Life') cautioned against admiration for western music and instructed Soviet songwriters not to emulate its 'endless repetition of vulgar themes from commercial beer-hall Bohemias'.[25] But it was too late. By the early 1950s, groups of youngsters began to congregate on the streets of Moscow and Leningrad dressed in brightly coloured suits and dresses, with elaborate haircuts unlike anything their countrymen had ever seen. Conspicuous and provocative, they strolled along Gorky Street and the Nevsky Prospekt, which they renamed 'Broadway', speaking a dialect peppered with words and phrases from their favourite records, unintelligible to the average Soviet citizen, and referring to themselves as *Shtatniki* ('United-Stateniks').

For the official Soviet media, it was all too much. *Pravda* coined another term for such misguided youth – *Stilyagi*, implying that they were all style and no substance, cretinous victims of vapid western consumerism.[26] They were depicted as amoral and potentially criminal, bent on undermining the social order of the USSR. The *stilyagi* were indeed rebelling against the conformity of Soviet society, but not from any desire to overthrow its political structures. Like teenagers the world over, they idealised individualism and unpredictability, values they found symbolised in American jazz. The future jazz musician Alexei Kozlov recalled the disconnect between the wondrous sounds he heard on western radio stations and the way such music was decried by the Soviet media. 'The radio was our only window to the West and neighbours could denounce you for listening to western stations. I bought a dictionary and tried to learn English by listening, because I wanted to understand what Nat King Cole was saying in songs like "Walkin' My Baby Back Home".'[27]

Jazz had long been proscribed in the Soviet Union. As early as 1928, Maxim Gorky had denounced it as the product of western degenerates, 'fat men's music', reducing listeners to animalistic states of sexual frenzy.[28] The Kremlin issued blood-curdling warnings about its effects on young people: 'It is only one step from a saxophone to a knife … Today he plays jazz, but tomorrow he will betray his homeland.' Komsomol, the young communist organisation, dispatched so-called 'Nightingale Squads' to harass the *stilyagi*, raiding dancehalls and clubs, cutting up their treasured drainpipe trousers, their colourful ties and dresses, shaving off their distinctive quiffs and long hair.[29]

For Vasily Aksyonov, later to become a notable dissident novelist, jazz represented a potentially transformative force, a means to challenge the authority of the state.

> For my generation of Russians it was the voice of America soaring over the iron curtain on the airwaves of the Voice of America. Why did we love it so? Perhaps for the same reason the Communists (and the Nazis before them) hated it. For its refusal to be pinned down, its improvisatory nature. Living as we did in a totalitarian society, we needed relief from the strictures of our minutely controlled everyday lives, of the five-year plans, of historical materialism. In Eastern Europe, jazz became more than music; it took on an ideology or, rather, an anti-ideology. Jazz was a rendezvous with freedom.[30]

Jazz had also ruffled feathers in the West,[31] and when rock and roll burst onto the scene in the mid 1950s, authorities on both sides of the Iron Curtain were united in their horror. Elvis 'the Pelvis' Presley offended conservative America to such an extent that *The Ed Sullivan Show* was allowed to film his performance only from the waist up. For the gerontocrats in the Kremlin, it was even more alarming: a concerted effort by the West, they declared, to undermine the health of our children. Young Russians latched onto the new music with such alacrity that it seemed to challenge the very foundations of Soviet society. Pirated western LPs sold for huge prices on the black market.[32] Enterprising teenagers developed ingenious methods of copying them, including the use of lathes to cut tunes into X-ray sheets pilfered from hospitals. Dealers would stand outside the GUM department store opposite the Kremlin with the makeshift recordings, known as 'rock on bones' (рок на костях), curled up inside their overcoats, surrounded by eager buyers.[33]

Even devoted young communists were not immune. Pavel Palazchenko, who would later serve as an interpreter for the Soviet politburo, fell for the charm of the Beatles as a student in the 1960s. 'We knew their songs by heart,' Palazchenko recalled in his memoirs. 'In the dusky years of the Brezhnev regime they were not only a source of musical relief. They helped us create a world of our own, a world different from the dull and senseless ideological liturgy that increasingly reminded one of Stalinism ... The Beatles were our quiet way of rejecting "the system" while conforming to most of its demands.'[34] The Beatles, banned in the Soviet bloc, enjoyed the appeal of forbidden fruit. Their records circulated as highly prized samizdat. When Paul McCartney wrote 'Back in the U.S.S.R.', it led to persistent rumours that the Fab Four had secretly stopped off in Moscow on their way to India and had played a private concert for the children of Soviet government ministers. McCartney himself recognised the ability of music to bridge the East–West divide. 'I wrote ['Back in the U.S.S.R.'] as a kind of Beach Boys parody,' he told *Playboy* magazine. 'It was also hands across the water, which I'm still conscious of. 'Cause they like us out there, even though the bosses in the Kremlin may not. The kids from there do. And that to me is very important for the future of the race.'[35]

Washington might have worried about the effect of rock and roll on America's teenagers, but the psychological warriors of the CIA recognised its potential to influence and subvert their socialist counterparts: music could be a 'means of seduction' towards western values, wrote Charles Montirian in the NATO-sponsored *General Military Review*.[36] The East German politburo agreed, accusing Radio Luxembourg of deliberately promoting the sort of music and dance that would corrupt East German youth. '[The] imperialists and militarists over the previous years have increased their efforts to bring the youth of the GDR under their influence,' concluded a 1960 report by the Department for Youth Affairs of the Central Committee. Western psychological warfare, the report claimed, was directly linked to a 60 per cent increase in juvenile delinquency between 1950 and 1959, while the level of other crime over same period had actually fallen.[37]

In West Germany, the Interior Ministry noted numerous violent incidents after concerts or movie screenings, referring to them as *Halbstarken* ('rocker' or 'beatnik') riots. The authorities turned to the educational psychologist Curt Werner Bondy, who played down the importance of cultural triggers, suggesting that rebellious behaviour was normal in male youths.[38] 'It is not easy for adults to accept that youngsters lean toward rebellion,' wrote the West Berlin minister for youth affairs, Ella Kay. 'But it is a [natural] step towards adulthood.'[39] East German politicians, by contrast, had little time for the intricacies of developmental psychology. Politburo member Paul Fröhlich was convinced that the GDR's children were being corrupted by the cultural machinations of the West, which aimed to foist 'bourgeois theories of a loneliness of man' on socialist youth, weakening their bond to the party. It was the West that was pushing them towards cynicism, scepticism and 'a need to question everything'.[40]

The question of youth identity has been a challenge to societies throughout history. Erik Erikson, like Curt Bondy, concluded that the adolescent identity crisis is an inherent, natural and universal stage of human development triggered by the individual's self-image coming into contact with the changing imperatives of existing society. It arises from developmental factors common to all humans; but its effects are especially acute in societies of strong ideological dependence. As young people search for an identity of their own, there is a natural tendency to achieve self-definition through the rejection of conventional majority views; questioning social orthodoxy is an important facilitator of individual validation. Such societal revolt may be disapproved of in the West, but it takes place there in a context of tolerance, where divergences from the cultural norm are, within limits, broadly accepted. In lands of ideological homogeneity, however, the path of individual differentiation can be treacherous. Divergences arouse suspicion and opprobrium, particularly when they are seen as turning to 'enemy' cultures for inspiration. Where the party is present in all aspects of life, there can be no apolitical actions; even a neutral search for identity is seen through the prism of ideology.

The ruling East German Socialist Unity Party (SED) drew up 'Ten Commandments of Socialist Morality', rules of personal conduct by which all citizens were expected to live. Rule 8 addressed the duty of families in raising their offspring: 'Thou shalt rear thy children in the spirit of peace and socialism to become citizens who are well-educated, strong in character, and physically healthy', and rule 9 laid out what was expected in return: 'Thou shalt live a clean and decent life and respect thy family.'[41] A Soviet propaganda film showed the damage that rock and roll could do to such ideals, using footage of young people in France: 'Young men and girls dance in ecstasy,' lamented the voiceover, 'mimicking the wild movements from across the ocean [i.e. from the USA]. Only when the dancehall is in danger of collapsing in total destruction do the police intervene. This is the export of western culture!'[42]

The worst example of such depraved dancing, it goes without saying, was the twist. Such was the twist's mind-subverting power that it could apparently be used to turn loyal Soviet citizens into traitors.

When Oleg Penkovsky was unmasked as a western spy, *Pravda* wrote, 'Not only had he learned Morse Code ... he had also mastered the fashionable Twist', as if one such suspicious activity inevitably led to the other.

The youths themselves were puzzled. In April 1962, a young communist member who'd been reprimanded for taking part in 'indecent modern dances' at the Kharkov House of Culture, wrote to the youth newspaper *Komsomolskaya Pravda*. 'Why,' he asked, 'even for good students with no disciplinary breaches on our records, is there such a strange attitude towards modern dances?' Lev Kassil, a popular children's author, provided the explanation. It was true, Kassil acknowledged, that times change and new forms of expression are inevitable, but these risqué modern dances were psychologically dangerous for young people and for the whole of Soviet society.

> Their heart-rending howls and monotonous rhythm and melody, insistently and endlessly repeated, bring onlookers and dancers to a state of frenzy that at times becomes mass hysteria. Dozens of cases are known in which possessed dancers of the twist, obsessed and infuriated, have demolished the buildings where they were gathered, have broken windows and chairs and, out in the street, have staged riots. There is no point in denying it – our country, too, has 'twisters' who cause loose manners and blatant posturing. These persons must be called to order![43]

Representatives of 'healthy' dance forms were especially vocal in decrying the twist. Igor Moiseyev, the leading Soviet choreographer of folk ballet, declared it sinful and unclean. It was, he said, a dangerous psychological weapon directed at innocent Soviet youngsters by a malign ideological foe.

> Dance is a method of upbringing, and if we do not make use of this method, our ideological enemy certainly will. ... But every person with healthy taste will be repelled by [western music's] sexuality, its indelicate intimacy, its isolation from everybody and everything and its demonstrative contempt for social principles. All this can be vanquished not through prohibition, but only by creating new dances.[44]

The 'new dances' advocated by Moiseyev would be the socialist bloc's Terpsichorean riposte to the West's dirty dancing, a wholesome, socialist weapon on the Cold War dancefloor. Walter Ulbricht tasked the GDR's choreographers with creating them. Socialist dances must 'reject the capitalist decadence', Ulbricht declared, 'fight against pulp fiction and petit bourgeois habits, speak out against "hot" music' and the ecstatic "singing" of someone like Presley. We have to offer something better!'[45] The problem, however, was the form that the socialist 'something' should take. Dancing close together was rejected as too highly sexualised, but dancing apart was no better because space between dancers allowed for suggestive thrusting and wiggling of the hips. In the end, the experts came up with an officially approved solution dubbed the Lipsi (after Leipzig), a sexless rumba with a spin, far too sedate to replace the twist, that left most socialist youths distinctly underwhelmed.

It wasn't just capitalist dancing which socialism had to combat; capitalist pop stars were an equally serious threat. In desperation, the socialist bloc set about recruiting its own. When home-grown singers failed to capture the imagination of the young, the Kremlin's psychological warriors looked abroad ... and came up with Dean Reed. Reed was a godsend. He was American, he had long hair, flared trousers and, most importantly, a fondness for socialism.

Reed had had some success in Hollywood but when his music became popular in South America, he moved to Chile. In Santiago, he got his own TV show, became involved in left-wing causes and attracted the sympathetic attention of the KGB. In 1966, he was invited to tour the USSR, offered a Soviet record deal and held up as proof that capitalism didn't have a monopoly on cool. In 1973, Reed settled permanently in East Berlin, where he released thirteen albums and starred in twenty films, seemingly fully committed to the socialist cause.

In a May 1986 interview on US national television, he defended the Soviet invasion of Afghanistan and the building of the Berlin Wall, comparing the policies of Ronald Reagan to the worst excesses of Stalinism. But six weeks later, Reed's lifeless body was discovered in a lake in East Berlin. In his car, he had left a letter to the then East German leader, Erich Honecker, apologising if his suicide was interpreted as reflecting badly on the GDR.

As the Cold War began to thaw, so did Moscow's freeze on

western music. By the 1980s, the *Great Soviet Encyclopaedia*, a reliable barometer of Kremlin thinking, was ready to concede that 'despite the increasing exploitation of pop music by businessmen in the bourgeois commercial music world, individual ensembles, including the Beatles and Chicago, have succeeded in creating a number of pop music works of genuine artistic value'.[46] In 1988, Dave Brubeck put the seal on the socialist rehabilitation of jazz by performing live at the Reagan–Gorbachev summit in Moscow. The US secretary of state, George Shultz, approached Brubeck the next day. 'Dave, you helped make the summit,' Schultz declared. 'And today everyone on both sides was talking about it. They found common ground. You broke the ice.'

Did music actually change the course of history? Brubeck himself just shrugged. 'I don't know … but they all started tapping their feet together. This was the first unity we'd seen. The whole audience was in there swingin'.'[47]

28

RELIGION

Between September and November 1945, the Roman Catholic newspaper *The Tablet* published a series of extended essays under the title 'God and the Atom'.[1] The author, Monsignor Ronald Knox, was Britain's leading Catholic thinker, active in formulating the Church's position on world events. His aim in his essays, Knox wrote, was to 'put something on record [to] give the curious historian a document of what the world felt like in September 1945'. From the outset, Knox's diagnosis makes clear that the world is suffering and afraid.

> Trauma. The news [of the bombing of Hiroshima] burst upon our breakfast-tables and left us numb. Our first reaction, probably, was one of fear … An indefinite period of universal peace, our confident assumption in 1918, is only a frantic aspiration in 1945; we pictured the next war, fought with such weapons as would make the rocket-bomb seem what in truth it was, last year's model … What hideous weapons, in a few years' time, might be within reach of the gunman and the hooligan! Was our civilization, after all, to turn Troglodyte?

'God and the Atom' is a flash-lit snapshot of the maelstrom of euphoria, guilt, horror and anxiety for the future that gripped British society in the days after the bombing of Hiroshima and Nagasaki. It is startlingly immediate, the thoughts of a sentient man picking up the newspaper that has dropped a moment before on his breakfast table, bearing the news of the most destructive act in the history of mankind. You can feel Knox struggling to remain calm as he contemplates the new world in which the Christian faith to which he has devoted his life will face unprecedented, existential challenges.

For those who professed religious belief, the bombing of Japan threw into sharp relief the vexed questions of faith, the benevolence of the deity and the assumption of divine omnipotence. Mankind had acquired a new power that conferred on it the means to unleash the apocalypse, a Promethean challenge to the supremacy of the gods and a source of anguish for religious men and women. What would it mean for morality? Would the atomic age drive people to hopelessness and nihilism or, conversely, bring them to the Church as a means of flight from the despair?

Christianity would become politicised, exploited by both sides in the Cold War. The West, and America in particular, had already turned to the forces of organised religion to battle the atheistic ideology of the Soviet Union. A succession of US presidents would deploy the Church at the forefront of their modern-day crusade against communism. Cognisant of the deep-seated religious faith that persisted in Soviet Russia, Stalin too would seek to co-opt religious leaders to his cause, playing on the Orthodox Church's historical animosity to Catholicism, promising rewards to the puppet priests who would lend their voice to the anti-western rhetoric of the Kremlin.

Ronald Knox is tormented by the big questions of the world's future and the future of organised religion, but his starting point is the individual. He ruminates on the effect that Hiroshima and the presence in the world of a frightening new force of destruction will have on the mental well-being of the man in the street. The spectre of the atomic threat weighs on people's thoughts, darkening their days. The lack of individual agency in the face of such might, the perception of a menacing external locus of control, has left humankind unnerved and demoralised. 'The imagination will make pictures for us,' Knox writes, 'and there are some which hardly bear thinking of … Our imaginations are threatened with a break-down of hope and they are threatened with a break-down of faith.'

'God and the Atom' is shot through with Freudian terminology, psychological concepts that had gained currency in the immediate pre-war years. Freud himself had died in London in September 1939 and it is striking that a man of the church should have absorbed so much of his thinking. Knox personifies atomic power as a malevolent genie, released from eternal slumber to sow confusion in the human subconscious.

This Force … stirred restless currents in the depths under the surface of the mind. Is there not reason to fear that a trauma (if that is the word the modern psychologists would have me use) may be set up by the rude impact of a decisive event, at once scientific and historical, like the coming of the atom-bomb? ... It strikes at our sense of cosmic discipline; it strikes at our optimism; it strikes at our confidence in the validity of our own moral judgements.

For the *croyant* Knox, personal fear is redoubled by moral horror at humanity's willingness to use the bomb, a feeling of collective guilt that civilised society could knowingly inflict such inhuman suffering, centuries of striving for progress and tolerance negated by a single act of barbarism. ('Sixty thousand people wiped out, with no moment to breathe a prayer!') Man's decision to drop the bomb prompts thoughts of a world abandoned by God. Knox wants to resist the idea, but it stays agonisingly with him. 'Across the bright sun of our believing a shadow fell; the shadow of an American airman, lackadaisically humming a tune, who carried such a freight as would make life impossible over four square miles of the earth's surface. He was the symbol of a catastrophic leap in the history of human achievement.' Christians in the post-Hiroshima age are prey to doubts about the fundamentals of religious faith: how could God allow this to happen? How could a Christian nation do such a thing? Has God despaired of the evil of the world He created? Knox toys with, before ultimately rejecting, the suggestion that the threat of atomic annihilation is a 'rebuke' sent by Heaven to punish mankind's impiety. 'Was God leaving the world to its own devices,' he asks, 'wearied at last by our long record of infidelity? ... There are more factors than one contributing to our present atmosphere of panic. But the imagination is most easily dominated by the threat of the Atom.'

It is not only faith in religion that has been shaken; the guilt of Hiroshima is enough to tarnish the achievement of victory in the war. Knox detects a poisonous undermining of the western psyche, a creeping loss of belief in the moral goodness of western democracy.

[A] man braces himself more readily for the moral struggle if he believes that the society to which he belongs adheres, at least in its major decisions, to the cause of right. Rouse in him the very suspicion that his country, when it goes to war, makes use of

> any and every expedient to achieve its end, and you tarnish the niceness of his own conscience ... The shadow of that American airman strikes him with a faint, simultaneous chill of doubt, of despair, and of guilt.

The destruction of Hiroshima and Nagasaki has undermined the world's duty of charity; the future is now in thrall to the whims of reckless politicians, heedless of moral constraints. 'Self-restraint,' Knox says, 'is a quality the Atomic Age will not find it easy to come by. [W]e shall feel vaguely, some of us at least, that the atom is the symbol of our release from every internal principle of self-control; the mind shall be a kingdom of its own, or rather, an anarchy of its own! ... We have conjured up the Atom, and the Atom henceforth is to be our master.' In this Nietzschean age of anxiety, the dictates of God and morality seem no longer to apply. 'Democracy labours for breath when the power of mass-murder is concentrated, for good or for evil, in the hands of a few.' Knox acknowledges that religious faith will diminish, with the rise of atheistic regimes in the East. All appears lost. But the essays end with a note of hope. Even in the darkest night of the soul, Knox suggests, Christian courage can be the bulwark that protects against the mind's despair. 'It may be that mankind is being called upon to exercise the virtue of hope; and if so, Christian people must think twice before they abandon themselves to the luxury of world-despair.'

'God and the Atom' captured the dilemmas that the nuclear age posed to religious thought in Britain. But it was not only in the West that the role of religion was at stake. Franklin Roosevelt had hoped that the Soviet Union would be swept by a religious revival during the war. When George Kennan returned to Moscow in 1944 he had reported that 'the development of the spiritual life of the Russian people' during the war was 'the most important change' to take place in his time away. The Bolshevik regime kept a keen eye on 'the souls of its human charges', Kennan noted, but it had signally failed to eradicate their religious sensibility. By the end of the war he felt that the Soviet government had 'lost moral dominion over the masses of the Russian population'.[2]

In Kennan's view, the persistence of religious faith in Russia was an opportunity. 'If the spiritual sources of human action were ever to be grasped and activated by outside influence,' he wrote, 'the danger to the [Soviet] regime would be incalculable.' The leaders of the

Orthodox Church held such sway over the Russian people that their authority, bolstered by the support of the West, could be fashioned into a powerful force of moral and political opposition, potentially even 'a match for the people in the Kremlin'.[3] The good opinion of the Orthodox Church was worth fighting for, and both Washington and Moscow would court it.

Ever since the Russian Revolution, the Church's leaders had been split over the question of its relationship with secular power. The majority had expressed horror at the anti-religious fervour of the Bolsheviks. In the years after 1917, priests had been murdered in their hundreds, churches destroyed or turned into museums of atheism, stables or public toilets. Public worship was banned and those who tried to hold services were harassed and attacked. Many of the leading Orthodox hierarchy, including the patriarch, were arrested. But others were willing to make an accommodation with the communists, creating a parallel 'official' Church that became effectively a tool of the state.

The Second World War afforded these pro-Kremlin clerics a prominent role. Facing the prospect of defeat by the invading Nazis, Stalin strove to enlist the forces of religion and nationalism that he had previously denounced as bourgeois relics. Priests were instructed to bless tanks and troops departing for the front; a new patriarch, installed by the Kremlin, declared the fight against Nazism a just war. A grateful Kremlin offered concessions, softening its atheist rhetoric and returning some ecclesiastical property.

At the end of hostilities, Church and State reached an unwritten accord. The Orthodox Church would be allowed to continue its work, but only under the direction of the Soviet authorities. Recognising the importance of the Church as a tool to shape popular opinion, Stalin facilitated the appointment and promotion of priests willing to toe the Kremlin line. One of his favourites, Metropolitan Nikolai, had signed the 1927 concordat pledging loyalty to the Bolshevik regime and disowning his fellow priests who were being tortured for their beliefs. In September 1943, Stalin called Nikolai to a secret meeting in the Kremlin. In return for unquestioning support, Stalin agreed to re-establish the Church's Moscow Patriarchate. Nikolai accepted. He would show his gratitude in countless loyal pronouncements over the coming years, lauding the Soviet regime and calling down God's vengeance on its enemies.

In the summer of 1949, he set out the position of the Orthodox Church on the challenges of the atomic age. Predictably, he was scathing in attributing blame. 'Common people the world over are alarmed by the ring of a knife, rusty with human blood,' Nikolai proclaimed. 'It is being sharpened by the hands of murderers. Death is again raising its merciless scythe over the fields of the earth, preparing to reap a bountiful harvest.' Nikolai was speaking just weeks before the USSR would conduct its first successful test of an atomic bomb. Since neither he nor his audience knew that this event was in the offing, the 'hands of murderers' could belong only to the capitalist warmongers in Washington, a fact that he was quick to point out.

> The same dark forces that ten years ago hurled humanity into the abyss of indescribable suffering again wish to hold a blood feast, for, being born to feed on human blood, they cannot live without it ... Who of us does not shudder at the lust possessing the new pretenders to world domination, the lust for re-embarking on a still more frightful campaign against the peace-loving democratic peoples, a campaign whose finale will be new, hard suffering for mankind?[4]

Denouncing the Pope as 'an agent of American imperialism',[5] Nikolai made clear that the good Christians were in Moscow, while the bad ones were in Washington, Rome and London.

Ronald Knox's rhetoric pales by comparison. But while Knox was expressing his personal, largely non-political opinions, Nikolai clearly is not. His remarks were made to the first USSR Conference for Peace and they parrot the official line of Soviet propaganda in the unipolar nuclear world of 1945–9. Disadvantaged by the US monopoly on atomic weaponry, the Kremlin mobilised every other weapon at its disposal, including the Orthodox Church. The theologian Reinhold Niebuhr noted that Moscow was adept at appropriating the templates and trappings of religious faith and applying them to its own messianic world mission. Through the intermediary of its tame prelates, the Kremlin was dictating God's message to the faithful.

The 1950s saw a surge in church attendance in the United States. It was natural that religious concerns should play a role in the shaping of Washington's view of the USSR. Regardless of all other considerations, Russia's 'godless communism' would continue to be regarded as inherently evil,[6] a fact of which Stalin was apparently well aware. In 1946, he instructed Andrei Gromyko, the newly appointed Soviet representative to the United Nations in New York, to attend church there every Sunday, in order to 'gain an insight into the American mind-set.'[7] Had Gromyko been at the Federal Council of Churches in Columbus, Ohio, on 6 March 1946, the day after Churchill's 'Sinews of Peace' address, he would have learned the views of the president himself. Harry Truman told the gathered churchmen that in order for the civilised world to survive, it would need to call on 'a spiritual strength of greater magnitude' than even the 'gigantic power ... of atomic energy'. Without a 'moral and spiritual awakening,' Truman declared, 'without a renewal and revival of religious faith ... we are lost!'[8] Five years later, in 1951, a homily delivered to the New York Avenue Presbyterian Church suggested that Truman had come to regard religion as America's trump card in the Cold War.

> Our religious faith gives us the answer to the false beliefs of communism. Surely, we can follow that faith with the same devotion and determination the Communists give to their godless creed! ... I have the feeling that God has created us and brought us to our present position of power and strength for some great purpose. And up to now we have been shirking it. Now we are assuming it, and now we must carry it through![9]

The claim of 'God on our side' has been the province of belligerent powers through the ages. The growth in politico-religious fervour alarmed the Russian-born philosopher Isaiah Berlin, by then a don in Oxford. His childhood experience of revolutionary Bolshevism had left him wary of any form of zealotry. He counselled against the West trying to fight communist fanaticism with a manufactured fanaticism of its own. 'I do not think that the answer to communism is a counter-faith, equally fervent, militant; to begin with, nothing is less likely to create a "faith" than perpetual reiteration of the fact that we are looking for one, must find one, are lost without one.'[10] But Berlin's caution fell on deaf ears. When the CIA's Psychological Strategy Board was formed at the request of President Truman in April 1951, one of its first initiatives was to investigate the scope for using religion in the struggle against the Reds.

The potentialities of religion as an instrument for combating Communism are universally tremendous. Religion is an established basic force which calls forth men's strongest emotions ... Our over-all objective in seeking the use of religion as a cold war instrumentality should be the furtherance of world spiritual health; for the Communist threat could not exist in a spiritually healthy world.[11]

For the capitalist world, religion was a means to create unity and rally opposition to the socialist bloc. For the Soviet Union, it was a tool to sow discord abroad.

Because the USSR had nailed its colours to the mast of atheism, Moscow had to find an indirect way to use the Church, and it did so through the auspices of the Soviet Peace Committee. The Peace Committee was presented to the world as a popular grassroots movement of ordinary Soviet citizens, spontaneously demanding international cooperation and disarmament. It was in fact a closely controlled instrument of state policy. Its coordinating body was the so-called World Peace Council, formed by the Kremlin in 1949 with the intention of moulding the 'drive for peace' into an anti-western force. Its activities would win the USSR the reputation of a peace-loving state, while at the same time pursuing its geopolitical goals – inhibiting western rearmament by mobilising western pacifist groups and individuals. The Soviet Peace Committee lent vociferous support to campaigns against western militarisation, but consistently failed to condemn similar actions by the USSR.

When western politicians denounced the one-sided nature of the Peace Committee, they were met with scepticism from many of their own citizens. The participation of the Orthodox Church added to the Peace Committee's credibility. Wrongly perceived as being above politics, the Church's pronouncements helped attract western churchmen, who naively viewed the Peace Council as a legitimate pacifist organisation. Metropolitan Nikolai was a natural leader of the enterprise. His 1949 speech echoed many of the charges that American liberals were themselves already levelling against their government.

The transatlantic sirens sing of 'liberty', but only a man with an evil conscience and a muddled intellect could think liberty exists in a country [the USA] where people are lynched ... workers

are bombarded with tear gas, bread is burned in the sight of
the hungry ... and guns are built to drench in human blood the
peaceful valleys of Greece, China, Indonesia and Vietnam. Their
liberty is liberty to rob, pillage and slaughter![12]

The Peace Committee took care to direct its accusations at politicians
and industrialists, and not at ordinary citizens. It was the 'capitalist
ruling circles' or the 'military–industrial complex' who were to blame
for the world's ills, while 'people of goodwill'– regular working folk
– were innocent victims, destined to suffer because of their leaders'
malevolence. Differentiating between institutional evil and individual benevolence played to the preconceptions that already existed in
western liberal minds.

When the Peace Council met in 1954, Metropolitan Nikolai
regaled delegates with tales of US 'war crimes'. To those Americans
who mistrusted their own government and believed that Washington
politicians lied about everything, even the most outlandish conspiracy theories were accepted as credible. 'The spirit of fascism has not
disappeared,' Nikolai fulminated. 'The criminal aggression of the
American neo-fascists is aimed at the bloodsucking extermination
of the "inferior" Korean race ... They brazenly carry out executions
without trial. They torture and mutilate, cutting off ears, noses and
breasts, gouging out eyes, breaking arms and legs, crucifying resistance fighters and burying alive both women and children.'[13]

To modern ears, even in the context of atrocities carried out
by western forces during the twentieth century, Nikolai's rhetoric
sounds deranged; but this was the tenor of much Soviet propaganda
at the time. Neither was he slow in accusing rival churches of participating in the US 'atrocities'. 'With the connivance of the highest
Catholic prelates,' he told the conference, 'the Christian religion
is being unscrupulously misused in the interests of European and
American capitalist powers to help oppress and exploit the masses,
preparing the way for another bloodbath. The Pope has revealed his
anti-Christian face in all its spiritual ugliness ...'[14]

It was indeed true that the papacy of the 1940s and 50s was a viru-
lent opponent of communism; but there is something of the pot and
the kettle in the Soviet indignation. The 'official' Orthodox Church
was more directly involved in supporting socialism than any western
church in supporting capitalism. And accusations of intolerance sat

uncomfortably in a country where freedom of worship was still curtailed and Christians continued to be persecuted. The persecution of priests in the Soviet Union endured for much of the twentieth century, spreading in the postwar years to the Soviet satellite states. The leaders of the Roman Catholic Church in Czechoslovakia (Cardinal František Tomášek), Poland (Cardinal Stefan Wyszyński) and Hungary (Cardinal József Mindszenty) were all imprisoned. As late as 1984, the Polish security forces were implicated in the brutal murder of Father Jerzy Popiełuszko, a Catholic priest who used his sermons to praise the Solidarity union.

At the height of the Cold War's battle of religion, the rhetoric escalated on both sides. When the words 'In God We Trust' were added to all US paper money and coins in 1955, the threat of communism was advanced as the reason behind the change. In 1956, 'In God We Trust' became the United States' official national motto. Dwight Eisenhower used Christianity as a go-to theme on the campaign trail. 'What is our battle against communism,' he challenged voters in 1952, 'if it is not a fight between anti-God and a belief in the Almighty? ... When God comes in, communism has to go.'[15]

Christianity had been co-opted as a tool of American politics, but not all clerics were comfortable with it. The ambivalence that existed among some of the faithful was highlighted in 'The Christian Conscience and Weapons of Mass Destruction', a 1950 report by a special commission of the Federal Council of Churches. Chaired by Angus Dun, Bishop of the Episcopal Diocese of Washington, the commission declared that 'Victory at any price is not worth having. If this price is for us to become utterly brutal, victory becomes a moral defeat. Victory is worth having only if it leaves us with enough reserves of decency, justice and mercy to build a better world.'[16] The commission's recommendations, though, stop short of unilateral nuclear disarmament. 'For the United States to abandon its atomic weapons, or to give the impression that they would not be used, would leave the non-Communist world with totally inadequate defense. For Christians to advocate such a policy would be for them to share responsibility for the worldwide tyranny that might result.'[17] In contrast to the stance of the pro-Kremlin Russian Church, the report offers no blanket endorsement of 'my country right or wrong'. There must be no first-use of atomic weapons, its authors conclude, no 'total war' and no 'preventative war'. Even their use in retaliation for a nuclear attack must conform to moral standards. Christians may prefer to perish unavenged rather than destroy other human beings, but the views of society as a whole must also be taken into account.

> We believe that it could be justifiable for our government to use them [atomic weapons] in retaliation, with all possible restraint, to prevent the triumph of an aggressor. Even if as individuals we would choose rather to be destroyed than to destroy in such measure, we do not believe it would be right for us to urge policies on our government which would expose others to such a fate.[18]

A decade later, with a new liberal-minded Pope in the Vatican, the Catholic Church also revised its position, going even further than the Episcopalians. 'Nuclear weapons must be banned,' declared Pope John XXIII in his 1963 encyclical, *'Pacem in Terris'*. The nuclear arms race was 'one of the greatest curses' facing mankind, 'an act of aggression against the poor and a folly which does not provide the security it promises ... Any act of war aimed indiscriminately at the destruction of entire cities along with their population is a crime against God and man himself. It merits unequivocal and unhesitating condemnation.'[19]

The complex relationship between religion and Cold War politics returned to the fore in 1980. Ronald Reagan made it clear that evangelical Christian belief would be a key driver in his policy towards the Soviet Union. For the next eight years he placed human rights, including the right to religious freedom, at the heart of Washington's negotiations with successive Soviet leaders. At times, some of his advisers and diplomats viewed it as a stumbling block, imperilling progress in other fields; but Reagan stuck to his guns. In 1983, he set out his understanding of East–West politics to the National Association of Evangelicals. 'Freedom prospers only where the blessings of God are avidly sought and humbly accepted,' he told his audience. 'The American experiment in democracy rests on this insight.'[20]

When Reagan came to Moscow for the 1988 summit with Mikhail Gorbachev, he asked the Soviet leader if they could hold a private discussion, to be excluded from the published record of the meeting. Gorbachev gave his agreement and was nonplussed to discover that Reagan was intent on converting him to Christianity. Reagan asked

Gorbachev if believed in God, if he had been baptised, if he would consider allowing religious freedom in the Soviet Union. Gorbachev initially waved away the questions, but Reagan persisted. He told the story of a wounded Soviet soldier in the Second World War who had been raised an atheist, but turned to God before he died and found salvation through his act of faith. When Gorbachev remained silent, Reagan told a more personal tale, this time about his own son, Ron, who he revealed was also a non-believer. The official note of the meeting, released years later, records that, 'the President concluded there was one thing he had long yearned to do for his atheist son. He wanted to serve his son the perfect gourmet dinner, to have him enjoy the meal, and then to ask him if he believed there was a cook ...'[21] When Reagan mused on what Ron Junior might answer, Gorbachev reportedly responded that there could be only one answer: Yes.[22]

The exchange hints at the inordinate power of personal interaction to nudge the course of history and the advantage it affords to a politician, like Reagan, who understands human psychology. An even more striking example came from another man of religion. Pope John Paul II, the Polish priest Karol Wojtyła, did more than anyone to ignite the flame of revolt that spread with such rapidity from his homeland to the whole of eastern Europe. The late 1980s was a time of discontent with Poland's Moscow-sponsored communist government as, encouraged by Mikhail Gorbachev's liberal reforms in Russia, the Solidarity union pushed at the boundaries of protest and civil unrest. I was proud to be in the Gdansk shipyards with Lech Wałęsa during the strikes that finally toppled the Jaruzelski regime in 1989. But two years earlier, things had looked very different. Solidarity was banned, its leaders silenced, the spirit of freedom seemingly crushed. In those dark days it was Poland's sense of religious devotion that sustained the nation's morale. The church of Jerzy Popiełuszko was close to my flat in the Żoliborz district of Warsaw and I witnessed the fervour of the congregation that overflowed into the church precincts. Wałęsa himself would call for prayers before every meeting. And in June 1987 John Paul's third visit to his homeland as pope reinvigorated the Polish people in a way no politician could have done. I was present in Gdansk when Poles congregated on a disused airfield to hear him say Mass. I saw the boost that his courage gave to the opposition movement. The authorities had done all in their power to disrupt the event, blocking roads and harassing people on their way there. But

The sheer number of people who congregated to hear the Pope speak
suggested that Poland was not the atheist paradise its leaders claimed.

the local churches had built a fifty-foot-high platform for the Pope to
speak from and a million Catholic faithful came to hear him, stretch-
ing nearly half a mile into the distance.[23]

In thinly disguised language, John Paul appealed for unity,
faith and resolution. To great cheers, he identified the most important quality people could show in this time of need: 'Solidarity,' he
said. '*Solidarność*. The greatest struggle can never be greater than
solidarity!'

> And so, my dear brothers and sisters, I finish with the promise of
> a prayer, an intimate bond, a spiritual bond with my homeland
> and with you; with the working people, with all those just and
> noble aims that make our lives more human and more dignified.
> I pray to the Holy Spirit to descend upon us and renew the face
> of this land ... the face of our Polish land![24]

And at the end of the mass, I was caught up in the emotion as a
million people sang the Polish national anthem, its words composed
during the eighteenth-century partitions when Russia and Prussia
invaded and occupied Poland, yet still poignantly relevant in those

days of Soviet domination: 'Poland has not perished so long as we still live. An alien power has seized her from us; But we shall reclaim her, sword in hand. Enough of this slavery! … The German and the Russian will never rest, So long as we remain united!' It was clear why Poles sang with such vigour. And the authorities were powerless to stop them: they could hardly ban the Polish people from singing their own national anthem. Together, a Polish pope, a nation's Christian piety and a devoutly Catholic trade union movement lit a spark that would ultimately consume the greatest empire of atheism the world had ever known.

29

FALLING DOMINOES

The concept of loss aversion was modelled in the 1980s in the field of consumer psychology. The American psychologist Daniel Kahneman was intrigued by the discrepancy between the value that subjects assign to a commodity they possess and one they do not. Owners of an object tended consistently to attach a higher worth to it than they did to an equivalent object not in their possession; losing it had a greater psychological impact than making an equivalent acquisition. Kahneman posited several explanations.[1] The concept of 'mere ownership' – the 'endowment effect' of attachment to a possession – was readily understandable. People feel more invested in an object they have grown to love, or have expended emotional capital in acquiring, than to an unowned object of the same empirical value.[2] Subsequent research explored deeper psychological processes, including the theory of self-referential memory. Things that we own are, in a manner of speaking, part of us, assimilated into our identity. The idea of losing something sets alarms ringing in the subconscious, which in turn conjures fears of depredations to follow, possibly involving existential threat to our sense of self.[3]

The psychological impact of loss aversion played its part in the Cold War. The average citizen behind the Iron Curtain kept silent for fear of losing the little freedom he or she possessed, clinging to a meagre luxury sooner than risk its loss by pushing for more. At the other end of the scale, it conditioned high-level decision-making. Both Moscow and Washington exhibited disproportionate fear of losing control over their acquired empires. A threat to one part of their sphere of influence was perceived as a threat to the whole, an augury of system collapse. Fear became a guiding principle; fear of loss, fear of looking weak, fear of the unknown. Both sides wanted to draw the countries of the developing world into their orbit but, having done so, suffered geopolitical nightmares of anticipated loss.

The spectre of the domino theory dragged the superpowers into debilitating conflicts in Korea and Vietnam, Hungary, Czechoslovakia and Afghanistan – wars that would complicate each power's self-image of moral integrity.

By the late 1940s, America was convinced that the communist bloc was intent on expanding into the 'free world', while the USSR had come to regard all opposition to Moscow's will as a capitalist plot to destroy socialism. Catastrophisation, the syndrome beloved of cognitive behavioural psychologists,[4] led imaginations to run wild. Dwight Eisenhower perceived a zero-sum game, in which only one national ideology could survive. 'Russia is definitely out to communize the world,' he wrote in his diary for September 1947. 'We face a battle to extinction between two systems.'[5] Having won the presidency, he gave a name to his fear: the 'falling domino' principle. 'You have a row of dominoes set up,' Eisenhower told the American media in an image that would haunt the western imagination. 'You knock over the first one, and what will happen to the last one is the certainty that it will go over very quickly.'[6] Since the last domino was the United States itself, Washington could permit no let-up in vigilance, no intimation of weakness that would encourage the enemy to nudge the other blocks in the chain.

Moscow reached the same conclusion. Unrest in Hungary in 1956 stirred fears of dominoes in the Soviet backyard, with Khrushchev warning that any sign of weakness would be exploited by the West.[7]

The cognitive distortion that leads to the universalising of individual threats convinced leaders East and West that the slightest lack of resolve was an invitation to the 'other' to trample on 'our' interests. Washington and Moscow conjured visions of a chain reaction culminating in annihilation. Both spoke of their mission to liberate the people of the world; but, challenged abroad, abandoned their lofty idealism and responded with force.

John Kennedy warned the US Congress that America was facing 'a very special moment in history' and needed to be alert to opportunity and to danger. 'The whole southern half of the world – Latin America, Africa, the Middle East, and Asia – are caught up in the adventures of asserting their independence and modernizing their old ways of life,' Kennedy said. '[We have] a moral obligation as a wise leader and good neighbor in the interdependent community of free nations ... and our political obligations as the single largest counter to the adversaries of freedom.' The message of moral duty was underpinned by the incentive of fear. 'Failure to meet those obligations now would be disastrous, and ... would inevitably invite the advance of totalitarianism into every weak and unstable area. Thus our own security would be endangered and our prosperity imperilled.'[8] The battlefield of the Cold War would henceforth be the world. At Kennedy's behest, America's youth was mobilised for the struggle. The US Peace Corps was created in 1961 to send thousands of 'our young men and women, dedicated to freedom ... fully capable of overcoming the efforts of Mr Khrushchev's missionaries who are dedicated to undermining that freedom', to work on development programmes across the globe.[9]

Unsurprisingly, Mr Khrushchev's interpretation of history's 'very special moment' was different. Far from bringing freedom to the world, America's emissaries were part of a capitalist plot. 'Everyone knows that the economies of the colonies,' Khrushchev told the UN in September 1960, 'are at present subordinated to the mercenary interests of foreign monopolies, and the industrialization of these countries is being deliberately impeded.' Only socialism, he suggested, could bring true liberation. 'Imagine that the situation has changed and that these countries and territories, having become independent, are in a position to make ample use of their rich natural resources and to proceed with their industrialization, and that a better life has begun for their peoples.'[10] Four months later, Kennedy responded in an inaugural speech that drew up the battle lines.

> Let every nation know, whether it wishes us well or ill, that we shall pay any price, bear any burden, meet any hardship, support any friend, oppose any foe to assure the survival and the success of liberty ... To those new states whom we welcome to the ranks of the free, we pledge our word that one form of colonial control shall not have passed away merely to be replaced by a far more iron tyranny ... The energy, the faith, the devotion which we bring to this endeavor will light our country and all who serve it.[11]

Soon America's youth were being called upon to do more than join the Peace Corps. Two and half million of them would find themselves 'defending freedom' in South East Asia. Philip Caputo was one of many to be inspired by Kennedy's 'rallying cry for my generation'; convinced that Vietnam was the first domino in a lethal chain where countries would be successively overrun by communist forces. 'We were the new Romans who faced the barbarians at the frontiers. I joined the Marines out of that sense of patriotism and once we were sent to Vietnam this was all considered to be right and fitting: this is what we were supposed to do.'[12]

But the reality was very different. 'No one [in power] knew anything about Vietnam,' recalled the Pentagon official Leslie Gelb. 'Vietnam was a piece on a chessboard, a strategic chessboard – not a place with a culture and a history that we would have an impossible time changing, even with the mighty force of the United States.'[13] The confidence of Kennedy's public persona differed from the private man. By the end of his first year in office, he had been weakened by the fiasco in the Bay of Pigs, the botched Vienna summit and the shock of the Berlin Wall. Even as he was sending Americans to die in Indo-China, he suspected it was a lost cause. 'It will be just like Berlin,' he told Arthur Schlesinger. 'The troops will march in, the bands will play, the crowds will cheer ... Then we will be told we have to send in more troops. It's like taking a drink. The effect wears off and you have to have another.'[14] Like many such decisions, the conviction that America must fight for Vietnam was driven by fear. 'If I tried to pull out,' he told Schlesinger later, 'we would have another Joe McCarthy Red Scare on our hands.'[15]

For much of the twentieth century, Washington had affected to recognise Vietnam's right to self-determination. In 1919, Ho Chi Minh (then known as Nguyen Ai Quoc) had written to President Woodrow Wilson, asking that colonised people be treated with respect. Receiving no reply, he gravitated to the doctrines of Karl Marx. In 1945, when he proclaimed Vietnam's independence from France, he prefaced his country's founding declaration with a quotation from the US Declaration of Independence: 'All men are created equal ... with certain inalienable rights; among these are Life, Liberty and the pursuit of Happiness.'[16] By the time of the 1954 Geneva Accords that divided Vietnam, Ho's nationalists looked certain to win the scheduled elections and Washington's alarm trumped its claims of respect for global liberty. Thousands of US military advisers poured into Vietnam, to be joined in 1965 by US Marines. America became the region's latest colonial power, following the Chinese, the Japanese and the French on the list of invaders. There was, though, a self-deluding refusal to accept the imperialist label. 'We thought we were the exceptions to history,' recalled the historian and journalist Neil Sheehan. 'We Americans … could never fight a bad war. We could never represent the wrong cause. We were Americans. Well, in Vietnam it proved that we were not an exception to history.'[17]

Vu Van Vinh was a teenager in the north when the American War, as it is known in Vietnam, began and the Cold War meant nothing to him and his countrymen. 'We were really confused why the Americans tried to invade our homeland. We hadn't done anything to them. … People didn't even know what communism was. They just knew what was going on with their lives.'[18] The Communist Party were leading the struggle, and controlling the supply of information. Their message was an easy one to sell to the population, even without recourse to ideology – a foreign force was yet again trying to impose its will on Vietnam. It was framed as an independence fight, a continuation of previous battles against foreigners.

A Viet Cong fighter captured by the Americans explained his reasons for joining the struggle, echoing the idealist rhetoric of US Marines like Philip Caputo: 'I wanted most to save my country and to be a hero. I wanted to change the present society. Everybody longed for justice and liberty. Nobody wanted to be oppressed.'[19]

By the time Lyndon Johnson decided to escalate an unwinnable conflict, America's priorities had strayed far from the ideals of freedom and respect that Kennedy proclaimed at his inauguration. The self-reinforcing nightmare of a war begun for ill-defined aims had become a struggle with no exit. A memorandum to Robert McNamara in 1965 acknowledged that the main reason for fighting was now to save face.

> US aims:
> 70% To avoid a humiliating US defeat (to our reputation as a guarantor).
> 20% To keep South Vietnam (and then adjacent) territory from Chinese hands.
> 10% To permit the people of SVN to enjoy a better, freer way of life.[20]

By 1968, there were over half a million American troops in Vietnam and any illusions that America might achieve the goals listed in McNamara's memorandum were vanishing. The same young people who had signed up for the ideals of JFK's Peace Corps were on the streets protesting against the war. The hope sparked by JFK's election in 1960 was extinguished, along with the crusading zeal of the first military volunteers. 'When I went to Vietnam, I believed both in Jesus Christ and John Wayne,' complained one veteran. 'After Vietnam, both went down the tubes. It didn't mean nothing.'[21] The poet Allen Ginsberg diagnosed the psychological damage that had been inflicted on American society. 'It felt like we were walking around in a large mass hallucination sustained by all the politicians, based on lies and secrecy, sustained by the media who couldn't conceive that the whole structure of the United States' mentality could be so wrong and so disastrous and so earth destroying.'[22]

The 'earth-destroying' nature of the war was evident, with the defoliant Agent Orange used to reduce swathes of jungle and agricultural land to bare earth, to be churned by American bombs. Tran Cong Thang, a soldier in the North Vietnamese Army, remembered the impact it had on the Vietnamese people's mental health. 'How could you not be afraid [of American bombs]? Nothing was left. An acrid stench and clouds of smoke hung in the air. In my unit some soldiers lost their nerve [and] deserted.'[23] The war in Vietnam would lead to a reassessment of the psychological impact combat has on those caught up in it. Post-traumatic stress disorder (PTSD) appeared for the first time in the third iteration of the American Psychiatric Association's *Diagnostic and Statistical Manual of Mental Disorders (DSM-III)*, published in 1980. It entered common parlance in the years that followed.[24]

While a 1990 report concluded that at least 480,000 of the 3.15 million Americans who served in Vietnam were still suffering from PTSD, far less research has been carried out on the people who suffered the most: the Vietnamese. The poet Nguyen Duy wrote that, 'In every war, whichever side wins, after all / It's the people who take the fall',[25] and the limited research available suggests that many in Vietnam continue to struggle with the aftermath of decades of war and division. One study pointed to 'a high burden of lifetime trauma and mental ill health', including depression, anxiety and PTSD in the adult population of central Vietnam, linked to the 'cumulative effect of multiple trauma'.[26]

Lyndon Johnson himself was showing signs of mental strain, bordering on paranoia. A poll taken in August 1968 revealed that more than half of Americans believed it had been a mistake to send troops to Vietnam; approval for the war would never again rise above 42 per cent. Johnson was increasingly convinced that communist agitators were behind the anti-war movement. The CIA were ordered to uncover the plot, illegally monitoring tens of thousands of Americans, but finding no evidence to support Johnson's suspicions.[27] In a private memorandum, McNamara warned the president that 'the picture of the world's greatest superpower killing or seriously injuring 1,000 non-combatants a week while trying to pound a tiny, backward nation into submission on an issue whose merits are hotly disputed is not a pretty one'.[28] After a brief moment of hope, fear had dragged America back into uncertainty about itself and its place in the world. 'We have fought great wars and made unprecedented sacrifices at home and abroad,' Robert Kennedy lamented. 'Yet we ourselves are uncertain of what we have achieved and whether we like what we have accomplished.'[29]

The year 1968 appeared pivotal for the future of liberal democracy. With demonstrations and demands for change in the US and western Europe, communist true believers sensed the onset of the crisis of capitalism they had been predicting since 1917. Conditions seemed ripe for the USSR to usher in the world revolution fervently desired by Lenin and Trotsky.

Unfortunately their own territories were in as much turmoil as the capitalist world. Trouble had been brewing since the end of 1964, when two students at Warsaw University, Jacek Kuroń and Karel Modzelewski, had published an academic critique of the political and economic system, titled 'An Open Letter to the Party: Marxism Against Stalinism'. In a closely argued dissection of the structures of the communist state, the authors assessed the effect of a flawed system of governance on the minds of the citizens it claimed to represent.[30] There were, said Kuroń and Modzelewski, bitter class divisions in a society that claimed to be classless; the state bureaucracy had become the equivalent of the capitalist rulers and the people felt they were being exploited as much as workers in the West. They had no say in how they were governed and no control over their own lives, which resulted in a sense of hopelessness and discontent.

Kuroń and Modzelewski were denounced and expelled from

the party. They responded with a scathing open letter to Warsaw University, decrying 'a bureaucratic, autocratic regime, deaf to the interests of all but the ruling elite it serves, ruling incompetently over an impoverished working population and censoring all criticism and commentary'.[31] The authorities' subsequent decision to sentence them to three years in jail for advocating the overthrow of the state did much to create an intellectual opposition in Poland that was previously non-existent.

Kuroń and Modzelewski's imprisonment was seen as the death knell of the reformist hopes kindled by Khrushchev's Thaw. Many Czechs and Slovaks identified with the Poles' experience of psychological oppression. As Milan Kundera would argue in his essay 'The Tragedy of Central Europe', in their minds Czechoslovakia was 'a kidnapped West', in which the Soviets strove to obliterate a history, a culture and a national mentality.[32] The suspicious, conservative Leonid Brezhnev, who considered Czechoslovakia the least ideologically reliable country in the Warsaw Pact, had his worries confirmed in January 1968. The pledge by the newly elected first secretary of the party, Alexander Dubček, to create 'socialism with a human face' was not simply a deviation from Soviet orthodoxy; it was a potential domino that presaged the socialist Armageddon of Brezhnev's catastrophising nightmares. Together with the leaders of Poland, Hungary, Bulgaria and East Germany, he sent a panicked letter to 'our brothers' in Prague warning that, 'The situation in Czechoslovakia jeopardizes the common vital interests of other socialist countries.'[33]

Dubček's hint that change was possible would again confirm the accuracy of de Tocqueville's maxim that 'the most critical moment for bad governments is the one which witnesses their first steps towards reform'.[34] Brezhnev could have offered sympathy and concessions, which might have contained the growing dissent. But he didn't. He issued threats and ultimatums. And de Tocqueville's prediction was borne out. Czechs and Slovaks duly seized the moment of change, demanding more radical and more far-reaching reforms than any the government had envisaged. A manifesto by the writer Ludvík Vaculík spoke of the people's alienation and loss of trust. His 'Two Thousand Words' made a powerful case for the Czechoslovak Communist Party to dismantle itself. 'After enjoying great popular confidence immediately after the war, the Party by degrees bartered this confidence away for office, until it had all the offices and nothing else ... Elections lost their significance, and the law carried no weight.' The corruption of the state led to the corruption of the human mind. Individuals internalised the distorted mentality of their rulers.

> We could not trust our representatives on any committee or, if we could, there was no point in asking them for anything because they were powerless. Worse still, we could scarcely trust one another. Personal and collective honour decayed. Honesty was a useless virtue. ... Personal relations were ruined, there was no more joy in work, and the nation, in short, entered a period that endangered its spiritual well-being and its character.[35]

The Dubček reforms were an opportunity not only for political renewal, Vaculík argued, but for the regeneration of the national psyche. The Czech spirit had been trampled and perverted; people were sick of the dishonesty and the humiliation. Many had given in to the mental oppression of the aggressor. But all of that could be about to change.

> Since the beginning of this year we have been experiencing a regenerative process of democratization. It started inside the communist party; that much we must admit. [But] there has been great alarm recently over the possibility that foreign forces will intervene in our development. Whatever superior forces may face us, all we can do is stick to our own positions, behave decently, and initiate nothing ourselves ... [We] have the chance to take into our own hands our common cause, which for working purposes we call socialism, and give it a form more appropriate to our once-good reputation and to the fairly good opinion we used to have of ourselves.[36]

Petr Pithart, later to become the first prime minister of the post-communist Czech Republic, remembered the spring of 1968 as 'wonderful', a resurrection of the true national character that had been repressed for so long. 'For the first time in history, the Czech people found themselves without their rulers. There was no one controlling them, no one giving them orders, and the nation was true to itself. The people were clever, resourceful, and they even showed a sense of humour.'[37] But Moscow found little to smile about. *Pravda*

Mutual incomprehension – Warsaw Pact troops thought they would
be greeted as heroes by their socialist brothers, but the locals couldn't
understand why they (and their tanks) were there at all.

denounced Vaculík's manifesto as ideological sabotage, initiated
by 'right-wing, antisocialist forces ... waging an attack against the
Czechoslovak Communist Party and the working class'. Their ultimate aim, Soviet citizens were told, was the restoration of capitalism.
'A situation has arisen which endangers the foundation of socialism in
Czechoslovakia and threatens the vital common interests of the other
socialist countries. The peoples of our countries would never forgive
us for indifference and carelessness in the face of such danger.'[38]
Just as Vietnam had been the first domino in an imagined chain for
America, so losing Czechoslovakia was considered too great a threat
to the socialist world. According to Petr Shelest, the first secretary of
the Ukrainian Communist Party,

> What we are talking about is not just the fate of socialism in one of
> the socialist countries, but the fate of socialism in the whole social-
> ist camp ... If we do not take tough action now, civil war could be
> unleashed in Czechoslovakia. We could lose her as a socialist state,
> creating an emergency situation in Europe, with serious military
> clashes, possibly even a war. It is not easy to decide to go to these
> lengths, but ... no other decision or way out exists.[39]

When TASS announced the invasion on 21 August, it described it as a
'rendering of fraternal assistance to the Czechoslovak people [against]
the threat to the security of the socialist community countries'. The

The people of Plzeň were unimpressed to see the Russian circus back in town.

imperative was to prevent a fissure in socialist unity that might lead to the disintegration of the monolith. 'The fraternal countries firmly and resolutely counterpose their unbreakable solidarity to any threat from outside,' TASS thundered. 'Nobody will ever be allowed to wrest a single link from the community of socialist states.'[40]

The half a million troops who took part in Operation Danube* were not welcomed as liberators. People refused to give them food or water; road signs were removed or replaced with ones pointing back to Moscow. Posters appeared, illustrating what Czechoslovaks felt about their 'brothers' coming to help. 'Lenin wake up, Brezhnev's gone mad!' read one of them.

Another, posted at the Park of Culture in Plzeň, announced the return of the 'Russian Circus', featuring 'Trained monkeys from the GDR, Hungary, Bulgaria, Poland' and 'a performance by a Russian dwarf, the biggest in the world', including a 'display of modern technology. Free entrance; sometimes you may pay with your life. Do not miss! One performance only!'[41]

The 'trained monkeys' were perplexed. They had been told they were rescuing the Czechoslovak people from the grip of capitalist enemies. '[We] were certain that someone was trying to knock

---

* Drawn largely from the Soviet Union, Poland, Bulgaria and Hungary, with only a small number from East Germany, because of the sensitive nature of deploying German troops on foreign soil.

Czechoslovakia off the correct path to socialism and create division in the unity of the socialist bloc,' recalled Eduard Vorobyov, who commanded a Russian motorised unit. 'We had no doubt about that. But as we advanced, unpleasant occurrences increased. An old lady yelled that if we wanted water from her house, then we'd have to shoot her first. People along the road shook their fists at us; one man even dropped his pants and showed us his behind. I didn't know what to think.' It was only with the passing of the years and the change in political mentalities that Vorobyov came to understand how his mind had been conditioned by decades of indoctrination. 'I was a total Soviet man back then,' he acknowledged. 'I was convinced that our intervention was necessary. So there was no space left in my mind for doubt.'[42]

A paratrooper, Boris Shmelev, recalled the intense political instruction that troops had been given before being deployed and the explicit parallels that were drawn with western efforts to prevent the splintering of the capitalist empire. 'They constantly reminded us of the ongoing American aggression in Vietnam. The events in Prague were explained to us in this context – that there was a threat to socialism and the whole Eastern Bloc.' Like his comrade, Shmelev would later conclude that his mind had been clouded by unchallenged state propaganda, describing himself as 'an unwilling participant in an intervention that strangled the Czechs' legitimate attempts to achieve democracy and freedom'.[43]

Many participants in Operation Danube, like many Americans who fought in Vietnam, however, continued to maintain that they were right to intervene. A lifetime of indoctrination is hard to overcome. A lifetime of devotion to a political ideology is hard to renounce without forfeiting something of one's personal self-worth. And, as Stanley Milgram demonstrated, a person may embark on a course of actions that he or she comes to recognise as unworthy, but cannot admit his or her error without having to accept an intolerable burden of guilt. In such cases, there is a powerful mental incentive to persevere with the ignominious conduct in order to maintain the pretence that one has done nothing wrong.

For those on the receiving end of the 'fraternal assistance', things were much clearer much more quickly. Radio journalist Ondřej Neff was twenty-three at the time of the invasion and not ill-disposed towards socialism until the Russians arrived. 'I remember very well the face of the first Russian soldier I saw,' he told BBC News in 2008.

'He was carrying a huge machine gun, and looked like he'd just stepped out of a film about the battle of Stalingrad. He was very dirty, and his face was full of sweat. I tried to talk to him, but it was pointless, he wouldn't speak to me. They were totally indoctrinated. They believed they had prevented the outbreak of World War III or something ... I believe that in August 1968, communism as a political and ideological movement lost its moral face.'[44]

Eduard Goldstücker, the communist author who would later become president of the Czech Writers' Union, felt the hurt of betrayal. 'I lived through Hitler's invasion ... but the Soviet invasion in 1968 was crueller, because Hitler was our declared enemy. We didn't expect anything from him but the worst; but here were those who for years and decades had preached that they were our best friends and brothers, the guarantors of our independence, and they came with an army of thousands to suppress our drive for a little bit more freedom.'[45]

Even in the Soviet Union, where unofficial demonstrations were unheard of, there was protest. On the morning of 25 August, eight young people sat down on Red Square and displayed slogans in Russian and Czech reading, 'For your freedom and ours' and 'We are losing our best friends'. They were arrested, beaten, and sentenced to five years in a labour camp. But popular unease at what had been done in Czechoslovakia was such that the party felt the need to justify itself. An article in *Pravda* on 26 September restated the Brezhnev doctrine of intervention in socialist countries, but struggled to excuse the blatant injustice of the invasion. 'One cannot ignore assertions heard here and there that [Operation Danube] seemed to contradict the Marxist–Leninist principles of the sovereignty and the right of nations to self-determination,' admitted the author, Sergey Kovalev.

> [Such] judgments ... are based on an abstract, non-class approach to the question of sovereignty and the right of nations to self-determination. The people of the socialist countries and their communist parties undoubtedly have and must have freedom for determining the path of development of their own countries. However, none of their decisions should damage either socialism in their country or the vital interests of the other socialist countries.[46]

Having read the article, the US ambassador George Ball quipped that 'the kind of fraternal assistance that the Soviet Union is according to Czechoslovakia is exactly the same kind that Cain gave to Abel'.[47] The West itself was not blameless. The megaphone diplomacy of the preceding twenty years had created an atmosphere of such febrile confrontation that many in eastern Europe were convinced the Americans would come to their aid if they were to rise up against their Soviet masters. Hana Laing felt as betrayed by the West as Eduard Goldstücker had by the USSR, describing how a 'terrible despair came over us' as they realised they could not 'expect anything from the West, that they would not come to our rescue'.[48] To Milan Kundera, it was a realisation that 'in the eyes of its beloved [Western] Europe, Central Europe is just a part of the Soviet Empire and nothing more, nothing more'.[49]

The years that followed 1968 would see an exercise in national psychological manipulation on an unprecedented scale. With Dubček and his reformers in exile or in prison, the new men in charge of the Czechoslovak Communist Party began what they termed a process of 'normalisation', a return to the old communist orthodoxy, with a purge of all 'unreliable' elements in the party and public life. Vast numbers of young people fled to the West. But normalisation was not just physical; the party was determined to alter people's minds. In an attempt to move on from the shame of being humiliated by their 'brothers' in Moscow, the Czech leadership embarked on a concerted rewriting of history, initiating a process of national forgetting. People were enjoined to renounce the hopes of the Prague Spring; references to it were removed from the record and individuals were punished for referring to it. Since it is impossible for the human mind to expunge memories that it has assimilated, the population had to enter a charade of 'forgetting'; playing a role of ignorance in public, while privately cradling the remembrance of things past in the inner chambers of their psyche. As the dissident author Milan Šimečka pointed out in his 1979 memoir, *The Restoration of Order: The Normalization of Czechoslovakia*, the process of enforced forgetting led to cognitive conflicts and feelings of shame.[50] Petr Pithart pinpointed the months of enforced forgetting as the onset of Czech society's mental and moral decline. 'How can people today remember those wonderful few months of the Prague Spring,' he asked in 2018, 'if almost everyone then renounced it? I think the defeat was irreversible, but the choice of how to endure it was in our own hands.'[51]

30

THEY TOOK AWAY YOUR MIND –
CONTROL THROUGH SILENCE

In Cold War eastern Europe, silence was a tool of control. Whole subjects became taboo; mentioning them put your freedom, perhaps your life, at risk. Punishment and oppression helped keep people silent. But the regimes developed more subtle tools. Manipulating minds became an art. *'Feind ist, wer anders denkt'* ('the enemy is he who thinks differently') was one of the catchier memos that the Stasi sent to its employees. 'Our motto was: psychology in use *for* the person, *with* the person and *against* the person,' recalled one of those who put it into practice.[1]

One of communism's discoveries was that people could be persuaded to renounce their freedom without force. Most would agree to alter their behaviour, even their way of thinking, if it made their existence easier. The socialist states offered a quiet life to those willing to give up their individuality and their right to influence society: a tacit contract in which citizens would compress their true thoughts into an inner world, while offering public obeisance to the regime. It worked for some; for others it became an intolerable burden.

Those who rebelled felt the weight of the powerful psychological armoury developed by the KGB, the Stasi and the StB. Even those not targeted assumed that they were, spreading mistrust through society and leading individuals to repress spontaneous thoughts, thinking and rethinking before speaking, using the 'official-speak' of socialist discourse in place of natural language. It was hard for westerners to truly understand the mental strain a totalitarian society placed on the individual.

I met Vlad Sobell in 1973, five years after he had fled his homeland, Czechoslovakia, for the life of an academic in the West. It took me a while to understand my new friend's way of thinking. Over the decades, I noticed how much he disliked being told what to do or how to act. He was suspicious of authority and attributed malign intentions to the most innocent of government initiatives. In 2016, when the UK voted to leave the European Union, I lamented the loss of solidarity with our European friends, but Vlad was happy. He denounced the EU as a dictatorship that needed to be thrown off, comparing the constitutionally defined powers of Brussels with the yoke of the USSR. Living under communism had left him with a lifelong aversion towards all outside tutelage. I asked him if he would delve a little deeper into the psychological processes that had brought him to where he now found himself.

Under communism, you didn't need to worry about basic social security (social care from cradle to grave), there was no unemployment (in fact, chronic labour shortages), you did not have to compete with anyone (because there was nothing to compete for), you didn't need to ponder what to buy or not to buy (because there was nothing to buy anyway), you didn't need to agonise about going abroad in search of work (because that was impossible) ... In short, you did not need to make any life-significant decisions whatsoever, because there was nothing one had to be deciding about: there were no options for anything, other than those laid down for everyone by the regime.

The end result is that under communism humans were reduced to the status of pigs in a pigsty, milling round a communal trough that (just) fed them with the essentials and kept them in contented ignorance, while everything concerning their lives was decided for them by the kind, 'benevolent' party ...

From this, I later deduced that communism was actually misunderstood in both the East and the West. It was not solely evil; it could also be regarded as good, depending on one's take. It was an ambiguous situation, like life itself.

In retrospect – and it was hard, for obvious reasons, to see this at the time – the most unpleasant consequence is the realisation that they took away one's mind. By reducing you to the level of a pig at the trough, they 'freed' you from the burden of possessing your own mind. They knew better than you what was good for you. And if you insisted on rejecting this notion

– against, as they understood it, your own best interests – then you were deemed to be mentally ill. You were classed as an individual who did not deserve to exist, a violation of the natural order that should be exterminated.

Incidentally, this is also very much part of my recent reasoning that we now live under a different form of totalitarianism …
I don't want to be like that. I want to think for myself.

Vlad Sobell rebelled against the communist dictatorship of the mind, but the majority of his compatriots did not. If your mind is controlled, you are by definition unaware of it. The American psychologist William James put it succinctly when he wrote of the difficulty of the mind trying to observe the workings of the mind: 'It is like *trying to turn up the gas quickly enough to see how the darkness looks.*'[2]

A 2010 documentary, *My Perestroika*, followed five schoolmates from the last generation to have been brought up in the USSR before communism collapsed. Lyuba, now in her forties, reflected on how strange the lost world of Soviet socialism, with its endless slogans and constant 'fight for peace', now appears, but how normal it seemed back then.

I can't say I consciously wanted to be like everyone else … I simply *was* like everyone else! I was completely satisfied with my beautiful Soviet reality. Life in the West didn't interest me at all. And when the TV showed shootings and protests over there, I would see that and think, 'Oh, my God! I am so lucky to live in the Soviet Union!' … The 'struggle for peace' meant the struggle against American Imperialism. They were the main provocateurs of war. Without them, there would be world peace! Even a hedgehog understood that … It all sounds like a joke now, but it was a fundamental part of my everyday life: I go to school, I eat my dinner, and I also sing songs for peace![3]

The Polish writer Czesław Miłosz rose to William James's challenge of 'turning up the gas to see the darkness' in his classic study of psychological manipulation in his homeland, *The Captive Mind*. Writing in 1953, shortly after he had defected to the West, Miłosz had acquired sufficient distance from the regime's mind games to assess them with clear-eyed objectivity. He marvelled at how effective the state had been in co-opting intellectuals to the socialist project and persuading others to silence themselves. 'My subject is the vulnerability of the twentieth-century mind to seduction by socio-political doctrines,' he wrote. 'I had the impression that I was participating in a demonstration of mass hypnosis.'[4] The lure of socialism lay in its certainty of its own perfection: the monolith of dialectical materialism, at once ultra-rational (its argument trumps all) and the acme of unreason (it is not open to question), won conformity as an act of faith, akin to that demanded by the Christian Church it so loudly denounced.

There was, though, a snag. People may have gone along with the regime's requirements, but in the minds of many there lingered the cognitive dissonance of not knowing *why*, the lurking suspicion of somehow being tricked or unwittingly compelled. To deal with the contradiction, Miłosz wrote, people became actors.

> [The stage] was the street, office, factory, meeting hall, or even the room one lives in. Such acting is a highly developed craft that places a premium upon mental alertness. Before it leaves the lips, every word must be evaluated as to its consequences. A smile that appears at the wrong moment, a glance that is not all it should be can occasion dangerous suspicions and accusations. Even one's gestures, tone of voice, or preference for certain kinds of neckties are interpreted as signs of one's political tendencies ... Acting in daily life differs from acting in the theatre in that everyone plays to everyone else, and everyone is fully aware that this is so.[5]

Nonetheless, 'it was necessary to act convincingly. The fact that a man acts is not to his prejudice, is no proof of unorthodoxy. But he must act well, for his ability to enter into his role skilfully proves that he has built his characterization upon an adequate foundation.' The problem was that such mental contortions practised over a prolonged period had a damaging effect on the psyche. 'After long acquaintance with his role, a man grows into it so closely that he can no longer differentiate his true self from the self he simulates, so that even the most intimate of individuals speak to each other in Party slogans.'[6] This was precisely the outcome the party desired: conditioning its subjects into permanent actors, it steered them away from the inner realm of human longings, of doubts and desire for autonomy.*

'In the people's democracies,' Miłosz wrote, 'a battle is being waged for mastery over the human spirit.' Its aim was to condition citizens not just to stop thinking for themselves, but to mould their thoughts until they *involuntarily* conformed to the directives of the party. The Czech film director Miloš Forman, who would also escape to the West, felt his own mind succumbing to it. 'The worst evil,' he recalled, 'was *self*-censorship, because that twists minds; that destroys your character ... That's what they wanted; they wanted everyone to feel guilty.'[7]

In practice, however, the human spirit could not be repressed forever. At unexpected times and in unexpected ways it burst through the ideological certainty with its very human *un*certainties and doubts.

Miłosz's own decision to flee was the result of a gradual dawning of disgust, accumulated glimpses of the regime's mendacity that finally turned his stomach. 'A man may persuade himself, by the most logical reasoning, that he will greatly benefit his health by swallowing live frogs; and, thus rationally convinced, he may swallow a first frog, then the second; but at the third his stomach will revolt. In the same way, the growing influence of the doctrine came up against the resistance of my whole nature.'[8]

Vlad Sobell fled because he too became aware of the contradictions at the heart of the doctrine. The subsequent realisation that the state was lying to its citizens, telling them what to think and what to do, redoubled his anger. As a young man in the early 1960s he witnessed an influx of West German tourists, allowed into the secretive Czechoslovakia to prop up the failing economy. Their smart clothes and modern cars planted the thought that people in the FRG were living 'normal', comfortable lives, contradicting the regime's

---

* Václav Havel commented that the worst part of the communist experience was the 'devastated moral environment. We are all morally sick, because we all got used to saying one thing and thinking another. All of us became accustomed to the totalitarian system, accepted it as an unalterable fact and therefore kept it running ... None of us is merely a victim of it, because all of us helped to create it together.' In T. Garton Ash, *We the People: The Revolution of '89 Witnessed in Warsaw, Budapest, Berlin & Prague*, Cambridge: Granta, 1990, pp. 137–8.

depiction of a backward, impoverished West. It stirred feelings of inferiority and resentment.

When it became too much to bear, Vlad Sobell used the brief window of the Prague Spring to travel abroad and remained in the UK. Soon after, in August 1968, the Soviet invasion reshaped the political and psychological landscape of his homeland. The new regime, under the pro-Moscow communist Gustáv Husák, was instructed to wipe out the spirit of liberal reform that had led to defiance and unrest.

The first step was the removal of choice. As Milan Šimečka pointed out, being free was mentally taxing – 'Pluralist systems require a lot of attention from the individual: it is not easy to ascertain one's actual place in society; competition makes heavy demands on one's own efficiency, and so on' – while the new society in post-1968 Czechoslovakia would be alluringly simple.

> In order to integrate into the new society, all the citizen had to do was to come to terms with a few very basic notions: that there is only one party of government; that there is only one truth; that everything belongs to the State which is also the sole employer; that the individual's fate rests on the favour of the State; that the world is divided into friends and foes; that assent is rewarded, dissent penalized; that it is senseless to kick against the pricks.[9]

State radio and television carried stories about Czechoslovak citizens who had committed the capital crime of 'abandonment of the republic' and quickly come to regret it. Returning émigrés spoke of a West that lacked job security, welfare, culture and a sense of community. Several highlighted the 'demanding tempo' of work there. When one young man was asked by a Czech journalist, 'Was this tempo a little unfamiliar after the way you worked here?', he replied, 'It was, because it's a fact – let's face it – that here I made enough money and I practically didn't do *any* work.'[10]

In the years of normalisation, the state backed away from demanding communist fervour, accepting instead that people could believe what they liked, as long as they kept it to themselves. Silence became the sine qua non of the quiet life that the majority of people desired more than everything.

In his 1978 book *The Soccer War*, the Polish journalist and author Ryszard Kapuściński examined the convoluted psychology of silence and the central role it played in oppressive regimes.

> Silence is necessary to tyrants and occupiers, who take pains to have their actions accompanied by quiet. Silence demands an enormous police apparatus with an army of informers. Silence demands that its enemies disappear suddenly and without a trace. Silence prefers that no voice – of complaint or protest or indignation – disturb its calm. Today one hears about noise pollution, but silence pollution is worse. Noise pollution affects the nerves; silence pollution is a matter of human lives. No one defends the maker of a loud noise, whereas those who establish silence in their own states are protected by an apparatus of repression. That is why the battle against silence is so difficult.[11]

Kapuściński presented his remarks as a description of repressive regimes in Africa and Latin America, but Polish readers readily understood them to be a commentary on their homeland. A characteristic ambiguity of the Alice in Wonderland world of the Soviet East is that the Polish authorities who allowed Kapuściński to be published almost certainly realised it, too. For all their brutal methods, the communist leaderships did not lack self-knowledge.

A common factor in the people's democracies was an awareness at the highest levels that communism was being imposed on a largely recalcitrant population. In East Germany, suspicion of the population tipped into paranoia. According to psychiatrist Hans-Joachim Maaz, 'East Germany began its existence as a nation with a huge mountain of guilt, humiliation, resentfulness, and alienation, which was never dealt with or treated ... From the outset, repression and projection were the basis of the ideological state doctrine.'[12] The GDR's postwar leadership channelled its misgivings into the most extensive secret police structure the world has known. The minister for state security, Erich Mielke, explained its purpose in his department's official handbook for 1958. 'The Ministry of State Security [commonly known as the Stasi] is entrusted with the task of preventing or throttling at the earliest stages – using whatever means and methods may be necessary – all attempts to delay or to hinder the victory of socialism.'[13]

At its peak, the Stasi had an agent or informer for every eighty-three

citizens. The majority of its informants, known as 'unofficial collaborators' (IMs), were men between twenty-five and forty. Their
handlers were instructed to form close bonds with them, blending
care and control, acting as father figures for young men whose real
parents may have died in the war, or whose Nazi pasts were shameful
to their sons.[14] Their regular meetings took on the aura of the confes-
sional, with no forbidden topics. According to one IM, 'This type of
discussion was the last modest remnant of a public discussion that
society was capable of.'[15] Informants felt valued as individuals in a
state that prioritised the collective and did not otherwise listen to the
views of its citizens.

With the building of the wall, the menace of western propaganda
and espionage campaigns receded. But, as with many powerful organisations, the Stasi took on a life of its own. Since its raison d'être was
the existence of a continuing threat, it was natural that it should insist
there was one. The organisation's bosses exaggerated the danger and
the political leadership internalised the fear, extending its remit to
grotesque proportions. According to the historian Mary Fulbrook,
the Stasi's activities began to spiral out of control in the 1970s, 'as …
paranoia became, in a sense, more institutionalized'.[16] It took literally
the slogan about the enemy being 'whoever thinks differently' and set
out to discover what was in people's heads. An expanding network of
agents provided more and more material until it swamped the organisation's ability to analyse it.

The more the Stasi invaded people's inner space, the more the
people withdrew into themselves. Joachim Gauck, who oversaw the
release of the Stasi's records after reunification, wrote that 'to be
caught in Stasi crosshairs normally meant years of psychic pressure
and … the constant feeling of being observed.' People dreamt they
were being followed; some were convinced that the Stasi was spying
on their dreams. The knowledge that any of one's fellow citizens
could be a Stasi spy was profoundly unsettling. According to the dissident author Jurek Becker, the reputed omniscience of the security
police meant people 'often presumed its representatives to be present
when in reality this wasn't the case. Many telephone conversations
took place only for the benefit of the person listening in … At public
gatherings (everyone's life was full of public gatherings) you even
made yourself sick with your applause at certain points.'[17]

The Soviet sociologist Vladimir Shlapentokh wrote eloquently of the effects that living in a police state can have on an individual. When he and his closest friends realised in their teens that they were the 'anti-Soviet elements' the KGB were seeking to unmask, they were terrified.

> When you recognize your own animosity toward the regime ... a fear that 'Big Brother' will understand who you really are deeply permeates your psyche. Fear may be a practical emotion, but it is also one of the most humiliating feelings ... Making people experience fear was one of the primary tasks of the Soviet rulers.[18]

After emigrating to America, Shlapentokh came to realise that his Soviet friendships were of an intensity few westerners could truly appreciate. He attributed this to the all-pervading 'fear of the totalitarian state', as it 'was only with friends that one could psychologically stand up against that monster; only among friends one could ease the tension from the constant self-control in communicating in the office or with unfamiliar people'. Shlapentokh and his pals forged bonds that the KGB were unable to break, with the 'main criterion of trust' among friends being the ability to reveal to them that you had been approached to spy on them by the secret police.[19]

The Stasi went to greater lengths than the KGB to undermine these bonds of trust. In the early years of the GDR, political opponents were arrested, tortured or executed. Later, the emphasis switched to psychological suppression. A Stasi directive of 1976 informed agents that hostile or oppositional citizens should be neutralised through 'coercive surveillance and systematic discrediting'. The new approach was dubbed *zersetzung* or 'decomposition'. The directive explained how this 'operative psychology' should be implemented.

> The systematic discrediting of public reputations, appearance and prestige on the basis of combining true, verifiable discrediting facts with false, but believable and unverifiable discrediting claims; systematic orchestration of career and social failures in order to undermine the self-confidence of individual persons ... the instigation of mistrust and mutual suspicion within groups of personal circles and organizations; instigation, exploitation and intensification of rivalries within personal circles, groups

and organizations through the use of personal weaknesses among individual members.[20]

Targets would be mentally destabilised by the undermining of their sense of self and their perception of reality. The recommended methods sounded like something out of a psychological thriller. Homes would be broken into and subtly altered; alarm clocks would be reset, sugar put in salt shakers, pictures moved. Items that had been thrown away would reappear, leading targets to question their memory and mental health. Stasi agents would seduce one member of a couple, creating emotional distress and discord. Where this was not possible, love affairs would be faked, with doctored pictures and forged letters. Family members and close friends would be arbitrarily punished, with the blame placed on the target. A number of cases ended in breakdowns and suicide.[21]

For the most obdurate subjects, the process of decomposition could be carried out in captivity. Erich Mielke established a faculty of operative psychology at Potsdam University, where Stasi men learned ways to undermine a prisoner's resistance. Agents studied the effects of sensory deprivation, mimicking controversial experiments carried out on rhesus macaques by the American psychologist Harry Harlow that left the monkeys severely psychologically disturbed.[22]

At the Hohenschönhausen prison in Berlin, Stasi psychologists were encouraged to use his methods on human beings. Dr Jochen Girke, the interrogator who revealed the Stasi motto of 'psychology in use for the person, with the person and against the person',[23] recalled how prisoners were isolated in 'submarine' cells with no natural light and referred to exclusively by number. Guards were trained to walk silently along the corridor so the prisoners never knew if and when they were being watched. A system of red and green lights ensured that prisoners being taken to interrogations never saw each other. It was a modern version of the panopticon prison devised by the eighteenth-century social theorist Jeremy Bentham. Bentham's aim had been to create an atmosphere of calm in which miscreants might reflect on and rethink their criminal ways. But in practice, the panopticon bred suspicion and paranoia, with inmates feeling they were being constantly observed by unseen eyes.

In Hohenschönhausen, Stasi guards were trained to spot the onset of psychological decomposition and offer their charges a chance to ease their isolation. The 'comfort' on offer was human contact with an interrogator, who would pose as the prisoner's friend, promising to help if only he would cooperate. The head of the prison, Siegfried Rataizick, kept note of when inmates started to become 'sad, perplexed, sullen, with despair and anxiety occurring'. Interrogators would then offer them small privileges, helping to lift their mood, co-opting them into collaboration with the system.[24]

Jürgen Fuchs, a psychologist who was arrested in the hope that he would inform on his friend, the dissident musician Wolf Biermann, spoke of the feelings of powerlessness, fear and despair that the Stasi sought to create in its prisoners. His account is reminiscent of the condition of DDD (debility, dependency and dread), which American psychologists believed the Chinese had used against US prisoners of war in Korea.

> They showed the power they exerted over you. You had no idea where you were, who was also imprisoned with you or when you would get out ... The tricks they played were designed to instill terror and hopelessness. Even though you know they are lying – for example, pretending to receive phone calls at key moments revealing that your mother or father had also been arrested – even though you could see they had a button that triggered the phone to ring, it could still have a deep psychological effect on you due to the effects of isolation ...*

The Stasi operatives who carried out the interrogations remembered things in a rosier light. Their conditioning as agents of the state had been thorough, their accounts shot through with the psychological disconnect they had been taught to internalise. The former Stasi official Peter Wolter continued to blame the opponents of the regime ('You have to ask why they were imprisoned at all. ... These were people who sabotaged the GDR and they were quite rightly punished ... I don't have to apologise for anything and I won't apologise for

---

*Fuchs's testimony is displayed at the Berlin-Hohenschönhausen Memorial Museum. He was able to 'record' his interrogations by 'writing' with his finger on the desk, baffling his interrogators and consigning details to memory, which he then wrote up in a feature-length article for *Der Spiegel* after he had been 'sold' to the West for foreign currency.

anything. I can only apologise for not having worked even more effi-
ciently') and western persecution of the GDR ('The GDR was the
weaker country, it had to react, it had to defend itself … by any means
and unfortunately many people had to suffer and to accept personal
restrictions').[25]

The majority of East Germans were never arrested and never had
any overt dealings with the Stasi. Millions of men and women toed
the party line, kept their mouths shut and applauded when they were
told to applaud. But even for the most ordinary of folk, the shadow
of surveillance was impossible to avoid. Psychoanalyst Hans-Joachim
Maaz believed the mind games of the GDR inflicted psychic trauma
on the entire population. Even the innocent fled the state's psychological pressure by retreating into isolated and intensely private lives.
The result, Maaz wrote, was 'a society of niches' ('*Nischengesellschaft*').

> The discipline and demagoguery along with the uncompromis-
> ing intolerance of any deviation had the effect of transforming
> external pressure into inner repression. Every single individual
> was worked over by the system until the psychological mecha-
> nism of self-enslavement and self-destruction was ensured. This
> process was particularly diabolical and sad because, in the end,
> the individual no longer realized his alienation. He no longer felt
> his actual suffering, and rationalized that his disturbed behav-
> iour was in the service of the 'great idea', a patriotic duty, to
> protect his country, for the triumph of socialism, and, of course,
> for the welfare of the people. You only had to hear our 'heroes'
> speak, as they thanked the Party and the government for their
> mental deformation and recast their psychological misery as a
> heroic deed.[26]

Maaz kept case notes on the patients who came to him for therapy. He
noticed that 'parents frequently admitted they felt frightened by the
spontaneity and emotionality of their children, because they themselves could lead only a compulsively narrow life'. In a society that
tracked every facet of its citizens' existence, mastery of one's feelings
was crucial. To avoid costly slips, people damned up their emotions
and 'talked about feelings instead of feeling them … the blockage of
our emotions controlled and determined our lives. We were walled
in emotionally as our country was blocked off physically from the

outside world by the Berlin Wall.'[27] Maaz recorded a new phenomenon of internally warring personalities, created by the conflicting
demands of public hypocrisy and private fear.

> It was clear to all that it was much too dangerous to show your
> true face or voice your honest opinion. As a result, the second
> face … eventually became a habit and was ultimately taken for
> granted as normal. There isn't a man or woman who can live a
> lie for a long period of time, and live well. As psychotherapists
> we know the mechanisms that help people to perceive the new
> 'identity' as their 'true' character, and at the slightest challenge,
> to defend their own false attitude with very sensible and seem-
> ingly believable arguments – splitting off the emotions makes
> this possible. They then lead lives controlled almost exclusively
> by the head or intellect. And the intellect turns every lie into a
> science.[28]

According to psychiatrist Uwe Peters, the symptoms of what he
called 'Stasi-Verfolgten-Syndrom' (Stasi Persecution Syndrome) endure
to this day. These include persistent fear and paranoid persecution
anxieties, depression, sleep disorders, exhaustion and social distrust
that can lead to suicidal ideation. The nature of the Stasi's operations,
permeating people's lives and existence, mean that these symptoms
can be triggered by seemingly banal daily events.[29]

While researching the effect the security services had on East
Germans' lives, anthropologist Ulrike Neuendorf interviewed Herr
K, a man who helped over fifty people escape East Berlin. When he
was caught, the Stasi exposed him to their full range of interrogatory
techniques, and even after his release to the West, continued to harass
him. Aware that someone must have denounced him but with no way
of knowing who, K severed all ties with family and friends. 'I grew
psychotic, I trusted no one.' Because of the surveillance 'I didn't know
where, in what place I was safe'. Only in recent years, following the
unwelcome revelation that his sister was the informant, has he been
able to reconnect with friends and some family members.[30] The pain
endures for political prisoners such as K; at least a third continue to
suffer with PTSD, as well as long-term mental health issues and social
difficulties.[31]

Ryszard Kapuściński was one of the very few authors able to

write openly about the mistrust and bitterness that constant suspicion inculcates in the citizens of a police state. Because he claimed to be describing the oppressive regime of the Shah of Iran, his account was passed by the censor, with the result that the real subjects of his narrative were allowed to see their reflection in the mirror of literature.

> The ubiquitous terror drove people crazy, made them so paranoid they couldn't credit anyone with being honest, pure, or courageous. After all, they considered themselves honest and yet they couldn't bring themselves to express an opinion or a judgement, to make any sort of accusation, because they knew punishment lay ruthlessly in wait for them ... Fear so debased people's thinking, they saw deceit in bravery, collaboration in courage.[32]

The division between the honesty of the 'natural' inner man and the imposed deceit of the external role was reinforced by socialism's approach to that most human of faculties, language. Psychologists have historically accepted that thinking cannot exist without words[33] and that thoughts are shaped by the words that make them manifest. Since the regimes of eastern Europe were striving to suppress the natural thoughts of the free individual, it was little surprise that they should also strive to suppress the natural language that gives them life.

According to the Soviet-born American anthropologist Alexei Yurchak, the state's 'authoritative discourse', the peculiar language people were enjoined to use in all public settings, was an extension of the campaign to control people's minds. The imposition of an idiolect that did not allow for the formulation of personal emotions was a psychological straitjacket designed to limit the population's ability to express themselves outside the parameters set by the state.

Yurchak traced the ways in which 'state speak' began to oust normal language in the young Soviet generation. 'Authoritative discourse' became progressively more convoluted, more rigidly formulaic and technical. It filled itself with quotations from Marx and Lenin, decreed that certain adjectives should accompany specific nouns, and structured phrases and arguments in specific ways. It became mandatory for people to learn and reproduce it mechanically, rarely engaging with the meaning of the words. Ritual and norms were more important than content; projecting proof of one's compliance was essential. Aspiring young communists would be taught the skills of writing and speaking in the genre of authoritative discourse. 'There were key phrases that we needed to use: the well-worn phrases (*izbitye frazy*) that everyone heard an endless number of times. They came to mind easily and were not difficult to reproduce.'[34]

For some young people, the act of mastering the intricacies of authoritative discourse was an enjoyable challenge that brought its own satisfaction, not unlike the 'code languages' that youngsters prize as unintelligible to outsiders. Yurchak quotes a Komsomol activist, Masha, who felt proud at being able to speak it, but unable to understand what it meant. 'Even as a child I was always impressed by such serious and unclear phraseology,' she boasts, but, despite learning to reproduce it brilliantly, 'often I would be unable to explain what I wrote in my own words.'[35]

The historian Stephen Kotkin described the shaping of language in Soviet Russia as 'speaking about oneself through the lens of Bolshevism'.[36] Peter Schneider noted a similar disconnect in the official discourse of the GDR. The posters erected in every street had a strange ring to them, a sense of a meaning that seemed to be there but which no one could pinpoint in human language. 'A few of the posted aspirations read like threats: SOVIET UNION – FRIENDS FOREVER. And one, IT WILL ALWAYS BE OCTOBER, has a kind of involuntary melancholy.'[37]

The Czech author Ivan Klíma dissected his country's version of official discourse in his scathingly bitter novel *Love and Garbage*. The narrator frames the problems of freedom, thinking and mind control against an underlying discussion of the choices that love imposes on us. While the latter takes place in the sphere of 'human' language, the intrusive overbearing state speaks 'Jerk-ish', a distorted, depleted jargon whose aim is to impoverish people's thoughts, not unlike the 'Newspeak' introduced by the ruling party in George Orwell's *Nineteen Eighty-Four*. In Newspeak, concepts that might threaten the ideology of the regime – individual identity, self-expression and free will – are stripped of the means by which they might be voiced. Complex thoughts are curtailed by simplistic terminology; unable to be formulated, they die.

To think and be unable to express one's thoughts is a source of anguish, a version of locked-in syndrome, a sentient brain imprisoned in an unresponsive body, tormented by the impossibility of communicating with its surroundings. For the citizens of Cold War eastern Europe, there were few ways to break the silence. The BBC's German service radio set itself three objectives: to reassure East Germans that they had not been forgotten, to fortify them against communist propaganda and to convince them of the spiritual and material superiority of life in the West.[38] A weekly programme, titled *Letters without Signatures*, invited East Germans to send anonymous letters to express their thoughts about the world. Thousands took up the offer. One regular letter-writer described it as 'coming up for air', as it provided an outlet for all he was unable to express in day-to-day life. But the Stasi did their best to cut the air off, opening 90,000 letters a day, collecting fingerprints and saliva samples from envelopes, laboriously comparing inks and handwriting. Those who were found faced prosecution, including a sixteen-year-old schoolboy, Karl-Heinz Borchardt, who wrote to the BBC in 1968.

> To the staff of Radio London's German service!
> I have only just started listening to your programme, 'Letters without signatures', but I like it a lot, since it airs opinions you don't find in our media. I am 16 years old. I will write to you regularly, mainly about young people and their views on world affairs. In my view, the West did not intervene strongly enough in Czechoslovakia. Does a country which fought so hard for its freedom have to carry on marching to the tune of the Soviets? Warm regards from a schoolboy.[39]

Borchardt was identified after his letter was compared with the handwriting in his school essays. He was arrested by the Stasi and sentenced to two years in a labour camp.

31

THE PSYCHOLOGY OF THE FRONT LINE

In his anguished assessment of religious faith in a post-Hiroshima age, Ronald Knox wrote of the 'American airman, lackadaisically humming a tune' who had dropped the bomb. The 'American airman' was in fact a team of pilots who flew seven B-29 bombers that August morning in 1945. The plane carrying the bomb that would destroy Hiroshima and kill 140,000 people was preceded by a weather reconnaissance aircraft sent to determine whether or not the bombing should go ahead; its pilot, Claude Eatherly, far from being lackadaisical, spent the rest of his life tormented by the consequences of what he had done.[1] He would make three suicide attempts and find himself committed to a psychiatric institution.

Others who took part in the bombing had different means of dealing with it. Some derided the tender conscience of their former comrade. But all faced the questions of guilt and responsibility that accompanied the new reality of war. Morality is a human impulse, felt equally in West and East, as sharply by the angst-ridden J. Robert Oppenheimer as by the future peace campaigner Andrei Sakharov. Questions of individual accountability – whether orders must always be obeyed, the impact of actions taken with no time to reflect – dogged the minds of men and women throughout the Cold War.

Moral agonising began at the top. Harry Truman claimed that he never regretted the decision to drop the Hiroshima and Nagasaki bombs, but the responsibility weighed on him. 'We ought not to use this thing unless we absolutely have to,' he told David Lilienthal, chairman of the Atomic Energy Commission, in 1948. 'It is a terrible thing to order the use of something … that is so terribly destructive … This isn't a military weapon. It is used to wipe out women and children and unarmed people.'[2]

Truman concluded that the use of atomic force should not be entrusted to the military; it had to be treated 'differently from rifles and cannons'.[3] The decision would rest on the shoulders of the president. He alone would take on the responsibility for all below him, all the men and women who would put his orders into effect, right down to the pilot whose plane would drop the bomb. The president would assume the role of guilt-bearer, the biblical scapegoat who would carry the sins of a nation.

The responsibility was embodied in the Biscuit, a small plastic receptacle containing a set of codes, handed to presidents at their inauguration, ready to be cracked open in time of crisis. Its data would be combined with the authentication codes contained in the Football, a heavy leather briefcase carried by an aide who accompanied the president at all times,* and the order would be transmitted to the bases from which the strike would be launched. According to Bruce Blair, missile launch officer at a bunker in Montana, 'It would take no more than about one minute to carry out a launch upon receipt of a valid launch order.'[4]

In the 1980s, the Soviet Union adopted a similar nuclear briefcase-based command and control system, known as Cheget, after a mountain in the Caucasus.

British prime ministers faced an additional complication: they must make their decision in advance about using nuclear weapons. If the UK were destroyed by a nuclear attack, the Royal Navy's Polaris submarines, roaming the oceans of the world, would be likely to survive, still capable of launching a nuclear response. With Westminster obliterated, the submarines' commanders would need to know what to do. Every British prime minister since Harold Wilson has prepared a sealed envelope soon after coming to power, to be stored in the submarines' secure safes, a 'letter of last resort' with handwritten instructions to launch or to desist.

For obvious reasons, no prime minister has explicitly revealed what he or she wrote. The decision is freighted with considerations of personal morality. A nuclear strike after the UK has been destroyed would serve no strategic purpose, merely ramping up the death and suffering. It could, though, be viewed as just retribution. And

---

* It is rumoured that Jimmy Carter sent his Biscuit to the dry cleaners in a trouser pocket, while Bill Clinton lost his for a week during the Monica Lewinsky scandal.

maintaining the possibility of retaliation is undoubtedly necessary if Britain's nuclear arsenal is to retain its value as a deterrent.*

Ambiguity keeps the opponent guessing. But it leaves the British submariners to suffer the strain of unknowing. At the HMS *Neptune* base in Faslane, the home of Britain's nuclear fleet, the 'Submariner's Prayer' is inscribed on the wall of the chapel.

> Lord, Thou commanded us saying 'thou shalt not kill'. Thou knowest that we prepare ourselves constantly to kill, not one but thousands, and that by this preparation we believe we help to preserve peace amongst nations.
>
> Do Thou, who gave man the knowledge to fashion this terrible weapon, give him also the sense of responsibility to control its use; so that fear for the consequences may indeed maintain peace until that day when love, not fear, shall control all men's actions.
>
> Give us the will, but never the wish, to obey the order to fire; oh God, if it is thy will, grant that that order may never need to be given.[5]

Lying dormant under the ocean, hidden for weeks, preparing to inflict unprecedented destruction called for steady nerves. Polaris commanding officer Tony Whetstone taught himself to live with the pressure. 'I can't say that I lost any sleep while on patrol thinking about the destructive power of these missiles. I think one had to sort it out well before you sailed for patrol and if you couldn't sort it out I don't think you've got any right to be there.'[6]

Rear Admiral John Gower joined the Royal Navy in 1978. His experience on board nuclear-capable frigates desensitised him to the terrible power of the weapons.

---

*James Callaghan did, however, hint at what his decision might have been. 'If it were to become necessary or vital [to fire], it would have meant the deterrent had failed, because the value of the nuclear weapon is frankly only as a deterrent. But if we had got to that point, where it was, I felt, necessary to do it, then I would have done it. I've had terrible doubts, of course, about this. I say to you, if I had lived after having pressed that button, I could never, ever have forgiven myself.' Garrett Graff, 'Theresa May's grim first task: Preparing for nuclear Armageddon', *Politico*, 15 July 2016. www.politico.eu/article/the-grim-task-awaiting-theresa-may-preparing-for-nuclear-armageddon-uk-prime-minister-british-defense-letter-of-last-resort/.

I slept within feet of the nuclear weapons storage. The continuous and permanent presence of a tactical nuclear weapon – as
we went about our peacetime business of exercises, training,
and port visits – subtly changed the relationship that the men
on board had with nuclear weapons. I would never say that it
bordered on the cavalier, but it was widely and tacitly accepted
that these tactical nuclear depth bombs would be the recourse in
any Atlantic battle with the Soviet Northern Fleet. The level of
shock and awe necessary to place nuclear weapons in the proper
context had been eroded at the front line.[7]

Very few people – thankfully – have actually hit the nuclear button.
One man who did so was the Soviet bomber pilot Mikhail Mokrinski,
who carried out air drops of Soviet test devices in Kazakhstan in 1961.
'I remember counting down the seconds, then dropping the bomb,'
Mokrinski recalled:

> We had to put on special glasses and pull-down curtains to protect
> us from the radiation. We'd put on the glasses, but 'forget' to
> draw the curtains as we wanted to have a peek. Suddenly there'd
> be something like a rising sun. The clouds dispersed and you'd
> see a beautiful, beautiful picture like in a fairy-tale, a mushroom
> growing up and up. It's on top of you and you're going under-
> neath. The instruments measuring the radiation go right off the
> scale, but of course we forgot about that, then suddenly there's
> a huge blow as the shockwave hits the plane. All the controls go
> crazy and you have to grab the joystick and quickly get it under
> control … We knew what a nuclear explosion was like.[8]

Mokrinski's description has an aura of romance and adventure, but
he was dropping his bombs on a closed site on the depopulated
steppe.* For the men who wiped out Hiroshima and Nagasaki, it took

---

* These tests were not without their human consequences, however. Subsequent
research has shown alarming rates of radiation in the surrounding population. See
for example S. Bauer, B. Gusev, et al., 'Radiation Exposure due to Local Fallout
from Soviet Atmospheric Nuclear Weapons Testing in Kazakhstan: Solid Cancer
Mortality in the Semipalatinsk Historical Cohort, 1960–1999', *Radiation Research*
164:4 (2005), 409–19.

a sterner effort of will to achieve detachment. Colonel Paul Tibbets, the pilot of the *Enola Gay*, compared his role to that of a surgeon who must distance himself emotionally from his patient, or put the whole operation at risk.

> If I get to thinking about some innocent person getting hit on the ground ... I won't be worth anything ... I made up my mind then that the morality of dropping that bomb was not my business. I was instructed to perform a military mission to drop the bomb. That was the thing that I was going to do to the best of my ability. Morality, there is no such thing in warfare.[9]

A common rationalisation by the men who flew with Tibbets – and by the politicians who gave them their orders – was that the bombing of Hiroshima saved American lives by avoiding the need for a ground invasion. Most claimed to feel little or no guilt about their part in it; but Claude Eatherly, the pilot of *Straight Flush*, the weather reconnaissance plane that gave the *Enola Gay* the go-ahead, found his life blighted by guilt and regret.

Eatherly left the air force in 1947, suffering problems with alcoholism and mental health. He became involved in petty criminality. When he was committed to a psychiatric institution, he began a correspondence with the German philosopher Günther Anders, who wrote that Eatherly was not insane; his crimes and his attempts at suicide were, rather, the natural actions of a man oppressed by an unbearable burden of guilt. Anders' book *Burning Conscience* positioned Eatherly as the 'antipode' of the Nazi war criminal Adolf Eichmann, whose trial in Jerusalem was being held while the two men were corresponding. Eichmann sought to defend himself as a mere cog in an unstoppable machine, arguing that he had no choice but to obey the commands of his superiors. He invoked the legal concept of *Befehl ist Befehl* ('orders are orders'), but Eatherly did the opposite. Rejecting the argument that the ends justified the means, Eatherly assumed his own guilt for participating in an action that cost many innocent lives.[10] 'In the past it has sometimes been possible for men to "coast along" without posing to themselves too many searching questions about the way they are accustomed to think and to act,' Eatherly wrote to Anders, 'but it is reasonably clear now that our age is not one of these. On the contrary, I believe that we are rapidly approaching a situation in which we shall be compelled to re-examine our willingness to surrender responsibility for our thoughts and actions to some social institution such as the political party, trade union, church or State.'[11]

In an act of contrition, Eatherly wrote to the *hibakusha*, the survivors of the Hiroshima bomb, many of whom were living with life-changing injuries. 'I asked them to forgive me. I told them that no human beings should fight ... It seems that those sleeping under the ashes of Hiroshima were crying for peace.' A reply, signed by thirty-one young survivors, proffered him the compassion of fellow sufferers.

> We are all girls who escaped death, but received injuries in our faces, limbs and/or bodies ... We heard that you have been tormented by a sense of guilt and that because of it you have been hospitalized for mental treatment. This letter comes to you to convey our sincere sympathy and to assure you that we now do not harbour any sense of enmity to you personally ... We have learned to feel towards you a fellow-feeling, thinking that you are also a victim of war, like us.[12]

Other *hibakusha* were less forgiving. Their suffering left little room for sympathy for those who had inflicted this pain upon them. Psychologist Robert Lifton interviewed many survivors and noted that feelings of guilt far outweighed anger. Yoko Ota believed that she had survived at the expense of others and 'was sorry for the people who died because I was living'. Lifton recalls:

> One man, a writer and manufacturer, told me, for instance, how he felt when watching his child dying: 'If it were possible, I wanted to sacrifice myself in place of my daughter.' The psychological difficulty is that one both wants to and is relieved that one cannot. To survive – and worse, to want to survive – is perceived as improper, wrong, inexcusable, even hateful.[13]

Some *hibakusha* suggested that Eatherly was literally haunted by what he had done, that his anguish and mental health problems were 'brought about by the souls of the dead which caused him this fate'.*

---

* This was reassuring to them as it indicated a balance in the world. The souls,

Paul Tibbets and his crew were equally reluctant to give Eatherly the benefit of the doubt. Tibbets wrote that he could not understand why Eatherly should feel guilty. 'Actually, Major Eatherly did not take part in the attack and did not see the bomb blast that was supposed to have haunted him through many sleepless nights.'[14] One of Eatherly's own crewmen suggested he was seeking fame and attention. But Bertrand Russell, who wrote the preface to *Burning Conscience*, was convinced of Eatherly's sincerity. 'No unbiased person, after reading Eatherly's letters, can honestly doubt his sanity ... He has been punished solely because he repented of his comparatively innocent participation in a wanton act of mass murder ... The world was prepared to honour him for his part in the massacre, but, when he repented, it turned against him, seeing in his act of repentance its own condemnation.'[15]

In the years that followed Hiroshima, thousands of servicemen and women would have to face questions of conscience similar to those that tormented Eatherly. They were the personnel who trained to implement the nuclear defence systems of the Cold War, when an exchange of bombs could potentially bring human existence to an end. Don Murray, the American journalist and author, described them in 1955 as 'those who are already living the strange, lonely war of tomorrow ... small bands of highly skilled men, armed with complex machines, scattered many miles from civilization. Their work will be vitally important – and deadly monotonous.'[16]

In the nuclear age, war would be waged at a distance, with telexes, radar screens and computers to depersonalise the process of killing. Günther Anders called it the 'technification' of human existence, a means of limiting voices of conscience, such as Eatherly's. A warlike society was dehumanising its warriors to ensure that, 'unknowingly and indirectly, like screws in a machine, we can be used in actions, the effects of which are beyond the horizon of our eyes and imagination, and of which, could we imagine them, we could not approve – this fact has changed the very foundation of our moral existence.' Man caught up in the stand-off of the Cold War, said Anders, had unwittingly become 'guiltlessly guilty'.[17]

---

considered eternal in Buddhism, 'had led something to pile up in his conscience and caused him to become insane'. R. Lifton, *Death in Life: Survivors of Hiroshima*, Chapel Hill: University of North Carolina Press, 1991, p. 341.

All felt the responsibility that lay on their shoulders and the choices they feared having to make. Those who were allocated places in the UK's nuclear bunkers knew they could not take their families with them. They knew, too, that a nuclear strike could destroy their homes and loved ones, while they survived underground. Like the Polaris crews, they would embark on their mission in the knowledge that they may have no homeland to return to.

'You could be called back on duty at any time of day or night and never knew if it was real or an exercise,' recalled Corporal Janet Huitt. Based at RAF Holmpton, an underground nuclear facility in East Yorkshire, she and her colleagues were responsible for alerting Westminster to an impending missile strike and keeping Britain running if Westminster were destroyed. 'We were drilled on procedure for a nuclear attack,' she said. 'We all knew if we were within range, we would not survive the fallout.'

Senior Aircraftwoman Janet Levesley, who served five years at the Holmpton bunker, came face to face with the human consequences of her position. 'I remember once ... I got a callout. I rushed upstairs to get my uniform on. My dad was tiling the kitchen at the time, and he said, "Is it worth me putting these tiles on?"'[18]

Many in the military used humour to deal with the danger. Michael Parker – later to become Sir Michael Parker – was a tank troop leader in 1960s Berlin.

> We were stationed in Spandau and down the road were the wire and the minefields and on the other side there were about 700 Russian tanks. One of my troopers said to me, 'Sir, I think we're farting against thunder here.' ... My personal position – the place I would put my tank if the Russians started anything – was on top of a BP petrol station. I said to my commanding officer, 'Do you think that's a good idea, sir, putting us on top of 40,000 gallons of fuel?' and he just said, 'Lad, you're not going to last long enough to worry about any of that.'[19]

The knowledge that the next war would be brutal, bloody and over very quickly was a constant presence in people's minds. The enormity of what lay ahead meant the thought was relegated to the subconscious or processed into a sort of newsreel running in the mind's eye, distancing the reality into fiction. 'In April 1965, the West German

Bundestag announced it was going to hold a session in the Reichstag
building in Berlin,' Sir Michael recalled.

> The building was just inside West Berlin, but the whole of the
> city was governed by the four-power agreement, which meant
> neither side could claim it as their capital. So the Bundestag was
> being very provocative by meeting there and suddenly we heard
> the sound of MiG fighters swooping down on the Reichstag
> from the east. We thought, 'This is it!' They were flying so fast
> that they broke the sound barrier and there were these almighty
> bangs that everyone could hear. Huge great bangs. It set a few
> hearts racing! And the bangs smashed a whole lot of windows,
> which is what they intended to happen. When the MiGs came
> in, our commander told us to grab our tanks and get out on the
> streets; so there we were, waving to the locals and shouting,
> 'Don't worry, chaps; we're on your side!' The whole thing was
> surreal. It was like something out of a B-movie: you kept expect-
> ing someone to come out and shout, 'Ok, cut!'[20]

Group Captain Brian Hoskins, who would go on to have a distinguished career as the leader of the Red Arrows, found himself at
the forefront of the Cold War in 1967. Stationed with 20 Squadron
in Singapore, he was called into action when organised mobs from
mainland China threatened to invade Hong Kong. Hundreds of
armed demonstrators, incited by Beijing, had crossed the frontier at
Sha Tau Kok, shooting at the Hong Kong police and killing several
of them. Hoskins was one of the pilots ordered to secure the border.

> The aim was to show determination, to tell China that the UK
> wasn't going to give ground. We were fully aware of the serious-
> ness of what was going on. It was the front line between East and
> West. But we'd been trained by the RAF and we knew what to do.
> I had the right personality for it, but it isn't a question of personal-
> ity: it's the training that kicks in. That's what gets you through.[21]

More than any previous conflict, the Cold War threw up situations
that put the future of the world at risk, where a miscalculation – a
simple slip of a finger, the unchecked actions of a single individual –
might lead to its end. The psychiatrist Jerome D. Frank examined the

pressure on people working on the front line at a time when advances in technology meant humanity had 'for the first time … reached the stage of the irretrievable mistake'.[22] The psychological toll on those in stressful jobs – stationed in remote military bases or confined on board ships – was reflected in higher rates of mental illness, drug dependency and alcohol abuse. A study commissioned by the US Navy in the 1960s found that even the most diligent psychological oversight could not predict how individuals would react under such stress. Indeed, 'the most potentially dangerous situations in the Navy,' the report concluded, 'have involved personnel who demonstrated no sign of psychiatric disturbance at the time of their initial assignment to militarily sensitive duties'.[23]

The mental strength of a Soviet naval crew was put to the test in October 1962. It was the height of the Cuban missile crisis and an American U-2 spy plane circling over the island was shot down by a Soviet-supplied ground-to-air missile. White House aides feared the Soviets had fired the first shot in a nuclear war. Off the Cuban coast, four Soviet Foxtrot class nuclear submarines were on patrol, each equipped with a nuclear torpedo. One of them, B-59, was commanded by Captain Valentin Savitsky, with the squadron's chief of staff, Vasily Arkhipov, also on board. The sub was diesel-powered, designed for the cold seas of the north. In the warm Caribbean, it needed to surface frequently to recharge its batteries, but now it was surrounded by American ships, spotter planes and helicopters. Unable to break cover, conditions on board were becoming desperate. The temperature was close to 50 degrees, the amount of CO_2 in the air was at critical levels and contact with Moscow had been lost. The submarines became the target of American depth charges, in an attempt to force them to the surface. 'We thought – that's it – the end,' recalled B-59's communications officer, Vadim Orlov.*

The totally exhausted Savitsky, who in addition to everything was not able to establish connection with the General Staff,

---

* Robert Kennedy says this was 'the time of greatest worry by the President'. His hand 'went up to his face and covered his mouth and he closed his fist. His eyes were tense, almost gray, and we just stared at each other across the table.' Had he known that the subs they were targeting were carrying nuclear torpedoes his fear would have been even greater. Fursenko and Naftali, *Khrushchev's Cold War*, p. 481.

got furious. He summoned the officer who was assigned to the
nuclear torpedo, and ordered him to assemble it to battle readiness. 'Maybe the war has already started up there, while we are
doing summersaults here,' [he] screamed ... 'We're gonna blast
them now! We will die, but we will sink them all. We will not
become the shame of the fleet!'[24]

For the first time in history, the US Strategic Air Command had raised
its threat level to DEFCON 2, defined as 'Next step to nuclear war'.
If Savitsky had launched his torpedoes, retaliation would have been
immediate, nuclear holocaust inevitable. But in spite of all his years
of ideological conditioning, Savitsky's chief of staff, Vasily Arkhipov,
had retained the capacity for what Russians call *inakomyslie*. 'Different
thinking' or 'independence of thought' was a dubious attribute in the
USSR. Arkhipov knew that military insubordination carried the sever-
est penalty but, remarkably, he made the right call. He argued with
Savitsky, persuaded him to hold fire then convinced him to come to
the surface. With communications restored, Savitsky radioed Moscow
to ask for confirmation that he should attack, but Moscow told him
not to.[25] Vasily Arkhipov's presence of mind, the 'human factor'
that should not, but did override the machine of war, had averted
the greatest of disasters. When he returned to the Soviet Union,
Arkhipov was severely reprimanded by Marshal Andrei Grechko for
allowing the Americans to force the submarine to surface. In later
life, Arkhipov rarely spoke of the incident. Even to his wife, he made
only coded allusions to what had happened. The truth of his exploit
emerged only after his death.

Analysis carried out by American anti-war medics in the 1980s concluded that the majority of potentially dangerous incidents involving
military or space exploration technology were the result of human
error. The hardware was considerably more reliable than the men or
women in charge of it.[26] But at crucial moments of potential conflagration, it has more than once been unpredictable, emotion-driven
human reflexes that have saved the world. Arkhipov's off-message
intervention was one example. Another came two decades later in
1983, one of the Cold War's hottest years.

In March 1983, Ronald Reagan denounced the Soviet Union as an
'evil empire'. Tensions rose over the summer and on 1 September,
the USSR shot down a Korean passenger plane that had strayed into

Soviet airspace. Three weeks later, warning signals flashed onto the computer screens of the Serpukhov-15 missile alert centre outside Moscow. Five US Minuteman missiles had been detected heading towards the Soviet capital; Washington had moved from rhetoric to action. The base commander, Lt Col. Stanislav Petrov, knew what he should do. The protocols for such an emergency stipulated that he should immediately call the Kremlin hotline so that General Secretary Yuri Andropov could authorise massive retaliation against the USA. Petrov didn't pick up the phone. He ran through thirty levels of supplementary checks and received confirmation that this was not a false alarm. The data indicated an attack from a single American base. Even then, Petrov hesitated. The rules told him to act; his gut told him to wait. He barely understood why he hadn't made the call, but there was something not quite right. It took him a moment to understand what it was. 'For two or three minutes, I didn't analyse anything. I was left with my intuition. I had two arguments. First of all, why would the US launch a rocket attack from a single base? They'd fire from everywhere. Secondly, the computer is an idiot. There's no telling what it might think is a launch.'[27] Petrov sensed the warning did not tally with the Cold War logic that if you are going to strike first, you annihilate your opponent with multiple launches so as to leave no scope for retaliation. And he was right. The system had confused the sun's glare reflecting off clouds for the fire trail of rockets.

Stanislav Petrov's instinctual understanding of human motivation – what the Americans would have been *thinking*, rather than what they had seemingly *done* – overrode the mechanistic juggernaut of war. The West knew nothing of what had happened in Serpukhov-15, but its analysts also appreciated the importance of the human factor. In May 1983, an operations officer at the Cheyenne Mountain Complex, the heavily fortified Colorado base of the North American Aerospace Defense Command (NORAD), had told *The New York Times* that 'people are the key'. Rather than judging solely by sensors and computers, 'the entire system relies on people and the people who are here are trained to be suspicious. They are discriminators.'[28]

It was a wise precaution that had saved America from disaster four years earlier. On 9 November 1979, the national security advisor, Zbigniew Brzezinski, was woken by a phone call informing him that Soviet missiles had been detected on their way to targets in the USA.

Robert Gates, then a member of the National Security Council, remembered the nightmare closeness of Brzezinski's response.

> Brzezinski was awakened at three in the morning by [military assistant William] Odom, who told him that some 250 Soviet missiles had been launched against the United States. Brzezinski knew that the President's decision time to order retaliation was *from three to seven minutes*. Thus, he told Odom he would stand by for a further call to confirm Soviet launch and the intended targets before calling the President ... When Odom called back, he reported that 2,200 missiles had been launched, it was an all-out attack. *One minute* before Brzezinski intended to call the President, Odom called a third time to say that other warning systems were not reporting Soviet launches. Sitting alone in the middle of the night, Brzezinski had not awakened his wife, reckoning that everyone would be dead in half an hour. It had been a false alarm. Someone had mistakenly put military exercise tapes into the computer system. Zbig just went back to bed. I doubt he slept much, though. Such were the terrors and nightmares of the Cold War.[29]

The US media ran garbled stories of the false alarm, prompting Leonid Brezhnev to send a triumphantly condescending message to Jimmy Carter. 'Reports have been received that recently, due to some erroneous actions, the US technical systems gave a signal of a nuclear missile attack on the United States which resulted in putting appropriate means on alert ... I think you will agree that there should be no errors in such matters. They must be completely excluded – not 99, but all 100 per cent.'[30]

The importance of the human factor would determine much of the course of the Cold War, and this included the men at the top. In the Cuban missile crisis of 1962, the leaders of both superpowers were subjected to sleepless nights and intense psychological strain, a combination that could have led to missteps. John Kennedy's adviser Ted Sorensen noted 'during the long days and nights of the Cuban crisis, how brutally physical and mental fatigue can numb the good sensc as well as the senses of normally articulate men'. Robert Kennedy concurred that 'crisis-induced pressure does strange things to a human being, even to brilliant, self-confident, mature, experienced men. For some it brings out characteristics and strengths that perhaps even they never knew they had, and for others the pressure is too overwhelming.'[31]

The Soviets had seen this at first hand. Stalin had crumbled in the days following the German invasion of 1941, rendered incapable of rational action. Leonid Brezhnev, too, seemed unnerved by the gravity of the decisions he was called upon to make. The Soviet general Andrian Danilevich witnessed the general secretary's intense anxiety during a military exercise to simulate the consequences of a nuclear exchange. According to Danilevich, Brezhnev was terrified when he was told that an American first strike would leave the Soviet Union with just one-thousandth of its military might intact and 80 million of its citizens dead.

> During the exercise, launches of ICBMs with dummy warheads were scheduled. Brezhnev was actually provided with a button and was expected to 'push the button' at the appropriate time ... When the time came, Brezhnev was visibly shaken and pale and his hand trembled and he asked [Marshal] Grechko several times for assurances that the action would not have any real-world consequences. 'Andrei Antonovich, are you sure this is just an exercise?'[32]

By the 1980s, 120,000 people had some role in the administration of nuclear weapons in the USA. The need to exclude unstable individuals from positions of responsibility was taken seriously. Stringent controls under the Personnel Reliability Program (PRP) were introduced 'to ensure that such weapons are not subject to loss, theft, sabotage, unauthorized use, unauthorized destruction, accidental damage or jettison ... Only those personnel who have demonstrated unswerving loyalty, integrity, trustworthiness, and discretion of the highest order shall be employed in nuclear weapon PRP positions.'[33] Just one person was exempted from such precautions – the commander-in-chief. The terms of the US Air Force Doctrine made it clear that if the president wishes to use nuclear weapons, he may do so and no one may hold him back.

> The President may direct the use of nuclear weapons through an execute order via the Chairman of the Joint Chiefs of Staff to the combatant commanders and, ultimately, to the forces in the field exercising direct control of the weapons.[34]

But what if a nuclear attack were ordered by a president who had become confused or mentally deranged? What safeguards could the world count on? And what was the position of American service personnel who felt they were being wrongly instructed to destroy it? During the presidency of Richard Nixon, a trainee missile crewman at Vandenberg Air Force Base in California tried to find his own answers to the problem. Major Harold Hering raised his hand at a training session and asked, 'How can I know that an order I receive to launch my missiles came from a sane president?', later writing to his superior officer, 'There's presently a degree of doubt in my mind as to whether I might one day be called upon to launch nuclear weapons as a result of an invalid or unlawful order. How can I be sure I'm participating in a just act?' Hering was no long-haired troublemaker. He had completed several tours as a helicopter pilot in Vietnam and always maintained that he would turn his key to trigger a launch if ordered to do so. He acknowledged that adequate checks existed at the operational level: missileers had always to work in pairs, to ensure that an individual could not act unilaterally. He was, though, troubled by the lack of oversight of the president. He wanted reassurance that an order from the top would be 'lawful'.[35]

> I feel I do have a need to know, because I am a human being. It is inherent in an officer's commission that he has to do what is right in terms of the needs of the nation despite any orders to the contrary. You really don't know at the time of key turning, whether you are complying with your oath of office.[36]

The Soviet Union and modern-day Russia have sought to remove such concerns by not disclosing to nuclear launch personnel whether the orders they receive relate to a genuine launch or simply an exercise. According to the Russian nuclear weapons specialist Igor Sutyagin, 'They will just receive the order "load flight plan number 2" and that is all that they know. The flight plan might be just training, but to avoid psychological difficulties for the crews they never know if it's a launch or not.'*

---

* An article in *Pravda* in 1985 quoted a launch officer: 'When an input comes in, in your soul there's an anxiety: is this combat, or is it training?' A. Gorokhov, 'Behind the controls of the strategic missiles', *Pravda*, 29 May 1985, p. 6, quoted in

Major Hering's concerns came at a time the White House was occupied by a president who did not always seem entirely in control of his impulses. 'I felt I had asked a very reasonable question that deserved an answer,' Hering wrote later, 'and it was not for me alone; it was for all of us.'[37] The only answer he received was the removal of his security clearance and an eventual discharge from the military.

H. Abrams, 'Sources of Human Instability in the Handling of Nuclear Weapons', in Frederic Solomon and Robert Q. Marston (eds.), *The Medical Implications of Nuclear War*, Symposium Papers, Washington DC: National Academy Press, 1986, pp. 510–11. See also 'The Inquiry: How do You Launch a Nuclear Missile?', BBC World Service. www.bbc.co.uk/programmes/po4pr36d.

32

THE MADMAN AND DÉTENTE

In the summer of 1974, Richard Nixon was under pressure. He had always been a drinker; now, infuriated by impeachment proceedings that threatened to curtail his second term as president, he was drinking to excess. In a conversation in the White House, he shocked two Democratic Congressmen by pointing to the door of his office and declaring, 'At any moment I could go into the next room, push a button and 20 minutes later 60 million people would be dead.'[1]

The remark might have been a regrettable outburst fuelled by stress and a surfeit of whisky. But Nixon had more than once tried to achieve key policy goals by playing psychological games on opponents, leveraging suspicions that he was unhinged, willing to do anything to get his own way – perhaps even start a nuclear war. It kept opponents on their toes, but opened the way for potentially fatal miscalculation. In a world where direct contact between the superpowers was curtailed, myths of the 'other' were quick to take root. Nixon had been prey to insecurity from early childhood; his need to prove himself, to be better than other presidents, had fostered paranoia. And in such flammable times, he was not the only one prone to ill-advised posturing, a willingness to gamble and bluff that drew both sides into high-stakes confrontations.

Nixon's 1968 campaign for the presidency coincided with the height of the Vietnam War. America's perceived humiliation by the Viet Cong had destroyed Lyndon Johnson's presidency and blighted his legacy. Nixon was determined not to share the same fate. He promised that he would win 'peace with honour' and he was prepared to break the rules, even the law, to do so. When LBJ came close to securing a peace deal in October 1968, Nixon put his personal interest ahead of the nation's, conspiring to undermine Johnson's negotiations by telling the South Vietnamese that, once in office, he would get them far better terms.[2] It was an act that bordered on treason, but Nixon had few qualms, apparently rationalising his conduct by equating America's future with his own success.

> What is on the line is more than South Vietnam. If we fail to end the war in a way that will not be an American defeat, and in a way that will deny the aggressor his goal, the hawks in Communist nations will push for even more and broader aggression … If a great power fails to meet its aims, it ceases to be a great power.[3]

Nixon, neurotic and insecure, formed an unlikely alliance with Henry Kissinger, his brilliant, duplicitous adviser and eventual secretary of state. 'Nixon was from California; a conservative, anti-Communist Republican from the grassroots of America,' wrote Kissinger's aide, Winston Lord. '[He was] distrustful and disdainful of the elite, the establishment, the northeast Ivy League and frankly with a heavy dose of anti-Semitism. And who does he pick as his National Security Advisor but Henry Kissinger, a Jewish immigrant from Harvard who had worked as a close advisor to Nelson Rockefeller, Nixon's strongest opponent. It was an amazing choice, and a brilliant one.'[4] The two men traded barbs behind each other's back. Nixon called Kissinger a 'cry-baby' and a 'dictator'; Kissinger dismissed Nixon as a 'drunk … unfit to be president'.[5] But they produced a unique combination of traits – overt aggression, discreet diplomacy, ruthless cunning and psychological trickery – that would alter the dynamic of Cold War politics.

Most who knew Nixon agreed that he possessed a high level of self-awareness, matched by a calculated willingness to adopt different personas in pursuit of his goals. Garry Wills called him 'the plastic man', 'the least authentic man alive, the late mover, the tester of responses … His aim has always been the detached mind, calculating, freed for observing the free play of political ideas, ready to go with the surviving one.'[6] At times, he seemed to lack any personal identity, coming alive only in his public role. 'I look in the mirror and it is as if there were nobody there,' Nixon told a psychiatrist in the 1950s.[7] 'This is a man of many masks,' jeered Adlai Stevenson, 'but who can say they have seen his real face?'[8] What Stevenson intended as a put-down, Nixon regarded as a trump. The more people struggled to pin down his identity, the more he could project a manufactured version of himself, up to and including the intimation of insanity. His chief of staff, Bob Haldeman, was taken aback by the audacity of it.

> We were walking along a foggy beach after a long day of speech-writing. He said, 'I call it the Madman Theory, Bob. I want the North Vietnamese to believe I've reached the point where I might do *anything* to stop the war. We'll just slip the word to them that, "for God's sake, you know Nixon is obsessed about Communism. We can't restrain him when he's angry – and he has his hand on the nuclear button" – and Ho Chi Minh himself will be in Paris in two days begging for peace.'[9]

Nixon's 'madman theory' chimed with Niccolò Machiavelli's advice that a prince might find it 'a very wise thing to simulate craziness' to wrong-foot his opponents, to persuade them that they 'should seek with all industry to make themselves friends to him'.[10] And Nixon was undoubtedly familiar with Dwight Eisenhower's tactics during the Korean War, when the president let the Chinese know in no uncertain terms that they must agree to peace talks or he would use the bomb. Nixon's defense secretary, Melvin Laird, said later, 'He never [publicly] used the term "madman", but he wanted adversaries to have the feeling that you could never put your finger on what he might do next. Nixon got this from Ike, who always felt this way.'[11] A more surprising source of inspiration for Nixon was the man he once called 'the most brilliant world leader I have ever met'. Nikita Khrushchev, the object of Nixon's admiration, had shamelessly exploited his own reputation for volatility and unpredictability, using the threat of irrational actions to manipulate opponents at home and abroad. Nixon had seen at first hand how '[Khrushchev] scared the hell out of people', and he adopted similar tactics himself.[12]

Faced with an escalating nuclear arms race, Nixon's response was to embrace risk, adopting Thomas Schelling's prescription of 'threats that leave something to chance'.[13] 'We've got to play it recklessly,' Nixon told Kissinger. 'That's the safest course.'[14] And Kissinger agreed. In order to convince the Chinese and Soviets to compel the North Vietnamese to sign a peace treaty, Nixon made a show of being willing to use the nuclear bomb. To give credence to his threats, DEFCON levels were randomly raised for days at a time, communications silence maintained and nuclear bombers dispersed to airfields around the country. The aim was to simulate preparations for large-scale offensive operations. '[These] actions should be discernible to the Soviets,' wrote the chairman of the US joint chiefs of staff, 'but not threatening in themselves.'[15]

The Madman Strategy became a startlingly accepted tactic in government circles. The White House consultant, Leonard Garment, was instructed by Henry Kissinger to take every opportunity to convince the Soviets that Nixon might actually be mad. 'If the chance comes your way,' Garment quoted Kissinger as saying, 'convey the impression that Nixon is somewhat crazy – immensely intelligent, well organized and experienced, to be sure, but at moments of stress or personal challenge unpredictable and capable of the bloodiest brutality.'[16] And it seemed to work. The Soviet ambassador in Washington, Anatoly Dobrynin, sent an anxious warning to his bosses in the Kremlin. 'Nixon is unable to control himself even in a conversation with a foreign ambassador. The vehemence of his remarks testified to his growing emotionalism and lack of balance.'[17]

The Soviets themselves had had experience of an unpredictable leader. Nikita Khrushchev had been ousted five years before Nixon came to power, partly as a result of his alarming volatility. His successor, Leonid Brezhnev, was valued as a safe pair of hands, uninspiring, but mercifully free of the 'hare-brained schemes' of his predecessor. An economically strapped USSR now desired stability and a reduction in tension with the West that would increase opportunities for trade. Their chastening experience with Khrushchev worked in Washington's favour, making Nixon's staged 'madness' seem credible and threatening.

'For deterrence, what the other side thinks is as important as what we think,' Kissinger told the National Security Council. In the nuclear age, the raised stakes meant that even a 'bluff is taken seriously'.[18]

The fraught relationship between East and West meant that both sides were hindered by a lack of perspective, their vision clouded by inculcated prejudice and an inability to inhabit the mind of the 'other'. One man who strove, with some success, to see through the ingrained distortions was the Kremlin adviser Georgy Arbatov. In 1967, he persuaded the Russian Academy of Sciences to establish an Institute for US and Canadian Studies (ISKRAN), which he headed for the next thirty years, declaring it 'an oasis of creative thought'.[19]

'The overwhelming majority of our specialists (and to some degree I include myself),' Arbatov recalled, 'were spoiled, overwhelmed, and deformed by the pervasive [Soviet] ideology and the dominance of propaganda, by the fear that has become an integral part of our national psyche, by timidity of thought, and by conformism.'[20]

For western correspondents in Moscow, Georgy Arbatov was a rare source of independent thinking, a man with close ties to the Kremlin but a mind of his own. We valued the infrequent interviews he granted us and sensed that he would have liked to be more critical of the suffocating dogma that warped his bosses' thinking. The 'high priests' of the Kremlin, Arbatov acknowledged many years later, were 'deeply steeped in myths and ideology'. They fed the soup of propaganda to the masses, while 'they themselves, ate completely different food, coldly and rationally calculating policy on the basis of some higher interests visible only to them'.

> The biggest and most harmful myth was the belief that we could ensure security and resolve, if not all, then almost all, political problems with military strength (a mirror image of the myth existed in the United States as well). At work here were the powerful forces of an inertia that dated back many years, even many centuries, and psychological baggage that was common to both of us. At fault were … wars that were almost always perceived as messianic, conducted in the name of a noble idea or cause.[21]

In order to reduce the scope for misunderstanding, Arbatov urged the leadership to boost contacts with the West; only then, he felt, would they begin 'gradually to understand how different types of people think, and no longer attribute our own stereotypes to another society'.[22] Nixon, too, favoured negotiation, but he framed his conciliatory rhetoric with continued threats of aggression, a 'strategy of ambiguity' that sought to initiate dialogue without appearing to give ground. 'After a period of confrontation,' Nixon had declared on taking office in 1969, 'we are entering an era of negotiation. Let all nations know that during this administration our lines of communication will always be open … [But] all those who would be tempted by weakness, let us leave no doubt that we will be as strong as we need to be for as long as we need to be.'[23]

The starting gun was fired by Willy Brandt's *Ostpolitik*. He was the first West German chancellor to visit the GDR, formally recognising the state-over-the-wall in 1970. It was a move that worried many conservative US politicians, but Henry Kissinger sensed the potential benefits. Increased contact with the socialist world, he reasoned, could be used 'to demonstrate to the American public that Vietnam was an aberration, that we had ideas for the construction of peace on a global scale'.[24] He and Nixon were willing to countenance arms control talks to help improve relations with the socialist world, but their conception of what came to be known as détente was not about making friends. Nixon explained to Kissinger the message they should give to the Soviets: 'Look, we'll divide up the world,' he said. 'But by God, you're going to respect our side or we won't respect your side!'[25] It was the voice of realpolitik and it found its echo in Moscow. The Soviet foreign minister, Andrei Gromyko, told a closed-door meeting of his staff that they too should demand respect: 'Our foreign policy is now conducted in a qualitatively new environment of genuine equilibrium. We have become a world power ... it took the hard work of two generations of Soviet people to reach that goal.'[26]

It was decided that communications would be conducted through a secret back-channel run by Anatoly Dobrynin and Henry Kissinger, unsupervised by the State Department and unseen by the wider world. Both sides had become entangled in international difficulties and each needed assistance from the other, but neither could admit it in public. The clandestine nature of the proposed negotiations would allow them greater freedom to compromise. Washington wanted Soviet assistance in ending the sapping US involvement in Vietnam. Moscow enjoyed the spectacle of the Americans' south-east Asian calvary, but feared North Vietnamese success would entrench China as the leading communist power in the region. Dobrynin noted wryly that both superpowers were trapped by the world they themselves had created: 'The situation was absurd,' he wrote. 'The behaviour of our allies systematically blocked any rational discussion of other problems that were really of key importance to both of us.'[27] Classified telephone conversations between the two sides underlined their broad commonality of interests. 'North Vietnam is a drag for us, as it is for you,' Nixon told Dobrynin in December 1972. 'What we're trying to do is to accomplish what you want and what we want – to remove this irritant between our relations. That's the real thing. We can't allow this damn place to interfere in relations between the

Soviet Union and the United States.' 'Yes,' Dobrynin replied. 'This is what our approach is, too.'[28]

Moscow had another irritant. China had troubled the Kremlin since the triumph of Mao Zedong in 1949, when Stalin came to resent Beijing's challenge to his primacy as the leader of world communism. The Great Leap Forward, the Cultural Revolution and China's acquisition of the atomic bomb had added to Moscow's concerns. Leonid Brezhnev was increasingly wary of a Chinese leadership that he suspected of unbridled ideological fanaticism. The Chinese, for their part, felt the crushing of the Prague Spring and the Brezhnev doctrine of intervention in eastern Europe were proof that the Soviets had become 'socio-imperialists'. Mao described Brezhnev's assumption of power in 1964 as 'a counter-revolution'. Tensions had boiled over in 1969 with fighting between Soviet and Chinese forces along the Ussuri River and on the Kazakh border. After seven months of clashes, with casualties in the hundreds, Mao acted on the old Chinese proverb advising the wise man to find 'the opportunity that exists in the crisis'. By putting out feelers to Washington, Mao decided, Beijing would 'become a wedge between the Soviets and Americans'.[29]

Mao's overtures were timely, allowing Nixon and Kissinger to play the two former socialist allies against one another. As early as 1967, Nixon had laid out his plans to use China as a counterweight to the USSR. 'We simply cannot afford to leave China forever outside the family of nations,' he wrote, '... there to nurture its fantasies, cherish its hates and threaten its neighbors ... The world cannot be safe until China changes. Thus our aim should be to induce change.'[30]

In July 1971, Kissinger secretly travelled to Beijing. Both parties agreed that a presidential visit would be in their mutual interest, but ending twenty-two years of enmity was a delicate task. Neither wanted to be seen as the supplicant; both needed to save face with their domestic audiences. The eventual announcement was a triumph of constructive ambiguity. 'Knowing of President Nixon's expressed desire to visit the People's Republic of China,' the communique read, 'Premier Chou Enlai, on behalf of the Government of the People's Republic of China, has extended an invitation to President Nixon to visit China at an appropriate date before May 1972. President Nixon has accepted the invitation with pleasure.'[31]

Nixon's visit, in February 1972, achieved its purpose. A joint announcement that both sides had pledged to improve Sino–US relations sent the desired message to Moscow. There was genuine worry in the Kremlin that the USSR was being surrounded. Kissinger assured the Soviets that the opening to China was not a threat to them, but did so in terms that he knew would be disbelieved. 'I stressed that it reflected no anti-Soviet intent. This was the conventional pacifier of diplomacy by which the target of a maneuver is given a formal reassurance intended to unnerve as much as to calm, and which would defeat its purpose if it were actually believed. Soviet diplomats are not known for their gullibility, but I thought that the implications spoke for themselves.'[32]

Having stoked the Soviet leadership's anxiety, Nixon and Kissinger moved to the next phase of their plan, proposing a presidential visit to Moscow that the Kremlin accepted at once. 'We've got their paranoia working for us,' Kissinger declared. 'They really think I'm a tricky bastard,' Nixon replied. 'And they're right.'[33] It would be the first visit by a US president to Moscow of the Cold War and Nixon was elated. 'An American president to visit Russia – do you realize what that's going to be? The damnedest show you ever saw in the world!'[34]

Somewhat disingenuously, Kissinger told Dobrynin that the summit, in May 1972, would be an opportunity for the two sides to overcome the 'psychological barrier' that existed between them, characterised by 'exaggerated mistrust'.[35] In fact, it was an opportunity for Washington to bully the Soviets. With the conflict in Vietnam dragging on, the North Vietnamese refusing to parley and the American public increasingly turning against the war, Nixon needed a way out. In the weeks before his trip to Moscow, he ramped up his madman image. He ordered a no-holds-barred bombing campaign, targeting Hanoi, seemingly unconcerned about civilian casualties, and threatening worse to come. 'Now, Henry,' he told Kissinger, 'we must not miss this chance. We're going to do it. I'm going to destroy the goddamn country, believe me, I mean destroy it if necessary. And let me say, even the nuclear weapon if necessary. It isn't necessary. But, you know, what I mean is, that shows you the extent to which I'm willing to go.'[36]

It worked. Nixon backed up his big stick with some soft speaking on his visit to Moscow and a few weeks later – under pressure now from both the Chinese and the Russians – the North Vietnamese agreed to reopen peace talks. In July, Le Duc Tho travelled to Paris for negotiations, culminating in a ceasefire in October.[37] In November's presidential election, Nixon won an unprecedented forty-nine states and 61 per cent of the popular vote. His inaugural address in January welled with triumphant optimism.

> This past year saw far-reaching results from our new policies for peace. By continuing to revitalize our traditional friendships, and by our missions to Peking and to Moscow, we were able to establish the base for a new and more durable pattern of relationships for the nations of the world. Because of America's bold initiative, 1972 will be long remembered as the year of the greatest progress since the end of World War II toward a lasting peace in the world.[38]

The clever management of Moscow and Beijing, said Kissinger, was proof that America could be creative and ingenious, using psychological levers to make a positive impact for peace. But, he added, 'It was not one of the least ironies of the period that it was a flawed man, so ungenerous in some of his human impulses, who took the initiative.'[39] Nixon may have achieved his goal, but his character defects remained. His life trajectory would be that of the Shakespearean tragic hero, raised high through worldly success, but undermined by personal flaws destined to trigger his downfall. An ingrained paranoia, a seemingly pathological inability to trust others, had already sowed the seeds of his demise. Within two years of his re-election he would be out of office, impeached for the use of dirty tricks in an election he would undoubtedly have won without them, and implicated in the cover-up that followed.

In public, Nixon scoffed at the growing numbers of Americans seeking psychiatric help, but he himself had been doing so for twenty years. He had been a client of the Austrian-American psychiatrist Dr Arnold Hutschnecker since the 1950s and kept up a regular correspondence with him while in office. The president 'didn't have a serious psychiatric diagnosis', Hutschnecker recalled, but he did have 'a good portion of neurotic symptoms'.[40] Nixon's nuanced self-awareness, verging on self-absorption, allowed him to trace his own insecurity back to an unfair childhood world, in which looks, popularity and riches were assigned to undeserving others. Speaking to his former communications director, Ken Clawson, in 1979, he embarked on a moment of revealing self-analysis.

What starts the process, really, are laughs and slights and snubs when you are a kid. But if you are reasonably intelligent and if your anger is deep enough and strong enough, you learn that you can change those attitudes by excellence, personal gut performance while those who have everything are sitting on their fat butts ... In your mind you have nothing to lose so you take plenty of chances, and if you do your homework many of them pay off. It is then you understand, for the first time, that you have an advantage because your competitors can't risk what they have already.[41]

Anger and resentment, an imbibed sense of life's unfairness and a willingness to take exaggerated risks drove the adult Nixon to prove himself – to be more famous, more successful, more admired and celebrated than those who had looked down on him. But ambition was an addiction that demanded ever greater highs. In the end, they became attainable only through the thrill of reckless gambles, covert actions that, if discovered, would mean personal ruin.

It's a piece of cake until you get to the top. [Then] you find you can't stop playing the game the way you've always played it because it is part of you and you need it as much as an arm or a leg. So you are lean and mean and resourceful and you continue to walk on the edge of the precipice because over the years you became fascinated by how close to the edge you can walk without losing your balance.[42]

Self-protection through aggression became a role that Nixon could not throw off. 'It was like one of those Greek things where a man is told his fate,' Kissinger reflected later, 'and fulfils it anyway, knowing exactly what is going to happen to him ... I sometimes had the impression that he invited crisis and that he couldn't stand normalcy. Triumph seemed to bring no surcease to this tortured man. It was hard to avoid the impression that Nixon, who thrived on crisis, also craved disasters.'[43]

In his final speech to the White House staff as he quit the presidency in disgrace, Nixon gave a forlorn diagnosis of the psychological obsession he himself had endured and which finally struck him down. 'Always remember,' he said, 'others may hate you – but those who hate you don't win unless you hate them, and then you destroy yourself.'[44] Even in his moment of gravest crisis, he had not lost his capacity for self-understanding. He understood the remedy for his self-destructive obsessions (not to hate one's enemies), but his inner demons had prevented him from adopting it. The faithful Bob Haldeman interpreted his boss's actions as a sacrifice of the self, accepted for the sake of America's security. 'Such a man, in the pressures of the political world, would see enemies – most of them real – everywhere; would be unable to defeat those enemies by a normal "easy" attitude that inspires popularity, would despair at his lack of natural charisma and realize that if he was to win he would have to attack and destroy.'[45] The constant battle to attack and destroy had conditioned Nixon's approach to human relations, blighting his personal as well as his political life. 'He was conscious every minute of self-discipline,' Haldeman wrote. 'Therefore he couldn't relax.' Nixon himself advanced the same analysis. 'I can't really let my hair down with anyone,' he told a journalist. 'Not even with my family.'[46] It is a charitable gloss of the paranoia that gripped the president in his last months in power. 'What happened to President Nixon is a human tragedy,' Kissinger concluded, less kindly. 'When I say tragedy, it doesn't mean that it wasn't deserved.'[47]

For their part, the Soviets found it hard to believe that Nixon had been forced to resign over the Watergate burglary. Anatoly Dobrynin recorded the shocked reaction of his masters in the Kremlin.

> They thought, 'How could the most powerful person in the United States, the most important person in the world, be forced to step down for stealing some silly documents?' It was so contrary to the Soviet mentality that someone in such a senior position could be removed by legal means. They simply couldn't understand it.[48]

If perceptions of inferiority and resentment can drive the behaviour of a man, they can to some extent drive the behaviour of a nation. Since its inception after 1917, the Soviet Union had imbibed the conviction that only 'excellence, personal gut performance and taking plenty of chances', to quote Nixon, would allow it to triumph over a hostile world. Allied military intervention on the side of the Bolsheviks' opponents, the western trade blockade and the Nazi invasion of 1941 reinforced the conviction that the USSR was despised, disrespected and threatened. 'The history of Russia is one of continual beatings she suffered because of her backwardness,' Stalin had declared in 1928. 'She was beaten by the Mongol khans, by Turkish beys, the Swedish lords, the Polish and Lithuanian nobles and by the British and French capitalists ... We are fifty or a hundred years behind the advanced countries. We must make up this distance in ten years. Either we do it, or they will crush us!'[49] Only by unwavering resolution and ruthless determination had the Soviet Union risen to the top table of international politics and it would do anything to stay there. Nixon understood this. An entry in his diary expressed empathy for the Soviets' 'Spartan' toughness, in contrast to the flabbiness of a West made soft by material wealth and comfort.

> If we fail it will be because the American way simply isn't as effective as the Communist way [in supporting countries abroad] ... we emphasize the material to the exclusion of the spiritual and the Spartan life ... On the other hand, the [Soviet] enemy emphasizes the Spartan life, not the material, emphasizes sacrifice ...[50]

Leonid Brezhnev's decision to embrace Washington's offer of détente raised concerns in some parts of the Kremlin. His hardline colleagues, wary of abandoning the long-standing ethos of unyielding defiance, demanded a stiffening of resistance in other areas, notably an extension of Soviet influence in the Third World. The politburo resolved 'to seek, without disclosing it publicly, a weakening of the US role in international affairs, including its position in western political–military alliances, as well as in strategically important regions in the world, Europe, Middle-East and Asia'.[51]

Things began well. The West's energy crisis of the early 1970s and the petrodollars flowing into Moscow's coffers increased the leadership's confidence, inflating its aspiration to dominate the Third World. 'The more that can be taken away from Washington the better,' wrote one architect of Soviet foreign policy.[52] But initial success led to overextended ambitions and unwise foreign involvements that sucked in more cash and manpower than had been bargained for. 'In Latin America and the Third World,' recalled General Nikolai Leonov, a former chief of analysis for Soviet Foreign Intelligence, 'the

Soviet leadership did not have strategic plans backed up by sufficient human, technical, and material resources.'[53] The Soviet ambassador to Damascus concluded that it was they who were being manipulated, exclaiming 'These damned Syrians, they will take anything except advice!'[54]

Georgy Arbatov's characterisation of the psychology of Soviet foreign policy was an uncanny echo of the path followed by Richard Nixon. 'As often happens in politics,' Arbatov wrote, 'if you get away with something and it looks as if you've been successful, you are practically doomed to repeat the policy. You do this until you blunder into a really serious mess.'[55]

By the end of the 1970s, the Soviets had made all the mistakes that America had made before them. The 1979 invasion of Afghanistan drew the USSR into a vicious, draining war in an alien land, with a growing wave of dissent at home, where their forces would toil to no avail for nearly a decade.

In post-Nixon America, détente became a dirty word, increasingly disparaged as a fruitless policy of appeasement that allowed the Soviets to thrive and caused America to fall back. The emerging truth about the illegal bombing of Cambodia and Laos fostered the feeling that America had abased itself. A crisis of confidence gripped the nation. The fallout from Watergate and Vietnam, unflattering revelations about the CIA, the economic downturn and a wave of youth unrest led Barry Goldwater to lament that Americans were 'losing our faith' in American principles and 'our national will to survive in freedom'.[56]

Seeking to pull the nation out of its Vietnam-induced malaise, Nixon had instead plunged it further into self-doubt. Détente was abandoned. Washington returned to the old Cold War policy of pressure against the Soviet Union. In 1980, America would turn to a movie star to revive its values of old.

33

REAGAN'S EPIPHANY

Ronald Reagan ascended to the White House on a tide of anti-Sovietism. His victorious 1980 presidential campaign was fuelled by a strident rejection of the incumbent Jimmy Carter's 'go-soft' in East–West relations. Carter may have confronted the Soviet Union over its human rights violations, but by agreeing strategic arms limitation measures with the USSR he allowed Reagan to paint him as a supporter of détente. 'Isn't it time that we made Carter understand we don't really care whether the Soviets like us or not?' candidate Reagan thundered. 'We want to be respected!'[1] Détente was a symptom of western weakness, an American crisis of confidence that had allowed the Soviets to grow stronger and more assertive; his task in office would be to crush the enemy he came to refer to as the 'evil empire'. Reagan had previously confided in Richard Allen, who would become his first national security advisor, that his Cold War strategy was a simple one: 'We win and they lose.'[2] How he would achieve it was less clear. The man with the reassuring charisma and soothing voice, honed by years of playing Hollywood good-guys, pledged to restore the nation's self-belief. He extolled America as the defender of world liberty and denounced Moscow's quest for 'world revolution and a one-world socialist or Communist state'. The globe was once again divided into 'us' and 'them'.

The adviser behind the president's thinking, the hawkish Richard Pipes, told him that Russians were different from 'us'. They were natural aggressors, convinced that they could start a nuclear war and win it. The psychology of mirror-imaging, Pipes argued, the projection of our own values onto a very different 'other', had led to critical failures in the evaluation of the Soviet threat. It was simply wrong to regard the USSR as peaceful and well-intentioned. The Soviets were not to be empathised with; they were to be stared down and defeated.

But if the start of Ronald Reagan's presidency presaged

confrontation, perhaps even war, its outcome was a surprise. Reagan would find his apotheosis as the man who helped end the struggle between East and West, not on the field of battle, but around the negotiating table. From being a sworn enemy of the Kremlin, his name would go down as one of the Cold War's peacemakers.

It is hard to imagine that Reagan foresaw the startling reversal that would transform him from crusader to conciliator. Early tales from his time in office suggested he was an unreformed Cold Warrior. The White House staffer Stefan Halper made notes of the president's first briefing by the US joint chiefs of staff.

> The service chiefs reported one by one that the Soviets had overwhelming strength; they had more aircraft, more surface combatants, more submarines, more tanks, more battalions and so on. With each report, the President said nothing. Eventually, the President turned to his old friend and new CIA Director, Bill Casey, and asked, 'Bill, what do we have more of?' Casey responded, 'We have more money.' The President said, 'Fine, we'll use that.' And that is what was done ... We more or less knew what we were doing from that point forward.[3]

Reagan and his vice president, later President George Herbert Walker Bush, would deploy America's unmatched spending power as a Cold War weapon. But more important than the military hardware it paid for was the honed understanding of human psychology – the art of bluff and double bluff – with which they manipulated economic power to edge their Soviet counterparts towards an acceptance of compromise. By the mid 1980s, Reagan's dedication to arms spending had made the holy grail of military supremacy the central measure of the East–West balance of power. America spent, so the USSR felt it must spend. Neither could allow the other to forge ahead. Dollars and roubles were lavished unstintingly. What Reagan knew, and Brezhnev strove to forget, was that Washington could afford it while Moscow could not. It was an asymmetry that would become critical as the decade wore on.

To justify the surge in military spending, the White House made public the views of the joint chiefs of staff expressed at the presidential briefing reported by Stefan Halper. The fear of Soviet military supremacy would be drummed into the anxious minds of the American people. But from the very outset, there was an element of pretence. 'The Soviets never really gained military superiority over us,' recalled the US assistant secretary of state, Leslie Gelb. 'It was just part of the psychodrama in America to use that issue to galvanise Americans about the larger legitimate question over the strategic competition between our two countries and philosophies.'[4]

The president's scare tactics about Soviet supremacy were a calculated ploy. But the psychodrama was no less dangerous for being calculated. Signals transmitted by one side could be – and frequently were – misinterpreted by the other. Part of Reagan's justification for reigniting the arms race was that the Soviets had ceased to fear the West. 'The Soviet leaders know full well,' Reagan declared in 1983, 'that there is no political constituency in the United States or anywhere in the West for aggressive military action against them.'[5]

But if Reagan believed – as he publicly declared – that Moscow was not motivated by fear, he could hardly have been more wrong. The Kremlin was haunted by it. Yuri Andropov, the then head of the KGB, had messaged his senior officers in 1981 that, 'Never before, starting from the Great Patriotic War and the Cold War years, has it been as acutely apparent as it is now: the imperialists are waging an arms race on an unprecedented scale and are expediting the preparations for war.'[6] In an interdepartmental collaboration with the GRU, the KGB launched Operation RYaN – an acronym for Ракетно-ядерное нападение or Nuclear Missile Attack – to try to predict the moment the West would push the nuclear button. 'The slogan of RYaN,' General Oleg Kalugin recalled, 'was "Do not miss the instant when the West is about to launch war!"'[7]

Soviet agents were instructed to gather intelligence that might give Moscow a moment of warning. Some were told to befriend western bankers, hoping they might have inside information on the build-up to war. Others monitored US blood banks to see if they were boosting their supplies; one was told to count the number of windows that stayed illuminated late at night at the Ministry of Defence in London. Oleg Gordievsky, a KGB agent who would later defect to the West, recognised the dangerously self-reinforcing feedback that sent Moscow's fear levels soaring. 'Because the political leadership was *expecting* to hear that the West was becoming more aggressive, more threatening and better armed, the KGB was obedient and reported:

Yes, the West *was* arming ... The Centre was duly alarmed by what they reported – and wanted more.'[8]

What began as propaganda was assimilated as the truth; ideology foisted on the public ended by infecting the leadership. Cool heads were in short supply. Tensions reached critical levels in 1983. A series of US PSYOP manoeuvres, including naval and submarine incursions into waters adjacent to Soviet military bases, set alarm bells ringing in the Kremlin. American bombers were dispatched to fly at high speed towards Soviet airspace, turning away at the last moment. According to the CIA historian Benjamin Fischer, the aim of the PSYOP actions was 'not so much to signal US intentions to the Soviets as to keep them guessing what might come next'.[9] Fischer quotes the former US under-secretary of state for military assistance and technology, William Schneider, as saying, 'It really got to them. They didn't know what it all meant. A squadron would fly straight at Soviet airspace, and other radars would light up and units would go on alert. Then at the last minute the squadron would peel off and return home.'[10]

On 8 March 1983, Reagan made his 'Evil Empire' speech, accusing the Soviet Union of being the 'focus of evil in the modern world'. The reply from Moscow was stark, accusing Reagan of reviving the 'worst rhetoric of the Cold War', motivated by a 'pathological hatred of Socialism' that led him to 'think only in terms of confrontation and bellicose, lunatic anti-Communism'.[11]

Tensions were further inflamed on 1 September, when a Soviet Sukhoi interceptor over the Sea of Japan shot down a Korean commercial jet that had strayed into Soviet airspace on its journey from New York to Seoul. And in November, NATO launched Operation Able Archer, a series of military manoeuvres in Europe involving hundreds of thousands of men, clearly aimed at intimidating the Soviets.

It achieved its aim. And more. According to Gordievsky, 'a potentially lethal combination of Reaganite rhetoric and Soviet paranoia' convinced the Kremlin that Washington was preparing to attack. Astonishingly, Reagan had failed to comprehend the effect his actions might produce. On being informed that the Soviets had come close to a military response to Able Archer, he wrote in his diary on 18 November, 'I feel the Soviets are so ... paranoid about being attacked that, without being in any way soft on them, we ought to tell them no one here has any intention of doing anything like that. What the hell have they got that anyone would want?'[12]

How could Washington and Moscow exhibit such an absence of insight into the way their actions were perceived? The behavioural historian Robert Jervis examined the psychology of Cold War misinterpretation in his influential study *Perception and Misperception in International Politics*. 'It takes great insight,' Jervis wrote, 'to realize that actions that one believes to be only the natural consequence of defending one's vital interests can appear to others as directed against them. The result is that when an actor believes he is not a threat to another, he usually assumes the other knows he is not hostile.'[13] When the future of the planet is at stake, such an assumption might be considered negligent, even dangerously myopic. Reagan, one of the worst offenders, was unable to grasp that America might be a source of fear for the Soviets. He later admitted that only in 1984 did he realise 'something surprising about the Russians'.

> [That] many people at the top of the Soviet hierarchy were genuinely afraid of America and Americans. Perhaps this shouldn't have surprised me, but it did. In fact, I had difficulty accepting my own conclusion at first. I'd always felt that from our deeds it must be clear to anyone that Americans were a moral people who starting at the birth of our nation had always used our power only as a force of good in the world. [Knowing this] I was even more anxious to get a top leader in a room alone and try to convince him we had no designs on the Soviet Union and the Russians had nothing to fear from us.[14]

The president's belated realisation was coloured by national self-representations ('power used only as a force for good') that were taken for granted at home but far from evident abroad. His secretary of state, George Shultz, recorded how hard it was to change Reagan's mind about anything, let along something as important as this. 'Many times I would try to correct the President on the particular facts of a favorite story. It rarely worked. Once a certain arrangement of facts was in his head, I could hardly ever get them out.'[15] Even after his light-bulb moment, Reagan was loth to abandon his alarmist rhetoric. His re-election campaign in 1984 was accompanied by a series of anti-Soviet television commercials. 'There is a bear in the woods,' proclaimed an ominous voiceover to video footage of a prowling grizzly. 'For some people, the bear is easy to see. Others don't see it at all. Some people say the bear is tame. Others say it's vicious and dangerous. Since no one can really be sure who's right, isn't it smart to be as strong as the bear?'

Reagan secured a landslide victory, but the public were far from convinced by his handling of the Cold War confrontation. A 1984 poll reported that 89 per cent of Americans believed 'there can be no winner in an all-out nuclear war; both the US and the Soviet Union would be completely destroyed'; 75 per cent of respondents agreed that Russians are understandably 'obsessed with their own military security' due to 'their homeland [being] invaded many, many times'; over half thought 'Soviet leaders believe that President Reagan is trying to humiliate them, and this is not a good climate for negotiating on matters of life and death'.[16]

The shift in polling data reflected the views of a younger generation less willing to accept the terrifying 'normality' of the Cold War nuclear stand-off. A 1982 study by the American Psychiatric Association on the 'Psychosocial Impact of Nuclear Advances' concluded that youngsters had

> not submerged or camouflaged their feelings of helplessness about the nuclear threat as most adults have learned to do. They may be showing us that growing up in a world dominated by the threat of imminent nuclear destruction is having an impact on the structure of personality itself. We may be raising a generation of young people denied a basis for making long-term commitments and serviceable ideals, given over, of necessity, to doctrines of impulsivity and immediacy in their personal relationships and their choice of activities, behaviours and occupations. How can we help our young people grow into some promise of certainty and fulfilment unless we adults address the apathy and helplessness we experience in the fact of the arms race and the threat of nuclear annihilation?[17]

Senior figures including McGeorge Bundy, George Kennan and Robert McNamara were more in tune with public opinion, warning that Reagan's aggressive military posture risked triggering an unwinnable conflict. In a collective article for the journal *Foreign Affairs*, they complained of 'a seeming callousness in some quarters in Washington toward nuclear dangers'.[18] Kennan went further. The commitment to the arms race, he wrote in his book, *The Nuclear Delusion*, was the result of a psychological obsession that had overtaken the minds of those who pursued it. 'We have gone on piling weapon upon weapon, missile upon missile, new levels of destructiveness upon old ones. We have done this helplessly, almost involuntarily, like the victims of some sort of hypnotism, like men in a dream, like lemmings heading for the sea.'[19]

Reagan himself was not unmindful of the flaws of deterrence theory. He disliked the idea of Mutually Assured Destruction, comparing it to 'two men standing in a saloon aiming their guns at each other's head – permanently'.[20] His Christian beliefs, with their vivid representation of Armageddon, made real the devastation that would ensue if one of the 'men in the saloon' let his trigger finger tighten. But the years of addiction to muscular militarism – endless threat countered by threat – had instilled a mental template that was hard to renounce. Taking the first step, being the first to lay down a weapon, with the attendant gamble that relaxing one's vigilance might invite destruction, seemed unpalatably counterintuitive. Freud described the locked behaviour that militates against change. Irrational, compulsive acts become an integral part of the psyche, he suggested, a way of attenuating neurotic anxiety. Sufferers cannot control themselves; when they try to desist from the behaviour or are made to stop 'they are forced by an appalling dread to yield to the compulsion and to carry out the act'.[21] Freud's observations would form the basis for the diagnosis of obsessive compulsive disorder, in which a person feels bound to perform repeated rituals (compulsions) by the conviction that doing so is the only means to stave off imagined consequences with catastrophic implications (obsessions).[22] For Reagan, nuclear weapons seemed to function in a similar way, as ritual objects that helped him fend off a monstrous, menacing danger. To dispense with them would require something to take their place; and for Ronald Reagan and his team, that 'something' would be SDI.

Reagan's Strategic Defense Initiative (SDI), or 'Star Wars' as it became known, advanced the theory of a revolutionary missile defence shield. Being able to destroy or deflect incoming ICBMs would change the dynamic of nuclear confrontation, creating a future in which the US would not rely 'solely on offensive retaliation for our security'. 'Wouldn't it be better,' Reagan asked with unarguable simplicity, 'to save lives than to avenge them?'[23] In practice, SDI – if proved practicable – would disrupt the precarious balance of nuclear forces that had been nurtured for three decades. It would negate Moscow's nuclear deterrent. The Kremlin, understandably, was horrified.

Even with SDI in development, Reagan hesitated to loosen the nuclear security blanket. His pronouncements vacillated between a desire to befriend and a compulsion to confront. Kenneth Adelman, the White House senior arms control negotiator, described him as 'a man singularly endowed with an ability to hold contradictory views without discomfort'.[24] Reagan's ambiguity confused and angered the Kremlin. Anatoly Dorbynin wrote that he had never seen the Soviet leadership 'so deeply set against an American president. It was a catastrophe in personal relations at the highest level.' Reagan's hesitation and confusion, and even his avowed desire for 'a fresh start', were interpreted as signs of duplicity and hostility.[25]

When Reagan eventually requested that a back-channel of negotiation be opened with the Kremlin, he did so in the face of opposition from his own advisers. The first problem was to find the right partner with whom to negotiate. The Kremlin leadership was as divided and confused as Reagan was. 'A group of troubled men,' George Kennan called them, 'prisoners of certain ingrained peculiarities of the Russian statesmanship of past ages – the congenital sense of insecurity, the lack of inner self-confidence.'[26] The 'senilocracy' that had emerged as a consequence of Brezhnev's aversion to renewal meant there was a rapid turnover of general secretaries during Reagan's first term. 'How am I supposed to get anyplace with the Russians,' he quipped to his wife Nancy, 'if they keep dying on me?'[27]

The obstacles were practical as well as psychological; but over the course of his two terms in office, Reagan discovered the trust he had once believed impossible. His epiphany on the road to Moscow owed much to the personal understanding that grew up between the men – and the woman – who led the world's great powers. By late 1983, British prime minister Margaret Thatcher had already begun moves to understand what was happening behind the scenes in the Kremlin and to make contact with possible future leaders. She had consulted with 'people who have really studied Russia – the Russian mind – and who have some experience of living there', to try to discover who might take the reins when the gerontocrats finally died

out. When the Oxford don, Archie Brown, reported that Mikhail Sergeyevich Gorbachev was 'open-minded, intelligent and anti-Stalinist'
and could potentially be at the root of 'a movement for democratiz-
ing change', Thatcher invited him to London.*

The Cabinet agreed that Gorbachev should be given 'insights into
American intentions and seriousness of purpose'. Cabinet and Foreign
Office briefing papers from December 1984 noted two priorities – to
reassure Moscow that the West had no aggressive intentions and, crucially, to discover if Moscow could say the same. 'Our message to him
should be that the West unquestionably wants better relations, but
not at any price. The world is not, as Soviet propaganda frequently
maintains, on the brink of nuclear catastrophe.'[28] The visit should
be used to 'teach him something about how a Western democracy
works and to emphasise the sincerity and willingness of the West ...
to negotiate substantial arms control agreements', as well as to 'get
an insight into Gorbachev's personality and qualities and through him
into current Soviet problems, priorities and intentions'.[29] Thatcher's
adviser Charles Powell added, 'This will be a unique opportunity to
try and get inside the minds of the next generation of Soviet leaders.'[30]

Gorbachev's arrival in mid December lifted a veil on an opaque
Kremlin. He was under the microscope both as a leader and as a
man, with the western media expressing an almost comic surprise
that he was human and – wonder of wonders – had brought his wife
with him. Mikhail and Raisa Gorbachev made the sort of favourable
impression as human beings that can – eventually did – change the
course of history. Tony Bishop, Thatcher's interpreter, saw in him
'the acceptable face of Communism'. 'He fitted his face to the tasks
in hand, refusing to be provoked by persistent demonstrators, by the
Prime Minister's challenging and probing examination of him, by the
clamorous and potentially embarrassing attentions of the media ...
His demeanour in addressing others can be summed up in the word
"naturalness".'[31]

'A roguish twinkle was never far from his eye,' Bishop added. 'He
even winked at me over his shoulder as I interpreted a neat parry

---

* W. Taubman, *Gorbachev*, p. 196. Invitations were sent to Gorbachev and two other
possible candidates, Grishin and Romanov. According to Charles Powell, '[it] was
pure chance that Gorbachev accepted first'. CNN, *Cold War, Episode 22: Star Wars*
produced by Pat Mitchell and Jeremy Isaacs, 1998.

The dull, grey ideologues in Downing Street were shocked to
discover that Gorbachev was no dull, grey ideologue.

of his to one of the Prime Minister's verbal thrusts.' But when the
question of imprisoned dissidents in the USSR was raised, 'the mask
slipped'. Challenged by the opposition Labour leader, Neil Kinnock,
Gorbachev gave way to 'an intemperate outburst of obscenities and
threats against "turds" and spies like [the dissident] Natan Sharansky
... He warned, with appropriate gestures, that Britain would "get it
in the teeth" in a merciless denunciation of its human rights crimes,
if that was the game it wanted to play ...' 'We had glimpsed beneath
the surface a man conscious of power,' Bishop concluded, 'and ready
if needs be to exploit it ruthlessly.'[32]

According to the British record, Gorbachev expressed himself
'very satisfied indeed with his talks with the Prime Minister. He had
arrived with preconceived ideas about her attitude towards the Soviet
Union. These had been proved wrong, and, to his great pleasure, he
had established a good understanding with her.'[33] The key element on
both sides – something that had been lacking for a long time – was
human warmth. Its potential to influence world events was evident
in Thatcher's spontaneous appreciation of her visitor not just as a
politician, but as a person.

His personality could not have been more different from the

wooden ventriloquism of the average Soviet apparatchik. He
smiled, laughed, used his hands for emphasis, modulated his
voice, followed an argument through and was a sharp debater
... As the day wore on I came to understand that it was the
style far more than the Marxist rhetoric which expressed the
substance of the personality beneath. I found myself liking him
... As he took his leave, I hoped I had been talking to the next
Soviet leader.[34]

Later that evening, Thatcher told the BBC's political editor, John Cole:

I like Mr. Gorbachev. We can do business together. We both
believe in our own political systems. He firmly believes in his;
I firmly believe in mine. We are never going to change one
another ... but we have two great interests in common: that we
should both do everything we can to see that war never starts
again, and therefore we go into the disarmament talks determined to make them succeed. And secondly, I think we both
believe that they are the more likely to succeed if we can build
up confidence in one another and trust in one another about
each other's approach.[35]

The message was communicated to President Reagan. An emphasis
on human contact and the psychology of personal confidence was
to be the key to improved international relations in the years ahead.
    When Gorbachev became general secretary in March 1985, fol-
lowing the death of the final interim leader, Konstantin Chernenko,
he inherited a Soviet Union in economic and spiritual decline. 'The
very system was dying away,' he would write in his memoirs. 'Its sluggish senile blood no longer contained any vital juices.'[36] Gorbachev
set out at once to change things. His aim was to reinvigorate Soviet
communism, to save the socialist system he loved and restore Soviet
influence in the world. His 'new thinking', as it quickly became
known, opened the door for better international relations – this was a
man the West felt it could talk to – but the sense of a USSR beginning
to rediscover its mojo was also a source of concern. 'When Gorbachev came to power he was initially seen as a threatening figure,'
recalled the British ambassador to Moscow, Rod Lyne. 'Unlike the
fossilized old men who had preceded him, he was actually trying to

reinvigorate the Communist system and get it working more effi-
ciently, which may have made things harder for the West if things had
taken a martial turn.'[37] Lyne's assessment reflected official thinking
in London. Gorbachev's visit there had convinced ministers that his
'combination of cleverness, modern-mindedness, Slav nationalism,
energy, charm, self-assurance and single-mindedness would make
him at worst a formidable adversary and at best an interlocutor to be
treated with the utmost respect and circumspection'.[38]

Gorbachev would have recognised the description. My own
impression of his character, formed in the course of several meetings with him during and after his time in power, was of a man who
was open and sincere but dedicated to the cause he believed to be
right. He had an avuncular charm – in manner and appearance he
reminded me of my own father – but he could surprise. Questioning the basis of his communist convictions resulted in unexpectedly
angry ripostes. And he could swear like a trooper.

His background explains much. His life had been shaped in the
harshest years of Stalinist repression. With neighbours disappearing
into labour camps, the Gorbachevs had been lucky. Both of his grand-
fathers, imprisoned during the brutal collectivisation of agriculture in
the 1930s, survived and returned to their home in the North Caucasus. His beloved father went to war and came back alive. In a stable,
loving household, Mikhail grew up trusting and optimistic.[39] He was
twenty-five when Nikita Khrushchev exposed the iniquities of Stalinism and initiated the years of Thaw. It imbued him with hope and a
belief that things could change. He studied law and seemed to believe
in the rule of law – not always the case in a capricious autocracy,
where absolute rulers flouted the rules at will. And he had a firm
confidence in his own abilities, even to the point of arrogance. The
ideal of the 'New Soviet Man', capable of confronting the biggest
challenges, had been drummed into Gorbachev's generation. In his
case, the challenges would be to heal the ruptures in Soviet society
and pave the way for peace in the world.

Gorbachev brought a can-do pragmatism to the Kremlin, a willingness to face up to reality that had long been missing. Brezhnev's
determined refusal to contemplate change had allowed problems to
accumulate in society and the economy. A popular joke had Stalin,
Khrushchev and Brezhnev travelling together in a railway carriage.
The train tracks run out and they shudder to a halt. Stalin has the

driver shot, but the train still doesn't move. Khrushchev rehabilitates the driver and suggests tearing up the rails from behind to lay tracks in front. Brezhnev shrugs and says, 'Comrades, let's draw the curtains and pretend we're moving ...'* The old guard had refused to accept that Marxist orthodoxy had failed – if the facts contradicted the theory, they simply ignored the facts – but Gorbachev wanted to know the truth about what was happening in the country and in the world. One of his first acts was to replace the old guard foreign minister, Andrei Gromyko, with a new generation of modern diplomats.

Like Gorbachev, Ronald Reagan was convinced that he too could achieve whatever he set his mind to. He was less interested (perhaps less capable) than his Soviet counterpart in mastering the technical details of policy-making, but he had a fixity of vision that allowed him to overcome setbacks and mistakes to press on towards his goal. Margaret Thatcher's first-hand assessment had bolstered his belief that Gorbachev was someone with whom he could work. 'Two men of good will,' Reagan ventured, 'could move the world together if they spoke as one human being to another.'[40]

The first of their five summit meetings would take place within eight months of Gorbachev assuming office. 'Time is short,' he told Dobrynin. 'We need to get to know Reagan and his plans, and most important, to launch a personal dialogue with the American president.' The emphasis on personal rapport was new. Previous general secretaries had lacked anything approaching a personality, and had been too sick, or their time in post too short, for a meeting to be arranged with Reagan. Meeting face to face, Gorbachev told Reagan, could 'create an atmosphere of trust between our countries ... For trust is an especially sensitive thing, keenly receptive to both deeds and words. It will not be enhanced if, for example, one were to talk as if in two languages: one – for private contacts, and the other ... for the audience.'[41]

Reagan echoed that message in a characteristically folksy parable

---

*The joke would later be included in the CIA's Soviet collection, with an additional line about Gorbachev, who calls a rally in front of the locomotive, encouraging the people to chant, 'No tracks! No tracks! No tracks!' www.cia.gov/readingroom/docs/CIA-RDP89G00720R000800040003-6.pdf. See also 'Gorbachev: his life and times', William Taubman in discussion with Vladislav Zubok, LSE, esp. 12:00–18:00. www.lse.ac.uk/ideas/podcasts/gorbachev.

of two fictional couples, the Soviets Ivan and Anya and the Americans Jim and Sally, who meet for the first time. To a worldwide television audience, Reagan asked,

> Would they debate the differences between their respective governments? Or would they find themselves comparing notes about their children and what each other did for a living? ... People want to raise their children in a world without fear and without war. They want to have some of the good things over and above bare subsistence that make life worth living ... Their common interests cross all borders. If the Soviet Government wants peace, then there will be peace.[42]

Reagan had written most of the speech himself. It may have been schmaltzy, but it sounded heartfelt. The Great Communicator understood how to appeal to the universal wellsprings of human emotion. But he knew little about ordinary Soviet people or the Soviet character. In advance of the impending summit, Reagan was given a crash course by Jack Matlock, the National Security Council's Soviet specialist. Matlock compiled a series of briefings on subjects such as 'Sources of Soviet Behavior' and 'The Soviet Union from the Inside', hoping to provide him with some psychological insight.[43] One point stressed by Matlock was that the president should not lend too much credence to widely touted notions of Soviet efficiency and monolithic invincibility. Moscow's propaganda – and western fears – needed to be taken with a grain of salt. 'Everything [in the Kremlin] is decided ad hoc. They don't know themselves what they are going to do next. But they will always claim that they had it in mind all along.' Matlock said Soviet diplomats admitted to saying things in public that they knew were absurd, simply because the ideology demanded they do so. There was, he said, room for negotiation and no need to get too worked up about the rhetoric.[44]

With the Geneva summit fixed for November 1985, the world's future seemed – optimistically – to be in the hands of two open, sincere and encouragingly emotional men. Gorbachev was most of those things. But according to those who knew him, Reagan, in spite of all appearances, was in private inscrutable, closed, frustratingly impenetrable. If Gorbachev thought he was truly going to get to 'know' Reagan, he was in for a shock. Edmund Morris, a Pulitzer

Prize-winning biographer, studied the man in the White House for several years. 'He was,' Morris concluded, 'one of the strangest men who's ever lived. Nobody around him understood him. Every person I interviewed, almost without exception, eventually would say, "You know, I could never really figure him out"'.[45] Reagan had 'a near-total lack of interest in people as individuals'; he was a man with no real close friends, keeping everyone except Nancy at a distance, even his own children.[46] In contrast to the charismatic public figure, the private Reagan was an empty vessel. He was an actor who came alive only when performing. As he once joked, motioning to the Oval Office, 'I've got the biggest theatre in the world right here.'[47] The biggest performance of his career would come in Geneva.

Like a true professional, Reagan arrived early, giving himself two days to adjust to the time difference and plan his stagecraft. He was twenty years older than Gorbachev and had recently undergone surgery, but he was determined to project a vigour commensurate with that of his nation. He pledged to 'get [Gorbachev] in a room alone and set him straight', to explain that America was not controlled by arms manufacturers, that it had a genuine desire to reduce the arms race, and that the American and Soviet people were not so different after all.[48]

His first piece of theatre was played to perfection. The opening morning of the talks on the shores of Lake Geneva was bitterly cold. Reagan found himself waiting in the entrance hall with his coat on. Seeing Gorbachev arrive in his limousine wrapped in an overcoat, a scarf and a hat, Reagan threw off his own coat and bounded down the steps wearing only his suit to greet the younger man.[49] At the initial get-to-know-you meeting, he deployed his actorly charm, riffing on their similar backgrounds – two boys who began their lives in small farming communities were now 'here with the fate of the world in their hands', the only men 'who could start World War III, but also the only two countries that can bring peace to the world'.[50] They spoke of building trust and improving communication, but their exchanges descended into finger-pointing. At the break, Reagan felt he'd come face to face with a 'diehard Bolshevik', while an exasperated Gorbachev told his colleagues he'd 'met a caveman, a real dinosaur!'[51] With hindsight, Gorbachev reflected that it had been inevitable: 'Number 1 communist and number 1 imperialist trying to out-argue each other,' he said, was a natural, perhaps even a necessary opening to such a high-stakes meeting.[52]

The personal relationship between Reagan and Gorbachev took time to thaw,
but their mutual empathy would help end the Cold War confrontation.

Hoping to defuse the tension, Reagan suggested they go for a
walk. They chatted about Reagan's film career then settled down by
the fire in the pool house, while the custodians of the nuclear foot-
balls stood guard outside. The main bone of contention emerged.
SDI, the unsettling missile defence shield that Moscow feared so
much, was the top of Gorbachev's agenda. If the US truly wanted
peace, he implored Reagan 'with some emotion', it should dispense with Star Wars. The official transcript of the exchange hints
at Gorbachev's appeal to personal empathy. 'To a certain extent he
[Gorbachev] could understand the President on a human level; he
could understand that the idea of strategic defense had captivated
the President's imagination. However, as a political leader he could
not possibly agree with the President with regard to this concept.'[53]

Gorbachev tried to explain how SDI would upset the delicate nuclear balance, but Reagan was unmoved. The US needed 'a shield as well as a spear', he said. Only in retrospect did the human factor begin to kick in. Gorbachev mused that they had had a 'genuinely human conversation' and Reagan's private rhetoric softened. He told his staff, almost regretfully, 'I can't just keep poking him in the eye ... You could almost just get to like the guy. I keep telling myself I mustn't do it ...'[54] He wanted 'no talk of winners and losers' in the Cold War any more, and under no circumstances should Gorbachev be forced to 'eat crow' by being made to look weak in negotiations.[55] Little was formally agreed at Geneva, but the ice was broken. The use of simultaneous interpretation through earphones had been a success, the first time it had been employed at a major summit. It synched words with tone and body language, a crucial precondition for a dialogue of empathy. They were, Reagan said, 'like a couple of fellows who had run into each other at the club and discovered they had a lot in common'. Both were optimists and both felt they had found a basis for understanding, just like Reagan's fictional Ivan and Jim.[56]

When they met again a year later, in Reykjavik in October 1986, they were pals, calling each other by their first names and – astoundingly – giving serious thought to the dismantling of all nuclear weapons within ten years.[57] The deal might have been struck, had Reagan not insisted on the right to continue the development of SDI. Gorbachev tried to look on the bright side. 'In spite of all its drama, Reykjavik is not a failure,' he told the final press conference. 'It is a breakthrough, which allowed us for the first time to look over the horizon.'[58]

The world might have wanted Reagan to set his weapons aside, but Margaret Thatcher, for one, was relieved. For all that she admired Gorbachev – probably more than she admired Reagan – she remained a firm proponent of nuclear deterrence.*

---

*For all the talk of Reagan and Thatcher's great friendship, they often did not see eye to eye. When she heard of the US invasion of Grenada in 1983, she was furious, calling the Americans 'worse than the Soviets! ... That man! After all I have done for him, he didn't even consult me.' R. Aldous, *Reagan and Thatcher: The Difficult Relationship*, London: Hutchinson, 2012, p. 156.

Thatcher regularly hectored the president over the phone, pushing him to see the world her way. At such times Reagan would hold the phone away from his ear so others could hear and whisper, 'Gee, isn't she wonderful?' to his staff. Jon

Progress, though, was being made. 'Reykjavik's resonance has been great,' Gorbachev told the politburo. 'It helped us in the critical process of realizing where we stand. Everyone saw that agreement is possible.'[59] And a cash-strapped Moscow needed agreement more than anyone. 'In order to get the country out on solid ground,' Gorbachev's chief foreign policy adviser, Anatoly Chernyaev, wrote in his diary, 'we have to relieve it of the burden of the arms race, which is a drain on more than just the economy ... My impression is that he [Gorbachev] has really decided to end the arms race no matter what.'[60]

The Reagan–Gorbachev relationship had shifted the dynamic of East–West relations further and faster in two years than their predecessors had in twenty. 'In Geneva, in Reykjavik, we were getting more and more open to each other,' wrote the Soviet deputy foreign minister, Alexander Bessmertnykh. 'One of the major elements of the Cold War was that we were changing ourselves. We were the products of the Cold War, all of us. But we became softened by the new realities.'[61]

When Reagan and Gorbachev signed the INF Treaty in Washington DC in December 1987, it was the first time the two sides had pledged to reduce, rather than merely limit, their nuclear arsenals. Gorbachev told an audience of assembled American luminaries that 'something very profound' had happened. He had earlier informed the Soviet people that 'we can't go on living like this' – things had to change in the domestic Soviet economy and almost certainly in politics, too. And now, in Washington, he was repeating the same message to the whole world. Now both sides had 'an awareness that we cannot go on as we are; we cannot leave as it is the state of relations between our peoples'.[62] There had been a tectonic shift and it had been effected through the personal trust that had been built between leaders. 'In Washington, perhaps for the first time, we understood so clearly how important the human factor is in international politics,' Gorbachev told the politburo. 'Before, we were content with the banal formula ... of "personal contacts", but meaning only encounters between the "representatives of two irreconcilable systems".' Now it had been

Meacham, 'Ronnie's Friend Maggie', *Time*, 22 April 2013. content.time.com/time/magazine/article/0,9171,2140783,00.html.

proved that statesmen 'can be guided by purely normal human feelings and aspirations'.*

When Reagan arrived in Moscow in May 1988 for their penultimate summit, Gorbachev's greeting had genuine warmth. 'It is better to see once, than to hear a hundred times,' he told his guest. When Reagan was asked if he still considered the Soviet Union to be an evil empire he replied, 'No, I was talking about another time, another era.' Looking back on it, Reagan felt there was 'a chemistry between Gorbachev and me that produced something very close to a friendship'. For a man who seemed to have no friends, the claim was significant.[63]

The Moscow summit saw the apogee of that Reagan-Gorbachev chemistry. Reagan charmed the Russians with a repertoire of Soviet jokes, delivered with an actor's timing and a cheeky grin. He parroted an old Russian proverb to characterise relations between the two sides: *Doveryai no proveryai!* – Trust, but check! – mangling the pronunciation, but comprehensible enough to delight the Russians. Watchful, cautious faith in the goodwill of human beings, from the lowliest to the most powerful, was a solid cornerstone for East–West rapprochement.

I was present at the Moscow State University on 31 May when Reagan, standing in front of a massive bust of Lenin, gave the keynote address of his visit to students in the university's great hall. Cynical journalist though I was, I felt myself swept along by the power of his rhetoric. Reagan used his charisma and human warmth to reach over the heads of the politicians to appeal directly to the young Russians before him, a new generation for whom his eulogy to freedom and his denunciation of political oppression had a personal, visceral appeal. 'Progress is not foreordained,' he boomed. 'The key is freedom – freedom of thought, freedom of information, freedom of communication.' He threw in every cultural reference from Tolstoy to Pasternak, from Yevgeny Yevtushenko to *Butch Cassidy and the Sundance Kid*. It wasn't always clear what it all meant – I think it was a variation of 'the only thing we have to fear is fear itself' – but the audience loved every minute.

---

*Many high officials struck up warm relations, too, in a way that was largely unthinkable in the recent past. The only people who did not get along were Raisa and Nancy. D. Reynolds, *Summits: Six Meetings that Shaped the Twentieth Century*, London, Allen Lane, 2007, p. 193.

There are some, I know, in your society who fear that change will bring only disruption and discontinuity, who fear to embrace the hope of the future – sometimes it takes faith. It's like that scene in the cowboy movie *Butch Cassidy and the Sundance Kid*, which some here in Moscow recently had a chance to see. The posse is closing in on the two outlaws, Butch and Sundance, who find themselves trapped on the edge of a cliff, with a sheer drop of hundreds of feet to the raging rapids below. Butch turns to Sundance and says their only hope is to jump into the river below, but Sundance refuses. He says he'd rather fight it out with the posse, even though they're hopelessly outnumbered. Butch says that's suicide and urges him to jump, but Sundance still refuses and finally admits, 'I can't swim.' Butch breaks up laughing and says, 'You crazy fool, the fall will probably kill you.' And, by the way, both Butch and Sundance made it, in case you didn't see the movie. I think what I've just been talking about is perestroika and what its goals are.[64]

Reagan never made it explicit, but his audience knew he was talking about himself and his friend Mikhail. Like Butch and Sundance, they too had made a courageous leap of faith, taking the risk of trusting each other's goodwill as they began to lay down their arms. They, too, seemed to have survived the jump into the unknown. Reagan would return to Washington with his stock high and his future bright. He would leave office in 1989 with the highest approval rating of any modern president. But Gorbachev's future – the future of his reforms and of the entire socialist bloc – were approaching their moment of greatest danger.

34

THE WALL TORN DOWN

In November 1989, Werner Krätschell, a Protestant minister in East Berlin, heard a rumour on the grapevine.

> I waste no time and drive quickly to reach our home. I find Konstanze, my twenty-year-old daughter and her friend Astrid, who is twenty-one. Rapidly we jump into the car and drive at great speed to the nearest border crossing: Bornholmer Strasse. Dream and reality become confused. The guards let us through: the girls cry. They cling together tightly on the back seat, as if they're expecting an air raid ... Astrid, suddenly, tells me to stop the car at the next intersection. She wants only to put her foot down on the street just once. Touching the ground. Armstrong after the moon landing. She has never been in the West before.[1]

Erich Honecker had promised that the Berlin Wall would 'be standing in fifty or a hundred years',[2] but suddenly it was gone, reuniting not just a city and a people, but changing the psychology of a generation. The new reality that so few had expected to experience would seize the imagination of the globe. If the Berlin Wall could go, so could all the other divisions that had riven the world.

When Ronald Reagan had stood at the Brandenburg Gate two years earlier, he had called on Mikhail Gorbachev to 'Tear down this wall!' But it took an unforeseeable concatenation of events to make it happen. Reagan's crusading rhetoric helped, as did Washington's unblinking commitment to a spiralling defence budget that would spend the USSR into the ground. But it would have been to no avail without the unique character of the man who was changing the face of Soviet communism. Mikhail Gorbachev had done his best to reinvigorate the moribund central command economy that for decades had hobbled the USSR with inefficient practices, chaotic management and worker apathy. He had departed from Marxist–Leninist orthodoxy by permitting a modicum of private enterprise – small 'cooperatives' that would run taxis, bakeries, hairdressers and similar businesses for personal profit – but nothing had worked. The Soviet Union continued to stagnate.

In December 1988, Gorbachev had become the first Soviet leader in twenty-eight years to appear before the General Assembly of the United Nations, giving an address that appeared to roll back Winston Churchill's 'Iron Curtain' speech. 'Our people want to live in peace with the Americans,' he told reporters in New York. 'I think we are now at the threshold, present at the birth of a new phase in our relationship.'[3]

The call for reconciliation was motivated by personal conviction and economic necessity. Gorbachev knew change was inevitable, even desirable. It was never his intention to set off the chain of tumbling dominoes his predecessors had struggled so long and so hard to avoid. But that is what his reforms would do. And the last domino in the chain would be the Soviet Union itself.

When he was appointed general secretary in March 1985, Gorbachev faced a challenge of unprecedented magnitude. He had been a member of the politburo for nearly five years, so he understood that the relentless propaganda of the Brezhnev years, with its claims of economic success and global influence, was a fiction. The era of stagnation had papered over the cracks with false illusions, and its leader was its poster boy.

Leonid Brezhnev, with his gaudy uniforms, banks of medals and glitzy Kremlin backdrops, was the incarnation of show without substance. His official biography eulogised him as a great leader, a brilliant economist and a war hero, but he was none of those. Brezhnev's empire had survived only because its gaping flaws were concealed behind the apparatus of centralised control, the repression and exploitation of its people, and mercifully high oil prices that staved off its incipient collapse.

That Gorbachev should undertake to restructure and revive a USSR in such peril was strikingly brave or myopically foolhardy. 'Marxism–Leninism had died a silent and unnoticed death at some point in the Brezhnev years,' wrote the political scientist Dmitry Furman. 'For someone in power to acknowledge this, let alone try

Like the society he led, Brezhnev the man was image over substance,
as the gently mocking poetry his appearance inspired suggests:
'His eyebrows are dark and dense,
His medal collection immense,
And his speeches long and without sense.'

to turn it around was nearly unimaginable ... [Gorbachev's project] was one of the least likely occurrences in history, akin to winning the lottery – it can happen, but the chances are so small as to make counting on it stupid.'[4]

It was Gorbachev's deep-seated belief in communism and in himself that convinced him change was possible. For his reforms to work, he would need to expose the fissures in the system to the whole world; he would need to explain that the propaganda had been lies, that things were far from well, that much needed fixing.

The irony was that many in Soviet society – ordinary citizens and top politicians alike – already knew that to be the case. The contrast between the claims the Kremlin made and the reality of daily life was so stark as to be absurd. Pointing it out, however, was fraught with danger. Those in the Brezhnev years who took the risk of criticising – who highlighted the lies the state was telling – were labelled insane. Andrei Snezhnevsky, the man who ruled Soviet psychiatry from the late Stalin years until his death in 1987, invented a new diagnosis of 'sluggish schizophrenia' to pathologise those who dared to think differently. Dissidents – the *inakomysliashchie* – were deemed to be mad because they opposed the perfect workers' state. Whole wards in psychiatric hospitals were turned into prisons, where offenders were dosed with sedatives and psychotropic medication.

When the distinguished mathematician Leonid Plyushch was forcibly hospitalised in 1973, his dissident colleagues in the Initiative Group for the Defence of Human Rights in the USSR wrote an open letter, commenting bitterly on the psychological distortions of Soviet reality: 'In our state only a crazy person dares stand against its shortcomings, only a madman speaks openly about the violation of his rights, only a schizophrenic acts against his own well-being but in accordance with his conscience and thought.'[5] Soviet reality, wrote Vladimir Bukovsky, was 'nothing more than an imaginary, schizophrenic world populated by made-up Soviet people building a mythical communism'.[6] If Gorbachev had expressed his reformist views ten years earlier, he might have found himself occupying a cell in Moscow's Serbsky Institute for Forensic Psychiatry.

Even in the post-Brezhnev 1980s, he knew he would have to 'restructure not just the way people work, but the psychological makeup of people. Without a perestroika of minds, there will be no restructuring of practical behaviour.'[7] He would find little support among the old dissidents. They shared his views on the need for change, but abhorred his plan to revivify the Soviet system. Why should they wish to save a state that had done so much to oppress them?

Neutral observers were more charitable. Coming after the feeble gerontocrats who had run the USSR for so long, Gorbachev brought a renewed energy and a respectable presence on the international stage. 'My whole outlook on the world changed,' wrote Dmitry Furman. 'Only under Gorbachev did I begin to feel the hitherto unknown sensation of pride in one's country and its leader. I remember how we spoke at home, watching the TV: "Oh my Lord, what is going on?! Our President is meeting the Americans, and it's obvious that ours is smarter and better."'[8]

Gorbachev's call to arms, summarised in the much-repeated phrase, 'We cannot go on living like this!', was a message that the majority of Soviet citizens welcomed. What they were not equipped to do was to take the next step and do something about it. The Russian people had lived for centuries under a centralised, autocratic system – in recent times the Bolsheviks, but also the tsars before them – that forbade independent thought and crushed initiative from below.

Individuals had been told for so long that they must not reason for themselves, and that the state would tell them how to live and how to think. As a result, an enduring learned helplessness had descended upon them. Untrained in taking decisions, few were ready to take a hand in deciding their future. Conditions were too hard, they complained; it was too little too late. Instead of seizing the chance for change, they railed against Gorbachev for opening the Pandora's box of choice. Gorbachev would lament the lack of patience the Soviet people showed for his reforms: 'Our Russian mentality required that the new life be served up on a silver platter immediately, then and there, without reforming society.'[9]

Unfortunately for Gorbachev, his reforms would necessitate a period of dismantling before society could be rebuilt; and dismantling meant temporary – but real – additional suffering. People complained that perestroika was depriving them of the only good things Soviet rule had brought: the pride they felt at living in one of just two superpowers in the world; the sense of self-righteousness that went with being the champion of the underdog in the fight against capitalist imperialism; the right to do little to no work and still be housed and fed. When Gorbachev tried to crack down on drunkenness, he was seen as stealing even the alcohol that allowed them to sustain their delusions.

Few in the USSR genuinely believed in the myth of 'the perfect workers' state'. But most of them shared the conviction that the Soviet Union was robust, imbued with a permanence that would allow it to survive the vicissitudes of time. The party itself was wasteful and disorganised, but it was the only unquestioned source of authority, not just in the Soviet Union, but across the Eastern Bloc. When Gorbachev opted to hold up the shortcomings of the party and the state to the eyes of the world, he somehow made them real. The old regime's denial of the nation's problems had allowed people to delude themselves, while simultaneously knowing they were deluding themselves. Gorbachev's frankness removed the possibility of delusion; it destroyed the sense of invulnerability that had attached to the party. The monolith was fractured at its base, the way opened for its collapse.

The first dominoes wobbled in the satellite states. In Poland, Solidarity undermined the communists' authority from within. 'This fight with the Communist monster was really impossible,' Lech

Wałęsa had concluded. 'We could only fight against it by using its own weapons because it pretended to be the people's system. The only effective way was for us to organise around bread-and-butter issues and use these concerns to gain our freedom. We set about using truth to conquer untruth.'[10]

The Baltic republics – not foreign countries, but constituents of the Soviet Union itself – were the next to be nudged. 'Nobody had any kind of seriousness concerning Soviet ideology anymore,' recalled Marju Lauristin, one of the leaders of the Estonian independence movement. 'It was a time of an almost absolute cynical attitude.'[11] When Gorbachev recognised the level of discontent and offered the possibility of change, it was a de Tocqueville moment. 'He expected people to come to him and discuss how to make Communism better, but people were not interested in that,' Lauristin said. 'Gorbachev opened these doors because, like all Communists of this era, he didn't have a clue what people were really thinking about the Soviet system. When he called people to glasnost, he didn't expect what these words and thoughts might be, what people really wanted to express.'[12]

What people wanted to express was not what Gorbachev wanted to hear. They didn't want to revitalise communism; they wanted to destroy it. And the man at the top had foolishly granted them the freedom to say so. 'The main achievement of Gorbachev's policies was that in the space of a year or two he made the fear disappear,' recalled Andrei Pavlov, then a student at Moscow University. 'As if by magic, people lost their fear of speaking and acting freely.'[13]

As foreign journalists in the USSR, we scrambled for pithy phrases to sum up what Gorbachev had done. 'He's let the genie of free expression out of the bottle,' some of us wrote, 'and he can't put it back in again.' He wanted to be 'a little bit pregnant,' opined others, 'but discovered it was all or nothing.' Gorbachev had 'tried to ride the tiger' of public opinion and now was being dragged along helplessly behind it. His glasnost policies had encouraged a free discussion of the problems facing Soviet society and the resulting outpouring of unhappiness had become a tsunami. Expectations had been raised that mere tinkering with the system could never satisfy.

In many ways, openness worked against Gorbachev. In order to circumvent the hardliners in the Kremlin and appeal directly to the Soviet people, he needed to allow them access to information, including more truth about life in the West. When Margaret

Thatcher visited the USSR in 1987, she was allowed to appear live on Soviet television. Three of the Soviet Union's top journalists were instructed to give her a hard time, beginning with a demand to know why Britain insisted on maintaining nuclear weapons. 'Well, you have more nuclear weapons in the Soviet Union than any other country in the world,' replied an unflustered Thatcher.

> You have more intercontinental ballistic missiles and warheads than the West. You have more than anyone else and you say there is a risk of a nuclear accident … All weapons of war are dangerous. Would it not be marvellous if we did not have to have them? But we can only get to that stage when we have more trust and confidence in one another. That means much more open societies.[14]

Unused to challenging debate, the journalists were trounced. Soviet viewers complained about their 'aggressive' and 'impolite' conduct. One of them, Vladimir Simonov of the Novosti press agency, admitted that he and his colleagues had been 'as ineffective as village chess players taking on Garry Kasparov'.[15]

Free elections to a new Congress of People's Deputies in 1989 were a genuine step towards democratisation. Gorbachev was convinced they would be welcomed by the Soviet people; that they would accustom the nation to unfettered political debate and win plaudits for his reform programme. Viewing figures for the televised live sessions of the congress were astonishingly high. The deputies were outspoken in their condemnation of the old way of doing things; they wanted change. But many were equally dismissive of Gorbachev's 'tinkering'. Calls for wholesale upheaval grew embarrassingly loud. Congress members including Andrei Sakharov, Gavriil Popov and Boris Yeltsin formed the so-called Inter-regional Group of Deputies, the first genuine opposition in Soviet history, calling for faster and more far-reaching reforms than Gorbachev could ever envisage. His ideas 'did not go beyond the existing order', wrote Anatoly Chernyaev, Gorbachev's aide and long-time friend. 'Hence the term "renovation" [обновление], which he clung to for a long time. It took years of torturous struggle for him to realise that it was impossible to renovate our society. It was doomed and had to be completely changed.'[16]

With the political momentum at home threatening to rip the reform process from his grasp, Gorbachev found reassurance in the praise he received from the West. He had made substantial unilateral cuts in the USSR's armed forces and his proposal for a 'common European home', in which neither the Warsaw Pact nor NATO would hold sway, was being listened to sympathetically. There was an eagerness about Gorbachev's desire to impress the West that echoed centuries of Russian striving to be accepted by the international community. 'For all Soviet people, including the higher echelons of the party, the West has always been an object of longing,' Dmitry Furman wrote. 'Trips to the West were a most important status symbol. There is nothing you can do about this; it is in the blood, in the culture.'[17] Gorbachev enjoyed his foreign trips considerably more than his appearances at home. He was mobbed by cheering crowds, greeted like a pop star in New York and London, Paris, Vienna and Bonn. But an under-current of national self-loathing – a sense that going cap-in-hand to a foreign power is undignified and humiliating – bred accusations that Gorbachev was sacrificing Soviet pride to his own search for fame. There was criticism of his wife, Raisa, who was (wrongly) alleged to be splashing government cash on a personal gold Amex card while millions of Russians were going hungry.

In January 1989, George H. W. Bush replaced Ronald Reagan in the White House. Lacking the conviction and self-belief of his predecessor, Bush opted to play safe, announcing that he would 'pause' the rapprochement between the superpowers. The US ambassador in Moscow, Jack Matlock, declared that America's priority 'should not be how can we help perestroika or Gorbachev, but how can we promote the interests of the United States'.[18] Gorbachev felt betrayed. He had given much ground in the horse-trading, in the belief that it would be reciprocated; now he was puzzled, angry and increasingly isolated.

Some in the Bush team suspected that Gorbachev's proposals for balanced arms reductions were a ploy to keep the Soviet Union competitive in the Cold War. They watched the flame of revolt spreading through eastern Europe and reasoned that the Soviet empire was weakening of its own accord. When Solidarity made gains in Poland's parliamentary elections in June 1989, Bush scheduled a visit to Warsaw. 'Democracy has captured the spirit of our times,' he declared in a speech to the Polish National Assembly in July. 'It is the destiny of man.'[19] Gorbachev bowed to what he himself had made inevitable. He acknowledged that Moscow could no longer halt the changes in eastern Europe – the USSR, he said, had hitherto been seen as a 'conservative power that hindered reforms that were ripe for implementation' – and would not use force to keep the Warsaw Pact countries in line.

Remarkably, though, Gorbachev persisted in the belief that when the people of eastern Europe were given a free choice, they would choose his brand of communism. Anatoly Chernyaev remembered his boss's misplaced optimism. 'He was convinced that when these countries got their freedom, they would choose socialism with a human face. He believed they would not turn away from Moscow nor run off to the West. He thought they would be grateful to Moscow and keep up ties of friendship to the Soviet Union.'* Gorbachev's naive faith in 'the people' reflected the blinkered self-delusion of a generation of Soviet apparatchiks. It explained why he, a committed communist, felt he could unleash a programme of profound liberal reform and not understand that it would lead to the collapse of the system.

On a visit to Berlin in October 1989 for the fortieth anniversary of the founding of the GDR, Gorbachev warned Erich Honecker that he must begin to liberalise the country or risk being overthrown. The political situation in Poland, Hungary and Czechoslovakia was turning dramatically against the communist old guard. Honecker dismissed his concerns, claiming that the necessary reforms had already been carried out.[20] When Gorbachev went walkabout, East Germans chanted, 'Gorby! Gorby! Help us!' It was reminiscent of 1956, when Khrushchev's Thaw convinced Poles and Hungarians that they could rise up against Moscow's tutelage without fear of reprisals. That had turned out to be a terrible mistake; but things were different now. The regime was losing its grip and both sides knew it.

'When you're twenty-two and you go on a demonstration with friends, wearing big boots and short hair, you feel invincible,' remembered Marion Loeffler, one of the young protestors. 'And there's so many people with you … it's such an exhilaration, and you feel you are in a tradition of revolutionaries.'[21] According to Günter Schabowski, the then first secretary of the SED in East Berlin, the leadership were 'rendered speechless because we were helpless; because this country and this leadership had never before experienced a conflict which was

---

* Honecker subsequently limited the availability of Soviet press in the GDR to stem the flow of Gorbachev's dangerous 'new thinking'.

so openly expressed'.[22] In a chaotic press conference on 9 November 1989, Schabowski mistakenly announced that the border between East and West Berlin was open. While the move had been discussed by the politburo, nothing was planned to happen until the following day. Border guards, with no instructions from the centre, were torn between letting people through or opening fire, eventually deciding to raise the barriers. The division of Berlin ended in a moment of human bumbling.

When Gorbachev was told what had happened, he replied that they had done the right thing, 'because, how could you shoot at Germans who walk across the border to meet Germans on the other side?'[23] Later the same day, Anatoly Chernyaev wrote in his diary that 'an entire era in the history of the "socialist system" has come to an end'.

> This is no longer a matter of socialism, but of a change in the world balance of powers, the end of Yalta, the end of Stalin's legacy and the defeat of Nazi Germany in the Great War. This is what Gorbachev has done! He is truly a great man because he sensed the footsteps of history and helped it to follow its natural course.[24]

Gorbachev himself was less sanguine. He had not expected – and could hardly approve of – the epochal collapse that his supposedly limited reforms had led to. 'I am doomed to go forward and only forward,' he told Chernyaev. 'For me, the path backwards is closed. If I retreat, I will perish.'[25]

In December 1989, Bush and Gorbachev met in Malta at the height of its winter storm season. Watching from the shore, we winced as they were ferried through raging seas on fragile naval barques between each other's warships off Marsaxlokk Bay. At a joint press conference, Bush announced that they had laid the foundation for 'a lasting peace to transform the East–West relationship to one of enduring co-operation', and Gorbachev concurred. 'The world is leaving one epoch and entering another,' he declared. 'The threat of force, mistrust, psychological and ideological struggle should all be things of the past.'*

---

*Gorbachev's Nobel Peace Prize earned him countless disparaging letters from

But Malta was a false dawn. Even as Gorbachev's standing rose in the West, his domestic popularity plummeted. He had relinquished Soviet control of central and eastern Europe with little in return. There had been no agreement from the West to integrate the USSR into the world community and no financial package to save the Soviet economy.[26] A popular joke likened the impact of his policies on the Russian people to lengthening a dog's chain by six feet while moving its bowl twelve feet away, then allowing it to bark as loud as it liked at whoever it wanted. Gorbachev's reforms were going too slowly for some, too fast for others. His tightrope act, trying to placate both camps, made him unpopular with everyone. He would later complain that 'there are no happy reformers'. The endless crises took their toll.[27] 'He had gone grey and his face was grey, too,' Raisa lamented. 'He seemed to have suffered a nervous shock – to have gone through a mental crisis.'[28]

Jack Matlock cabled the US State Department that the crises enveloping Gorbachev were 'of his making, if not of his design'.

> Five years of perestroika have undermined the key institution of political power in the Soviet Union, the Communist Party, without replacing it with a coherent system of legitimate power around new state institutions ... The powerful social forces his reforms have unleashed [are] a threat to him and to communism in the Soviet Union as a whole.[29]

George Bush exhibited a woeful lack of understanding for the man he had cosseted at Malta. He lacked Reagan's empathy, refusing to act on notions of friendship or emotional intuition. When his secretary of state, James Baker, suggested the US might provide guarantees that NATO would not encroach on the former Soviet sphere of influence, Bush jibbed. 'The Soviets are not in a position to dictate ... To hell with that! We prevailed. They didn't.'[30]

It was the first of many occasions on which Bush and other western leaders would trample on Soviet sensitivities. Yet again, their inability – or unwillingness – to fathom the complex psychology of the Russian mind would have far-reaching consequences.

Soviet citizens, who associated such awards with selling out to the West, thanks to the state's past hounding of Pasternak, Sakharov, Solzhenitsyn and Brodsky.

35

THE EVIL EMPIRE IS NO MORE

Gorbachev had gambled on his relationship with the West. He had banked on securing concessions for the Soviet Union in exchange for allowing the peaceful collapse of socialism in eastern Europe. But he had misread the psychology of the Cold War. The brief inter- lude of warm personal relations with Ronald Reagan and Margaret Thatcher persuaded him that the West might offer the USSR a way out of its dire economic and social predicament. But four decades of entrenched hostility could not be wiped away. With the communist monster at their mercy, the western powers were hardly going to take their foot off its throat.

Gorbachev was surprised and affronted when the Americans rejected his request for big loans to help perestroika succeed. He com- plained that Bush had left him and the Soviet Union 'to stew'. But Gorbachev's indignation, Anatoly Chernyaev wrote, was 'the wail of a desperate man whose control over his country was visibly slipping away – of one who no longer understood what he was trying to achieve'.[1]

The Soviet prime minister, Nikolai Ryzhkov, told the Central Committee that they should be worried not about the future of Germany, but about the Soviet Union itself. 'What we should fear is not the Baltics, but Russia and Ukraine. I smell an overall collapse. And then there will be another government, another leadership of the country, already a different country.'[2]

It is clear that Gorbachev had failed to anticipate the conse- quences his reform process would unleash. In retrospect, it is easy to conclude that that he misunderstood the mood of the country and the psychology of the Russian people. But at the time, things were less clear-cut, the future much harder to discern through the fog of claim and counterclaim. The dramatic events of 1991 would cause the fog to lift.

From the beginning of 1991, old-style communists in the party structures began to ramp up their attacks on Gorbachev's reforms, denouncing them as a betrayal of the revolution. His weakening of centralised Soviet control had encouraged independence movements in the republics, which became the target of threats – sometimes escalating into armed attacks – from the hardliners. Perestroika was tottering. Violence loomed. For months, Gorbachev tried to placate everyone, swinging uncomfortably between the two sides, with the result that he pleased no one. His thinking was muddled; he had no clear strategy to secure the union's future, other than trying to stay afloat from one crisis to the next. At the same time, Boris Yeltsin was consolidating his reputation for decisiveness; he was brash and radical, promising clear solutions – an end to the old ways of communism and a fresh start as a democratic state.

By early summer, the threat of unrest had moved from the outlying republics to Moscow itself. There were warnings, including from the Americans, of plots to overthrow Gorbachev. On the morning of Monday 19 August, I awoke to find state radio playing martial music, and *Swan Lake* on the television instead of the news, a turn of events usually reserved for the death of a high-ranking official.* In between the music, the newsreader was repeating an official communique.

In view of Mikhail Sergeyevich Gorbachev's inability, for health reasons, to perform the duties of the U.S.S.R. President and of the transfer of the U.S.S.R. President's powers, in keeping with Paragraph 7, Article 127 of the U.S.S.R. Constitution, to U.S.S.R. Vice President Gennadi Ivanovich Yanayev, with the aim of overcoming the profound and comprehensive crisis, political, ethnic and civil strife, chaos and anarchy that threaten the lives and security of the Soviet Union's citizens and the sovereignty, territory integrity, freedom and independence of our fatherland, we resolve to adopt the most decisive measures to prevent society from sliding into national catastrophe and insure law and order ... to form a State Committee for the State of Emergency in the U.S.S.R. in order to run the country and effectively exercise the state-of-emergency regime.

---

*Such was the impact of the broadcast that morning that a whole generation of Russians have since been unable to hear the delicate music of *Swan Lake* without thinking that something dramatic, potentially terrible, must be happening.

If there was any doubt that this was a coup, it was quickly dispelled. As I sped into town, I was met by columns of tanks descending the broad avenues towards the Kremlin. They had been sent by the hardline communists of the State Emergency Committee who had put Gorbachev under arrest and now claimed to be running the country. When I spoke to the tank crews, they told me they had live ammunition in their guns and were ready to use it if they were ordered to do so. But in the days that followed, ordinary Russians stood in the way of the tanks; some of them were shot or crushed to death for their determination to defend democracy. I was there when Boris Yeltsin, liberalism's last champion now that Gorbachev was in captivity, climbed on the back of a tank to dramatise his defiance of the coup. For two days and nights, we waited with Yeltsin in the Russian White House for the attack to begin.

The dramatic events of those August days resolved the confrontation between the forces of reform and hardline autocracy in the Soviet Union. In the face of vociferous public opposition, the hardliners lost their nerve, the coup collapsed and its leaders were arrested. Both the vacillating Gorbachev and the Communist Party he had championed for so long were hopelessly delegitimised. Boris Yeltsin was the hero of the moment, the coming man.

The downfall of the USSR played out around a clash of personalities. Gorbachev and Yeltsin had begun as allies in the cause of reform, but personal differences, competing ambition and perceived slights had turned them into acrimonious rivals. The personal antagonism between them would influence the course of history.

Mikhail Gorbachev's perestroika-driven policy of devolving powers to the presidents of the individual Soviet republics had had the unintended consequence of boosting the profile of his now sworn enemy. Boris Yeltsin, the president of Russia, had become a rival to his nominal superior, the Soviet president, Mikhail Gorbachev. Yeltsin was genuinely popular, not least because he eschewed Gorbachev's tinkering and commitment to communism, calling instead for systemic change.

From August to December 1991 – the period between the failed coup and the collapse of the USSR – the two presidents led an uneasy coexistence. But Yeltsin had the whip hand and was determined to wrest total power. At the beginning of December, he called the leaders of Belarus and Ukraine to a meeting in a state hunting lodge in the Belovezhskaya Forest. His purpose was to destroy Gorbachev's power base, by dissolving the Soviet Union itself – and he did it behind Gorbachev's back.

The three leaders – Yeltsin, Shushkevich and Kravchuk – retired to the *banya*, the sauna, while their officials drew up a pseudo-legal fig-leaf of a declaration. 'We, the Republic of Belarus, the Russian Federation and Ukraine, as originators of the USSR on the basis of the Union Treaty of 1922, confirm that the USSR, as a subject of international law and a geopolitical reality, ceases its existence.'[3]

History often includes an element of farce. The declaration, written out in longhand, was finished in the early hours of the morning and pushed under the door of the typist's room. But when the cleaning lady found it the next morning, she put it in the bin. The three leaders were busy toasting each of the dozen protocols in the document with cognac. When a few reporters were brought in to witness the signing, no one had anything to write with. They had to borrow pens from a journalist. Yeltsin was so drunk that his security guard wouldn't let him talk to the reporters and warned the photographers to stay away.[4]

He was drunk again a day or two later when he called Gorbachev from his car. 'Nothing's going to come out of your Union now,' Yeltsin crowed. 'What you have done behind my back with the consent of the US President is a crying shame, a disgrace!' Gorbachev replied angrily.[5] 'Where is the place for me? … I'm not going to float like a piece of shit in an ice hole … You are going to scupper all the reforms … Everything depends on the two of us to a great degree.' 'We'll think about you,' said Yeltsin. 'We'll find some job you can do.' But he was lying. He had no intention of letting Gorbachev stay on at all.

At midday on 23 December, without notice, Yeltsin arrived at the Kremlin to dictate the terms of the handover of power. The meeting went on for nine hours. Drink was brought in – cognac for Gorbachev; vodka for Yeltsin. The Soviet Union was expiring on a sea of alcohol. They agreed that Gorbachev would abdicate two days later, on 25 December, with his resignation speech broadcast to the nation. Yeltsin made a series of promises: Gorbachev and his staff could continue using their Kremlin offices for a further four days, after which Yeltsin would move in; Gorbachev could keep his presidential dacha for another week; the Soviet red flag would stay in place above the

Kremlin until 31 December. Yeltsin was free with his promises – but he had no intention of keeping them.[6]

At six o'clock, an already tipsy Gorbachev took a scheduled call from John Major and kept him talking for over half an hour. He was in denial, hoping against hope that he could remain in power. Then he went to find his long-time adviser, Alexander Yakovlev, and more drink was consumed. Eventually, Gorbachev could take it no longer. He went to lie down in an adjacent office. When Yakovlev found him later, Gorbachev had been crying. 'You see, Sasha,' he said. 'That's it.' Yakovlev himself had a lump in his throat.[7]

Yeltsin, meanwhile, gloated with his aides. 'It's over,' he told them. 'That's the last time I will ever have to go and see *him*.' The following afternoon, Gorbachev got a phone call from his wife at the presidential dacha. Raisa was in hysterics: Yeltsin had sent his security guards to evict them; they were tossing the Gorbachevs' possessions out of the building. Gorbachev got the head of Yeltsin's security on the line. He cursed and swore at him and threatened to call the media. He got a few more hours' grace, but the point had been made. He said later that he came home to find 'heaps of clothes, books, dishes, folders, newspapers, letters, and God knows what lying all over the floor'.[8]

Before his resignation speech, Gorbachev had another lie-down in his resting room. When he emerged, Anatoly Chernyaev noted that he had again been crying. Gorbachev said he had decided to sign his resignation decree straight away, rather than doing it live on television. But his Soviet-made pen wouldn't work. The image sums up the strange mixture that was the Soviet Union: both mighty and powerful and rickety and incompetent. To the rescue came Tom Johnson, an official from CNN who was there to oversee the live broadcast. He handed Gorbachev his Mont Blanc pen, a birthday present from his wife. Just as had happened at Belovezhskaya Pushcha, a pen borrowed from a journalist was used to sign away the communist superpower.[9]

A downbeat Gorbachev gave his farewell address sitting at an empty desk with a red flag hanging limply behind him. 'When I found myself at the helm of this state,' he told a shocked television audience, 'it already was clear that something was wrong in this country.'

This country was suffocating in the shackles of the bureaucratic command system. Doomed to cater to ideology, and suffer and carry the onerous burden of the arms race, it found itself at the breaking point ... The process of renovating this country and bringing about drastic change in the international community has proven to be much more complicated than anyone could imagine.

Gorbachev was admitting defeat. He had failed to revitalise the Soviet system and the USSR was about to pass into history. His dreamed-of 'communism with a human face' – indeed, any form of communism – had become a thing of the past.

> However, let us give its due to what has been done so far. This society has acquired freedom. It has been freed politically and spiritually, and this is the most important achievement ... An end has been put to the Cold War and to the arms race, as well as to the mad militarization of the country, which has crippled our economy, public attitudes and morals. The threat of nuclear war has been removed ... We opened up ourselves to the rest of the world, abandoned the practices of interfering in others' internal affairs and using troops outside this country, and we were reciprocated with trust, solidarity, and respect.

Gorbachev was putting a brave face on a moment of bitter failure. His claim that his concessions to the West had been met with 'trust ... and respect' must have stuck in his throat.

> All this change has taken a lot of strain, and took place in the context of fierce struggle against the background of increasing resistance by the reactionary forces, as well as our ideological baggage and the psychology of dependency [i.e. the Russian tradition of dependence on the state; the lack of personal initiative]. Change ran up against our intolerance, a low level of political culture and fear of change. That is why we have wasted so much time. The old system fell apart even before the new system began to work.[10]

As Yeltsin watched the speech on television, he became increasingly irritated that Gorbachev took all the credit for the reforms in Russia and didn't mention him or wish him well. Despite his agreement with Gorbachev, he gave orders for the Red Flag to be taken down from the Kremlin immediately and the white, blue and red flag of Russia to be hoisted. Diplomats and the media were taken by surprise. All had understood that the Red Flag would be flying until 31 December. But Yeltsin ordered a workman to take it down, fold it up and put it away in a Kremlin basement.

The day ended with Gorbachev and his closest aides knocking off two bottles of cognac in an empty Kremlin. He complained bitterly about the leaders of the republics – men he had put in power by introducing free elections – who now, he said, were 'all in a state of euphoria, squabbling over their inheritance'.

Looking back, Gorbachev conceded that he should have been more decisive. He should have moved more quickly to reform the economy, ended totalitarianism faster and pushed more firmly for a union treaty binding the republics to the USSR. But ultimately, he thought, 'I helped the country to change.'[11]

There is a dose of imposed rationalisation in Gorbachev's assessment. He had set out to rescue and strengthen the USSR, but ended up by destroying it. In his post facto appraisal, he adopted the pretence that the actual outcome had been his intention all along. The psychiatrist Aron Belkin speculated that Gorbachev's self-image was as 'a winner, who always achieved his aims. And if that meant retrospectively altering those aims, then so be it.'[12] It explains why Gorbachev could list his achievements as ending the Cold War and introducing democracy to the former Soviet republics, while ignoring the fact that the Soviet empire collapsed on his watch.

Dmitry Furman was more generous, acknowledging that Gorbachev had operated 'in the name of principled moral values'. He had created the conditions whereby millions of people were able to gain independence and personal freedom from a hitherto authoritarian state. In that context, his 'final defeat was a victory'.*

The dissolution of the USSR after seven decades of communism was a moment of unprecedented opportunity for West and East to

---

* W. Taubman, *Gorbachev: His Life and Times*, London: Simon & Schuster, 2018, p. 2. In 1998, Gorbachev would claim that 'if I hadn't promoted the reforms, if I hadn't tried to let the people breathe freely, opened the door to glasnost and democracy, to stir the society to get it thinking and acting, I would probably still be in my Secretary General's armchair today. I could have stayed there a lot longer.' CNN, *Cold War, Episode 19: Freeze*, produced by Pat Mitchell and Jeremy Isaacs, 1998.

come together in an enduring partnership of cooperation and friendship. It was a time of remarkable deference and openness by Russia to the West. James Baker marvelled at what he called 'the uniform, intense desire to satisfy the United States'. The first call Boris Yeltsin made after signing the document abolishing the USSR was to George Bush. 'Dear George,' he said. 'Because of the friendship between us, I couldn't wait even ten minutes to call you.'[13] Russia and all the emerging new countries agreed to accept a list of democratic principles laid down by the Bush administration, including peaceful self-determination, respect for existing borders, respect for democracy and the rule of law, respect for human rights and respect for international law.

Fulfilment of those promises would prove to be patchy, to say the least; but in the dying days of the Soviet Union, American diplomats and Russia's political figures enjoyed genuinely close relations. Both Gorbachev and Yeltsin addressed the US ambassador as 'Comrade'. The KGB even pointed American officials to where they had placed their listening devices in the US embassy. As the Soviet Union collapsed, the Kremlin leadership measured their standing in the world by the quality of their relations with the West.

But Washington and London would also misjudge the psychology of the times. Soon after Mikhail Gorbachev made his final televised address on Christmas Day 1991, President George H. W. Bush spoke to the American nation. Bush's Christmas message had none of the sadness and trepidation that permeated Gorbachev's; instead, it had the elation of a baseball manager whose team has won the World Series.

> Good evening, and Merry Christmas to all Americans across our great country ... For over forty years, the United States led the West in the struggle against Communism and the threat it posed to our most precious values. This struggle shaped the lives of all Americans ... But the confrontation is now over. The nuclear threat is receding. Eastern Europe is free. The Soviet Union itself is no more. This is a victory for democracy and freedom. It is a victory for the moral force of our values. Every American can take pride in this victory![14]

It was a remarkable display of hubris and insensitivity. Bush celebrated 'winning the Cold War' as if the United States had single-handedly wiped out autocracy in Russia. Bush was saying that 'American values' had triumphed and Russia and the other post-Soviet states would henceforth adopt them. This blinkered confidence that its leaders could simply be instructed in the art of becoming good capitalists 'like us' would be a hallmark of how the West would treat Russia for the next ten years.

But the Russian psyche, forged through centuries of abuse by the country's rulers and enemies alike, is not 'like us'. Sensitivity and understanding can elicit rational, constructive responses; but in the years following 1991, the West trod on every one of Russia's exposed nerves. Western triumphalism had something of the vindictiveness of 1919 Versailles, and the long-term consequences proved catastrophic.

In 1991, after decades of misery under communism, the Russian people were willing to do almost anything to share in the freedoms and economic success of the West. There was a rush to slough off the remaining trappings of communism to make way for the new capitalist society: a new national anthem was commissioned, a new flag, and old names became new again – Leningrad became St Petersburg, Gorky Street in Moscow reverted to its old name of Tverskaya, Marx Prospekt became Okhotny Ryad, and so on across the country. I attended a bizarre event in Gorky Park, where Moscow's communist-era statues – all the Lenins and Brezhnevs, and the towering monument to 'Iron' Felix Dzerzhinsky, symbol of the KGB, that the crowds had toppled in Lubyanka Square – were dumped unceremoniously on a plot of scrubby grass. The Moscow mayor, Gavriil Popov, declared that this would be an 'open-air museum of social history'. 'One era of history has ended,' he told the crowds. 'Now we must build the new one.'[15] But the exorcism of communism from Russian society and Russian minds would not be easy. The Communist Party of the Soviet Union was far more than just a political party; over the course of seventy years it had virtually become the state. Gorbachev's spokesman, Vitaly Ignatenko, spoke of the 'void' it left in the running of the country and in the psyche of its citizens.

> This was a society whose resources had been allocated and whose needs had been supplied for decades by the Party. Every-thing was done by and through the Party. I even remember a poem by a young girl in the Communist youth newspaper. It said, 'Winter has gone; summer has come – thanks be to the

Party.' It sounds naive and funny today. But in those days we had
the Party to thank for everything. And all of a sudden to realise
that the Party is no longer there to tell you how to live your life,
how to build your future.[16]

To tackle the problems it faced – to remake the psychology of its
people at the same time as it remade its system of governance, Russia
needed the West's assistance. People were going hungry. There were
shortages of everything – meat, bread, rice. In retrospect, it would
have been in the West's interest to provide all the help Russia needed.
It was the only way to preserve the cordial relationship that was
emerging with Moscow. And Bush did organise a Berlin airlift-type
operation, with fifty-four transport planes bringing in 38 million
pounds of food and medicine. But it was not nearly enough. And
the Russian people were humiliated by having to accept food parcels
from the West, including from the Germans. One woman, a widow
of the Second World War, opened a parcel from the Red Cross and
found it contained marzipan and cigarettes. 'And we defeated Hitler,'
she said.[17] The large quantities of chicken legs sent by the USA
(quickly dubbed «ножки Буша» or 'Bush Legs') were widely believed
to contain bacteria that were dangerous to people's health.

Yeltsin had known for a long time that the Soviet model was
broken. He wanted to dismantle the communist command economy
and substitute it with neoliberal economics. The United States had
some Cold War experience in engineering the transformation of a
socialist to capitalist economy in Chile. Now Washington sent its
experts to Russia. They were known as the Chicago Boys, inspired
by Milton Friedman, and they urged Yeltsin to make the switch in
one fell swoop, in a process known as shock therapy: abolish controls
and subsidies, trust in market forces and let the market decide prices.
It was a disaster. Inflation roared out of control and living standards
plummeted. As one analyst concluded, the new reality involved 'too
much shock, and too little therapy', leaving millions of people finan-
cially crippled, and bereft of the psychological supports on which
they had long depended.[18] From a society of relatively low inequality,
where one could rely on state salaries and trading goods and services
with colleagues to get by, people were now confronted by extended
periods of unpaid salaries, unemployment and massive income
inequality, with a few resourceful, often corrupt and unscrupulous,

The nadir of the post-Soviet 'democratic' experiment came in the
form of army tanks shelling the Russian parliament in 1993.

operators seizing control of what had hitherto been communally
owned industries and natural resources.

Roman Kutuzov had a young family at the time, and remembers

> [how every] Monday and Tuesday would be spent desperately
> trying to think who we could visit on Wednesday, Thursday and
> Friday in order to scrounge a meal, as all our food and money
> would run out. Once, having seen the TV adverts for the new,
> foreign 'Snickers' bar, we bought this delicacy for a ridiculous
> sum from a kiosk and carefully divided it up on a plate with a
> knife so that the whole family could try it, in order to become
> acquainted with European values, as it were![19]

The heralded abundance of capitalism was nowhere to be seen.
Deputies in the Russian parliament seethed with discontent. Yeltsin's
economic programme was increasingly portrayed as western sabotage. The parliamentary speaker, Ruslan Khasbulatov, attacked the
'vile' monetarist policy imposed by the Americans. The result would
be the revolt of deputies in 1993 that was put down with force by
Yeltsin, with Russian tanks shelling the Russian parliament, the very

building Yeltsin had defended during the coup two years earlier. Was this the democracy Russians had been promised? The West didn't blink as Yeltsin used violence to get his way. US secretary of state, Warren Christopher, even praised the 'superb handling' of a crisis that critically weakened Russia's nascent democracy and recentralised power in the Kremlin and the presidential office.[20]

The West still professed a desire to help Russia, but the economic recession of the early 1990s meant priorities lay elsewhere. George Bush's Christmas message of 1991 had promised an end to worry about Russia, not an expensive campaign to support its government, however pro-western it might be. In his 1992 re-election campaign, he bigged up the 'victory' he had achieved over the communist adversary. 'The Berlin Wall came tumbling down,' Bush crowed, 'and the Soviet Union collapsed. Imperial communism became a four-letter word: D-E-A-D, dead. And today, because we stood firm, because we did the right things, America stands alone the undisputed leader of the world. We put an end to decades of cold war and reaped a springtime harvest of peace. The American people should be proud of what together we have achieved.'[21] This 'rare great moment in history', declared US National Security Advisor Brent Scowcroft, put America in 'a unique position, without experience, without precedent, and standing alone at the height of power. It was, and is, an unparalleled situation in history, one which presents us with the rarest opportunity to shape the world.'[22]

Russia had been admitted as a member of the G7 and the International Monetary Fund had granted it an economic stimulus package worth around $10 billion. But further aid was slow to come. As early as October 1992, Yeltsin had begun to signal Moscow's frustration at the lack of western support. 'Russia is not a country that can be kept waiting in the ante-room,'[23] he said, as the Kremlin expressed a desire for quick integration into the western system. At various times, Yeltsin suggested that Russia could become a member of the European Union, the World Trade Organization and even NATO.

Friendship was the name of the game; but the West blew it. NATO continued its expansion into the former Soviet satellites in central Europe, signing up Poland, Hungary and the Czech Republic while leaving Russia with little more than a cooperation agreement. Moscow became alarmed at suggestions that former Soviet republics including Ukraine, Georgia and the Baltic states might also be recruited.

By the end of the 1990s, relations were frosty. Yeltsin denounced NATO's intervention in Serbia and Kosovo without a UN mandate; and Bill Clinton responded by attacking the Kremlin's renewed military activity in Chechnya. At a meeting of the Organization for Security and Co-operation in Europe, President Clinton jabbed his finger at the Russian president and demanded he halt the bombing of Grozny; Yeltsin stormed out of the conference. Shortly afterwards he gave vent to his frustration. 'Yesterday,' he said, 'President Clinton sought to put pressure on Russia. He forgot for a moment, for a second, that Russia has a full arsenal of nuclear weapons. He has forgotten about that.'[24] It was a disturbing recrudescence of the acrimony of the Khrushchev and Kennedy era.*

In the West, Yeltsin is remembered as a buffoon, notwithstanding his bravery during the coup of August 1991, while Gorbachev is widely regarded as a great man, a reformer whose policies transformed the world. In Russia, though, both Yeltsin and Gorbachev are widely reviled. Russians blame them both for bringing a great nation to its knees, for leaving Russia humbled and diminished. Vladimir Putin enjoyed a decade of great popularity largely on the basis that he *wasn't* Yeltsin and he *wasn't* Gorbachev, and that he was undoing much of what they had done.

Looking back to the dramatic events of 1991, I am struck by how futile it was – and is – to predict the future of Russia. After the collapse of the coup, I was convinced – and said so in my reports for the BBC – that the downfall of the communist dinosaurs, together with the dissolution of the Communist Party after seventy years in power, meant that autocracy was dead in Russia, that centuries of repression would be thrown off and replaced with freedom and democracy. But I was wrong. For the next decade, Russia tried to turn itself into a western-style market democracy but slid instead into

---

* Yeltsin also gave Clinton's deputy secretary of state, Strobe Talbott, a piece of his mind. 'My impression is that the US doesn't quite know what to do with Russia now, from your current position of superiority. But Russia isn't Haiti, and we won't be treated as though we were ... I don't like it when the US flaunts its superiority. Russia's difficulties are only temporary, and not only because we have nuclear weapons, but also because of our economy, our culture, our spiritual strength. All that amounts to a legitimate, undeniable basis for equal treatment. Russia will rise again! I repeat: Russia will rise again!' S. Talbott, *The Russia Hand: A Memoir of Presidential Diplomacy*, New York: Random House, 2002, p. 197.

runaway inflation, ethnic violence and chaos. Primitive, unchecked capitalism came to Moscow, bringing corruption, depravity and business disputes settled with machine guns on the streets. Crime was endemic. Russians had had enough. If this was western democracy, they didn't want it. The following decade, from 2000 onwards, saw the process of democratisation largely reversed. After the infatuation with western values in the 1990s, the pendulum swung. The tone from the Kremlin became distinctly anti-western. Putin courted the worst extremes of Russian nationalism and blamed America for everything, from Russia's economic woes to anti-Kremlin demonstrations in Moscow and St Petersburg. He understood his countrymen's thoughts and desires.

Under Putin, Russia returned to its default model of governance – centralised autocracy – and its default mode of behaviour. Such was the animosity arising from the lost decade of the 1990s and from the perception that the West had used and abused the country's goodwill, that the new era of East–West tension seemed almost a foregone conclusion. Moscow once again blustered and threatened, flexing its muscles on the international stage, eliminating its enemies at home and abroad. The country became stable and relatively prosperous, but democracy and freedom again took second place to the demands of the state.

36

THE MISUSES OF MEMORY

In December 2000, Vladimir Putin marked the first anniversary of his ascent to the Russian presidency by bringing back the old Soviet national anthem. It is a rousing patriotic hymn that stirs the emotions, but its identification with the era of communism meant there were protests at its reinstatement, albeit with new words.[1] Putin justified his decision in a long-unpublished interview with the filmmaker Vitaly Mansky. 'I was in Ulyanovsk,' Putin says on camera,

> when a woman suddenly spoke up and said, 'Please! Return our previous life to us – as it was twenty years ago!' Well, what can you say to that? To go back is impossible. Neither our youth nor the old days can ever return. But it is essential to rebuild people's trust in their leaders. You need to make people feel that not everything has been snatched away from them. The vast majority of the population feel nostalgic for that time [the Soviet era]. You can't simply take everything away from them. I think of my parents, this part of their lives. Can we just throw all this away, root and branch, as if they never lived?*

---

*Mansky's interview with Putin was recorded in 2000 and included in his 2018 film *Svideteli Putina* ('Putin's Witnesses'). Putin was fond of repeating a phrase from his political mentor, former St Petersburg mayor Anatoly Sobchak. 'Revolutions are all well and good, but why pull down memorials?' 'Putin schitaeyet ugolovniye dela protiv Sobchak "podtasovkami"' ('Putin considers the criminal cases against Sobchak to be "distortions"'), *RIA Novosti*, 6 September 2013. ria.ru/spb/20130906/961401636.html.

In his speech reintroducing the old anthem, Putin told a television audience, 'Neither in my heart nor my head could I accept the rejection of Russia's past; doing so would mean that the lives of our mothers and fathers were meaningless, worthless and lived in vain.' Shireen Hunter, *Islam in Russia: The Politics of Identity and Security*, Abingdon: Routledge, 2004, p. 195.

The old certainties were gone. The old world had vanished. In East and West alike, people faced an unsettling psychological challenge of adaptation. When Bill Clinton struggled with the ambiguities of modern international relations during the 1993 Somalia crisis, he exclaimed, 'Gosh, I miss the Cold War!'[2] In the new era of uncertainty, memories of the past would be recast and at times manipulated. They would be deployed by politicians, writers and agitators for purposes of reassurance and of deception.

George Kennan proved to be a shrewd analyst of the Russian character. As early as 1947, he had suggested that it had become distorted under the Soviet system, leaving precarious psychological foundations. 'The present generation of Russians have never known spontaneity of collective action,' Kennan warned in his article 'The Sources of Soviet Conduct'. 'If, consequently, anything were ever to occur to disrupt the unity and efficacy of the Party as a political instrument, Soviet Russia might be changed overnight from one of the strongest to one of the weakest and most pitiable of national societies.'[3] The end of the Cold War and the collapse of the Communist Party of the Soviet Union would demonstrate how right Kennan had been. Millions in Russia were left without savings, without jobs and without hope, bereft of any conception of what their lives now meant. The land they had called their home, the social and political ideals to which they had dedicated their existence, had vanished overnight. 'It seems to me that we lack an aim,' lamented Natalya Pronina, one of many who felt lost in the new Russia. 'If before we had a goal, communism – even if it was an unobtainable one – we at least had a purpose. However, there's none now.'[4] Their society had failed, so they too had failed. Memories became meaningless – bitter reminders that they had been part of an evil age. It is not hard to understand why so many of the older generation clung forlornly to an idealised version of the past, desperate to rehabilitate it – and themselves.

The man they blamed for destroying their country and blighting their lives struggled to rationalise what he had done. Mikhail Gorbachev was torn between the adulation he received from a grateful West and contrition for the suffering of his countrymen. In 1992, he spoke from the same podium in Fulton, Missouri, where Winston Churchill had given his 'Iron Curtain' speech forty-six years earlier.

In uncertain times, many Russians turned back to the idealised
certainty and successes of Stalin's reign for comfort.

The end of the Cold War, Gorbachev suggested, could offer an
opportunity for worldwide reconciliation, a new paradigm in which
'the idea that certain states or groups of states could monopolize the
international arena is no longer valid'. To reach 'the exalted goal' of
peace and progress for all, however, would require greater wisdom
than had been shown in 1945. The Cold War had been presented
to people in East and West as 'the inevitable opposition between
good and evil – with all the evil, of course, being attributed to the
opponent'. Now both sides would need to 'dispense with egoistic
considerations' in order to secure a better future.[5]

Gorbachev was in denial. Haunted by the harsh fate his actions
had inflicted on his homeland, he was appealing for the same concessions from the West that he had failed to win when he had cards to
play and reciprocal concessions to offer. Now he was out of power
and impotent: America was hardly likely to 'dispense with egoistic
considerations', however eloquently Gorby pleaded. On the contrary, George H. W. Bush had placed national egotism and a world
in which 'certain states [i.e. the USA] would monopolize the international arena' at the top of his to-do list. 'For the Cold War didn't end;
it was won,' Bush told the US Congress. 'We are the United States
of America, the leader of the West that has become the leader of
the world … Moods come and go, but greatness endures.'[6] In Bush's
telling, humanity had reached the End of History: American ideals

Gorbachev's speech from Fulton was as well received in
Russia as Churchill's had been forty-six years earlier.

of liberal democracy and capitalism had triumphed; from now on, it
would be a unipolar world.

The political analyst and psychiatrist Charles Krauthammer spoke
for the American right when he wrote that Gorbachev's self-justifying
characterisation of the Cold War was 'an affront to Churchill's
memory', an attempt to reshape the world's memory of what he had
done and falsely define his legacy as a success.

> Mikhail Gorbachev is given the Fulton podium from which he
> declares, to warm applause, that the Cold War was (a) a great
> misunderstanding and (b) as much our fault as Stalin's ... This
> was the wrong speech given by the wrong man. It was given by
> the man who *accidentally* destroyed communism. It should have
> been given by someone who *intended* to, someone like Havel or
> Walesa or Sharansky or even Yeltsin.[7]

Gorbachev was not alone in appealing to Washington to be magnani-
mous in victory. Pope John Paul II, himself a long-standing opponent
of communist oppression in his Polish homeland, called on the West
to respond constructively to the end of the Cold War, to 'avoid seeing
this collapse of communism as a one-sided victory of their own economic system and thereby failing to make the necessary corrections
in that system'.[8] The independent-minded East German novelist

Christa Wolf agreed: lessons needed to be learned by both sides if the mistakes of the past were not to be repeated. '[Often] the defeated can see more than a victor, and perhaps can see what is essential, if they are clearheaded without self-pity and self-indulgence, and capable of learning.' But sadly, she wrote, 'the Gods despise losers'[9] and in the post-Cold War world, the gods were the countries of the West, chiefly the Americans. It was not for the 'saved' to tell their 'liberators' that they too are slaves to delusions and false beliefs that distort their thinking and control their lives.

America was constructing an idealised national narrative of the Cold War, a collective memory that excluded mistakes, lies, defeats and brutalities in favour of a uniform chronicle of success. The former CIA director Robert Gates summed it up in his memoirs as 'a glorious crusade', in which 'the American people paid the price … to keep the hope of freedom alive'.[10]

But the problem with viewing the past as a righteous crusade is that it suggests there are no lessons to learn from it. And a gloriously celebrated triumph makes what follows a disappointment. Western figures whose formative years were lived in the good-versus-evil world of the Cold War found it hard to adapt. All knew that those who forget the past are condemned to repeat it, but many struggled accurately to remember it. Those like Bill Clinton who lamented the passing of the Cold War fell into the trap of the 'peak-end rule': the innate human tendency to judge an experience on how we perceive it at its most intense point and at its end, demonstrated by Daniel Kahneman and others. Even an unpleasant experience can be looked back on with fondness if it concludes on a positive note. The Cold War was a time of tension, fear and danger, but because it ended in 'victory' for the West, it came to be viewed with nostalgia. Other information about the experience is not lost, Kahneman observed, but it is set aside in the process of remembering.[11] As early as 1990, with the USSR still in existence, John Mearsheimer had prophesied a future in which the Cold War would become an object of western nostalgia. '[While we] will not wake up one day to discover fresh wisdom in the collected fulminations of John Foster Dulles,' he wrote in his essay 'Why We Will Soon Miss the Cold War', 'we may, however, wake up one day lamenting the loss of the order that the Cold War gave to the anarchy of international relations … Deductively, a bipolar system is more peaceful for the simple reason that under it only two major powers are in contention.'[12]

Nostalgia for the old twin-track world was not confined to the West. Like many socialists who had clashed with the GDR authorities, Christa Wolf remained nonetheless committed to the aspirations that had underpinned the socialist state, with its emphasis on community, equality and collective solidarity. As the process of German reunification gathered pace, millions who had supported the regime moved to deny their past, becoming so-called 'weathervanes', eager now to champion western values. Wolf feared the psychological dislocation that would result from such a precipitately imposed rethinking. 'You can't develop an identity or acquire a new one if you simply throw the old one away,' she wrote. 'A lot of people from the former GDR may feel that they are actually being asked to deny their lives. And that's dangerous in the long run. You can't work through things that you exclude, that you can't admit to.'[13] Wolf and others who clung to their East German identity felt themselves tainted, shunned by the outside world.[14]

The 2003 film *Good Bye Lenin!* was a humorous take on the displacement felt by a generation of East Germans. The mother of the film's hero, Alex, is a committed communist who falls into a coma just before Erich Honecker resigns and the Berlin Wall comes down. When she wakes, the world has changed. Her doctor tells Alex that his mother's health is fragile and any shock might be fatal. Knowing her devotion to the GDR, Alex devises ever more complicated ways to conceal its collapse from her. He dresses in old East German fashions, uses Ostmarks and produces videos of fake television news reports to keep up the pretence that the GDR is alive and well. When his mother sees footage of crowds rushing through the breached wall, Alex tells her that they are West Germans fleeing to the East to escape the long-awaited crisis of capitalism.

For many in the real world, the GDR had become a life-enveloping mentality that was not easy to throw off. The East German comic, Uwe Steimle, called it 'Ostalgie',[15] a yearning for the old life-experiences, memories and values that had been lost in the new, reunified world. In a psychological exegesis of the aetiology of 'Ostalgia', Dominic Boyer offered several narratives, including the minimalist explanation that we all yearn for a past in which we were younger and more able. East Germans might simply be confusing their youth for a non-existent utopia. But he also examined the inheritance of German war-guilt (*Vergangenheitsbelastung* – the burden of the past), from which citizens

of East Germany felt themselves at least partially excused because of
their socialist – 'anti-fascist' – present. And he argued that both Ger-
manies, East and West, had embraced Ostalgia: just as East Germans
strove to preserve an image of their past, so West Germans needed
to preserve an image of the now-departed enemy.[16]

The West showed little understanding for the psychological
turmoil of the former GDR. Socialism had failed – the radical 'future'
had been consigned to the past – and the East should simply be grateful for its new freedoms. Katharina Herrmann was one of many who
resented the simplistic dismissal of her past. 'It felt a bit like being
colonised,' she recalled.

> There was an assumption that you would immediately accept
> West was good, East was bad. There was a lot of deliberate mis-
> interpretation about what had been going on in East Germany.
> There was a lot of very negative propaganda about people …
> who had spent their lives trying to build on something very
> worthwhile and positive – an egalitarian social experiment, no
> matter how flawed.[17]

East Germans became fixated on their Stasi files, fearing revelations of
past collaboration or hoping to demonstrate that they had stood up to
the regime.* When Christa Wolf's file was released, it contained records
of the extensive surveillance to which she was subjected because of her
willingness to criticise the authorities. But there was also a folder listing
several meetings she was said to have had with Stasi handlers in the late
1950s and early 1960s. The file was insubstantial, because Wolf lacked
what her handler called 'the proper devotion to the business'. But in
1992 Wolf was widely criticised, with a media campaign accusing her
of hypocrisy and lying about her past. What troubled her more was
that she had no recollection of the meetings listed in the dossier.

---

* The fact that Stasi observation was often arbitrary was ignored, as were the
details of individual cases. At times, subjects 'collaborated' with the Stasi in order
to provide deliberately false information to protect the people around them. At
others, Stasi agents invented contacts with people in order to satisfy their superiors. These subtleties do not appear in the black-and-white documents released in
the years following reunification, sometimes leading to the vilification of innocent
individuals.

The all-important memories [Wolf wrote], namely, that I had a cover name, that I once met these people in Berlin in an apartment used for undercover work, and that I composed a handwritten report – things for which it is hard for me to forgive myself – have not resurfaced [in my memory]. I can neither confirm nor deny whether I made the statements attributed to me in the Stasi reports, which are written in 'Stasi prose'. I break out in a sweat when I read this kind of language, but I know it's how we used to talk back then.[18]

In her novel *City of Angels or, The Overcoat of Dr. Freud*, Wolf set out to probe how she could have 'forgotten' her dalliance with the Stasi. Her namesake character visits a psychiatrist, who asks her, 'Don't you know that line from Freud: We cannot live without forgetting?' Wolf toys with the explanation of Freudian repression, but ends by declaring that 'ruthless self-examination is the prerequisite for the right to judge others'.[19]

Soviet society had followed the pattern of denial to the very last moments of its existence. The Brezhnev years were founded on blocking out the legacy of the past and the decay of the present. By the time Mikhail Gorbachev came to power, ready to face reality, it was too late. The USSR experienced the fate that Karl Marx had predicted for bourgeois capitalism. 'All that is solid melts into air,' Marx and Engels had written in their *Communist Manifesto*. 'And man is at last compelled to face with sober senses his real conditions of life, and his relations with his kind.'[20]

The man who set about restoring Russia to what he deemed its rightful place at the top table of international politics also had a Stasi file. But Vladimir Putin's record was as a perpetrator, not a victim. Putin had been a KGB representative in East Germany in the late 1980s, posted in Dresden in the so-called 'Valley of the Clueless' where West German TV could not be received.*

He would remember the disintegration of the Soviet empire as a formative time in his life. His official biography, produced in short order in 2000 to give the Russian people an idea who their new

---

*The suggestion is that Putin must have slipped up to end up in such a relatively unimportant post, and by his own admission he spent much of his time drinking beer. www.bbc.co.uk/news/world-europe-46525543.

Vladimir Putin's personal experience of the end of the Cold War has been
central to the development of the Russian state under his watch.

president was, helped explain why. It described a dramatic episode
in late 1989, when a baying crowd threatened to invade the KGB's
Dresden headquarters. Putin, then a lieutenant colonel, tried des-
perately to contact Moscow for guidance on what to do, only to be
told that Gorbachev was asleep and 'we cannot do anything without
orders'. 'I got the feeling that the country no longer existed,' Putin
recalled.

> That it had disappeared. It was clear that the Union was ailing.
> And it had a terminal disease without a cure – a paralysis of
> power. Intellectually I understood that a position based on
> walls and dividers could not last. But I wanted something dif-
> ferent to rise in its place. And nothing different was proposed.
> That's what hurt. They just dropped everything and went
> away.[21]

Putin had lived through events that can trigger what German psychiatrist Michael Linden described as Post-Traumatic Embitterment
Disorder (PTED). Closely related to PTSD, PTED causes bitterness,
hostility and aggression in sufferers following sudden upheavals in
their lives.

> Almost everybody had to cope with fundamental changes in
> their work situation and in their families, and many saw their

value systems called into question. There are men and women who feel that much of their life has been wasted because of the old system, and even those who hoped for a new beginning in the new system often found that they were cheated, let down, or set aside.[22]

Deprived of the cognitive schemata that had given shape to their lives, millions of people had been left unable to find their place in the world.

Such emotions about the chaotic state of post-Soviet Russian society may throw light on Vladimir Putin's behaviour since coming to power at the end of 1999. Motivated by anger at Gorbachev's 'betrayal', he concluded that it was imperative to find 'something different' if Russia were to survive one of the hardest periods in its history.'[23] He feared that, without a vast effort, Russia would lose its place in the top tier of global powers.[24]

Putin's initial instinct was to follow the lead of his mentor, Boris Yeltsin, and strive for reconciliation with the West. When the self-declared Islamic martyrs of Al-Qaeda destroyed the World Trade Center in September 2001, Putin was the first foreign leader to call the American president to offer support. He allowed US fighter-bombers to use Russian airbases in central Asia and provided maps and advice on Afghanistan. With Russia struggling against Muslim separatists in Chechnya, Putin suggested that Moscow and Washington become allies in the global war against Islamic terrorism. But the alliance was short lived. Russia received little in the way of reciprocal support and the West continued to criticise Russian human rights abuses in Chechnya. By the time of the Munich Security Conference of 2007, Putin's tone had changed. 'I am here to say what I really think about international security problems,' he told his fellow world leaders.

> Just like any war, the Cold War left us with live ammunition, figuratively speaking. I am referring to ideological stereotypes, double standards and other typical aspects of Cold War bloc thinking. The unipolar world that had been proposed after the Cold War is one in which there is one master, one sovereign ... the United States has overstepped its national borders in every way. This is visible in the economic, political, cultural and

educational policies it imposes on other nations. Well, who likes this? Who is happy about this?[25]

A world order dominated by the US was bad for Russia, Putin said, but it was equally harmful for America itself. He listed areas of concern including western interference in other states, the West's development of strategic conventional military capabilities, US missile defence plans and NATO expansion and 'aggression'. 'At the end of the day this is pernicious not only for all those within this system,' he concluded, 'but also for the sovereign itself … because it destroys itself from within.'[26] Seven years later, when the West complained about Russia's seizure of Crimea, Putin commented acidly, 'It's a good thing they at least remember that there exists such a thing as international law – better late than never!'[27]

The western 'other' returned as an instrument of validation for a new era of Russian nationalism. 'The policy of containment was not invented yesterday,' Putin said in 2014, when international outcry over the annexation of Crimea was at its peak. 'It has been carried out against our country for many years, always, for decades if not centuries. In short, whenever someone thinks Russia has become too strong or independent, these tools are quickly put to use.'[28] Memory was co-opted as an instrument of policy-making, with Cold War grudges invoked to blame the US for Russia's ills. A poll carried out in 2018 found that two-thirds of those asked regretted the collapse of the Soviet Union.* It was, wrote the historian, playwright and novelist Svetlana Boym, 'a *restorative nostalgia* that … does not think of itself as nostalgia, but rather as truth and tradition. It knows two main plots – the return to origins and the conspiracy.'[29] Putin's approach claimed to be more nuanced. 'Whoever does not miss the Soviet Union has no heart,' he wrote in 2010. 'Whoever wants it back has no brain.'[30]

---

* The replies suggest that the nostalgia people feel for the Soviet Union is less to do with military power and confronting the West than with the sense of security they had about their lives. They missed a time when the price of ice creams and sausages didn't change. The 1990s, by contrast, brought runaway inflation, and the pension reforms of 2018 heaped added misery on the already straitened lives of elderly people. In the USSR, people felt they lived in a superpower, in which their lives would not be upended from one day to the next (except, of course, that they eventually were). 'Nostalgiya po SSSR' ('Nostalgia for the USSR'), *Levada Center*, 19 December 2018. www.levada.ru/2018/12/19/nostalgiya-po-sssr-2/.

It was a formula that allowed a dubious past to be utilised without questioning its true character. 'It becomes clear,' Boym wrote, 'that in spite of great social transformation and the publication of revealing documents and onslaught of personal memoirs, short-lived public reflection on the experience of communism and, particularly, state repression, failed to produce any institutional change.'

> The collective trauma of the past was hardly acknowledged, or if it was, everyone was seen as an innocent victim or a cog in the system only following orders. The campaign for recovery of memory gave way to a new longing for the imaginary ahistorical past, the age of stability and normalcy. This mass nostalgia is a kind of nationwide midlife crisis; many are longing for the time of their childhood and youth, projecting personal affective memories onto the larger historical picture and partaking in a selective forgetting.[31]

Memory became a tool of aggression, too. Politicians in both East and West resurrected tropes of the old Cold War to magnify fears of a new one. Christa Wolf had warned that 'denied, repressed reality disappears into the blind spot in our consciousness, where it engulfs activity and creativity and generates myths, aggressiveness, delusion'.[32] When a Russian fighter in the so-called Donetsk People's Republic in eastern Ukraine was asked what he was fighting for, he instinctively reached for the memory myth that Putin and others had done much to create. 'We need to rebuild the country,' he told the *Guardian*'s Shaun Walker. 'The Soviet Union, the Russian Empire, it doesn't matter what you call it. I want a Russian idea for the Russian people; I don't want the Americans to teach us how to live. I want a strong country, one you can be proud of. I want life to have some meaning again.'[33]

The practice of defining oneself in opposition to an external enemy was common to both sides. 'Many in the West,' noted Lyle Goldstein of the US Naval War College, 'seemed to have succumbed to "enemy deprivation syndrome" after the Cold War. Many national security specialists seem to yearn for a more simple threat that is easily characterised.'* Moscow's acts of cyberterrorism and interference in

---

*In 1987, Georgy Arbatov wrote, 'We warned the Americans that the worst thing we could do to them would be to deprive them of their enemy. I didn't add

western elections in the 2010s slotted easily into the erstwhile Cold War narrative. James Clapper, a former director of national intelligence, drew on the preposterous excesses of the McCarthy era when he declared in 2017 that 'Russians are almost genetically driven to co-opt, penetrate, gain favour. It's in their genes to be opposed, diametrically opposed, to the United States and western democracies.'[34]

Attributing America's troubles to malevolent Russian penetration avoided the need to reflect on inherent domestic weaknesses, while also fuelling Russian paranoia about a West motivated by Russophobia. The Kremlin was convinced – and told the Russian people – that the unrest in Ukraine, Georgia and elsewhere that occurred throughout the 2010s was stoked by the CIA. Whether the distortion of memory by the new Cold Warriors stemmed from conviction or was the result of deliberate role-playing,* its real-world consequences were the same. Putin no longer pretended that his Russia was a liberal democracy. He painted the West as corrupt, with bogus elections and no freedom of speech, a stark contrast to the moral righteousness of his homeland. He based his legitimacy and his international swagger on confronting the decadent 'other', and it made him very popular.†

----

something that I understood all along: that by doing so we would be depriving ourselves of an enemy as well.' Georgi Arbatov, *The System: An Insider's Life in Soviet Politics*, New York: Random House, 1992, p. vi. See also Jonathan Marcus, 'Russia v the West: Is this a new Cold War?', BBC News, 1 April 2018. www.bbc.co.uk/news/world-europe-43581449.

* Primo Levi examined the interface between belief and pretence, highlighting the tendency for actors to assimilate the lies they peddle: 'Anyone who has sufficient experience of human affairs knows that the distinction good faith/bad faith is optimistic and illuminist ... There are, it is true, those who lie consciously, coldly falsifying reality itself, but more numerous are those who weigh anchor, move off, momentarily or forever, from genuine memories, and fabricate for themselves a convenient reality ... The distinction between true and false progressively loses its contours, and man ends by fully believing the story he has told so many times and still continues to tell, polishing and retouching here and there ... initial bad faith has become good faith. The silent transition from falsehood to sly deception is useful: anyone who lies in good faith is better off; he recites his part better, is more easily believed by the judge, the historian, the reader, his wife and his children. The further events fade into the past, the more the construction of convenient truth grows and is perfected.' Primo Levi, *The Drowned and the Saved*, London: Michael Joseph, 1988, p. 14.

† Although Putin's approval rating dropped markedly in late 2018, his 66 per cent support would make any Western leader jealous. www.levada.ru/indikatory/odobrenie-organov-vlasti/.

A Russian journalist, Mikhail Zygar, wrote that 'Putin has restored a sense of pride'.

> It's like what you feel when your favourite football team wins. Nothing actually changes: You don't become smarter, healthier, or richer; your personal life doesn't improve. You simply, irrationally, feel happier, proud of an accomplishment in which you played no role. To millions of Russians, Putin is that football team. And all he does is win.[35]

Although Russia can no longer credibly claim superpower status, and China has emerged as the real global threat to American hegemony, the two Cold War rivals are still drawn to one another. Both nations claim to believe in their unique position in the world, claiming the moral high ground, and each accusing the other of interfering in their internal affairs. In his 2018 address to the Federal Assembly, delivered shortly before he was elected president for the fourth time, Putin reprised Stalin's warning from 1931 that Russia needed to catch up with the West or face destruction. He had, he said, offered friendship to the United States but had been rebuffed.

> At one point, I thought that a compromise was possible, but this was not to be. All our proposals, absolutely all of them, were rejected ... Despite our numerous protests and pleas, the American machine has been set into motion, the conveyer belt is moving forward ... To those who in the past 15 years have tried to accelerate an arms race and seek unilateral advantage against Russia, I will say this: No one has managed to restrain Russia. We have to be aware of this reality and be aware that everything I have said today is not a bluff.[36]

The rhetoric was menacing, but it had a discernible logic. Putin was vaunting Russian military strength in order to dissuade the Americans from pursuing their destabilising missile defence plans. The logic of the man in the White House was less easy to discern. Donald Trump began his presidency with declarations of awed admiration for nuclear weapons and the destructive power they would put at his disposal. In the final Republican candidate debate in December 2015, he was asked what his nuclear priorities would be as president. 'For me,' Trump replied, 'nuclear – just the power, the devastation – is very important to me.'[37] During the election campaign of the following year, he seemed to endorse the premise of Nixon's 'madman theory', telling an interviewer, 'I'm never going to rule anything out. Even if I wasn't, I wouldn't want to tell you that because at a minimum, I want them to think maybe we would use [nuclear weapons], OK?'[38] As Trump's presidency ended in January 2021, after a disastrous riot that saw the Capitol building overrun by his supporters, the madman theory seemed perilously close to reality, with house speaker, Nancy Pelosi, calling General Mark Milley, the chairman of the joint chiefs of staff, 'to discuss available precautions for preventing an unstable president from initiating military hostilities or accessing the launch codes and ordering a nuclear strike'.[39]

The unpredictability of the man in the White House made it harder – and all the more crucial – for each side correctly to read the signals coming from the other. Rear Admiral John Gower, a former head of the British Ministry of Defence's nuclear weapons policy team, was tasked with examining the psychology of how East and West project their military intentions to each other. Writing in 2018, he identified a growing potential for misunderstanding.

> Nuclear signalling is the core of responsible nuclear weapon ownership. It was a difficult task during the Cold War, and shaping perceptions and communication of nuclear weapon intent has become more complex, nuanced and important in a world with multiple nuclear powers and rising tensions [increasing] the risk of misperception or unwanted escalation. These risks are higher than they have been for several decades and are rising.[40]

The Duke of Wellington's maxim that '[All] the business of war is … guessing at what [is] at the other side of the hill' was true before the Battle of Waterloo and remains true into the third decade of the twenty-first century. We still live in a world where decision-makers neglect to examine their own psychological motivations and assumptions, where we fear and project onto 'the other', where decisions that affect the lives of millions turn on the quirks, paranoias and anxieties of the men and women who lead us. Neither side will make informed decisions under these conditions. The risk of unleashing a war from which the globe will not recover remains real, long after the Cold War is supposed to have ended.

NOTES AND SELECTED BIBLIOGRAPHY

The notes and selected bibliography of this book are available online at www.profilebooks.com/work/the-war-of-nerves/.

ILLUSTRATION CREDITS

11 Cartoon by Cargill in the Kansas City *Journal Post*, reprinted in *The Literary Digest*, 14 April 1923. Public domain; **22** CORBIS/Corbis via Getty Images; **27** National Archives, London. Crown copyright under the Open Government Licence; **30** Poster by Alexei Koreikin, 1944. Public domain; **36** Keystone-France/Gamma-Keystone via Getty Images; **39** Keystone/Getty Images; **45** Still from *Seventeen Moments of Spring*, 1973. Public domain; **49** Bettmann/Getty Images; **68** Valery Sharifulin/TASS via Getty Images; **103** Keystone-France/Gamma-Rapho via Getty Images; **112** 'Re-education' poster, US Defense Department, 1947. Wikimedia Commons; **119** Soviet propaganda poster, 1940s. Public domain; **127** Wikicommons; **149** Soviet propaganda poster, Viktor Ivanov, 1947. Public domain; **160** Creative Commons/Bundesarchiv, B 285 Bild-14676/Unknown author/CC-BY-SA 3.0; **174** United States Information Agency poster, 1951. Public domain; **187** Freedom Train publicity poster, 1948. Public domain; **193** Keep America Committee, Los Angeles, 1955. Public domain; **222** Heritage Image Partnership Ltd/Alamy Stock Photo; **225** *Pravda*, 6 October 1957. Public domain; **229** Bettmann/Getty Images; **238** Universal History Archive/Universal Images Group via Getty Images; **246** From a 1950s Soviet magazine. Public domain; **254** Underwood Archives/Getty Images; **259** Everett Collection Historical/Alamy Stock Photo; **260** Bettmann/Getty Images; **262** dpa picture alliance/Alamy Stock Photo; **265** Photograph courtesy of the author; **267** Heritage Image Partnership Ltd/Alamy Stock Photo; **270** Bettmann/Getty Images; **271** *Izvestiya*, 14 April 1961. Public domain; **273** Universal Images Group North America LLC/Alamy Stock Photo; **308** CORBIS/Corbis via Getty Images; **309** Bettmann/Getty Images; **316** Department of Civil Defense, City of Boston, official US government booklet, 1951. Public domain; **320** Soviet civil defence posters, circa 1955, photographed by Nanette van der Laan; **321** Soviet poster from the series 'Civil defense & fire service', poster no. 3. From the installation 'Fire & Rescue Museum', 2009, by Jussi Kivi. Photo by Filippo Zambon; **333** Cartoon by D. Agayev, *Pravda*, 31 Oct 1986; **340** Department of the Army, March 1955; **352** Dasvedanya Images/Alamy Stock Photo; **359** CIA archives; **395** Photo12/Archives Snark/Alamy Stock Photo; **402** Scott's Porage Oats advert, 1967; **412** Bettmann/Getty Images; **434** Keystone/Getty Images; **445** AFP via Getty Images; **446** UCL Library Services, from 'The Prague Spring Through the Lens of Frank Carter' exhibition at UCL SSEES, London, June 2018. Licensed under a Creative Commons licence; **504** Peter Jordan/Alamy Stock Photo; **510** REUTERS/Alamy Stock Photo; **517** Laski Diffusion/Getty Images; **536** Peter Turnley/Corbis/VCG via Getty Images; **542** Oleg Nikishin/Getty Images; **543** James A. Finley/AP/Shutterstock; **548** Bundesarchiv.

While every effort has been made to contact copyright-holders of illustrations, the author and publishers would be grateful for information about any illustrations where they have been unable to trace them, and would be glad to make amendments in further editions.

INDEX

Page references in *italics* indicate images.